Collins
French
School
Dictio

D0806879

HarperCollins Publishers
Westerhill Road
Bishopbriggs
Glasgow G64 2QT

Fifth Edition 2018, 2019

10 9 8 7 6 5 4 3

© HarperCollins Publishers 2005,
2006, 2011, 2015, 2018, 2019

ISBN 978-0-00-825796-5

Collins® is a registered trademark of
HarperCollins Publishers Limited

schools.collinsdictionary.com
collins.co.uk/dictionaries

Typeset by Davidson Publishing
Solutions, Glasgow

Printed in Italy by Grafica Veneta
S.p.A.

All rights reserved. No part of this
book may be reproduced, stored in
a retrieval system, or transmitted
in any form or by any means,
electronic, mechanical, photocopying,
recording or otherwise, without the
prior permission in writing of the
Publisher. This book is sold subject to
the conditions that it shall not, by way
of trade or otherwise, be lent, re-sold,
hired out or otherwise circulated
without the Publisher's prior consent
in any form of binding or cover other
than that in which it is published and
without a similar condition including
this condition being imposed on the
subsequent purchaser.

Entered words that we have reason to
believe constitute trademarks have
been designated as such. However,
neither the presence nor absence of
such designation should be regarded
as affecting the legal status of any
trademark.

The contents of this publication
are believed correct at the time of
printing. Nevertheless the publisher
can accept no responsibility for
errors or omissions, changes in the
detail given or for any expense or loss
thereby caused.

HarperCollins does not warrant that
any website mentioned in this title
will be provided uninterrupted, that
any website will be error free, that
defects will be corrected, or that the
website or the server that makes it
available are free of viruses or bugs.
For full terms and conditions please
refer to the site terms provided on
the website.

A catalogue record for this book is
available from the British Library.

Acknowledgements
We would like to thank those authors
and publishers who kindly gave
permission for copyright material to be
used in the Collins Corpus. We would
also like to thank Times Newspapers
Ltd for providing valuable data.

EDITOR
Susie Beattie

CONTRIBUTORS
Val McNulty
Phyllis Buchanan
Maggie Seaton
Marie Ollivier-Caudray
Anna Stevenson

FOR THE PUBLISHER
Gillian Bowman
Laura Waddell
Sarah Woods

TECHNICAL SUPPORT
Agnieszka Urbanowicz

CONTENTS

Acknowledgements

We are grateful to all those teachers and students who have contributed to the development of the *Collins French School Dictionary* by advising us on how to tailor it to their needs. We also gratefully acknowledge the help of the examining boards.

USING THIS DICTIONARY

The *Collins French School Dictionary* is designed specifically for anyone starting to learn French, and has been carefully researched with teachers and students. It is very straightforward, with an accessible layout that is easy on the eye, guiding students quickly to the right translation. It also offers essential help on French culture.

This section gives useful tips on how to use the *Collins French School Dictionary* effectively.

▷ Make sure you look in the right side of the dictionary

There are two sides in a bilingual dictionary. Here, the **French–English** side comes first, and the second part is **English–French**. At the top of each page there is a reminder of which side of the dictionary you have open. The middle pages of the book have a grey border so you can see where one side finishes and the other one starts.

▷ Finding the word you want

To help you find a word more quickly, use the **alphabet tabs** down the side of the page, then look at the words in **bold** at the top of pages. They show the first and last words on the two pages where the dictionary is open.

▷ Make sure you use the right part of speech

Some entries are split into several parts of speech. For example **'glue'** can either be a noun ("Can I borrow your **glue**?") or a verb ("**Glue** this into your exercise book"). Parts of speech within an entry are separated by a black triangle ▶ and are given on a new line. They are given in their abbreviated form (*n* for noun, *adj* for adjective, etc). For the full list of abbreviations, look at page viii.

> **glue** *n* colle *f*
> ▶ *vb* coller [**28**]

▷ Choosing the right translation

The main translation of a word is underlined and is shown after the part of speech. If there is more than one main translation for a word, each one is numbered. You may also sometimes find bracketed words in *italics* which give you some context. They help you to choose the translation you want.

> **pool** n ❶ *(puddle)* <u>flaque</u> f ❷ *(pond)*
> <u>étang</u> m ❸ *(for swimming)* <u>piscine</u> f
> ❹ *(game)* <u>billard américain</u> m …

Often you will see phrases in *italics*, preceded by a white triangle ▷. These are examples of the word being used in context.

> **numérique** *adj* <u>digital</u> ▷ *un appareil*
> *photo numérique* a digital camera

Phrases in **bold type** are phrases which are particularly common and important. Sometimes these phrases have a completely different translation.

> **chausson** *nm* <u>slipper</u>; **un**
> **chausson aux pommes** an apple
> turnover

Once you have found the right translation, remember that you may need to adapt the French word you have found. You may need to make a **noun** plural, or make an **adjective** feminine or plural. Remember that the feminine form is given for nouns and adjectives, and that irregular plural forms are given also.

> **dancer** *n* <u>danseur</u> *m*, <u>danseuse</u> *f*
> **horse** *n* <u>cheval</u> *m* (*pl* chevaux)
> **salty** *adj* <u>salé(e)</u>

You may also need to adapt the **verb**. Verbs are given in the infinitive form, but you may want to use them in the present, past or future tense. To do this, use the **verb tables** in the last section of the dictionary. French verbs on both sides are usually followed by a number in square brackets. This number corresponds to a verb table number in the verb tables at the back of the dictionary.

In the following example, **imprimer** follows the same pattern as **donner**, which is verb number **28** in the verb tables.

imprimer *vb* [**28**] to print

▷ Find out more

In the *Collins French School Dictionary*, you will find lots of extra information about the French language. These **usage notes** help you understand how the language works, draw your attention to false friends (words which look similar but have a different meaning), and give you some word-for-word translations.

te *pron*
> **te** changes to **t'** before a vowel and most words beginning with 'h'.

librairie *nf* bookshop
> Be careful! **librairie** does not mean **library**.

chauve-souris (*pl* **chauves-souris**) *nf (animal)* bat
> Word for word, this means 'bald mouse'.

You can also find out more about life in France and French-speaking countries by reading the **cultural notes**.

half-term *n* petites vacances *fpl*
> - There are two half-term holidays
> - in France: **les vacances de la**
> - **Toussaint** (in October/
> - November) and **les vacances**
> - **de février** (in February).

▷ Remember!

Never take the first translation you see without looking at the others. Always look to see if there is more than one translation, or more than one part of speech.

ABBREVIATIONS USED IN THIS DICTIONARY

abbr	abbreviation
adj	adjective
adv	adverb
art	article
conj	conjunction
excl	exclamation
f	feminine
n	noun
nf	feminine noun
nm	masculine noun
nmf	masculine and feminine noun
nm/f	masculine or feminine noun
npl	plural noun
num	number
prep	preposition
pron	pronoun
vb	verb

SYMBOLS

▷	example
▶	new part of speech
②	new meaning
[29]	verb table number (see Verb Tables section at the back of the dictionary)
accident	Key words which you need for your GCSE or other exams of a similar level are highlighted in light grey throughout both sides of the dictionary to help you find them more easily.

Note that to help you decide whether to use **le, la** or **l'** in front of a word starting with 'h', the article is given for all the nouns in letter **H** on the **French–English** side of the dictionary.

TIME

Quelle heure est-il? **What time is it?**   **À quelle heure?** **At what time?**
Il est…   **It's…**

une heure

une heure dix

une heure et quart

une heure et demie

deux heures moins vingt

deux heures moins le quart

à minuit

à midi

à une heure (de l'après-midi)

à huit heures (du soir)

*In French times are often given using the
24-hour clock.*

à onze heures quinze (11h15)

à vingt heures quarante-cinq
(20h45)

DATES

▷ Days of the Week

lundi	Monday
mardi	Tuesday
mercredi	Wednesday
jeudi	Thursday
vendredi	Friday
samedi	Saturday
dimanche	Sunday

▷ Months of the Year

janvier	January	**juillet**	July
février	February	**août**	August
mars	March	**septembre**	September
avril	April	**octobre**	October
mai	May	**novembre**	November
juin	June	**décembre**	December

▷ Quand?

en février
le 1er décembre
le premier décembre
en 2019
en deux mille dix-neuf

▷ When?

in February
on 1 December
on the first of December
in 2019
in two thousand and nineteen

▷ Quel jour sommes nous?

Nous sommes le…
dimanche 1er octobre *or*
dimanche premier octobre
lundi 10 février *or*
lundi dix février

▷ What day is it?

It's…
Sunday 1 October *or*
Sunday, the first of October
Monday, 10 February *or*
Monday, the tenth of February

NUMBERS

▷ Cardinal numbers

1	un (une)	21	vingt et un (une)
2	deux	22	vingt-deux
3	trois	30	trente
4	quatre	40	quarante
5	cinq	50	cinquante
6	six	60	soixante
7	sept	70	soixante-dix
8	huit	71	soixante et onze
9	neuf	72	soixante-douze
10	dix	80	quatre-vingts
11	onze	81	quatre-vingt-un (-une)
12	douze	90	quatre-vingt-dix
13	treize	91	quatre-vingt-onze
14	quatorze	100	cent
15	quinze	101	cent un (une)
16	seize	200	deux cents
17	dix-sept	201	deux cent un (une)
18	dix-huit	300	trois cents
19	dix-neuf	1000	mille
20	vingt	1,000,000	un million

▷ Fractions

1/2	un demi, une demie	1/5	un cinquième
1/3	un tiers	0.5	zéro virgule cinq (0,5)
2/3	deux tiers	10%	dix pour cent
1/4	un quart	100%	cent pour cent
3/4	trois quarts		

NUMBERS

▷ Ordinal numbers

1st	premier (1er), première (1re)
2nd	deuxième (2e or 2ème)
3rd	troisième (3e or 3ème)
4th	quatrième (4e or 4ème)
5th	cinquième (5e or 5ème)
6th	sixième (6e or 6ème)
7th	septième (7e or 7ème)
8th	huitième (8e or 8ème)
9th	neuvième (9e or 9ème)
10th	dixième (10e or 10ème)
11th	onzième (11e or 11ème)
12th	douzième (12e or 12ème)
13th	treizième (13e or 13ème)
14th	quatorzième (14e or 14ème)
15th	quinzième (15e or 15ème)
16th	seizième (16e or 16ème)
17th	dix-septième (17e or 17ème)
18th	dix-huitième (18e or 18ème)
19th	dix-neuvième (19e or 19ème)
20th	vingtième (20e or 20ème)
21st	vingt et unième (21e or 21ème)
22nd	vingt-deuxième (22e or 22ème)
30th	trentième (30e or 30ème)
100th	centième (100e or 100ème)
101st	cent-unième (101e or 101ème)
1000th	millième (1000e or 1000ème)

a

a *vb see* **avoir**

> **a** should not be confused with the preposition **à**.

Il a beaucoup d'amis. He has a lot of friends.; **Il a mangé des frites.** He had some chips.; **Il a neigé pendant la nuit.** It snowed during the night.; **il y a (1)** there is ▷ *Il y a un bon film à la télé.* There's a good film on TV. **(2)** there are ▷ *Il y a beaucoup de monde.* There are lots of people.

à *prep*

> **à** should not be confused with the verb form **a**. See also **au (=à + le)** and **aux (=à + les)**.

❶ to ▷ *être à la maison* to be at home ▷ *à trois heures* at 3 o'clock **❷** in ▷ *être à Paris* to be in Paris ▷ *habiter au Portugal* to live in Portugal ▷ *habiter à la campagne* to live in the country ▷ *au printemps* in the spring ▷ *au mois de juin* in June **❸** to ▷ *aller à Paris* to go to Paris ▷ *aller au Portugal* to go to Portugal ▷ *aller à la campagne* to go to the country ▷ *donner quelque chose à quelqu'un* to give something to somebody ▷ *Cette veste appartient à Marie.* This jacket belongs to Marie. ▷ *Je n'ai rien à faire.* I've got nothing to do.; **Ce livre est à Paul.** This book is Paul's.; **Cette voiture est à nous.** This car is ours. **❹** by ▷ *à bicyclette* by bicycle ▷ *être payé à l'heure* to be paid by the hour; **à pied** on foot; **C'est à côté de chez moi.** It's near my house.; **C'est à dix kilomètres d'ici.** It's 10 kilometres from here.; **C'est à dix minutes d'ici.** It's 10 minutes from here.; **cent kilomètres à l'heure** 100 kilometres an hour; **À bientôt!** See you soon! ▷ *À demain!* See you tomorrow! ▷ *À samedi!* See you on Saturday! ▷ *À tout à l'heure!* See you later!

abandonner *vb* [28] **❶** to abandon **❷** to give up ▷ *J'ai décidé d'abandonner la natation.* I've decided to give up swimming.

abeille *nf* bee

abîmer *vb* [28] to damage; **s'abîmer** to get damaged

abonnement *nm* **❶** season ticket **❷** *(to magazine)* subscription

s'**abonner** *vb* [28] **s'abonner à une revue** to take out a subscription to a magazine; **être abonné sur**

Twitter to be on Twitter
abord nm d'abord first
aboyer vb [53] to bark
abri nm shelter; **être à l'abri** to be under cover; **se mettre à l'abri** to shelter
abricot nm apricot
s' **abriter** vb [28] to shelter
absence nf absence; **Il est passé pendant ton absence.** He came while you were away.
absent, e adj absent
absolument adv absolutely
abus nm abuse; **abus de confiance** breach of trust; **abus de pouvoir** abuse of power; **abus sexuels** sexual abuse
accélérateur nm accelerator
accélérer vb [34] to accelerate
accent nm accent ▷ Il a l'accent de Marseille. He has a Marseilles accent.; **un accent aigu** an acute accent; **un accent grave** a grave accent; **un accent circonflexe** a circumflex
accentuer vb [28] to stress
accepter vb [28] to accept; **accepter de faire quelque chose** to agree to do something
accès nm access ▷ avoir accès à quelque chose to have access to something; **'Accès aux quais'** 'To the trains'
accessoire nm ❶ accessory ❷ prop
accident nm accident; **par accident** by chance
accompagner vb [28] to accompany
accomplir vb [38] to carry out ▷ Il n'a pas réussi à accomplir cette tâche. He didn't manage to carry out this task.
accord nm agreement; **être**

d'accord to agree ▷ Tu es d'accord avec moi? Do you agree with me?; **se mettre d'accord** to come to an agreement; **D'accord!** OK!
accordéon nm accordion
accoudoir nm armrest
accrochage nm collision
accrocher vb [28] accrocher **quelque chose à (1)** to hang something on ▷ Il a accroché sa veste au portemanteau. He hung his jacket on the coat rack. **(2)** to hitch something up to ▷ Ils ont accroché la remorque à leur voiture. They hitched the trailer up to their car.; **s'accrocher à quelque chose** to get caught on something ▷ Sa jupe s'est accrochée aux ronces. Her skirt got caught on the brambles.
s' **accroupir** vb [38] to squat down
accueil nm welcome; **Elle s'occupe de l'accueil des visiteurs.** She's in charge of looking after visitors.; **'Accueil'** 'Reception'
accueillant, e adj welcoming
accueillir vb [22] to welcome
accumuler vb [28] to accumulate; **s'accumuler** to pile up
accusation nf accusation
accusé nm accused; **un accusé de réception** an acknowledgement of receipt
accusée nf accused
accuser vb [28] to accuse ▷ accuser quelqu'un de quelque chose to accuse somebody of something
achat nm purchase; **faire des achats** to do some shopping
acheter vb [1] to buy ▷ J'ai acheté des

gâteaux à la pâtisserie. I bought some cakes at the cake shop.;
acheter quelque chose à quelqu'un (1) to buy something for somebody ▷ *Qu'est-ce que tu lui as acheté pour son anniversaire?* What did you buy him for his birthday? **(2)** to buy something from somebody ▷ *J'ai acheté des œufs au fermier.* I bought some eggs from the farmer.

acide *adj* acid
  ▸ *nm* acid

acier *nm* steel

acné *nf* acne

acquérir *vb* [2] to acquire

acquis *vb* see **acquérir**

acquitter *vb* [28] to acquit
  ▷ *L'accusé a été acquitté.* The accused was acquitted.

acte *nm* act; **un acte de naissance** a birth certificate

acteur *nm* actor

actif (*f* **active**) *adj* active; **la population active** the working population

action *nf* action; **une bonne action** a good deed

s'**activer** *vb* [28] ❶ to bustle about ▷ *Elle s'activait à préparer le repas.* She bustled about preparing the meal. ❷ to get moving ▷ *Allez! Active-toi!* Come on! Get moving!

activité *nf* activity

actrice *nf* actress

actualité *nf* current events; **un problème d'actualité** a topical issue; **les actualités** the news

actuel (*f* **actuelle**) *adj* present; à **l'heure actuelle** at the present time

> Be careful! **actuel** does not mean **actual**.

actuellement *adv* at present

> Be careful! **actuellement** does not mean **actually**.

adaptateur *nm* adaptor

addition *nf* ❶ addition ❷ bill ▷ *L'addition, s'il vous plaît!* Can we have the bill, please?

additionner *vb* [28] to add up

adhérent *nm* member

adhérente *nf* member

adhésif (*f* **adhésive**) *adj* **le ruban adhésif** sticky tape

adieu *excl* farewell!

adjectif *nm* adjective

admettre *vb* [47] ❶ to admit ▷ *Il refuse d'admettre qu'il s'est trompé.* He won't admit that he made a mistake. ❷ to allow ▷ *Les chiens ne sont pas admis dans le restaurant.* Dogs are not allowed in the restaurant.

administration *nf* administration; **l'Administration** the Civil Service

admirable *adj* wonderful

admirateur *nm* admirer

admiratrice *nf* admirer

admirer *vb* [28] to admire

admis *vb* see **admettre**

adolescence *nf* adolescence

adolescent *nm* teenager

adolescente *nf* teenager

adopter *vb* [28] to adopt

adorable *adj* lovely

adorer *vb* [28] to love ▷ *Elle adore le*

a
b
c
d
e
f
g
h
i
j
k
l
m
n
o
p
q
r
s
t
u
v
w
x
y
z

chocolat. She loves chocolate.
▷ *J'adore jouer au tennis.* I love
playing tennis.

adresse *nf* address; **une adresse
web** a Web address; **mon adresse
électronique** my email address

adresser *vb* [28] **adresser la
parole à quelqu'un** to speak to
someone; **s'adresser à quelqu'un
(1)** to speak to somebody ▷ *C'est à
toi que je m'adresse.* It's you I'm
speaking to. **(2)** to go and see
somebody ▷ *Adressez-vous au
patron.* Go and see the boss. **(3)** to
be aimed at somebody ▷ *Ce film
s'adresse surtout aux enfants.* This
film is aimed mainly at children.

adulte *nmf* adult

adverbe *nm* adverb

adversaire *nmf* opponent

aérien (*f* **aérienne**) *adj* **une
compagnie aérienne** an airline

aérobic *nm* aerobics

aérogare *nf* terminal

aéroglisseur *nm* hovercraft

aéroport *nm* airport

affaire *nf* ❶ case ▷ *une affaire de
drogue* a drugs case ❷ business
▷ *Son affaire marche bien.* His
business is doing well.; **une bonne
affaire** a real bargain; **Ça fera
l'affaire.** This will do nicely.; **avoir
affaire à quelqu'un** to deal with
somebody

affaires *nfpl* ❶ things ▷ *Va chercher
tes affaires!* Go and get your things!
❷ business ▷ *Les affaires marchent
bien en ce moment.* Business is good
at the moment.; **un homme**

d'affaires a businessman

affection *nf* affection

affectueusement *adv*
affectionately

affectueux (*f* **affectueuse**) *adj*
affectionate

affiche *nf* poster

afficher *vb* [28] to put up ▷ *Ils ont
affiché les résultats dehors.* They've
put the results up outside.;
'Défense d'afficher' 'Post no bills'

affilée: **d'affilée** *adv* at a stretch

affirmation *nf* assertion

affirmer *vb* [28] to claim ▷ *Il a
affirmé que c'était la vérité.* He
claimed it was the truth.;
s'affirmer to assert oneself ▷ *Il est
trop timide, il faut qu'il s'affirme.* He's
too shy, he should assert himself.

affluence *nf* **les heures
d'affluence** the rush hour

s'**affoler** *vb* [28] to panic ▷ *Ne
t'affole pas!* Don't panic!

affranchir *vb* [38] to stamp

affreux (*f* **affreuse**) *adj* awful

affronter *vb* [28] to face
▷ *L'Allemagne affrontera l'Italie en
finale.* Germany will face Italy in the
final.

afin de *conj* **afin de faire quelque
chose** so as to do something ▷ *Je
me suis levé très tôt afin d'être prêt à
temps.* I got up very early so as to be
ready on time.

afin que *conj* so that

afin que is followed by a verb in
the subjunctive.

▷ *Il m'a téléphoné afin que je sois prêt à
temps.* He phoned me so that I'd be

ready on time.

africain, e *adj, nm/f* African; **un Africain** *(man)* an African; **une Africaine** *(woman)* an African

Afrique *nf* Africa; **en Afrique (1)** in Africa **(2)** to Africa; **l'Afrique du Sud** South Africa

agacer *vb* [12] **agacer quelqu'un** to get on somebody's nerves ▷ *Tu m'agaces avec tes questions!* You're getting on my nerves with all your questions!

âge *nm* age; **Quel âge as-tu?** How old are you?

âgé, e *adj* old; **les personnes âgées** elderly people

agence *nf* ❶ agency ▷ *l'agence pour l'emploi* the employment agency; **une agence de voyages** a travel agency ❷ office; **une agence immobilière** an estate agent's

agenda *nm* diary ▷ *J'ai perdu mon agenda.* I have lost my diary.

> Be careful! The French word **agenda** does not mean **agenda**.

s'**agenouiller** *vb* [28] to kneel down

agent *nm* **un agent de police** a police officer; **un agent d'entretien** a cleaner

agglomération *nf* town; **l'agglomération parisienne** Greater Paris

aggraver *vb* [28] to make worse; **s'aggraver** to worsen

agir *vb* [38] to act ▷ *Il a agi par vengeance.* He acted out of vengeance.; **Il s'agit de ...** It's

about ... ▷ *Il s'agit du club de sport.* It's about the sports club. ▷ *De quoi s'agit-il?* What is it about?; **Il s'agit de faire attention.** We must be careful.

agité, e *adj* ❶ restless ❷ rough; **un sommeil agité** broken sleep

agiter *vb* [28] to shake ▷ *Agitez la bouteille.* Shake the bottle.

agneau *(pl* **agneaux)** *nm* lamb

agrafe *nf (for papers)* staple

agrafeuse *nf* stapler

agrandir *vb* [38] ❶ to enlarge ▷ *J'ai fait agrandir mes photos.* I've had my photos enlarged. ❷ to extend ▷ *Ils ont agrandi leur jardin.* They've extended their garden.; **s'agrandir** to expand ▷ *Leur magasin s'est agrandi.* Their shop has expanded.

agréable *adj* nice

agréer *vb* [18] **Veuillez agréer, Monsieur, l'expression de mes sentiments les meilleurs. Jean Ormal.** Yours sincerely, Jean Ormal.

agressif *(f* **agressive)** *adj* aggressive

agressivité *nf* aggression; **faire preuve d'agressivité envers quelqu'un** to be aggressive to somebody; **l'agressivité au volant** road rage

agricole *adj* agricultural; **une exploitation agricole** a farm

agriculteur *nm* farmer ▷ *Il est agriculteur.* He's a farmer.

agricultrice *nf* farmer

agriculture *nf* farming

ai *vb* see **avoir**; **J'ai deux chats.**

a
b
c
d
e
f
g
h
i
j
k
l
m
n
o
p
q
r
s
t
u
v
w
x
y
z

I have two cats.; **J'ai bien dormi.**
I slept well.
aide *nf* ❶ help; **À l'aide!** Help!
❷ aid; **à l'aide de** using
aider *vb* [28] to help
aide-soignant (*pl* **aides-soignants**) *nm* auxiliary nurse
aide-soignante (*pl* **aides-soignantes**) *nf* auxiliary nurse
aie *vb see* **avoir**
aïe *excl* ouch!
aigre *adj* sour
aigu (*f* **aiguë**) *adj* (pain) sharp;
e accent aigu e acute
aiguille *nf* needle; **les aiguilles d'une montre** the hands of a watch
ail *nm* garlic
aile *nf* wing
aille *vb see* **aller**
ailleurs *adv* somewhere else;
partout ailleurs everywhere else;
nulle part ailleurs nowhere else;
d'ailleurs besides
aimable *adj* kind
aimant *nm* magnet
aimer *vb* [28] ❶ to love ▷ *Elle aime ses enfants.* She loves her children.
❷ to like ▷ *Tu aimes le chocolat?* Do you like chocolate? ▷ *J'aime bien ce garçon.* I like this boy. ▷ *J'aime bien jouer au tennis.* I like playing tennis.
▷ *J'aimerais aller en Grèce.* I'd like to go to Greece.; **J'aimerais mieux ne pas y aller.** I'd rather not go.
aîné, e *adj* elder ▷ *mon frère aîné* my big brother
aîné *nm* oldest child ▷ *C'est l'aîné.*
He's the oldest child.
aînée *nf* oldest child

ainsi *adv* in this way; **C'est ainsi qu'il a réussi.** That's how he succeeded.; **ainsi que** as well as;
et ainsi de suite and so on
air *nm* ❶ air; **prendre l'air** to get some fresh air ❷ tune ▷ *Elle a joué un air au piano.* She played a tune on the piano.; **Elle a l'air fatiguée.**
She looks tired.; **Il a l'air d'un clown.** He looks like a clown.
aire de jeux *nf* playground
aire de repos *nf* (on motorway) rest area
aise *nf* **être à l'aise** to be at ease;
être mal à l'aise to be ill at ease; **se mettre à l'aise** to make oneself comfortable
ait *vb see* **avoir**
ajouter *vb* [28] to add
alarme *nf* alarm
Albanie *nf* Albania
album *nm* album
alcool *nm* alcohol ▷ *Je ne bois pas d'alcool.* I don't drink alcohol.
alcoolisé, e *adj* alcoholic; **une boisson non alcoolisée** a soft drink
alentours *nmpl* **dans les alentours** in the area; **aux alentours de Paris** in the Paris area; **aux alentours de cinq heures** around 5 o'clock
algèbre *nf* algebra
Alger *n* Algiers
Algérie *nf* Algeria
algérien (*f* **algérienne**) *adj, nm/f* Algerian; **un Algérien** (*man*) an Algerian; **une Algérienne** (*woman*) an Algerian

algue *nf* seaweed

aliment *nm* food

alimentation *nf* ❶ groceries ▷ *le rayon alimentation du supermarché* the grocery department in the supermarket ❷ diet ▷ *Elle a une alimentation saine.* She has a healthy diet.

allée *nf* ❶ path ❷ (*in street names*) drive

allégé, e *adj* low-fat

Allemagne *nf* Germany; **en Allemagne (1)** in Germany **(2)** to Germany

allemand, e *adj, n* German ▷ *Elle parle allemand.* She speaks German.; **un Allemand** (*man*) a German; **une Allemande** (*woman*) a German; **les Allemands** the Germans

aller *vb* [**3**] to go ▷ *Je suis allé à Londres.* I went to London. ▷ *Je vais me fâcher.* I'm going to get angry.; **s'en aller** to go away ▷ *Je m'en vais demain.* I'm going tomorrow.; **aller bien à quelqu'un** to suit somebody ▷ *Cette robe te va bien.* This dress suits you.; **Allez! Dépêche-toi!** Come on! Hurry up!; **Comment allez-vous? — Je vais bien.** How are you? — I'm fine.; **Comment ça va? — Ça va bien.** How are you? — I'm fine.; **aller mieux** to be better ▶ *nm* ❶ outward journey ❷ (*ticket*) single; **un aller simple** a single; **un aller retour (1)** a return ticket **(2)** a round trip

allergique *adj* allergique à allergic to

allô *excl* hello! ▷ *Allô! Je voudrais parler à Monsieur Simon.* Hello! I'd like to speak to Mr Simon.

allô is only used when talking to someone on the phone.

allocation *nf* allowance; **les allocations chômage** unemployment benefit

s'**allonger** *vb* [**45**] to lie down ▷ *Il s'est allongé sur son lit.* He lay down on his bed.

allumer *vb* [**28**] ❶ to switch on ▷ *Tu peux allumer la lumière?* Can you put the light on? ▷ *Allume la radio.* Switch on the radio. ❷ to light ▷ *Elle a allumé une cigarette.* She lit a cigarette.; **s'allumer** (*light*) to come on ▷ *La lumière s'est allumée.* The light came on.

allumette *nf* match ▷ *une boîte d'allumettes* a box of matches

allure *nf* ❶ speed ❷ look ▷ *avoir une drôle d'allure* to look odd

allusion *nf* reference

alors *adv* ❶ then ▷ *Tu as fini? Alors je m'en vais.* Have you finished? I'm going then. ❷ so ▷ *Alors je lui ai dit de partir.* So I told him to leave.; **Et alors?** So what? ❸ at that time; **alors que (1)** as ▷ *Il est arrivé alors que je partais.* He arrived just as I was leaving. **(2)** while ▷ *Alors que je travaillais dur, lui se reposait.* While I was working hard, he was resting.

Alpes *nfpl* Alps

alphabet *nm* alphabet

alphabétique *adj* alphabetical

alpinisme *nm* mountaineering

alpiniste *nmf* mountaineer

Alsace nf Alsace

amande nf almond; **la pâte d'amandes** marzipan

amant nm lover

amateur (f **amatrice**) adj amateur

amateur nm amateur; **en amateur** as a hobby; **C'est un amateur de musique.** He's a music lover.

amatrice nf amateur

ambassade nf embassy

ambassadeur nm ambassador

ambiance nf atmosphere; **la musique d'ambiance** background music

ambitieux (f **ambitieuse**) adj ambitious

ambition nf ambition; **Il a beaucoup d'ambition.** He's very ambitious.

ambulance nf ambulance

âme nf soul

amélioration nf improvement

améliorer vb [28] to improve; **s'améliorer** to improve ▷ Le temps s'améliore. The weather's improving.

amende nf fine

amener vb [43] to bring ▷ Qu'est-ce qui t'amène? What brings you here? ▷ Est-ce que je peux amener un ami? Can I bring a friend?

amer (f **amère**) adj bitter

américain, e adj, nm/f American; **un Américain** (man) an American; **une Américaine** (woman) an American

Amérique nf America; **en Amérique (1)** in America **(2)** to America; **l'Amérique du Nord** North America; **l'Amérique du Sud** South America

ami nm friend; **C'est son petit ami.** He's her boyfriend.; **ajouter quelqu'un à sa liste d'amis** (social networks) to friend somebody; **supprimer quelqu'un de sa liste d'amis** (social networks) to unfriend somebody

amical, e (mpl **amicaux**) adj friendly

amicalement adv in a friendly way; **Amicalement, Pierre.** (in letter) Best wishes, Pierre.

amie nf friend; **C'est sa petite amie.** She's his girlfriend.

amitié nf friendship; **Fais mes amitiés à Paul.** Give my regards to Paul.; **Amitiés, Christèle.** (in letter) Best wishes, Christèle.

amour nm love; **faire l'amour** to make love

amoureux (f **amoureuse**) adj in love ▷ être amoureux de quelqu'un to be in love with somebody

amour-propre nm self-esteem

amphithéâtre nm lecture theatre

amplement adv **Nous avons amplement le temps.** We have plenty of time.

ampoule nf ❶ light bulb ❷ blister

amusant, e adj amusing

amuse-gueule nmpl party nibbles

amuser vb [28] to amuse; **s'amuser (1)** to play ▷ Les enfants s'amusent dehors. The children are playing outside. **(2)** to enjoy oneself ▷ On s'est bien amusés. We really enjoyed ourselves.

an nm year; **le premier de l'an** New Year's Day; **le nouvel an** New Year

analyse nf ❶ analysis ❷ (medical) test

ananas nm pineapple

ancêtre nmf ancestor

anchois nm anchovy

ancien (f **ancienne**) adj ❶ former ▷ C'est une ancienne élève. She's a former pupil. ❷ old ▷ notre ancienne voiture our old car ❸ antique

ancre nf anchor

Andorre nf Andorra

âne nm donkey

ange nm angel; **être aux anges** to be over the moon

angine nf throat infection

anglais, e adj, n English ▷ Est-ce que vous parlez anglais? Do you speak English?; **un Anglais** an Englishman; **une Anglaise** an Englishwoman; **les Anglais** the English

angle nm ❶ angle ❷ corner

Angleterre nf England; **en Angleterre (1)** in England ▷ J'habite en Angleterre. I live in England. **(2)** to England ▷ Je suis allée en Angleterre le mois dernier. I went to England last month.

anglo- prefix anglo-; **les îles Anglo-Normandes** the Channel Islands

anglophone adj English-speaking

angoissé, e adj stressed

animal (pl **animaux**) nm animal

animateur nm ❶ host ❷ youth leader

animatrice nf ❶ host ❷ youth leader

animé, e adj lively ▷ Cette rue est très animée. This is a very lively street.; **un dessin animé** a cartoon

anis nm aniseed

anneau (pl **anneaux**) nm ring

année nf year

anniversaire nm ❶ birthday ❷ anniversary

annonce nf advert; **les petites annonces** the small ads

annoncer vb [12] to announce ▷ Ils ont annoncé leurs fiançailles. They've announced their engagement.

annuaire nm phone book

annuel (f **annuelle**) adj annual

annuler vb [28] to cancel

anonyme adj anonymous

anorak nm anorak

ANPE nf (= Agence nationale pour l'emploi) job centre

Antarctique nm Antarctic

antenne nf ❶ aerial; **antenne parabolique** satellite dish; **être à l'antenne** to be on the air ❷ antenna

antibiotique nm antibiotic

antidépresseur nm antidepressant

antigel nm antifreeze

Antilles nfpl West Indies; **aux Antilles (1)** in the West Indies **(2)** to the West Indies

antipathique adj unpleasant

antiquaire nmf antique dealer

antiquité nf antique; **pendant l'antiquité** in classical times

antiseptique adj antiseptic ▶ nm antiseptic

antivirus nm antivirus (program)

antivol nm ❶ (on bike) lock ❷ (on car) steering lock

anxieux (f **anxieuse**) adj anxious

a
b
c
d
e
f
g
h
i
j
k
l
m
n
o
p
q
r
s
t
u
v
w
x
y
z

août nm August; **en août** in August

apercevoir vb [67] to see
▷ *J'aperçois la côte.* I can see the shore.; **s'apercevoir de quelque chose** to notice something; **s'apercevoir que ...** to notice that ...

apéritif nm aperitif

apparaître vb [56] to appear

appareil nm device; **un appareil dentaire** (for teeth) a brace; **les appareils ménagers** domestic appliances; **un appareil photo** a camera; **Qui est à l'appareil?** (on phone) Who's speaking?

apparemment adv apparently

apparence nf appearance

apparition nf appearance

appartement nm flat

appartenir vb [83] **appartenir à quelqu'un** to belong to somebody

apparu vb see **apparaître**

appel nm ❶ cry ▷ *un appel au secours* a cry for help ❷ phone call; **faire appel à quelqu'un** to appeal to somebody; **faire l'appel** (in school) to call the register; **faire un appel de phares** to flash one's headlights

appeler vb [4] to call; **s'appeler** to be called ▷ *Elle s'appelle Muriel.* Her name's Muriel. ▷ *Comment tu t'appelles?* What's your name?

appendicite nf appendicitis

appétissant, e adj appetizing

appétit nm appetite; **Bon appétit!** Enjoy your meal!

applaudir vb [38] (applaud) to clap

applaudissements nmpl applause sg

appliquer vb [28] ❶ to apply ❷ to enforce ▷ *appliquer la loi* to enforce the law; **s'appliquer** to apply oneself

apporter vb [28] to bring

apprécier vb [19] to appreciate

appréhender vb [28] to dread
▷ *J'appréhende cette réunion.* I'm dreading this meeting.

apprendre vb [65] ❶ to learn
▷ *apprendre quelque chose par cœur* to learn something by heart; **apprendre à faire quelque chose** to learn to do something
▷ *J'apprends à faire la cuisine.* I'm learning to cook. ❷ to hear ▷ *J'ai appris son départ.* I heard that she had left.; **apprendre quelque chose à quelqu'un (1)** to teach somebody something ▷ *Ma mère m'a appris l'anglais.* My mother taught me English. **(2)** to tell somebody something ▷ *Jean-Pierre m'a appris la nouvelle.* Jean-Pierre told me the news.

apprentissage nm learning

appris vb see **apprendre**

approbation nf approval

approcher vb [28] **approcher de** to approach ▷ *Nous approchons de Paris.* We are approaching Paris.; **s'approcher** to come closer to ▷ *Ne t'approche pas, j'ai la grippe!* Don't get too close to me, I've got flu!

approprié, e adj suitable

approuver vb [28] to approve of
▷ *Je n'approuve pas ses méthodes.* I don't approve of his methods.

approximatif (f **approximative**)
adj ① approximate ② rough

appui nm support

appuyer vb [**53**] ① to press
▷ appuyer sur un bouton to press a
button ② to lean ▷ Elle a appuyé son
vélo contre la porte. She leaned her
bike against the door.; **s'appuyer**
to lean ▷ Elle s'est appuyée contre le
mur. She leaned against the wall.

après prep, adv ① after ▷ après le
déjeuner after lunch ▷ après son
départ after he had left
② afterwards ▷ aussitôt après
immediately afterwards; **après
coup** afterwards ▷ J'y ai repensé
après coup. I thought about it again
afterwards.; **d'après** according to
▷ D'après lui, c'est une erreur.
According to him, that's a
mistake.; **après tout** after all

après-demain adv the day after
tomorrow

après-midi nmf afternoon

après-rasage nm aftershave

aquarium nm aquarium

arabe adj, nmf ① Arab ② Arabic ▷ Il
parle arabe. He speaks Arabic.; **un
Arabe** (man) an Arab; **une Arabe**
(woman) an Arab

Arabie Saoudite nf Saudi Arabia

araignée nf spider

arbitre nm ① referee ② umpire

arbre nm tree; **un arbre
généalogique** a family tree

arbuste nm shrub

arc nm bow

arc-en-ciel (pl **arcs-en-ciel**) nm
rainbow

archéologie nf archaeology

archéologue nmf archaeologist

archipel nm archipelago

architecte nmf architect

architecture nf architecture

Arctique nm Arctic

ardoise nf slate

arène nf bullring; **des arènes
romaines** a Roman amphitheatre;
l'arène politique the political
arena

arête nf fish bone

argent nm ① silver ② money ▷ Je
n'ai plus d'argent. I haven't got any
more money.; **l'argent de poche**
pocket money; **l'argent liquide**
cash

argentin, e adj, nm/f Argentinian;
un Argentin (man) an Argentinian;
une Argentine (woman) an
Argentinian

Argentine nf Argentina

argile nf clay

argot nm slang

arme nf weapon; **une arme à feu** a
firearm

armée nf army; **l'armée de l'air** the
Air Force

armistice nm armistice

armoire nf wardrobe

armure nf armour

arnaquer vb [**28**] (informal) to con

arobase nf @ symbol

aromatisé, e adj flavoured

arôme nm ① aroma ② (added to
food) flavouring

arpenter vb [**28**] to pace up and
down ▷ Il arpentait le couloir. He was
pacing up and down the corridor.

a
b
c
d
e
f
g
h
i
j
k
l
m
n
o
p
q
r
s
t
u
v
w
x
y
z

arrache-pied: d'arrache-pied *adv* furiously

arracher *vb* [**28**] ❶ to take out ▷ *Le dentiste m'a arraché une dent.* The dentiste took one of my teeth out. ❷ to tear out ▷ *Arrachez la page.* Tear the page out. ❸ to pull up ▷ *Elle a arraché les mauvaises herbes.* She pulled up the weeds.; **arracher quelque chose à quelqu'un** to snatch something from somebody

arranger *vb* [**45**] ❶ to arrange ▷ *arranger des fleurs dans un vase* to arrange flowers in a vase ❷ to suit ▷ *Ça m'arrange de partir plus tôt.* It suits me to leave earlier.; **s'arranger** to come to an agreement; **Je vais m'arranger pour venir.** I'll organize things so that I can come.; **Ça va s'arranger.** Things will work themselves out.

arrestation *nf* arrest

arrêt *nm* stop; **sans arrêt** (1) non-stop (2) continually

arrêter *vb* [**28**] ❶ to stop; **Arrête!** Stop it!; **arrêter de faire quelque chose** to stop doing something ❷ to switch off ▷ *Il a arrêté le moteur.* He switched the engine off. ❸ to arrest ▷ *Mon voisin a été arrêté.* My neighbour's been arrested.; **s'arrêter** to stop ▷ *Elle s'est arrêtée devant une vitrine.* She stopped in front of a shop window.; **s'arrêter de faire quelque chose** to stop doing something ▷ *s'arrêter de fumer* to stop smoking

arrhes *nfpl* deposit *sg* ▷ *verser des*

arrhes to pay a deposit

arrière *nm* back; **à l'arrière** at the back; **en arrière** behind
▶ *adj* back ▷ *le siège arrière* the back seat

arrière-grand-mère (*pl* **arrière-grands-mères**) *nf* great-grandmother

arrière-grand-père (*pl* **arrière-grands-pères**) *nm* great-grandfather

arrivée *nf* arrival

arriver *vb* [**5**] ❶ to arrive ▷ *J'arrive à l'école à huit heures.* I arrive at school at 8 o'clock. ❷ to happen ▷ *Qu'est-ce qui est arrivé à Christian?* What happened to Christian?; **arriver à faire quelque chose** to manage to do something ▷ *J'espère que je vais y arriver.* I hope I'll manage it.; **Il m'arrive de dormir jusqu'à midi.** I sometimes sleep till midday.

arrogant, e *adj* arrogant

arrondissement *nm* district
● Paris, Lyons and Marseilles are
● divided into numbered districts
● called **arrondissements**.

arroser *vb* [**28**] to water ▷ *Daphne arrose ses tomates.* Daphne is watering her tomatoes.; **Ils ont arrosé leur victoire.** They had a drink to celebrate their victory.

arrosoir *nm* watering can

art *nm* art

artère *nf* ❶ artery ❷ thoroughfare

artichaut *nm* artichoke

article *nm* ❶ article ❷ item

articulation *nf* joint

articuler vb [**28**] to pronounce clearly

artificiel (f **artificielle**) adj artificial

artisan nm self-employed craftsman

artiste nmf ❶ artist ❷ performer

artistique adj artistic

as vb see **avoir**; **Tu as de beaux cheveux.** You've got nice hair.
  ▶ nm ace

ascenseur nm lift

Ascension nf Ascension

asiatique adj Asiatic

Asie nf Asia; **en Asie** (1) in Asia (2) to Asia

aspect nm appearance

asperge nf asparagus

aspirateur nm vacuum cleaner; **passer l'aspirateur** to vacuum

aspirine nf aspirin

assaisonner vb [**28**] to season

assassin nm murderer

assassiner vb [**28**] to murder

assembler vb [**28**] to assemble; **s'assembler** to gather ▷ Une foule énorme s'était assemblée. A huge crowd had gathered.

s'**asseoir** vb [**6**] to sit down
  ▷ Asseyez-vous! Sit down!
  ▷ Assieds-toi! Sit down!

assez adv ❶ enough; **J'en ai assez!** I've had enough! ❷ quite ▷ Il faisait assez beau. The weather was quite nice.

assiette nf plate; **une assiette anglaise** assorted cold meats

assis, e adj sitting
  ▶ vb see **asseoir**

assistance nf ❶ audience ❷ aid ▷ l'assistance humanitaire humanitarian aid ❸ assistance

assistant nm assistant; **un assistant social** a social worker

assistante nf assistant

assister vb [**28**] **assister à un accident** to witness an accident; **assister à un cours** to attend a class; **assister à un concert** to be at a concert

association nf association

associé nm (in business) partner

associée nf (in business) partner

s'**associer** vb [**19**] to go into partnership

assommer vb [**28**] to knock out ▷ Il l'a assommé avec une bouteille. He knocked him out with a bottle.

Assomption nf Assumption

assorti, e adj ❶ matching ❷ assorted; **être assorti à quelque chose** to match something

assortiment nm assortment

assurance nf ❶ insurance ❷ confidence

assurer vb [**28**] ❶ to insure ▷ La maison est assurée. The house is insured. ▷ être assuré contre quelque chose to be insured against something ❷ to assure ▷ Je t'assure que c'est vrai! I assure you it's true!; **s'assurer de quelque chose** to make sure of something ▷ Il s'est assuré que la porte était fermée. He made sure the door was shut.

asthme nm asthma

astronaute nmf astronaut

astronomie nf astronomy

astucieux (astucieuse) adj clever

atelier nm ❶ workshop ❷ (artist's) studio

Athènes n Athens

athlète nmf athlete

athlétisme nm athletics

Atlantique nm Atlantic

atlas nm atlas

atmosphère nf atmosphere

atomique adj atomic

atout nm ❶ asset ❷ trump card

atroce adj terrible

attachant, e adj lovable

attacher vb [28] to tie up ▷ Elle a attaché ses cheveux avec un élastique. She tied her hair up with an elastic band.; **s'attacher à quelqu'un** to become attached to somebody; **une poêle qui n'attache pas** a non-stick frying pan

attaquer vb [28] to attack

atteindre vb [60] to reach

attendant: **en attendant** adv in the meantime

attendre vb [7] to wait ▷ attendre quelqu'un to wait for someone; **attendre un enfant** to be expecting a baby; **s'attendre à** to expect ▷ Je m'attends à une surprise. I'm expecting a surprise.

> Be careful! **attendre** does not mean to attend.

attentat nm **un attentat à la bombe** a terrorist bombing

attente nf wait; **la salle d'attente** the waiting room

attentif (attentive) adj attentive

attention nf attention; **faire**

attention to be careful; **Attention!** Watch out!

attentionné, e adj thoughtful

atterrir vb [38] to land

atterrissage nm (of plane) landing

attirant, e adj attractive

attirer vb [28] to attract ▷ attirer l'attention de quelqu'un to attract somebody's attention; **s'attirer des ennuis** to get into trouble ▷ Si tu continues, tu vas t'attirer des ennuis. If you keep on like that, you'll get yourself into trouble.

attitude nf attitude

attraction nf **un parc d'attractions** an amusement park

attraper vb [28] to catch

attrayant, e adj attractive

attrister vb [28] to sadden

au prep see **à**

> **au** is the contracted form of **à + le**.

▷ **au printemps** in the spring

aube nf dawn ▷ **à l'aube** at dawn

auberge nf inn; **une auberge de jeunesse** a youth hostel

aubergine nf aubergine

aucun, e adj, pron ❶ no ▷ Il n'a aucun ami. He's got no friends. ❷ none ▷ Aucun d'entre eux n'est venu. None of them came.; **sans aucun doute** without any doubt

au-delà adv **au-delà de** beyond

au-dessous adv ❶ downstairs ▷ Ils habitent au-dessous. They live downstairs. ❷ underneath; **au-dessous de** under

au-dessus adv ❶ upstairs ▷ J'habite au-dessus. I live upstairs. ❷ above;

au-dessus de above
audiovisuel (f **audiovisuelle**) adj
audiovisual
auditeur nm (to radio) listener
auditrice nf (to radio) listener
augmentation nf rise
augmenter vb [28] to increase
aujourd'hui adv today
auparavant adv first
auquel (mpl **auxquels**, fpl
auxquelles) pron

▌ **auquel** is the contracted form
of à + lequel.

▷ l'homme auquel j'ai parlé the man I
spoke to
aura, aurai, auras, aurez,
aurons, auront vb see **avoir**
aurore nf daybreak
ausculter vb [28] Le médecin l'a
ausculté. The doctor listened to
his chest.
aussi adv ❶ too ▷ Dors bien. — Toi
aussi. Sleep well. — You too. ❷ also
▷ Je parle anglais et aussi allemand. I
speak English and also German.;
aussi ... que as ... as ▷ aussi grand
que moi as big as me
aussitôt adv straight away;
aussitôt que as soon as
Australie nf Australia; **en**
Australie (1) in Australia **(2)** to
Australia
australien (f **australienne**) adj,
nm/f Australian; **un Australien**
(man) an Australian; **une**
Australienne (woman) an
Australian
autant adv **autant de (1)** so much
(2) so many; **autant ... que (1)** as

much ... as **(2)** as many ... as;
d'autant plus que all the more
since; **d'autant moins que** even
less since
auteur nm author
auto nf car
autobus nm bus
autocar nm coach
autocollant, e adj self-adhesive;
une enveloppe autocollante a
self-seal envelope
▶ nm sticker
auto-école nf driving school
automatique adj automatic
automne nm autumn; **en**
automne in autumn
automobile adj **une course**
automobile a motor race
▶ nf car
automobiliste nmf motorist
autoradio nm car radio
autorisation nf ❶ permission
❷ permit
autoriser vb [28] to give
permission for ▷ Il m'a autorisé à en
parler. He's given me permission to
talk about it.
autoritaire adj authoritarian
autorité nf authority
autoroute nf motorway
auto-stop nm **faire de l'auto-stop**
to hitchhike
auto-stoppeur nm hitchhiker
autour adv around
autre adj, pron other ▷ J'ai d'autres
projets. I've got other plans.; **autre**
chose something else; **autre part**
somewhere else; **un autre** another
▷ Tu veux un autre morceau de gâteau?

a
b
c
d
e
f
g
h
i
j
k
l
m
n
o
p
q
r
s
t
u
v
w
x
y
z

Would you like another piece of cake?; **l'autre** the other; **d'autres** others; **les autres** the others; **ni l'un ni l'autre** neither of them; **entre autres** among other things

autrefois adv in the old days

autrement adv ❶ differently ❷ otherwise; **autrement dit** in other words

Autriche nf Austria; **en Autriche** (1) in Austria (2) to Austria

autrichien (f **autrichienne**) adj, nm/f Austrian; **un Autrichien** (man) an Austrian; **une Autrichienne** (woman) an Austrian

autruche nf ostrich

aux prep see **à**

> **aux** is the contracted form of **à** + **les**.

▷ J'ai dit aux enfants d'aller jouer. I told the children to go and play.

auxquelles pron pl

> **auxquelles** is the contracted form of **à** + **lesquelles**.

▷ les revues auxquelles il est abonné the magazines to which he subscribes

auxquels pron pl

> **auxquels** is the contracted form of **à** + **lesquels**.

▷ les enfants auxquels il a parlé the children he spoke to

avaient, avais, avait vb see **avoir**; Il y avait beaucoup de monde. There were lots of people.

avalanche nf avalanche

avaler vb [28] to swallow

avance nf être en avance to be early; à l'avance beforehand;

d'avance in advance

avancé, e adj advanced; **bien avancé** well under way

avancer vb [12] ❶ to move forward ❷ to bring forward ▷ La date de l'examen a été avancée. The date of the exam has been brought forward. ❸ to put forward ▷ Il a avancé sa montre d'une heure. He put his watch forward an hour. ❹ (watch) to be fast ▷ Ma montre avance d'une heure. My watch is an hour fast. ❺ to lend ▷ Peux-tu m'avancer dix euros? Can you lend me 10 euros?

avant prep, adj ❶ before ▷ avant qu'il ne pleuve before it rains ▷ avant de partir before leaving ❷ front ▷ le siège avant the front seat; **avant tout** above all ▶ nm front; à l'avant in front; en avant forward

avantage nm advantage

avant-bras (pl **avant-bras**) nm forearm

avant-dernier (f **avant-dernière**, mpl **avant-derniers**) adj last but one

avant-hier adv the day before yesterday

avare adj miserly ▶ nmf miser

avec prep with ▷ avec mon père with my father; **Et avec ça?** (in shop) Anything else?

avenir nm future; à l'avenir in future; dans un proche avenir in the near future

aventure nf adventure

avenue nf avenue

averse nf (of rain) shower

avertir vb [38] to warn; **avertir quelqu'un de quelque chose** to warn somebody about something

avertissement nm warning

aveugle adj blind

avion nm plane; **aller en avion** to fly; **par avion** by airmail

aviron nm rowing

avis nm ❶ opinion; **à mon avis** in my opinion ❷ notice; **changer d'avis** to change one's mind

avocat nm ❶ lawyer ❷ avocado

avocate nf lawyer

avoine nf oats

avoir vb [8] ❶ to have ▷ Ils ont deux enfants. They have two children. ▷ Il a les yeux bleus. He's got blue eyes. ▷ J'ai déjà mangé. I've already eaten.; **On t'a bien eu!** (informal) You've been had! ❷ to be ▷ Il a trois ans. He's three.; **il y a (1)** there is ▷ Il y a quelqu'un à la porte. There's somebody at the door. **(2)** there are ▷ Il y a des chocolats sur la table. There are some chocolates on the table. **(3)** ago ▷ Je l'ai rencontré il y a deux ans. I met him two years ago.; **Qu'est-ce qu'il y a?** What's the matter?; **Il n'y a qu'à partir plus tôt.** We'll just have to leave earlier.

avortement nm abortion

avouer vb [28] to admit

avril nm April; **en avril** in April

ayez, ayons vb see **avoir**

baby-foot nm table football

baby-sitting nm **faire du baby-sitting** to babysit

bac nm = **baccalauréat**

baccalauréat nm A levels

- The French **baccalauréat**, or
- **bac** for short, is taken at the age
- of 17 or 18. Students have to sit
- one of a variety of set subject
- combinations, rather than being
- able to choose any combination
- of subjects they want. If you
- pass you have the right to a
- place at university.

bâcler vb [28] to botch up

bagage nm luggage; **faire ses bagages** to pack; **les bagages à main** hand luggage

bagarre nf fight

se **bagarrer** vb [28] to fight

bagnole nf (informal) car
bague nf ring
baguette nf ① stick of French bread ② chopstick; **une baguette magique** a magic wand
baie nf bay
baignade nf 'baignade interdite' 'no swimming'
se **baigner** vb [28] to go swimming ▷ Si on allait se baigner? Shall we go swimming?
baignoire nf (bathtub) bath
bâiller vb [28] to yawn
bain nm bath ▷ prendre un bain to take a bath ▷ prendre un bain de soleil to sunbathe
baiser nm kiss
baisse nf fall; **être en baisse** to be falling; **revoir les chiffres à la baisse** to revise figures downwards
baisser vb [28] ① to turn down ▷ Il fait moins froid, tu peux baisser le chauffage. It's not so cold, you can turn down the heating. ② to fall ▷ Le prix des CD a baissé. The price of CDs has fallen.; **se baisser** to bend down
bal nm dance
balade nf (informal) walk
se **balader** vb [28] (informal) to wander around
baladeur nm
balai nm broom
balance nf (for weighing) scales pl; **la Balance** Libra
se **balancer** vb [12] to swing
balançoire nf swing
balayer vb [59] ① to sweep ② to sweep up

balayeur nm roadsweeper
balbutier vb [19] to stammer
balcon nm balcony
baleine nf whale
balle nf ① ball ▷ une balle de tennis a tennis ball ② bullet
ballerine nf ① ballet dancer ② ballet shoe
ballet nm ballet
ballon nm ① ball ▷ lancer le ballon to throw the ball; **un ballon de foot** a football ② balloon
balnéaire adj **une station balnéaire** a seaside resort
banal, e adj ① commonplace ② hackneyed
banane nf ① banana ② bumbag
banc nm bench
bancaire adj **une carte bancaire** a bank card
bandage nm bandage
bande nf ① gang ▷ une bande de voyous a gang of louts ② bunch ▷ C'est une bande d'idiots! They are a bunch of idiots! ③ bandage; **une bande dessinée** a comic strip
　● Comic strips are very popular in
　● France with people of all ages.
une bande magnétique a tape; **la bande sonore** the sound track; **Elle fait toujours bande à part.** She always keeps to herself.
bandeau (pl **bandeaux**) nm headband
bander vb [28] to bandage ▷ L'infirmière lui a bandé la jambe. The nurse bandaged his leg.
bandit nm bandit
banlieue nf suburbs; **les lignes de**

banlieue suburban lines; **les trains de banlieue** commuter trains

banque nf bank

banquet nm dinner

banquette nf seat

banquier nm banker

baptême nm christening; **C'était mon baptême de l'air.** It was the first time I had flown.

baquet nm tub

bar nm bar

baraque nf (informal) house

barbant, e adj (informal) boring

barbare adj barbaric

barbe nf beard ▷ *Il porte la barbe.* He's got a beard.; **Quelle barbe!** (informal) What a drag!; **la barbe à papa** candyfloss

barbecue nm barbecue

barbouiller vb [28] to daub ▷ *Les murs étaient barbouillés de graffitis.* The walls were daubed with graffiti.; **J'ai l'estomac barbouillé.** (informal) I'm feeling queasy.

barbu, e adj bearded

barder vb [28] (informal) **Ça va barder!** There's going to be trouble!

baromètre nm barometer

barque nf rowing boat

barrage nm dam; **un barrage de police** a police roadblock

barre nf (metal) bar

barreau (pl **barreaux**) nm (on window) bar

barrer vb [28] to block ▷ *Il y a un tronc d'arbre qui barre la route.* There's a tree trunk blocking the road.; **se barrer** (informal) to clear off ▷ *Barre-toi!* Clear off!

barrette nf hair slide

barrière nf fence

bar-tabac (pl **bars-tabacs**) nm
  ● A **bar-tabac** is a bar which also
  ● sells cigarettes and stamps; you
  ● can tell a **bar-tabac** by the red
  ● diamond-shaped sign outside it.

bas (f **basse**) adj, adv low ▷ *parler à voix basse* to speak in a low voice; **en bas (1)** down ▷ *Ça me donne le vertige de regarder en bas.* I get dizzy if I look down. **(2)** (down) at the bottom ▷ *Son nom est tout en bas.* His name is down at the bottom. **(3)** downstairs ▷ *Elle habite en bas.* She lives downstairs.
  ▶ nm ❶ bottom ▷ *en bas de la page* at the bottom of the page ❷ stocking

bas-côté nm verge

bascule nf **un fauteuil à bascule** a rocking chair

base nf base; **de base** basic; **à base de** made from; **une base de données** a database

basilic nm basil

basket nm basketball

baskets nfpl trainers ▷ *une paire de baskets* a pair of trainers

basque adj, n Basque ▷ *Elle parle basque.* She speaks Basque.; **un Basque** (man) a Basque; **une Basque** (woman) a Basque

basse adj f see **bas**

basse-cour (pl **basses-cours**) nf farmyard

bassin nm ❶ pond ❷ pelvis

bassine nf (for washing) bowl

a
b
c
d
e
f
g
h
i
j
k
l
m
n
o
p
q
r
s
t
u
v
w
x
y
z

bas-ventre nm lower abdomen
bataille nf battle
bateau (pl **bateaux**) nm boat
bateau-mouche (pl **bateaux-mouches**) nm pleasure boat
bâti, e adj **bien bâti** well-built
bâtiment nm building
bâtir vb [38] to build
bâton nm stick
battement nm **J'ai dix minutes de battement.** I've got ten minutes free.
batterie nf ❶ battery ❷ drums; **la batterie de cuisine** the pots and pans
batteur nm drummer
battre vb [9] to beat ▷ Quand je le vois, mon cœur bat plus vite. When I see him, my heart beats faster.; **se battre** to fight ▷ Je me bats souvent avec mon frère. I fight a lot with my brother.; **battre les cartes** to shuffle the cards; **Battre les blancs en neige.** Beat the egg whites until stiff.; **battre son plein** to be in full swing
bavard, e adj talkative
bavarder vb [28] to chat
baver vb [28] to dribble
baveux (f **baveuse**) adj runny
bavure nf blunder
bazar nm general store; **Quel bazar!** (informal) What a mess!
BCBG adj (= bon chic bon genre) posh
BD (pl **BD**) nf (= bande dessinée) comic strip
béant, e adj gaping
beau (f **belle**, mpl **beaux**) adj, adv

▌ The masculine singular form **beau** changes to **bel** before a vowel and most words beginning with 'h'.

❶ lovely ❷ beautiful ❸ good-looking ❹ handsome; **Il fait beau aujourd'hui.** It's a nice day today.; **J'ai beau essayer, je n'y arrive pas.** However hard I try, I just can't do it.

beaucoup adv ❶ a lot ▷ Il boit beaucoup. He drinks a lot. ❷ much ▷ Elle n'a pas beaucoup d'argent. She hasn't got much money.; **beaucoup de** a lot of; **J'ai eu beaucoup de chance.** I was very lucky.
beau-fils (pl **beaux-fils**) nm ❶ son-in-law ❷ stepson
beau-frère (pl **beaux-frères**) nm brother-in-law
beau-père (pl **beaux-pères**) nm ❶ father-in-law ❷ stepfather
beauté nf beauty
beaux-arts nmpl fine arts
beaux-parents nmpl in-laws
bébé nm baby
bec nm beak
bécane nf (informal) bike
bêche nf spade
bêcher vb [28] to dig ▷ Il bêchait son jardin. He was digging the garden.
bégayer vb [59] to stammer
beige adj beige
beignet nm fritter
bel adj m see **beau**
belge adj, nmf Belgian; **un Belge** (man) a Belgian; **une Belge** (woman) a Belgian

Belgique *nf* Belgium; **en Belgique (1)** in Belgium **(2)** to Belgium
bélier *nm* ram; **le Bélier** Aries
belle *adj f see* **beau**
belle-famille (*pl* **belles-familles**) *nf* in-laws
belle-fille (*pl* **belles-filles**) *nf* ❶ daughter-in-law ❷ stepdaughter
belle-mère (*pl* **belles-mères**) *nf* ❶ mother-in-law ❷ stepmother
belle-sœur (*pl* **belles-sœurs**) *nf* sister-in-law
bénédiction *nf* blessing
bénéfice *nm* profit
bénévole *adj* voluntary ▷ *du travail bénévole* voluntary work
bénir *vb* [38] to bless
bénit, e *adj* consecrated; **l'eau bénite** holy water
béquille *nf* crutch
berceau (*pl* **berceaux**) *nm* cradle
bercer *vb* [12] to rock
berceuse *nf* lullaby
béret *nm* beret
berge *nf* (of river) bank
berger *nm* shepherd
bergère *nf* shepherdess
besoin *nm* need; **avoir besoin de quelque chose** to need something ▷ *J'ai besoin d'argent.* I need some money.; **une famille dans le besoin** a needy family
bétail *nm* livestock
bête *adj* stupid
▶ *nf* animal
bêtise *nf* **faire une bêtise** to do something stupid; **dire des bêtises** to talk nonsense

béton *nm* concrete; **un alibi en béton** a cast-iron alibi
betterave *nf* beetroot
beur *nmf* (informal)
- A **beur** is a young person of
- North African origin born in
- France.
beurre *nm* butter
beurrer *vb* [28] to butter
Beyrouth *n* Beirut
bibelot *nm* ornament
biberon *nm* baby's bottle
Bible *nf* Bible
bibliothécaire *nmf* librarian
bibliothèque *nf* ❶ library ❷ bookcase
bic® *nm* Biro®
biche *nf* doe
bicyclette *nf* bicycle
bidet *nm* bidet
bidon *nm* can
▶ *adj* (informal) phoney
bidonville *nm* shanty town
Biélorussie *nf* Belarus
bien *adj, adv* ❶ well ▷ *Daphne travaille bien.* Daphne works well. ▷ *Je ne me sens pas bien.* I don't feel well. ❷ good ▷ *Ce restaurant est vraiment bien.* This restaurant is really good. ❸ quite; **Je veux bien le faire.** I'm quite willing to do it.; **bien mieux** much better; **J'espère bien y aller.** I very much hope to go. ❹ right; **C'est bien fait pour lui!** It serves him right!
▶ *nm* ❶ good; **faire du bien à quelqu'un** to do somebody good ❷ possession
bien-être *nm* well-being

bienfaisance nf charity; **une œuvre de bienfaisance** a charity

bien que conj although

> **bien que** is followed by a verb in the subjunctive.
>
> ▷ Il fait assez chaud bien qu'il n'y ait pas de soleil. It's quite warm although there's no sun.

bien sûr adv of course

bientôt adv soon

bienvenu nm **Vous êtes le bienvenu!** You're welcome!

bienvenue nf welcome ▷ Bienvenue à Paris! Welcome to Paris!

bière nf beer; **la bière blonde** lager; **la bière brune** brown ale; **la bière pression** draught beer

bifteck nm steak

bigoudi nm (in hair) roller

bijou (pl **bijoux**) nm jewel

bijouterie nf jeweller's

bijoutier nm jeweller

bilan nm **faire le bilan de quelque chose** to assess something

bilingue adj bilingual

billard nm billiards; **le billard américain** pool

bille nf (toy) marble

billet nm ❶ ticket ▷ un billet d'avion a plane ticket ❷ banknote ▷ un billet de dix euros a 10 euro note

biodégradable adj biodegradable

biographie nf biography

biologie nf biology

biologique adj ❶ organic ❷ biological

bip nm beep; **bip sonore** tone

Birmanie nf Burma

bis adv ▷ Il habite au douze bis rue des Fleurs. He lives at 12A rue des Fleurs.

▶ nm encore

biscotte nf (sold in packets) toasted bread

biscuit nm biscuit; **un biscuit de Savoie** a sponge cake

bise nf (informal) kiss ▷ Grosses bises de Bretagne. Big kisses from Brittany.; **faire la bise à quelqu'un** to give somebody a peck on the cheek

- Between girls and boys, and between girls, the normal French way of saying hello and goodbye is with kisses, usually one on each cheek. Boys shake hands with each other instead.

bisou nm (informal) kiss

bissextile adj **une année bissextile** a leap year

bistrot nm (informal) café

- Cafés in France sell both alcoholic and non-alcoholic drinks.

bizarre adj strange

blague nf (informal) ❶ joke ▷ raconter une blague to tell a joke; **Sans blague!** No kidding! ❷ trick

blaguer vb [**28**] (informal) to joke

blaireau (pl **blaireaux**) nm ❶ badger ❷ shaving brush

blâmer vb [**28**] to blame

blanc (f **blanche**) adj ❶ white ❷ blank ▷ une page blanche a blank page

▶ nm ❶ white ❷ white wine; **un blanc d'œuf** an egg white; **un blanc de poulet** a chicken breast

blanche adj f see **blanc**
blanchisserie nf laundry
blé nm wheat
blessé, e adj injured
blessé nm injured person
blessée nf injured person
blesser vb [28] ❶ to injure ▷ Il a été
blessé dans un accident de voiture. He
was injured in a car accident. ❷ to
hurt ▷ Il a fait exprès de le blesser. He
hurt him on purpose.; **se blesser**
to hurt oneself
blessure nf injury
bleu, e adj ❶ blue; **bleu marine**
navy blue ❷ (steak) very rare
▶ nm ❶ blue ❷ bruise
bleuet nm cornflower
bloc nm pad; **le bloc opératoire** the
operating theatre
bloc-notes (pl **blocs-notes**) nm
note pad
blog nm blog
bloggeur nm blogger
bloguer vb [28] to blog
blond, e adj blond; **blond cendré**
ash blond
bloquer vb [28] to block ▷ bloquer le
passage to block the way; **être
bloqué dans un embouteillage** to
be stuck in a traffic jam
se **blottir** vb [38] to huddle
blouse nf overall
blouson nm jacket
bob nm cotton sunhat
bobine nf reel
bocal (pl **bocaux**) nm jar
bœuf nm ❶ ox ❷ beef
bof excl (informal) Le film t'a plu?
— Bof! C'était pas terrible! Did you

like the film? — Well ... it wasn't
that great!; **Comment ça va?
— Bof! Pas terrible.** How is it
going? — Oh ... not too well
actually.
bohémien nm gipsy
bohémienne nf gipsy
boire vb [10] to drink; **boire un
coup** (informal) to have a drink
bois nm wood; **en bois** wooden;
avoir la gueule de bois (informal)
to have a hangover
boisson nf drink
boîte nf ❶ box ▷ une boîte
d'allumettes a box of matches; **une
boîte aux lettres** a letter box; **une
boîte postale** a PO Box ❷ tin; **une
boîte de conserve** a tin; **en boîte**
tinned; **une boîte de nuit** a night
club; **sortir en boîte** to go
clubbing
boiter vb [28] to limp
bol nm bowl; **en avoir ras le bol**
(informal) to be fed up
bombarder vb [28] to bomb
bombe nf ❶ bomb ❷ aerosol
bon (f **bonne**) adj, adv ❶ good
▷ un bon restaurant a good
restaurant ▷ Le tabac n'est pas bon
pour la santé. Smoking isn't good
for you. ▷ être bon en maths to be
good at maths; **sentir bon** to
smell nice; **Bon anniversaire!**
Happy birthday!; **Bon courage!**
Good luck!; **Bon voyage!** Have a
good trip!; **Bon week-end!** Have a
nice weekend!; **Bonne chance!**
Good luck!; **Bonne journée!** Have
a nice day!; **Bonne nuit!** Good

night!; **Bonne année!** Happy New
Year!; **Bonnes vacances!** Have a
good holiday! ❷ right ▷ *Il est arrivé
au bon moment.* He arrived at the
right moment. ▷ *Ce n'est pas la
bonne réponse.* That's not the right
answer.; **Il fait bon aujourd'hui.**
It's nice today.; **de bonne heure**
early; **bon marché** cheap ▷ *Les
fraises ne sont pas bon marché en
hiver.* Strawberries aren't cheap in
winter.; **Ah bon?** Really? ▷ *Je pars
aux États-Unis la semaine prochaine.
— Ah bon?* I'm going to the States
next week. — Really?; **J'aimerais
vraiment que tu viennes! — Bon,
d'accord.** I'd really like you to
come! — OK then, I will.; **Est-ce
que ce yaourt est encore bon?** Is
this yoghurt still OK?
  ▶ *nm* voucher ▷ *un bon d'achat* a
voucher; **pour de bon (1)** for good
▷ *Il est parti pour de bon.* He's gone
for good. **(2)** for real ▷ *Cette fois, on
le fait pour de bon.* Let's do it for real
this time.

bonbon *nm* sweet
bondé, e *adj* crowded
bondir *vb* [38] to leap
bonheur *nm* happiness; **porter
bonheur** to bring luck
bonhomme (*pl* **bonshommes**)
nm **un bonhomme de neige** a
snowman
bonjour *excl* ❶ hello! ▷ *Donne le
bonjour à tes parents de ma part.* Say
hello to your parents for me.
❷ good morning! ❸ good
afternoon!

bonjour is used in the morning
and afternoon; in the evening
bonsoir is used instead.
C'est simple comme bonjour! It's
easy as pie!
bonne *adj f see* **bon**
bonnet *nm* hat; **un bonnet de
bain** a bathing cap
bonsoir *excl* good evening!
bonté *nf* kindness
bord *nm* ❶ edge ❷ side; **au bord de
la mer** at the seaside; **au bord de
l'eau** by the water; **monter à bord**
to go on board; **être au bord des
larmes** to be on the verge of tears
bordeaux *nm* Bordeaux wine; **du
bordeaux rouge** claret
  ▶ *adj* burgundy
border *vb* [28] ❶ to line ▷ *une route
bordée d'arbres* a tree-lined street
❷ to trim ▷ *un col bordé de dentelle* a
collar trimmed with lace ❸ to tuck
up ▷ *Sa mère vient la border tous les
soirs.* Her mother comes and tucks
her up every night.
bordure *nf* border; **une villa en
bordure de mer** a villa right by the
sea
borne *nf* (*of computer*) terminal
Bosnie *nf* Bosnia; **la Bosnie-
Herzégovine** Bosnia-Herzegovina
bosse *nf* bump
bosser *vb* [28] (*informal*) to work;
bosser un examen to study for an
exam
bossu *nm* hunchback
botanique *adj* botanic
  ▶ *nf* botany
botte *nf* ❶ boot ▷ *une paire de bottes*

a pair of boots; **les bottes en caoutchouc** Wellington boots ❷ bunch ▷ *une botte de radis* a bunch of radishes

bottin® *nm* phone book

bouc *nm* ❶ goatee beard ❷ billy goat; **un bouc émissaire** a scapegoat

bouche *nf* mouth; **le bouche à bouche** the kiss of life; **une bouche d'égout** a manhole; **une bouche de métro** an entrance to the underground

bouchée *nf* mouthful; **une bouchée à la reine** a chicken vol-au-vent

boucher *vb* [28] ❶ to fill ▷ *boucher un trou* to fill a hole ❷ to block ▷ *L'évier est bouché.* The sink is blocked. ▷ *J'ai le nez bouché.* My nose is blocked.
▶ *nm* butcher

bouchère *nf* butcher

boucherie *nf* butcher's

bouchon *nm* ❶ (of plastic bottle) top ❷ (of wine bottle) cork ❸ hold-up

boucle *nf* (of hair) curl; **une boucle d'oreille** an earring

bouclé, e *adj* curly

bouclier *nm* shield

bouddhiste *nmf* Buddhist

bouder *vb* [28] to sulk

boudin *nm* **le boudin noir** black pudding; **le boudin blanc** white pudding

boue *nf* mud

bouée *nf* buoy; **une bouée de sauvetage** a life buoy

boueux (*f* **boueuse**) *adj* muddy

bouffe *nf* (informal) food

bouffée *nf* **une bouffée d'air frais** a breath of fresh air

bouffer *vb* [28] (informal) to eat

bougeoir *nm* candlestick

bouger *vb* [45] to move

bougie *nf* candle

bouillabaisse *nf* fish soup

bouillant, e *adj* ❶ boiling ❷ piping hot

bouillir *vb* [11] to boil ▷ *L'eau bout.* The water's boiling.; **Je bous d'impatience.** I'm bursting with impatience.

bouilloire *nf* kettle

bouillon *nm* stock

bouillotte *nf* hot-water bottle

boulanger *nm* baker

boulangère *nf* baker

boulangerie *nf* baker's

boule *nf* ball; **une boule de neige** a snowball; **jouer aux boules** to play bowls

boulevard *nm* boulevard

bouleverser *vb* [28] ❶ to move deeply ❷ to shatter ▷ *La mort de son ami l'a bouleversé.* He was shattered by the death of his friend. ❸ to turn upside down ▷ *Cette rencontre a bouleversé sa vie.* This meeting turned his life upside down.

boulot *nm* (informal) ❶ job ❷ work

boum *nf* (informal) party

bouquet *nm* bunch of flowers

bouquin *nm* (informal) book

bouquiner *vb* [28] (informal) to read

bourdonner *vb* [28] to buzz

bourg *nm* small market town

a
b
c
d
e
f
g
h
i
j
k
l
m
n
o
p
q
r
s
t
u
v
w
x
y
z

bourgeois, e *adj* middle-class
bourgeon *nm* bud
Bourgogne *nf* Burgundy
bourré, e *adj* **bourré de** stuffed
with; **être bourré** *(informal)* to be
plastered
bourreau *(pl* **bourreaux)** *nm*
executioner; **C'est un véritable
bourreau de travail.** He's a real
workaholic.
bourrer *vb* [28] to stuff
bourse *nf* grant; **la Bourse** the
Stock Exchange
bous *vb see* **bouillir**
bousculade *nf* crush
bousculer *vb* [28] ❶ to jostle
▷ *être bousculé par la foule* to be
jostled by the crowd ❷ to rush
▷ *Je n'aime pas qu'on me bouscule.*
I don't like to be rushed.
boussole *nf* compass
bout *vb see* **bouillir**
▶ *nm* ❶ end ▷ *Elle habite au bout
de la rue.* She lives at the end of the
street. ❷ tip ▷ *le bout du nez* the tip
of the nose ❸ bit; **un bout de
papier** a scrap of paper; **au bout
de** after; **Elle est à bout.** She's at
the end of her tether.
bouteille *nf* bottle; **une bouteille
de gaz** a gas cylinder
boutique *nf* shop
bouton *nm* ❶ button ❷ *(on skin)*
spot ❸ bud; **un bouton d'or** a
buttercup
bowling *nm* ❶ tenpin bowling
❷ bowling alley
boxe *nf* boxing
boxeur *nm* boxer

bracelet *nm* bracelet
bracelet-montre *(pl*
bracelets-montres) *nm*
wristwatch
brancard *nm* stretcher
brancardier *nm* stretcher-bearer
branche *nf* branch
branché, e *adj (informal)* trendy
brancher *vb* [28] ❶ to connect
▷ *Le téléphone est branché?* Is the
phone connected? ❷ to plug in
▷ *L'aspirateur n'est pas branché.*
The hoover isn't plugged in.
bras *nm* arm
brasse *nf* breaststroke
brasserie *nf* café-restaurant
brave *adj* nice
bravo *excl* bravo!
break *nm* estate car
brebis *nf* ewe; **le fromage de
brebis** sheep's cheese
bref *(f* **brève)** *adj, adv* short; **en bref**
in brief; **... bref, ça s'est bien
terminé.** ... to cut a long story
short, it turned out all right in the
end.
Brésil *nm* Brazil
Bretagne *nf* Brittany
bretelle *nf* strap; **les bretelles**
braces
breton *(f* **bretonne)** *adj, nm/f*
Breton ▷ *Ils parlent breton.*
They speak Breton.; **un Breton**
(man) a Breton; **une Bretonne**
(woman) a Breton; **les Bretons**
the Bretons
brève *adj f see* **bref**
brevet *nm* certificate
brevet des collèges *nm*

The **brevet des collèges** is an exam you take at the end of **collège**, at the age of 15.

bricolage nm do-it-yourself

bricole nf (informal) J'ai acheté une bricole pour le bébé de Sabine. I've bought a little something for Sabine's baby.; J'ai encore quelques bricoles à faire avant de partir. I've still got a few things to do before I go.

bricoler vb [28] to do DIY ▷ Pascal aime bricoler. Pascal loves doing DIY.

bricoleur nm DIY enthusiast

bricoleuse nf DIY enthusiast

bridge nm (game) bridge

brièvement adv briefly

brigade nf (of police) squad

brillamment adv brilliantly

brillant, e adj ❶ brilliant ❷ shiny

briller vb [28] to shine

brin nm un brin d'herbe a blade of grass; un brin de muguet a sprig of lily of the valley

brindille nf twig

brioche nf brioche bun

brique nf brick

briquet nm cigarette lighter

brise nf breeze

se **briser** vb [28] to break ▷ Le vase s'est brisé en mille morceaux. The vase broke into a thousand pieces.

Britannique nmf Briton; les Britanniques the British

britannique adj British

brocante nf junk

brocanteur nm dealer in second-hand goods

broche nf brooch; à la broche spit-roasted

brochette nf skewer; les brochettes d'agneau lamb kebabs

brochure nf brochure

broder vb [28] to embroider

broderie nf embroidery

bronchite nf bronchitis

bronze nm bronze

bronzer vb [28] to get a tan ▷ Il est bien bronzé. He's got a good tan.; se bronzer to sunbathe

brosse nf brush; une brosse à cheveux a hairbrush; une brosse à dents a toothbrush; Il est coiffé en brosse. He's got a crew cut.

brosser vb [28] to brush; se brosser les dents to brush one's teeth ▷ Je me brosse les dents tous les soirs. I brush my teeth every night.

brouette nf wheelbarrow

brouillard nm fog

brouillon nm first draft

broussailles nfpl undergrowth sg

brouter vb [28] (animals) to graze

broyer vb [53] to crush; broyer du noir to be down in the dumps

brugnon nm nectarine

bruit nm ❶ noise ▷ faire du bruit to make a noise; sans bruit without a sound ❷ rumour

brûlant, e adj ❶ blazing ❷ boiling hot

brûlé nm smell of burning

brûler vb [28] to burn; se brûler to burn oneself

brûlure nf burn; des brûlures d'estomac heartburn

brume nf mist

a
b
c
d
e
f
g
h
i
j
k
l
m
n
o
p
q
r
s
t
u
v
w
x
y
z

brumeux (f **brumeuse**) adj misty
brun, e adj brown; **Elle est brune.**
　She's got dark hair.
brushing nm blow-dry
brusque adj abrupt; **d'un ton**
　brusque brusquely
brusquer vb [**28**] to rush
brut, e adj **le champagne brut** dry
　champagne; **le pétrole brut** crude
　oil; **son salaire brut** his gross
　salary
brutal, e (mpl **brutaux**) adj brutal
brutaliser vb [**28**] to knock about
　▷ Il a été brutalisé par la police. He
　was treated roughly by the police.
Bruxelles n Brussels
bruyamment adv noisily
bruyant, e adj noisy
bruyère nf heather
bu vb see **boire**
bûche nf log; **la bûche de Noël** the
　Yule log
　● **la bûche de Noël** is what is
　　usually eaten in France instead
　● of Christmas pudding.
bûcheron nm woodcutter
budget nm budget
buffet nm ❶ sideboard ❷ buffet
　▷ un buffet de gare a station buffet
buisson nm bush
Bulgarie nf Bulgaria
bulle nf bubble
bulletin nm ❶ bulletin; **le bulletin**
　d'informations the news bulletin
　❷ report; **le bulletin**
　météorologique the weather
　report; **un bulletin de salaire** a
　pay slip; **un bulletin de vote** a
　ballot paper

bureau (pl **bureaux**) nm ❶ desk
　❷ office; **un bureau de change** a
　bureau de change; **le bureau de**
　poste the post office; **le bureau de**
　tabac the tobacconist's; **le bureau**
　de vote the polling station
bus vb see **boire**
　▶ nm bus
buste nm bust
but vb see **boire**
　▶ nm ❶ aim; **Quel est le but de**
　votre visite? What's the reason for
　your visit?; **dans le but de** with the
　intention of ❷ goal ▷ marquer un
　but to score a goal
butane nm Calor gas®
butin nm loot
buvais, buvait vb see **boire**
buvard nm blotter

C

c' *pron see* **ce**

ça *pron* ❶ this ▷ *Est-ce que vous pouvez me donner un peu de ça?* Can you give me a bit of this? ❷ that ▷ *Regarde ça là-bas.* Look at that over there. ❸ it ▷ *Ça ne fait rien.* It doesn't matter.; **Comment ça va?** How are you?; **Ça alors!** Well, well!; **C'est ça.** That's right.; **Ça y est!** That's it!

çà *adv* çà et là here and there

cabane *nf* hut

cabillaud *nm* cod

cabine *nf (on a ship)* cabin; **une cabine d'essayage** a fitting room; **une cabine téléphonique** a phone box

cabinet *nm (of doctor, dentist)* surgery; **une chambre avec cabinet de toilette** a room with washing facilities

cabinets *nmpl* toilet *sg*

câble *nm* cable; **la télévision par câble** cable television

cabosser *vb* [28] to dent

cacahuète *nf* peanut; **le beurre de cacahuète** peanut butter

cacao *nm* cocoa; **le beurre de cacao** cocoa butter

cache-cache *nm* jouer à cache-cache to play hide-and-seek

cachemire *nm* cashmere

cache-nez *(pl* **cache-nez***)* *nm* long woollen scarf

cacher *vb* [28] to hide ▷ *J'ai caché les cadeaux sous le lit.* I hid the presents under the bed.; **se cacher** to hide

cachet *nm* ❶ tablet; **un cachet d'aspirine** an aspirin ❷ *(for performer)* fee; **le cachet de la poste** the postmark

cachette *nf* hiding place; **en cachette** on the sly

cachot *nm* dungeon

cactus *nm* cactus

cadavre *nm* corpse

Caddie® *nm* supermarket trolley

cadeau *(pl* **cadeaux***)* *nm* present ▷ *un cadeau d'anniversaire* a birthday present ▷ *un cadeau de Noël* a Christmas present; **faire un cadeau à quelqu'un** to give somebody a present

cadenas *nm* padlock

cadet *(f* **cadette***)* *adj* ❶ *(brother, sister)* younger ❷ *(son, daughter)* youngest

cadet *nm* youngest ▷ *C'est le cadet*

de la famille. He's the youngest of the family.

cadette *nf* youngest

cadre *nm* ❶ frame ❷ surroundings ❸ executive ▷ *un cadre supérieur* a senior executive

cafard *nm* cockroach; **avoir le cafard** *(informal)* to be feeling down

café *nm* ❶ coffee ▷ *un café au lait* a white coffee ▷ *un café crème* a strong white coffee ❷ café
   Cafés in France sell both alcoholic and non-alcoholic drinks.

café-tabac *(pl* **cafés-tabacs***) nm*
   A **café-tabac** is a bar which also sells cigarettes and stamps; you can tell a **café-tabac** by the red diamond-shaped sign outside it.

cafétéria *nf* cafeteria

cafetière *nf* ❶ coffee maker ❷ coffeepot

cage *nf* cage; **la cage d'escalier** the stairwell

cagoule *nf* balaclava

cahier *nm* exercise book

caille *nf* quail

caillou *(pl* **cailloux***) nm* pebble

caisse *nf* ❶ box ❷ till ▷ *le ticket de caisse* the till receipt ❸ checkout

caissier *nm* cashier

cake *nm* fruit cake

calcul *nm* ❶ calculation ❷ arithmetic

calculatrice *nf* calculator

calculer *vb* [28] to work out ▷ *J'ai calculé combien ça allait coûter.* I worked out how much it was going to cost.

calculette *nf* pocket calculator

cale *nf* wedge

calé, e *adj (informal)*; **Elle est calée en histoire.** She's really good at history.

caleçon *nm* ❶ boxer shorts ❷ leggings

calendrier *nm* calendar

calepin *nm* notebook

caler *vb* [28] to stall

câlin, e *adj* cuddly
   ▶ *nm* cuddle

calmant *nm* tranquillizer

calme *adj* ❶ quiet ❷ calm
   ▶ *nm* peace and quiet

calmer *vb* [28] to soothe; **se calmer** to calm down ▷ *Calme-toi!* Calm down!

calorie *nf* calorie

camarade *nmf* friend; **un camarade de classe** a school friend

cambriolage *nm* burglary

cambrioler *vb* [28] to burgle

cambrioleur *nm* burglar

camelote *nf (informal)* junk

caméra *nf (cinema, TV)* camera; **une caméra numérique** a digital camera

caméscope® *nm* camcorder

camion *nm* lorry

camionnette *nf* van

camionneur *nm* lorry driver

camomille *nf* camomile tea

camp *nm* camp

campagne *nf* ❶ country; **à la campagne** in the country ❷ campaign

camper *vb* [28] to camp

campeur nm camper
campeuse nf camper
camping nm camping ▷ faire du camping to go camping; **un (terrain de) camping** a campsite
Canada nm Canada; **au Canada (1)** in Canada **(2)** to Canada
canadien (f **canadienne**) adj, nm/f Canadian; **un Canadien** (man) a Canadian; **une Canadienne** (woman) a Canadian
canal (pl **canaux**) nm canal
canapé nm ❶ sofa ❷ open sandwich
canard nm duck
canari nm canary
cancer nm cancer; **le Cancer** Cancer
candidat nm ❶ (in exam, election) candidate ❷ (for job) applicant
candidature nf poser sa candidature à un poste to apply for a job
caneton nm duckling
canette nf une canette de bière a small bottle of beer
caniche nm poodle
canicule nf scorching heat
canif nm penknife
caniveau (pl **caniveaux**) nm gutter
canne nf walking stick; **une canne à pêche** a fishing rod
cannelle nf cinnamon
canoë nm ❶ canoe ❷ canoeing
canon nm ❶ gun ❷ cannon
canot nm dinghy; **un canot de sauvetage** a lifeboat
cantatrice nf opera singer

cantine nf canteen
caoutchouc nm rubber; **des bottes en caoutchouc** Wellington boots
cap nm (land) cape
capable adj Elle est capable de marcher pendant des heures. She can walk for hours.; **Il est capable de changer d'avis au dernier moment.** He's capable of changing his mind at the last minute.
cape nf (garment) cape
capitaine nm captain
capitale nf capital
capot nm (of car) bonnet
capote nf (informal) condom
câpre nf (food) caper
caprice nm faire des caprices to make a fuss
capricieux (f **capricieuse**) adj un enfant capricieux an awkward child
Capricorne nm Capricorn
captivant, e adj fascinating
captivité nf captivity
capturer vb [28] to capture
capuche nf hood
capuchon nm (of pen) cap
capucine nf nasturtium
car nm coach ▷ un car scolaire a school bus
▶ conj because ▷ Réfléchis bien car c'est important. Think carefully because it's important.
carabine nf rifle
caractère nm personality; **Il a bon caractère.** He's good-natured.; **Elle a mauvais caractère.** She's

a b c d e f g h i j k l m n o p q r s t u v w x y z

bad-tempered.; **Il n'a pas un caractère facile.** He isn't easy to get on with.

caractéristique adj characteristic
▶ nf characteristic

carafe nf jug

Caraïbes nfpl Caribbean Islands

caramel nm ❶ caramel ❷ toffee

caravane nf caravan

carbonique adj **le gaz carbonique** carbon dioxide

carburant nm fuel

cardiaque adj **une crise cardiaque** a heart attack; **Ma tante est cardiaque.** My aunt has heart trouble.

cardigan nm cardigan

cardiologue nmf heart specialist

carême nm Lent

caresse nf stroke

caresser vb [28] to stroke

carie nf tooth decay

caritatif (f **caritative**) adj **une organisation caritative** a charity

carnaval nm carnival

carnet nm ❶ notebook ❷ book
▷ un carnet d'adresses an address book ▷ un carnet de chèques a cheque book ▷ un carnet de timbres a book of stamps ▷ un carnet de tickets a book of tickets
● In the Paris metro it is cheaper to buy tickets in a book of ten, known as a **carnet**.
mon carnet de notes my school report

carotte nf carrot

carré, e adj square; **un mètre carré** a square metre

▶ nm square

carreau (pl **carreaux**) nm ❶ check ❷ (on floor, wall) tile ❸ pane ❹ (cards) diamonds

carrefour nm junction

carrelage nm tiled floor

carrément adv ❶ completely ❷ straight out

carrière nf career; **un militaire de carrière** a professional soldier

carrure nf build

cartable nm satchel

carte nf ❶ card; **une carte d'anniversaire** a birthday card; **une carte postale** a postcard; **une carte de vœux** a Christmas card
● The French send greetings cards (**les cartes de vœux**) in January rather than at Christmas, with best wishes for the New Year.
une carte de vœux électronique an e-card; **une carte bancaire** a cash card; **une carte bleue**
● **Carte bleue** is a major French debit card.
une carte de crédit a credit card; **une carte de fidélité** a loyalty card; **une carte d'embarquement** a boarding card; **une carte d'identité** an identity card; **une carte de séjour** a residence permit; **une carte téléphonique** a phonecard; **un jeu de cartes (1)** a pack of cards **(2)** a card game ❷ map ▷ une carte de France a map of France ▷ une carte routière a road map ❸ menu ▷ la carte des vins the wine list; **manger à la carte** to eat à la carte ▷ Nous allons manger à la

carte. We'll choose from the à la carte menu.

carton *nm* ❶ cardboard ❷ cardboard box

cartouche *nf* cartridge

cas (*pl* **cas**) *nm* case; **ne faire aucun cas de** to take no notice of; **en aucun cas** on no account; **en tout cas** at any rate; **au cas où** in case; **en cas de** in case of

cascade *nf* waterfall

cascadeur *nm* stuntman

case *nf* ❶ (*in board game*) square ❷ (*on form*) box

caserne *nf* barracks

cash *adv* **payer cash** to pay cash

casier *nm* locker

casque *nm* ❶ helmet ❷ headphones

casquette *nf* cap

cassant, e *adj* **Il m'a parlé d'un ton cassant.** He spoke to me curtly.

casse-croûte (*pl* **casse-croûte**) *nm* snack

casse-noix (*pl* **casse-noix**) *nm* nutcrackers

casse-pieds *adj* (*informal*) **Il est vraiment casse-pieds!** He's a real pain in the neck!

casser *vb* [**28**] to break ▷ *J'ai cassé un verre.* I've broken a glass.; **se casser** to break ▷ *Il s'est cassé la jambe au ski.* He broke his leg when he was skiing.; **se casser la tête** (*informal*) to go to a lot of trouble

casserole *nf* saucepan

casse-tête (*pl* **casse-tête**) *nm* **C'est un vrai casse-tête!** It's a real headache!

cassette *nf* cassette

cassis *nm* blackcurrant

castor *nm* beaver

catalogue *nm* catalogue

catastrophe *nf* disaster

catch *nm* wrestling

catéchisme *nm* catechism

catégorie *nf* category

catégorique *adj* firm

cathédrale *nf* cathedral

catholique *adj* Catholic
▶ *nmf* Catholic

cauchemar *nm* nightmare

cause *nf* cause; **à cause de** because of

causer *vb* [**28**] ❶ to cause ▷ *La tempête a causé beaucoup de dégâts.* The storm caused a lot of damage. ❷ to chat

caution *nf* ❶ bail ❷ deposit

cavalier *nm* ❶ rider ❷ (*at dance*) partner

cavalière *nf* rider

cave *nf* cellar

caverne *nf* cave

CD (*pl* **CD**) *nm* CD

CDD *nm* (= *contrat de durée déterminée*) temporary contract

CDI *nm* (= *contrat de durée indéterminée*) permanent contract

ce (*f* **cette**, *pl* **ces**) *adj*

▮ The masculine singular form **ce** changes to **cet** before a vowel and most words beginning with 'h'.

❶ this ▷ *Tu peux prendre ce livre.* You can take this book. ▷ *cet après-midi* this afternoon ▷ *cet hiver* this winter; **ce livre-ci** this book; **cette voiture-ci** this car ❷ that ▷ *Je n'aime pas du tout ce film.* I don't like that film at all.; **ce livre-là** that book; **cette voiture-là** that car ▶ *pron*

▌ **ce** changes to **c'** before the vowel in **est**, **était** and **étaient**.

it ▷ *Ce n'est pas facile.* It's not easy.; **c'est** (1) it is ▷ *C'est vraiment trop cher.* It's really too expensive. ▷ *Ouvre, c'est moi!* Open the door, it's me! (2) he is ▷ *C'est un peintre du début du siècle.* He's a painter from the turn of the century. (3) she is ▷ *C'est une actrice très célèbre.* She's a very famous actress.; **ce sont** they are ▷ *Ce sont des amis de mes parents.* They're friends of my parents'.; **Qui est-ce?** Who is it?; **Qu'est-ce que c'est?** What is it?; **ce qui** what ▷ *C'est ce qui compte.* That's what matters.; **tout ce qui** everything that ▷ *J'ai rangé tout ce qui traînait par terre.* I've tidied up everything that was on the floor.; **ce que** what ▷ *Je vais lui dire ce que je pense.* I'm going to tell him what I think.; **tout ce que** everything ▷ *Tu peux avoir tout ce que tu veux.* You can have everything you want.

ceci *pron* this ▷ *Prends ceci, tu en auras besoin.* Take this, you'll need it.

céder *vb* [**34**] to give in ▷ *Elle a tellement insisté qu'il a fini par céder.* She went on so much that he eventually gave in.; **céder à** to give in to

cédérom *nm* CD-ROM
cédille *nf* cedilla
ceinture *nf* belt; **une ceinture de sauvetage** a lifebelt; **votre ceinture de sécurité** your seatbelt
cela *pron* ❶ it ▷ *Cela dépend.* It depends. ❷ that ▷ *Je n'aime pas cela.* I don't like that.; **C'est cela.** That's right.; **à part cela** apart from that
célèbre *adj* famous
célébrer *vb* [**34**] to celebrate
céleri *nm* le céleri-rave celeriac; **le céleri (en branche)** celery
célibataire *adj* single
célibataire *nmf* single person; **un célibataire** a bachelor; **une célibataire** a single woman
celle *pron* see **celui**
celles *pron* see **ceux**
cellule *nf* cell
celui (*f* celle, *mpl* ceux, *fpl* celles) *pron* the one ▷ *Prends celui que tu préfères.* Take the one you like best. ▷ *Je n'ai pas d'appareil photo mais je peux emprunter celui de ma sœur.* I haven't got a camera but I can borrow my sister's. ▷ *Je n'ai pas de webcam mais je peux emprunter celle de mon frère.* I haven't got a webcam but I can borrow my brother's.; **celui-ci** this one; **celle-ci** this one; **celui-là** that one; **celle-là** that one
cendre *nf* ash
cendrier *nm* ashtray
censé, e *adj* être censé faire quelque chose to be supposed to do something ▷ *Vous êtes censé arriver à l'heure.* You're supposed to get here on time.

cent *num* a hundred ▷ *cent euros* a hundred euros

> **cent** is spelt with an **-s** when there are two or more hundreds, but not when it is followed by another number, as in 'four hundred and two'.

▷ *trois cents ans* three hundred years ▷ *trois cent cinquante kilomètres* three hundred and fifty kilometres

▶ *nm* (currency) cent

centaine *nf* about a hundred; **des centaines de** hundreds of

centenaire *nm* centenary

centième *adj* hundredth

centilitre *nm* centilitre

centime *nm* ❶ (one hundredth of a euro) cent

> The euro is divided into 100 **centimes**.

❷ (one hundredth of a franc) centime

centimètre *nm* centimetre

central, e (*mpl* **centraux**) *adj* central

centrale *nf* power station

centre *nm* centre; **un centre commercial** a shopping centre; **un centre d'appels** a call centre

centre-ville (*pl* **centres-villes**) *nm* town centre

cependant *adv* however

cercle *nm* circle; **un cercle vicieux** a vicious circle

cercueil *nm* coffin

céréale *nf* cereal; **un pain aux cinq céréales** a multigrain loaf

cérémonie *nf* ceremony

cerf *nm* stag

cerf-volant (*pl* **cerfs-volants**) *nm* kite

cerise *nf* cherry

cerisier *nm* cherry tree

cerné, e *adj* **avoir les yeux cernés** to have shadows under one's eyes

cerner *vb* [28] **J'ai du mal à le cerner.** I can't figure him out.

certain, e *adj* ❶ certain ❷ some; **un certain temps** quite some time

certainement *adv* ❶ definitely ❷ of course

certains (*f* **certaines**) *pron pl* ❶ some ▷ *certains d'entre vous* some of you ▷ *certaines de ses amies* some of his friends ❷ some people ▷ *Certains pensent que le film est meilleur que le roman.* Some people think that the film is better than the novel.

certes *adv* certainly

certificat *nm* certificate

cerveau (*pl* **cerveaux**) *nm* brain

cervelle *nf* brain; **se creuser la cervelle** (*informal*) to rack one's brains

CES *nm* (= *collège d'enseignement secondaire*) secondary school

ces *adj pl* ❶ these; **ces photos-ci** these photos ❷ those; **ces livres-là** those books

cesse: **sans cesse** *adv* continually ▷ *Elle me dérange sans cesse.* She continually interrupts me.

cesser *vb* [28] to stop ▷ *cesser de faire quelque chose* to stop doing something

cessez-le-feu (*pl* **cessez-le-feu**) *nm* ceasefire

c'est-à-dire *adv* that is

cet *adj see* **ce**

a
b
c
d
e
f
g
h
i
j
k
l
m
n
o
p
q
r
s
t
u
v
w
x
y
z

cette adj see **ce**

ceux (fpl **celles**) pron pl the ones
▷ Prends ceux que tu préfères. Take
the ones you like best.; **ceux-ci**
these ones; **celles-ci** these ones;
ceux-là those ones; **celles-là**
those ones

chacun (f **chacune**) pron ❶ each
▷ Il nous a donné un cadeau à chacun.
He gave us each a present. ▷ Nous
avons chacune donné dix euros. We
each gave 10 euros. ❷ everyone
▷ Chacun fait ce qu'il veut. Everyone
does what they like.

chagrin nm avoir du chagrin to be
very upset

chahut nm bedlam

chaîne nf ❶ chain ▷ une chaîne en or
a gold chain ❷ (on TV) channel ▷ Le
film passe sur quelle chaîne? Which
channel is the film on?; **une chaîne
hi-fi** a hi-fi system; **une chaîne
stéréo** a music centre; **travailler à
la chaîne** to work on an assembly
line

chair nf flesh; **en chair et en os** in
the flesh; **avoir la chair de poule**
to have goose pimples

chaise nf chair; **une chaise longue**
a deckchair

châle nm shawl

chaleur nf ❶ heat ❷ warmth

chaleureux (f **chaleureuse**) adj
warm

se **chamailler** vb [**28**] (informal) to
squabble ▷ Elle se chamaille sans
cesse avec son frère. She's always
squabbling with her brother.

chambre nf room; **une chambre à**

coucher a bedroom; **une
chambre d'amis** a spare room;
une chambre à un lit a single
room; **une chambre pour une
personne** a single room; **une
chambre pour deux personnes** a
double room; **'Chambres d'hôte'**
'Bed and Breakfast'

chameau (pl **chameaux**) nm
camel

champ nm field

champagne nm champagne

champignon nm mushroom; **un
champignon de Paris** a button
mushroom

champion nm champion

championnat nm championship

chance nf ❶ luck; **Bonne chance!**
Good luck!; **par chance** luckily;
avoir de la chance to be lucky
❷ chance

change nm exchange

changement nm change

changer vb [**45**] to change ▷ Il n'a
pas beaucoup changé. He hasn't
changed much.; **se changer** to get
changed; **changer de** to change
▷ Je change de chaussures et j'arrive!
I'll change my shoes and then I'll be
ready!; **changer d'avis** to change
one's mind ▷ Appelle-moi si tu
changes d'avis. Give me a ring if you
change your mind.; **changer de
chaîne** to change the channel

chanson nf song

chant nm singing; **un chant de
Noël** a Christmas carol

chantage nm blackmail

chanter vb [**28**] to sing

chanteur nm singer
chanteuse nf singer
chantier nm building site
chantonner vb [28] to hum
chapeau (pl **chapeaux**) nm hat
chapelle nf chapel
chapitre nm chapter
chaque adj ① every ② each
char nm (military) tank
charabia nm (informal) gibberish
charade nf ① riddle ② charade
charbon nm coal; **le charbon de bois** charcoal
charcuterie nf ① pork butcher's
  ● A **charcuterie** sells cuts of pork
  ● and pork products such as
  ● sausages, salami and pâté, as
  ● well as various cooked dishes
  ● and salads.
  ② cold meats
charcutier nm pork butcher
chardon nm thistle
charger vb [45] to load; **charger quelqu'un de faire quelque chose** to tell somebody to do something
chariot nm (at supermarket) trolley
charmant, e adj charming
charme nm charm
charmer vb [28] to charm
charrue nf plough
chasse nf ① hunting ② shooting; **tirer la chasse d'eau** to flush the toilet
chasse-neige (pl **chasse-neige**) nm snowplough
chasser vb [28] ① to hunt ▷ *Mon père chasse le lapin.* My father hunts rabbits. ② to chase away ▷ *Ils ont chassé les cambrioleurs.* They chased

away the robbers. ③ to get rid of
chasseur nm hunter
chat nm ① cat ② chat
châtaigne nf chestnut
châtaignier nm chestnut tree
châtain adj brown
château (pl **châteaux**) nm ① castle; **un château fort** a castle ② palace
chaton nm kitten
chatouiller vb [28] to tickle
chatouilleux (f **chatouilleuse**) adj ticklish
chatte nf (female) cat
chatter vb [28] (on the internet) to chat
chaud, e adj ① warm; **avoir chaud** to be warm ② hot ▷ *Il fait chaud aujourd'hui.* It's hot today.
chauffage nm heating; **le chauffage central** central heating
chauffe-eau (pl **chauffe-eau**) nm water heater
chauffer vb [28] to heat ▷ *Je vais mettre de l'eau à chauffer pour faire du thé.* I'm going to heat some water to make tea.
chauffeur nm driver
chaume nm **un toit de chaume** a thatched roof
chaussée nf road surface
chausser vb [28] **Vous chaussez du combien?** What size shoe do you take?
chaussette nf sock
chausson nm slipper; **un chausson aux pommes** an apple turnover
chaussure nf shoe; **les**

chaussures de ski ski boots
chauve adj bald
chauve-souris (pl **chauves-souris**) nf (animal) bat

> Word for word, this means 'bald mouse'.

chef nm ❶ head; **le chef de l'État** the Head of State ❷ boss; **un chef d'entreprise** a company director ❸ chef; **un chef d'orchestre** a conductor
chef-d'œuvre (pl **chefs-d'œuvre**) nm masterpiece
chemin nm ❶ path ❷ way; **en chemin** on the way; **le chemin de fer** the railway
cheminée nf ❶ chimney ❷ fireplace
chemise nf ❶ shirt; **une chemise de nuit** a nightdress ❷ folder
chemisier nm blouse
chêne nm oak
chenil nm kennels
chenille nf caterpillar
chèque nm cheque; **les chèques de voyage** traveller's cheques
chéquier nm cheque book
cher (f **chère**) adj, adv ❶ dear
> Chère Mélusine ... Dear Mélusine ... ❷ expensive ▷ C'est trop cher. It's too expensive. ▷ coûter cher to be expensive
chercher vb [28] ❶ to look for ▷ Je cherche mes clés. I'm looking for my keys. ❷ to look up ▷ chercher un mot dans le dictionnaire to look up a word in the dictionary; **aller chercher** (1) to go to get ▷ Elle est allée chercher du pain. She's gone to

get some bread. (2) to pick up ▷ J'irai te chercher à la gare. I'll pick you up at the station.
chercheur nm scientist
chercheuse nf scientist
chère adj f see **cher**
chéri, e adj darling ▷ ma petite fille chérie my darling daughter
chéri nm darling; **mon chéri** darling
chérie nf darling
cheval (pl **chevaux**) nm horse; **un cheval de course** a racehorse; **à cheval** on horseback; **faire du cheval** to go riding
chevalier nm knight
chevalière nf signet ring
chevalin, e adj **une boucherie chevaline** a horsemeat butcher's
chevaux nmpl see **cheval**
chevet nm **une table de chevet** a bedside table; **une lampe de chevet** a bedside lamp
cheveux nmpl hair sg ▷ Elle a les cheveux courts. She's got short hair.
cheville nf ankle
chèvre nf goat; **le fromage de chèvre** goat's cheese
chevreau (pl **chevreaux**) nm (animal, leather) kid
chèvrefeuille nm honeysuckle
chevreuil nm ❶ roe deer ❷ venison
chewing-gum nm chewing gum
chez prep **chez Pierre** (1) at Pierre's house (2) to Pierre's house; **chez moi** (1) at my house ▷ Mes amis sont restés chez moi. My friends stayed at my house. (2) to my house ▷ Allons chez moi. Let's go to my house.; **je**

rentre chez moi. I'm going home.; **chez le dentiste (1)** at the dentist's ▷ *J'ai rendez-vous chez le dentiste demain matin.* I've got an appointment at the dentist's tomorrow morning. **(2)** to the dentist's ▷ *Je vais chez le dentiste.* I'm going to the dentist's.

chic *adj* ❶ smart ❷ nice

chicorée *nf* endive

chien *nm* dog; 'Attention, chien méchant' 'Beware of the dog'

chienne *nf* (dog) bitch

chiffon *nm* cloth

chiffonner *vb* [28] to crease

chiffre *nm* figure; **les chiffres romains** Roman numerals

chignon *nm* (in hair) bun

Chili *nm* Chile

chimie *nf* chemistry

chimique *adj* chemical; **les produits chimiques** chemicals

Chine *nf* China

chinois, e *adj, n* Chinese ▷ *Il apprend le chinois.* He's learning Chinese.; **un Chinois** (man) a Chinese; **une Chinoise** (woman) a Chinese; **les Chinois** the Chinese

chiot *nm* puppy

chips *nfpl* crisps

chirurgical, e (*mpl* **chirurgicaux**) *adj* **une intervention chirurgicale** an operation

chirurgie *nf* surgery; **la chirurgie esthétique** plastic surgery

chirurgien *nm* surgeon

choc *nm* shock; **Elle est encore sous le choc.** She's still in shock.

chocolat *nm* chocolate; **un chocolat chaud** a hot chocolate; **le chocolat à croquer** dark chocolate

chœur *nm* choir

choisir *vb* [38] to choose

choix *nm* ❶ choice; **avoir le choix** to have the choice ❷ selection

chômage *nm* unemployment; **être au chômage** to be unemployed

chômeur *nm* unemployed person

chômeuse *nf* unemployed woman

choquer *vb* [28] to shock

chorale *nf* choir

chose *nf* thing; **C'est peu de chose.** It's nothing really.

chou (*pl* **choux**) *nm* cabbage; **les choux de Bruxelles** Brussels sprouts; **un chou à la crème** a choux bun

chouchou *nm* (informal) teacher's pet

choucroute *nf* (with sausages and ham) sauerkraut

chouette *nf* owl

▶ *adj* (informal) brilliant

chou-fleur (*pl* **choux-fleurs**) *nm* cauliflower

chrétien (*f* **chrétienne**) *adj* Christian

Christ *nm* Christ

chronologique *adj* chronological

chronomètre *nm* stopwatch

chronométrer *vb* [34] to time

chrysanthème *nm* chrysanthemum

- Chrysanthemums are strongly associated with funerals in
- France.

a
b
c
d
e
f
g
h
i
j
k
l
m
n
o
p
q
r
s
t
u
v
w
x
y
z

chuchoter vb [**28**] to whisper
chut excl shh!
chute nf fall; **faire une chute** to fall; **une chute d'eau** a waterfall; **la chute des cheveux** hair loss; **les chutes de neige** snowfalls
Chypre n Cyprus
-ci adv **ce livre-ci** this book; **ces bottes-ci** these boots
cible nf target
ciboulette nf chives
cicatrice nf scar
se cicatriser vb [**28**] to heal up
  ▷ *Cette plaie s'est vite cicatrisée.* This wound has healed up quickly.
ci-contre adv opposite
ci-dessous adv below
ci-dessus adv above
cidre nm cider
ciel nm ❶ sky ❷ heaven
cierge nm (in church) candle
cigale nf cicada
cigare nm cigar
cigarette nf cigarette
cigogne nf stork
ci-joint adv attached ▷ *Veuillez trouver ci-joint mon curriculum vitae.* Please find attached my CV.
cil nm eyelash
ciment nm cement
cimetière nm cemetery
cinéaste nmf film-maker
cinéma nm cinema
cinq num five ▷ *Il a cinq ans.* He's five.; **le cinq février** the fifth of February
cinquantaine nf about fifty; **Il a la cinquantaine.** He's in his fifties.
cinquante num fifty ▷ *Il a cinquante ans.* He's fifty.; **cinquante et un**

fifty-one; **cinquante-deux** fifty-two
cinquième adj fifth
  ▶ nf year 8
  ● In French secondary schools,
  ● years are counted from the
  ● **sixième** (youngest) to **première**
  ● and **terminale** (oldest).
cintre nm coat hanger
cirage nm shoe polish
circonflexe adj **un accent circonflexe** a circumflex
circonstance nf circumstance
circulation nf ❶ traffic ❷ circulation
circuler vb [**28**] to run ▷ *Il n'y a qu'un bus sur trois qui circule.* Only one bus in three is running.
cire nf wax
ciré nm oilskin jacket
cirer vb [**28**] (shoes, floor) to polish
cirque nm circus
ciseaux nmpl **une paire de ciseaux** a pair of scissors
citadin nm city dweller
citation nf quotation
cité nf estate ▷ *J'habite dans une cité.* I live on an estate.; **une cité universitaire** halls of residence; **une cité-dortoir** a dormitory town
citer vb [**28**] to quote
citoyen nm citizen
citoyenne nf citizen
citoyenneté nf citizenship
citron nm lemon; **un citron vert** a lime; **un citron pressé** a fresh lemon juice
citronnade nf still lemonade
citrouille nf pumpkin

civet nm stew

civil, e adj civilian; **en civil** in civilian clothes

civilisation nf civilization

civique adj **l'instruction civique** PSHE

clair, e adj, adv ① light ② (water) clear; **voir clair** to see clearly; **le clair de lune** moonlight

clairement adv clearly

clairière nf clearing

clandestin, e adj **un passager clandestin** a stowaway

claque nf slap

claquer vb [28] ① to bang ▷ On entend des volets qui claquent. You can hear shutters banging. ② to slam ▷ Elle est partie en claquant la porte. She left, slamming the door behind her.

claquettes nfpl **faire des claquettes** to tap-dance

clarinette nf clarinet

classe nf ① class ② classroom

classer vb [28] to arrange ▷ Les livres sont classés par ordre alphabétique. The books are arranged in alphabetical order.

classeur nm ring binder

classique adj ① classical ② classic

clavier nm (of computer, typewriter) keyboard

clé nf ① key ② clef

clef nf = **clé**

client nm customer

cliente nf customer

clientèle nf customers

cligner vb [28] **cligner des yeux** to blink

clignotant nm indicator

climat nm climate

climatisation nf air conditioning

climatisé, e adj air-conditioned

clin d'œil (pl **clins d'œil**) nm wink; **en un clin d'œil** in a flash

clinique nf private hospital

cliquer vb [28] to click ▷ cliquer sur une icône to click on an icon

clochard nm tramp

cloche nf bell

clocher nm ① church tower ② steeple

clone nm clone

cloner vb [28] to clone

clou nm nail; **un clou de girofle** a clove

clown nm clown

club nm club

cobaye nm guinea pig

coca nm Coke®

cocaïne nf cocaine

coccinelle nf ladybird

cocher vb [28] to tick ▷ Cochez la bonne réponse. Tick the right answer.

cochon (f **cochonne**) adj (informal) dirty
▶ nm pig; **un cochon d'Inde** a guinea pig

cocktail nm ① cocktail ② cocktail party

coco nm **une noix de coco** a coconut

cocorico excl ① cock-a-doodle-doo! ② three cheers for France!
* The symbol of France is the cockerel and so **cocorico!** is sometimes used as an expression of French national pride.

a b c d e f g h i j k l m n o p q r s t u v w x y z

cocotte nf (pan) casserole; **une cocotte-minute**® a pressure cooker

code nm code; **le code de la route** the highway code; **le code postal** the postcode

cœur nm heart; **avoir bon cœur** to be kind-hearted; **la dame de cœur** the queen of hearts; **avoir mal au cœur** to feel sick; **par cœur** by heart ▷ apprendre quelque chose par cœur to learn something by heart

coffre nm ❶ (of car) boot ❷ (furniture) chest

coffre-fort (pl **coffres-forts**) nm safe

coffret nm **un coffret à bijoux** a jewellery box

cognac nm brandy

se **cogner** vb [28] **se cogner à quelque chose** to bang into something

coiffé, e adj **Tu es bien coiffée.** Your hair looks nice.

coiffer vb [28] **se coiffer** to do one's hair

coiffeur nm hairdresser

coiffure nf hairstyle; **un salon de coiffure** a hairdresser's

coin nm corner ▷ au coin de la rue on the corner of the street; **Tu habites dans le coin?** Do you live near here?; **Je ne suis pas du coin.** I'm not from here.; **le bistrot du coin** the local pub

coincé, e adj ❶ stuck ❷ stuffy

coincer vb [12] to jam ▷ La porte est coincée. The door's jammed.

coïncidence nf coincidence

col nm ❶ collar ❷ (of mountain) pass

colère nf anger; **Je suis en colère.** I'm angry.; **se mettre en colère** to get angry

colin nm hake

colique nf diarrhoea

colis nm parcel

collaborer vb [28] to collaborate

collant, e adj ❶ sticky ❷ clingy ▶ nm tights

colle nf ❶ glue ❷ detention; **Je n'en sais rien: tu me poses une colle.** I really don't know: you've got me there.

collecte nf (of money) collection

collection nf collection

collectionner vb [28] to collect

collège nm secondary school
  ● In France pupils go to a **collège**
  ● between the ages of 11 and 15,
  ● and then to a **lycée** until the age
  ● of 18.

collégien nm schoolboy

collégienne nf schoolgirl

collègue nmf colleague

coller vb [28] ❶ to stick ▷ Il y a un chewing-gum collé sous la chaise. There's a bit of chewing gum stuck under the chair. ▷ Ce timbre ne colle plus. This stamp won't stick on. ❷ to press ▷ J'ai collé mon oreille au mur. I pressed my ear against the wall.

collier nm ❶ necklace ❷ (of dog, cat) collar

colline nf hill

collision nf crash

colombe nf dove

colonie nf **aller en colonie de**

vacances to go to summer camp

colonne nf column; **la colonne vertébrale** the spine

colorant nm colouring

coloris nm colour

coma nm coma ▷ être dans le coma to be in a coma

combat nm fighting; **un combat de boxe** a boxing match

combattant nm un ancien combattant a war veteran

combattre vb [**9**] to fight

combien adv ❶ how much ▷ Vous en voulez combien? Un kilo? How much do you want? One kilo?; **C'est combien?** How much is that? ▷ Combien est-ce que ça coûte? How much does it cost? ▷ Combien ça fait? How much does it come to? ❷ how many ▷ Tu en veux combien? Deux? How many do you want? Two?; **combien de (1)** how much ▷ Combien de purée est-ce que je vous sers? How much mashed potato shall I give you? **(2)** how many ▷ Combien de personnes as-tu invitées? How many people have you invited?; **combien de temps** how long ▷ Combien de temps est-ce que tu seras absente? How long will you be away?; **Il y a combien de temps?** How long ago? ▷ Il est parti il y a combien de temps? How long ago did he leave?; **On est le combien aujourd'hui? — On est le vingt.** What's the date today? — It's the 20th.

combinaison nf❶ combination ❷ (petticoat) slip; **une**

combinaison de plongée a wetsuit; **une combinaison de ski** a ski suit

comble nm Alors ça, c'est le comble! That's the last straw!

comédie nf comedy; **une comédie musicale** a musical

comédien nm actor

comédienne nf actress

comestible adj edible

comique adj comical ▶ nmf comedian

comité nm committee

commande nf order; **être aux commandes** to be at the controls

commander vb [**28**] ❶ to order ▷ J'ai commandé une robe sur catalogue. I've ordered a dress from a catalogue. ❷ to give orders ▷ C'est moi qui commande ici, pas vous! I give the orders here, not you!

comme conj, adv ❶ like ▷ Il est comme son père. He's like his father. ❷ for ▷ Qu'est-ce que tu veux comme dessert? What would you like for pudding? ❸ as ▷ J'ai travaillé comme serveuse cet été. I worked as a waitress this summer. ▷ Faites comme vous voulez. Do as you like.; **comme ça** like this ▷ Ça se plie comme ça. You fold it like this.; **comme il faut** properly ▷ Mets le couvert comme il faut! Set the table properly!; **Comme tu as grandi!** How you've grown!; **Regarde comme c'est beau!** Look, isn't it lovely!; **comme ci comme ça** so-so

commencement nm beginning

commencer vb [**12**] to start ▷ *Les cours commencent à huit heures.* Lessons start at 8 o'clock.

comment adv how; **Comment allez-vous?** How are you?; **Comment dit-on 'pomme' en anglais?** How do you say 'pomme' in English?; **Comment s'appelle-t-il?** What's his name?; **Comment?** What did you say?

commentaire nm comment

commérages nmpl gossip sg

commerçant nm shopkeeper

commerce nm ❶ trade ▷ *le commerce extérieur* foreign trade; **le commerce électronique** e-commerce ❷ business ▷ *Il fait des études de commerce.* He's studying business. ❸ shop ▷ *tenir un commerce* to have a shop; **On trouve ça dans le commerce.** You can find it in the shops.

commercial, e (mpl **commerciaux**) adj **un centre commercial** a shopping centre

commettre vb [**47**] to commit

commissaire nmf police superintendent

commissariat nm police station

commissions nfpl shopping sg

commode nf chest of drawers ▷ adj handy; **Son père n'est pas commode.** His father is a difficult character.

commun, e adj shared; **en commun** in common; **les**

transports en commun public transport; **mettre quelque chose en commun** to share something

communauté nf community

communication nf communication; **une communication téléphonique** a telephone call

communion nf communion

communiquer vb [**28**] to communicate

communiste adj communist

compact, e adj compact; **un disque compact** a compact disc

compagne nf ❶ companion ❷ (living together) partner

compagnie nf company; **une compagnie d'assurances** an insurance company; **une compagnie aérienne** an airline

compagnon nm ❶ companion ❷ (living together) partner

comparaison nf comparison

comparer vb [**28**] to compare

compartiment nm (on train) compartment

compas nm (for drawing circles) compass

compatible adj compatible

compétence nf competence

compétent, e adj competent

compétitif (f **compétitive**) adj competitive

compétition nf competition; **avoir l'esprit de compétition** to be competitive

complet (f **complète**) adj ❶ complete ❷ full; **'complet'** no vacancies'; **le pain complet**

wholemeal bread
▶ *nm (for man)* suit
complètement *adv* completely
compléter *vb* [**34**] to complete
▷ *Complétez les phrases suivantes.*
Complete the following sentences.
complexe *adj* complex
complexé, e *adj* hung up
complication *nf* complication
complice *nmf* accomplice
compliqué, e *adj* complicated
complot *nm* plot
comportement *nm* behaviour
comporter *vb* [**28**] ❶ to consist of
▷ *Le château comporte trois parties.*
The castle consists of three parts.
❷ to have ▷ *Ce modèle comporte un*
écran couleur. This model has a
colour screen.; **se comporter** to
behave
composer *vb* [**28**] *(music, text)* to
compose; **composer un numéro**
to dial a number; **se composer de**
to consist of
compositeur *nm* composer
composition *nf* test
compostage *nm* date stamping
composter *vb* [**28**] to punch
▷ *N'oublie pas de composter ton billet*
avant de monter dans le train.
Remember to punch your ticket
before you get on the train.
● In France you have to punch
  your ticket on the platform to
  validate it before getting onto
● the train.

compote *nf* stewed fruit; **la**
compote de prunes stewed
plums

compréhensible *adj*
understandable
compréhensif (*f* **compréhensive**)
adj understanding

> Be careful! **compréhensif** does
> not mean **comprehensive**.

compréhension *nf*
❶ comprehension ❷ sympathy
▷ *Elle a fait preuve de beaucoup de*
compréhension à mon égard. She
showed a lot of sympathy for me.
comprendre *vb* [**65**] ❶ to
understand ▷ *Je ne comprends pas ce*
que vous dites. I don't understand
what you're saying. ❷ to include
▷ *Le forfait ne comprend pas la*
location des skis. The price doesn't
include ski hire.
comprimé *nm* tablet
compris, e *adj* included ▷ *Le service*
n'est pas compris. Service is not
included.; **y compris** including;
non compris excluding; **cent**
euros tout compris 100 euros
all-inclusive
compromettre *vb* [**47**] to
compromise
compromis *nm* compromise
comptabilité *nf* accounting
comptable *nmf* accountant
comptant *adv* **payer comptant** to
pay cash
compte *nm* account; **Le compte**
est bon. That's the right amount.;
tenir compte de (1) to take into
account **(2)** to take notice of;
travailler à son compte to be
self-employed; **en fin de compte**
all things considered

compter vb [28] to count
compte rendu (pl **comptes rendus**) nm report
compteur nm meter
comptoir nm bar
se **concentrer** vb [28] to concentrate
conception nf design
concernant prep regarding
concerner vb [28] to concern ▷ en ce qui me concerne as far as I'm concerned; **Je ne me sens pas concerné.** I don't feel it's anything to do with me.
concert nm concert
concierge nmf caretaker
conclure vb [13] to conclude
conclusion nf conclusion
concombre nm cucumber
concorder vb [28] to tally ▷ Les dates concordent. The dates tally.
concours nm ❶ competition ❷ (for a job or a place in a school) competitive exam
concret (f **concrète**) adj concrete
conçu vb designed ▷ Ces appartements sont très mal conçus. These flats are very badly designed.
concurrence nf competition
concurrent nm competitor
condamner vb [28] ❶ to sentence ▷ condamner à mort to sentence to death ❷ to condemn ▷ Le gouvernement a condamné cette décision. The government condemned this decision.
condition nf condition; **à condition que** provided that; **les**

conditions de travail working conditions
conditionnel nm conditional tense
conducteur nm driver
conductrice nf driver
conduire vb [23] to drive ▷ Est-ce que tu sais conduire? Can you drive?; **se conduire** to behave ▷ Il s'est mal conduit. He behaved badly.
conduite nf behaviour
conférence nf ❶ lecture ❷ conference
se **confesser** vb [28] to go to confession
confettis nmpl confetti
confiance nf ❶ trust; **avoir confiance en quelqu'un** to trust somebody ❷ confidence; **Tu peux avoir confiance. Il sera à l'heure.** You don't need to worry. He'll be on time.; **confiance en soi** self-confidence
confiant, e adj confident
confidences nfpl **faire des confidences à quelqu'un** to confide in someone
confidentiel (f **confidentielle**) adj confidential
confier vb [19] **se confier à quelqu'un** to confide in somebody ▷ Elle s'est confiée à sa meilleure amie. She confided in her best friend.
confirmer vb [28] to confirm
confiserie nf sweet shop
confisquer vb [28] to confiscate
confit, e adj **des fruits confits** crystallized fruits
confiture nf jam; **la confiture**

d'oranges marmalade

conflit nm conflict

confondre vb [69] to mix up ▷ On le confond souvent avec son frère. People often mix him up with his brother.

confort nm comfort; **tout confort** with all mod cons

confortable adj comfortable

confus, e adj ❶ unclear ❷ embarrassed

confusion nf ❶ confusion ❷ embarrassment

congé nm holiday; **en congé** on holiday; **un congé de maladie** sick leave

congélateur nm freezer

congeler vb [1] to freeze

conjonction nf conjunction

conjonctivite nf conjunctivitis

conjugaison nf conjugation

connaissance nf ❶ knowledge ❷ acquaintance; **perdre connaissance** to lose consciousness; **faire la connaissance de quelqu'un** to meet somebody

connaître vb [14] to know ▷ Je ne connais pas du tout cette région. I don't know this area at all.; **Ils se sont connus à Nantes.** They first met in Nantes.; **s'y connaître en quelque chose** to know about something ▷ Je ne m'y connais pas beaucoup en musique classique. I don't know much about classical music.

connecté, e adj (computer) online

se **connecter** vb [28] to log on

connu, e adj well-known

conquérir vb [2] to conquer

consacrer vb [28] to devote ▷ Il consacre beaucoup de temps à ses enfants. He devotes a lot of time to his children.

conscience nf conscience; **prendre conscience de** to become aware of

consciencieux (f **consciencieuse**) adj conscientious

conscient, e adj conscious

consécutif (f **consécutive**) adj consecutive

conseil nm advice; **un conseil** a piece of advice

conseiller vb [28] ❶ to advise ▷ Il a été mal conseillé. He has been badly advised. ❷ to recommend ▷ Il m'a conseillé ce livre. He recommended this book to me.
▶ nm ❶ (political) councillor ❷ adviser ▷ le conseiller d'orientation the careers adviser

consentement nm consent

consentir vb [77] to agree ▷ consentir à quelque chose to agree to something

conséquence nf consequence; **en conséquence** consequently

conséquent (f **conséquente**) adj par conséquent consequently

conservatoire nm school of music

conserve nf tin; **une boîte de conserve** a tin; **les conserves** tinned food; **en conserve** tinned

conserver vb [28] to keep ▷ J'ai conservé toutes ses lettres. I've kept all her letters.; **se conserver** to keep ▷ Ce pain se conserve plus d'une

a
b
c
d
e
f
g
h
i
j
k
l
m
n
o
p
q
r
s
t
u
v
w
x
y
z

semaine. This bread will keep for
more than a week.

considérable *adj* considerable

considération *nf* **prendre
quelque chose en considération**
to take something into
consideration

considérer *vb* [**34**] **considérer que**
to believe that ▷ *Je considère que le
gouvernement devrait investir
davantage dans l'éducation.* I believe
that the government should invest
more money in education.

consigne *nf* left-luggage office;
une consigne automatique a
left-luggage locker

consistant, e *adj* substantial

consister *vb* [**28**] **consister à** to
consist of; **En quoi consiste votre
travail?** What does your job
involve?

console de jeu *nf* games console

consoler *vb* [**28**] to console

consommateur *nm* ❶ consumer
❷ *(in café)* customer

consommation *nf*
❶ consumption ❷ drink

consommer *vb* [**28**] ❶ to use ▷ *Ces
grosses voitures consomment
beaucoup d'essence.* These big cars
use a lot of petrol. ❷ to have a
drink ▷ *Est-ce qu'on peut consommer
à la terrasse?* Can we have drinks
outside?

consonne *nf* consonant

constamment *adv* constantly

constant, e *adj* constant

constater *vb* [**28**] to notice

constipé, e *adj* constipated

constitué, e *adj* **être constitué de**
to consist of

constituer *vb* [**28**] to make up ▷ *les
États qui constituent la Fédération
russe* the states which make up the
Russian Federation

construction *nf* building; **une
maison en construction** a house
being built

construire *vb* [**23**] to build ▷ *Ils font
construire une maison neuve.* They're
having a new house built.

consulat *nm* consulate

consultation *nf* **les heures de
consultation** surgery hours

consulter *vb* [**28**] ❶ to consult ▷ *Il
vaut toujours mieux consulter un
médecin.* It's always best to consult
a doctor. ❷ to see patients ▷ *Le
docteur ne consulte pas le samedi.* The
doctor doesn't see patients on
Saturdays.

contact *nm* contact; **Il a le
contact facile.** He's very
approachable.; **garder le contact
avec quelqu'un** to keep in touch
with somebody

contacter *vb* [**28**] to get in touch
with ▷ *Je te contacterai dès que j'aurai
des nouvelles.* I'll get in touch with
you as soon as I have some news.

contagieux *(f* **contagieuse)** *adj*
infectious

contaminer *vb* [**28**] to contaminate

conte de fées *(pl* **contes de fées)**
nm fairy tale

contempler *vb* [**28**] to gaze at

contemporain, e *adj*
contemporary; **un auteur**

contemporain a modern writer
contenir vb [83] to contain ▷ *un portefeuille contenant de l'argent* a wallet containing money
content, e adj glad ▷ *Je suis content que tu sois venu.* I'm glad you've come.; **content de** pleased with
contenter vb [28] to please ▷ *Il est difficile à contenter.* He's hard to please.; **Je me contente de peu.** I can make do with very little.
contesté, e adj controversial
continent nm continent
continu, e adj continuous; **faire la journée continue** to work without taking a full lunch break
continuellement adv constantly
continuer vb [28] to carry on ▷ *Continuez sans moi!* Carry on without me! ▷ *Il ne veut pas continuer ses études.* He doesn't want to carry on studying.; **continuer à faire quelque chose** to go on doing something ▷ *Ils ont continué à regarder la télé sans me dire bonjour.* They went on watching TV without saying hello to me.; **continuer de faire quelque chose** to keep on doing something ▷ *Il continue de fumer malgré son asthme.* He keeps on smoking, despite his asthma.
contourner vb [28] to go round ▷ *La route contourne la ville.* The road goes round the town.
contraceptif nm contraceptive
contraception nf contraception
contractuel nm traffic warden
contradiction nf contradiction;

par esprit de contradiction just to be awkward
contraire nm opposite; **au contraire** on the contrary
contrarier vb [19] ❶ to annoy ▷ *Il avait l'air contrarié.* He looked annoyed. ❷ to upset ▷ *Est-ce que tu serais contrariée si je ne venais pas?* Would you be upset if I didn't come?
contraste nm contrast
contrat nm contract
contravention nf parking ticket
contre prep ❶ against ▷ *Ne mets pas ton vélo contre le mur.* Don't put your bike against the wall. ▷ *Tu es pour ou contre ce projet?* Are you for or against this plan? ❷ for ▷ *échanger quelque chose contre quelque chose* to swap something for something; **par contre** on the other hand
contrebande nf smuggling; **des produits de contrebande** smuggled goods
contrebasse nf double bass
contrecœur: **à contrecœur** adv reluctantly
contredire vb [27] to contradict ▷ *Il ne supporte pas d'être contredit.* He can't stand being contradicted.
contre-indication nf 'Contre-indication en cas d'eczéma' 'Not to be used by people with eczema'
contresens nm mistranslation
contretemps nm Désolé d'être en retard: j'ai eu un contretemps. Sorry I'm late: I was held up.
contribuer vb [28] contribuer à to

contribute to ▷ *Est-ce que tu veux contribuer au cadeau pour Marie? Do you want to contribute to Marie's present?*

contrôle nm ❶ control ▷ *le contrôle des passeports* passport control ❷ check; **un contrôle d'identité** an identity check; **le contrôle des billets** ticket inspection ❸ test ▷ *un contrôle antidopage* a drugs test; **le contrôle continu** continuous assessment

contrôler vb [28] to check ▷ *Personne n'a contrôlé mon billet.* Nobody checked my ticket.

contrôleur nm ticket inspector

controversé, e adj controversial

convaincre vb [86] ❶ to persuade ▷ *Il a essayé de me convaincre de rester.* He tried to persuade me to stay. ❷ to convince ▷ *Tu n'as pas l'air convaincu.* You don't look convinced.

convalescence nf convalescence

convenable adj decent; **Ce n'est pas convenable.** It's bad manners.

convenir vb [89] **convenir à** to suit ▷ *Est-ce que cette date te convient?* Does this date suit you?; **convenir de** to agree on ▷ *Nous avons convenu d'une date.* We've agreed on a date.

conventionné, e adj **un médecin conventionné** a Health Service doctor

● All doctors in France charge for treatment, but patients of Health Service doctors get their money refunded by the government.

convenu, e adj agreed

conversation nf conversation

convocation nf notification

convoquer vb [28] **convoquer quelqu'un à une réunion** to invite somebody to a meeting

cool adj (informal) cool

coopération nf co-operation

coopérer vb [34] to co-operate

coordonnées nfpl contact details

copain nm (informal) ❶ friend ❷ boyfriend

copie nf ❶ copy ❷ paper ▷ *Il a des copies à corriger ce week-end.* He's got some papers to mark this weekend.

copier vb [19] to copy; **copier-coller** to copy and paste

copieux (f **copieuse**) adj hearty

copine nf (informal) ❶ friend ❷ girlfriend

coq nm cockerel

coque nf (of boat) hull; **un œuf à la coque** a soft-boiled egg

coquelicot nm poppy

coqueluche nf whooping cough

coquillage nm ❶ shellfish ❷ shell

coquille nf shell; **une coquille d'œuf** an eggshell; **une coquille Saint-Jacques** a scallop

coquin, e adj cheeky

cor nm horn

corbeau (pl **corbeaux**) nm crow

corbeille nf ❶ basket ❷ (of a computer) recycle bin; **une corbeille à papier** a wastepaper basket

corde nf ❶ rope ❷ (of violin, tennis racket) string; **une corde à linge**

a clothes line

cordonnerie nf shoe repair shop

cordonnier nm cobbler

coriace adj tough

corne nf horn

cornemuse nf bagpipes

cornet nm un cornet de frites a bag of chips; **un cornet de glace** an ice cream cone

cornichon nm gherkin

Cornouailles nf Cornwall

corps nm body

correct, e adj ❶ correct ❷ reasonable ▷ un salaire correct a reasonable salary

correction nf correction

correspondance nf ❶ correspondence; **un cours par correspondance** a correspondence course ❷ (train, plane) connection

correspondant nm penfriend

correspondre vb [69] to correspond; **Faites correspondre les phrases.** Match the sentences together.

corridor nm corridor

corriger vb [45] to mark ▷ Vous pouvez corriger mon test? Can you mark my test?

corsage nm blouse

corse adj, nmf Corsican; **un Corse** (man) a Corsican; **une Corse** (woman) a Corsican

corvée nf chore

costaud, e adj brawny

costume nm ❶ (man's) suit ❷ (theatre) costume

côte nf ❶ coastline; **la Côte d'Azur** the French Riviera ❷ hill ❸ rib ❹ chop; **une côte de bœuf** a rib of beef; **côte à côte** side by side

côté nm side; **à côté de** (1) next to ▷ Le café est à côté du sucre. The coffee's next to the sugar. (2) next door to ▷ Il habite à côté de chez moi. He lives next door to me.; **de l'autre côté** on the other side; **De quel côté est-il parti?** Which way did he go?; **mettre quelque chose de côté** to save something

côtelette nf chop

cotisation nf ❶ (to club, union) subscription ❷ (to pension, national insurance) contributions; **cotisations sociales** social security contributions

coton nm cotton; **le coton hydrophile** cotton wool

Coton-tige® (pl **Cotons-tiges**) nm cotton bud

cou nm neck

couchant adj le soleil couchant the setting sun

couche nf ❶ layer ▷ la couche d'ozone the ozone layer ❷ (of paint, varnish) coat ❸ nappy

couché, e adj ❶ lying down ▷ Il était couché sur le tapis. He was lying on the carpet. ❷ in bed ▷ Il est déjà couché. He's already in bed.

coucher nm un coucher de soleil a sunset

se **coucher** vb [28] ❶ to go to bed ❷ (sun) to set

couchette nf ❶ (on train) couchette ❷ (on boat) bunk

coude nm elbow

a b c d e f g h i j k l m n o p q r s t u v w x y z

coudre vb [15] ❶ to sew ▷ J'aime coudre. I like sewing. ❷ to sew on ▷ Il ne sait même pas coudre un bouton. He can't even sew a button on.

couette nf duvet

couettes nfpl bunches

couler vb [28] ❶ to run ▷ Ne laissez pas couler les robinets. Don't leave the taps running. ❷ to flow ▷ La rivière coulait lentement. The river was flowing slowly. ❸ to leak ▷ Mon stylo coule. My pen's leaking. ❹ to sink ▷ Le bateau a coulé. The boat sank.

couleur nf colour; Tu as pris des couleurs. You've got a tan.

couleuvre nf grass snake

coulisses nfpl (in theatre) wings; dans les coulisses behind the scenes

couloir nm corridor

coup nm ❶ knock ▷ donner un coup à quelque chose to give something a knock ❷ blow; Il m'a donné un coup! He hit me!; un coup de pied a kick; un coup de poing a punch ❸ shock; un coup de feu a shot; un coup de fil (informal) a ring; donner un coup de main à quelqu'un to give somebody a hand; un coup d'œil a quick look; attraper un coup de soleil to get sunburnt; un coup de téléphone a phone call; un coup de tonnerre a clap of thunder; boire un coup (informal) to have a drink; après coup afterwards; à tous les coups (informal) every time; du premier

coup first time; sur le coup at first

coupable adj guilty
▶ nmf culprit

coupe nf (sport) cup; une coupe de cheveux a haircut; une coupe de champagne a glass of champagne

coupe-ongle (pl coupe-ongles) nm nail clippers

couper vb [28] ❶ to cut ❷ to turn off ▷ couper le courant to turn off the electricity ❸ to take a short-cut ▷ On peut couper par la forêt. We could take a short-cut through the woods.; couper l'appétit to spoil one's appetite; se couper to cut oneself ▷ Je me suis coupé le doigt avec une boîte de conserve. I cut my finger on a tin.; couper la parole à quelqu'un to interrupt somebody

couple nm couple

couplet nm verse

coupure nf cut; une coupure de courant a power cut

cour nf ❶ yard ▷ la cour de l'école the school yard ❷ court

courage nm courage

courageux (f courageuse) adj brave

couramment adv ❶ fluently ❷ commonly

courant, e adj ❶ common ❷ standard
▶ nm ❶ (of river) current; un courant d'air a draught ❷ power ▷ une panne de courant a power cut; Je le ferai dans le courant de la semaine. I'll do it some time during the week.; être au courant de quelque chose to know about

something; **mettre quelqu'un au courant de quelque chose** to tell somebody about something; **Tu es au courant?** Have you heard about it?; **se tenir au courant de quelque chose** to keep up with something

coureur nm runner; **un coureur à pied** a runner; **un coureur cycliste** a racing cyclist; **un coureur automobile** a racing driver

coureuse nf runner

courgette nf courgette

courir vb [**16**] to run ▷ Elle a traversé la rue en courant. She ran across the street.; **courir un risque** to run a risk

couronne nf crown

courons, courez vb see **courir**

courriel nm email

courrier nm mail; **N'oublie pas de poster le courrier.** Don't forget to post the letters.; **le courrier électronique** email

> Be careful! The French word **courrier** does not mean **courier**.

courroie nf **la courroie du ventilateur** fan belt

cours nm ❶ lesson ▷ un cours d'espagnol a Spanish lesson ❷ course ▷ un cours intensif a crash course ❸ rate; **au cours de** during

course nf ❶ running ▷ la course de fond long-distance running ❷ race ▷ une course hippique a horse race ❸ shopping ▷ J'ai juste une course à faire. I've just got a bit of shopping to do.; **faire les courses** to go shopping

court, e adj short
> nm **un court de tennis** a tennis court

couru vb see **courir**

couscous nm couscous

> couscous is a spicy North African dish made with meat, vegetables and steamed semolina.

cousin nm cousin

cousine nf cousin

coussin nm cushion

coût nm cost

couteau (pl **couteaux**) nm knife

coûter vb [**28**] to cost ▷ Est-ce que ça coûte cher? Does it cost a lot?; **Combien ça coûte?** How much is it?

coûteux (f **coûteuse**) adj expensive

coutume nf custom

couture nf ❶ sewing; **faire de la couture** to sew ❷ seam

couturier nm fashion designer

couturière nf dressmaker

couvercle nm ❶ (of pan) lid ❷ (of tube, jar, spray can) top

couvert, e adj ❶ covered; **couvert de** covered with ❷ (sky) overcast
> vb see **couvrir**
> nm **mettre le couvert** to lay the table

couverts nmpl cutlery sg

couverture nf blanket

couvre-lit nm bedspread

couvrir vb [**55**] to cover ▷ Le chien est revenu couvert de boue. The dog came back covered with mud.; **se couvrir (1)** to wrap up ▷ Couvre-toi

a
b
c
d
e
f
g
h
i
j
k
l
m
n
o
p
q
r
s
t
u
v
w
x
y
z

bien: il fait très froid dehors. Wrap up well: it's very cold outside. **(2)** to cloud over ▷ *Le ciel se couvre.* The sky's clouding over.

covoiturage *nm* car sharing

crabe *nm* crab

cracher *vb* [28] to spit

crachin *nm* drizzle

craie *nf* chalk

craindre *vb* [17] to fear ▷ *Tu n'as rien à craindre.* You've got nothing to fear.

crainte *nf* fear; **de crainte de** for fear of

craintif (*f* **craintive**) *adj* timid

crampe *nf* cramp

cran *nm* (*in belt*) hole; **avoir du cran** (*informal*) to have guts

crâne *nm* skull

crâner *vb* [28] (*informal*) to show off

crapaud *nm* toad

craquer *vb* [28] ❶ to creak ▷ *Le plancher craque.* The floor creaks. ❷ to burst ▷ *Ma fermeture éclair a craqué.* My zip's burst. ❸ to crack up ▷ *Je vais finir par craquer!* (*informal*) I'm going to crack up at this rate!; **Quand j'ai vu cette robe, j'ai craqué!** (*informal*) When I saw that dress, I couldn't resist it!

crasse *nf* filth

cravate *nf* tie

crawl *nm* crawl

crayon *nm* pencil ▷ *un crayon de couleur* a coloured pencil; **un crayon feutre** a felt-tip pen

création *nf* creation

crèche *nf* ❶ nursery ❷ nativity scene

crédit *nm* credit

créer *vb* [18] to create

crémaillère *nf* pendre la crémaillère to have a house-warming party

crème *nf* cream; **la crème anglaise** custard; **la crème Chantilly** whipped cream; **la crème fouettée** whipped cream; **une crème caramel** a crème caramel; **une crème au chocolat** a chocolate dessert ▶ *nm* white coffee

crémerie *nf* cheese shop

crémeux (*f* **crémeuse**) *adj* creamy

crêpe *nf* pancake

crêperie *nf* pancake restaurant

crépuscule *nm* dusk

cresson *nm* watercress

Crète *nf* Crete

creuser *vb* [28] (*a hole*) to dig; **Ça creuse!** That gives you a real appetite!; **se creuser la cervelle** (*informal*) to rack one's brains

creux (*f* **creuse**) *adj* hollow

crevaison *nf* puncture

crevé, e *adj* ❶ punctured ▷ *un pneu crevé* a puncture ❷ knackered

crever *vb* [43] ❶ (*balloon*) to burst ❷ (*motorist*) to have a puncture ▷ *J'ai crevé sur l'autoroute.* I had a puncture on the motorway.; **Je crève de faim!** (*informal*) I'm starving!; **Je crève de froid!** (*informal*) I'm freezing!

crevette *nf* prawn; **une crevette rose** a prawn; **une crevette grise** a shrimp

cri *nm* ❶ scream ❷ call; **C'est le dernier cri.** It's the latest fashion.

criard, e *adj (colours)* garish

cric *nm (for car)* jack

crier *vb* [**19**] to shout; **crier de douleur** to scream with pain

crime *nm* ❶ crime ❷ murder

criminel *nm* ❶ criminal ❷ murderer

crin *nm* horsehair

crinière *nf* mane

criquet *nm* grasshopper

crise *nf* ❶ crisis; **la crise économique** the recession ❷ attack ▷ *une crise d'asthme* an asthma attack ▷ *une crise cardiaque* a heart attack; **une crise de foie** an upset stomach; **piquer une crise de nerfs** to go hysterical; **avoir une crise de fou rire** to have a fit of the giggles

cristal (*pl* **cristaux**) *nm* crystal

critère *nm* criterion

critique *adj* critical
   ▶ *nm* critic
   ▶ *nf* ❶ criticism ❷ review

critiquer *vb* [**28**] to criticize

Croatie *nf* Croatia

crochet *nm* ❶ hook ❷ detour ▷ *faire un crochet* to make a detour ❸ crochet

crocodile *nm* crocodile

croire *vb* [**20**] to believe; **croire que** to think that ▷ *Tu crois qu'il fera meilleur demain?* Do you think the weather will be better tomorrow?; **croire à quelque chose** to believe in something; **croire en Dieu** to believe in God

crois *vb see* **croire**

croîs *vb see* **croître**

croisement *nm* crossroads

croiser *vb* [**28**] **J'ai croisé Anne-Laure dans la rue.** I bumped into Anne-Laure in the street.; **croiser les bras** to fold one's arms; **croiser les jambes** to cross one's legs; **se croiser** to pass each other

croisière *nf* cruise

croissance *nf* growth

croissant *nm* croissant

croit *vb see* **croire**

croître *vb* [**21**] to grow

croix *nf* cross; **la Croix-Rouge** the Red Cross

croque-madame (*pl* **croque-madame**) *nm* toasted ham and cheese sandwich with fried egg on top

croque-monsieur (*pl* **croque-monsieur**) *nm* toasted ham and cheese sandwich

croquer *vb* [**28**] to munch; **le chocolat à croquer** plain chocolate

croquis *nm* sketch

crotte *nf* **une crotte de chien** dog dirt

crottin *nm* ❶ manure ❷ small goat's cheese

croustillant, e *adj* crusty

croûte *nf* ❶ *(of bread)* crust; **en croûte** in pastry ❷ *(of cheese)* rind ❸ *(on skin)* scab

croûton *nm* ❶ *(end of loaf)* crust ❷ crouton

croyons, croyez *vb see* **croire**

CRS *nmpl* French riot police

cru, e *adj* raw; **le jambon cru** Parma ham
   ▶ *vb see* **croire**

a
b
c
d
e
f
g
h
i
j
k
l
m
n
o
p
q
r
s
t
u
v
w
x
y
z

crû vb see **croître**
cruauté nf cruelty
cruche nf jug
crudités nfpl assorted raw vegetables
cruel (f **cruelle**) adj cruel
crustacés nmpl shellfish
cube nm cube; **un mètre cube** a cubic metre
cueillette nf picking
cueillir vb [22] (flowers, fruit) to pick
cuiller nf spoon; **une cuiller à café** a teaspoon; **une cuiller à soupe** a soup spoon
cuillerée nf spoonful
cuir nm leather; **le cuir chevelu** the scalp
cuire vb [23] to cook ▷ cuire quelque chose à feu vif to cook something on a high heat; **cuire quelque chose au four** to bake something; **cuire quelque chose à la vapeur** to steam something; **faire cuire** to cook ▷ 'Faire cuire pendant une heure' 'Cook for one hour'; **bien cuit** well done; **trop cuit** overdone
cuisine nf ❶ kitchen ❷ cooking; **faire la cuisine** to cook
cuisiné, e adj un plat cuisiné a ready-made meal
cuisiner vb [28] to cook ▷ J'aime beaucoup cuisiner. I love cooking.
cuisinier nm cook
cuisinière nf ❶ cook ❷ cooker
cuisse nf thigh; **une cuisse de poulet** a chicken leg
cuisson nf cooking ▷ 'une heure de cuisson' 'cooking time: one hour'
cuit vb see **cuire**

cuivre nm copper
culot nm (informal) cheek
culotte nf knickers
culpabilité nf guilt
cultivateur nm farmer
cultivatrice nf farmer
cultivé, e adj cultured
cultiver vb [28] to grow ▷ Il cultive la vigne. He grows grapes.; **cultiver la terre** to farm the land
culture nf ❶ farming ❷ education; **la culture physique** physical education
culturisme nm body-building
curé nm parish priest
cure-dent nm toothpick
curieux (f **curieuse**) adj curious
curiosité nf curiosity
curriculum vitae nm CV
curseur nm cursor
cuvette nf bowl
CV nm (= curriculum vitae) CV
cyberattaque nf cyberattack
cybercafé nm internet café
cyclable adj une piste cyclable a cycle track
cycle nm cycle
cyclisme nm cycling
cycliste nmf cyclist
cyclomoteur nm moped
cyclone nm hurricane
cygne nm swan

d' prep, art see **de**

dactylo nf ❶ typist ▷ Elle est dactylo. She's a typist. ❷ typing

daim nm suede

dame nf ❶ lady ❷ (in cards, chess) queen

dames nfpl draughts

Danemark nm Denmark

danger nm danger; **être en danger** to be in danger; **'Danger de mort'** 'Extremely dangerous'

dangereux (f **dangereuse**) adj dangerous

danois, e adj, n Danish ▷ Il parle danois. He speaks Danish.; **un Danois** (man) a Dane; **une Danoise** (woman) a Dane; **les Danois** the Danish

dans prep ❶ in ▷ Il est dans sa chambre. He's in his bedroom.

▷ dans deux mois in two months' time ❷ into ▷ Il est entré dans mon bureau. He came into my office. ❸ out of ▷ On a bu dans des verres en plastique. We drank out of plastic glasses.

danse nf ❶ dance; **la danse classique** ballet ❷ dancing

danser vb [28] to dance

danseur nm dancer

danseuse nf dancer

date nf date; **un ami de longue date** an old friend

dater vb [28] **dater de** to date from

datte nf (fruit) date

dauphin nm dolphin

davantage adv **davantage de** more

de prep, art

> See also **du** (=**de** + **le**) and **des** (=**de** + **les**). **de** changes to **d'** before a vowel and most words beginning with 'h'.

❶ of ▷ le toit de la maison the roof of the house ▷ la voiture de Paul Paul's car ▷ la voiture d'Hélène Hélène's car ▷ deux bouteilles de vin two bottles of wine ▷ un litre d'essence a litre of petrol; **un bébé d'un an** a one-year-old baby; **un billet de cinquante euros** a 50-euro note ❷ from ▷ de Londres à Paris from London to Paris ▷ Il vient de Londres. He comes from London. ▷ une lettre de Victor a letter from Victor ❸ by ▷ augmenter de dix euros to increase by ten euros

> You use **de** to form expressions with the meaning of 'some' and 'any'.

Je voudrais de l'eau. I'd like some water.; **du pain et de la confiture** bread and jam; **Il n'a pas de famille.** He hasn't got any family.; **Il n'y a plus de biscuits.** There aren't any more biscuits.

dé nm ❶ dice ❷ thimble

dealer nm (informal) drug-pusher

déballer vb [28] to unpack

débardeur nm tank top

débarquer vb [28] to disembark ▷ Nous avons dû débarquer à Marseille. We had to disembark at Marseilles.; **débarquer chez quelqu'un** (informal) to descend on somebody

débarras nm junk room; **Bon débarras!** Good riddance!

débarrasser vb [28] to clear ▷ Tu peux débarrasser la table, s'il te plaît? Can you clear the table please?; se **débarrasser de quelque chose** to get rid of something ▷ Je me suis débarrassé de mon vieux frigo. I got rid of my old fridge.

débat nm debate

se **débattre** vb [9] to struggle

débile adj crazy

débordé, e adj être débordé to be snowed under

déborder vb [28] (river) to overflow; **déborder d'énergie** to be full of energy

débouché nm job prospect

déboucher vb [28] ❶ (sink, pipe) to unblock ❷ (bottle) to open; **déboucher sur** to lead into ▷ La rue débouche sur une place. The street leads into a square.

debout adv ❶ standing up ▷ Il a mangé ses céréales debout. He ate his cereal standing up. ❷ upright ▷ Mets les livres debout sur l'étagère. Put the books upright on the shelf. ❸ up ▷ Tu es déjà debout? Are you up already?; **Debout!** Get up!

déboutonner vb [28] to unbutton

débraillé, e adj sloppily dressed

débrancher vb [28] to unplug

débris nm des débris de verre bits of glass

débrouillard, e adj streetwise

se **débrouiller** vb [28] to manage ▷ C'était difficile, mais je ne me suis pas trop mal débrouillé. It was difficult, but I managed OK.; **Débrouille-toi tout seul.** Sort things out for yourself.

début nm beginning ▷ au début at the beginning; **début mai** in early May

débutant nm beginner

débuter vb [28] to start

décaféiné, e adj decaffeinated

décalage horaire nm (between time zones) time difference

décalquer vb [28] to trace

décapiter vb [28] to behead

décapotable adj convertible

décapsuler vb [28] décapsuler une bouteille to take the top off a bottle

décapsuleur nm bottle-opener

décéder vb [34] to die ▷ Son père est décédé il y a trois ans. His father died three years ago.

décembre nm December; **en décembre** in December

décemment adv decently

décent, e adj decent

déception nf disappointment

décerner vb [28] to award

décès nm death

décevant, e adj disappointing

décevoir vb [67] to disappoint

décharger vb [45] to unload

se **déchausser** vb [28] to take off one's shoes

déchets nmpl waste sg

déchiffrer vb [28] to decipher

déchirant, e adj heart-rending

déchirer vb [28] ❶ (clothes) to tear ❷ to tear up ▷ déchirer une lettre to tear up a letter ❸ to tear out ▷ déchirer une page d'un livre to tear a page out of a book; se **déchirer** to tear ▷ se déchirer un muscle to tear a muscle

déchirure nf (rip) tear; une déchirure musculaire a torn muscle

décidé, e adj determined; C'est décidé. It's decided.

décidément adv certainly

décider vb [28] to decide; décider de faire quelque chose to decide to do something; se **décider** to make up one's mind ▷ Elle n'arrive pas à se décider. She can't make up her mind.

décisif (f décisive) adj decisive

décision nf decision

déclaration nf statement; faire une déclaration de vol to report something as stolen

déclarer vb [28] to declare ▷ déclarer la guerre à un pays to declare war on a country; se **déclarer** to break out ▷ Le feu s'est déclaré dans la cantine. The fire broke out in the canteen.

déclencher vb [28] (alarm, explosion) to set off; se **déclencher** to go off

déclic nm click

décoiffé, e adj Elle était toute décoiffée. Her hair was in a real mess.

décollage nm (of plane) takeoff

décollé, e adj avoir les oreilles décollées to have sticking-out ears

décoller vb [28] ❶ to unstick ▷ décoller une étiquette to unstick a label; se **décoller** to come unstuck ❷ to take off ▷ L'avion a décollé avec dix minutes de retard. The plane took off ten minutes late.

décolleté, e adj low-cut ▶ nm un décolleté plongeant a plunging neckline

se **décolorer** vb [28] to fade ▷ Ce T-shirt s'est décoloré au lavage. This T-shirt has faded in the wash.; se faire décolorer les cheveux to have one's hair bleached

décombres nmpl rubble sg

se **décommander** vb [28] to cry off ▷ Elle devait venir mais elle s'est décommandée à la dernière minute. She was supposed to be coming, but she cried off at the last minute.

déconcerté, e adj disconcerted

décongeler vb [1] to thaw

se **déconnecter** vb [28] to log out

déconnection nf disconnection

déconseiller vb [28] déconseiller à quelqu'un de faire quelque

a b c d e f g h i j k l m n o p q r s t u v w x y z

chose to advise somebody not to do something ▷ *Je lui ai déconseillé d'y aller.* I advised him not to go.; **C'est déconseillé.** It's not recommended.

décontenancé, e *adj* disconcerted

décontracté, e *adj* relaxed; **s'habiller décontracté** to dress casually

se **décontracter** *vb* [28] to relax ▷ *Il est allé faire du footing pour se décontracter.* He went jogging to relax.

décor *nm* décor

décorateur *nm* interior decorator

décoration *nf* decoration

décorer *vb* [28] to decorate

décors *nmpl* ❶ *(in play)* scenery *sg* ❷ *(in film)* set

décortiquer *vb* [28] to shell; **des crevettes décortiquées** peeled shrimps

découdre *vb* [15] to unpick; **se découdre** to come unstitched

découper *vb* [28] ❶ to cut out ▷ *J'ai découpé cet article dans le journal.* I cut this article out of the paper. ❷ *(meat)* to carve

décourageant, e *adj* discouraging

décourager *vb* [45] to discourage; **se décourager** to get discouraged; **Ne te décourage pas!** Don't give up!

décousu, e *adj* unstitched

découvert *nm* overdraft

découverte *nf* discovery

découvrir *vb* [55] to discover

décrire *vb* [30] to describe

décrocher *vb* [28] ❶ to take down ▷ *Tu peux m'aider à décrocher les rideaux?* Can you help me take down the curtains? ❷ to pick up the phone ▷ *Il a décroché et a composé le numéro.* He picked up the phone and dialled the number.; **décrocher le téléphone** to take the phone off the hook

déçu *vb* disappointed

dédaigneux *(f* **dédaigneuse)** *adj* disdainful

dédain *nm* disdain

dedans *adv* inside; **là-dedans (1)** in there ▷ *J'ai trouvé les clés là-dedans.* I found the keys in there. **(2)** in that ▷ *Il y a du vrai là-dedans.* There's some truth in that.

dédicacé, e *adj* **un exemplaire dédicacé** a signed copy

dédier *vb* [19] to dedicate

déduire *vb* [23] to take off ▷ *Tu as déduit les vingt euros que je te devais?* Did you take off the twenty euros I owed you?; **J'en déduis qu'il m'a menti.** That means he must have been lying.

défaire *vb* [36] to undo; **défaire sa valise** to unpack; **se défaire** to come undone

défaite *nf* defeat

défaut *nm* fault

défavorable *adj* unfavourable

défavorisé, e *adj* underprivileged

défectueux *(f* **défectueuse)** *adj* faulty

défendre *vb* [88] ❶ to forbid; **défendre à quelqu'un de faire**

quelque chose to forbid somebody to do something ▷ *Sa mère lui a défendu de le revoir.* Her mother forbade her to see him again. ❷ to defend ▷ *défendre quelqu'un* to defend somebody

défendu, e *adj* forbidden ▷ *C'est défendu.* It's forbidden.

défense *nf* ❶ defence; 'défense de fumer' 'no smoking' ❷ (*of elephant*) tusk

défi *nm* challenge; **d'un air de défi** defiantly; **sur un ton de défi** defiantly

défier *vb* [19] ❶ to challenge ▷ *Je te défie de trouver un meilleur exemple.* I challenge you to find a better example. ❷ to dare ▷ *Il m'a défié d'aller à l'école en pyjama.* He dared me to go to school in my pyjamas.

défigurer *vb* [28] to disfigure

défilé *nm* ❶ parade; **un défilé de mode** a fashion show ❷ march

défiler *vb* [28] to march

définir *vb* [38] to define

définitif (*f* **définitive**) *adj* final; **en définitive** in the end

définitivement *adv* for good

déformer *vb* [28] to stretch ▷ *Ne tire pas sur ton pull, tu vas le déformer.* Don't pull at your sweater, you'll stretch it.; **se déformer** to stretch ▷ *Ce T-shirt s'est déformé au lavage.* This T-shirt has stretched in the wash.

se défouler *vb* [28] to unwind

dégagé, e *adj* **d'un air dégagé** casually; **sur un ton dégagé** casually

dégager *vb* [45] ❶ to free ▷ *Ils ont mis une heure à dégager les victimes.* They took an hour to free the victims. ❷ to clear ▷ *des gouttes qui dégagent le nez* drops to clear your nose; **Ça se dégage.** (*weather*) It's clearing up.

se dégarnir *vb* [38] to go bald

dégâts *nmpl* damage

dégel *nm* thaw

dégeler *vb* [1] to thaw

dégivrer *vb* [28] ❶ to defrost ❷ to de-ice

dégonfler *vb* [28] to let down ▷ *Quelqu'un a dégonflé mes pneus.* Somebody let down my tyres.; **se dégonfler** (*informal*) to chicken out

dégouliner *vb* [28] to trickle

dégourdi, e *adj* smart

dégourdir *vb* [38] **se dégourdir les jambes** to stretch one's legs

dégoût *nm* disgust; **avec dégoût** disgustedly

dégoûtant, e *adj* disgusting

dégoûté, e *adj* disgusted; **être dégoûté de tout** to be sick of everything

dégoûter *vb* [28] to disgust; **dégoûter quelqu'un de quelque chose** to put somebody off something ▷ *Ça m'a dégoûté de la viande.* That put me off meat.

se dégrader *vb* [28] to deteriorate

degré *nm* degree; **de l'alcool à 90 degrés** surgical spirit

dégringoler *vb* [28] ❶ to rush down ▷ *Il a dégringolé l'escalier.* He rushed down the stairs. ❷ to collapse ▷ *Elle a fait dégringoler la* *pile de livres*. She knocked over the stack of books.

déguisement nm disguise

déguiser vb [28] **se déguiser en quelque chose** to dress up as something ▷ *Elle s'était déguisée en vampire.* She was dressed up as a vampire.

dégustation nf tasting

déguster vb [28] ❶ (*food, wine*) to taste ❷ to enjoy

dehors adv outside ▷ *Je t'attends dehors.* I'll wait for you outside.; **jeter quelqu'un dehors** to throw somebody out; **en dehors de** apart from

déjà adv ❶ already ▷ *J'ai déjà fini.* I've already finished. ❷ before ▷ *Tu es déjà venu en France?* Have you been to France before?

déjeuner vb [28] to have lunch ▶ nm lunch

délai nm ❶ extension ❷ time limit
 Be careful! **délai** does not mean **delay**.

délasser vb [28] to relax ▷ *La lecture délasse.* Reading's relaxing.; **se délasser** to relax ▷ *J'ai pris un bain pour me délasser.* I had a bath to relax.

délavé, e adj faded

délégué nm representative ▷ *les délégués de classe* the class representatives
 In French schools, each class elects two representatives or **délégués de classe**, one boy and one girl.

déléguée nf representative

déléguer vb [34] to delegate

délibéré, e adj deliberate

délicat, e adj ❶ delicate ❷ tricky ❸ tactful ❹ thoughtful

délicatement adv ❶ gently ❷ tactfully

délice nm delight; *Ce gâteau est un vrai délice.* This cake's a real treat.

délicieux (f **délicieuse**) adj delicious

délinquance nf crime

délinquant nm criminal

délirer vb [28] **Mais tu délires!** (*informal*) You're crazy!

délit nm criminal offence

délivrer vb [28] (*prisoner*) to set free

deltaplane nm hang-glider; **faire du deltaplane** to go hang-gliding

demain adv tomorrow; **À demain!** See you tomorrow!

demande nf request; **une demande en mariage** an offer of marriage; **'demandes d'emploi'** 'situations wanted'

demandé, e adj très demandé very much in demand

demander vb [28] ❶ to ask for ▷ *J'ai demandé la permission.* I've asked for permission. ❷ to require ▷ *un travail qui demande beaucoup de temps* a job that requires a lot of time; **se demander** to wonder ▷ *Je me demande à quelle heure il va venir.* I wonder what time he'll come.
 Be careful! **demander** does not mean **to demand**.

demandeur d'asile nm asylum seeker

demandeur d'emploi nm job-seeker

démangeaison nf itching

démanger vb [45] to itch ▷ Ça me démange. It itches.

démaquillant nm make-up remover

démaquiller vb [28] se démaquiller to remove one's make-up

démarche nf ❶ walk ❷ step ▷ faire les démarches nécessaires pour obtenir quelque chose to take the necessary steps to obtain something

démarrer vb [28] (car) to start

démêler vb [28] to untangle

déménagement nm move; un camion de déménagement a removal van

déménager vb [45] to move house

déménageur nm removal man

dément, e adj crazy

démentiel (f démentielle) adj insane

demeurer vb [28] to live

demi, e adj, adv half ▷ Il a trois ans et demi. He's three and a half.; Il est trois heures et demie. It's half past three.; Il est midi et demi. It's half past twelve.; à demi endormi half-asleep
▶ nm half pint of beer; Un demi, s'il vous plaît! A beer please!

demi-baguette nf half a baguette

demi-cercle nm semicircle

demi-douzaine nf half-dozen

demie nf half-hour ▷ Le bus passe à la demie. The bus comes by on the half-hour.

demi-écrémé, e adj semi-skimmed

demi-finale nf semi-final

demi-frère nm half-brother

demi-heure nf half an hour ▷ dans une demi-heure in half an hour

demi-journée nf half-day

demi-litre nm half litre

demi-livre nf half-pound

demi-pension nf half board ▷ Cet hôtel propose des tarifs raisonnables en demi-pension. This hotel has reasonable rates for half board.

demi-pensionnaire nmf être demi-pensionnaire to have school lunches

demi-sel adj du beurre demi-sel slightly salted butter

demi-sœur nf half-sister

démission nf resignation; donner sa démission to resign

démissionner vb [28] to resign

demi-tarif nm ❶ half-price ❷ half-fare

demi-tour nm faire demi-tour to turn back

démocratie nf democracy

démocratique adj democratic

démodé, e adj old-fashioned

demoiselle nf young lady; une demoiselle d'honneur a bridesmaid

démolir vb [38] to demolish

démon nm devil

démonter vb [28] ❶ (tent) to take down ❷ (machine) to take apart

démontrer vb [28] to show

dénoncer vb [12] to denounce; se dénoncer to give oneself up

a
b
c
d
e
f
g
h
i
j
k
l
m
n
o
p
q
r
s
t
u
v
w
x
y
z

dénouement nm outcome
densité nf density
dent nf tooth ▷ *une dent de lait* a milk tooth ▷ *une dent de sagesse* a wisdom tooth
dentaire adj dental
dentelle nf lace
dentier nm denture
dentifrice nm toothpaste
dentiste nmf dentist
déodorant nm deodorant
dépannage nm un service de dépannage a breakdown service
dépanner vb [28] ❶ to fix ▷ *Il a dépanné la voiture en cinq minutes.* He fixed the car in five minutes. ❷ to help out ▷ *Il m'a prêté dix euros pour me dépanner.* (informal) He lent me 10 euros to help me out.
dépanneuse nf breakdown lorry
départ nm departure; **Je lui téléphonerai la veille de son départ.** I'll phone him the day before he leaves.
département nm ❶ department ❷ administrative area
  • France is divided into 96
  • **départements**, administrative
  • areas rather like counties.
dépasser vb [58] ❶ to overtake ❷ to pass ▷ *Nous avons dépassé Dijon.* We've passed Dijon. ❸ (sum, limit) to exceed
dépaysé, e adj se sentir un peu dépaysé to feel a bit lost
se **dépêcher** vb [28] to hurry ▷ *Dépêche-toi!* Hurry up!
dépendre vb [88] dépendre de to depend on ▷ *Ça dépend du temps.* It

depends on the weather.; **dépendre de quelqu'un** to be dependent on somebody; **Ça dépend.** It depends.
dépenser vb [28] (money) to spend
dépensier (f dépensière) adj Il est dépensier. He's a big spender.; **Elle n'est pas dépensière.** She's not exactly extravagant.
dépilatoire adj une crème dépilatoire a hair-removing cream
dépit nm en dépit de in spite of
déplacé, e adj uncalled-for
déplacement nm trip
déplacer vb [12] ❶ to move ▷ *Tu peux m'aider à déplacer la table?* Can you help me move the table? ❷ to put off ▷ *déplacer un rendez-vous* to put off an appointment; **se déplacer (1)** to travel around ▷ *Il se déplace beaucoup pour son travail.* He travels around a lot for his work. **(2)** to get around ▷ *Il a du mal à se déplacer.* He has difficulty getting around.; **se déplacer une vertèbre** to slip a disc
déplaire vb [62] Cela me déplaît. I dislike this.
déplaisant, e adj unpleasant
dépliant nm leaflet
déplier vb [19] to unfold
déposer vb [28] ❶ to leave ▷ *J'ai déposé mon sac à la consigne.* I left my bag at the left-luggage office. ❷ to put down ▷ *Déposez le paquet sur la table.* Put the parcel down on the table.; **déposer quelqu'un** to drop somebody off
dépourvu, e adj prendre

quelqu'un au dépourvu to take somebody by surprise

dépression nf depression; **faire de la dépression** to be suffering from depression; **faire une dépression** to have a breakdown

déprimant, e adj depressing

déprimer vb [28] to get depressed ▷ *Ce genre de temps me déprime.* This kind of weather makes me depressed.

depuis prep, adv ❶ since ▷ *Il habite Paris depuis 2003.* He's been living in Paris since 2003.; **depuis que** since ❷ for ▷ *Il habite Paris depuis cinq ans.* He's been living in Paris for five years.; **Depuis combien de temps?** How long? ▷ *Depuis combien de temps est-ce que vous le connaissez?* How long have you known him?; **Depuis quand?** How long? ▷ *Depuis quand est-ce que vous le connaissez?* How long have you known him?

député nm Member of Parliament

députée nf Member of Parliament

déraciner vb [28] to uproot

dérangement nm **en dérangement** out of order

déranger vb [45] ❶ to bother ▷ *Excusez-moi de vous déranger.* I'm sorry to bother you.; **Ne vous dérangez pas, je vais répondre au téléphone.** You stay there, I'll answer the phone. ❷ to mess up ▷ *Ne dérange pas mes livres, s'il te plaît.* Don't mess up my books, please.

déraper vb [28] to skid

dermatologue nmf dermatologist

dernier (f **dernière**) adj ❶ last ▷ *la dernière fois* the last time ❷ latest ▷ *le dernier film de Spielberg* Spielberg's latest film; **en dernier** last

dernièrement adv recently

dérouler vb [28] ❶ to unroll ❷ to unwind; **se dérouler** to take place; **Tout s'est déroulé comme prévu.** Everything went as planned.

derrière adv, prep behind
▶ nm ❶ back ▷ *la porte de derrière* the back door ❷ backside

des art

des is the contracted form of de + les.

❶ some ▷ *Tu veux des chips?* Would you like some crisps?

des is sometimes not translated.

▷ *J'ai des cousins en France.* I have cousins in France. ❷ any ▷ *Tu as des frères?* Have you got any brothers? ▷ *la fin des vacances* the end of the holidays ▷ *la voiture des Durand* the Durands' car ▷ *Il arrive des États-Unis.* He's arriving from the United States.

dès prep as early as; **dès le mois de novembre** from November; **dès le début** right from the start; **Il vous appellera dès son retour.** He'll call you as soon as he gets back.; **dès que** as soon as ▷ *Il m'a reconnu dès qu'il m'a vu.* He recognized me as soon as he saw me.

désabusé, e adj disillusioned

désaccord nm disagreement

a
b
c
d
e
f
g
h
i
j
k
l
m
n
o
p
q
r
s
t
u
v
w
x
y
z

désagréable adj unpleasant

désaltérer vb [34] **L'eau gazeuse désaltère bien.** Sparkling water is very thirst-quenching.; **se désaltérer** to quench one's thirst

désapprobateur (f **désapprobatrice**) adj disapproving

désastre nm disaster

désavantage nm disadvantage

désavantager vb [45] **désavantager quelqu'un** to put somebody at a disadvantage

descendre vb [24] **①** to go down ▷ Je suis tombé en descendant l'escalier. I fell as I was going down the stairs. **②** to come down ▷ Attends en bas; je descends! Wait downstairs; I'm coming down! **③** to get down ▷ Vous pouvez descendre ma valise, s'il vous plaît? Can you get my suitcase down, please? **④** to get off ▷ Nous descendons à la prochaine station. We're getting off at the next station.

descente nf way down ▷ Je t'attendrai au bas de la descente. I'll wait for you at the bottom of the hill.; **une descente de police** a police raid

description nf description

déséquilibré, e adj unbalanced

déséquilibrer vb [28] **déséquilibrer quelqu'un** to throw somebody off balance

désert, e adj deserted; **une île déserte** a desert island
▶ nm desert

déserter vb [28] to desert

désertique adj desert ▷ une région désertique a desert region

désespéré, e adj desperate

désespérer vb [34] to despair ▷ Il ne faut pas désespérer. Don't despair.

désespoir nm despair

déshabiller vb [28] to undress; **se déshabiller** to get undressed

déshériter vb [28] to disinherit; **les déshérités** the underprivileged

déshydraté, e adj dehydrated

désigner vb [28] to choose ▷ On l'a désignée pour remettre le prix. She was chosen to present the prize.; **désigner quelque chose du doigt** to point at something

désinfectant nm disinfectant

désinfecter vb [28] to disinfect

désintéressé, e adj **①** unselfish ▷ un acte désintéressé an unselfish action **②** impartial ▷ un conseil désintéressé impartial advice

désintéresser vb [28] se **désintéresser de quelque chose** to lose interest in something

désir nm **①** wish ▷ Vos désirs sont des ordres. Your wish is my command. **②** will ▷ le désir de réussir the will to succeed **③** desire

désirer vb [28] to want ▷ Vous désirez? (in shop) What would you like?

désobéir vb [38] **désobéir à quelqu'un** to disobey somebody

désobéissant, e adj disobedient

désobligeant, e adj unpleasant

désodorisant nm air freshener

désolé, e adj sorry; **Désolé!** Sorry!

désopilant, e *adj* hilarious
désordonné, e *adj* untidy
désordre *nm* untidiness; **Quel désordre!** What a mess!; **en désordre** untidy
désormais *adv* from now on
desquelles *pron pl*

desquelles is the contracted form of **de** + **lesquelles**.
▷ *des négociations au cours desquelles les patrons ont fait des concessions* negotiations during which the employers made concessions

desquels *pron pl*

desquels is the contracted form of **de** + **lesquels**.
▷ *les lacs au bord desquels nous avons campé* the lakes on the banks of which we camped

dessécher *vb* [**34**] to dry out ▷ *Le soleil dessèche la peau.* The sun dries your skin out.
desserrer *vb* [**28**] to loosen
dessert *nm* pudding
dessin *nm* drawing; **un dessin animé** (*film*) a cartoon; **un dessin humoristique** (*drawing*) a cartoon
dessinateur *nm* **un dessinateur industriel** a draughtsman
dessiner *vb* [**28**] to draw
dessous *adv* underneath; **en dessous** underneath; **par-dessous** underneath; **là-dessous** under there; **ci-dessous** below ▷ *Complétez les phrases ci-dessous.* Complete the sentences below.; **au-dessous de** below

▶ *nm* underneath; **les voisins du dessous** the downstairs neighbours; **les dessous** underwear
dessous-de-plat (*pl* **dessous-de-plat**) *nm* tablemat
dessus *adv* on top; **par-dessus** over; **au-dessus** above ▷ *la taille au-dessus* the size above ▷ *au-dessus du lit* above the bed; **là-dessus** (1) on there ▷ *Tu peux écrire là-dessus.* You can write on there. (2) with that ▷ *'Je démissionne!' Là-dessus, il est parti.* 'I resign!' With that, he left.; **ci-dessus** above ▷ *l'exemple ci-dessus* the example above

▶ *nm* top; **les voisins du dessus** the upstairs neighbours; **avoir le dessus** to have the upper hand
destinataire *nmf* addressee
destination *nf* destination; **les passagers à destination de Paris** passengers travelling to Paris
destiné, e *adj* intended; **Elle était destinée à faire ce métier.** She was destined to go into that job.
destruction *nf* destruction
détachant *nm* stain remover
détacher *vb* [**28**] to undo; **se détacher** (1) to come off ▷ *La poignée de la porte s'est détachée.* The door handle came off. (2) to break away ▷ *Un wagon s'est détaché du reste du train.* A carriage broke away from the rest of the train.
détail *nm* detail; **en détail** in detail
détective *nm* detective
déteindre *vb* [**60**] (*in wash*) to fade
détendre *vb* [**88**] to relax ▷ *La*

lecture, ça me détend. I find reading relaxing.; **se détendre** to relax ▷ *Il est allé prendre un bain pour se détendre.* He's gone to have a bath to relax.

détente *nf* relaxation

détenu *nm* prisoner

détenue *nf* prisoner

se **détériorer** *vb* [28] to deteriorate

déterminé, e *adj* ❶ determined ❷ specific ▷ *un but déterminé* a specific aim

détestable *adj* horrible

détester *vb* [28] to hate

détonation *nf* bang

détour *nm* detour; **Ça vaut le détour.** It's worth the trip.

détournement *nm* un détournement d'avion a hijacking

détrempé, e *adj* waterlogged

détritus *nmpl* litter *sg*

détruire *vb* [23] to destroy

dette *nf* debt

deuil *nm* **être en deuil** to be in mourning

deux *num* two ▷ *Elle a deux ans.* She's two.; **deux fois** twice; **deux-points** colon; **tous les deux** both; **le deux février** the second of February

deuxième *adj* second ▷ *au deuxième étage* on the second floor

deuxièmement *adv* secondly

devais, devait, devaient *vb see* **devoir**

dévaliser *vb* [28] to rob

devant *adv*, *prep* ❶ in front ❷ in front of; **passer devant** to go past ▶ *nm* front ▷ *le devant de la maison*

the front of the house; **les pattes de devant** the front legs

développement *nm* development; **les pays en voie de développement** developing countries

développer *vb* [28] to develop; **se développer** to develop

devenir *vb* [25] to become

devez *vb see* **devoir**

déviation *nf* diversion

deviez *vb see* **devoir**

deviner *vb* [28] to guess

devinette *nf* riddle

devions *vb see* **devoir**

dévisager *vb* [45] dévisager quelqu'un to stare at somebody

devise *nf* currency

dévisser *vb* [28] to unscrew

dévoiler *vb* [28] to unveil

devoir *vb* [26] ❶ to have to ▷ *Je dois partir.* I've got to go. ❷ must ▷ *Tu dois être fatigué.* You must be tired. ❸ to be due to ▷ *Le nouveau centre commercial doit ouvrir en mai.* The new shopping centre is due to open in May.; **devoir quelque chose à quelqu'un** to owe somebody something ▷ *Combien est-ce que je vous dois?* How much do I owe you?
▶ *nm* ❶ exercise; **les devoirs** homework; **un devoir sur table** a written test ❷ duty

devons *vb see* **devoir**

dévorer *vb* [28] to devour

dévoué, e *adj* devoted

devra, devrai, devras, devrez, devrons, devront *vb see* **devoir**

diabète nm diabetes
diabétique adj diabetic
diable nm devil
diabolo nm fruit cordial and lemonade; **un diabolo menthe** a mint cordial and lemonade
diagonal, e (mpl **diagonaux**) adj diagonal
diagonale nf diagonal; **en diagonale** diagonally
diagramme nm diagram
dialecte nm dialect
dialogue nm dialogue
diamant nm diamond
diamètre nm diameter
diapo nf (informal) (image) slide
diapositive nf slide
diarrhée nf diarrhoea
dictateur nm dictator
dictature nf dictatorship
dictée nf dictation
dicter vb [28] to dictate
dictionnaire nm dictionary
diététique adj **un magasin diététique** a health food shop
dieu (pl **dieux**) nm god; **Dieu** God ▷ Mon Dieu! Oh my God!
différé nm **une émission en différé** a recording
différence nf difference; **la différence d'âge** the age difference; **à la différence de** unlike
différent, e adj ❶ different ❷ various; **différent de** different from
difficile adj difficult
difficilement adv **faire quelque chose difficilement** to have

trouble doing something; **Je pouvais difficilement refuser.** It was difficult for me to refuse.
difficulté nf difficulty ▷ **avec difficulté** with difficulty; **élève en difficulté (scolaire)** a student who is struggling
digérer vb [34] to digest
digestif nm after-dinner liqueur
digne adj **digne de** worthy of ▷ **digne de confiance** trustworthy
dignité nf dignity
dilemme nm dilemma
diluer vb [28] to dilute
dimanche nm ❶ Sunday ▷ Aujourd'hui, on est dimanche. It's Sunday today. ❷ on Sunday; **le dimanche** on Sundays; **tous les dimanches** every Sunday; **dimanche dernier** last Sunday; **dimanche prochain** next Sunday
diminuer vb [28] to decrease
diminutif nm pet name
diminution nf ❶ reduction ❷ decrease
dinde nf (meat) turkey
dindon nm (bird) turkey
dîner nm (evening meal) dinner ▶ vb [28] (evening meal) to have dinner
dingue adj (informal) crazy
diplomate adj diplomatic ▶ nmf diplomat
diplomatie nf diplomacy
diplôme nm qualification
diplômé, e adj qualified
dire vb [27] ❶ to say ▷ Il a dit qu'il ne viendrait pas. He said he wouldn't come.; **on dit que ...** they say

a
b
c
d
e
f
g
h
i
j
k
l
m
n
o
p
q
r
s
t
u
v
w
x
y
z

that ... ❷ to tell; **dire quelque chose à quelqu'un** to tell somebody something ▷ *Elle m'a dit la vérité.* She told me the truth.; **On dirait qu'il va pleuvoir.** It looks as if it's going to rain.; **se dire quelque chose** to think something ▷ *Quand je l'ai vu, je me suis dit qu'il avait vieilli.* When I saw him, I thought to myself that he'd aged.; **Est-ce que ça se dit?** Can you say that?; **Ça ne me dit rien.** (1) That doesn't appeal to me. (2) It doesn't ring a bell.

direct, e adj direct; **en direct** live
directement adv straight
directeur nm ❶ headteacher ❷ manager
direction nf ❶ management ❷ direction
directrice nf manager ▷ *Elle est directrice commerciale.* She's a sales manager.
dirent vb see **dire**
dirigeant nm leader
dirigeante nf leader
diriger vb [45] to manage ▷ *Il dirige une petite entreprise.* He manages a small company.; **se diriger vers** to head for ▷ *Il se dirigeait vers la gare.* He was heading for the station.
dis vb see **dire**; **Dis-moi la vérité!** Tell me the truth!; **dis donc** hey ▷ *Dis donc, tu te souviens de Sam?* Hey, do you remember Sam?
disaient, disais, disait vb see **dire**
discothèque nf (club) disco
discours nm speech

discret (f **discrète**) adj discreet
discrimination nf discrimination
discussion nf discussion
discutable adj debatable
discuter vb [28] ❶ to talk ▷ *Nous avons discuté pendant des heures.* We talked for hours. ❷ to argue ▷ *C'est ce que j'ai décidé, alors ne discutez pas!* That's what I've decided, so don't argue!
disent, disiez, disions vb see **dire**
disons vb see **dire** let's say ▷ *C'est à, disons, une demi-heure à pied.* It's half an hour's walk, say.
disparaître vb [56] to disappear; **faire disparaître quelque chose** (1) to make something disappear (2) to get rid of something
disparition nf disappearance; **une espèce en voie de disparition** an endangered species
disparu, e adj **être porté disparu** to be reported missing
dispensaire nm community clinic
dispensé, e adj **être dispensé de quelque chose** to be excused something ▷ *Elle est dispensée de gymnastique.* She's excused gym.
disperser vb [28] to break up ▷ *La police a dispersé les manifestants.* The police broke up the demonstrators.; **se disperser** to break up ▷ *Une fois l'ambulance partie, la foule s'est dispersée.* Once the ambulance had left, the crowd broke up.
disponible adj available
disposé, e adj **être disposé à faire quelque chose** to be willing to do

something ▷ *Il était disposé à m'aider.* He was willing to help me.

disposer *vb* [28] **disposer de quelque chose** to have access to something ▷ *Je dispose d'un ordinateur.* I have access to a computer.

disposition *nf* **prendre ses dispositions** to make arrangements; **avoir quelque chose à sa disposition** to have something at one's disposal; **Je suis à votre disposition.** I am at your service.; **Je tiens ces livres à votre disposition.** The books are at your disposal.

dispute *nf* argument

se **disputer** *vb* [28] to argue

disquaire *nm* record dealer

disque *nm* record; **un disque compact** a compact disc; **le disque dur** hard disk

disséminé, e *adj* scattered

disséquer *vb* [34] to dissect

dissertation *nf* essay

dissimuler *vb* [28] to conceal

se **dissiper** *vb* [28] to clear ▷ *Le brouillard va se dissiper dans l'après-midi.* The fog will clear during the afternoon.

dissolvant *nm* nail polish remover

dissoudre *vb* [70] to dissolve; **se dissoudre** to dissolve

dissuader *vb* [28] **dissuader quelqu'un de faire quelque chose** to dissuade somebody from doing something

distance *nf* distance

distillerie *nf* distillery

distingué, e *adj* distinguished

distinguer *vb* [28] to distinguish

distraction *nf* entertainment

distraire *vb* [85] *Va voir un film, ça te distraira.* Go and see a film, it'll take your mind off things.

distrait, e *adj* absent-minded

distribuer *vb* [28] ❶ to give out ▷ *Distribue les livres, s'il te plaît.* Give out the books, please. ❷ *(cards)* to deal

distributeur *nm* **un distributeur automatique** a vending machine; **un distributeur de billets** a cash machine

dit, e *adj* known as ▷ *Pierre, dit Pierrot* Pierre, known as Pierrot ▶ *vb* see **dire**

dites *vb* see **dire**; **Dites-moi ce que vous pensez.** Tell me what you think.; **dites donc** hey ▷ *Dites donc, vous, là-bas!* Hey, you there!

divers, e *adj* diverse; **pour diverses raisons** for various reasons

se **divertir** *vb* [38] to enjoy oneself

divin, e *adj* divine

diviser *vb* [28] to divide ▷ *Quatre divisé par deux égale deux.* 4 divided by 2 equals 2.

divorcé *nm* divorcee

divorcer *vb* [12] to get divorced

dix *num* ten ▷ *Elle a dix ans.* She's ten.; **le dix février** the tenth of February

dix-huit *num* eighteen ▷ *Elle a dix-huit ans.* She's eighteen. ▷ *à dix-huit heures* at 6 p.m.

dixième *adj* tenth

a
b
c
d
e
f
g
h
i
j
k
l
m
n
o
p
q
r
s
t
u
v
w
x
y
z

dix-neuf num nineteen ▷ Elle a
dix-neuf ans. She's nineteen. ▷ à
dix-neuf heures at 7 p.m.
dix-sept num seventeen ▷ Elle a
dix-sept ans. She's seventeen.
▷ à dix-sept heures at 5 p.m.
dizaine nf about ten
do nm ❶ C ❷ do
docteur nm doctor
document nm document
documentaire nm documentary
documentaliste nmf librarian
documentation nf
documentation
documenter vb [28] se
documenter sur quelque chose
to gather information on
something
dodu, e adj plump
doigt nm finger; **les doigts de pied**
the toes
dois, doit, doivent vb see **devoir**
domaine nm ❶ estate ▷ Il possède
un immense domaine en Normandie.
He owns a huge estate in
Normandy. ❷ field ▷ La chimie n'est
pas mon domaine. Chemistry's not
my field.
domestique adj domestic; **les
animaux domestiques** pets
▶ nmf servant
domicile nm place of residence; **à
domicile** at home ▷ Il travaille à
domicile. He works at home.
domicilié, e adj 'domicilié à: ...'
'address: ...'
dominer vb [28] to dominate; **se
dominer** to control oneself
dominos nmpl dominoes

dommage nm damage; **C'est
dommage.** It's a shame.
dompter vb [28] to tame
dompteur nm animal tamer
don nm ❶ donation ❷ gift; **Elle a le
don de m'énerver.** She's got a
knack of getting on my nerves.
donc conj so
donjon nm (of castle) keep
données nfpl data
donner vb [28] ❶ to give; **donner
quelque chose à quelqu'un** to
give somebody something ▷ Elle
m'a donné son adresse. She gave me
her address.; **Ça m'a donné faim.**
That made me feel hungry. ❷ to
give away; **donner sur quelque
chose** to overlook something ▷ une
fenêtre qui donne sur la mer a
window overlooking the sea
dont pron ❶ of which ▷ deux livres,
dont l'un est en anglais two books,
one of which is in English ▷ le prix
dont il est si fier the prize he's so
proud of ❷ of whom ▷ trois
candidats, dont deux parlent italien
three candidates, two of whom
speak Italian ▷ la fille dont je t'ai
parlé the girl I told you about
doré, e adj golden
dorénavant adv from now on
dorloter vb [28] to pamper
dormir vb [29] ❶ to sleep ▷ Tu as
bien dormi? Did you sleep well? ❷ to
be asleep ▷ Tu dors? Are you asleep?
dortoir nm dormitory
dos nm back; **faire quelque chose
dans le dos de quelqu'un** to do
something behind somebody's

back; **de dos** from behind; **nager
le dos crawlé** to swim backstroke;
'voir au dos' 'see over'

dose *nf* dose

dossier *nm* ❶ file ▷ *une pile de
dossiers* a stack of files ❷ report
▷ *un bon dossier scolaire* a good
school report ❸ *(in magazine)*
feature ❹ *(of chair)* back

douane *nf* customs

douanier *nm* customs officer

double *nm* **le double** twice as much;
en double in duplicate; **le double
messieurs** *(tennis)* the men's doubles

double-clic *(pl* **doubles-clics)** *nm*
double-click

double-cliquer *vb* [**28**] to
double-click ▷ *double-cliquer sur une
icône* to double-click on an icon

doubler *vb* [**28**] ❶ to double ▷ *Le prix a
doublé en dix ans.* The price has
doubled in 10 years. ❷ to overtake ▷ *Il
est dangereux de doubler sur cette route.*
It's dangerous to overtake on this
road.; **un film doublé** a dubbed film

douce *adj f see* **doux**

doucement *adv* ❶ gently ❷ slowly
▷ *Je ne comprends pas, parle plus
doucement.* I don't understand,
speak more slowly.

douceur *nf* ❶ softness
❷ gentleness; **L'avion a atterri en
douceur.** The plane made a
smooth landing.

douche *nf* shower; **les douches**
the shower room; **prendre une
douche** to have a shower

se doucher *vb* [**28**] to have a shower

doudou *nm* *(informal)* ❶ *(piece of*

fabric) comfort blanket ❷ *(toy)*
cuddly toy

doué, e *adj* talented; **être doué en
quelque chose** to be good at
something

douillet *(f* **douillette)** *adj* ❶ cosy
❷ soft

douleur *nf* pain

douloureux *(f* **douloureuse)** *adj*
painful

doute *nm* doubt; **sans doute**
probably

douter *vb* [**28**] to doubt; **douter de
quelque chose** to have doubts
about something ▷ *Je doute de sa
sincérité.* I have my doubts about his
sincerity.; **se douter de quelque
chose** to suspect something; **Je
m'en doutais.** I suspected as much.

douteux *(f* **douteuse)** *adj*
❶ dubious ❷ suspicious-looking

Douvres *n* Dover

doux *(f* **douce,** *mpl* **doux)** *adj* ❶ soft
▷ *un tissu doux* soft material ❷ sweet
▷ *du cidre doux* sweet cider ❸ mild
▷ *Il fait doux aujourd'hui.* It's mild
today. ❹ gentle ▷ *C'est quelqu'un de
très doux.* He's a very gentle
person.; **en douce** on the quiet

douzaine *nf* dozen; **une douzaine
de personnes** about twelve people

douze *num* twelve ▷ *Il a douze ans.*
He's twelve.; **le douze février** the
twelfth of February

douzième *adj* twelfth ▷ *au
douzième étage* on the twelfth floor

dragée *nf* sugared almond

draguer *vb* [**28**] *(informal)* **draguer
quelqu'un** to chat somebody up;

se faire draguer to get chatted up
dragueur nm (informal) (person) flirt
dramatique adj tragic; **l'art dramatique** drama
drame nm (incident) drama; **Ça n'est pas un drame si tu ne viens pas.** It's not the end of the world if you don't come.
drap nm (for bed) sheet
drapeau (pl **drapeaux**) nm flag
dressé, e adj trained
dresser vb [28] ❶ to draw up
▷ *dresser une liste* to draw up a list ❷ to train ▷ *dresser un chien* to train a dog; **dresser l'oreille** to prick up one's ears
drogue nf drug; **les drogues douces** soft drugs; **les drogues dures** hard drugs
drogué nm drug addict
droguer vb [28] **droguer quelqu'un** to drug somebody; **se droguer** to take drugs
droguerie nf hardware shop
droit, e adj, adv ❶ right ▷ *le côté droit* the right-hand side ❷ straight ▷ *Tiens-toi droite!* Stand up straight!; **tout droit** straight on ▶ nm ❶ right ▷ *les droits de l'homme* human rights; **avoir le droit de faire quelque chose** to be allowed to do something ❷ law ▷ *un étudiant en droit* a law student
droite nf right ▷ *sur votre droite* on your right; **à droite (1)** on the right ▷ *la troisième rue à droite* the third street on the right **(2)** to the right ▷ *à droite de la fenêtre* to the right of the window; **Tournez à droite.**

Turn right.; **la voie de droite** the right-hand lane; **la droite** (in politics) the right
droitier (f **droitière**) adj right-handed
drôle adj funny; **un drôle de temps** funny weather
drôlement adv (informal) really
drone nm drone
du art
  du is the contracted form of **de + le**.
❶ some ▷ *Tu veux du fromage?* Would you like some cheese? ❷ any ▷ *Tu as du chocolat?* Have you got any chocolate? ❸ of the ▷ *la porte du garage* the door of the garage ▷ *la femme du directeur* the headmaster's wife
dû (f **due**, mpl **dus**) adj **dû à** due to ▶ vb see **devoir**; **Nous avons dû nous arrêter.** We had to stop.
duc nm duke
duchesse nf duchess
dupe adj **Elle me ment mais je ne suis pas dupe.** She lies to me but I'm not taken in by that.
duquel (mpl **desquels**, fpl **desquelles**) pron
  duquel is the contracted form of **de + lequel**.
▷ *l'homme duquel il parle* the man he is talking about
dur, e adj, adv hard
durant prep ❶ during ▷ *durant la nuit* during the night ❷ for ▷ *durant des années* for years
durée nf length; **pour une durée de quinze jours** for a period of two

weeks; **de courte durée** short; **de
longue durée** long
durement *adv* harshly
durer *vb* [**28**] to last
dureté *nf* harshness
DVD *nm* DVD
dynamique *adj* dynamic
dyslexique *adj* dyslexic

eau (*pl* **eaux**) *nf* water; **l'eau
minérale** mineral water; **l'eau
plate** still water; **tomber à l'eau**
to fall through
ébahi, e *adj* amazed
éblouir *vb* [**38**] to dazzle
éboueur *nm* dustman
ébouillanter *vb* [**28**] to scald
écaille *nf* (*of fish*) scale
s' **écailler** *vb* [**28**] to flake
écart *nm* gap; **à l'écart de** away
from
écarté, e *adj* remote; **les bras
écartés** arms outstretched; **les
jambes écartées** legs apart
écarter *vb* [**28**] (*arms, legs*) to open
wide; **s'écarter** to move ▷ *Ils se
sont écartés pour le laisser passer.*
They moved to let him pass.
échafaudage *nm* scaffolding

échalote nf shallot

échange nm exchange

échanger vb [**45**] to swap ▷ Je t'échange ce timbre contre celui-là. I'll swap you this stamp for that one.

échantillon nm sample

échapper vb [**28**] **échapper à** to escape from ▷ Le prisonnier a réussi à échapper à la police. The prisoner managed to escape from the police.; **s'échapper** to escape ▷ Il s'est échappé de prison. He escaped from prison.; **l'échapper belle** to have a narrow escape ▷ Nous l'avons échappé belle. We had a narrow escape.

écharde nf splinter of wood

écharpe nf scarf

s'**échauffer** vb [**28**] (before exercise) to warm up

échec nm failure

échecs nmpl chess sg

échelle nf ❶ ladder ❷ (of map) scale

échevelé, e adj dishevelled

écho nm echo

échouer vb [**28**] **échouer à un examen** to fail an exam

éclabousser vb [**28**] to splash

éclair nm flash of lightning; **un éclair au chocolat** a chocolate éclair

éclairage nm lighting

éclaircie nf bright interval

éclairer vb [**28**] **Cette lampe éclaire bien.** This lamp gives a good light.

éclat nm ❶ (of glass) piece ❷ (of sun, colour) brightness; **des éclats de rire** roars of laughter

éclatant, e adj brilliant

éclater vb [**28**] ❶ (tyre, balloon) to burst; **éclater de rire** to burst out laughing; **éclater en sanglots** to burst into tears ❷ to break out ▷ La Seconde Guerre mondiale a éclaté en 1939. The Second World War broke out in 1939.

écœurant, e adj sickly

écœurer vb [**28**] **Tous ces mensonges m'écœurent.** All these lies make me sick.

école nf school ▷ aller à l'école to go to school ▷ une école publique a state school ▷ une école maternelle a nursery school

     The **école maternelle** is a state school for 2–6 year-olds.

écolier nm schoolboy

écolière nf schoolgirl

écologie nf ecology

écologique adj ecological

économie nf ❶ economy ❷ economics ▷ un cours d'économie an economics class

économies nfpl savings; **faire des économies** to save up

économique adj ❶ economic ❷ economical

économiser vb [**28**] to save

économiseur d'écran nm screen saver

écorce nf ❶ (of tree) bark ❷ (of orange, lemon) peel

s'**écorcher** vb [**28**] **Je me suis écorché le genou.** I've grazed my knee.

écossais, e adj, nm/f ❶ Scottish; **un Écossais** (man) a Scot; **une**

Écossaise *(woman)* a Scot; **les Écossais** the Scots ❷ tartan

Écosse *nf* Scotland; **en Écosse** (1) in Scotland (2) to Scotland

s' **écouler** *vb* [28] ❶ *(water)* to flow out ❷ to pass ▷ *Le temps s'écoule trop vite.* Time passes too quickly.

écouter *vb* [28] to listen to ▷ *J'aime écouter de la musique.* I like listening to music.; **Écoute-moi!** Listen!

écouteur *nm* *(of phone)* earpiece

écran *nm* screen; **le petit écran** television; **l'écran total** sunblock

écraser *vb* [28] ❶ to crush ▷ *Écrasez une gousse d'ail.* Crush a clove of garlic. ❷ to run over ▷ *Mon chien s'est fait écraser par une voiture.* My dog got run over by a car.; **s'écraser** to crash ▷ *L'avion s'est écrasé dans le désert.* The plane crashed in the desert.

écrémé, e *adj* skimmed

écrevisse *nf* crayfish

écrire *vb* [30] to write ▷ *Nous nous écrivons régulièrement.* We write to each other regularly.; **Ça s'écrit comment?** How do you spell that?

écrit *nm* written paper; **par écrit** in writing

écriteau *(pl* **écriteaux)** *nm* notice

écriture *nf* writing

écrivain *nm* writer

écrou *nm* *(metal)* nut

s' **écrouler** *vb* [28] to collapse

écru, e *adj* off-white

écureuil *nm* squirrel

écurie *nf* stable

Édimbourg *n* Edinburgh

éditer *vb* [28] to publish

éditeur *nm* publisher

édition *nf* ❶ edition ❷ publishing

édredon *nm* eiderdown

éducateur *nm* *(of people with special needs)* teacher

éducatif *(f* **éducative)** *adj* educational

éducation *nf* ❶ education ❷ upbringing

éducatrice *nf* *(of people with special needs)* teacher

éduquer *vb* [28] to educate

effacer *vb* [12] to rub out

effarant, e *adj* amazing

effectivement *adv* indeed

> Be careful! **effectivement** does not mean **effectively**.

effectuer *vb* [28] ❶ to make ❷ to do

effervescent, e *adj* effervescent

effet *nm* effect; **faire de l'effet** to take effect; **Ça m'a fait un drôle d'effet de le revoir.** It gave me a strange feeling to see him again.; **en effet** yes indeed

efficace *adj* ❶ efficient ❷ effective ▷ *un médicament efficace* an effective medicine

s' **effondrer** *vb* [28] to collapse

s' **efforcer** *vb* [12] **s'efforcer de faire quelque chose** to try hard to do something

effort *nm* effort

effrayant, e *adj* frightening

effrayer *vb* [59] to frighten

effronté, e *adj* cheeky

effroyable *adj* horrifying

égal, e *(mpl* **égaux)** *adj* equal; **Ça m'est égal.** (1) I don't mind.

a
b
c
d
e
f
g
h
i
j
k
l
m
n
o
p
q
r
s
t
u
v
w
x
y
z

(2) I don't care.

également *adv* also

égaler *vb* [28] to equal

égalité *nf* equality; **être à égalité** to be level

égard *nm* **à cet égard** in this respect

égarer *vb* [28] to mislay ▷ *J'ai égaré mes clés.* I've mislaid my keys.; **s'égarer** to get lost ▷ *Ils se sont égarés dans la forêt.* They got lost in the forest.

église *nf* church

égoïsme *nm* selfishness

égoïste *adj* selfish

égout *nm* sewer

égratignure *nf* scratch

Égypte *nf* Egypt

égyptien (f **égyptienne**) *adj* Egyptian

eh *excl* hey!; **eh bien** well

élan *nm* **prendre de l'élan** to gather speed

s' **élancer** *vb* [12] to hurl oneself

élargir *vb* [38] to widen

élastique *nm* rubber band

électeur *nm* (man) voter

élection *nf* election

électrice *nf* (woman) voter

électricien *nm* electrician

électricité *nf* electricity ▷ *une facture d'électricité* an electricity bill

électrique *adj* electric

électronique *adj* electronic
▶ *nf* electronics

élégant, e *adj* smart

élémentaire *adj* elementary

éléphant *nm* elephant

élevage *nm* cattle rearing; **un**

élevage de porcs a pig farm; **un élevage de poulets** a chicken farm; **les truites d'élevage** farmed trout

élevé, e *adj* high; **être bien élevé** to have good manners; **être mal élevé** to have bad manners

élève *nmf* pupil

élever *vb* [43] ❶ to bring up ▷ *Il a été élevé par sa grand-mère.* He was brought up by his grandmother. ❷ to breed ▷ *Son oncle élève des chevaux.* His uncle breeds horses.; **élever la voix** to raise one's voice; **s'élever à** to come to

éleveur *nm* breeder

éliminatoire *adj* **une note éliminatoire** a fail mark; **une épreuve éliminatoire** (sport) a qualifying round

éliminer *vb* [28] to eliminate

élire *vb* [44] to elect

elle *pron* ❶ she ▷ *Elle est institutrice.* She is a primary school teacher. ❷ her ▷ *Vous pouvez avoir confiance en elle.* You can trust her. ❸ it ▷ *Prends cette chaise: elle est plus confortable.* Take this chair: it's more comfortable.

  elle is also used for emphasis. ▷ *Elle, elle est toujours en retard!* Oh, SHE's always late!; **elle-même** herself ▷ *Elle l'a choisi elle-même.* She chose it herself.

elles *pron pl* they ▷ *Où sont Anne et Rachel? — Elles sont allées au cinéma.* Where are Anne and Rachel? — They've gone to the cinema.; **elles-mêmes** themselves

élogieux (f **élogieuse**) adj complimentary

éloigné, e adj distant

s'**éloigner** vb [28] to go far away ▷ Ne vous éloignez pas: le dîner est bientôt prêt! Don't go far away: dinner will soon be ready!; **Vous vous éloignez du sujet.** You are getting off the point.

Élysée nm Élysée Palace
  The **Élysée** is the residence of the French president.

e-mail nm email

emballage nm le papier d'emballage wrapping paper

emballer vb [28] to wrap; s'**emballer** (informal) to get excited ▷ Il s'est emballé pour ce projet. He got really excited about this plan.

embarquement nm boarding

embarras nm embarrassment; **Vous n'avez que l'embarras du choix.** The only problem is choosing.

embarrassant, e adj embarrassing

embarrasser vb [28] to embarrass ▷ Cela m'embarrasse de vous demander encore un service. I feel embarrassed to ask you to do something more for me.

embaucher vb [28] to take on ▷ L'entreprise vient d'embaucher cinquante ouvriers. The firm has just taken on fifty workers.

embêtant, e adj annoying

embêtements nmpl trouble sg

embêter vb [28] to bother; s'**embêter** to be bored ▷ Qu'est-ce qu'on s'embête ici! Isn't it boring here!

embouteillage nm traffic jam

embrasser vb [28] to kiss ▷ Ils se sont embrassés. They kissed each other.

s'**embrouiller** vb [28] to get confused ▷ Il s'embrouille dans ses explications. He gets confused when he explains things.

émerveiller vb [28] to dazzle

émeute nf riot

émigrer vb [28] to emigrate

émission nf programme ▷ une émission de télévision a TV programme

s'**emmêler** vb [28] to get tangled

emménager vb [45] to move in ▷ Nous venons d'emménager dans une nouvelle maison. We've just moved into a new house.

emmener vb [43] to take ▷ Ils m'ont emmené au cinéma pour mon anniversaire. They took me to the cinema for my birthday.

émoticon nm (computing) smiley

émotif (f **émotive**) adj emotional

émotion nf emotion

émouvoir vb [31] to move ▷ Sa lettre l'a beaucoup émue. She was deeply moved by his letter.

s'**emparer** vb [28] s'emparer de to grab ▷ Il s'est emparé de ma valise. He grabbed my case.

empêchement nm Nous avons eu un empêchement de dernière minute. We were held up at the last minute.

empêcher vb [28] to prevent ▷ Le

café le soir m'empêche de dormir.
Coffee at night keeps me awake.;
Il n'a pas pu s'empêcher de rire.
He couldn't help laughing.
empereur *nm* emperor
s'**empiffrer** *vb* [28] *(informal)* to
stuff one's face
empiler *vb* [28] to pile up
empirer *vb* [28] to worsen ▷ *La*
situation a encore empiré. The
situation got even worse.
emplacement *nm* site
emploi *nm* ❶ use; **le mode**
d'emploi directions for use ❷ job;
un emploi du temps a timetable
employé *nm* employee; **un employé**
de bureau an office worker
employée *nf* employee
employer *vb* [53] ❶ to use ▷ *Quelle*
méthode employez-vous? What
method do you use? ❷ to employ
▷ *L'entreprise emploie dix ingénieurs.*
The firm employs ten engineers.
employeur *nm* employer
empoisonner *vb* [28] to poison
emporter *vb* [28] to take
▷ *N'emportez que le strict nécessaire.*
Only take the bare minimum.;
plats à emporter take-away
meals; **s'emporter** to lose one's
temper ▷ *Je m'emporte facilement.*
I'm quick to lose my temper.
empreinte *nf* footprint; **l'empreinte**
carbone carbon footprint; **une**
empreinte digitale a fingerprint
s'**empresser** *vb* [28] s'empresser
de faire quelque chose to be quick
to do something
emprisonner *vb* [28] to imprison

emprunt *nm* loan
emprunter *vb* [28] to borrow;
emprunter quelque chose à
quelqu'un to borrow something
from somebody ▷ *Je peux*
t'emprunter dix euros? Can I borrow
ten euros from you?
EMT *nf* (= éducation manuelle
technique) technology
ému, e *adj* touched
en *prep, pron* ❶ in ▷ *Il habite en*
France. He lives in France. ▷ *La*
mariée est en blanc. The bride is in
white. ▷ *Je le verrai en mai.* I'll see
him in May. ❷ to ▷ *Je vais en France*
cet été. I'm going to France this
summer. ❸ by ▷ *C'est plus rapide en*
voiture. It's quicker by car. ❹ made
of ▷ *C'est en verre.* It's made of glass.
▷ *un collier en argent* a silver
necklace ❺ while ▷ *Il s'est coupé le*
doigt en ouvrant une boîte de conserve.
He cut his finger while opening a
tin.; **Elle est sortie en courant.**
She ran out.

When **en** is used with **avoir** and
il y a, it is not translated in
English.
▷ *Est-ce que tu as un dictionnaire?*
— *Oui, j'en ai un.* Have you got a
dictionary? — Yes, I've got one.
▷ *Combien d'élèves y a-t-il dans ta*
classe? — *Il y en a trente.* How many
pupils are there in your class?
— There are 30.

en is also used with verbs and
expressions normally followed
by **de** to avoid repeating the
same word.

▷ *Si tu as un problème, tu peux m'en parler.* If you've got a problem, you can talk to me about it. ▷ *Est-ce que tu peux me rendre ce livre? J'en ai besoin.* Can you give me back that book? I need it. ▷ *Il a un beau jardin et il en est très fier.* He's got a beautiful garden and is very proud of it.; **J'en ai assez.** I've had enough.

encaisser vb [28] *(money)* to cash
enceinte adj f pregnant
enchanté, e adj delighted; **Enchanté!** Pleased to meet you!
encombrant, e adj bulky
encombrer vb [28] to clutter
encore adv ❶ still ▷ *Il est encore au travail.* He's still at work. ❷ even ❸ again ▷ *Il m'a encore demandé de l'argent.* He asked me for money again.; **encore une fois** once again; **pas encore** not yet
encourager vb [45] to encourage
encre nf ink
encyclopédie nf encyclopaedia
endive nf chicory
endommager vb [45] to damage
endormi, e adj asleep
endormir vb [29] to deaden ▷ *Cette piqûre sert à endormir le nerf.* This injection is to deaden the nerve.; **s'endormir** to go to sleep
endroit nm place; **à l'endroit** (1) the right way out (2) the right way up
endurant, e adj *(person)* tough
endurcir vb [38] to toughen up; **s'endurcir** to become hardened
endurer vb [28] to endure

énergie nf ❶ energy ❷ power; **avec énergie** vigorously
énergique adj energetic; **des mesures énergiques** strong measures
énerver vb [28] **Il m'énerve!** He gets on my nerves!; **Ce bruit m'énerve.** This noise gets on my nerves.; **s'énerver** to get worked up; **Ne t'énerve pas!** Take it easy!
enfance nf childhood ▷ *Je le connais depuis l'enfance.* I've known him since I was a child.
enfant nmf child
enfer nm hell
s'enfermer vb [28] **Il s'est enfermé dans sa chambre.** He shut himself up in his bedroom.
enfiler vb [28] ❶ to put on ▷ *J'ai rapidement enfilé un pull avant de sortir.* I quickly put on a sweater before going out. ❷ to thread ▷ *J'ai du mal à enfiler cette aiguille.* I am having difficulty threading this needle.
enfin adv at last
enflé, e adj swollen
enfler vb [28] to swell
enfoncer vb [12] **Il marchait, les mains enfoncées dans les poches.** He was walking with his hands thrust into his pockets.; **s'enfoncer** to sink
s'enfuir vb [39] to run off
engagement nm commitment
engager vb [45] *(person)* to take on
s'engager vb [45] to commit oneself ▷ *Le Premier ministre s'est engagé à combattre le chômage.* The

a
b
c
d
e
f
g
h
i
j
k
l
m
n
o
p
q
r
s
t
u
v
w
x
y
z

Prime Minister has committed himself to fighting unemployment.; **Il s'est engagé dans l'armée à dix-huit ans.** He joined the army when he was 18.

engelures *nfpl* chilblains

engin *nm* device

> Be careful! The French word **engin** does not mean **engine**.

s' **engourdir** *vb* [**38**] to go numb

engueuler *vb* [**28**] (*informal*) **engueuler quelqu'un** to tell somebody off

énigme *nf* riddle

s' **enivrer** *vb* [**28**] to get drunk

enjamber *vb* [**28**] to stride over
> *enjamber une barrière* to stride over a fence

enlèvement *nm* kidnapping

enlever *vb* [**43**] ❶ to take off
> *Enlève donc ton manteau!* Take off your coat! ❷ to kidnap

enneigé, e *adj* snowed up

ennemi *nm* enemy

ennui *nm* ❶ boredom ❷ problem
> *avoir des ennuis* to have problems

ennuyer *vb* [**53**] to bother ▷ *J'espère que cela ne vous ennuie pas trop.* I hope it doesn't bother you too much.; **s'ennuyer** to be bored

ennuyeux (f **ennuyeuse**) *adj* ❶ boring ❷ awkward

énorme *adj* huge

énormément *adv* **Il a énormément grossi.** He's put on an awful lot of weight.; **Il y a énormément de neige.** There's an enormous amount of snow.

enquête *nf* ❶ investigation ❷ survey

enquêter *vb* [**28**] to investigate
> *La police enquête actuellement sur le crime.* The police are currently investigating the crime.

enrageant, e *adj* infuriating

enrager *vb* [**45**] to be furious

enregistrement *nm* recording; **l'enregistrement des bagages** baggage check-in

enregistrer *vb* [**28**] ❶ to record
> *Ils viennent d'enregistrer un nouvel album.* They've just recorded a new album. ❷ to check in ▷ *Vous pouvez enregistrer plusieurs valises.* You can check in several cases.

s' **enrhumer** *vb* [**28**] to catch a cold
> *Je suis enrhumé.* I've got a cold.

s' **enrichir** *vb* [**38**] to get rich

enrouler *vb* [**28**] to wind ▷ *Enroulez le fil autour de la bobine.* Wind the thread round the bobbin.

enseignant *nm* teacher

enseignante *nf* teacher

enseignement *nm* ❶ education
> *les réformes de l'enseignement* education reforms ❷ teaching
> *l'enseignement des langues étrangères* the teaching of foreign languages

enseigner *vb* [**28**] to teach

ensemble *adv* together ▷ *tous ensemble* all together
> *nm* outfit; **l'ensemble de** the whole of; **dans l'ensemble** on the whole

ensoleillé, e *adj* sunny

ensuite *adv* then

entamer *vb* [**28**] to start ▷ *Qui a*

entamé le gâteau? Who's started the cake?

s'**entasser** *vb* [**28**] to cram ▷ *Ils se sont tous entassés dans ma voiture.* They all crammed into my car.

entendre *vb* [**88**] ❶ to hear ▷ *Je ne t'entends pas.* I can't hear you.; **J'ai entendu dire qu'il est dangereux de nager ici.** I've heard that it's dangerous to swim here. ❷ to mean ▷ *Qu'est-ce que tu entends par là?* What do you mean by that?; **s'entendre** to get on ▷ *Il s'entend bien avec sa sœur.* He gets on well with his sister.

entendu, e *adj* **C'est entendu!** Agreed!; **bien entendu** of course

enterrement *nm* (burial) funeral

enterrer *vb* [**28**] to bury

entêté, e *adj* stubborn

s'**entêter** *vb* [**28**] to persist ▷ *Il s'entête à refuser de voir le médecin.* He persists in refusing to go to the doctor.

enthousiasme *nm* enthusiasm

s'**enthousiasmer** *vb* [**28**] to get enthusiastic ▷ *Il s'enthousiasme facilement.* He gets very enthusiastic about things.

entier (*f* **entière**) *adj* whole ▷ *Il a mangé une quiche entière.* He ate a whole quiche.; **le lait entier** full fat milk

entièrement *adv* completely

entorse *nf* sprain ▷ *Il s'est fait une entorse à la cheville.* He's sprained his ankle.

entourer *vb* [**28**] to surround

entracte *nm* interval

entraînement *nm* training

entraîner *vb* [**28**] ❶ to lead ▷ *Il se laisse facilement entraîner par les autres.* He's easily led. ❷ to train ▷ *Il entraîne l'équipe de France depuis cinq ans.* He's been training the French team for five years. ❸ to involve ▷ *Un mariage entraîne beaucoup de dépenses.* A wedding involves a lot of expense.; **s'entraîner** to train ▷ *Il s'entraîne au foot tous les samedis matins.* He does football training every Saturday morning.

entraîneur *nm* trainer

entre *prep* between ▷ *Il est assis entre son père et son oncle.* He's sitting between his father and his uncle.; **entre eux** among themselves; **l'un d'entre eux** one of them

entrecôte *nf* rib steak

entrée *nf* ❶ entrance ❷ (of meal) starter ▷ *Qu'est ce que vous prenez comme entrée?* What would you like for the starter?

entreprendre *vb* [**65**] to start on ▷ *Elle a entrepris des démarches pour adopter un enfant.* She's started on the procedures for adopting a child.

entrepreneur *nm* contractor

entreprise *nf* firm

entrer *vb* [**32**] ❶ to come in ▷ *Entrez donc!* Come on in! ❷ to go in ▷ *Ils sont tous entrés dans la maison.* They all went into the house.; **entrer à l'hôpital** to go into hospital; **entrer des données** to enter data

entre-temps *adv* meanwhile

a
b
c
d
e
f
g
h
i
j
k
l
m
n
o
p
q
r
s
t
u
v
w
x
y
z

entretien nm ❶ maintenance ❷ interview

entrevue nf interview

entrouvert, e adj half open

envahir vb [38] to invade

enveloppe nf envelope

envelopper vb [28] to wrap

envers prep towards ▷ Il est bien disposé envers elle. He's well disposed towards her.
▶ nm à l'**envers** inside out

envie nf avoir envie de faire quelque chose to feel like doing something ▷ J'avais envie de pleurer. I felt like crying. ▷ J'ai envie d'aller aux toilettes. I want to go to the toilet.; **Cette glace me fait envie.** I fancy some of that ice cream.

envier vb [19] to envy

environ adv about ▷ C'est à soixante kilomètres environ. It's about 60 kilometres.

environnement nm environment

environs nmpl area sg ▷ Il y a beaucoup de choses intéressantes à voir dans les environs. There are a lot of interesting things to see in the area.; **aux environs de dix-neuf heures** around 7 p.m.

envisager vb [45] to consider

s'**envoler** vb [28] ❶ to fly away ▷ Le papillon s'est envolé. The butterfly flew away. ❷ to blow away ▷ Toutes mes feuilles de cours se sont envolées. All my lecture notes blew away.

envoyer vb [33] to send ▷ Ma tante m'a envoyé une carte pour mon anniversaire. My aunt sent me a

card for my birthday.; **envoyer quelqu'un chercher quelque chose** to send somebody to get something ▷ Sa mère l'a envoyé chercher du pain. His mother sent him to get some bread.; **envoyer un e-mail à quelqu'un** to send somebody an email

épais (f **épaisse**) adj thick

épaisseur nf thickness

épatant, e adj (informal) great

épaule nf shoulder

épée nf sword

épeler vb [4] to spell ▷ Est-ce que vous pouvez épeler votre nom, s'il vous plaît? Can you spell your name, please?

épice nf spice

épicé, e adj spicy

épicerie nf grocer's shop

épicier nm grocer

épidémie nf epidemic

épiler vb [28] s'épiler les jambes to wax one's legs; s'épiler les sourcils to pluck one's eyebrows

épinards nmpl spinach sg

épine nf thorn

épingle nf pin; une épingle de sûreté a safety pin

épisode nm episode

éplucher vb [28] to peel

éponge nf sponge

époque nf time ▷ à cette époque de l'année at this time of year; **à l'époque** at that time

épouse nf wife

épouser vb [28] to marry

épouvantable adj awful

épouvante nf terror; un film

d'épouvante a horror film

épouvanter vb [28] to terrify

époux nm husband; **les nouveaux époux** the newly-weds

épreuve nf ❶ test ▷ une épreuve écrite a written test ❷ (sport) event

éprouver vb [28] to feel ▷ Qu'est-ce que vous avez éprouvé à ce moment-là? What did you feel at that moment?

EPS nf (= éducation physique et sportive) PE (= physical education)

épuisé, e adj exhausted

épuiser vb [28] to wear out ▷ Ce travail m'a complètement épuisé. This job has completely worn me out.; **s'épuiser** to wear oneself out ▷ Il s'épuise à garder un jardin impeccable. He wears himself out keeping his garden immaculate.

Équateur nm Ecuador

équateur nm equator

équation nf equation

équerre nf set square

équilibre nm balance ▷ J'ai failli perdre l'équilibre. I nearly lost my balance.

équilibré, e adj well-balanced

équipage nm crew

équipe nf team

équipé, e adj bien équipé well-equipped

équipement nm equipment

équipements nmpl facilities ▷ les équipements sportifs sports facilities

équitation nf riding

équivalent nm equivalent

erreur nf mistake; **faire erreur** to be mistaken

es vb see **être**; **Tu es très gentille.**

You're very kind.

escabeau (pl **escabeaux**) nm stepladder

escalade nf climbing

escalader vb [28] to climb

escale nf faire escale to stop off

escalier nm stairs

escargot nm snail

esclavage nm slavery

esclave nmf slave

escrime nf fencing

escroc nm crook

espace nm space; **espace de travail** workspace

s'**espacer** vb [12] to become less frequent ▷ Ses visites se sont peu à peu espacées. His visits became less and less frequent.

espadrille nf rope-soled sandal

Espagne nf Spain; **en Espagne (1)** in Spain **(2)** to Spain

espagnol, e adj, n Spanish ▷ J'apprends l'espagnol. I'm learning Spanish.; **un Espagnol** (man) a Spaniard; **une Espagnole** (woman) a Spaniard

espèce nf ❶ sort ❷ species ▷ une espèce en voie de disparition an endangered species; **Espèce d'idiot!** You idiot!

espèces nfpl cash sg

espérer vb [34] to hope; **J'espère bien.** I hope so. ▷ Tu penses avoir réussi? — Oui, j'espère bien. Do you think you've passed? — Yes, I hope so.

espiègle adj mischievous

espion nm spy

espionnage nm spying; **un roman**

a
b
c
d
e
f
g
h
i
j
k
l
m
n
o
p
q
r
s
t
u
v
w
x
y
z

d'espionnage a spy novel

espoir nm hope

esprit nm mind ▷ *Ça ne m'est pas venu à l'esprit.* It didn't cross my mind.; **avoir de l'esprit** to be witty

esquimau® (pl **esquimaux**) nm ice lolly

essai nm attempt; **prendre quelqu'un à l'essai** to take somebody on for a trial period

essayer vb [59] ❶ to try ▷ *Essaie de rentrer de bonne heure.* Try to come home early. ❷ to try on ▷ *Essaie ce pull: il devrait bien t'aller.* Try this sweater on: it ought to look good on you.

essence nf petrol

essentiel (f **essentielle**) adj essential; **Tu es là: c'est l'essentiel.** You're here: that's the main thing.

s'**essouffler** vb [28] to get out of breath

essuie-glace nm windscreen wiper

essuyer vb [53] to wipe; **essuyer la vaisselle** to dry the dishes; **s'essuyer** to dry oneself ▷ *Vous pouvez vous essuyer les mains avec cette serviette.* You can dry your hands on this towel.

est vb see **être**; **Elle est merveilleuse.** She's marvellous.
▶ adj ❶ east ❷ eastern
▶ nm east; **vers l'est** eastwards; **à l'est de Paris** east of Paris; **l'Europe de l'Est** Eastern Europe; **le vent d'est** the east wind

est-ce que adv **Est-ce que c'est**

cher? Is it expensive?; **Quand est-ce qu'il part?** When is he leaving?

esthéticienne nf beautician

estime nf J'ai beaucoup d'estime pour elle. I think a lot of her.

estimer vb [28] **estimer quelqu'un** to have great respect for somebody; **estimer que** to consider that ▷ *J'estime que c'est de sa faute.* I consider that it's his fault.

estivant nm holiday-maker

estomac nm stomach

Estonie nf Estonia

estrade nf platform

et conj and

établir vb [38] to establish; **s'établir à son compte** to set up in business

établissement nm establishment; **un établissement scolaire** a school

étage nm floor ▷ *au premier étage* on the first floor; **à l'étage** upstairs

étagère nf shelf

étaient vb see **être**

étain nm tin

étais, était vb see **être**; **Il était très jeune.** He was very young.

étalage nm display

étaler vb [28] to spread

étanche adj ❶ watertight ❷ (watch) waterproof

étang nm pond

étant vb see **être**; **Mes revenus étant limités ...** My income being limited ...

étape nf stage; **faire étape** to stop off

État nm (nation) state

état nm condition ▷ en mauvais état in poor condition; **remettre quelque chose en état** to repair something; **le bureau d'état civil** the registry office

États-Unis nmpl United States; **aux États-Unis (1)** in the United States **(2)** to the United States

été vb see **être**; **Il a été licencié.** He's been made redundant. ▶ nm summer; **en été** in the summer

éteindre vb [60] ❶ to switch off ▷ Éteins la lumière. Switch the light off. ❷ (cigarette) to put out

étendre vb [88] to spread ▷ Elle a étendu une nappe propre sur la table. She spread a clean cloth on the table.; **étendre le linge** to hang out the washing; **s'étendre** to lie down ▷ Je vais m'étendre cinq minutes. I'm going to lie down for five minutes.

éternité nf J'ai attendu une éternité chez le médecin. I waited for ages at the doctor's.

éternuer vb [28] to sneeze

êtes vb see **être**; **Vous êtes en retard.** You're late.

étiez vb see **être**

étinceler vb [4] to sparkle

étions vb see **être**

étiquette nf label

s'**étirer** vb [28] to stretch ▷ Elle s'est étirée paresseusement. She stretched lazily.

étoile nf star; **une étoile de mer** a starfish; **une étoile filante** a

shooting star; **dormir à la belle étoile** to sleep under the stars

étonnant, e adj amazing

étonner vb [28] to surprise ▷ Cela m'étonnerait que le colis soit déjà arrivé. I'd be surprised if the parcel had arrived yet.

étouffer vb [28] On étouffe ici: ouvre donc les fenêtres. It's stifling in here: open the windows.; **s'étouffer** to choke ▷ Ne mange pas si vite: tu vas t'étouffer! Don't eat so fast: you'll choke!

étourderie nf absent-mindedness; **une erreur d'étourderie** a slip

étourdi, e adj scatterbrained

étourdissement nm avoir des étourdissements to feel dizzy

étrange adj strange

étranger (f étrangère) adj foreign; **une personne étrangère** a stranger

étranger nm ❶ foreigner ❷ stranger; **à l'étranger** abroad

étrangère nf ❶ foreigner ❷ stranger

étrangler vb [28] to strangle; **s'étrangler** to choke ▷ s'étrangler avec quelque chose to choke on something

être nm un être humain a human being ▶ vb [35] ❶ to be ▷ Je suis heureux. I'm happy. ▷ Il est dix heures. It's 10 o'clock. ❷ to have ▷ Il n'est pas encore arrivé. He hasn't arrived yet.

étrennes nfpl Nous avons donné des étrennes à la gardienne. We

a
b
c
d
e
f
g
h
i
j
k
l
m
n
o
p
q
r
s
t
u
v
w
x
y
z

gave the caretaker a New Year gift.

étroit, e adj narrow; **être à l'étroit** to be cramped

étude nf study; **faire des études** to be studying ▷ Il fait des études de droit. He's studying law.

étudiant nm student

étudiante nf student

étudier vb [19] to study

étui nm case ▷ un étui à lunettes a glasses case

eu vb see **avoir**; J'ai eu une bonne note. I got a good mark.

euh excl er ▷ Euh ... je ne m'en souviens pas. Er ... I can't remember.

euro nm euro

Europe nf Europe; **en Europe (1)** in Europe **(2)** to Europe

européen (f **européenne**) adj European

eux pron pl them ▷ Je pense souvent à eux. I often think of them.

▋ eux is also used for emphasis. ▷ Elle a accepté l'invitation, mais eux, ils ont refusé. She accepted the invitation, but THEY refused.

évacuer vb [28] to evacuate

s'**évader** vb [28] to escape

évangile nm gospel

s'**évanouir** vb [38] to faint

s'**évaporer** vb [28] to evaporate

évasif (f **évasive**) adj evasive

évasion nf escape

éveillé, e adj ❶ awake ▷ Il est resté éveillé toute la nuit. He stayed awake all night. ❷ bright ▷ C'est un enfant très éveillé pour son âge. He's very bright for his age.

s'**éveiller** vb [28] to awaken

événement nm event

éventail nm (hand-held) fan; **un large éventail de prix** a wide range of prices

éventualité nf dans l'éventualité d'un retard in the event of a delay

éventuel (f **éventuelle**) adj possible

▋ Be careful! **éventuel** does not mean **eventual**.

éventuellement adv possibly

▋ Be careful! **éventuellement** does not mean **eventually**.

évêque nm bishop

évidemment adv ❶ obviously ❷ of course

évidence nf C'est une évidence. It's quite obvious.; **de toute évidence** obviously; **être en évidence** to be clearly visible; **mettre en évidence** to reveal

évident, e adj obvious

évier nm sink

éviter vb [28] to avoid

évolué, e adj advanced

évoluer vb [28] to progress ▷ La chirurgie esthétique a beaucoup évolué. Cosmetic surgery has progressed a great deal.; **Il a beaucoup évolué.** He has come on a great deal.

évolution nf ❶ development ❷ evolution

évoquer vb [28] to mention ▷ Il a évoqué divers problèmes dans son discours. He mentioned various problems in his speech.

exact, e adj ❶ right ❷ exact

exactement adv exactly

ex aequo adj Ils sont arrivés ex aequo. They finished neck and neck.

exagérer vb [34] **①** to exaggerate ▷ Vous exagérez! You're exaggerating! **②** to go too far ▷ Ça fait trois fois que tu arrives en retard: tu exagères! That's three times you've been late: you really go too far sometimes!

examen nm exam; **un examen médical** a medical

examiner vb [28] to examine

exaspérant, e adj infuriating

exaspérer vb [34] to infuriate

excédent nm l'excédent de bagages excess baggage

excéder vb [34] to exceed ▷ un contrat dont la durée n'excède pas deux ans a contract for a period not exceeding two years; **excéder quelqu'un** to drive somebody mad ▷ Les cris des enfants l'excédaient. The noise of the children was driving her mad.

excellent, e adj excellent

excentrique adj eccentric

excepté prep except ▷ Toutes les chaussures excepté les sandales sont en solde. All the shoes except sandals are reduced.

exception nf exception; **à l'exception de** except

exceptionnel (f **exceptionnelle**) adj exceptional

excès nm faire des excès to overindulge; **les excès de vitesse** speeding

excessif (f **excessive**) adj excessive

excitant, e adj exciting ▶ nm stimulant

excitation nf excitement

exciter vb [28] to excite ▷ Il était tout excité à l'idée de revoir ses cousins. He was all excited about seeing his cousins again.; **s'exciter** (informal) to get excited ▷ Ne t'excite pas trop vite: ça ne va peut-être pas marcher! Don't get excited too soon: it may not work!

exclamation nf exclamation

exclu, e adj Il n'est pas exclu que ... It's not impossible that ...

exclusif (f **exclusive**) adj exclusive

excursion nf **①** trip **②** walk ▷ une excursion dans la montagne a walk in the hills

excuse nf **①** excuse **②** apology ▷ présenter ses excuses to offer one's apologies; **un mot d'excuse** a note ▷ Vous devez apporter un mot d'excuse signé par vos parents. You have to bring a note signed by your parents.

excuser vb [28] to excuse; **Excusez-moi.** (1) Sorry. ▷ Excusez-moi, je ne vous avais pas vu. Sorry, I didn't see you. (2) Excuse me. ▷ Excusez-moi, est-ce que vous avez l'heure? Excuse me, have you got the time?; **s'excuser** to apologize

exécuter vb [28] **①** to execute ▷ Le prisonnier a été exécuté à l'aube. The prisoner was executed at dawn. **②** to perform ▷ Le pianiste va maintenant exécuter une valse de Chopin. The pianist is now going to

a
b
c
d
e
f
g
h
i
j
k
l
m
n
o
p
q
r
s
t
u
v
w
x
y
z

perform a waltz by Chopin.

exemplaire nm copy

exemple nm example ▷ donner l'exemple to set an example; **par exemple** for example

s'**exercer** vb [12] to practise

exercice nm exercise

exhiber vb [28] to show off ▷ Il aime bien exhiber ses décorations. He likes showing off his medals.; **s'exhiber** to expose oneself

exhibitionniste nm flasher

exigeant, e adj hard to please

exiger vb [45] ❶ to demand ▷ Le propriétaire exige d'être payé immédiatement. The landlord is demanding to be paid immediately. ❷ to require ▷ Ce travail exige beaucoup de patience. This job requires a lot of patience.

exil nm exile

exister vb [28] to exist ▷ Ça n'existe pas. It doesn't exist.

exotique adj exotic; **un yaourt aux fruits exotiques** a tropical fruit yoghurt

expédier vb [19] to send ▷ expédier un colis to send a parcel

expéditeur nm sender

expédition nf expedition; **l'expédition du courrier** the dispatch of the mail

expérience nf ❶ experience ❷ experiment

expérimenter vb [28] to test ▷ Ces produits de beauté n'ont pas été expérimentés sur des animaux. These cosmetics have not been tested on animals.

experimenté, e adj experienced

expert nm expert

expirer vb [28] ❶ (document, passport) to expire ❷ (time allowed) to run out ❸ (person) to breathe out

explication nf explanation; **une explication de texte** (of a text) a critical analysis

expliquer vb [28] to explain ▷ Il m'a expliqué comment faire. He explained to me how to do it.; **Ça s'explique.** It's understandable.

exploit nm achievement

exploitation nf exploitation; **une exploitation agricole** a farm

exploiter vb [28] to exploit

explorer vb [28] to explore

exploser vb [28] to explode

explosif nm explosive

explosion nf explosion

exportateur nm exporter

exportation nf export

exporter vb [28] to export

exposé nm talk ▷ un exposé sur l'environnement a talk on the environment

exposer vb [28] ❶ to show ▷ Il expose ses peintures dans une galerie d'art. He shows his paintings in a private art gallery. ❷ to expose ▷ N'exposez pas la pellicule à la lumière. Don't expose the film to light. ❸ to set out ▷ Il nous a exposé les raisons de son départ. He set out the reasons for his departure.; **s'exposer au soleil** to stay out in the sun

exposition nf exhibition

exprès adv ❶ on purpose

❷ specially

express *nm* **❶** *(coffee)* espresso
  ❷ fast train

expression *nf* **❶** expression
  ❷ phrase

exprimer *vb* **[28]** to express;
  s'exprimer to express oneself

exquis, e *adj* exquisite

extérieur, e *adj* outside
  ▶ *nm* outside; **à l'extérieur** outside
  ▷ *Les toilettes sont à l'extérieur.* The
  toilet is outside.

externat *nm* day school

externe *nmf* day pupil

extincteur *nm* fire extinguisher

extra *adj* excellent

extraire *vb* **[85]** to extract

extrait *nm* extract

extraordinaire *adj* extraordinary

extravagant, e *adj* extravagant

extrême *adj* extreme
  ▶ *nm* extreme

extrêmement *adv* extremely

Extrême-Orient *nm* the Far East

extrémité *nf* end ▷ *La gare est à*
  l'autre extrémité de la ville. The
  station is at the other end of the
  town.

F *abbr (currency in Switzerland and*
  many former French colonies) franc

fa *nm* F

fabrication *nf* manufacture

fabriquer *vb* **[28]** to make
  ▷ *fabriqué en France* made in France;
  Qu'est-ce qu'il fabrique? *(informal)*
  What's he up to?

fac *nf (informal)* university; **à la fac**
  at university

face *nf* face **à face** face to face; **en**
  face de opposite ▷ *Le bus s'arrête en*
  face de chez moi. The bus stops
  opposite my house.; **faire face à**
  quelque chose to face something;
  Pile ou face? — Face. Heads or
  tails? — Heads.

fâché, e *adj* angry; **être fâché**
  contre quelqu'un to be angry with
  somebody; **être fâché avec**

quelqu'un to be on bad terms with somebody

se fâcher vb [**28**] **se fâcher contre quelqu'un** to lose one's temper with somebody; **se fâcher avec quelqu'un** to fall out with somebody

facile adj easy; **facile à faire** easy to do

facilement adv easily

facilité nf **un logiciel d'une grande facilité d'utilisation** a very user-friendly piece of software; **Il a des facilités en langues.** He has a gift for languages.

▌Be careful! **facilité** does not mean **facility**.

façon nf way ▷ *De quelle façon?* In what way?; **de toute façon** anyway

facteur nm postman

facture nf bill ▷ *une facture de gaz* a gas bill

facultatif (f **facultative**) adj optional

faculté nf faculty; **avoir une grande faculté de concentration** to have great powers of concentration

fade adj tasteless

faible adj weak; **Il est faible en maths.** He's not very good at maths.

faiblesse nf weakness

faïence nf pottery

faillir vb [**12**] **J'ai failli tomber.** I nearly fell down.

faillite nf bankruptcy; **une entreprise en faillite** a bankrupt

business; **faire faillite** to go bankrupt

faim nf hunger; **avoir faim** to be hungry

fainéant, e adj lazy

faire vb [**36**] ❶ to make ▷ *Je vais faire un gâteau pour ce soir.* I'm going to make a cake for tonight. ▷ *Ils font trop de bruit.* They're making too much noise. ❷ to do ▷ *Qu'est-ce que tu fais?* What are you doing? ▷ *Il fait de l'italien.* He's doing Italian. ❸ to play ▷ *Il fait du piano.* He plays the piano. ❹ to be ▷ *Qu'est-ce qu'il fait chaud!* Isn't it hot! ▷ *Espérons qu'il fera beau demain.* Let's hope it'll be nice weather tomorrow.; **Ça ne fait rien.** It doesn't matter.; **Ça fait cinquante-trois euros en tout.** That makes fifty-three euros in all.; **Ça fait trois ans qu'il habite à Paris.** He's lived in Paris for three years.; **faire tomber** to knock over ▷ *Le chat a fait tomber le vase.* The cat knocked over the vase.; **faire faire quelque chose** to get something done ▷ *Je dois faire réparer ma voiture.* I've got to get my car repaired.; **Je vais me faire couper les cheveux.** I'm going to get my hair cut.; **Ne t'en fais pas!** Don't worry!

fais, faisaient, faisais, faisait vb see **faire**

faisan nm pheasant

faisiez, faisions, faisons, fait vb see **faire**

fait nm fact; **un fait divers** a news item; **au fait** by the way; **en fait** actually

faites *vb see* **faire**

falaise *nf* cliff

falloir *vb* [37] *see* **faut**; **faudra**; **faudrait**

famé, e *adj* un quartier mal famé a rough area

fameux (*f* **fameuse**) *adj* Ce n'est pas fameux. It's not great.

familial, e (*mpl* **familiaux**) *adj* family; **les allocations familiales** child benefit

familier (*f* **familière**) *adj* familiar

famille *nf* ❶ family ▷ *une famille nombreuse* a big family ❷ relatives ▷ *Il a de la famille à Paris.* He's got relatives in Paris.

famine *nf* famine

fanatique *adj* fanatical
▶ *nmf* fanatic

fanfare *nf* brass band

fantaisie *adj* des bijoux fantaisie costume jewellery

fantastique *adj* fantastic

fantôme *nm* ghost

farce *nf* ❶ (for chicken, turkey) stuffing ❷ practical joke

farci, e *adj* stuffed ▷ *des tomates farcies* stuffed tomatoes

farine *nf* flour

fascinant, e *adj* fascinating

fasciner *vb* [28] to fascinate

fascisme *nm* fascism

fasse, fassent, fasses, fassiez, fassions *vb see* **faire**; Pourvu qu'il fasse beau demain! Let's hope it'll be fine tomorrow!

fatal, e *adj* fatal; C'était fatal. It was bound to happen.

fatalité *nf* fate

fatigant, e *adj* tiring

fatigue *nf* tiredness

fatigué, e *adj* tired

se **fatiguer** *vb* [28] to get tired

fauché, e *adj* (informal) hard up

faudra *vb*
⏐ faudra is the future tense of falloir.
Il faudra qu'on soit plus rapide. We'll have to be quicker.

faudrait *vb*
⏐ faudrait is the conditional tense of falloir.
Il faudrait qu'on fasse attention. We ought to be careful.

se **faufiler** *vb* [28] Il s'est faufilé à travers la foule. He made his way through the crowd.

faune *nf* wildlife

fausse *adj see* **faux**

faut *vb*
⏐ faut is the present tense of falloir.
Il faut faire attention. You've got to be careful.; Nous n'avons pas le choix, il faut y aller. We've no choice, we've got to go.; Il faut que je parte. I've got to go.; Il faut du courage pour faire ce métier. It takes courage to do that job.; Il me faut de l'argent. I need money.

faute *nf* ❶ mistake ▷ *faire une faute* to make a mistake ❷ fault ▷ *Ce n'est pas de ma faute.* It's not my fault.; **sans faute** without fail

fauteuil *nm* armchair; **un fauteuil roulant** a wheelchair

faux (*f* **fausse**) *adj, adv* untrue;

a b c d e f g h i j k l m n o p q r s t u v w x y z

faire un faux pas to trip; **Il chante faux.** He sings out of tune.
▶ *nm* fake ▷ *Ce tableau est un faux.* This painting is a fake.

faveur *nf* favour

favori (f **favorite**) *adj* favourite

favoriser *vb* [28] to favour

fax *nm* fax

faxer *vb* [28] to fax; **faxer un document à quelqu'un** to fax somebody a document

fée *nf* fairy

feignant, e *adj* (informal) lazy

félicitations *nfpl* congratulations

féliciter *vb* [28] to congratulate

femelle *nf* (animal) female

féminin, e *adj* ❶ female ▷ *les personnages féminins du roman* the female characters in the novel ❷ feminine ▷ *Elle est très féminine.* She's very feminine. ❸ women's ▷ *Elle joue dans l'équipe féminine de France.* She plays in the French women's team.

féministe *adj* feminist

femme *nf* ❶ woman ❷ wife; **une femme au foyer** a housewife; **une femme de ménage** a cleaning woman; **une femme d'affaires** a business woman

se **fendre** *vb* [88] to crack

fenêtre *nf* window

fenouil *nm* fennel

fente *nf* slot

fer *nm* iron; **un fer à cheval** a horseshoe; **un fer à repasser** an iron

fera, ferai, feras, ferez *vb* see **faire**

férié, e *adj* **un jour férié** a public holiday

feriez, ferions *vb* see **faire**

ferme *adj* firm
▶ *nf* farm

fermé, e *adj* ❶ closed ▷ *La pharmacie est fermée.* The chemist's is closed. ❷ off ▷ *Est-ce que le gaz est fermé?* Is the gas off?

fermer *vb* [28] ❶ to close ▷ *Ferme la fenêtre.* Close the window. ❷ to turn off ▷ *As-tu bien fermé le robinet?* Have you turned the tap off?; **fermer à clé** to lock ▷ *N'oublie pas de fermer la porte à clé!* Don't forget to lock the door!

fermeture *nf* **les heures de fermeture** closing times; **une fermeture éclair®** a zip

fermier *nm* farmer

fermière *nf* ❶ (woman) farmer ❷ farmer's wife

féroce *adj* fierce

ferons, feront *vb* see **faire**

fesses *nfpl* buttocks

festival *nm* festival

festivités *nfpl* festivities

fête *nf* ❶ party; **faire la fête** to party ❷ name day ▷ *C'est sa fête aujourd'hui.* It's his name day today.; **une fête foraine** a funfair; **la Fête Nationale** Bastille Day; **les fêtes de fin d'année** the festive season

fêter *vb* [28] to celebrate

feu (*pl* **feux**) *nm* ❶ fire ▷ *prendre feu* to catch fire ▷ *faire du feu* to make a fire; **Au feu!** Fire!; **un feu de joie** a bonfire ❷ traffic light ▷ *un feu rouge* a red light ▷ *Tournez à gauche aux feux.* Turn left at the lights.; **Avez-vous du feu?** Have you got a light? ❸ heat ▷ *... mijoter à feu doux* ... simmer over a gentle heat; **un feu d'artifice** a firework display

feuillage *nm* leaves

feuille *nf* ❶ leaf ▷ *des feuilles mortes* fallen leaves ❷ sheet ▷ *une feuille de papier* a sheet of paper; **une feuille de maladie** a claim form for medical expenses

feuilleté, e *adj* de la pâte **feuilletée** flaky pastry

feuilleter *vb* [**41**] to leaf through

feuilleton *nm* serial

feutre *nm* felt; **un stylo-feutre** a felt-tip pen

fève *nf* broad bean

février *nm* February; **en février** in February

fiable *adj* reliable

fiançailles *nfpl* engagement *sg*

fiancé, e *adj* **être fiancé à quelqu'un** to be engaged to somebody

se **fiancer** *vb* [**12**] to get engaged

ficelle *nf* ❶ string ❷ (*bread*) thin baguette

fiche *nf* form

se **ficher** *vb* [**28**] (*informal*) **Je m'en fiche!** I don't care!; **Quoi, tu n'as fait que ça? Tu te fiches de moi!** You've only done that much? You can't be serious!

fichier *nm* file

fichu, e *adj* (*informal*) **Ce parapluie est fichu.** This umbrella's knackered.

fidèle *adj* faithful

fier (*f* **fière**) *adj* proud

fierté *nf* pride

fièvre *nf* fever

fiévreux (*f* **fiévreuse**) *adj* feverish

figue *nf* fig

figure *nf* ❶ face ▷ *Il a reçu le ballon en pleine figure.* The ball hit him smack in the face. ❷ (*illustration*) figure ▷ *Voir figure 2.1, page 32.* See figure 2.1, page 32.

fil *nm* thread; **le fil de fer** wire; **un coup de fil** a phone call

file *nf* (*of people, objects*) line; **une file d'attente** a queue; **à la file** one after the other; **en file indienne** in single file

filer *vb* [**28**] to speed along; **File dans ta chambre!** Off to your room with you!

filet *nm* net

fille *nf* ❶ girl ▷ *C'est une école de filles.* It's a girls' school. ❷ daughter ▷ *C'est leur fille aînée.* She's their oldest daughter.

fillette *nf* little girl

filleul *nm* godson

filleule *nf* goddaughter

film *nm* film; **un film policier** a thriller; **un film d'aventures** an adventure film; **un film d'épouvante** a horror film; **le film alimentaire** Clingfilm®

fils *nm* son

fin *nf* end ▷ *À la fin, il a réussi à se décider.* In the end he managed to make up his mind.; **'Fin'** 'The End'; **Il sera en vacances fin juin.** He'll be on holiday at the end of June.;

en fin de journée at the end of the day; **en fin de compte** when all's said and done; **sans fin** endless
▶ adj fine; **des fines herbes** mixed herbs

finale nf final

finalement adv ❶ at last ▷ Nous sommes finalement arrivés. At last we arrived. ❷ after all ▷ Finalement, tu avais raison. You were right after all.

fini, e adj finished

finir vb [38] to finish ▷ Le cours finit à onze heures. The lesson finishes at 11 o'clock.; **Il a fini par se décider.** He made up his mind in the end.

finlandais, e adj, nm/f Finnish ▷ Ils parlent finlandais. They speak Finnish.; **un Finlandais** (man) a Finn; **une Finlandaise** (woman) a Finn; **les Finlandais** the Finns

Finlande nf Finland

firme nf firm

fis vb see **faire**

fissure nf crack

fit vb see **faire**

fixe adj ❶ steady ▷ Il n'a pas d'emploi fixe. He hasn't got a steady job. ❷ set ▷ Il mange toujours à heures fixes. He always eats at set times.; **un menu à prix fixe** a set menu

fixer vb [28] ❶ to fix ▷ Nous avons fixé une heure pour nous retrouver. We fixed a time to meet. ❷ to stare at ▷ Ne fixe pas les gens comme ça! Don't stare at people like that!

flacon nm bottle

flageolet nm small haricot bean

flamand, e adj, nm/f Flemish ▷ Il

parle flamand chez lui. He speaks Flemish at home.; **les Flamands** the Dutch-speaking Belgians

flambé, e adj **des bananes flambées** flambéed bananas

flamme nf flame; **en flammes** on fire

flan nm baked custard

flâner vb [28] to stroll

flaque nf (of water) puddle

flash (pl **flashes**) nm (of camera) flash; **un flash d'information** a newsflash

flatter vb [28] to flatter

flèche nf arrow

fléchettes nfpl darts

fleur nf flower

fleuri, e adj ❶ full of flowers ❷ flowery

fleurir vb [38] to flower ▷ Cette plante fleurit en automne. This plant flowers in autumn.

fleuriste nmf florist

fleuve nm river

flic nm (informal) cop

flipper nm pinball machine

flirter vb [28] to flirt

flocon nm flake

flotter vb [28] to float

flou, e adj blurred

fluor nm **le dentifrice au fluor** fluoride toothpaste

flûte nf flute; **une flûte à bec** a recorder; **Flûte!** (informal) Heck!

foi nf faith

foie nm liver; **une crise de foie** a stomach upset

foin nm hay; **le rhume des foins** hay fever

foire nf fair

fois nf time ▷ *la première fois* the first time ▷ *à chaque fois* each time ▷ *Deux fois deux font quatre.* 2 times 2 is 4.; **une fois** once; **deux fois** twice ▷ *deux fois plus de gens* twice as many people; **une fois que** once; **à la fois** at once ▷ *Je ne peux pas faire deux choses à la fois.* I can't do two things at once.

folie nf madness; **faire une folie** to be extravagant

folklorique adj folk

folle adj f see **fou**

foncé, e adj dark

foncer vb [12] (informal) *Je vais foncer à la boulangerie.* I'm just going to dash to the baker's.

fonction nf function; **une voiture de fonction** a company car

fonctionnaire nmf civil servant

fonctionner vb [28] to work

fond nm ❶ bottom ▷ *Mon porte-monnaie est au fond de mon sac.* My purse is at the bottom of my bag. ❷ end ▷ *Les toilettes sont au fond du couloir.* The toilets are at the end of the corridor.; **dans le fond** all things considered

fonder vb [28] to found

fondre vb [69] to melt; **fondre en larmes** to burst into tears

fondu, e adj **du beurre fondu** melted butter

font vb see **faire**

fontaine nf fountain

foot nm football

football nm football

footballeur nm footballer

footing nm jogging

forain, e adj **une fête foraine** a funfair

▶ nm fairground worker

force nf strength; **à force de** by ▷ *Il a grossi à force de manger autant.* He got fat by eating so much.; **de force** by force

forcé, e adj forced; **C'est forcé.** (informal) It's inevitable.

forcément adv **Ça devait forcément arriver.** That was bound to happen.; **pas forcément** not necessarily

forêt nf forest

forfait nm all-in price; **C'est compris dans le forfait.** It's included in the price.

forgeron nm blacksmith

formalité nf formality

format nm size

formation nf training; **la formation continue** continuing education; **Il a une formation d'ingénieur.** He is a trained engineer.

forme nf shape; **être en forme** to be in good shape; **Je ne suis pas en forme aujourd'hui.** I'm not feeling too good today.; **Tu as l'air en forme.** You're looking well.

formellement adv strictly

former vb [28] ❶ to form ❷ to train

formidable adj great

formulaire nm form

fort, e adj, adv ❶ strong ▷ *Le café est trop fort.* The coffee's too strong. ❷ good ▷ *Il est très fort en espagnol.* He's very good at Spanish. ❸ loud

a
b
c
d
e
f
g
h
i
j
k
l
m
n
o
p
q
r
s
t
u
v
w
x
y
z

▷ *Est-ce vous pouvez parler plus fort?*
Can you speak louder?; **frapper
fort** to hit hard

fortifiant nm (medicine) tonic

fortune nf fortune; **de fortune**
makeshift

forum de discussion nm (for
discussion) forum

fossé nm ditch

fou (f **folle**) adj mad; **Il y a un
monde fou sur la plage!** (informal)
There are loads of people on the
beach!; **attraper le fou rire** to get
the giggles

foudre nf lightning

foudroyant, e adj instant

fouet nm whisk

fougère nf fern

fouiller vb [28] to rummage

fouillis nm mess ▷ *Il y a du fouillis
dans sa chambre.* His bedroom is a
mess.

foulard nm scarf

foule nf crowd; **une foule de**
masses of

se **fouler** vb [28] se fouler la
cheville to sprain one's ankle

four nm oven ▷ *un four à micro-ondes*
a microwave oven

fourchette nf fork

fourmi nf ant; **avoir des fourmis
dans les jambes** to have pins and
needles

> Word for word, this means 'to
> have ants in one's legs'.

fourneau (pl **fourneaux**) nm stove

fourni, e adj (beard, hair) thick

fournir vb [38] to supply

fournisseur nm supplier; **un**

fournisseur d'accès à Internet an
internet service provider

fournitures nfpl les fournitures
scolaires school stationery

fourré, e adj filled

fourrer vb [28] (informal) to put
▷ *Où as-tu fourré mon sac?* Where
have you put my bag?

fourre-tout (pl **fourre-tout**) nm
holdall

fourrure nf fur

foyer nm home; **un foyer de
jeunes** a youth club

fracture nf fracture

fragile adj fragile

fragilité nf fragility

fraîche adj f see **frais**

fraîcheur nf ❶ cool ❷ freshness

frais (f **fraîche**) adj ❶ fresh ▷ *des
œufs frais* fresh eggs ❷ chilly ▷ *Il fait
un peu frais ce soir.* It's a bit chilly this
evening. ❸ cool ▷ *des boissons
fraîches* cool drinks; **'servir frais'**
'serve chilled'; **mettre au frais** to
put in a cool place
▶ nmpl expenses

fraise nf strawberry

framboise nf raspberry

franc (f **franche**) adj frank
▶ nm franc

● The **franc** is the unit of currency
: in Switzerland and many former
● French colonies.

français, e adj, n French
▷ *Il parle français couramment.*
He speaks French fluently.;
un Français a Frenchman;
une Française a Frenchwoman;
les Français the French

France nf France; **en France (1)** in France ▷ Je suis né en France. I was born in France. **(2)** to France ▷ Je pars en France pour Noël. I'm going to France for Christmas.

franche adj f see **franc**

franchement adv ❶ frankly ❷ really

franchir vb [38] to get over

franchise nf frankness

francophone adj French-speaking

frange nf fringe

frangipane nf almond cream

frapper vb [28] to strike ▷ Il l'a frappée au visage. He struck her in the face.

fredonner vb [28] to hum

freezer nm freezing compartment

frein nm brake; **le frein à main** handbrake

freiner vb [28] to brake

frêle adj frail

frelon nm hornet

frémir vb [38] shudder

fréquemment adv frequently

fréquent, e adj frequent

fréquenté, e adj busy ▷ une rue très fréquentée a very busy street; **un bar mal fréquenté** a rough pub

fréquenter vb [28] (person) to see ▷ Je ne le fréquente pas beaucoup. I don't see him often.

frère nm brother

friand nm **un friand au fromage** a cheese puff

friandise nf sweet

fric nm (informal) cash

frigidaire® nm refrigerator

frigo nm (informal) fridge

frileux (f **frileuse**) adj être frileux to feel the cold ▷ Je suis très frileuse. I really feel the cold.

frimer vb [28] (informal) to show off

fringues nfpl (informal) clothes

fripé, e adj crumpled

frire vb [80] faire frire to fry

frisé, e adj curly

frisson nm shiver

frissonner vb [28] to shiver

frit, e adj fried

frites nfpl chips

friture nf ❶ fried food ❷ fried fish

froid, e adj cold
▶ nm cold; **Il fait froid.** It's cold.; **avoir froid** to be cold ▷ Est-ce que tu as froid? Are you cold?

se froisser vb [28] ❶ to crease ▷ Ce tissu se froisse très facilement. This material creases very easily. ❷ to take offence ▷ Paul se froisse très facilement. Paul's very quick to take offence.; **se froisser un muscle** to strain a muscle

frôler vb [28] ❶ to brush against ▷ Le chat m'a frôlé au passage. The cat brushed against me as it went past. ❷ to narrowly avoid ▷ Nous avons frôlé la catastrophe. We narrowly avoided disaster.

fromage nm cheese

froment nm wheat; **une crêpe de froment** (made with wheat flour) a pancake

froncer vb [12] froncer les sourcils to frown

front nm forehead

frontière nf border

frotter vb [28] to rub ▷ se frotter les

a
b
c
d
e
f
g
h
i
j
k
l
m
n
o
p
q
r
s
t
u
v
w
x
y
z

yeux to rub one's eyes; **frotter une allumette** to strike a match

fruit *nm* fruit; **un fruit** a piece of fruit; **les fruits de mer** seafood

fruité, e *adj* fruity

frustrer *vb* [28] to frustrate

fugue *nf* **faire une fugue** to run away

fuir *vb* [39] ❶ to flee ▷ *fuir devant un danger* to flee from danger ❷ to drip ▷ *Le robinet fuit.* The tap's dripping.

fuite *nf* ❶ leak ❷ (*escape*) flight; **être en fuite** to be on the run

fumé, e *adj* smoked ▷ *du saumon fumé* smoked salmon

fumée *nf* smoke

fumer *vb* [28] to smoke

fumeur *nm* smoker

fur *nm* **au fur et à mesure** as you go along ▷ *Je vérifie mon travail au fur et à mesure.* I check my work as I go along.; **au fur et à mesure que** as ▷ *Je réponds à mon courrier au fur et à mesure que je le reçois.* I answer my mail as I receive it.

furet *nm* ferret

fureur *nf* fury; **faire fureur** to be all the rage

furieux (*f* **furieuse**) *adj* furious

furoncle *nm* (*on skin*) boil

fus *vb see* **être**

fuseau (*pl* **fuseaux**) *nm* ski pants

fusée *nf* rocket

fusil *nm* gun

fut *vb see* **être**

futé, e *adj* crafty

futur *nm* future

g

gâcher *vb* [28] to waste ▷ *Je n'aime pas gâcher la nourriture.* I don't like to waste food.

gâchis *nm* waste

gaffe *nf* **faire une gaffe** to do something stupid; **Fais gaffe!** (*informal*) Watch out!

gage *nm* (*in a game*) forfeit

gagnant *nm* winner

gagner *vb* [28] to win ▷ *Qui a gagné?* Who won?; **gagner du temps** to save time; **Il gagne bien sa vie.** He makes a good living.

gai, e *adj* cheerful

gaieté *nf* cheerfulness

galerie *nf* gallery; **une galerie marchande** a shopping arcade; **une galerie de jeux d'arcade** an amusement arcade

galet *nm* pebble

galette nf ❶ round flat cake; **une galette de blé noir** a buckwheat pancake ❷ biscuit ▷ *des galettes pur beurre* shortbread biscuits; **la galette des Rois**

● A **galette des Rois** is a cake
● eaten on Twelfth Night
● containing a figurine. The
● person who finds it is the king (or
● queen) and gets a paper crown.
● They then choose someone else
● to be their queen (or king).

Galles nf **le pays de Galles** Wales; **le prince de Galles** the Prince of Wales

gallois, e adj, n Welsh; **un Gallois** a Welshman; **une Galloise** a Welshwoman; **les Gallois** the Welsh

galop nm gallop

galoper vb [28] to gallop

gamin nm (informal) kid

gamine nf (informal) kid

gamme nf (in music) scale; **une gamme de produits** a range of products

gammée adj **la croix gammée** the swastika

gant nm glove; **un gant de toilette** a face cloth

garage nm garage

garagiste nmf ❶ garage owner ❷ mechanic

garantie nf guarantee

garantir vb [38] to guarantee

garçon nm boy; **un vieux garçon** a bachelor

garde nm ❶ (in prison) warder ❷ security man; **un garde du corps** a bodyguard
▶ nf ❶ guarding ❷ guard; **être de garde** to be on duty ▷ *La pharmacie de garde ce week-end est …* The duty chemist this weekend is …; **mettre en garde** to warn

garde-côte (pl **garde-côtes**) nm coastguard

garder vb [28] ❶ to keep ▷ *Tu as gardé toutes ses lettres?* Have you kept all his letters? ❷ to look after ▷ *Je garde ma nièce samedi après-midi.* I'm looking after my niece on Saturday afternoon. ❸ to guard ▷ *Ils ont pris un gros chien pour garder la maison.* They got a big dog to guard the house.; **garder le lit** to stay in bed; **se garder** to keep ▷ *Ces crêpes se gardent bien.* These pancakes keep well.

garderie nf nursery

garde-robe nf (clothes) wardrobe

gardien nm ❶ caretaker ❷ (in a museum) attendant; **un gardien de but** a goalkeeper

gare nf station ▷ *la gare routière* the bus station
▶ excl **Gare aux serpents!** Watch out for snakes!

garer vb [28] to park; **se garer** to park

garni, e adj **un plat garni** (vegetables, chips, rice etc) a dish served with accompaniments

gars nm (informal) guy

gaspiller vb [28] to waste

gâteau (pl **gâteaux**) nm cake; **les gâteaux secs** biscuits

gâter vb [28] to spoil ▷ *Il aime gâter*

a
b
c
d
e
f
g
h
i
j
k
l
m
n
o
p
q
r
s
t
u
v
w
x
y
z

ses petits-enfants. He likes to spoil his grandchildren.; **se gâter** to go bad; **Le temps va se gâter.** The weather's going to break.

gauche *adj* left ▷ *le côté gauche* the left-hand side

▶ *nf* left ▷ *sur votre gauche* on your left; **à gauche (1)** on the left ▷ *la deuxième rue à gauche* the second street on the left **(2)** to the left ▷ *à gauche de l'armoire* to the left of the cupboard; **Tournez à gauche.** Turn left.; **la voie de gauche** the left-hand lane; **la gauche** (*in politics*) the left

gaucher (*f* **gauchère**) *adj* left-handed

gaufre *nf* waffle

gaufrette *nf* wafer

Gaulois *nm* Gaul ▷ *Astérix le Gaulois* Asterix the Gaul

gaulois, e *adj* Gallic

gaz *nm* gas

gazeux (*f* **gazeuse**) *adj* **une boisson gazeuse** a fizzy drink; **de l'eau gazeuse** sparkling water

gazole *nm* (*fuel*) diesel

gazon *nm* lawn

géant *nm* giant

gel *nm* frost

gelée *nf* ❶ jelly ❷ frost

geler *vb* [43] to freeze; **Il a gelé cette nuit.** There was a frost last night.

gélule *nf* (*containing medicine*) capsule

Gémeaux *nmpl* Gemini

gémir *vb* [38] to moan

gênant, e *adj* awkward

gencive *nf* (*in mouth*) gum

gendarme *nm* police officer

gendarmerie *nf* ❶ police force ❷ police station

gendre *nm* son-in-law

gêné, e *adj* embarrassed

gêner *vb* [28] ❶ to bother ▷ *Je ne voudrais pas vous gêner.* I don't want to bother you. ❷ to feel awkward ▷ *Son regard la gênait.* The way he was looking at her made her feel awkward.

général, e (*mpl* **généraux**) *adj* general; **en général** usually

▶ *nm* general

généralement *adv* generally

généraliste *nmf* family doctor

génération *nf* generation

généreux (*f* **généreuse**) *adj* generous

générosité *nf* generosity

genêt *nm* (*bush*) broom

génétique *nf* genetics

génétiquement *adv* genetically ▷ *les aliments génétiquement modifiés* GM foods

Genève *n* Geneva

génial, e (*mpl* **géniaux**) *adj* (*informal*) great

genou (*pl* **genoux**) *nm* knee

genre *nm* kind

gens *nmpl* people

gentil (*f* **gentille**) *adj* ❶ nice ❷ kind

gentillesse *nf* kindness

gentiment *adv* ❶ nicely ❷ kindly

géographie *nf* geography

géolocalisation *nf* geolocation

géométrie *nf* geometry

gérant *nm* manager

gérer *vb* [34] to manage

germain, e adj un cousin germain a first cousin

geste nm geste; Ne faites pas un geste! Don't move!

gestion nf management

gestionnaire de site nmf webmaster

gifle nf slap across the face

gifler vb [28] to slap across the face

gigantesque adj gigantic

gigot nm leg of lamb

gilet nm ❶ waistcoat ❷ cardigan; un gilet de sauvetage a life jacket

gingembre nm ginger

girafe nf giraffe

gitan nm gipsy

gitane nf gipsy

gîte nm un gîte rural a holiday house

glace nf ❶ ice ❷ ice cream ▷ une glace à la fraise a strawberry ice cream ❸ mirror

glacé, e adj ❶ icy ❷ iced ▷ un thé glacé an iced tea

glacial, e (mpl glaciaux) adj icy

glaçon nm ice cube

glissant, e adj slippery

glisser vb [28] ❶ to slip ❷ to be slippery

global, e (mpl globaux) adj total

gloire nf glory

godasse nf (informal) shoe

goéland nm seagull

golf nm ❶ golf ❷ golf course

golfe nm gulf; le golfe de Gascogne the Bay of Biscay

gomme nf rubber

gommer vb [28] to rub out

gonflé, e adj ❶ (arm, finger, stomach) swollen ❷ (ball, tyre) inflated; Il est gonflé! (informal) He's got a nerve!

gonfler vb [28] ❶ to blow up ▷ gonfler un ballon to blow up a balloon ❷ to pump up ▷ gonfler un pneu to pump up a tyre

gorge nf ❶ throat ▷ J'ai mal à la gorge. I've got a sore throat. ❷ gorge ▷ les gorges du Tarn the Tarn gorges

gorgée nf sip

gorille nm gorilla

gosse nmf (informal) kid

goudron nm tar

gouffre nm chasm; Cette voiture est un vrai gouffre! This car eats up money!

gourde nf water bottle

gourmand, e adj greedy

gourmandise nf greed

gousse nf une gousse d'ail a clove of garlic

goût nm taste

goûter vb [28] ❶ to taste ❷ (in the afternoon) to have a snack ▷ Les enfants goûtent généralement vers quatre heures. The children usually have a snack around 4 o'clock. ▶ nm afternoon snack

goutte nf drop

gouvernement nm government

gouverner vb [28] to govern

grâce nf grâce à thanks to

gracieux (f gracieuse) adj graceful

gradins nmpl (in stadium) terraces

graduel (f graduelle) adj gradual

graffiti nmpl graffiti sg

grain nm grain; un grain de

a b c d e f **g** h i j k l m n o p q r s t u v w x y z

beauté a beauty spot; **un grain de café** a coffee bean; **un grain de raisin** a grape

graine nf seed

graisse nf fat

grammaire nf grammar

gramme nm gram

grand, e adj, adv ❶ tall ▷ *Il est grand pour son âge.* He's tall for his age. ❷ big ▷ *C'est sa grande sœur.* She's his big sister.; **une grande personne** a grown-up ❸ long ▷ *un grand voyage* a long journey; **les grandes vacances** the summer holidays ❹ great ▷ *C'est un grand ami à moi.* He's a great friend of mine.; **un grand magasin** a department store; **une grande surface** a hypermarket; **les grandes écoles** *(at university level)* top ranking colleges; **au grand air** out in the open air; **grand ouvert** wide open

grand-chose pron **pas grand-chose** not much

Grande-Bretagne nf Britain

grandeur nf size

grandir vb [38] to grow ▷ *Il a beaucoup grandi.* He's grown a lot.

grand-mère *(pl* **grands-mères***)* nf grandmother

grand-peine: **à grand-peine** adv with great difficulty

grand-père *(pl* **grands-pères***)* nm grandfather

grands-parents nmpl grandparents

grange nf barn

grappe nf **une grappe de raisin** a bunch of grapes

gras *(f* **grasse***)* adj ❶ *(food)* fatty ❷ greasy ❸ oily; **faire la grasse matinée** to have a lie-in

gratis adj, adv free

gratte-ciel *(pl* **gratte-ciel***)* nm skyscraper

gratter vb [28] ❶ to scratch ❷ to be itchy

gratuit, e adj free ▷ *entrée gratuite* entrance free

grave adj ❶ serious ❷ deep ▷ *Il a une voix grave.* He's got a deep voice.; **Ce n'est pas grave.** It doesn't matter.

gravement adv seriously

graveur nm **un graveur de CD** a CD burner

grec *(f* **grecque***)* adj, nm/f Greek ▷ *J'apprends le grec.* I'm learning Greek.; **un Grec** *(man)* a Greek; **une Grecque** *(woman)* a Greek; **les Grecs** the Greeks

Grèce nf Greece; **en Grèce (1)** in Greece **(2)** to Greece

grêle nf hail

grêler vb [28] **Il grêle.** It's hailing.

grelotter vb [28] to shiver

grenade nf ❶ pomegranate ❷ grenade

grenier nm attic

grenouille nf frog

grève nf ❶ strike; **en grève** on strike; **faire grève** to be on strike ❷ shore

gréviste nmf striker

grièvement adv **grièvement blessé** seriously injured

griffe nf ❶ claw ❷ label

griffer vb [28] to scratch ▷ Le chat m'a griffé. The cat scratched me.

grignoter vb [28] to nibble

grillade nf grilled food

grille nf ❶ wire fence ❷ metal gate

grille-pain (pl grille-pain) nm toaster

griller vb [28] ❶ to toast; du pain grillé toast ❷ to grill ▷ des saucisses grillées grilled sausages

grimace nf faire des grimaces to make faces

grimper vb [28] to climb

grincer vb [12] to creak

grincheux (f grincheuse) adj grumpy

grippe nf flu; avoir la grippe to have flu

grippé, e adj être grippé to have flu

gris, e adj grey

Groenland nm Greenland

grogner vb [28] ❶ to growl ❷ to complain

gronder vb [28] to tell off; se faire gronder to get a telling-off ▷ Tu vas te faire gronder par ton père! You're going to get a telling-off from your father!

gros (f grosse) adj ❶ big ▷ une grosse pomme a big apple ❷ fat ▷ Je suis trop grosse pour porter ça! I'm too fat to wear that!

groseille nf la groseille rouge redcurrant; la groseille à maquereau gooseberry

grossesse nf pregnancy

grossier (f grossière) adj rude; une erreur grossière a bad mistake

grossir vb [38] to put on weight ▷ Il a beaucoup grossi. He's put on a lot of weight.

grosso modo adv roughly

grotte nf cave

groupe nm group

grouper vb [28] to group; se grouper to gather ▷ Nous nous sommes groupés autour du feu. We gathered round the fire.

guépard nm cheetah

guêpe nf wasp

guérir vb [38] to recover ▷ Il est maintenant complètement guéri. He's now completely recovered.

guérison nf recovery

guerre nf war ▷ la Deuxième Guerre mondiale the Second World War

guetter vb [28] to look out for

gueule nf mouth; Ta gueule! (rude) Shut your face!; avoir la gueule de bois (informal) to have a hangover

gueuler vb [28] (informal) to bawl

guichet nm (in bank, booking office) counter

guide nm guide

guider vb [28] to guide

guidon nm handlebars

guillemets nmpl inverted commas

guirlande nf tinsel; des guirlandes en papier paper chains

guitare nf guitar

gym nf (informal) PE

gymnase nm gym

gymnastique nf gymnastics

h

habile *adj* skilful

habillé, e *adj* ❶ dressed ▷ *Il n'est pas encore habillé.* He's not dressed yet. ❷ smart ▷ *Cette robe fait très habillé.* This dress looks very smart.

s' **habiller** *vb* [**28**] ❶ to get dressed ▷ *Je me suis rapidement habillé.* I got dressed quickly. ❷ to dress up ▷ *Est-ce qu'il faut s'habiller pour la réception?* Do you have to dress up to go to the party?

habitant *nm* inhabitant

habiter *vb* [**28**] to live ▷ *Il habite à Montpellier.* He lives in Montpellier.

habits *nmpl* clothes

habitude *nf* habit; **avoir l'habitude de quelque chose** to be used to something; **d'habitude** usually; **comme d'habitude** as usual

habituel (*f* **habituelle**) *adj* usual

s' **habituer** *vb* [**28**] **s'habituer à quelque chose** to get used to something

hachis *nm* mince; **le hachis Parmentier** shepherd's pie

haie *nf* hedge

haine *nf* hatred

haïr *vb* [**40**] to hate

haleine *nf* breath ▷ *être hors d'haleine* to be out of breath

halles *nfpl* covered market *sg*

halte *nf* stop; **Halte!** Stop!

haltérophilie *nf* weightlifting

hamburger *nm* hamburger

hameçon *nm* fish hook

hamster *nm* hamster

hanche *nf* hip

handicap *nm* ❶ (*medical problem*) disability ❷ (*in sport*) handicap

handicapé *nm* disabled man

handicapée *nf* disabled woman

harcèlement *nm* harassment

harceler *vb* to bully

hareng *nm* herring; **un hareng saur** a kipper

haricot *nm* bean; **les haricots verts** runner beans; **les haricots blancs** haricot beans

harmonica *nm* mouth organ

harpe *nf* harp

hasard *nm* coincidence; **au hasard** at random; **par hasard** by chance; **à tout hasard (1)** just in case **(2)** on the off chance

hâte *nf* **à la hâte** hurriedly; **J'ai hâte de te voir.** I can't wait to see you.

hausse *nf* ❶ increase ❷ rise

hausser *vb* [**28**] **hausser les épaules** to shrug one's shoulders

haut, e adj, adv ❶ high ▷ une haute montagne a high mountain ❷ aloud ▷ penser tout haut to think aloud ▶ nm top; **un mur de trois mètres de haut** a wall 3 metres high; **en haut (1)** upstairs **(2)** at the top

hauteur nf height

haut-parleur (pl **haut-parleurs**) nm loudspeaker

hebdomadaire nm (magazine) weekly

hébergement nm accommodation

héberger vb [**45**] to put up ▷ Mon cousin a dit qu'il nous hébergerait. My cousin said he would put us up.

hein? excl eh? ▷ Hein? Qu'est-ce que tu dis? Eh? What did you say?

hélas adv unfortunately

hélicoptère nm helicopter

hémorragie nf haemorrhage

herbe nf grass; **les herbes de Provence** mixed herbs

hérisson nm hedgehog

hériter vb [**28**] to inherit

héritier nm heir

héritière nf heiress

hermétique adj airtight

héroïne nf ❶ heroine ❷ (drug) heroin

héros nm hero

hésitation nf hesitation

hésiter vb [**28**] to hesitate; **J'ai hésité entre le pull vert et le cardigan jaune.** I couldn't decide between the green pullover and the yellow cardigan.; **sans hésiter** without hesitating

heure nf ❶ hour ▷ Le trajet dure six heures. The journey lasts six hours. ❷ time ▷ Vous avez l'heure? Have you got the time?; **Quelle heure est-il?** What time is it?; **À quelle heure?** What time?; **deux heures du matin** 2 o'clock in the morning; **être à l'heure** to be on time; **une heure de français** a period of French

heureusement adv luckily

heureux (f **heureuse**) adj happy

heurter vb [**28**] to hit

hexagone nm hexagon; **l'Hexagone** France

● France is often referred to as
● **l'Hexagone** because of its
● six-sided shape.

hibou (pl **hiboux**) nm owl

hier adv yesterday; **avant-hier** the day before yesterday

hi-fi nf stereo; **une chaîne hi-fi** a stereo system

hippique adj **un club hippique** a riding centre; **un concours hippique** a horse show

hippopotame nm hippopotamus

hirondelle nf (bird) swallow

histoire nf ❶ history ▷ un cours d'histoire a history lesson ❷ story ▷ C'est l'histoire de deux enfants. It's the story of two children.; **Ne fais pas d'histoires!** Don't make a fuss!

historique adj historic

hiver nm winter; **en hiver** in winter

HLM nmf (= habitation à loyer modéré) council flat; **des HLM** council housing

hockey nm hockey; **le hockey sur glace** ice hockey

a
b
c
d
e
f
g
h
i
j
k
l
m
n
o
p
q
r
s
t
u
v
w
x
y
z

hollandais, e adj, n Dutch
▷ J'apprends le hollandais. I'm
learning Dutch.; **un Hollandais**
a Dutch man; **une Hollandaise**
a Dutch woman; **les Hollandais**
the Dutch

Hollande nf Holland; **en Hollande
(1)** in Holland **(2)** to Holland

homard nm lobster

homéopathique adj
homeopathic

hommage nm tribute

homme nm man; **un homme
d'affaires** a businessman

homoparental, e (mpl
homoparentaux) adj **une famille
homoparentale** a same-sex-
parent family

homosexuel (f **homosexuelle**)
adj homosexual

Hongrie nf Hungary

hongrois, e adj, n Hungarian

honnête adj honest

honnêteté nf honesty

honneur nm honour

honte nf shame; **avoir honte de
quelque chose** to be ashamed of
something

hôpital (pl **hôpitaux**) nm hospital

hoquet nm **avoir le hoquet** to have
hiccups

horaire nm timetable; **les horaires
de train** the train timetable

horizon nm horizon

horizontal, e (mpl **horizontaux**)
adj horizontal

horloge nf clock

horreur nf horror ▷ un film d'horreur
a horror film; **avoir horreur de**

to hate ▷ J'ai horreur du chou. I hate
cabbage.

horrible adj horrible

hors prep **hors de** out of ▷ Elle est
hors de danger maintenant. She's out
of danger now.; **hors taxes**
duty-free

hors-d'œuvre (pl **hors-d'œuvre**)
nm (food) starter

hospitalier (f **hospitalière**) adj
hospitable; **les services
hospitaliers** hospital services

hospitalité nf hospitality

hostile adj hostile

hôte nmf ❶ host ❷ guest

hôtel nm hotel; **l'hôtel de ville** the
town hall

hôtesse nf hostess; **une hôtesse
de l'air** a stewardess

housse nf cover ▷ une housse de
couette a quilt cover ▷ une housse de
téléphone a phone cover

houx nm holly

huile nf oil; **l'huile solaire** suntan
oil

huit num eight ▷ Il a huit ans. He's
eight.; **le huit février** the eighth of
February; **dans huit jours** in a
week's time

huitaine nf **une huitaine de jours**
about a week

huitième adj eighth ▷ au huitième
étage on the eighth floor

huître nf oyster

humain, e adj human
▶ nm human being

humeur nf mood ▷ Il est de bonne
humeur. He's in a good mood.

humide adj damp

humilier *vb* [**19**] to humiliate
humoristique *adj* humorous; **des dessins humoristiques** cartoons
humour *nm* humour ▷ *Il n'a pas beaucoup d'humour.* He hasn't got much of a sense of humour.
hurler *vb* [**28**] ❶ to howl ❷ to scream
hutte *nf* hut
hydratant, e *adj* **une crème hydratante** a moisturizing cream
hygiène *nf* hygiene
hygiénique *adj* hygienic; **une serviette hygiénique** a sanitary towel; **le papier hygiénique** toilet paper
hymne *nm* **l'hymne national** the national anthem
hypermarché *nm* hypermarket
hypermétrope *adj* long-sighted
hypocrite *adj* hypocritical
hypothèse *nf* hypothesis

iceberg *nm* iceberg
ici *adv* here ▷ *Les assiettes sont ici.* The plates are here.; **La mer monte parfois jusqu'ici.** The sea sometimes comes in as far as this.; **Jusqu'ici nous n'avons eu aucun problème avec la voiture.** So far we haven't had any problems with the car.
icône *nf* icon
idéal, e (*mpl* **idéaux**) *adj* ideal
idée *nf* idea
identifiant *nm* (*on a computer*) login
identifier *vb* [**19**] to identify
identique *adj* identical
identité *nf* identity; **une pièce d'identité** a form of identification
idiot, e *adj* ❶ stupid ❷ silly
idiot *nm* idiot
idiote *nf* idiot

ignoble adj horrible
ignorant, e adj ignorant
ignorer vb [**28**] ❶ not to know
▷ *J'ignore son nom.* I don't know his
name. ❷ to ignore ▷ *Il m'a
complètement ignoré.* He completely
ignored me.
il pron ❶ he ▷ *Il est parti ce matin de
bonne heure.* He left early this
morning. ❷ it ▷ *Méfie-toi de ce chien:
il mord.* Be careful of that dog: it
bites. ▷ *Il pleut.* It's raining.
île nf island; **les îles Anglo-
Normandes** the Channel Islands;
les îles Britanniques the British
Isles; **les îles Féroé** the Faroe Islands
illégal, e (mpl **illégaux**) adj illegal
illettrisme nm illiteracy
illimité, e adj unlimited
illisible adj illegible
illuminer vb [**28**] to floodlight
illusion nf illusion
illustration nf illustration
illustré, e adj illustrated
   ▶ nm comic
illustrer vb [**28**] to illustrate
ils pron pl they ▷ *Ils nous ont appelés
hier soir.* They phoned us last night.
image nf picture
imagination nf imagination
imaginer vb [**28**] to imagine
imbécile nmf idiot
imitation nf imitation
imiter vb [**28**] to imitate
immatriculation nf une plaque
   d'immatriculation (of car) a
   numberplate
immédiat nm dans l'immédiat for
   the moment

immédiatement adv
   immediately
immense adj ❶ huge
   ❷ tremendous
immeuble nm block of flats
immigration nf immigration
immigré nm immigrant
immigrée nf immigrant
immobile adj motionless
immobilier (f **immobilière**) adj
   une agence immobilière an
   estate agent's
immobiliser vb [**28**] to immobilize
immunisé, e adj immunized
impact nm impact
impair, e adj odd
impardonnable adj unforgivable
impasse nf cul-de-sac
impatience nf impatience
impatient, e adj impatient
impeccable adj ❶ immaculate
   ❷ perfect
imper nm (informal) mac
impératif nm imperative
impératrice nf empress
imperméable nm raincoat
impertinent, e adj cheeky
impitoyable adj merciless
impliquer vb [**28**] to mean ▷ *Son
silence implique qu'il est d'accord.* His
silence means he agrees.; **être
impliqué dans** to be involved in
▷ *Il est impliqué dans un scandale
financier.* He's involved in a financial
scandal.
impoli, e adj rude
importance nf importance
important, e adj ❶ important
   ❷ considerable

importation nf import
importer vb [**28**] see also
n'importe 1 (goods) to import
2 to matter ▷ Peu importe. It
doesn't matter.
imposant, e adj imposing
imposer vb [**28**] to impose; **La
direction leur impose des
horaires impossibles.** The
managers are making them work
ridiculous hours.
impossible adj impossible
▶ nm **Nous ferons l'impossible
pour finir à temps.** We'll do our
utmost to finish on time.
impôt nm tax
imprécis, e adj imprecise
impression nf impression
impressionnant, e adj impressive
impressionner vb [**28**] to impress
imprévisible adj unpredictable
imprévu, e adj unexpected
imprimante nf (for computer)
printer
imprimé, e adj printed
imprimer vb [**28**] to print
impropre adj **impropre à la
consommation** unfit for human
consumption
improviser vb [**28**] to improvise
improviste adv **arriver à
l'improviste** to arrive
unexpectedly
imprudence nf carelessness; **Ne
fais pas d'imprudences!** Don't do
anything silly!
imprudent, e adj **1** unwise
2 careless
impuissant, e adj helpless

impulsif (f **impulsive**) adj
impulsive
inabordable adj prohibitive
inaccessible adj inaccessible
inachevé, e adj unfinished
inadmissible adj intolerable
inanimé, e adj unconscious
inaperçu, e adj **passer inaperçu**
to go unnoticed
inattendu, e adj unexpected
inattention nf **une faute
d'inattention** a careless mistake
inaugurer vb [**28**] (an exhibition) to
open
incapable adj incapable
incassable adj unbreakable
incendie nm fire ▷ un incendie de
forêt a forest fire
incertain, e adj **1** uncertain
2 unsettled ▷ Le temps est incertain.
The weather is unsettled.
incident nm incident
inciter vb [**28**] **inciter quelqu'un à
faire quelque chose** to encourage
somebody to do something
inclure vb [**13**] to enclose ▷ Veuillez
inclure une enveloppe timbrée libellée
à votre adresse. Please enclose a
stamped addressed envelope.;
jusqu'au dix mars inclus until
10th March inclusive
incohérent, e adj incoherent
incollable adj **être incollable sur
quelque chose** (informal) to know
everything there is to know about
something; **le riz incollable**
non-stick rice
incolore adj colourless
incompétent, e adj incompetent

a
b
c
d
e
f
g
h
i
j
k
l
m
n
o
p
q
r
s
t
u
v
w
x
y
z

incompris, e *adj* misunderstood
inconnu *nm* stranger; **l'inconnu** the unknown
inconsciemment *adv* unconsciously
inconscient, e *adj* ❶ unconscious ❷ unaware
incontestable *adj* indisputable
incontournable *adj* inevitable
inconvénient *nm* disadvantage; **si vous n'y voyez pas d'inconvénient** if you have no objection
incorrect, e *adj* ❶ incorrect ❷ rude
incroyable *adj* incredible
inculper *vb* [28] **inculper de** to charge with
Inde *nf* India
indécis, e *adj* ❶ indecisive ❷ undecided
indéfiniment *adv* indefinitely
indélicat, e *adj* tactless
indemne *adj* unharmed
indemniser *vb* [28] to compensate
indépendamment *adv* independently; **indépendamment de** irrespective of
indépendance *nf* independence
indépendant, e *adj* independent
index *nm* ❶ index finger ❷ (in book) index
indicatif (f **indicative**) *adj* **à titre indicatif** for your information ▷ *nm* ❶ dialling code ❷ (of verb) indicative ❸ (of TV programme) theme tune
indications *nfpl* instructions
indice *nm* clue

indien (f **indienne**) *adj, nm/f* Indian; **un Indien** (*man*) an Indian; **une Indienne** (*woman*) an Indian
indifférence *nf* indifference
indifférent, e *adj* indifferent
indigène *nmf* native
indigeste *adj* indigestible
indigestion *nf* indigestion
indigne *adj* unworthy
indigner *vb* [28] **s'indigner de quelque chose** to get indignant about something
indiqué, e *adj* advisable
indiquer *vb* [28] to point out ▷ *Il m'a indiqué la mairie.* He pointed out the town hall.
indirect, e *adj* indirect
indiscipliné, e *adj* unruly
indiscret (f **indiscrète**) *adj* indiscreet
indispensable *adj* indispensable
indisposé, e *adj* indisposed; **être indisposée** to be having one's period
individu *nm* individual
individuel (f **individuelle**) *adj* individual; **Vous aurez une chambre individuelle.** You'll have a room of your own.
indolore *adj* painless
Indonésie *nf* Indonesia
indulgent, e *adj* indulgent; **Elle est trop indulgente avec son fils.** She's not firm enough with her son.
industrie *nf* industry
industriel (f **industrielle**) *adj* industrial ▷ *nm* industrialist

inédit, e *adj* unpublished

inefficace *adj* ① (treatment) ineffective ② inefficient

inégal, e (*mpl* **inégaux**) *adj* ① unequal ② uneven

inévitable *adj* unavoidable; **C'était inévitable!** That was bound to happen!

inexact, e *adj* inaccurate

in extremis *adv* Il a réussi à attraper son train in extremis. He just managed to catch his train.; **Ils ont évité un accident in extremis.** They avoided an accident by the skin of their teeth.

infarctus *nm* coronary

infatigable *adj* indefatigable

infect, e *adj* (meal) revolting

s'**infecter** *vb* [28] to go septic

infection *nf* infection

inférieur, e *adj* lower

infernal, e (*mpl* **infernaux**) *adj* terrible

infini *nm* à l'infini indefinitely

infinitif *nm* infinitive

infirme *nmf* disabled person

infirmerie *nf* medical room

infirmier *nm* nurse

inflammable *adj* inflammable

influence *nf* influence

influencer *vb* [12] to influence

informaticien *nm* computer scientist

informaticienne *nf* computer scientist

informations *nfpl* ① (on TV) news ▷ les informations de vingt heures the 8 o'clock news ② information ▷ Je voudrais quelques informations, s'il vous plaît. I'd like some information, please.; **une information** a piece of information

informatique *nf* computing

informer *vb* [28] to inform; s'informer to find out

infuser *vb* [28] ① (tea) to brew ② (herbal tea) to infuse

infusion *nf* herbal tea

ingénieur *nmf* engineer

ingrat, e *adj* ungrateful

ingrédient *nm* ingredient

inhabituel (*f* **inhabituelle**) *adj* unusual

inhumain, e *adj* inhuman

initial, e (*mpl* **initiaux**) *adj* initial

initiale *nf* initial

initiation *nf* introduction

initiative *nf* initiative ▷ avoir de l'initiative to have initiative

injecter *vb* [28] to inject

injection *nf* injection

injure *nf* ① insult ② abuse

injurier *vb* [19] to insult

injurieux (*f* **injurieuse**) *adj* (language) abusive

injuste *adj* unfair

innocent, e *adj* innocent

innombrable *adj* innumerable

innover *vb* [28] to break new ground

inoccupé, e *adj* empty ▷ un appartement inoccupé an empty flat

inoffensif (*f* **inoffensive**) *adj* harmless

inondation *nf* flood

inoubliable *adj* unforgettable

inoxydable *adj* l'acier inoxydable

stainless steel

inquiet (f **inquiète**) adj worried

inquiétant, e adj worrying

s'**inquiéter** vb [**34**] to worry ▷ Ne t'inquiète pas! Don't worry!

inquiétude nf anxiety

insatisfait, e adj dissatisfied

inscription nf (for school, course) registration

s'**inscrire** vb [**30**] s'inscrire à (1) to join ▷ Je me suis inscrit au club de tennis. I've joined the tennis club. (2) to register ▷ N'attends pas trop pour t'inscrire à la fac. Don't leave it too long to register at the university.

insecte nm insect

insensible adj insensitive

insigne nm badge

insignifiant, e adj insignificant

insister vb [**28**] to insist; N'insiste pas! Don't keep on!

insolation nf sunstroke

insolent, e adj cheeky

insouciant, e adj carefree

insoutenable adj unbearable

inspecter vb [**28**] to inspect

inspecteur nm inspector

inspection nf inspection

inspirer vb [**28**] ❶ to inspire; s'inspirer de to take one's inspiration from ❷ to breathe in ▷ Inspirez! Expirez! Breathe in! Breathe out!

instable adj ❶ (piece of furniture) unsteady ❷ (person) unstable

installations nfpl facilities

installer vb [**28**] ❶ (shelves) to put up ❷ (gas, telephone) to install;

s'**installer** to settle in; Installez-vous, je vous en prie. Have a seat, please.

instant nm moment ▷ pour l'instant for the moment

instantané, e adj instant ▷ du café instantané instant coffee

instinct nm instinct

institut nm institute

instituteur nm primary school teacher

institution nf institution

institutrice nf primary school teacher

instruction nf ❶ instruction ❷ education

s'**instruire** vb [**23**] to educate oneself

instruit, e adj educated

instrument nm instrument ▷ un instrument de musique a musical instrument

insuffisant, e adj insufficient; 'travail insuffisant' (on school report) 'must try harder'

insuline nf insulin

insultant, e adj insulting

insulte nf insult

insulter vb [**28**] to insult

insupportable adj unbearable

intact, e adj intact

intégral, e (mpl **intégraux**) adj le texte intégral unabridged version; un remboursement intégral a full refund

intégrisme nm fundamentalism

intelligence nf intelligence

intelligent, e adj intelligent

intense adj intense

intensif (f **intensive**) adj intensive; **un cours intensif** a crash course

intention nf intention; **avoir l'intention de faire quelque chose** to intend to do something

interdiction nf 'interdiction de stationner' 'no parking'; 'interdiction de fumer' 'no smoking'

interdire vb [27] to forbid

interdit, e adj forbidden

intéressant, e adj interesting; On lui a fait une offre intéressante. They made him an attractive offer.; **On trouve des CD à des prix très intéressants dans ce magasin.** You can get very cheap CDs in this shop.

intéresser vb [28] to interest; **s'intéresser à** to be interested in

intérêt nm interest; **avoir intérêt à faire quelque chose** to do well to do something

intérieur nm inside

interlocuteur nm son interlocuteur the man he's speaking to

intermédiaire nm intermediary; **par l'intermédiaire de** through

internat nm boarding school

international, e (mpl **internationaux**) adj international

internaute nmf internet user

interne nmf boarder

Internet nm internet ▷ sur Internet on the internet

interphone nm intercom

interprète nmf interpreter

interpréter vb [34] to interpret

interrogatif (f **interrogative**) adj interrogative

interrogation nf ❶ question ❷ test ▷ une interrogation écrite a written test

interrogatoire nm questioning; C'est un interrogatoire ou quoi? Am I being cross-examined?

interroger vb [45] to question

interrompre vb [75] to interrupt

interrupteur nm switch

interruption nf interruption; **sans interruption** without stopping

intervalle nm interval; **dans l'intervalle** in the meantime

intervenir vb [89] ❶ to intervene ❷ to take action ▷ La police est intervenue. The police took action.

intervention nf intervention; **une intervention chirurgicale** a surgical operation

interview nf (on radio, TV) interview

intestin nm intestine

intime adj intimate; **un journal intime** a diary

intimider vb [28] to intimidate

intimité nf dans l'intimité in private; **Le mariage a eu lieu dans l'intimité.** The wedding ceremony was private.

intitulé, e adj entitled

intolérable adj intolerable

intoxication nf une intoxication alimentaire food poisoning

Intranet nm Intranet

a b c d e f g h i j k l m n o p q r s t u v w x y z

intransigeant, e *adj* uncompromising

intrigue *nf (of book, film)* plot

introduction *nf* introduction

introduire *vb* [**23**] to introduce

intuition *nf* intuition

inusable *adj* hard-wearing

inutile *adj* useless

invalide *nmf* disabled person

invasion *nf* invasion

inventer *vb* [**28**] ❶ to invent ❷ to make up ▷ *inventer une excuse* to make up an excuse

inventeur *nm* inventor

invention *nf* invention

inverse *adj* dans l'ordre inverse in reverse order; **en sens inverse** in the opposite direction
▷ *nm* reverse; **Tu t'es trompé, c'est l'inverse.** You've got it wrong, it's the other way round.

investissement *nm* investment

invisible *adj* invisible

invitation *nf* invitation

invité *nm* guest

inviter *vb* [**28**] to invite

involontaire *adj* unintentional

invraisemblable *adj* unlikely

ira, irai, iraient, irais *vb see* **aller**; J'irai demain au supermarché. I'll go to the supermarket tomorrow.

Irak *nm* Iraq

Iran *nm* Iran

iras, irez *vb see* **aller**

irlandais, e *adj, n* Irish; **un Irlandais** an Irishman; **une Irlandaise** an Irishwoman; **les Irlandais** the Irish

Irlande *nf* Ireland; **en Irlande (1)** in Ireland **(2)** to Ireland; **la République d'Irlande** the Irish Republic; **l'Irlande du Nord** Northern Ireland

ironie *nf* irony

ironique *adj* ironical

irons, iront *vb see* **aller**; Nous irons à la plage cet après-midi. We'll go to the beach this afternoon.

irrationnel (f irrationnelle) *adj* irrational

irréel (f irréelle) *adj* unreal

irrégulier (f irrégulière) *adj* irregular

irrésistible *adj* irresistible

irritable *adj* irritable

irriter *vb* [**28**] to irritate

islamique *adj* Islamic

Islande *nf* Iceland

isolé, e *adj* isolated

Israël *nm* Israel

israélien (f israélienne) *adj, nm/f* Israeli; **un Israélien** *(man)* an Israeli; **une Israélienne** *(woman)* an Israeli; **les Israéliens** the Israelis

issue *nf* une voie sans issue a dead end; **l'issue de secours** emergency exit

Italie *nf* Italy; **en Italie (1)** in Italy **(2)** to Italy

italien (f italienne) *adj, n* Italian ▷ *J'apprends l'italien.* I'm learning Italian.; **un Italien** *(man)* an Italian; **une Italienne** *(woman)* an Italian; **les Italiens** the Italians

itinéraire *nm* route
IUT *nm* (= Institut universitaire de technologie) (at university level) institute of technology
ivre *adj* drunk
ivrogne *nmf* drunkard

j

j' *pron see* **je**
jalousie *nf* jealousy
jaloux (*f* **jalouse**) *adj* jealous
jamais *adv* ❶ never ▷ *Il ne boit jamais d'alcool.* He never drinks alcohol. ❷ ever

> Phrases with **jamais** meaning 'ever' are followed by a verb in the subjunctive.

▷ *C'est la plus belle chose que j'aie jamais vue.* It's the most beautiful thing I've ever seen.
jambe *nf* leg
jambon *nm* ham; **le jambon cru** Parma ham
jambonneau (*pl* **jambonneaux**) *nm* knuckle of ham
janvier *nm* January; **en janvier** in January
Japon *nm* Japan; **au Japon (1)** in

Japan (2) to Japan

japonais, e adj, n Japanese ▷ Elle parle japonais. She speaks Japanese.; **un Japonais** (man) a Japanese; **une Japonaise** (woman) a Japanese; **les Japonais** the Japanese

jardin nm garden ▷ un jardin potager a vegetable garden

jardinage nm gardening

jardinier nm gardener

jaune adj yellow
  ▶ nm yellow; **un jaune d'œuf** an egg yolk

jaunir vb [**38**] to turn yellow

jaunisse nf jaundice

Javel n l'eau de Javel bleach

jazz nm jazz

J.-C. abbr (= Jésus-Christ) 44 avant J.-C. 44 BC; **115 après J.-C.** 115 AD

je pron

> je changes to **j'** before a vowel and most words beginning with 'h'.

I ▷ Je t'appellerai ce soir. I'll phone you this evening. ▷ J'arrive! I'm coming! ▷ J'hésite. I'm not sure.

jean nm jeans

jeannette nf Brownie

Jésus-Christ nm Jesus Christ

jet nm ❶ (of water) jet; **un jet d'eau** a fountain ❷ jet plane

jetable adj disposable

jetée nf jetty

jeter vb [**41**] ❶ to throw ▷ Il a jeté son sac sur le lit. He threw his bag onto the bed. ❷ to throw away ▷ Ils ne jettent jamais rien. They never throw anything away.; **jeter un coup**

d'œil to have a look

jeton nm (in board game) counter

jeu (pl **jeux**) nm game ▷ Les enfants jouaient à un jeu. The children were playing a game.; **un jeu d'arcade** an arcade video game; **un jeu de cartes** (1) a pack of cards (2) a card game; **un jeu de mots** a pun; **un jeu de société** a board game; **un jeu électronique** an electronic game; **les jeux sur ordinateur** computer gaming; **les jeux sur téléphone portable** mobile gaming; **les jeux vidéo** video games; **en jeu** at stake ▷ Des vies humaines sont en jeu. Human lives are at stake.

jeudi nm ❶ Thursday ▷ Aujourd'hui, nous sommes jeudi. It's Thursday today. ❷ on Thursday; **le jeudi** on Thursdays; **tous les jeudis** every Thursday; **jeudi dernier** last Thursday; **jeudi prochain** next Thursday

jeun: **à jeun** adv on an empty stomach

jeune adj young ▷ un jeune homme a young man; **une jeune fille** a girl
  ▶ nmf young person ▷ les jeunes young people

jeunesse nf youth

job nm (informal) job

jogging nm ❶ jogging ❷ tracksuit

joie nf joy

joindre vb [**42**] ❶ to put together ▷ On va joindre les deux tables. We're going to put the two tables together. ❷ to contact ▷ Vous pouvez le joindre chez lui. You can contact him at home.

joint, e *adj* une pièce jointe *(in email)* an attachment

joli, e *adj* pretty

jonc *nm* rush

jonquille *nf* daffodil

joue *nf* cheek

jouer *vb* [**28**] ❶ to play; **jouer de** *(instrument)* to play ▷ *Il joue de la guitare et du piano.* He plays the guitar and the piano.; **jouer à** *(sport, game)* to play ▷ *Elle joue au tennis.* She plays tennis. ▷ *jouer aux cartes* to play cards ❷ to act ▷ *Je trouve qu'il joue très bien dans ce film.* I think he acts very well in this film.; **On joue Hamlet au Théâtre de la Ville.** Hamlet is on at the Théâtre de la Ville.

jouet *nm* toy

joueur *nm* player; **être mauvais joueur** to be a bad loser

joueuse *nf* player

jour *nm* day; **Il fait jour.** It's daylight.; **mettre quelque chose à jour** to update something; **le jour de l'An** New Year's Day; **un jour de congé** a day off; **un jour férié** a public holiday; **dans huit jours** in a week; **dans quinze jours** in a fortnight

journal *(pl* **journaux**) *nm* ❶ newspaper; **le journal télévisé** the television news ❷ diary

journalier *(f* **journalière**) *adj* daily

journalisme *nm* journalism

journaliste *nmf* journalist

journée *nf* day

joyeux *(f* **joyeuse**) *adj* happy;

Joyeux anniversaire! Happy birthday!; **Joyeux Noël!** Merry Christmas!

judo *nm* judo

juge *nm* judge

juger *vb* [**45**] to judge

juif *(f* **juive**) *adj, nm/f* Jewish; **un Juif** *(man)* a Jew; **une Juive** *(woman)* a Jew

juillet *nm* July; **en juillet** in July

juin *nm* June; **en juin** in June

jumeau *(pl* **jumeaux**) *nm* twin

jumeler *vb* [**4**] to twin ▷ *Saint-Brieuc est jumelée avec Aberystwyth.* Saint-Brieuc is twinned with Aberystwyth.

jumelle *nf* twin

jumelles *nfpl* binoculars

jument *nf* mare

jungle *nf* jungle

jupe *nf* skirt

jurer *vb* [**28**] to swear ▷ *Je jure que c'est vrai!* I swear it's true!

juridique *adj* legal

jury *nm* jury

jus *nm* juice; **un jus de fruit** a fruit juice

jusqu'à *prep* ❶ as far as ▷ *Nous avons marché jusqu'au village.* We walked as far as the village. ❷ until ▷ *Il fait généralement chaud jusqu'à la mi-août.* It's usually hot until mid-August.; **jusqu'à ce que** until; **jusqu'à présent** so far

jusque *prep* as far as ▷ *Je l'ai raccompagnée jusque chez elle.* I went with her as far as her house.

juste *adj, adv* ❶ fair ▷ *Il est sévère, mais juste.* He's strict but fair.

a
b
c
d
e
f
g
h
i
j
k
l
m
n
o
p
q
r
s
t
u
v
w
x
y
z

② tight ▷ *Cette veste est un peu juste.* This jacket is a bit tight.; **juste assez** just enough; **chanter juste** to sing in tune

justement *adv* just

justesse *nf* **de justesse** only just

justice *nf* justice

justifier *vb* [**19**] to justify

juteux (*f* **juteuse**) *adj* juicy

juvénile *adj* youthful

kaki *adj* khaki

kangourou *nm* kangaroo

karaté *nm* karate

kermesse *nf* fair

kidnapper *vb* [**28**] to kidnap

kiffer *vb* [**28**] (*informal*) to like, be into

kilo *nm* kilo

kilogramme *nm* kilogram

kilomètre *nm* kilometre

kinésithérapeute *nmf* physiotherapist

kiosque *nm* **un kiosque à journaux** a news stand

kit *nm* kit ▷ *en kit* in kit form ▷ *un kit mains libres* a hands-free kit

klaxon *nm* (*of car*) horn

klaxonner *vb* [**28**] to sound the horn

km *abbr* (= *kilomètre*) km (= *kilometre*)

KO *adj* knocked out; **mettre quelqu'un KO** to knock somebody out; **Je suis complètement KO.** *(informal)* I'm completely knackered.

K-way® *nm* cagoule

l' *art, pron see* **la**; **le**

la *art, pron*

> la changes to **l'** before a vowel and most words beginning with 'h'.

① the ▷ *la maison* the house ▷ *l'actrice* the actress ▷ *l'herbe* the grass **②** her ▷ *Je la connais depuis longtemps.* I've known her for a long time. **③** it ▷ *C'est une bonne émission: je la regarde tous les jours.* It's a good programme: I watch it every day. **④** one's; **se mordre la langue** to bite one's tongue ▷ *Je me suis mordu la langue.* I've bitten my tongue.; **six euros la douzaine** six euros a dozen

▶ *nm* **①** A ▷ *en la bémol* in A flat **②** la ▷ *sol, la, si, do* so, la, ti, do

là *adv* **①** there ▷ *Ton livre est là, sur la*

table. Your book's there, on the table. ❷ here ▷ *Elle n'est pas là.* She isn't here.; **C'est là que … (1)** That's where … ▷ *C'est là que je suis né.* That's where I was born. **(2)** That's when … ▷ *C'est là que j'ai réalisé que je m'étais trompé.* That's when I realized that I had made a mistake.

là-bas *adv* over there

labo *nm (informal)* lab

laboratoire *nm* laboratory

labourer *vb* [28] to plough

labyrinthe *nm* maze

lac *nm* lake

lacer *vb* [12] *(shoes)* to do up

lacet *nm* lace; **des chaussures à lacets** lace-up shoes

lâche *adj* ❶ loose ▷ *Le nœud est trop lâche.* The knot's too loose. ❷ cowardly; **Il est lâche.** He's a coward.
▶ *nmf* coward

lâcher *vb* [28] ❶ to let go of ▷ *Il n'a pas lâché ma main de tout le film.* He didn't let go of my hand until the end of the film. ❷ to drop ▷ *Il a été tellement surpris qu'il a lâché son verre.* He was so surprised that he dropped his glass. ❸ to fail ▷ *Les freins ont lâché.* The brakes failed.

lâcheté *nf* cowardice

lacrymogène *adj* **le gaz lacrymogène** tear gas

lacune *nf* gap

là-dedans *adv* in there

là-dessous *adv* ❶ under there ❷ behind it

là-dessus *adv* on there

là-haut *adv* up there

laïcité *nf* secularity, secularism

laid, e *adj* ugly

laideur *nf* ugliness

lainage *nm* woollen garment

laine *nf* wool; **une laine polaire** *(jacket)* a fleece

laïque *adj* **une école laïque** a state school

laisse *nf* lead ▷ *Tenez votre chien en laisse.* Keep your dog on a lead.

laisser *vb* [28] ❶ to leave ▷ *J'ai laissé mon parapluie à la maison.* I've left my umbrella at home. ❷ to let ▷ *Laisse-le parler.* Let him speak.; **Il se laisse aller.** He's letting himself go.

laisser-aller *nm* carelessness

lait *nm* milk; **un café au lait** a white coffee

laitue *nf* lettuce

lambeaux *nmpl* **en lambeaux** tattered

lame *nf* blade

lamelle *nf* thin strip

lamentable *adj* appalling

se lamenter *vb* [28] to moan

lampadaire *nm* standard lamp

lampe *nf* lamp; **une lampe de poche** a torch

lance *nf* spear

lancement *nm* launch

lancer *vb* [12] ❶ to throw ▷ *Lance-moi le ballon!* Throw me the ball! ❷ to launch ▷ *Ils viennent de lancer un nouveau modèle.* They've just launched a new model.; **se lancer dans** to embark on ▷ *Il s'est lancé là-dedans sans bien réfléchir.* He embarked on it without thinking properly.

▶ *nm* **le lancer de poids** putting the shot

lancinant, e *adj* **une douleur lancinante** a shooting pain

landau *nm* pram

lande *nf* moor

langage *nm* language

langouste *nf* crayfish

langue *nf* ❶ tongue; **sa langue maternelle** his mother tongue ❷ language ▷ *une langue étrangère* a foreign language

lanière *nf* strap

lapin *nm* rabbit

laps *nm* **un laps de temps** a space of time

laque *nf* hair spray

laquelle (*pl* **lesquelles**) *pron f* ❶ which ▷ *Laquelle de ces photos préfères-tu?* Which of these photos do you prefer? ❷ whom ▷ *la personne à laquelle vous faites référence* the person to whom you are referring

 laquelle is often not translated in English.

▷ *la personne à laquelle je pense* the person I'm thinking of

lard *nm* streaky bacon

lardons *nmpl* chunks of bacon

large *adj, adv* wide; **voir large** to allow a bit extra

▶ *nm* **cinq mètres de large** 5 m wide; **le large** the open sea; **au large de** off the coast of

largement *adv* **Vous avez largement le temps.** You have plenty of time.; **C'est largement suffisant.** That's ample.

largeur *nf* width

larme *nf* tear

laryngite *nf* laryngitis

laser *nm* laser; **une platine laser** a compact disc player; **un disque laser** a compact disc

lasser *vb* [28] **se lasser de** to get tired of

latin *nm* Latin

laurier *nm* laurel tree ▷ *une feuille de laurier* a bay leaf

lavable *adj* washable

lavabo *nm* washbasin

lavage *nm* wash

lavande *nf* lavender

lave-linge (*pl* **lave-linge**) *nm* washing machine

laver *vb* [28] to wash; **se laver** to wash ▷ *se laver les mains* to wash one's hands

laverie *nf* **une laverie automatique** a launderette

lave-vaisselle (*pl* **lave-vaisselle**) *nm* dishwasher

le *art, pron*

 le changes to **l'** before a vowel and most words beginning with 'h'.

❶ the ▷ *le livre* the book ▷ *l'arbre* the tree ▷ *l'hélicoptère* the helicopter ❷ him ▷ *Daniel est un vieil ami: je le connais depuis plus de vingt ans.* Daniel is an old friend: I've known him for over 20 years. ❸ it ▷ *Où est mon stylo? Je ne le trouve plus.* Where's my pen? I can't find it. ❹ one's; **se laver le visage** to wash one's face ▷ *Évitez de vous laver le visage avec du savon.* Avoid washing

your face with soap.; **dix euros le kilo** 10 euros a kilo; **Il est arrivé le douze mai.** He arrived on 12 May.
lécher vb [**34**] to lick
lèche-vitrine nm **faire du lèche-vitrine** to go window-shopping
leçon nf lesson
lecteur nm ❶ reader ❷ (at a university) foreign language assistant; **un lecteur de CD** a CD player; **un lecteur de DVD** a DVD player; **un lecteur MP3** an MP3 player
lectrice nf ❶ reader ❷ (at a university) foreign language assistant
lecture nf reading

> Be careful! The French word **lecture** does not mean **lecture**.

légal, e (mpl **légaux**) adj legal
légende nf ❶ legend ❷ (of map) key ❸ (of picture) caption
léger (f **légère**) adj ❶ light ❷ slight; **à la légère** thoughtlessly
légèrement adv ❶ lightly ❷ slightly ▷ Il est légèrement plus grand que son frère. He's slightly taller than his brother.
leggings mpl leggings
législatives nfpl general election sg
légume nm vegetable
lendemain nm next day ▷ le lendemain de son arrivée the day after he arrived; **le lendemain matin** the next morning
lent, e adj slow
lentement adv slowly
lenteur nf slowness
lentille nf ❶ contact lens ❷ lentil
léopard nm leopard

LEP mpl (= lycée d'enseignement professionnel) vocational school
lequel (f **laquelle**, mpl **lesquels**, fpl **lesquelles**) pron ❶ which ▷ Lequel de ces films as-tu préféré? Which of the films did you prefer? ❷ whom ▷ l'homme avec lequel elle a été vue pour la dernière fois the man with whom she was last seen

> **lequel** is often not translated in English.

▷ le garçon avec lequel elle est sortie the boy she went out with
les art, pron ❶ the ▷ les arbres the trees ❷ them ▷ Elle les a invités à dîner. She invited them to dinner. ❸ one's; **se brosser les dents** to brush one's teeth ▷ Elle s'est brossé les dents. She brushed her teeth.; **dix euros les cinq** 10 euros for 5
lesbienne nf lesbian
lesquels (f **lesquelles**) pron pl ❶ which ▷ Lesquelles de ces photos préfères-tu? Which of the photos do you prefer? ❷ whom ▷ les personnes avec lesquelles il est associé the people with whom he is in partnership

> **lesquels** is often not translated in English.

▷ les gens chez lesquels nous avons dîné the people we had dinner with
lessive nf ❶ washing powder ❷ washing; **faire la lessive** to do the washing
leste adj nimble
Lettonie nf Latvia
lettre nf letter
lettres nfpl arts ▷ la faculté de lettres

the Faculty of Arts

leur adj, pron ❶ their ▷ leur ami their friend ❷ them ▷ Je leur ai dit la vérité. I told them the truth.; **le leur** theirs ▷ Ma voiture est rouge, la leur est bleue. My car's red, theirs is blue.

leurs (f **leurs**) adj pl, pron pl their ▷ leurs amis their friends; **les leurs** theirs ▷ tes livres et les leurs your books and theirs

levé, e adj **être levé** to be up ▷ Est-ce qu'il est levé? Is he up?

levée nf (of mail) collection

lever vb [43] to raise; **Levez la main!** Put your hand up!; **lever les yeux** to look up; **se lever (1)** to get up ▷ Il se lève tous les jours à six heures. He gets up at 6 o'clock every day. ▷ Lève-toi! Get up! **(2)** to rise ▷ Le soleil se lève actuellement à cinq heures. At the moment the sun rises at 5 o'clock. **(3)** to stand up ▷ Levez-vous! Stand up!
▶ nm **le lever du soleil** sunrise

levier nm lever

lèvre nf lip

lévrier nm greyhound

levure nf yeast; **la levure chimique** baking powder

lexique nm word list

lézard nm lizard

liaison nf affair

libellule nf dragonfly

libérer vb [34] to free; **se libérer** to find time

liberté nf freedom; **mettre en liberté** to release

libraire nmf bookseller

librairie nf bookshop

Be careful! **librairie** does not mean **library**.

libre adj ❶ free ▷ Tu es libre de faire ce que tu veux. You are free to do as you wish. ▷ Est-ce que cette place est libre? Is this seat free?; **Avez-vous une chambre de libre?** Have you got a free room? ❷ clear ▷ La route est libre: vous pouvez traverser. The road is clear: you can cross.

libre-service (pl **libres-services**) nm self-service store

Libye nf Libya

licence nf ❶ degree ❷ licence

licencié nm graduate

licenciée nf graduate

licenciement nm redundancy

licencier vb [19] to make redundant

liège nm cork; **un bouchon en liège** (for bottle) a cork

lien nm ❶ connection; **un lien de parenté** a family tie ❷ (in computing) link

lier vb [19] **lier conversation avec quelqu'un** to get into conversation with somebody; **se lier avec quelqu'un** to make friends with somebody

lierre nm ivy

lieu (pl **lieux**) nm place; **avoir lieu** to take place ▷ La cérémonie a eu lieu dans la salle des fêtes. The ceremony took place in the village hall.; **au lieu de** instead of

lièvre nm hare

ligne nf ❶ (phone, train) line ▷ la ligne de bus numéro six the number 6 bus; **en ligne** (computing) online

a b c d e f g h i j k l m n o p q r s t u v w x y z

❷ figure ▷ *C'est mauvais pour la ligne.* It's bad for your figure.

ligoter *vb* [**28**] to tie up

ligue *nf* league

lilas *nm* lilac

limace *nf* slug

lime *nf* une lime à ongles a nail file

limitation *nf* la limitation de vitesse the speed limit

limite *nf* ❶ (*of property, football pitch*) boundary ❷ limit; **À la limite, on pourrait prendre le bus.** At a pinch we could go by bus.; **la date limite** the deadline; **la date limite de vente** the sell-by date

limiter *vb* [**28**] to limit

limonade *nf* lemonade

lin *nm* linen

linge *nm* ❶ linen ❷ washing ▷ *laver le linge* to do the washing; **du linge de corps** underwear

lingerie *nf* (*women's*) underwear

lion *nm* lion; **le Lion** Leo

lionne *nf* lioness

liqueur *nf* liqueur

liquide *adj* liquid
▶ *nm* liquid; **payer quelque chose en liquide** to pay cash for something

lire *vb* [**44**] to read ▷ *Tu as lu 'Madame Bovary'?* Have you read 'Madame Bovary'?

lis, lisent, lisez *vb see* **lire**; *Je lis beaucoup.* I read a lot.

lisible *adj* legible

lisse *adj* smooth

liste *nf* list; **faire la liste de** to make a list of

lit *nm* bed ▷ *un grand lit* a double bed ▷ *aller au lit* to go to bed; **faire son lit** to make one's bed; **un lit de camp** a campbed
▶ *vb see* **lire**

literie *nf* bedding

litière *nf* ❶ (*for cat*) litter ❷ (*of caged pet*) bedding

litre *nm* litre

littéraire *adj* une œuvre littéraire a work of literature

littérature *nf* literature

littoral (*pl* **littoraux**) *nm* coast

Lituanie *nf* Lithuania

livraison *nf* delivery; **la livraison des bagages** baggage reclaim

livre *nm* book; **un livre de poche** a paperback

> Word for word, **livre de poche** means 'pocket book'.

▶ *nf* pound

● The French **livre** is 500 grams.

▷ *une livre de beurre* a pound of butter; **la livre sterling** the pound sterling

livrer *vb* [**28**] to deliver

livret *nm* booklet; **le livret scolaire** the school report book

livreur *nm* delivery man

local, e (*mpl* **locaux**) *adj* local
▶ *nm* premises

locataire *nmf* ❶ tenant ❷ lodger

location *nf* location de voitures car rental; **location de skis** ski hire

> Be careful! The French word **location** does not mean **location**.

locomotive *nf* locomotive

loge *nf* dressing room

logement nm ❶ housing ❷ accommodation

loger vb [45] to stay; **trouver à se loger** to find somewhere to live

logiciel nm software

logique adj logical
▶ nf logic

loi nf law

loin adv ❶ far ▷ *La gare n'est pas très loin d'ici.* The station is not very far from here. ❷ far off ▷ *Noël n'est plus tellement loin.* Christmas isn't far off now. ❸ a long time ago ▷ *Les vacances paraissent déjà tellement loin!* The holidays already seem such a long time ago!; **au loin** in the distance; **de loin (1)** from a long way away ▷ *On voit l'église de loin.* You can see the church from a long way away. **(2)** by far ▷ *C'est de loin l'élève la plus brillante.* She is by far the brightest pupil.; **C'est plus loin que la gare.** It's further on than the station.

lointain, e adj distant
▶ nm **dans le lointain** in the distance

loir nm dormouse; **dormir comme un loir** to sleep like a log

loisirs nmpl ❶ free time sg ▷ *Qu'est-ce que vous faites pendant vos loisirs?* What do you do in your free time? ❷ hobby

Londonien nm Londoner

Londres n London; **à Londres (1)** in London **(2)** to London

long (f **longue**) adj long
▶ nm **un bateau de trois mètres de long** a boat 3 m long; **tout le**

long de all along; **marcher de long en large** to walk up and down

longer vb [45] **La route longe la forêt.** The road runs along the edge of the forest.; **Nous avons longé la Seine à pied.** We walked along the Seine.

longtemps adv a long time; **pendant longtemps** for a long time; **mettre longtemps à faire quelque chose** to take a long time to do something

longue nf **à la longue** in the end

longuement adv at length

longueur nf length; **à longueur de journée** all day long

look nm look

loques nfpl **être en loques** to be torn to bits

lors de prep during

lorsque conj when

lot nm prize; **le gros lot** the jackpot

loterie nf ❶ lottery ❷ raffle

lotion nf lotion; **une lotion après-rasage** an aftershave; **une lotion démaquillante** cleansing milk

lotissement nm housing estate

loto nm lottery; **le loto sportif** the pools

loubard nm (informal) lout

louche adj fishy
▶ nf ladle

loucher vb [28] to squint

louer vb [28] ❶ to let; **'à louer'** 'to let' ❷ to rent ▷ *Je loue un petit appartement au centre-ville.* I rent a little flat in the centre of town. ❸ to hire ▷ *Nous allons louer une*

a
b
c
d
e
f
g
h
i
j
k
l
m
n
o
p
q
r
s
t
u
v
w
x
y
z

voiture. We're going to hire a car.
❹ to praise
loup *nm* wolf
loupe *nf* magnifying glass
louper *vb* [**28**] *(informal)* to miss
lourd, e *adj* heavy
▶ *adv (weather)* close
loutre *nf* otter
loyauté *nf* loyalty
loyer *nm* rent
lu *vb see* lire
lucarne *nf* skylight
luge *nf* sledge
lugubre *adj* gloomy
lui *pron* ❶ him ▷ *Il a été très content
du cadeau que je lui ai offert.* He was
very pleased with the present I
gave him. ▷ *C'est bien lui!* It's
definitely him! ▷ *J'ai pensé à lui toute
la journée.* I thought about him all
day long. ❷ to him ▷ *Mon père est
d'accord: je lui ai parlé ce matin.* My
father said yes: I spoke to him this
morning. ❸ her ▷ *Elle a été très
contente du cadeau que je lui ai offert.*
She was very pleased with the
present I gave her. ❹ to her ▷ *Ma
mère est d'accord: je lui ai parlé ce
matin.* My mother said yes: I spoke
to her this morning. ❺ it ▷ *Qu'est-ce
que tu donnes à ton chat? — Je lui
donne de la viande crue.* What do you
give your cat? — I give it raw meat.
▰ **lui** is also used for emphasis.
▷ *Lui, il est toujours en retard!* Oh
him, he's always late!; **lui-même**
himself ▷ *Il a construit son bateau
lui-même.* He built his boat himself.
lumière *nf* light; **la lumière du**

jour daylight
lumineux (*f* **lumineuse**) *adj* une
enseigne lumineuse a neon sign
lunatique *adj* temperamental
lundi *nm* ❶ Monday ▷ *Aujourd'hui,
nous sommes lundi.* It's Monday
today. ❷ on Monday; **le lundi** on
Mondays; **tous les lundis** every
Monday; **lundi dernier** last
Monday; **lundi prochain** next
Monday; **le lundi de Pâques**
Easter Monday
lune *nf* moon; **la lune de miel**
honeymoon
lunettes *nfpl* glasses; **des lunettes
de soleil** sunglasses; **des lunettes
de plongée** swimming goggles
lutte *nf* ❶ fight ❷ wrestling
lutter *vb* [**28**] to fight
luxe *nm* luxury; **de luxe** luxury
luxueux (*f* **luxueuse**) *adj* luxurious
lycée *nm* secondary school; **lycée
technique** technical college
  ● In France pupils go to a **collège**
  ● between the ages of 11 and 15,
  ● and then to a **lycée** until the age
  ● of 18.
lycéen *nm* secondary school pupil
lycéenne *nf* secondary school
pupil

m

M. *abbr* (= *Monsieur*) Mr ▷ *M. Bernard* Mr Bernard

m' *pron see* **me**

ma *adj f* my ▷ *ma mère* my mother ▷ *ma montre* my watch

macaronis *nmpl* macaroni *sg*

Macédoine *nf* Macedonia

macédoine *nf* **la macédoine de fruits** fruit salad; **la macédoine de légumes** mixed vegetables

mâcher *vb* [**28**] to chew

machin *nm* (*informal*) thingy

machinalement *adv* **Elle a regardé sa montre machinalement.** She looked at her watch without thinking.

machine *nf* machine; **une machine à laver** a washing machine; **une machine à écrire** a typewriter; **une machine à coudre** a sewing machine; **une machine à sous** a fruit machine

machiste *nm* male chauvinist

macho *nm* (*informal*) male chauvinist pig

mâchoire *nf* jaw

mâchonner *vb* [**28**] to chew

maçon *nm* bricklayer

Madame (*pl* **Mesdames**) *nf* ❶ Mrs ▷ *Madame Legall* Mrs Legall ❷ lady ▷ *Occupez-vous de Madame.* Could you look after this lady? ❸ Madam ▷ *Madame, ...* (*in letter*) Dear Madam, ...

Mademoiselle (*pl* **Mesdemoiselles**) *nf* ❶ Miss ▷ *Mademoiselle Martin* Miss Martin ❷ Madam ▷ *Mademoiselle, ...* (*in letter*) Dear Madam, ...

magasin *nm* shop; **faire les magasins** to go shopping

magazine *nm* magazine

magicien *nm* magician

magie *nf* magic ▷ *un tour de magie* a magic trick

magique *adj* magic ▷ *une baguette magique* a magic wand

magistral, e (*mpl* **magistraux**) *adj* **un cours magistral** (*at university*) a lecture

magnétique *adj* magnetic

magnétophone *nm* tape recorder; **un magnétophone à cassettes** a cassette recorder

magnétoscope *nm* video recorder

magnifique *adj* superb

mai *nm* May; **en mai** in May

maigre *adj* ❶ skinny ❷ (*meat*) lean ❸ (*cheese, yoghurt*) low-fat

maigrir vb [**38**] to lose weight
maillot de bain nm ① swimsuit
② swimming trunks
main nf hand; **serrer la main à quelqu'un** to shake hands with somebody; **se serrer la main** to shake hands; **sous la main** to hand
main-d'œuvre nf workforce; **la main-d'œuvre immigrée** immigrant labour
maintenant adv ① now ▷ Qu'est-ce que tu veux faire maintenant? What do you want to do now? ② nowadays
maintenir vb [**83**] to maintain; **se maintenir** to hold
maire nm mayor
mairie nf town hall
mais conj but ▷ C'est cher mais de très bonne qualité. It's expensive, but very good quality.
maïs nm ① maize ② sweetcorn
maison nf house; **une maison des jeunes** a youth club; **des maisons mitoyennes (1)** semi-detached houses **(2)** terraced houses; **à la maison (1)** at home ▷ Je serai à la maison cet après-midi. I'll be at home this afternoon. **(2)** home ▷ Elle est rentrée à la maison. She's gone home.
▶ adj home-made
maître nm ① (in primary school) teacher ② (of dog) master; **un maître d'hôtel** (in restaurant) a head waiter; **un maître nageur** a lifeguard
maîtresse nf ① (in primary school)

teacher ② mistress
maîtrise nf master's degree; **la maîtrise de soi** self-control
maîtriser vb [**28**] **se maîtriser** to control oneself
majestueux (f **majestueuse**) adj majestic
majeur, e adj **être majeur** to be 18 ▷ Tu feras ce que tu voudras quand tu seras majeure. You can do what you like once you're 18. ▷ Elle sera majeure en août. She will be 18 in August.; **la majeure partie** most ▷ la majeure partie de mon salaire most of my salary
majorité nf majority; **la majorité et l'opposition** the government and the opposition
Majorque nf Majorca
majuscule nf capital letter
mal adv, adj ① badly ② wrong ▷ C'est mal de mentir. It's wrong to tell lies.; **aller mal** to be ill; **pas mal** quite good
▶ nm ① ache ▷ J'ai mal à la tête. I've got a headache. ▷ J'ai mal aux dents. I've got toothache. ▷ J'ai mal au dos. My back hurts. ▷ Est-ce que vous avez mal à la gorge? Have you got a sore throat?; **Ça fait mal.** It hurts.; **Où est-ce que tu as mal?** Where does it hurt?; **faire mal à quelqu'un** to hurt somebody; **se faire mal** to hurt oneself ▷ Je me suis fait mal au bras. I hurt my arm.; **se donner du mal pour faire quelque chose** to go to a lot of trouble to do something; **avoir le mal de mer** to be seasick; **avoir le**

mal du pays to be homesick ❷ evil;
dire du mal de quelqu'un to speak
ill of somebody
malade *adj* ill; **tomber malade** to
fall ill
▶ *nmf* patient
maladie *nf* illness
maladif (*f* **maladive**) *adj* sickly
maladresse *nf* clumsiness
maladroit, e *adj* clumsy
malaise *nm* **avoir un malaise** to
feel faint; **Son arrivée a créé un
malaise parmi les invités.** Her
arrival made the guests feel
uncomfortable.
malchance *nf* bad luck
mâle *adj* male
malédiction *nf* curse
mal en point *adj* **Il avait l'air mal
en point quand je l'ai vu hier soir.**
He didn't look too good when I saw
him last night.
malentendu *nm*
misunderstanding
malfaiteur *nm* criminal
mal famé, e (*mpl* **mal famés**) *adj*
un quartier mal famé a seedy area
malgache *adj* from Madagascar
malgré *prep* in spite of; **malgré
tout** all the same
malheur *nm* tragedy; **faire un
malheur** (*informal*) to be a smash
hit
malheureusement *adv*
unfortunately
malheureux (*f* **malheureuse**) *adj*
miserable
malhonnête *adj* dishonest
malice *nf* mischief

malicieux (*f* **malicieuse**) *adj*
mischievous
   ■ Be careful! **malicieux** does not
   mean **malicious**.
malin (*f* **maligne**) *adj* crafty; **C'est
malin!** (*informal*) That's clever!
malle *nf* trunk
malodorant, e *adj* foul-smelling
malpropre *adj* dirty
malsain, e *adj* unhealthy
Malte *nm* Malta
maltraiter *vb* [28] to ill-treat; **des
enfants maltraités** battered
children
malveillant, e *adj* malicious
maman *nf* mum
mamie *nf* granny
mammifère *nm* mammal
manche *nf* ❶ (*of clothes*) sleeve
❷ (*of game*) leg; **la Manche** the
Channel
▶ *nm* (*of pan*) handle
mandarine *nf* mandarin orange
manège *nm* merry-go-round
manette *nf* lever
mangeable *adj* edible
manger *vb* [45] to eat
mangue *nf* mango
maniaque *adj* fussy
manie *nf* ❶ obsession; **avoir la
manie de** to be obsessive about
❷ habit
manier *vb* [19] to handle
maniéré, e *adj* affected
manière *nf* way; **de manière à** so
as to; **de toute manière** in any
case
manières *nfpl* ❶ manners ❷ fuss
▷ *Ne fais pas de manières: mange ta*

soupe! Don't make a fuss: eat your
soup!

manifestant nm demonstrator

manifestation nf demonstration

manifester vb [28] to
demonstrate

manipuler vb [28] ❶ to handle
❷ to manipulate

mannequin nmf model

manœuvrer vb [28] to manœuvre

manque nm le manque de lack of

manqué, e adj un garçon manqué
a tomboy

manquer vb [28] to miss ▷ *Il
manque des pages à ce livre.* There are
some pages missing from this
book.; **Mes parents me
manquent.** I miss my parents.;
Ma sœur me manque. I miss my
sister.; **Il manque encore dix
euros.** We are still 10 euros short.;
manquer de to lack; **Il a manqué
se tuer.** He nearly got killed.

manteau (pl **manteaux**) nm coat

manuel (f **manuelle**) adj manual
▶ nm ❶ textbook ❷ handbook

maquereau (pl **maquereaux**) nm
mackerel

maquette nf model

maquillage nm make-up

se **maquiller** vb [28] to put on one's
make-up

marais nm marsh

marbre nm marble

marchand nm ❶ shopkeeper; **un
marchand de journaux** a
newsagent ❷ stallholder (*in
market*)

marchander vb [28] to haggle

marchandise nf goods

marche nf ❶ step ▷ *Fais attention à
la marche!* Mind the step!
❷ walking ▷ *La marche me fait du
bien.* Walking does me good.; **être
en état de marche** to be in
working order; **Ne montez jamais
dans un train en marche.** Never
try to get onto a moving train.;
mettre en marche to start; **la
marche arrière** reverse gear; **faire
marche arrière** to reverse
❸ march ▷ *une marche militaire* a
military march

marché nm market; **un marché
aux puces** a flea market; **le
marché noir** the black market

marcher vb [28] ❶ to walk ▷ *Elle
marche cinq kilomètres par jour.* She
walks 5 kilometres every day.
❷ to run ▷ *Le métro marche
normalement aujourd'hui.* The
underground is running normally
today. ❸ to work ▷ *Est-ce que
l'ascenseur marche?* Is the lift
working? ❹ to go well; **Alors les
études, ça marche?** (*informal*)
How are you getting on at school?;
faire marcher quelqu'un to pull
somebody's leg

marcheur nm walker

mardi nm ❶ Tuesday ▷ *Aujourd'hui,
nous sommes mardi.* It's Tuesday
today. ❷ on Tuesday; **le mardi** on
Tuesdays; **tous les mardis** every
Tuesday; **mardi dernier** last
Tuesday; **mardi prochain** next
Tuesday; **Mardi gras** Shrove
Tuesday

mare *nf* pond

marécage *nm* marsh

marée *nf* tide; **une marée noire** an oil slick

margarine *nf* margarine

marge *nf* margin

mari *nm* husband

mariage *nm* ❶ marriage ❷ wedding

marié, e *adj* married

marié *nm* bridegroom; **les mariés** the bride and groom

mariée *nf* bride

se **marier** *vb* [**19**] to marry

marin, e *adj* sea; **un pull marin** a sailor's jersey
  ▶ *nm* sailor

marine *adj* bleu marine navy-blue
  ▶ *nf* navy; **la marine nationale** the French navy

marionnette *nf* puppet

marketing *nm* marketing

marmelade *nf* stewed fruit; **la marmelade de pommes** stewed apple; **la marmelade d'oranges** marmalade

marmite *nf* cooking pot

marmonner *vb* [**28**] to mumble

Maroc *nm* Morocco

marocain, e *adj, nm/f* Moroccan

maroquinerie *nf* leather goods shop

marquant, e *adj* significant

marque *nf* ❶ mark ▷ *des marques de doigts* fingermarks ❷ make ▷ *De quelle marque est ton jean?* What make are your jeans? ❸ brand ▷ *une grande marque de cognac* a well-known brand of cognac;

l'image de marque the public image ▷ *Le ministre tient à son image de marque.* The minister cares about his public image.; **une marque déposée** a registered trademark; **À vos marques! Prêts! Partez!** Ready, steady, go!

marquer *vb* [**28**] ❶ to mark ❷ to score ▷ *L'équipe irlandaise a marqué dix points.* The Irish team scored ten points. ❸ to celebrate ▷ *On va sortir au restaurant pour marquer ton anniversaire.* We'll eat out to celebrate your birthday.

marraine *nf* godmother

marrant, e *adj* (informal) funny

marre *adv* (informal); **en avoir marre de quelque chose** to be fed up with something

se **marrer** *vb* [**28**] (informal) to have a good laugh

marron *nm* chestnut ▷ *la crème de marrons* chestnut purée
  ▶ *adj* brown

marronnier *nm* chestnut tree

mars *nm* March; **en mars** in March

marteau (*pl* **marteaux**) *nm* hammer

martyriser *vb* [**28**] to batter

masculin, e *adj* ❶ men's ▷ *la mode masculine* men's fashion ❷ masculine ▷ *'Chat' est un nom masculin.* 'Chat' is a masculine noun.

masque *nm* mask

massacre *nm* massacre

massacrer *vb* [**28**] to massacre

massage *nm* massage

masse *nf* **une masse de** (informal)

masses of; **produire en masse**
to mass-produce; **venir en masse**
to come en masse

masser vb [**28**] to massage; **se masser** to gather

massif (f **massive**) adj ❶ (gold, silver, wood) solid ❷ massive ▷ une dose massive d'antibiotiques a massive dose of antibiotics ❸ mass ▷ des départs massifs a mass exodus

mat, e adj matt; **être mat** (chess) to be checkmate

match nm match; **le match aller** the first leg; **le match retour** the second leg; **faire match nul** to draw

matelas nm mattress; **un matelas pneumatique** an air bed

matelassé, e adj quilted

matelot nm sailor

matériaux nmpl materials

matériel nm ❶ equipment ❷ gear

maternel (f **maternelle**) adj motherly; **ma grand-mère maternelle** my mother's mother; **mon oncle maternel** my mother's brother

maternelle nf nursery school
  ● The **maternelle** is a state school
  ● for 2–6 year-olds.

maternité nf **le congé de maternité** maternity leave

mathématiques nfpl mathematics

maths nfpl (informal) maths

matière nf subject ▷ Le latin est une matière facultative. Latin is an optional subject.; **sans matières**

grasses fat-free; **les matières premières** raw materials

matin nm morning ▷ à trois heures du matin at 3 o'clock in the morning; **Je suis du matin.** I'm at my best in the morning.; **de bon matin** early in the morning

matinal, e (mpl **matinaux**) adj morning; **être matinal** to be up early

matinée nf morning

matou nm tomcat

matrimonial, e (mpl **matrimoniaux**) adj **une agence matrimoniale** a marriage bureau

maudire vb [**46**] to curse

maudit, e adj (informal) blasted

maussade adj sullen

mauvais, e adj, adv ❶ bad ▷ une mauvaise note a bad mark; **Il fait mauvais.** The weather's bad.; **être mauvais en** to be bad at ▷ Je suis mauvais en allemand. I'm bad at German. ❷ poor ▷ Il est en mauvaise santé. His health is poor.; **Tu as mauvaise mine.** You don't look well. ❸ wrong ▷ Vous avez fait le mauvais numéro. You've dialled the wrong number.; **des mauvaises herbes** weeds; **sentir mauvais** to smell

maux nmpl **des maux de ventre** stomachache; **des maux de tête** headache

maximal, e (mpl **maximaux**) adj maximum

maximum nm maximum; **au maximum (1)** as much as one can **(2)** at the very most

mayonnaise *nf* mayonnaise
mazout *nm* fuel oil
me *pron*

> me changes to **m'** before a vowel and most words beginning with 'h'.

❶ me ▷ *Elle me téléphone tous les jours.* She phones me every day. ▷ *Il m'attend depuis une heure.* He's been waiting for me for an hour. ❷ to me ▷ *Il me parle en allemand.* He talks to me in German. ❸ myself ▷ *Je vais me préparer quelque chose à manger.* I'm going to make myself something to eat.

> With reflexive verbs, **me** is often not translated.

▷ *Je me lève à sept heures tous les matins.* I get up at 7 every morning.
mec *nm* (informal) guy
mécanicien *nm* mechanic
mécanique *nf* ❶ mechanics ❷ (of watch, clock) mechanism
mécanisme *nm* mechanism
méchamment *adv* nastily
méchanceté *nf* nastiness
méchant, e *adj* nasty; 'Attention, chien méchant' 'Beware of the dog'
mèche *nf* (of hair) lock
mécontent, e *adj* mécontent de unhappy with
mécontentement *nm* displeasure
médaille *nf* medal
médecin *nm* doctor
médecine *nf* (subject) medicine
médias *nmpl* media sg
médical, e (*mpl* **médicaux**) *adj*

medical; **passer une visite médicale** to have a medical
médicament *nm* (drug) medicine
médiéval, e (*mpl* **médiévaux**) *adj* medieval
médiocre *adj* poor
Méditerranée *nf* Mediterranean
méditerranéen (*f* **méditerranéenne**) *adj* Mediterranean
méduse *nf* jellyfish
méfiance *nf* mistrust
méfiant, e *adj* mistrustful
se **méfier** *vb* [**19**] se méfier de quelqu'un to distrust somebody
mégarde *nf* par mégarde by mistake
mégot *nm* cigarette end
meilleur, e *adj, adv, n* better; **le meilleur** the best; **le meilleur des deux** the better of the two; **meilleur marché** cheaper
mél *nm* email
mélancolique *adj* melancholy
mélange *nm* mixture
mélanger *vb* [**45**] ❶ to mix ❷ to muddle up
mêlée *nf* scrum
mêler *vb* [**28**] se mêler to mix; **Mêle-toi de ce qui te regarde!** (informal) Mind your own business!
mélodie *nf* melody
melon *nm* melon
membre *nm* ❶ limb ❷ member ▷ *un membre de la famille* a member of the family
mémé *nf* (informal) granny
même *adj, adv, pron* ❶ same; **en même temps** at the same time;

a b c d e f g h i j k l m n o p q r s t u v w x y z

moi-même myself ▷ *Je l'ai fait moi-même.* I did it myself.;
toi-même yourself; **eux-mêmes** themselves ❷ even ▷ *Il n'a même pas pleuré.* He didn't even cry.
mémoire *nf* memory
menace *nf* threat
menacer *vb* [**12**] to threaten
ménage *nm* housework; **une femme de ménage** a cleaning woman
ménager (*f* **ménagère**) *adj* **les travaux ménagers** housework
ménagère *nf* housewife
mendiant *nm* beggar
mendier *vb* [**19**] to beg
mener *vb* [**43**] to lead; **Cela ne vous mènera à rien!** That will get you nowhere!
méningite *nf* meningitis
menottes *nfpl* handcuffs
mensonge *nm* lie
mensualité *nf* monthly payment
mensuel (*f* **mensuelle**) *adj* monthly
mensurations *nfpl* measurements
mentalité *nf* mentality
menteur *nm* liar
menteuse *nf* liar
menthe *nf* mint
mention *nf* grade
mentionner *vb* [**28**] to mention
mentir *vb* [**77**] to lie ▷ *Tu mens!* You're lying!
menton *nm* chin
menu, e *adj, adv* ❶ slim ▷ *Elle est menue.* She's slim. ❷ very fine ▷ *Les oignons doivent être coupés menu.*

The onions have to be cut up very fine.
▶ *nm* menu ▷ *le menu du jour* today's menu
menuiserie *nf* woodwork
menuisier *nm* joiner
mépris *nm* contempt
méprisant, e *adj* contemptuous
mépriser *vb* [**28**] to despise
mer *nf* ❶ sea; **au bord de la mer** at the seaside; **la mer du Nord** the North Sea ❷ tide
mercerie *nf* ❶ haberdashery ❷ haberdasher's shop
merci *excl* thank you ▷ *Merci de m'avoir raccompagné.* Thank you for taking me home.; **merci beaucoup** thank you very much
mercredi *nm* ❶ Wednesday ▷ *Aujourd'hui, nous sommes mercredi.* It's Wednesday today. ❷ on Wednesday; **le mercredi** on Wednesdays; **tous les mercredis** every Wednesday; **mercredi dernier** last Wednesday; **mercredi prochain** next Wednesday
mère *nf* mother
merguez *nf* spicy sausage
méridional, e (*mpl* **méridionaux**) *adj* southern
meringue *nf* meringue
mériter *vb* [**28**] to deserve
merlan *nm* whiting
merle *nm* blackbird
merveille *nf* **Cet ordinateur est une vraie merveille!** This computer's really wonderful!; **à merveille** wonderfully
merveilleux (*f* **merveilleuse**) *adj*

marvellous

mes *adj pl* my ▷ *mes parents* my parents

Mesdames *nfpl* ladies

Mesdemoiselles *nfpl* ladies

mesquin, e *adj* mean

message *nm* message; **un message SMS** a text message

messagerie *nf* **une messagerie vocale** voice mail; **la messagerie électronique** email

messe *nf* mass

messieurs *nmpl* gentlemen; **Messieurs, ...** *(in letter)* Dear Sirs, ...

mesure *nf* ❶ measurement; **sur mesure** tailor-made ❷ measure; **au fur et à mesure** as one goes along; **être en mesure de faire quelque chose** to be in a position to do something

mesurer *vb* [28] to measure; **Il mesure un mètre quatre-vingts.** He's 1 m 80 tall.

met *vb see* **mettre**

métal *(pl* **métaux**) *nm* metal

métallique *adj* metallic

météo *nf* weather forecast

méthode *nf* ❶ method ❷ tutor ▷ *une méthode de guitare* a guitar tutor

métier *nm* job

mètre *nm* metre; **un mètre ruban** a tape measure

métro *nm* underground

mets *vb see* **mettre**

metteur en scène *(pl* **metteurs en scène**) *nm (of film or play)* director

mettre *vb* [47] ❶ to put ▷ *Où est-ce*

que tu as mis les clés? Where have you put the keys? ❷ to put on ▷ *Je mets mon manteau et j'arrive.* I'll put on my coat and then I'll be ready. ❸ to wear ▷ *Elle ne met pas souvent de jupe.* She doesn't often wear a skirt. ❹ to take ▷ *Combien de temps as-tu mis pour aller à Lille?* How long did it take you to get to Lille?; **mettre en marche** to start; **Vous pouvez vous mettre là.** You can sit there.; **se mettre au lit** to get into bed; **se mettre en maillot de bain** to put on one's swimsuit; **se mettre à** to start

meuble *nm* piece of furniture

meublé *nm* ❶ furnished flat ❷ furnished room

meubler *vb* [28] to furnish

meurtre *nm* murder

meurtrier *nm* murderer

meurtrière *nf* murderess

Mexico *n* Mexico City

Mexique *nm* Mexico

mi *nm* ❶ E ▷ *mi bémol* E flat ❷ mi ▷ *do, ré, mi ...* do, re, mi ...

mi- *prefix* ❶ half- ▷ *mi-clos* half-shut ❷ mid- ▷ *à la mi-janvier* in mid-January

miauler *vb* [28] to mew

miche *nf* loaf

mi-chemin: **à mi-chemin** *adv* halfway

micro *nm* microphone

microbe *nm* germ

micro-ondes *nm* microwave oven

micro-ordinateur *nm* microcomputer

microscope *nm* microscope

midi nm ❶ midday ▷ à midi at midday;
midi et demi half past twelve
❷ lunchtime ▷ On a bien mangé à midi.
We had a good meal at lunchtime.;
le Midi the South of France

mie nf breadcrumbs

miel nm honey

mien pron m **le mien** mine

mienne pron f **la mienne** mine

miennes pron fpl **les miennes** mine

miens pron mpl **les miens** mine

miette nf (of bread, cake) crumb

mieux adv, adj, n better; **Il vaut
mieux que tu appelles ta mère.**
You'd better phone your mother.;
le mieux the best; **faire de son
mieux** to do one's best; **de mieux
en mieux** better and better; **au
mieux** at best

mignon (f **mignonne**) adj sweet

migraine nf migraine

mijoter vb [28] to simmer

milieu (pl **milieux**) nm ❶ middle;
au milieu de in the middle of; **au
beau milieu de** in the middle of
❷ background ▷ le milieu familial
the family background
❸ environment ▷ le milieu marin the
marine environment

militaire adj military
▶ nm serviceman; **un militaire de
carrière** a professional soldier

mille num a thousand ▷ mille euros a
thousand euros ▷ deux mille
personnes two thousand people

millefeuille nm vanilla slice

millénaire nm millennium

milliard nm billion

milliardaire nmf billionaire

millier nm thousand; **par milliers**
by the thousand

milligramme nm milligram

millimètre nm millimetre

million nm million

millionnaire nmf millionaire

mi-long (f **mi-longue**) adj
medium-length

mime nmf mime artist

mimer vb [28] to mimic

minable adj ❶ shabby ❷ pathetic

mince adj ❶ thin ❷ slim; **Mince
alors!** (informal) Oh bother!

minceur nf ❶ thinness ❷ slimness

mine nf ❶ expression ❷ look ▷ Tu as
bonne mine. You look well. ▷ Il a
mauvaise mine. He doesn't look
well. ▷ Elle avait une mine fatiguée.
She was looking tired.
❸ appearance ▷ Il ne faut pas juger
les gens d'après leur mine. You
shouldn't judge people by their
appearance. ❹ (of pencil) lead
❺ mine ▷ une mine de charbon a coal
mine; **faire mine de faire quelque
chose** to pretend to do something
▷ Elle a fait mine de le croire. She
pretended to believe him.

minéral, e (mpl **minéraux**) adj
mineral

minéralogique adj **une plaque
minéralogique** a number plate

minet nm pussycat

minette nf (female) pussycat

mineur, e adj minor

mineur nm ❶ boy under 18; **les
mineurs** the under-18s ❷ miner

mineure nf girl under 18

minijupe nf miniskirt

minimal, e (*mpl* **minimaux**) *adj* minimum

minimum *nm* minimum; **au minimum** at the very least

ministère *nm* ministry

ministre *nm* minister

Minitel® *nm*

   Minitel was a system for getting
   information online which
   pre-dated the internet.

minorité *nf* minority

Minorque *nf* Minorca

minuit *nm* midnight ▷ *à minuit et quart* at a quarter past midnight

minuscule *adj* tiny
   ▶ *nf* small letter

minute *nf* minute; **à la minute** just this minute

minutieux (*f* **minutieuse**) *adj* meticulous; **C'est un travail minutieux.** It's a fiddly job.

mirabelle *nf* small yellow plum

miracle *nm* miracle

miroir *nm* mirror

mis, e *adj* **bien mis** well turned out
   ▶ *vb see* **mettre**

miser *vb* [28] (*informal*) to bank on

misérable *adj* shabby-looking

misère *nf* extreme poverty; **un salaire de misère** starvation wages

missionnaire *nmf* missionary

mit *vb see* **mettre**

mi-temps *nf* ❶ (*of match*) half ▷ *la première mi-temps* the first half ❷ half-time; **travailler à mi-temps** to work part-time

mi-trimestre *nm* half-term

mixte *adj* **une école mixte** a mixed school

Mlle (*pl* **Mlles**) *abbr* (= *Mademoiselle*) Miss ▷ *Mlle Renoir* Miss Renoir

Mme (*pl* **Mmes**) *abbr* (= *Madame*) Mrs ▷ *Mme Leroy* Mrs Leroy

mobile *nm* ❶ motive ❷ mobile phone

mobilier *nm* furniture

mobylette® *nf* moped

moche *adj* (*informal*) ❶ awful ❷ rotten

mode *nf* fashion
   ▶ *nm* **le mode d'emploi** directions for use; **le mode de vie** the way of life

modèle *nm* ❶ model ❷ (*of clothes*) style

modéré, e *adj* moderate

moderne *adj* modern

moderniser *vb* [28] to modernize

modeste *adj* modest

modestie *nf* modesty

moelleux (*f* **moelleuse**) *adj* soft

mœurs *nfpl* social attitudes; **l'évolution des mœurs** changing attitudes

moi *pron* me ▷ *Coucou, c'est moi!* Hello, it's me!; **Moi, je pense que tu as tort.** I personally think you're wrong.; **à moi** mine ▷ *Ce livre n'est pas à moi.* This book isn't mine. ▷ *un ami à moi* a friend of mine

moi-même *pron* myself

moindre *adj* **le moindre** the slightest

moine *nm* monk

moineau (*pl* **moineaux**) *nm* sparrow

moins *adv, prep* ❶ less ▷ *Ça coûte moins de deux cents euros.* It costs less than 200 euros. ❷ <u>fewer</u> ▷ *Il y a moins de gens aujourd'hui.* There are fewer people today.; **Il est cinq heures moins dix.** It's 10 to 5. ❸ <u>minus</u> ▷ *quatre moins trois* 4 minus 3; **le moins** the least; **de moins en moins** less and less; **Il a trois ans de moins que moi.** He's three years younger than me.; **au moins** at least; **à moins que** unless

▌ **à moins que** is followed by a verb in the subjunctive.

▷ *Je te retrouverai à dix heures à moins que le train n'ait du retard.* I'll meet you at 10 o'clock unless the train's late.

mois *nm* <u>month</u>

moisi *nm* **Ça sent le moisi.** It smells musty.

moisir *vb* [**38**] <u>to go mouldy</u>

moisson *nf* <u>harvest</u>

moite *adj* <u>sweaty</u>

moitié *nf* <u>half</u> ▷ *Il a mangé la moitié du gâteau.* He ate half the cake.; **la moitié du temps** half the time; **à la moitié de** halfway through ▷ *Elle est partie à la moitié du film.* She left halfway through the film.; **à moitié** half ▷ *Ton verre est encore à moitié plein.* Your glass is still half-full. ▷ *Ce sac était à moitié prix.* This bag was half-price.; **partager moitié moitié** to go halves ▷ *On partage moitié moitié, d'accord?* We'll go halves, OK?

molaire *nf* <u>back tooth</u>

Moldavie *nf* <u>Moldova</u>

molle *adj f see* **mou**

mollet *nm* (*of leg*) <u>calf</u>
  ▶ *adj* **un œuf mollet** a soft-boiled egg

môme *nmf* (*informal*) <u>kid</u>

moment *nm* <u>moment</u>; **en ce moment** at the moment; **pour le moment** for the moment; **au moment où** just as; **à ce moment-là** (1) at that point (2) in that case; **à tout moment** (1) at any moment (2) constantly; **sur le moment** at the time; **par moments** at times

momentané, e *adj* <u>momentary</u>

momie *nf* (*Egyptian*) <u>mummy</u>

mon (*f* **ma**, *pl* **mes**) *adj* <u>my</u> ▷ *mon ami* my friend

monarchie *nf* <u>monarchy</u>

monastère *nm* <u>monastery</u>

monde *nm* <u>world</u>; **Il y a du monde.** There are a lot of people.; **beaucoup de monde** a lot of people; **peu de monde** not many people

mondial, e (*mpl* **mondiaux**) *adj* ❶ <u>world</u> ▷ *la population mondiale* the world population ❷ <u>world-wide</u>

moniteur *nm* ❶ <u>instructor</u> ❷ <u>monitor</u>

monitrice *nf* <u>instructor</u>

monnaie *nf* **une pièce de monnaie** a coin; **avoir de la monnaie** to have change; **rendre la monnaie à quelqu'un** to give somebody their change

monoparental, e (*mpl* **monoparentaux**) *adj* **une famille monoparentale** a <u>single-parent family</u>

monotone *adj* <u>monotonous</u>

Monsieur (*pl* **Messieurs**) *nm* ❶ <u>Mr</u> ▷ *Monsieur Dupont* Mr Dupont

❷ man ▷ *Il y a un monsieur qui veut te voir.* There's a man to see you. **❸** Sir ▷ *Monsieur, ... (in letter)* Dear Sir, ...

monstre nm monster

▶ adj **Nous avons un travail monstre.** We've got a terrific amount of work.

mont nm mount; **le mont Everest** Mount Everest; **le mont Blanc** Mont Blanc

montagne nf mountain; **les montagnes russes** roller coaster

montagneux (f **montagneuse**) adj mountainous

montant, e adj **❶** rising ▷ *la marée montante* the rising tide **❷** high

monter vb [48] **❶** to go up ▷ *Elle a du mal à monter les escaliers.* She has difficulty going upstairs. **❷** to assemble ▷ *Est-ce que ces étagères sont difficiles à monter?* Are these shelves difficult to assemble?; **monter dans** to get on; **monter sur** to stand on; **monter à cheval** to ride

montre nf watch

montrer vb [28] to show

monture nf (of glasses) frames

monument nm monument

se **moquer** vb [28] **se moquer de (1)** to make fun of **(2)** (informal) not to care about

moquette nf fitted carpet

moqueur (f **moqueuse**) adj mocking

moral nm **Elle a le moral.** She's in good spirits.; **J'ai le moral à zéro.** I'm feeling really down.

morale nf moral; **faire la morale à**

quelqu'un to lecture somebody

morceau (pl **morceaux**) nm piece

mordre vb [49] to bite

mordu, e adj **Il est mordu de jazz.** (informal) He's crazy about jazz.

morgue nf mortuary

morse nm walrus

morsure nf bite

mort nf death

mort, e adj dead; **Il était mort de peur.** He was scared to death.; **Je suis morte de fatigue.** I'm dead tired.

mortel (f **mortelle**) adj **❶** deadly **❷** fatal

morue nf cod

Moscou n Moscow

mosquée nf mosque

mot nm **❶** word ▷ *mot à mot* word for word; **des mots croisés** a crossword; **le mot de passe** the password **❷** note

motard nm **❶** biker **❷** (informal) motorcycle cop

moteur nm engine; **un bateau à moteur** a motor boat; **un moteur de recherche** a search engine

motif nm pattern; **sans motif** for no reason

motivé, e adj motivated

moto nf motorbike

motocycliste nmf motorcyclist

mou (f **molle**) adj **❶** soft **❷** lethargic

mouche nf fly; **prendre la mouche** to get into a huff

se **moucher** vb [28] to blow one's nose

moucheron nm midge

mouchoir nm handkerchief; **un**

a
b
c
d
e
f
g
h
i
j
k
l
m
n
o
p
q
r
s
t
u
v
w
x
y
z

mouchoir en papier a tissue

moudre vb [**50**] to grind

moue nf pout; **faire la moue** to pout

mouette nf seagull

moufle nf mitt

mouillé, e adj wet

mouiller vb [**28**] to get wet; **se mouiller** to get wet

moulant, e adj figure-hugging

moule nf mussel
▶ nm **un moule à gâteaux** a cake tin

moulin nm mill

moulu vb see **moudre**

mourir vb [**51**] to die; **mourir de faim** to starve to death; **Je meurs de faim!** I'm starving!; **mourir de froid** to die of exposure; **Je meurs de froid!** I'm freezing!; **mourir d'envie de faire quelque chose** to be dying to do something

mousse nf ❶ moss ❷ (on beer) froth ❸ (of soap, shampoo) lather ❹ mousse ▷ **une mousse au chocolat** a chocolate mousse; **la mousse à raser** shaving foam

mousseux (f **mousseuse**) adj **un vin mousseux** a sparkling wine

moustache nf moustache; **les moustaches** (of a cat) whiskers

moustique nm mosquito

moutarde nf mustard

mouton nm ❶ sheep ❷ mutton

mouvement nm movement

mouvementé, e adj eventful

moyen (f **moyenne**) adj ❶ average ❷ medium ▷ **Elle est de taille moyenne.** She's of medium height.;

le Moyen Âge the Middle Ages
▶ nm way ▷ **Quel est le meilleur moyen de le convaincre?** What's the best way of convincing him?; **Je n'en ai pas les moyens.** I can't afford it.; **un moyen de transport** a means of transport; **par tous les moyens** by every possible means

moyenne nf **avoir la moyenne** to get a pass mark; **en moyenne** on average; **la moyenne d'âge** the average age

Moyen-Orient nm Middle East

muet (f **muette**) adj (not speaking) with a speech impairment; **un film muet** a silent film

muguet nm lily of the valley

multiple adj numerous

multiplier vb [**19**] to multiply

multitâche adj (also for computer) multitasking

municipal, e (mpl **municipaux**) adj **la bibliothèque municipale** the public library

municipalité nf town council

munir vb [**38**] **munir quelqu'un de** to equip someone with; **se munir de** to equip oneself with

munitions nfpl ammunition sg

mur nm wall

mûr, e adj ❶ (fruit) ripe ❷ (person) mature

mûre nf bramble

mûrir vb [**38**] ❶ to ripen ❷ to make mature ▷ **Cette expérience l'a beaucoup mûrie.** That experience has made her much more mature.

murmurer vb [**28**] to whisper

muscade nf nutmeg

muscat *nm* **①** muscat grape
② (*wine*) muscatel
muscle *nm* muscle
musclé, e *adj* muscular
museau (*pl* **museaux**) *nm* muzzle
musée *nm* museum
musical, e (*mpl* **musicaux**) *adj*
musical; **avoir l'oreille musicale**
to be musical
music-hall *nm* variety
musicien *nm* musician
musique *nf* music
musulman, e *adj, nm/f* Muslim;
un musulman (*man*) a Muslim;
une musulmane (*woman*) a
Muslim
mutation *nf* transfer
mutuelle *nf* private health
insurance
myope *adj* short-sighted
mystère *nm* mystery
mystérieux (*f* **mystérieuse**) *adj*
mysterious
mythe *nm* myth

n

n' *pron see* **ne**
nage *nf* **traverser une rivière à
la nage** to swim across a river;
être en nage to be sweating
profusely
nageoire *nf* fin
nager *vb* [**45**] to swim
nageur *nm* swimmer
naïf (*f* **naïve**) *adj* naïve
naissance *nf* birth; **votre date de
naissance** your date of birth
naître *vb* [**52**] to be born; **Il est né
en 1992.** He was born in 1992.
naïve *adj f see* **naïf**
nana *nf* (*informal*) girl
nappe *nf* tablecloth
narine *nf* nostril
natal, e *adj* native
natation *nf* swimming; **faire de la
natation** to go swimming

nation *nf* nation

national, e (*mpl* **nationaux**) *adj* national; **la fête nationale espagnole** the national day of Spain

nationale *nf* main road

nationalité *nf* nationality

natte *nf* plait

nature *nf* nature
▶ *adj* plain

naturel (*f* **naturelle**) *adj* natural

naturellement *adv* of course

naufrage *nm* shipwreck

nautique *adj* water; **les sports nautiques** water sports; **le ski nautique** water-skiing

navet *nm* turnip

navette *nf* shuttle; **faire la navette** to commute

navigateur *nm* (on computer) browser

navigation *nf* La navigation est interdite ici. Boats are not allowed here.

naviguer *vb* [28] to sail

navire *nm* ship

ne *adv*

　ne is combined with words such as **pas, personne, plus** and **jamais** to form negative phrases.
　▷ *Je ne peux pas venir.* I can't come.
　ne changes to **n'** before a vowel and most words beginning with 'h'.
　▷ *Je n'ai pas d'argent.* I haven't got any money.
　ne is sometimes not translated.

▷ *C'est plus loin que je ne le croyais.* It's further than I thought.

né *vb see* **naître** born ▷ *Elle est née en 1980.* She was born in 1980.

néanmoins *adv* nevertheless

nécessaire *adj* necessary

nectar *nm* **le nectar d'abricot** apricot drink

néerlandais, e *adj, nm/f* Dutch
▷ *Manon parle néerlandais.* Manon speaks Dutch.; **un Néerlandais** a Dutchman; **une Néerlandaise** a Dutchwoman; **les Néerlandais** the Dutch

négatif (*f* **négative**) *adj* negative
▶ *nm* (of photo) negative

négligé, e *adj* scruffy

négliger *vb* [45] to neglect

négocier *vb* [19] to negotiate

neige *nf* snow; **un bonhomme de neige** a snowman

neiger *vb* [45] to snow

nénuphar *nm* water lily

néon *nm* neon

néo-zélandais, e *adj, nm/f* New Zealand; **un Néo-Zélandais** (*man*) a New Zealander; **une Néo-Zélandaise** (*woman*) a New Zealander

nerf *nm* nerve; **taper sur les nerfs de quelqu'un** to get on somebody's nerves

nerveux (*f* **nerveuse**) *adj* nervous

nervosité *nf* nervousness

n'est-ce pas *adv*

　n'est-ce pas is used to check that something is true.
　▷ *Nous sommes le douze aujourd'hui, n'est-ce pas?* It's the 12th today, isn't

it? ▷ *Elle aura dix-huit ans en octobre, n'est-ce pas?* She'll be 18 in October, won't she?

Net nm the Net

net (f **nette**) adj, adv ❶ clear ❷ net ▷ *Poids net: 500 g.* Net weight: 500 g. ❸ flatly ▷ *Il a refusé net de nous aider.* He flatly refused to help us.; **s'arrêter net** to stop dead

nettement adv much

nettoyage nm cleaning; **le nettoyage à sec** dry cleaning

nettoyer vb [53] to clean

neuf (f **neuve**) adj new
▶ num nine ▷ *Claire a neuf ans.* Claire's nine.; **le neuf février** the ninth of February

neutre adj neutral

neuve adj f see **neuf**

neuvième adj ninth

neveu (pl **neveux**) nm nephew

nez nm nose; **se trouver nez à nez avec quelqu'un** to come face to face with somebody

ni conj ni ... ni ... neither ... nor ...

niche nf kennel

nid nm nest

nièce nf niece

nier vb [19] to deny

n'importe adv **n'importe quel** any old; **n'importe qui** anybody; **n'importe quoi** anything; **Tu dis n'importe quoi.** You're talking rubbish.; **n'importe où** anywhere; **Ne laisse pas tes affaires n'importe où.** Don't leave your things lying everywhere.; **n'importe quand** any time; **n'importe comment** any old how

niveau (pl **niveaux**) nm ❶ level ❷ standard; **le niveau de vie** the standard of living

noble adj noble

noblesse nf nobility

noce nf wedding; **un repas de noce** a wedding reception; **leurs noces d'or** their golden wedding anniversary

nocif (f **nocive**) adj harmful

nocturne adj ❶ nocturnal ❷ by night ▷ *Découvrez le Paris nocturne!* Discover Paris by night!
▶ nf late-night opening

Noël nm Christmas; **Joyeux Noël!** Merry Christmas!

nœud nm ❶ knot ❷ bow; **un nœud papillon** a bow tie
    Word for word, this means 'a butterfly bow'.

Noir nm black man

noir, e adj ❶ black ❷ dark ▷ *Il fait noir dehors.* It's dark outside.
▶ nm dark ▷ *J'ai peur du noir.* I'm afraid of the dark.; **le travail au noir** moonlighting

Noire nf black woman

noisette nf hazelnut

noix (pl **noix**) nf walnut; **une noix de coco** a coconut; **les noix de cajou** cashew nuts; **une noix de beurre** a knob of butter

nom nm ❶ name; **mon nom de famille** my surname; **son nom de jeune fille** her maiden name ❷ (in grammar) noun

nombre nm number

nombreux (f **nombreuse**) adj

a b c d e f g h i j k l m **n** o p q r s t u v w x y z

1 many **2** large ▷ *une famille nombreuse* a large family; **peu nombreux** few

nombril *nm* navel

nommer *vb* [28] **1** to name **2** to appoint

non *adv* no; **non seulement** not only; **Moi non plus.** Neither do I.

non alcoolisé, e *adj* non-alcoholic

non-fumeur *nm* non-smoker; **une voiture non-fumeurs** a no-smoking carriage

nord *nm* north; **vers le nord** northwards; **au nord de Paris** north of Paris; **l'Afrique du Nord** North Africa; **le vent du nord** the north wind

▶ *adj* **1** north; **le pôle Nord** the North Pole **2** northern

nord-est *nm* north-east

nord-ouest *nm* north-west

normal, e (*mpl* **normaux**) *adj* **1** normal **2** natural ▷ *C'est tout à fait normal.* It's perfectly natural.; **Vous trouvez que c'est normal?** Does that seem right to you?

normalement *adv* normally; **Normalement, elle doit arriver à huit heures.** She's supposed to arrive at 8 o'clock.

normand, e *adj* **un village normand** a village in Normandy; **la côte normande** the coast of Normandy

Normandie *nf* Normandy

Norvège *nf* Norway

norvégien (*f* **norvégienne**) *adj*, *nm/f* Norwegian ▷ *Elle parle norvégien.* She speaks Norwegian.; **un Norvégien** (*man*) a Norwegian; **une Norvégienne** (*woman*) a Norwegian

nos *adj pl* our ▷ *Où sont nos affaires?* Where are our things?

notaire *nm* solicitor

note *nf* **1** note ▷ *J'ai pris des notes pendant la conférence.* I took notes at the lecture. **2** mark ▷ *Vincent a de bonnes notes en maths.* Vincent's got good marks in maths. **3** bill ▷ *Il n'a pas payé sa note.* He didn't pay his bill.

noter *vb* [28] to make a note of

notions *nfpl* basics

notre (*pl* **nos**) *adj* our ▷ *Voici notre maison.* Here's our house.

nôtre *pron* **le nôtre** ours

nôtres *pron pl* **les nôtres** ours

nouer *vb* [28] to tie

nouilles *nfpl* noodles

nounours *nm* teddy bear

nourrir *vb* [38] to feed

nourriture *nf* food

nous *pron pl* **1** we ▷ *Nous avons deux enfants.* We have two children. **2** us ▷ *Viens avec nous.* Come with us.; **nous-mêmes** ourselves

nouveau (*f* **nouvelle**, *mpl* **nouveaux**) *adj* new ▷ *Elle a une nouvelle voiture.* She's got a new car.

> The masculine singular form **nouveau** changes to **nouvel** before a vowel and most words beginning with 'h'.
> ▷ *le nouvel élève dans ma classe* The

new boy in my class; **le nouvel an**
New Year
▶ *nm* new pupil; **de nouveau**
again
nouveau-né *nm* newborn child
nouveauté *nf* novelty
nouvel, nouvelle *adj see*
nouveau
nouvelle *nf* ❶ news ❷ short story;
les nouvelles the news; **avoir des
nouvelles de quelqu'un** to hear
from somebody
Nouvelle-Zélande *nf* New
Zealand
novembre *nm* November; **en
novembre** in November
noyau (*pl* **noyaux**) *nm* (*of fruit*)
stone
noyer *nm* walnut tree
se noyer *vb* [**53**] to drown
nu, e *adj* ❶ naked ❷ bare
nuage *nm* cloud; **un nuage de lait**
a drop of milk
nuageux (*f* **nuageuse**) *adj*
cloudy
nucléaire *adj* nuclear
nudiste *nmf* nudist
nuit *nf* night; **Il fait nuit.** It's dark.;
cette nuit tonight; **Bonne nuit!**
Good night!; **de nuit** by night
nul (*f* **nulle**) *adj* rubbish ▷ *Ce film est
nul.* (*informal*) This film's rubbish.);
être nul to be no good ▷ *Je suis nul
en maths.* I'm no good at maths.;
un match nul (*in sport*) a draw;
nulle part nowhere
numérique *adj* digital ▷ *un
appareil photo numérique* a digital
camera

numéro *nm* number; **mon
numéro de téléphone** my phone
number; **le numéro de compte**
the account number
nu-pieds *adj, adv* barefoot
nuque *nf* nape of the neck
nylon *nm* nylon

O

obéir *vb* [**38**] to obey; **obéir à quelqu'un** to obey somebody

obéissant, e *adj* obedient

objet *nm* object; **les objets de valeur** valuables; **les objets trouvés** the lost property office

obligatoire *adj* compulsory

obliger *vb* [**45**] **obliger quelqu'un à faire quelque chose** to force somebody to do something; **Je suis bien obligé d'accepter.** I can't really refuse.

obscur, e *adj* dark

obscurité *nf* darkness

obsédé *nm* sex maniac; **un obsédé sexuel** a sex maniac

obséder *vb* [**34**] to obsess

observation *nf* comment

observer *vb* [**28**] ❶ to watch ▷ *Il observait les canards sur le lac.* He watched the ducks on the lake. ❷ to observe

obstacle *nm* ❶ obstacle ❷ (*in show jumping*) fence; **une course d'obstacles** an obstacle race

obstiné, e *adj* stubborn

obtenir *vb* [**83**] ❶ to get ▷ *Ils ont obtenu cinquante pour cent des voix.* They got 50% of the votes. ❷ to achieve ▷ *Nous avons obtenu de bons résultats.* We achieved good results.

occasion *nf* ❶ opportunity ❷ occasion ❸ bargain; **d'occasion** second-hand

Occident *nm* West ▷ *en Occident* in the West

occidental, e (*mpl* **occidentaux**) *adj* western; **les pays occidentaux** the West

occupation *nf* occupation

occupé, e *adj* ❶ busy ❷ taken ▷ *Est-ce que cette place est occupée?* Is this seat taken? ❸ engaged ▷ *Les toilettes sont occupées.* The toilet's engaged.

occuper *vb* [**28**] to occupy; **s'occuper de quelque chose** (1) to be in charge of something (2) to deal with something; **On s'occupe de vous?** (*in a shop*) Are you being attended to?

océan *nm* ocean

octobre *nm* October; **en octobre** in October

odeur *nf* smell

odieux (*f* **odieuse**) *adj* horrible

œil (*pl* **yeux**) *nm* eye; **à l'œil** (*informal*) for free

œillet *nm* carnation

œuf *nm* egg; **un œuf à la coque** a soft-boiled egg; **un œuf dur** a hard-boiled egg; **un œuf au plat** a fried egg; **les œufs brouillés** scrambled eggs; **un œuf de Pâques** an Easter egg

œuvre *nf* work; **une œuvre d'art** a work of art

offert *vb* see **offrir**

office *nm* **un office du tourisme** a tourist office

officiel (*f* **officielle**) *adj* official

officier *nm* officer

offre *nf* offer; **'offres d'emploi'** 'situations vacant'

offrir *vb* [54] **offrir quelque chose (1)** to offer something ▷ *Elle lui a offert à boire.* She offered him a drink. **(2)** to give something ▷ *Il lui a offert des roses.* He gave her roses.; **s'offrir quelque chose** to treat oneself to something

oie *nf* goose

oignon *nm* onion

oiseau (*pl* **oiseaux**) *nm* bird

olive *nf* olive

olympique *adj* **les Jeux olympiques** the Olympic Games®

ombre *nf* ❶ shade ❷ shadow; **l'ombre à paupières** eye shadow

omelette *nf* omelette

omnibus *nm* local train

on *pron* ❶ we ▷ *On va à la plage demain.* We're going to the beach tomorrow. ❷ someone ▷ *On m'a volé mon sac.* Someone has stolen my bag.; **On m'a dit d'attendre.** I was told to wait.; **On vous**

demande au téléphone. There's a phone call for you. ❸ you ▷ *On peut visiter le château en été.* You can visit the castle in the summer.

oncle *nm* uncle

onde *nf* (on radio) wave

ongle *nm* nail; **se couper les ongles** to cut one's nails

ont *vb* see **avoir**; **Ils ont beaucoup d'argent.** They've got lots of money.; **Elles ont passé de bonnes vacances.** They had a good holiday.

ONU *nf* (= *Organisation des Nations Unies*) UN (= *United Nations*)

onze *num* eleven ▷ *Elle a onze ans.* She's eleven.; **le onze février** the eleventh of February

onzième *adj* eleventh

opéra *nm* opera

opération *nf* operation

opérer *vb* [34] to operate on ▷ *Elle a été opérée de l'appendicite.* She was operated on for appendicitis.; **se faire opérer** to have an operation

opinion *nf* opinion

opposé, e *adj* opposite; **être opposé à quelque chose** to be opposed to something
▶ *nm* the opposite

opposer *vb* [28] **opposer quelqu'un à quelqu'un** to pit somebody against somebody; **s'opposer** to conflict ▷ *Ces deux points de vue s'opposent.* These two points of view conflict.; **s'opposer à quelque chose** to oppose something

opposition *nf* opposition; **par**

opposition à as opposed to; **faire opposition à un chèque** to stop a cheque

opticien nm optician

optimiste adj optimistic

option nf option; **une matière à option** an optional subject

or nm gold ▷ *un bracelet en or* a gold bracelet
▶ conj and yet ▷ *Il était sûr de gagner, or il a perdu.* He was sure he would win, and yet he lost.

orage nm thunderstorm

orageux (f **orageuse**) adj stormy

oral, e (mpl **oraux**) adj **une épreuve orale** an oral exam; **à prendre par voie orale** to be taken orally
▶ nm (exam) oral

orange nf (fruit) orange
▶ adj (in colour) orange

orchestre nm ❶ orchestra ❷ band

ordinaire adj ❶ ordinary ❷ standard
▶ nm two-star (petrol); **sortir de l'ordinaire** to be out of the ordinary

ordinateur nm computer

ordonnance nf prescription

ordonné, e adj tidy

ordonner vb [28] **ordonner à quelqu'un de faire quelque chose** to order somebody to do something

ordre nm order; **dans l'ordre** in order; **mettre en ordre** to tidy up; **jusqu'à nouvel ordre** until further notice

ordures nfpl rubbish sg; **jeter quelque chose aux ordures** to throw something in the bin

oreille nf ear

oreiller nm pillow

oreillons nmpl mumps

organe nm (in body) organ

organisateur nm organizer

organisation nf organization

organiser vb [28] to organize; **s'organiser** to get organized

organisme nm (organization) body

orgue nm organ

orgueilleux (f **orgueilleuse**) adj proud

Orient nm East ▷ *en Orient* in the East

oriental, e (mpl **orientaux**) adj ❶ oriental ❷ eastern

orientation nf orientation; **avoir le sens de l'orientation** to have a good sense of direction; **l'orientation professionnelle** careers advice

originaire adj **Elle est originaire de Paris.** She's from Paris.

original, e (mpl **originaux**) adj original
▶ nm original; **un vieil original** an old eccentric

origine nf origin; **à l'origine** originally

orphelin nm orphan

orteil nm toe

orthographe nf spelling

os nm bone

oser vb [28] to dare; **oser faire quelque chose** to dare to do something

otage nm hostage

ôter vb [28] ❶ to take off ▷ *Elle a ôté*

son manteau. She took off her coat.
❷ to take away

ou *conj* or; **ou ... ou ...** either ... or ...;
ou bien or else ▷ *On pourrait aller au cinéma ou bien rentrer directement.* We could go to the cinema or else go straight home.

où *pron, adv* ❶ where ▷ *Où est Nick?* Where's Nick? ▷ *Où allez-vous?* Where are you going? ▷ *Je sais où il est.* I know where he is. ❷ that ▷ *Le jour où il est parti, tout le monde a pleuré.* The day that he left, everyone cried.; **Par où allons-nous passer?** Which way are we going to go?

ouate *nf* cotton wool

oublier *vb* [**19**] ❶ to forget ▷ *N'oublie pas de fermer la porte.* Don't forget to shut the door. ❷ to leave ▷ *J'ai oublié mon sac chez Sabine.* I left my bag at Sabine's.

ouest *nm* west; **à l'ouest de Paris** west of Paris; **vers l'ouest** westwards; **l'Europe de l'Ouest** Western Europe; **le vent d'ouest** the west wind
▸ *adj* ❶ west ❷ western

ouf *excl* phew!

oui *adv* yes

ouragan *nm* hurricane

ourlet *nm* seam

ours *nm* bear; **un ours en peluche** a teddy bear

outil *nm* tool

outré, e *adj* outraged

ouvert, e *adj* ❶ open ▷ *Le magasin est ouvert.* The shop's open. ❷ on ▷ *Il a laissé le robinet ouvert.* He left

the tap on.; **avoir l'esprit ouvert** to be open-minded
▸ *vb see* **ouvrir**

ouverture *nf* opening

ouvre-boîte *nm* tin opener

ouvre-bouteille *nm* bottle-opener

ouvreuse *nf* usherette

ouvrier *nm* worker

ouvrière *nf* worker

ouvrir *vb* [**55**] to open ▷ *Ouvrez!* Open up! ▷ *Elle a ouvert la porte.* She opened the door.; **s'ouvrir** to open

ovale *adj* oval

ovni *nm* (= *objet volant non identifié*) UFO

oxygène *nm* oxygen

ozone *nm* ozone

p

Pacifique nm Pacific

pacifiste nm pacifist

PACS nm (= pacte civil de solidarité) civil partnership

pagaille nf mess sg

page nf page; **la page d'accueil** (on internet) the home page

paie nf wages

paiement nm payment

paillasson nm doormat

paille nf straw

pain nm ❶ bread ❷ loaf; **le pain complet** wholemeal bread; **le pain d'épice** gingerbread; **le pain de mie** sandwich loaf; **le pain grillé** toast

pair, e adj even ▷ un nombre pair an even number; **une jeune fille au pair** an au pair

paire nf pair

paisible adj peaceful

paix nf peace; **faire la paix (1)** to make peace ▷ Les deux pays ont fait la paix. The two countries have made peace with each other. **(2)** to make it up ▷ Laure a fait la paix avec son frère. Laure made it up with her brother.; **avoir la paix** to have peace and quiet ▷ J'aimerais bien avoir la paix. I'd like to have a bit of peace and quiet.; **Fiche-moi la paix!** (informal) Leave me alone!

palais nm ❶ palace ❷ (in mouth) palate

pâle adj pale

Palestine nf Palestine

pâleur nf paleness

palier nm landing

pâlir vb [38] to go pale

palme nf (for swimming) flipper

palmé, e adj webbed

palmier nm palm tree

palpitant, e adj thrilling

pamplemousse nm grapefruit

panaché nm shandy

pancarte nf sign

pané, e adj fried in breadcrumbs

panier nm basket

panique nf panic

paniquer vb [28] to panic

panne nf breakdown; **être en panne** to have broken down; **tomber en panne** to break down; **une panne de courant** a power cut

panneau (pl **panneaux**) nm sign; **panneau d'affichage (1)** advertising hoarding **(2)** (in station) arrivals and departures board **(3)** (on internet) bulletin board

panorama nm panorama

pansement nm ❶ (bandage) dressing ❷ sticking plaster

pantalon nm trousers pl; **un pantalon de ski** a pair of ski pants

panthère nf panther

pantoufle nf slipper

PAO abbr (= publication assistée par ordinateur) DTP (= desktop publishing)

paon nm peacock

papa nm dad

pape nm pope

papeterie nf stationer's

papi nm (informal) granddad

papier nm paper; **Vos papiers, s'il vous plaît.** Your identity papers, please.; **les papiers d'identité** identity papers; **le papier à lettres** writing paper; **le papier hygiénique** toilet paper; **le papier peint** wallpaper

papillon nm butterfly

paquebot nm liner

pâquerette nf daisy

Pâques nm Easter; **les œufs de Pâques** Easter eggs

  ⁕ In France, Easter eggs are said to
  ⁕ be brought by the Easter bells or
  ⁕ **cloches de Pâques** which fly
  ⁕ from Rome and drop them in
  ⁕ people's gardens.

paquet nm ❶ packet ❷ parcel

paquet-cadeau (pl **paquets-cadeaux**) nm gift-wrapped parcel

par prep ❶ by ▷ L'Amérique a été découverte par Christophe Colomb. America was discovered by Christopher Columbus.; **deux par deux** two by two ❷ with ▷ Son nom commence par un H. His name begins with H. ❸ out of ▷ Elle regardait par la fenêtre. She was looking out of the window. ❹ via ▷ Nous sommes passés par Lyon pour aller à Grenoble. We went via Lyons to Grenoble. ❺ through ▷ Il faut passer par la douane avant de prendre l'avion. You have to go through customs before boarding the plane. ❻ per ▷ Prenez trois cachets par jour. Take three tablets per day.; **par ici (1)** this way ▷ Il faut passer par ici pour y arriver. You have to go this way to get there. **(2)** round here ▷ Il y a beaucoup de touristes par ici. There are lots of tourists round here.; **par-ci, par-là** here and there

parachute nm parachute

parachutiste nmf parachutist

paradis nm heaven

parages nmpl **dans les parages** in the area

paragraphe nm paragraph

paraître vb [56] ❶ to seem ▷ Ça paraît incroyable. It seems unbelievable. ❷ to look ▷ Elle paraît plus jeune que son frère. She looks younger than her brother.; **il paraît que** it seems that

parallèle nm parallel
  ▶ nf parallel line

paralympique adj Paralympic

paralysé, e adj paralysed

parapluie nm umbrella

parasol nm parasol

parc nm ❶ park; **un parc d'attractions** an amusement park ❷ grounds

a
b
c
d
e
f
g
h
i
j
k
l
m
n
o
p
q
r
s
t
u
v
w
x
y
z

parce que conj because ▷ Il n'est pas
venu parce qu'il n'avait pas de voiture.
He didn't come because he didn't
have a car.

parcmètre nm parking meter

parcourir vb [16] **1** to cover
▷ Gavin a parcouru cinquante
kilomètres à vélo. Gavin covered 50
kilometres on his bike. **2** to glance
through ▷ J'ai parcouru le journal
d'aujourd'hui. I glanced through
today's newspaper.

parcours nm journey

par-dessous adv underneath

pardessus nm overcoat

par-dessus adv, prep **1** on top
2 over ▷ Elle a sauté par-dessus le
mur. She jumped over the wall.; **en
avoir par-dessus la tête** to have
had enough

pardon nm forgiveness
▶ excl **sorry!** ▷ Oh, pardon! J'espère
que je ne vous ai pas fait mal. Oh,
sorry! I hope I didn't hurt you.;
demander pardon à quelqu'un to
apologize to somebody; **Je vous
demande pardon.** I'm sorry.
2 excuse me! ▷ Pardon, madame!
Pouvez-vous me dire où se trouve la
poste? Excuse me! Could you tell me
where the post office is? **3** pardon?
▷ Pardon? Je n'ai pas compris ce que
vous avez dit. Pardon? I didn't
understand what you said.

pardonner vb [28] to forgive

pare-brise (pl **pare-brise**) nm
windscreen

pare-chocs nm bumper

pareil (f **pareille**) adj **1** the same

▷ Ces deux maisons ne sont pas
pareilles. These two houses aren't
the same. **2** like that ▷ J'aime bien
sa voiture. J'en voudrais une pareille. I
like his car. I'd like one like that.
3 such ▷ Je refuse d'écouter des
bêtises pareilles. I won't listen to
such nonsense.; **sans pareil**
unequalled

parenthèse nf bracket

parents nmpl **1** (mother and father)
parents **2** relatives

paresse nf laziness

paresseux (f **paresseuse**) adj lazy

parfait, e adj perfect

parfaitement adv perfectly

parfois adv sometimes

parfum nm **1** perfume **2** flavour

parfumé, e adj **1** fragrant
2 flavoured

parfumerie nf perfume shop

pari nm bet

parier vb [19] to bet

Paris n Paris; **à Paris (1)** in Paris
(2) to Paris

parisien (f **parisienne**) adj, nm/f
1 Parisian **2** Paris ▷ le métro
parisien the Paris metro; **un
Parisien** (man) a Parisian; **une
Parisienne** (woman) a Parisian

parking nm car park

Be careful! The French word
parking does not mean
parking.

parlement nm parliament

parler vb [28] **1** to speak ▷ Vous
parlez français? Do you speak
French? **2** to talk ▷ Nous étions en
train de parler quand le directeur est

entré. We were talking when the headmaster came in.; **parler de quelque chose à quelqu'un** to tell somebody about something

parmi *prep* among ▷ *Ils étaient parmi les meilleurs de la classe.* They were among the best pupils in the class.

paroi *nf* wall

paroisse *nf* parish

parole *nf* ❶ speech ❷ word; **les paroles** lyrics

parquet *nm (wooden) floor*

parrain *nm* godfather

parrainer *vb* [**28**] to sponsor ▷ *Cette entreprise parraine notre équipe de rugby.* This firm is sponsoring our rugby team.

pars *vb see* **partir**

part *nf* ❶ share ❷ piece ▷ *une part de gâteau* a piece of cake; **prendre part à quelque chose** to take part in something; **de la part de (1)** on behalf of **(2)** from; **à part** except

partager *vb* [**45**] ❶ to share ▷ *Ils partagent un appartement.* They share a flat. ❷ to divide ▷ *Janet a partagé le gâteau en quatre.* Janet divided the cake into four.

partenaire *nmf* partner

parti *nm* party

participant *nm* participant

participation *nf* participation

participe *nm* participle; **le participe passé** the past participle; **le participe présent** the present participle

participer *vb* [**28**] **participer à quelque chose (1)** to take part in something ▷ *André va participer à la*

course. André is going to take part in the race. **(2)** to contribute to something ▷ *Je voudrais participer aux frais.* I would like to contribute to the cost.

particularité *nf* characteristic

particule *nf* particle; **particules fines** fine particulate matter

particulier (*f* **particulière**) *adj* ❶ private ▷ *une maison particulière* a private house ❷ distinctive ❸ particular; **en particulier (1)** particularly **(2)** in private

particulièrement *adv* particularly

partie *nf* ❶ part ▷ *Une partie du groupe partira en Italie.* Part of the group will go to Italy. ❷ game ▷ *une partie de cartes* a game of cards; **en partie** partly; **en grande partie** largely; **faire partie de** to be part of

partiel (*f* **partielle**) *adj* partial

partir *vb* [**57**] to go ▷ *Je lui ai téléphoné mais il était déjà parti.* I phoned him but he'd already gone.; **partir en vacances** to go on holiday; **partir de** to leave ▷ *Il est parti de Nice à sept heures.* He left Nice at 7.

partition *nf (in music)* score

partout *adv* everywhere

paru *vb see* **paraître**

parution *nf* publication

parvenir *vb* [**89**] **parvenir à faire quelque chose** to manage to do something; **faire parvenir quelque chose à quelqu'un** to send something to somebody

pas *adv* **ne ... pas** not ▷ *Il ne pleut pas.* It's not raining. ▷ *Elle n'est pas*

a
b
c
d
e
f
g
h
i
j
k
l
m
n
o
p
q
r
s
t
u
v
w
x
y
z

venue. She didn't come.; **Vous viendrez à notre soirée, n'est-ce pas?** You're coming to our party, aren't you?; **pas moi** not me; **pas du tout** not at all; **pas mal** not bad; **pas mal de** quite a lot of ▸ *nm* ❶ pace ❷ step ❸ footstep; **au pas** at walking pace; **faire les cent pas** to pace up and down

passage *nm* passage; **Il a été éclaboussé au passage de la voiture.** He was soaked by a passing car.; **de passage** passing through; **un passage à niveau** a level crossing; **un passage clouté** a pedestrian crossing; **un passage protégé** a pedestrian crossing; **un passage souterrain** a subway

passager (*f* **passagère**) *adj* temporary

passager *nm* passenger; **un passager clandestin** a stowaway

passagère *nf* passenger

passant *nm* passer-by

passé, e *adj* ❶ last ▸ *Je l'ai vu la semaine passée.* I saw him last week. ❷ past ▸ *Il est minuit passé.* It's past midnight.
▸ *nm* ❶ past ❷ past tense; **le passé composé** the perfect tense; **le passé simple** the past historic

passeport *nm* passport

passer *vb* [58] ❶ to cross ▸ *Nous avons passé la frontière belge.* We crossed the Belgian border. ❷ to go through ▸ *Il faut passer la douane en sortant.* You have to go through customs on the way out. ❸ to spend ▸ *Ils passent toujours leurs*

vacances au Danemark. They always spend their holidays in Denmark. ❹ to take ▸ *Gordon a passé ses examens la semaine dernière.* Gordon took his exams last week.

> Be careful! **passer un examen** does not mean **to pass an exam**.

❺ to pass ▸ *Passe-moi le sel, s'il te plaît.* Pass me the salt, please. ❻ to show ▸ *On passe 'Le Kid' au cinéma cette semaine.* They're showing 'The Kid' at the cinema this week. ❼ to call in ▸ *Je passerai chez vous ce soir.* I'll call in this evening.; **passer à la radio** to be on the radio; **passer à la télévision** to be on the television; **Ne quittez pas, je vous passe Madame Chevalier.** Hold on please, I'm putting you through to Mrs Chevalier.; **passer par** to go through ▸ *Ils sont passés par Paris pour aller à Tours.* They went through Paris to get to Tours.; **en passant** in passing; **laisser passer** to let through ▸ *Il m'a laissé passer.* He let me through.; **se passer (1)** to take place ▸ *Cette histoire se passe au Moyen Âge.* This story takes place in the Middle Ages. **(2)** to go ▸ *Comment se sont passés tes examens?* How did your exams go? **(3)** to happen ▸ *Que s'est-il passé? Un accident?* What happened? Was there an accident?; **Qu'est-ce qui se passe? Pourquoi est-ce qu'elle pleure?** What's the matter? Why is she crying?; **se passer de** to do without

passerelle nf ➊ (over river) footbridge ➋ (onto plane, boat) gangway

passe-temps nm pastime

passif (f **passive**) adj passive ▶ nm passive

passion nf passion

passionnant, e adj fascinating

passionné, e adj keen; **Il est passionné de voile.** He's a sailing fanatic.

passionner vb [28] **Son travail le passionne.** He's passionate about his work.; **se passionner pour quelque chose** to have a passion for something

passoire nf sieve

pastèque nf watermelon

pasteur nm (priest) minister

pastille nf cough sweet

patate nf (informal) potato; **une patate douce** a sweet potato

pâte nf ➊ pastry ➋ dough ➌ cake mixture; **la pâte à crêpes** pancake batter; **la pâte à modeler** Plasticine®; **la pâte d'amandes** marzipan

pâté nm pâté; **un pâté de maisons** (of houses) a block

paternel (f **paternelle**) adj **ma grand-mère paternelle** my father's mother; **mon oncle paternel** my father's brother

pâtes nfpl pasta sg

patience nf patience

patient, e adj patient

patient nm patient

patiente nf patient

patienter vb [28] to wait ▷ **Veuillez**

patienter un instant, s'il vous plaît. Please wait a moment.

patin nm ➊ skate ➋ skating; **les patins à glace** ice skates; **les patins en ligne** Rollerblades®; **les patins à roulettes** roller skates

patinage nm skating; **le patinage artistique** figure skating

patiner vb [28] to skate

patineur nm skater

patinoire nf ice rink

pâtisserie nf cake shop; **faire de la pâtisserie** to bake; **les pâtisseries** cakes

pâtissier nm confectioner

patrie nf homeland

patron nm ➊ boss ➋ (for dressmaking) pattern

patronne nf boss; **Elle est patronne de café.** She runs a café.

patronner vb [28] to sponsor ▷ **Le festival est patronné par des entreprises locales.** The festival is sponsored by local businesses.

patrouille nf patrol

patte nf ➊ (of dog, cat) paw ➋ (of bird, animal) leg

paumer vb [28] (informal) to lose ▷ **J'ai paumé mes clés.** I've lost my keys.

paupière nf eyelid

pause nf ➊ break ▷ **une pause de midi** a lunch break ➋ pause

pauvre adj poor

pauvreté nf poverty

pavé, e adj cobbled

pavillon nm house

payant, e adj paying; **C'est payant.** You have to pay.

a
b
c
d
e
f
g
h
i
j
k
l
m
n
o
p
q
r
s
t
u
v
w
x
y
z

paye nf wages

payer vb [59] ❶ to pay for
▷ *Combien as-tu payé ta voiture?* How
much did you pay for your car?; **J'ai
payé ce T-shirt vingt euros.** I paid
20 euros for this T-shirt. ❷ to pay
▷ *Elle a été payée aujourd'hui.* She got
paid today.; **faire payer quelque
chose à quelqu'un** to charge
somebody for something ▷ *Il me l'a
fait payer dix euros.* He charged me
10 euros for it.; **payer quelque
chose à quelqu'un** to buy
somebody something ▷ *Allez, je
vous paye un verre.* Come on, I'll buy
you a drink.

pays nm country; **du pays** local

paysage nm landscape

paysan nm farmer

Pays-Bas nmpl Netherlands; **aux
Pays-Bas (1)** in the Netherlands
(2) to the Netherlands

pays de Galles nm Wales; **au pays
de Galles (1)** in Wales **(2)** to Wales

PC nm PC (= *personal computer*)
▶ abbr (= *Parti communiste*)
Communist Party

PDG nm (= *président-directeur
général*) MD (= *managing director*)

péage nm ❶ toll ▷ *Nous avons payé
vingt euros de péage.* We paid a toll of
20 euros. ❷ tollbooth
⁝ French motorways charge a toll.

peau (pl **peaux**) nf skin

Peau-Rouge (pl **Peaux-Rouges**)
nmf Red Indian

péché nm sin

pêche nf ❶ peach ❷ fishing; **aller à
la pêche** to go fishing; **la pêche à**

la ligne angling

pêcher vb [28] ❶ to fish for ▷ *Ils sont
partis pêcher la truite.* They've gone
fishing for trout. ❷ to catch
▷ *Jacques a pêché deux saumons.*
Jacques caught two salmon.

pêcheur nm fisherman; **un
pêcheur à la ligne** an angler

pédagogique adj educational

pédale nf pedal

pédalo nm pedalo

pédestre adj une randonnée
pédestre a ramble

peigne nm comb

peigner vb [28] to comb ▷ *Elle
peigne sa poupée.* She's combing her
doll's hair.; **se peigner** to comb
one's hair

peignoir nm dressing gown; **un
peignoir de bain** a bathrobe

peindre vb [60] to paint

peine nf ❶ trouble; **avoir de la peine
à faire quelque chose** to have
trouble doing something; **se
donner de la peine** to make a real
effort; **prendre la peine de faire
quelque chose** to go to the trouble
of doing something; **faire de la
peine à quelqu'un** to upset
somebody; **ce n'est pas la peine**
there's no point; **à peine (1)** hardly
(2) only just

peintre nm painter

peinture nf ❶ painting ❷ paint;
'peinture fraîche' 'wet paint'

pêle-mêle adv higgledy-piggledy

peler vb [43] to peel

pelle nf ❶ shovel ❷ spade

pellicule nf film

pellicules nfpl dandruff sg

pelote nf ball

pelouse nf lawn

peluche nf un animal en peluche a soft toy

penchant nm avoir un penchant pour quelque chose to have a liking for something

pencher vb [28] to tilt ▷ Ce tableau penche vers la droite. The picture's tilting to the right.; **se pencher** (1) to lean over ▷ Françoise s'est penchée sur son cahier. Françoise leant over her exercise book. (2) to bend down ▷ Il s'est penché pour ramasser sa casquette. He bent down to pick his cap up. (3) to lean out ▷ Annick s'est penchée par la fenêtre. Annick leant out of the window.

pendant prep during ▷ Ça s'est passé pendant l'été. It happened during the summer.; **pendant que** while

pendentif nm pendant

penderie nf (for hanging clothes) wardrobe

pendre vb [88] to hang ▷ Il a pendu sa veste dans l'armoire. He hung his jacket in the wardrobe.; **pendre quelqu'un** to hang somebody ▷ L'assassin a été pendu. The murderer was hanged.

pendule nf clock

pénétrer vb [34] ❶ to enter ▷ Ils ont pénétré dans la maison en passant par le jardin. They entered the house through the garden. ❷ to penetrate ▷ L'armée a pénétré sur le territoire ennemi. The army penetrated enemy territory.

pénible adj hard; **Il est vraiment pénible.** He's a real nuisance.

péniblement adv with difficulty

péniche nf barge

pénis nm penis

pénombre nf half-light

pensée nf thought

penser vb [28] to think ▷ Je pense que Yann a eu raison de partir. I think Yann was right to leave.; **penser à quelque chose** to think about something; **faire penser quelqu'un à quelque chose** to remind someone of something ▷ Cette photo me fait penser à la Grèce. This photo reminds me of Greece.; **faire penser quelqu'un à faire quelque chose** to remind someone to do something ▷ Fais-moi penser à téléphoner à Claire. Remind me to phone Claire.; **penser faire quelque chose** to be planning to do something ▷ Ils pensent partir en Espagne en juillet. They're planning to go to Spain in July.

pension nf ❶ boarding school ❷ pension ❸ boarding house; **la pension complète** full board

pensionnaire nmf boarder

pensionnat nm boarding school

pente nf slope; **en pente** sloping

Pentecôte nf Whitsun

pépin nm ❶ pip ❷ problem ▷ avoir un pépin (informal) to have a slight problem

perçant, e adj ❶ sharp ▷ Il a une vue perçante. He has very sharp eyes.

❷ piercing ▷ *un cri perçant* a
piercing cry

percer vb [**12**] to pierce ▷ *Elle s'est
fait percer les oreilles.* She's had her
ears pierced.

percuter vb [**28**] to smash into

perdant nm loser

perdre vb [**61**] to lose ▷ *Cécile a perdu
ses clés.* Cécile's lost her keys.; **J'ai
perdu mon chemin.** I've lost my
way.; **perdre un match** to lose a
match; **perdre du temps** to waste
time ▷ *J'ai perdu beaucoup de temps
ce matin.* I've wasted a lot of time
this morning.; **se perdre** to get
lost ▷ *Je me suis perdu en route.* I got
lost on the way here.

perdu vb see **perdre**

père nm father; **le père Noël** Father
Christmas

perfectionné, e adj sophisticated

perfectionner vb [**28**] to improve
▷ *Elle a besoin de perfectionner son
anglais.* She needs to improve her
English.

périmé, e adj out-of-date; **Ces
yaourts sont périmés.** These
yoghurts are past their use-by
date.

période nf period

périodique adj periodic

périphérique adj outlying
▶ nm ring road

perle nf pearl

permanence nf assurer une
permanence to operate a basic
service; **être de permanence** to be
on duty; **en permanence**
permanently

permanent, e adj ❶ permanent
❷ continuous

permanente nf perm

permettre vb [**47**] to allow;
**permettre à quelqu'un de faire
quelque chose** to allow somebody
to do something ▷ *Sa mère lui
permet de sortir le soir.* His mother
allows him to go out at night.

permis nm permit; **le permis de
conduire** driving licence; **un
permis de séjour** a residence
permit; **un permis de travail** a
work permit

permission nf permission; **avoir
la permission de faire quelque
chose** to have permission to do
something; **être en permission**
(*from the army*) to be on leave

Pérou nm Peru

perpétuel (f **perpétuelle**) adj
perpetual

perplexe adj puzzled

perroquet nm parrot

perruche nf budgie

perruque nf wig

persil nm parsley

personnage nm ❶ figure ▷ *les
grands personnages de l'histoire de
France* the important figures in
French history ❷ character ▷ *le
personnage principal du film* the
main character in the film

personnalité nf ❶ personality
❷ prominent figure

personne nf person ▷ *une personne
âgée* an elderly person; **en
personne** in person
▶ pron ❶ nobody ▷ *Il n'y a personne à*

la maison. There's nobody at home.
❷ anybody ▷ *Elle ne veut voir
personne.* She doesn't want to see
anybody.
personnel (*f* **personnelle**) *adj*
personal
▶ *nm* staff; **le service du
personnel** the personnel
department
personnellement *adv* personally
perspective *nf* prospect;
perspectives d'avenir prospects;
en perspective (1) in prospect
(2) in perspective
persuader *vb* [28] to persuade;
**persuader quelqu'un de faire
quelque chose** to persuade
somebody to do something
perte *nf* ❶ loss ❷ waste
perturber *vb* [28] to disrupt
pèse-personne *nm* bathroom
scales *pl*
peser *vb* [43] to weigh ▷ *Elle pèse
cent kilos.* She weighs 100 kilos.
pessimiste *adj* pessimistic
pétale *nm* petal
pétanque *nf*

  ● **pétanque** is a type of bowls
  ● played in France, especially in
  ● the south.

pétard *nm* firecracker
péter *vb* [34] (*rude*) to fart
pétillant, e *adj* sparkling
petit, e *adj* ❶ small ▷ *Sonia habite
une petite ville.* Sonia lives in a small
town. ❷ little ▷ *Elle a une jolie petite
maison.* She has a nice little house.;
petit à petit bit by bit; **un petit
ami** a boyfriend; **une petite amie**

a girlfriend; **le petit déjeuner**
breakfast ▷ *prendre le petit déjeuner*
to have breakfast; **un petit pain** a
bread roll; **les petites annonces**
the small ads; **des petits pois**
garden peas; **les petits** (*of animal*)
young
petite-fille (*pl* **petites-filles**) *nf*
granddaughter
petit-fils (*pl* **petits-fils**) *nm*
grandson
petits-enfants *nmpl*
grandchildren
pétrole *nm* oil

  ▌ Be careful! **pétrole** does not
  ▌ mean **petrol**.

peu *adv, n* not much; **un peu** a bit;
un petit peu a little bit; **peu de
(1)** not many **(2)** not much; **à peu
près (1)** more or less **(2)** about; **peu
à peu** little by little; **peu avant**
shortly before; **peu après** shortly
afterwards; **de peu** only just
peuple *nm* people
peur *nf* fear; **avoir peur de** to be
afraid of; **avoir peur de faire
quelque chose** to be frightened of
doing something; **faire peur à
quelqu'un** to frighten somebody
peureux (*f* **peureuse**) *adj* fearful
peut *vb* see **pouvoir**; **Il ne peut pas
venir.** He can't come.
peut-être *adv* perhaps; **peut-être
que** perhaps
peuvent, peux *vb* see **pouvoir**; **Je
ne peux pas le faire.** I can't do it.
p. ex. *abbr* (= *par exemple*) e.g.
phare *nm* ❶ lighthouse ▷ *On voit le
phare depuis le pont du bateau.* You

a b c d e f g h i j k l m n o **p** q r s t u v w x y z

can see the lighthouse from the ship's deck. ❷ headlight ▷ *Elle a laissé ses phares allumés.* She left her headlights on.

pharmacie *nf* chemist's
   • Chemists' shops in France are
   • identified by a special green
   • cross outside the shop.

pharmacien *nm* pharmacist

phasme *nm* stick insect

phénomène *nm* phenomenon

philosophie *nf* philosophy

phoque *nm* (*animal*) seal

photo *nf* photograph; **en photo** in photographs; **prendre quelqu'un en photo** to take a photo of somebody; **une photo d'identité** a passport photograph

photocopie *nf* photocopy

photocopier *vb* [**19**] to photocopy

photocopieuse *nf* photocopier

photographe *nmf* photographer

photographie *nf* ❶ photography
   ❷ photograph

photographier *vb* [**19**] to photograph

phrase *nf* sentence

physique *adj* physical
   ▶ *nm* **Il a un physique agréable.** He's quite good-looking.
   ▶ *nf* physics

pianiste *nmf* pianist

piano *nm* piano

pic *nm* peak; **à pic (1)** vertically ▷ *La falaise tombe à pic dans la mer.* The cliff drops vertically into the sea. **(2)** just at the right time ▷ *Tu es arrivé à pic.* You arrived just at the right time.

pièce *nf* ❶ room ▷ *Mon lit est au centre de la pièce.* My bed is in the middle of the room.; **un cinq-pièces** a five-roomed flat ❷ play ▷ *On joue une pièce de Shakespeare au théâtre.* There's a play by Shakespeare on at the theatre. ❸ part ▷ *Il faut changer une pièce du moteur.* There's an engine part which needs changing. ❹ coin ▷ *des pièces d'un euro* some one-euro coins; **cinquante euros pièce** 50 euros each ▷ *J'ai acheté ces T-shirts dix euros pièce.* I bought these T-shirts for ten euros each.; **un maillot une pièce** a one-piece swimsuit; **un maillot deux-pièces** a bikini; **Avez-vous une pièce d'identité?** Have you got any identification?; **une pièce jointe** an email attachment

pied *nm* foot; **à pied** on foot; **avoir pied** to be able to touch the bottom

pied-noir (*pl* **pieds-noirs**) *nm*
   • A **pied-noir** is a French person
   • born in Algeria; most of them
   • moved to France during the
   • Algerian war in the 1950s.

piège *nm* trap; **prendre quelqu'un au piège** to trap somebody

piéger *vb* [**66**] to trap; **un colis piégé** a parcel bomb; **une voiture piégée** a car bomb

pierre *nf* stone; **une pierre précieuse** a precious stone

piéton *nm* pedestrian

piétonnier (*f* **piétonnière**) *adj* **une rue piétonnière** a pedestrianized street; **un quartier piétonnier** a pedestrianized area

pieuvre nf octopus

pigeon nm pigeon

piger vb [45] (informal) to understand

pile nf ❶ pile ▷ Il y a une pile de disques sur la table. There's a pile of records on the table. ❷ battery ▷ La pile de ma montre est usée. The battery in my watch has run out.
▶ adv **à deux heures pile** at two on the dot; **jouer à pile ou face** to toss up; **Pile ou face?** Heads or tails?

pilote nm pilot; **un pilote de course** a racing driver; **un pilote de ligne** an airline pilot

piloter vb [28] (a plane) to fly

pilule nf pill; **prendre la pilule** to be on the pill

piment nm chilli

pin nm pine

pinard nm (informal) wine

pince nf ❶ (tool) pliers pl ❷ (of crab) pincer; **une pince à épiler** tweezers; **une pince à linge** a clothes peg

pinceau (pl **pinceaux**) nm paintbrush

pincée nf **une pincée de sel** a pinch of salt

pincer vb [12] to pinch

pingouin nm penguin

ping-pong nm table tennis

pintade nf guinea fowl

pion nm ❶ (in chess) pawn ❷ (in draughts) piece ❸ (man) supervisor

In French secondary schools, the teachers are not responsible for supervising the pupils outside class. This job is done by people called **pions** or **surveillants**.

pionne nf (woman) supervisor

pipe nf pipe

piquant, e adj ❶ prickly ❷ spicy

pique nm spades pl
▶ nf cutting remark

pique-nique nm picnic

piquer vb [28] ❶ to bite ▷ Nous avons été piqués par les moustiques. We were bitten by mosquitoes. ❷ to burn ▷ Cette sauce me pique la langue. This sauce is burning my tongue. ❸ to steal ▷ On m'a piqué mon porte-monnaie. (informal) I've had my purse stolen.; **se piquer** to prick oneself

piquet nm ❶ post ❷ peg ▷ Il nous manque un des piquets de la tente. One of our tent pegs is missing.

piqûre nf ❶ injection ❷ bite ❸ sting

pirate nm pirate; **un pirate informatique** a hacker

pire adj, n worse; **le pire** the worst; **le pire de** the worst of

piscine nf swimming pool

pisser vb [28] (informal) to have a pee

pistache nf pistachio

piste nf ❶ lead ▷ La police est sur une piste. The police are following a lead. ❷ runway ❸ ski run; **une piste artificielle** a dry ski slope; **la piste de danse** the dance floor; **une piste cyclable** a cycle lane

a
b
c
d
e
f
g
h
i
j
k
l
m
n
o
p
q
r
s
t
u
v
w
x
y
z

pistolet nm pistol

pistonner vb [28] Il a été pistonné pour avoir ce travail. They pulled some strings to get him this job.

pitié nf pity; Il me fait pitié. I feel sorry for him.; avoir pitié de quelqu'un to feel sorry for somebody

pittoresque adj picturesque

pizza nf pizza

placard nm cupboard

place nf ❶ place ❷ square ❸ space ▷ Il ne reste plus de place pour se garer. There's no more space to park. ❹ seat ▷ Il y a vingt places assises. There are 20 seats.; remettre quelque chose en place to put something back in its place; sur place on the spot; à la place instead; à la place de instead of

placer vb [12] ❶ to seat ▷ Nous étions placés à côté du directeur. We were seated next to the manager. ❷ to invest ▷ Il a placé ses économies en Bourse. He invested his money on the Stock Exchange.

plafond nm ceiling

plage nf beach

plaie nf wound

plaindre vb [17] plaindre quelqu'un to feel sorry for somebody ▷ Je te plains. I feel sorry for you.; se plaindre to complain ▷ Il n'arrête pas de se plaindre. He never stops complaining.; se plaindre à quelqu'un to complain to somebody; se plaindre de quelque chose to complain about something

plaine nf (level area) plain

plainte nf complaint; porter plainte to lodge a complaint

plaire vb [62] Ce cadeau me plaît beaucoup. I like this present a lot.; Ce film plaît beaucoup aux jeunes. The film is very popular with young people.; Ça t'a plu d'aller en Italie? Did you enjoy going to Italy?; Elle lui plaît. He fancies her.; s'il te plaît please; s'il vous plaît please

plaisanter vb [28] to joke

plaisanterie nf joke

plaisir nm pleasure; faire plaisir à quelqu'un to please somebody

plaît vb see plaire

plan nm plan; un plan de la ville a street map; au premier plan in the foreground

planche nf plank; une planche à repasser an ironing board; une planche à roulettes a skateboard; une planche à voile a sailboard

plancher nm floor

planer vb [28] ❶ to glide ▷ L'avion planait dans le ciel. The plane was gliding in the sky. ❷ to have one's head in the clouds ▷ Ce garçon plane complètement. (informal) He's not with us at all.

planète nf planet

plante nf plant

planter vb [28] ❶ to plant ❷ to hammer in ▷ Jean-Pierre a planté un clou dans le mur. Jean-Pierre hammered a nail into the wall. ❸ to pitch ▷ André a planté sa tente au bord du lac. André pitched his tent next to the lake.; **Ne reste pas planté là!** Don't just stand there!; **se planter** (informal) to fail

plaque nf (metal) plate; **une plaque de verglas** a patch of ice; **une plaque de chocolat** a bar of chocolate

plaqué, e adj plaqué or gold-plated; **plaqué argent** silver-plated

plaquer vb [28] (informal) ❶ to ditch ▷ Elle a plaqué son copain. She ditched her boyfriend. ❷ to pack in ▷ Il a plaqué son boulot. He packed in his job.

plaquette nf **une plaquette de chocolat** a bar of chocolate; **une plaquette de beurre** a pack of butter

plastique nm plastic

plat, e adj flat; **être à plat ventre** to be lying face down; **l'eau plate** still water
▶ nm ❶ dish ❷ course ▷ le plat principal the main course; **un plat cuisiné** a pre-cooked meal; **le plat de résistance** the main course; **le plat du jour** the dish of the day

platane nm plane tree

plateau (pl **plateaux**) nm ❶ tray; **un plateau de fromages** a selection of cheeses ❷ plateau

platine nm platinum
▶ nf (of record player) turntable; **une platine laser** a CD player

plâtre nm plaster

plein, e adj full; **à plein temps** full-time; **plein de** (informal) lots of; **Il y a plein de gens dans la rue.**

The street is full of people.; **en plein air** in the open air; **en pleine nuit** in the middle of the night; **en plein jour** in broad daylight
▶ nm **faire le plein** (petrol tank) to fill up

pleurer vb [28] to cry

pleut vb see **pleuvoir**

pleuvoir vb [63] to rain ▷ Il pleut. It's raining.

pli nm ❶ fold ❷ pleat ❸ crease

pliant, e adj folding

plier vb [19] ❶ to fold ▷ Elle a plié sa serviette. She folded her towel. ❷ to bend ▷ Elle a plié le bras. She bent her arm.

plomb nm ❶ lead ❷ fuse; **l'essence sans plomb** unleaded petrol

plombier nm plumber; **Il est plombier.** He's a plumber.

plongée nf diving

plongeoir nm diving board

plongeon nm dive

plonger vb [45] to dive; **J'ai plongé ma main dans l'eau.** I plunged my hand into the water.; **être plongé dans son travail** to be absorbed in your work; **se plonger dans un livre** to get absorbed in a book

plu vb see **plaire**; **pleuvoir**

pluie nf rain

plume nf feather; **un stylo à plume** a fountain pen

plupart: **la plupart** pron most (of them) ▷ La plupart ont moins de quinze ans. Most of them are under 15.; **la plupart des** most ▷ La plupart des gens ont vu ce film. Most people have seen this film.; **la**

a b c d e f g h i j k l m n o p q r s t u v w x y z

plupart du temps most of the time

pluriel *nm* plural; **au pluriel** in the plural

plus *adv, prep* **ne … plus (1)** not … any more ▷ *Je ne veux plus le voir.* I don't want to see him any more. **(2)** no longer ▷ *Il ne travaille plus ici.* He's no longer working here.; **Je n'ai plus de pain.** I've got no bread left.; **plus … que** more … than ▷ *Il est plus intelligent que son frère.* He's more intelligent than his brother.; **C'est le plus grand de la famille.** He's the tallest in his family.; **plus … plus …** the more … the more …; **plus de (1)** more ▷ *Il nous faut plus de pain.* We need more bread. **(2)** more than ▷ *Il y avait plus de dix personnes.* There were more than 10 people.; **de plus** more ▷ *Il nous faut un joueur de plus.* We need one more player.; **en plus** more ▷ *J'ai apporté quelques gâteaux en plus.* I brought a few more cakes.; **de plus en plus** more and more; **un peu plus difficile** a bit more difficult; **plus ou moins** more or less; **Quatre plus deux égalent six.** 4 plus 2 is 6.

plusieurs *pron pl* several ▷ *Elle a acheté plusieurs chemises.* She bought several shirts.

plus-que-parfait *nm* pluperfect

plutôt *adv* ❶ quite ▷ *Elle est plutôt jolie.* She's quite pretty. ❷ rather ▷ *L'eau est plutôt froide.* The water's rather cold. ❸ instead ▷ *Demande-leur plutôt de venir avec*

toi. Ask them to come with you instead.; **plutôt que** rather than

pluvieux (*f* **pluvieuse**) *adj* rainy

pneu *nm* tyre

pneumonie *nf* pneumonia

poche *nf* pocket; **l'argent de poche** pocket money; **un livre de poche** a paperback

podcast *nm* podcast

podcaster *vb* [28] to podcast

poêle *nf* frying pan; **une poêle à frire** a frying pan

poème *nm* poem

poésie *nf* ❶ poetry ❷ poem

poète *nm* poet

poids *nm* weight; **prendre du poids** to put on weight; **perdre du poids** to lose weight; **un poids lourd** a lorry

poignée *nf* ❶ handful ❷ handle; **une poignée de main** a handshake

poignet *nm* ❶ wrist ❷ (*of shirt*) cuff

poil *nm* ❶ hair ❷ fur; **à poil** (*informal*) stark naked

poilu, e *adj* hairy

poinçonner *vb* [28] to punch ▷ *Le contrôleur a poinçonné les billets.* The conductor punched the tickets.

poing *nm* fist; **un coup de poing** a punch

point *nm* ❶ point ▷ *Je ne suis pas d'accord sur ce point.* I don't agree with this point. ▷ *Son point faible, c'est qu'elle est trop gentille.* Her weak point is she's too nice.; **point de vue** point of view ❷ full stop; **être sur le point de faire quelque chose** to be just about to do something ▷ *J'étais sur le point de te* *téléphoner.* I was just about to phone you.; **mettre au point** to finalize; **Ce n'est pas encore au point.** It's not finalized yet.; **à point** medium ▷ *Comment voulez-vous votre steak? — À point.* How would you like your steak? — Medium.; **un point d'exclamation** an exclamation mark; **un point d'interrogation** a question mark; **un point noir** a blackhead

pointe *nf* point; **être à la pointe du progrès** to be in the forefront of progress; **sur la pointe des pieds** on tiptoe; **les heures de pointe** peak hours

pointillé *nm* dotted line

pointu, e *adj* pointed

pointure *nf* size (of shoes) ▷ *Quelle est votre pointure?* What size shoes do you take?

point-virgule (*pl* **points-virgules**) *nm* semicolon

poire *nf* pear

poireau (*pl* **poireaux**) *nm* leek

pois *nm* pea; **les petits pois** peas; **les pois chiches** chickpeas; **à pois** spotted

poison *nm* poison

poisson *nm* fish; **les Poissons** Pisces; **Poisson d'avril!** April fool!

* Pinning a paper fish to somebody's back is a traditional April fool joke in France.

un poisson rouge a goldfish

poissonnerie *nf* fish shop

poissonnier *nm* fishmonger

poitrine *nf* ❶ chest ❷ bust

poivre *nm* (spice) pepper

poivron *nm* (vegetable) pepper

pôle *nm* pole; **le pôle Nord** the North Pole; **le pôle Sud** the South Pole

poli, e *adj* polite

police *nf* police; **police secours** emergency services; **une police d'assurance** an insurance policy

policier (*f* **policière**) *adj* **un roman policier** a detective novel
▶ *nm* police officer

politesse *nf* politeness

politique *nf* politics ▷ *La politique ne l'intéresse pas du tout.* He's not at all interested in politics.

pollué, e *adj* polluted

polluer *vb* [28] to pollute

pollution *nf* pollution

polo *nm* polo shirt

Pologne *nf* Poland

polonais, e *adj, nm/f* Polish ▷ *Elle parle polonais.* She speaks Polish.; **un Polonais** (man) a Pole; **une Polonaise** (woman) a Pole; **les Polonais** the Poles

Polynésie *nf* Polynesia

pommade *nf* ointment

pomme *nf* apple; **les pommes de terre** potatoes; **les pommes frites** chips; **les pommes vapeur** boiled potatoes

pompe *nf* pump; **une pompe à essence** a petrol pump; **les pompes funèbres** undertakers

pompier *nm* firefighter

pompiste *nm* petrol pump attendant

ponctuel (*f* **ponctuelle**) *adj* ❶ punctual ❷ occasional; **On a**

rencontré quelques problèmes ponctuels. We've had the occasional problem.

pondre vb [**69**] (eggs) to lay

pont nm ❶ bridge ❷ (of ship) deck; **faire le pont** to take a long weekend

populaire adj ❶ popular ❷ working-class

population nf population

porc nm ❶ pig ❷ pork

port nm ❶ harbour ❷ port

portable adj (telephone) mobile ▶ nm ❶ mobile phone ❷ laptop

portail nm gate

portatif (f portative) adj portable

porte nf ❶ door; **la porte d'entrée** the front door ❷ gate; **mettre quelqu'un à la porte** to sack somebody

porte-bagages nm luggage rack

porte-clés nm key ring

portée nf à portée de main within arm's reach; **hors de portée** out of reach

portefeuille nm wallet

portemanteau (pl **portemanteaux**) nm ❶ coat hanger ❷ coat rack

porte-monnaie (pl **porte-monnaie**) nm purse

porte-parole (pl porte-parole) nm spokesperson

porter vb [**28**] ❶ to carry ▷ Il portait une valise. He was carrying a suitcase. ❷ to wear ▷ Elle porte une robe bleue. She's wearing a blue dress.; **se porter bien** to be well; **se porter mal** to be unwell

porteur nm porter

portière nf (of car) door

portion nf portion

porto nm (wine) port

portrait nm portrait

portugais, e adj, n Portuguese ▷ Il parle portugais. He speaks Portuguese.; **un Portugais** (man) a Portuguese; **une Portugaise** (woman) a Portuguese; **les Portugais** the Portuguese

Portugal nm Portugal; **au Portugal (1)** in Portugal **(2)** to Portugal

poser vb [**28**] ❶ to put down ▷ J'ai posé la cafetière sur la table. I put the coffee pot down on the table. ❷ to pose ▷ Cela pose un problème. That poses a problem.; **poser une question à quelqu'un** to ask somebody a question; **se poser** to land

positif (f positive) adj positive

position nf position

posséder vb [**34**] to own ▷ Ils possèdent une jolie maison. They own a lovely house.

possibilité nf possibility

possible adj possible; **le plus de gens possible** as many people as possible; **le plus tôt possible** as early as possible; **le moins d'argent possible** as little money as possible; **Il travaille le moins possible.** He works as little as possible.; **dès que possible** as soon as possible; **faire son possible** to do all one can

poste nf ❶ post ❷ post office;

mettre une lettre à la poste to post a letter
▶ nm ❶ post ❷ (phone) extension ❸ set ▷ un poste de radio a radio set; **un poste de police** a police station

poster vb [28] to post
▶ nm poster

postérieur, e adj ❶ later ❷ back

pot nm jar; **prendre un pot** (informal) to have a drink; **un pot de fleurs** a plant pot

potable adj eau potable drinking water; 'eau non potable' 'not drinking water'

potage nm soup

potager nm vegetable garden

pot-au-feu (pl **pot-au-feu**) nm beef stew

pot-de-vin (pl **pots-de-vin**) nm bribe

pote nm (informal) mate

poteau (pl **poteaux**) nm post; un **poteau indicateur** a signpost

potentiel (f **potentielle**) adj potential

poterie nf ❶ pottery ❷ piece of pottery

potier nm potter

pou (pl **poux**) nm louse

poubelle nf dustbin

pouce nm ❶ thumb ❷ inch; **manger sur le pouce** to have a quick snack

poudre nf ❶ powder ❷ face powder; **la poudre à laver** washing powder; **le lait en poudre** powdered milk; **le café en poudre** instant coffee

poulain nm foal

poule nf hen

poulet nm ❶ chicken ❷ cop

pouls nm pulse

poumon nm lung

poupée nf doll

pour prep for ▷ Qu'est-ce que tu veux pour ton petit déjeuner? What would you like for breakfast?; **pour faire quelque chose** to do something ▷ Je lui ai téléphoné pour l'inviter. I phoned him to invite him.; **Pour aller à Strasbourg, s'il vous plaît?** Which way is it to Strasbourg, please?; **pour que** so that

▌ **pour que** is followed by a verb in the subjunctive.

▷ Je lui ai prêté mon pull pour qu'elle n'ait pas froid. I lent her my jumper so that she wouldn't be cold.; **pour cent** per cent

pourboire nm tip

pourcentage nm percentage

pourquoi adv, conj why

pourra, pourras, pourrai, pourrez vb see **pouvoir**

pourri, e adj rotten

pourrir vb [38] to go bad ▷ Ces poires ont pourri. These pears have gone bad.

pourrons, pourront vb see **pouvoir**

poursuite nf chase; **se lancer à la poursuite de quelqu'un** to chase after somebody

poursuivre vb [81] to carry on with ▷ Ils ont poursuivi leur travail. They carried on with their work.; **se poursuivre** to go on ▷ Le concert

a b c d e f g h i j k l m n o p q r s t u v w x y z

s'est poursuivi très tard. The concert went on very late.

pourtant *adv* yet; **C'est pourtant facile!** But it's easy!

pourvu (*f* **pourvue**) *adj* **pourvu que ...** let's hope that ...

▌ **pourvu que** is followed by a verb in the subjunctive.

▷ *Pourvu qu'il ne pleuve pas!* Let's hope it doesn't rain!

pousser *vb* [**28**] ❶ to push ▷ *Ils ont dû pousser la voiture.* They had to push the car. ❷ to grow ▷ *Mes cheveux poussent vite.* My hair grows quickly.; **pousser un cri** to give a cry; **se pousser** to move over ▷ *Pousse-toi, je ne vois rien.* Move over, I can't see a thing.

poussette *nf* pushchair

poussière *nf* ❶ dust ❷ speck of dust

poussiéreux (*f* **poussiéreuse**) *adj* dusty

poussin *nm* chick

pouvoir *vb* [**64**] can ▷ *Je peux lui téléphoner si tu veux.* I can phone her if you want. ▷ *J'ai fait tout ce que j'ai pu.* I did all I could.; **Je n'en peux plus.** I'm exhausted.; **Il se peut que ...** It's possible that ...

▌ **il se peut que** is followed by a verb in the subjunctive.

▷ *Il se peut que j'y aille.* I might go.

▶ *nm* power

prairie *nf* meadow

pratique *nf* practice

▶ *adj* practical

pratiquement *adv* virtually

pratiquer *vb* [**28**] to practise; **Pratiquez-vous un sport?** Do you do any sport?

pré *nm* meadow

précarité *nf* (*of a situation*) precariousness; (*in economics*) **la précarité (de l'emploi)** job insecurity, lack of job security

précaution *nf* precaution; **par précaution** as a precaution; **avec précaution** cautiously; '**à manipuler avec précaution**' 'handle with care'

précédemment *adv* previously

précédent, e *adj* previous

précieux (*f* **précieuse**) *adj* precious; **une pierre précieuse** a precious stone; **de précieux conseils** invaluable advice

précipice *nm* ravine

précipitamment *adv* hurriedly

précipitation *nf* haste

se précipiter *vb* [**28**] to rush

précis, e *adj* precise; **à huit heures précises** at exactly eight o'clock

précisément *adv* precisely

préciser *vb* [**28**] ❶ to be more specific about ▷ *Pouvez-vous préciser ce que vous voulez dire?* Can you be more specific about what you want to say? ❷ to specify

précision *nf* ❶ precision ❷ detail

préfecture *nf*

● A **préfecture** is the headquarters of a **département**, one of the 96 administrative areas of France.

la préfecture de police the police headquarters

préférable *adj* preferable

préféré, e *adj* favourite

préférence *nf* preference; **de préférence** preferably

préférer vb [34] to prefer ▷ Je préfère manger à la cantine. I prefer to eat in the canteen.; **Je préférerais du thé.** I'd rather have tea.; **préférer quelqu'un à quelqu'un** to prefer somebody to somebody ▷ Je le préfère à son frère. I prefer him to his brother.

préhistorique adj prehistoric

préjugé nm prejudice

premier (f **première**) adj first ▷ au premier étage on the first floor ▷ C'est notre premier jour de vacances. It's the first day of our holiday. ▷ C'est la première fois que je viens ici. It's the first time I've been here. ▷ le premier mai the first of May ▷ Il est arrivé premier. He came first.; **le Premier ministre** the Prime Minister

premièrement adv firstly

prendre vb [65] to take ▷ Prends tes affaires et viens avec moi. Take your things and come with me.; **prendre quelque chose à quelqu'un** to take something from somebody; **Nous avons pris le train de huit heures.** We took the eight o'clock train.; **Je prends toujours le train pour aller à Paris.** I always go to Paris by train.; **passer prendre** to pick up ▷ Je dois passer prendre Richard. I have to pick up Richard.; **prendre à gauche** to turn left ▷ Prenez à gauche en arrivant au rond-point. Turn left at the roundabout.; **Il se prend pour Napoléon.** He thinks he's Napoleon.; **s'en prendre à quelqu'un** (verbally) to lay into somebody; **s'y prendre** to set

about it ▷ Tu t'y prends mal! You're setting about it the wrong way!

prénom nm first name

préoccupé, e adj worried

préparation nf preparation

préparer vb [28] ① to prepare ▷ Elle prépare le dîner. She's preparing dinner. ② to make ▷ Je vais préparer le café. I'm going to make the coffee. ③ to prepare for ▷ Laure prépare son examen d'économie. Laure's preparing for her economics exam.; **se préparer** to get ready

préposition nf preposition

près adv **tout près** nearby; **près de** (1) near (to) (2) next to (3) nearly; **de près** closely; **à peu de chose près** more or less

présence nf ① presence ② attendance

présent, e adj present ▶ nm present tense; **à présent** now

présentation nf presentation; **faire les présentations** to do the introductions

présenter vb [28] to present; **présenter quelqu'un à quelqu'un** to introduce somebody to somebody ▷ Il m'a présenté à sa sœur. He introduced me to his sister.; **Marc, je te présente Anaïs.** Marc, this is Anaïs.; **se présenter (1)** to introduce oneself ▷ Elle s'est présentée à ses collègues. She introduced herself to her colleagues. **(2)** to arise ▷ Si l'occasion se présente, nous irons en

Écosse. If the chance arises, we'll go to Scotland. **(3)** to stand ▷ *Monsieur Legros se présente encore aux élections.* Mr Legros is standing for election again.

préservatif *nm* condom

préserver *vb* [28] to protect

président *nm* ❶ president ❷ chairman; **le président-directeur général** the chairman and managing director

présidente *nf* ❶ president ❷ chairwoman

présider *vb* [28] ❶ to chair ❷ to be the guest of honour

presque *adv* nearly; **presque rien** hardly anything; **presque pas** hardly at all; **presque pas de** hardly any

presqu'île *nf* peninsula

presse *nf* press

pressé, e *adj* ❶ in a hurry ❷ urgent; **une orange pressée** a fresh orange juice

presser *vb* [28] ❶ to squeeze ❷ to be urgent ▷ *Est-ce que ça presse?* Is it urgent?; **se presser** to hurry up; **Rien ne presse.** There's no hurry.

pressing *nm* dry-cleaner's

pression *nf* ❶ pressure; **faire pression sur quelqu'un** to put pressure on somebody ❷ (*informal*) draught beer

prêt, e *adj* ready
▶ *nm* loan

prêt-à-porter *nm* ready-to-wear clothes *pl*

prétendre *vb* [88] **prétendre que** to claim that ▷ *Il prétend qu'il ne la connaît pas.* He claims he doesn't know her.

  Be careful! **prétendre** does not mean **to pretend**.

prétendu, e *adj* so-called

prétentieux (*f* **prétentieuse**) *adj* pretentious

prêter *vb* [28] **prêter quelque chose à quelqu'un** to lend something to someone ▷ *Il m'a prêté sa voiture.* He lent me his car.; **prêter attention à quelque chose** to pay attention to something

prétexte *nm* excuse; **sous aucun prétexte** on no account

prétexter *vb* [28] to give as an excuse

prêtre *nm* priest

preuve *nf* ❶ evidence ❷ proof; **faire preuve de courage** to show courage; **faire ses preuves** to prove oneself

prévenir *vb* [89] **prévenir quelqu'un** to warn somebody ▷ *Je te préviens, il est de mauvaise humeur.* I'm warning you, he's in a bad mood.

prévention *nf* prevention; **des mesures de prévention** preventative measures; **la prévention routière** road safety

prévision *nf* **les prévisions météorologiques** the weather forecast; **en prévision de quelque chose** in anticipation of something

prévoir *vb* [92] ❶ to plan ▷ *Nous prévoyons un pique-nique pour dimanche.* We're planning to have a picnic on Sunday.; **Le départ est**

prévu pour dix heures. The departure's scheduled for 10 o'clock. ❷ to allow ▷ *J'ai prévu assez à manger pour quatre.* I allowed enough food for four. ❸ to foresee ▷ *J'avais prévu qu'il serait en retard.* I'd foreseen that he'd be late.; **Je prévois qu'il me faudra une heure de plus.** I reckon on it taking me another hour.

prier *vb* [19] to pray to ▷ *Les Grecs priaient Dionysos.* The Greeks prayed to Dionysos.; **prier quelqu'un de faire quelque chose** to ask somebody to do something ▷ *Elle l'a prié de sortir.* She asked him to leave.; **je vous en prie (1)** please do ▷ *Je peux m'asseoir? — Je vous en prie.* May I sit down? — Please do. **(2)** please ▷ *Je vous en prie, ne me laissez pas seule.* Please, don't leave me alone. **(3)** don't mention it ▷ *Merci pour votre aide. — Je vous en prie.* Thanks for your help. — Don't mention it.

prière *nf* prayer; **'prière de ne pas fumer'** 'no smoking please'

primaire *nm* primary education; **l'école primaire** primary school

prime *nf* ❶ bonus ❷ free gift ❸ premium

primevère *nf* primrose

prince *nm* prince

princesse *nf* princess

principal, e (*mpl* **principaux**) *adj* main
  ▶ *nm* ❶ head teacher ❷ main thing ▷ *Personne n'a été blessé; c'est le principal.* Nobody was injured;

that's the main thing.

principe *nm* principle; **pour le principe** on principle; **en principe (1)** as a rule **(2)** in theory

printemps *nm* spring; **au printemps** in spring

priorité *nf* ❶ priority ❷ right of way

pris, e *adj* ❶ taken ▷ *Est-ce que cette place est prise?* Is this seat taken? ❷ busy ▷ *Je serai très pris la semaine prochaine.* I'll be very busy next week.; **avoir le nez pris** to have a stuffy nose; **être pris de panique** to be panic-stricken
  ▶ *vb see* **prendre**

prise *nf* ❶ plug ❷ socket; **une prise de courant** a power point; **une prise multiple** an adaptor; **une prise de sang** a blood test

prison *nf* prison

prisonnier (*f* **prisonnière**) *adj* captive

prisonnier *nm* prisoner

prisonnière *nf* prisoner

prit *vb see* **prendre**

privé, e *adj* private; **en privé** in private

priver *vb* [28] **priver quelqu'un de quelque chose** to deprive somebody of something; **Tu seras privé de dessert!** You won't get any pudding!

prix *nm* ❶ price ❷ prize; **hors de prix** exorbitantly priced; **à aucun prix** not at any price; **à tout prix** at all costs

probable *adj* likely; **C'est peu probable.** That's unlikely.

a
b
c
d
e
f
g
h
i
j
k
l
m
n
o
p
q
r
s
t
u
v
w
x
y
z

probablement adv probably

problème nm problem

procédé nm process

procès nm trial; **Il est en procès avec son employeur.** He's involved in a lawsuit with his employer.

prochain, e adj next; **la prochaine fois** next time; **la semaine prochaine** next week; **À la prochaine!** See you!

prochainement adv soon

proche adj ❶ near ❷ close; **proche de** near to; **le Proche-Orient** the Middle East

proches nmpl close relatives

proclamer vb [28] to proclaim

procréation nf procreation; **procréation médicalement assistée, assistance médicale à la procréation** assisted reproduction

procurer vb [28] **procurer quelque chose à quelqu'un** to get something for somebody; **se procurer quelque chose** to get something

producteur nm producer

production nf production

produire vb [23] to produce; **se produire** to take place

produit nm product

prof nmf (informal) teacher

professeur nm ❶ teacher ❷ professor; **un professeur de faculté** a university lecturer

profession nf profession; **'sans profession'** 'unemployed'

professionnel (f **professionnelle**) adj professional

profil nm ❶ (of person) profile ❷ (of object) contours

profit nm profit; **tirer profit de quelque chose** to profit from something; **au profit de** in aid of

profiter vb [28] **profiter de quelque chose** to take advantage of something; **Profitez-en bien!** Make the most of it!

profond, e adj deep; **peu profond** shallow

profondeur nf depth

programme nm ❶ programme ❷ syllabus ❸ program ▷ un programme informatique a computer program

programmer vb [28] ❶ to show ▷ Ce film est programmé dimanche soir. The film is showing on Sunday evening. ❷ to program

programmeur nm programmer

programmeuse nf programmer

progrès nm progress

progresser vb [28] to progress

progressif (f **progressive**) adj progressive

projecteur nm ❶ projector ❷ spotlight

projet nm ❶ plan ❷ draft; **un projet de loi** (in parliament) a bill

projeter vb [41] ❶ to plan ▷ Ils projettent d'acheter une maison. They're planning to buy a house. ❷ to cast ▷ une ombre projetée sur le mur a shadow cast onto the wall; **Elle a été projetée hors de la voiture.** She was thrown out of the car.

prolonger vb [45] ❶ to prolong ❷ to extend ▷ Je vais prolonger mon abonnement. I'm going to extend my subscription.; **se prolonger** to go on ▷ *La réunion s'est prolongée tard.* The meeting went on late.

promenade *nf* walk; **faire une promenade** to go for a walk; **faire une promenade en voiture** to go for a drive; **faire une promenade à vélo** to go for a bike ride

promener *vb* [**43**] to take for a walk ▷ *Cordelia promène son chien tous les jours.* Cordelia takes her dog for a walk every day.; **se promener** to go for a walk

promesse *nf* promise

promettre *vb* [**47**] to promise

promotion *nf* promotion; **être en promotion** to be on special offer

pronom *nm* pronoun

prononcer *vb* [**12**] ① to pronounce ▷ *Le russe est difficile à prononcer.* Russian is difficult to pronounce. ② to deliver ▷ *prononcer un discours* to deliver a speech; **se prononcer** to be pronounced ▷ *Le 'e' final ne se prononce pas.* The final 'e' isn't pronounced.

prononciation *nf* pronunciation

propagande *nf* propaganda

se **propager** *vb* [**45**] to spread

proportion *nf* proportion

propos *nm* **à propos** by the way; **à propos de quelque chose** about something

proposer *vb* [**28**] **proposer quelque chose à quelqu'un (1)** to suggest something to somebody ▷ *Nous lui avons proposé une promenade en bateau.* We suggested going on a boat ride to him. **(2)** to

offer somebody something ▷ *Ils m'ont proposé des chocolats.* They offered me some chocolates.

proposition *nf* offer

propre *adj* ① clean ② own ▷ *Gordon l'a fabriqué de ses propres mains.* Gordon made it with his own hands.; **propre à** characteristic of ▶ *nm* **recopier quelque chose au propre** to make a fair copy of something

proprement *adv* properly; **le village proprement dit** the village itself; **à proprement parler** strictly speaking

propreté *nf* cleanliness

propriétaire *nm* ① owner ② landlord ▶ *nf* ① owner ② landlady

propriété *nf* property

prospectus *nm* leaflet

prospère *adj* prosperous

prostituée *nf* prostitute

protecteur (*f* **protectrice**) *adj* ① protective ② patronizing

protection *nf* protection

protéger *vb* [**66**] to protect

protéine *nf* protein

protestant, e *adj* Protestant; **Il est protestant.** He's a Protestant.

protestation *nf* protest

protester *vb* [**28**] to protest ▷ *Ils protestent contre leurs conditions de travail.* They're protesting about their working conditions.

prouver *vb* [**28**] to prove

provenance *nf* origin; **un avion en provenance de Berlin** a plane arriving from Berlin

provenir vb [89] provenir de (1) to come from ▷ Ces tomates proviennent d'Espagne. These tomatoes come from Spain. (2) to be the result of ▷ Cela provient d'un manque d'organisation. This is the result of a lack of organization.

proverbe nm proverb

province nf province; **en province** in the provinces

proviseur nm (of state secondary school) headteacher

provision nf supply

provisions nfpl food

provisoire adj temporary

provoquer vb [28] ❶ to provoke ❷ to cause ▷ Cet accident a provoqué la mort de quarante personnes. The accident caused the death of 40 people.

proximité nf proximity; **à proximité** nearby

prudemment adv ❶ carefully ❷ wisely ❸ cautiously

prudence nf caution; **avec prudence** carefully

prudent, e adj ❶ careful ❷ wise

prune nf plum

pruneau (pl pruneaux) nm prune

psychiatre nmf psychiatrist

psychologie nf psychology

psychologique adj psychological

psychologue nmf psychologist

pu vb see **pouvoir**; Je n'ai pas pu venir. I couldn't come.

pub nf (informal) ❶ advertising ❷ adverts

public (f **publique**) adj public; **une école publique** a state school

▶ nm ❶ public ❷ audience; **en public** in public

publicitaire adj **une agence publicitaire** an advertising agency; **un film publicitaire** a publicity film

publicité nf ❶ advertising ❷ advert; **faire de la publicité pour quelque chose** to publicize something

publier vb [19] to publish

publique adj f see **public**

puce nf ❶ flea ❷ chip; **une carte à puce** a smart card

puces nfpl flea market sg

puer vb [28] to stink

puéril, e adj childish

puis vb see **pouvoir**; Puis-je venir vous voir samedi? May I come and see you on Saturday?
▶ adv then

puisque conj since

puissance nf power

puissant, e adj powerful

puits nm well

pull nm jumper

pull-over nm jumper

pulvérisateur nm spray

pulvériser vb [28] ❶ to pulverize ❷ to spray

punaise nf drawing pin

punir vb [38] to punish ▷ Il a été puni pour avoir menti. He was punished for lying.

punition nf punishment

pupitre nm (for pupil) desk

pur, e adj ❶ pure ❷ (undiluted) neat; C'est de la folie pure. It's sheer madness.

purée *nf* mashed potatoes; **la purée de marrons** chestnut purée

puzzle *nm* jigsaw puzzle

PV *nm* (= *procès-verbal*) parking ticket

pyjama *nm* pyjamas *pl*

pyramide *nf* pyramid

Pyrénées *nfpl* Pyrenees; **dans les Pyrénées** in the Pyrenees

QI *nm* (= *quotient intellectuel*) IQ

quai *nm* ❶ quay ❷ platform

qualifié, e *adj* qualified

qualifier *vb* [19] **se qualifier** to qualify ▷ *Bob s'est qualifié pour la demi-finale.* Bob has qualified for the semifinal.

qualité *nf* quality

quand *conj, adv* when ▷ *Quand est-ce que tu pars en vacances?* When are you going on holiday?; **quand même** all the same ▷ *Je ne voulais pas de dessert, mais j'en ai mangé quand même.* I didn't want any dessert, but I had some all the same.

quant à *prep* regarding ▷ *Quant au problème de chauffage ...* Regarding the problem with the heating ... ▷ *Quant à moi, je n'arriverai qu'à dix* *heures.* As for me, I won't be arriving till 10 o'clock.

quantité *nf* amount; **des quantités de** a great deal of

quarantaine *nf* about forty; **Elle a la quarantaine.** She's in her forties.

quarante *num* forty; **quarante et un** forty-one; **quarante-deux** forty-two

quart *nm* quarter; **le quart de** a quarter of; **trois quarts** three quarters; **un quart d'heure** a quarter of an hour; **deux heures et quart** a quarter past two; **dix heures moins le quart** a quarter to ten; **Un quart d'eau minérale, s'il vous plaît.** A small bottle of mineral water, please.

quartier *nm* ❶ (*of town*) area; **un cinéma de quartier** a local cinema ❷ piece ▷ *un quartier d'orange* a piece of orange

quartz *nm* **une montre à quartz** a quartz watch

quasi *adv* nearly

quasiment *adv* nearly; **quasiment jamais** hardly ever

quatorze *num* fourteen; **le quatorze février** the fourteenth of February

quatre *num* four ▷ *Il a quatre ans.* He's four.; **le quatre février** the fourth of February; **faire les quatre cents coups** to be a bit wild

quatre-vingts *num* eighty

> quatre-vingts is spelt with an **-s** when it is followed by a noun, but not when it is followed by another number.

▷ *quatre-vingts euros* eighty euros ▷ *Elle a quatre-vingt-deux ans.* She's eighty-two.; **quatre-vingt-dix** ninety; **quatre-vingt-onze** ninety-one; **quatre-vingt-quinze** ninety-five; **quatre-vingt-dix-huit** ninety-eight

> Word for word, **quatre-vingts** means 'four twenties'.

quatrième *adj* fourth ▷ *au quatrième étage* on the fourth floor ▶ *nf* year 9 ▷ *Mon frère est en quatrième.* My brother's in year 9.

● In French secondary schools, years are counted from the **sixième** (youngest) to **première** and **terminale** (oldest).

que *conj, pron, adv* ❶ that ▷ *Il sait que tu es là.* He knows that you're here.; **Je veux que tu viennes.** I want you to come. ❷ what ▷ *Que fais-tu?* What are you doing?; **Qu'est-ce que ...?** What ...? ▷ *Qu'est-ce que tu fais?* What are you doing? ▷ *Qu'est-ce que c'est?* What's that?; **plus ... que** more ... than ▷ *Il est plus grand que moi.* He's bigger than me.; **aussi ... que** as ... as ▷ *Elle est aussi jolie que sa sœur.* She's as pretty as her sister.; **ne ... que** only ▷ *Il ne boit que de l'eau.* He only drinks water.; **Qu'il est bête!** He's so silly!

quel (*f* **quelle**) *adj* ❶ who ▷ *Quel est ton chanteur préféré?* Who's your favourite singer? ❷ what ▷ *Quelle heure est-il?* What time is it? ❸ which ▷ *Quel groupe préfères-tu?* Which band do you like best?; **quel que soit (1)** whoever **(2)** whatever

quelle adj f see **quel**

quelque adj, adv ❶ some ▷ Il a quelques amis à Paris. He has some friends in Paris. ❷ a few ▷ Il reste quelques bouteilles. There are a few bottles left. ❸ few ▷ Ils ont fini les quelques bouteilles qui restaient. They finished the few bottles that were left.; **quelque chose (1)** something ▷ J'ai quelque chose pour toi. I've got something for you. **(2)** anything ▷ Avez-vous quelque chose à déclarer? Have you got anything to declare?; **quelque part (1)** somewhere **(2)** anywhere

quelquefois adv sometimes

quelques-uns (f **quelques-unes**) pron pl some ▷ As-tu vu ses films? J'en ai vu quelques-uns. Have you seen his films? I've seen some of them.

quelqu'un pron ❶ somebody ▷ Il y a quelqu'un à la porte. There's somebody at the door. ❷ anybody ▷ Est-ce que quelqu'un a vu mon parapluie? Has anybody seen my umbrella?

querelle nf quarrel

qu'est-ce que see **que**

qu'est-ce qui see **qui**

question nf ❶ question ❷ matter; **Il n'en est pas question.** There's no question of it.; **De quoi est-il question?** What's it about? ▷ Il est question de l'organisation du concert. It's about the organization of the concert.; **hors de question** out of the question

questionnaire nm questionnaire

questionner vb [28] to question

queue nf ❶ tail; **faire la queue** to queue; **une queue de cheval** a ponytail ❷ rear ❸ bottom ❹ (of fruit, leaf) stalk

qui pron ❶ who ▷ Qui a téléphoné? Who phoned? ❷ whom ▷ C'est la personne à qui j'ai parlé hier. It's the person who I spoke to yesterday. ❸ that ▷ Donne-moi la veste qui est sur la chaise. Give me the jacket that's on the chair.; **Qui est-ce qui ...?** Who ...? ▷ Qui est-ce qui t'emmène au spectacle? Who's taking you to the show?; **Qui est-ce que ...?** Who ...? ▷ Qui est-ce que tu as vu à cette soirée? Who did you see at the party?; **Qu'est-ce qui ...?** What ...? ▷ Qu'est-ce qui est sur la table? What's on the table? ▷ Qu'est-ce qui te prend? What's the matter with you?; **À qui est ce sac?** Whose bag is this?; **À qui parlais-tu?** Who were you talking to?

quille nf un jeu de quilles skittles

quincaillerie nf ironmonger's (shop)

quinquennat nm

   ● **le quinquennat** is the five-year
   ● term of office of the French
   ● President.

quinzaine nf about fifteen; **une quinzaine de jours** a fortnight

quinze num fifteen; **le quinze février** the fifteenth of February; **dans quinze jours** in a fortnight's time

quittance nf ❶ receipt ❷ bill

quitter vb [28] to leave ▷ J'ai quitté

la maison à huit heures. I left the house at 8 o'clock.; **se quitter** to part ▷ *Les deux amis se sont quittés devant le café.* The two friends parted in front of the café.; **Ne quittez pas.** *(on telephone)* Hold the line.

quoi *pron* <u>what?</u> ▷ *À quoi penses-tu?* What are you thinking about?; **Quoi de neuf?** What's new?; **As-tu de quoi écrire?** Have you got anything to write with?; **Je n'ai pas de quoi acheter une voiture.** I can't afford to buy a car.; **Quoi qu'il arrive.** Whatever happens.; **Il n'y a pas de quoi.** Don't mention it.; **Il n'y a pas de quoi s'énerver.** There's no reason for getting worked up.; **En quoi puis-je vous aider?** How may I help you?

quoique *conj* <u>even though</u>

　quoique is followed by a verb in the subjunctive.

▷ *Il va l'acheter quoique ce soit cher.* He's going to buy it even though it's expensive.

quotidien (*f* **quotidienne**) *adj* <u>daily</u>; **la vie quotidienne** everyday life
　▶ *nm* <u>daily paper</u>

rab *nm (informal) (of meal)* <u>seconds</u>

rabais *nm (in price)* <u>reduction</u>; **au rabais** at a discount

racaille *nf* <u>riff-raff</u>

raccompagner *vb* [28] <u>to take home</u> ▷ *Tu peux me raccompagner?* Can you take me home?

raccourci *nm* <u>shortcut</u>

raccrocher *vb* [28] <u>to hang up</u> *(telephone)*

race *nf* ❶ <u>race</u> ❷ <u>breed</u>; **de race** pedigree

racheter *vb* [1] ❶ <u>to buy another</u> ▷ *J'ai racheté un portefeuille.* I've bought another wallet. ▷ *racheter du lait* to buy more milk ❷ <u>to buy</u> ▷ *Il m'a racheté ma moto.* He bought my bike from me.

racine *nf* <u>root</u>

racisme *nm* <u>racism</u>

raciste *adj* racist

raconter *vb* [28] raconter quelque chose à quelqu'un to tell somebody about something; **Qu'est-ce que tu racontes?** What are you talking about?

radar *nm* radar

radiateur *nm* radiator; **un radiateur électrique** an electric heater

radin, e *adj* (informal) stingy

radio *nf* ❶ radio ❷ X-ray; **passer une radio** to have an X-ray

radio-réveil (*pl* **radios-réveils**) *nm* clock radio

radis *nm* radish

raffoler *vb* [28] raffoler de to be crazy about

rafraîchir *vb* [38] to cool down; **se rafraîchir (1)** to get cooler ▷ *Le temps se rafraîchit.* The weather's getting cooler. **(2)** to freshen up ▷ *Il a pris une douche pour se rafraîchir.* He had a shower to freshen up.

rafraîchissant, e *adj* refreshing

rage *nf* rabies; **une rage de dents** raging toothache

ragoût *nm* stew

raide *adj* ❶ steep ❷ straight ▷ *Laure a les cheveux raides.* Laure has straight hair. ❸ stiff ❹ flat broke

raie *nf* ❶ (fish) skate ❷ (in hair) parting

rail *nm* rail

raisin *nm* grapes; **des raisins secs** raisins

raison *nf* reason; **Ce n'est pas une raison.** That's no excuse.; **avoir raison** to be right; **en raison de** because of

raisonnable *adj* sensible

raisonnement *nm* reasoning

rajouter *vb* [28] to add

ralentir *vb* [38] to slow down

râler *vb* [28] (informal) to moan

ramassage *nm* le ramassage scolaire the school bus service

ramasser *vb* [28] ❶ to pick up ▷ *Il a ramassé son crayon.* He picked up his pencil. ❷ to take in ▷ *Il a ramassé les copies.* He took in the exam papers.

rame *nf* ❶ (of boat) oar ❷ (on the underground) train

rameau (*pl* **rameaux**) *nm* branch; **le dimanche des Rameaux** Palm Sunday

ramener *vb* [43] ❶ to bring back ▷ *Je t'ai ramené un souvenir de Grèce.* I've brought you back a present from Greece. ❷ to take home ▷ *Tu me ramènes?* Will you take me home?

ramer *vb* [28] to row

rampe *nf* banister

rancune *nf* garder rancune à quelqu'un to bear somebody a grudge; **Sans rancune!** No hard feelings!

rancunier (*f* **rancunière**) *adj* vindictive

randonnée *nf* une randonnée à vélo a bike ride; **une randonnée pédestre** a ramble; **faire de la randonnée** to go hiking

randonneur *nm* hiker

rang *nm* (line) row

rangée *nf* (line) row

ranger vb [**45**] ❶ to put away ▷ *J'ai rangé tes affaires.* I've put your things away. ❷ to tidy up ▷ *Va ranger ta chambre.* Go and tidy up your room.

rap nm rap

râper vb [**28**] to grate ▷ *le fromage râpé* grated cheese

rapide adj ❶ fast ❷ quick

rapidement adv quickly

rappel nm ❶ (vaccination) booster ❷ curtain call

rappeler vb [**4**] to call back ▷ *Je te rappelle dans cinq minutes.* I'll call you back in 5 minutes.; **rappeler quelque chose à quelqu'un** to remind somebody of something; **rappeler à quelqu'un de faire quelque chose** to remind somebody to do something; **se rappeler** to remember ▷ *Il s'est rappelé qu'il avait une course à faire.* He remembered he had some shopping to do.

rapport nm ❶ report ▷ *Il a écrit un rapport.* He wrote a report. ❷ connection ▷ *Je ne vois pas le rapport.* I can't see the connection.; **par rapport à** in comparison with

rapporter vb [**28**] to bring back

rapporteur nm telltale

rapprocher vb [**28**] ❶ to bring together ▷ *Cet accident a rapproché les deux frères.* The accident brought the two brothers together. ❷ to bring closer ▷ *Il a rapproché le fauteuil de la télé.* He brought the armchair closer to the TV.; **se rapprocher** to come closer

▷ *Rapproche-toi, tu verras mieux.* Come closer, you'll see better.

raquette nf ❶ (tennis) racket ❷ (table tennis) bat

rare adj rare

rarement adv rarely

ras, e adj, adv short; **à ras bords** to the brim; **en avoir ras le bol de quelque chose** (informal) to be fed up with something; **un pull ras du cou** a crew-neck jumper

raser vb [**28**] to shave off; **se raser** to shave

rasoir nm razor
▶ adj (informal) dead boring

rassembler vb [**28**] to assemble ▷ *Il a rassemblé les enfants dans la cour.* He assembled the children in the playground.; **se rassembler** to gather together

rassurer vb [**28**] to reassure; **Je suis rassuré.** I don't need to worry any more.; **se rassurer** to be reassured; **Rassure-toi!** Don't worry!

rat nm rat

raté, e adj failed

râteau (pl **râteaux**) nm rake

rater vb [**28**] ❶ to miss ▷ *Chantal a raté son train.* Chantal missed her train. ❷ to fail ▷ *J'ai raté mon examen de maths.* I failed my maths exam.

RATP nf Paris transport authority

rattacher vb [**28**] to tie up again

rattraper vb [**28**] ❶ to recapture ❷ to catch up with ▷ *Je vais rattraper Cécile.* I'll catch up with Cécile. ❸ to make up for ▷ *Il faut rattraper le temps perdu.* We must make up for lost time.; **se rattraper** to make up for it

rature nf correction

ravi, e adj **être ravi** to be delighted ▷ Ils étaient ravis de nous voir. They were delighted to see us. ▷ Je suis ravi que vous puissiez venir. I'm delighted that you can come.

se **raviser** vb [28] to change your mind ▷ Il allait accepter, mais il s'est ravisé. He was going to accept, but he changed his mind.

ravissant, e adj lovely

rayé, e adj striped

rayer vb [59] ❶ to scratch ❷ to cross off ▷ Son nom a été rayé de la liste. His name has been crossed off the list.

rayon nm ❶ ray ▷ un rayon de soleil a ray of sunshine ❷ radius ❸ shelf ▷ les rayons d'une bibliothèque the shelves of a bookcase ❹ department ▷ le rayon hi-fi vidéo the hi-fi and video department; **les rayons X** X-rays

rayure nf stripe

ré nm ❶ D ❷ re

réaction nf reaction

réagir vb [38] to react

réalisateur nm director (of film)

réaliser vb [28] ❶ to carry out ▷ Ils ont réalisé leur projet. They carried out their plan. ❷ to fulfil ▷ Il a réalisé son rêve. He has fulfilled his dream. ❸ to realize ❹ to make ▷ réaliser un film to make a film; **se réaliser** to come true

réaliste adj realistic

réalité nf reality; **en réalité** in fact; **dans la réalité** in reality; **réalité augmentée** augmented reality

rebelle nm rebel

rebondir vb [38] to bounce

rebord nm edge; **le rebord de la fenêtre** the window ledge

recaler vb [28] (informal) **J'ai été recalé en maths.** I failed maths.

récemment adv recently

récent, e adj recent

récepteur nm receiver

réception nf reception desk

réceptionniste nmf receptionist

recette nf recipe

recevoir vb [67] ❶ to receive ▷ J'ai reçu une lettre. I received a letter. ❷ to see ▷ Il a déjà reçu trois clients. He has already seen three clients. ❸ to have round ▷ Je reçois des amis à dîner. I'm having friends round for dinner.; **être reçu à un examen** to pass an exam

rechange nm **de rechange** (battery, bulb) spare

recharge nf refill

réchaud nm stove

réchauffer vb [28] ❶ to reheat ▷ Je vais réchauffer les légumes. I'll reheat the vegetables. ❷ to warm up ▷ Un bon café va te réchauffer. A nice cup of coffee will warm you up.; **se réchauffer** to warm oneself

recherche nf research; **être à la recherche de quelque chose** to be looking for something; **les recherches** search

recherché, e adj much sought-after

rechercher vb [28] to look for ▷ La police recherche l'assassin. The police are looking for the killer.

rechute nf relapse

a
b
c
d
e
f
g
h
i
j
k
l
m
n
o
p
q
r
s
t
u
v
w
x
y
z

récipient nm container

récit nm story

réciter vb [28] to recite

réclamation nf complaint; **les réclamations** the complaints department

réclame nf advert; **en réclame** on special offer

réclamer vb [28] ❶ to demand ▷ Nous réclamons la semaine de trente heures. We demand a 30-hour week. ❷ to complain ▷ Elles sont toujours en train de réclamer. They're always complaining about something.

reçois vb see **recevoir**

récolte nf harvest

récolter vb [28] ❶ to harvest ❷ to collect ▷ Ils ont récolté deux cents euros. They collected 200 euros. ❸ to get ▷ Il a récolté une amende. (informal) He got a fine.

recommandé nm **en recommandé** by registered mail

recommander vb [28] to recommend

recommencer vb [12] ❶ to start again ▷ Il a recommencé à pleuvoir. It's started raining again. ❷ to do again ▷ S'il n'est pas puni, il va recommencer. If he's not punished he'll do it again.

récompense nf reward

récompenser vb [28] to reward

réconcilier vb [19] **se réconcilier avec quelqu'un** to make it up with somebody ▷ Il s'est réconcilié avec sa sœur. He has made it up with his sister.

reconnaissant, e adj grateful

reconnaître vb [14] ❶ to recognize ▷ Je ne l'ai pas reconnu. I didn't recognize him. ❷ to admit ▷ Je reconnais que j'ai eu tort. I admit I was wrong.

reconstruire vb [23] to rebuild

record nm record

recouvrir vb [55] to cover ▷ La neige recouvre le sol. The ground is covered in snow.

récréation nf break; **la cour de récréation** the playground (of school)

rectangle nm rectangle

rectangulaire adj rectangular

rectifier vb [19] to correct

reçu nm receipt

▶ vb see **recevoir**; **J'ai reçu un colis ce matin.** I received a parcel this morning.; **être reçu à un examen** to pass an exam

reculer vb [28] ❶ to step back ▷ Il a reculé pour la laisser entrer. He stepped back to let her in. ❷ to reverse ▷ J'ai reculé pour laisser passer le camion. I reversed to let the lorry past. ❸ to postpone ▷ Ils ont reculé la date du spectacle. They postponed the show.

reculons: **à reculons** adv backwards

récupérer vb [34] ❶ to get back ▷ Je vais récupérer ma voiture au garage. I'm going to get my car back from the garage. ❷ to make up ▷ J'ai des heures à récupérer. I've got time to make up. ❸ to recover ▷ J'ai besoin de récupérer. I need to recover.

recyclage nm recycling

recycler vb [28] to recycle
rédaction nf essay
redemander vb [28] ❶ to ask again for ▷ Je vais lui redemander son adresse. I'll ask him for his address again. ❷ to ask for more ▷ Je vais redemander des carottes. I'm going to ask for more carrots.
redescendre vb [24] ❶ to go back down ▷ Il est redescendu au premier étage. He went back down to the first floor. ▷ Elle a redescendu l'escalier. She went back down the stairs.
rédiger vb [45] (an essay) to write
redoubler vb [28] to repeat a year ▷ Il a raté son examen et doit redoubler. He's failed his exam and will have to repeat the year.
réduction nf ❶ reduction ❷ discount
réduire vb [23] to cut ▷ Ils ont réduit leurs prix. They've cut their prices.
réel (f **réelle**) adj real
réellement adv really
refaire vb [36] ❶ to do again ▷ Je dois refaire ce rapport. I've got to do this report again. ❷ to take up again ▷ Je voudrais refaire de la gym. I'd like to take up gymnastics again.
réfectoire nm refectory
référence nf reference; **faire référence à quelque chose** to refer to something; **Ce n'est pas une référence!** That's no recommendation!
réfléchi, e adj (verb) reflexive; **C'est tout réfléchi.** My mind's made up.

réfléchir vb [38] to think ▷ Il est en train de réfléchir. He's thinking.; **réfléchir à quelque chose** to think about something
reflet nm reflection
refléter vb [34] to reflect
réflexe nm reflex
réflexion nf ❶ thought ❷ remark; **réflexion faite** on reflection
refrain nm chorus (of song)
réfrigérateur nm refrigerator
refroidir vb [38] to cool ▷ Laissez le gâteau refroidir. Leave the cake to cool.; **se refroidir** to get colder ▷ Le temps se refroidit. It's getting colder.
se **réfugier** vb [19] to take shelter
refus nm refusal; **Ce n'est pas de refus.** I wouldn't say no.
refuser vb [28] to refuse ▷ Il a refusé de payer sa part. He refused to pay his share.; **Je refuse qu'on me parle ainsi!** I won't let anybody talk to me like that!
se **régaler** vb [28] **Merci beaucoup: je me suis régalé!** Thank you very much: it was absolutely delicious!
regard nm look; **Tous les regards se sont tournés vers lui.** All eyes turned towards him.
regarder vb [28] ❶ to look at ▷ Il regardait ses photos de vacances. He was looking at his holiday photos. ❷ to watch ▷ Je regarde la télévision. I'm watching television. ❸ to concern ▷ Ça ne nous regarde pas. It doesn't concern us.; **ne pas regarder à la dépense** to spare no expense
régime nm ❶ régime (of a country)

❷ diet; **un régime de bananes** a bunch of bananas

région nf region

régional, e (mpl **régionaux**) adj regional

registre nm register

règle nf ❶ ruler ❷ rule; **être en règle** to be in order; **les règles** (menstruation) period

règlement nm rules

régler vb [34] ❶ to adjust ❷ to tune ▷ J'ai réglé ma radio sur 476 FM. I tuned my radio to 476 FM. ❸ to set ▷ J'ai réglé le thermostat à vingt degrés. I've set the thermostat to 20 degrees. ❹ to solve ▷ Le problème est réglé. The problem's solved. ❺ to settle ▷ Elle a réglé sa facture. She's settled her bill.

réglisse nf liquorice

règne nm reign

régner vb [34] to reign

regret nm regret; **à regret** reluctantly

regretter vb [28] ❶ to regret; **Je regrette.** I'm sorry. ▷ Je regrette, je ne peux pas vous aider. I'm sorry, I can't help you. ❷ to miss ▷ Je regrette mon ancien travail. I miss my old job.

regrouper vb [28] to group together; **se regrouper** to gather together

régulier (f **régulière**) adj ❶ regular ❷ steady ▷ à un rythme régulier at a steady rate ❸ scheduled ▷ des vols réguliers pour Marseille scheduled flights to Marseilles

régulièrement adv regularly

rein nm kidney; **les reins** (of body) back

reine nf queen

rejoindre vb [42] to go back to ▷ J'ai rejoint mes amis. I went back to my friends.; **Je te rejoins au café.** I'll see you at the café.; **se rejoindre** to meet up ▷ Elles se sont rejointes une heure après. They met up an hour later.

relâcher vb [28] (prisoner, animal) to release; **se relâcher** to get slack ▷ Il se relâche dans son travail. He is slacking in his work.

relais nm relay race; **prendre le relais** to take over

relation nf relationship; **les relations franco-britanniques** Anglo-French relations

se **relaxer** vb [28] to relax

se **relayer** vb [59] **se relayer pour faire quelque chose** to take it in turns to do something

relevé nm **un relevé de compte** a bank statement

relever vb [43] ❶ to collect ▷ Je relève les copies dans cinq minutes. I'll collect the papers in five minutes. ❷ to react to ▷ Je n'ai pas relevé sa réflexion. I didn't react to his remark.; **relever la tête** to look up; **se relever** to get up ▷ Il est tombé mais s'est relevé aussitôt. He fell, but got up immediately.

religieuse nf ❶ nun ❷ choux cream bun

religieux (f **religieuse**) adj religious

religion nf religion

relire vb [44] ❶ to read over ❷ to read again

remarquable adj remarkable

remarque nf ❶ remark ❷ comment

remarquer vb [28] to notice ▷ J'ai remarqué qu'elle avait l'air triste. I noticed she was looking sad.; **faire remarquer quelque chose à quelqu'un** to point something out to somebody ▷ Je lui ai fait remarquer que c'était un peu cher. I pointed out to him that it was rather expensive.; **Remarquez, il n'est pas si bête que ça.** Mind you, he's not as stupid as all that.; **se remarquer** to be noticeable; **se faire remarquer** to call attention to oneself

remboursement nm refund

rembourser vb [28] to pay back ▷ Il m'a remboursé l'argent qu'il me devait. He paid me back the money he owed me.; **'satisfait ou remboursé'** 'satisfaction or your money back'

remède nm ❶ medicine ❷ cure

remercier vb [19] to thank ▷ Je te remercie pour ton cadeau. Thank you for your present.; **remercier quelqu'un d'avoir fait quelque chose** to thank somebody for doing something ▷ Je vous remercie de m'avoir invité. Thank you for inviting me.

remettre vb [47] ❶ to put back on ▷ Il a remis son pull. He put his sweater back on. ❷ to put back ▷ Il a remis sa veste dans l'armoire. He put

his jacket back in the wardrobe. ❸ to put off ▷ J'ai dû remettre mon rendez-vous. I've had to put my appointment off.; **se remettre** (from illness) to recover

remonte-pente nm ski-lift

remonter vb [48] ❶ to go back up ▷ Il est remonté au premier étage. He has gone back up to the first floor. ❷ to go up ▷ Ils ont remonté la pente. They went up the hill. ❸ to buck up ▷ Cette nouvelle m'a un peu remontée. The news bucked me up a bit.; **remonter le moral à quelqu'un** to cheer somebody up

remords nm avoir des remords to feel remorse

remorque nf (of car) trailer

remparts nmpl city walls

remplaçant nm supply teacher

remplacer vb [12] to replace ▷ Il remplace le prof de maths. He's replacing the maths teacher.; **remplacer par** to replace with

rempli, e adj busy; **rempli de** full of

remplir vb [38] ❶ to fill up ▷ Elle a rempli son verre de vin. She filled her glass up with wine. ❷ to fill in ▷ Tu as rempli ton formulaire? Have you filled in your form?; **se remplir** to fill up

remuer vb [28] ❶ to move ▷ Elle a remué le bras. She moved her arm. ❷ to stir ▷ Remuez la sauce pendant deux minutes. Stir the sauce for two minutes.; **se remuer** (informal) to go to a lot of trouble ▷ Ils se sont beaucoup remués pour organiser cette soirée. They went to a lot of trouble organizing this party.

a
b
c
d
e
f
g
h
i
j
k
l
m
n
o
p
q
r
s
t
u
v
w
x
y
z

renard nm fox

rencontre nf **faire la rencontre de quelqu'un** to meet somebody; **aller à la rencontre de quelqu'un** to go and meet somebody

rencontrer vb [28] to meet; **se rencontrer** to meet ▷ *Ils se sont rencontrés il y a deux ans.* They met two years ago.

rendez-vous nm ❶ appointment ▷ *J'ai rendez-vous chez le coiffeur.* I've got an appointment at the hairdresser's. ▷ *prendre rendez-vous avec quelqu'un* to make an appointment with somebody ❷ date ▷ *Tu sors ce soir? — Oui, j'ai un rendez-vous.* Are you going out tonight? — Yes, I've got a date.; **donner rendez-vous à quelqu'un** to arrange to meet somebody

rendre vb [7] ❶ to give back ▷ *J'ai rendu ses CD à Christine.* I've given Christine her CDs back. ❷ to take back ▷ *J'ai rendu mes livres à la bibliothèque.* I've taken my books back to the library.; **rendre quelqu'un célèbre** to make somebody famous; **se rendre** to give oneself up ▷ *Le meurtrier s'est rendu à la police.* The murderer gave himself up to the police.; **se rendre compte de quelque chose** to realize something

renfermé nm **sentir le renfermé** to smell stuffy

renifler vb [28] to sniff

renne nm reindeer

renommé, e adj renowned

renoncer vb [12] **renoncer à** to give up ▷ *Ils ont renoncé à leur projet.* They've given up their plan.; **renoncer à faire quelque chose** to give up the idea of doing something

renouvelable adj renewable

renouveler vb [4] (passport, contract) to renew; **se renouveler** to happen again ▷ *J'espère que ça ne se renouvellera pas.* I hope that won't happen again.

renseignement nm piece of information; **les renseignements** (1) information ▷ *Il m'a donné des renseignements.* He gave me some information. (2) information desk (3) directory inquiries

renseigner vb [28] **renseigner quelqu'un sur quelque chose** to give somebody information about something; **Est-ce que je peux vous renseigner?** Can I help you?; **se renseigner** to find out

rentable adj profitable

rentrée nf **la rentrée (des classes)** the start of the new school year

rentrer vb [68] ❶ to come in ▷ *Rentre, tu vas prendre froid.* Come in, you'll catch cold. ❷ to go in ▷ *Elle est rentrée dans le magasin.* She went into the shop. ❸ to get home ▷ *Je suis rentré à sept heures hier soir.* I got home at 7 o'clock last night. ❹ to put away ▷ *Tu as rentré la voiture?* Have you put the car away?; **rentrer dans** to crash into ▷ *Sa voiture est rentrée dans un arbre.* He crashed into a tree.; **rentrer dans l'ordre** to get back to normal

renverse nf tomber à la renverse to fall backwards

renverser vb [**28**] **①** to knock over ▷ J'ai renversé mon verre. I knocked my glass over. **②** to knock down ▷ Elle a été renversée par une voiture. She was knocked down by a car. **③** to spill ▷ Il a renversé de l'eau partout. He has spilt water everywhere.; **se renverser** (glass, vase) to fall over

renvoyer vb [**33**] **①** to send back ▷ Je t'ai renvoyé ton courrier. I've sent your mail back to you. **②** to dismiss ▷ On a renvoyé deux employés. Two employees have been dismissed.

répandu, e adj common; du vin répandu sur la table wine spilt on the table; des papiers répandus sur le sol papers scattered over the floor

réparateur nm repairman

réparation nf repair

réparer vb [**28**] to repair

repartir vb [**57**] to set off again ▷ Il était là tout à l'heure, mais il est reparti. He was here a moment ago, but he's gone again.; **repartir à zéro** to start again from scratch

repas nm meal; **le repas de midi** lunch; **le repas du soir** dinner

repassage nm ironing

repasser vb [**28**] **①** to come back ▷ Je repasserai demain. I'll come back tomorrow. **②** to go back ▷ Je dois repasser au magasin. I've got to go back to the shop. **③** to iron ▷ J'ai repassé ma chemise. I've ironed my shirt. **④** to resit ▷ Elle doit repasser son examen. She's got to resit her exam.

repérer vb [**34**] to spot ▷ J'ai repéré deux fautes. I spotted two mistakes.; **se repérer** to find one's way around ▷ J'ai du mal à me repérer de nuit. I have difficulty finding my way around when it's dark.

répertoire nm directory

répéter vb [**34**] **①** to repeat ▷ Elle répète toujours la même chose. She keeps repeating the same thing. **②** to rehearse ▷ Les acteurs répètent une scène. The actors are rehearsing a scene.; **se répéter** to happen again ▷ J'espère que cela ne se répétera pas! I hope this won't happen again!

répétition nf **①** repetition; **des grèves à répétition** repeated strikes **②** rehearsal; **la répétition générale** the dress rehearsal

répondeur nm answering machine

répondre vb [**69**] to answer ▷ répondre à quelqu'un to answer somebody

réponse nf answer

reportage nm **①** report **②** story

reporter nm reporter

repos nm rest

reposer vb [**28**] **①** to put back down ▷ Elle a reposé son verre sur la table. She put her glass back down on the table.; **se reposer** to have a rest ▷ Tu pourras te reposer demain. You'll be able to have a rest tomorrow.

repousser vb [**28**] **①** to grow again ▷ Ses cheveux ont repoussé. Her hair

a
b
c
d
e
f
g
h
i
j
k
l
m
n
o
p
q
r
s
t
u
v
w
x
y
z

has grown again. ❷ **to postpone**
▷ *Le voyage est repoussé.* The trip's
been postponed.

reprendre *vb* [**65**] ❶ to take back
▷ *Il a repris son livre.* He's taken his
book back. ❷ to go back to ▷ *Elle a
repris le travail.* She went back to
work. ❸ to start again ▷ *La réunion
reprendra à deux heures.* The meeting
will start again at 2 o'clock.;
reprendre du pain to take more
bread; **reprendre la route** to set
off again; **reprendre son souffle**
to get one's breath back

représentant *nm* rep

représentation *nf* performance

représenter *vb* [**28**] to show ▷ *Le
tableau représente un enfant et un
chat.* The picture shows a child
with a cat.; **se représenter** to arise
again ▷ *Cette occasion ne se
représentera pas.* This opportunity
won't arise again.

reproche *nm* **faire des reproches à
quelqu'un** to reproach somebody

reprocher *vb* [**28**] **reprocher
quelque chose à quelqu'un** to
reproach somebody for
something; **Qu'est-ce que tu lui
reproches?** What have you got
against him?

reproduction *nf* reproduction

reproduire *vb* [**23**] to reproduce;
se reproduire to happen again ▷ *Je
te promets que ça ne se reproduira pas!*
I promise it won't happen again!

républicain, e *adj* republican

république *nf* republic

répugnant, e *adj* repulsive

réputation *nf* reputation

requin *nm* shark

RER *nm* Greater Paris high-speed
train service

réseau (*pl* **réseaux**) *nm* network

réservation *nf* reservation

réserve *nf* stock; **mettre quelque
chose en réserve** to put
something aside

réservé, e *adj* reserved

réserver *vb* [**28**] ❶ to reserve ▷ *Je
voudrais réserver une table.* I'd like to
reserve a table. ❷ to book ▷ *Nous
avons réservé une chambre.* We've
booked a room. ❸ to save ▷ *Je t'ai
réservé une part de gâteau.* I've saved
you a piece of cake.

réservoir *nm* petrol tank

résidence *nf* block of flats; **une
résidence secondaire** a second
home

résistant, e *adj* ❶ hard-wearing
❷ robust

résister *vb* [**28**] to resist

résolu, e *adj* **Le problème est
résolu.** The problem's solved.

résoudre *vb* [**70**] to solve

respect *nm* respect

respecter *vb* [**28**] to respect

respiration *nf* breathing

respirer *vb* [**28**] to breathe

responsabilité *nf* responsibility

responsable *adj* responsible ▷ *être
responsable de quelque chose* to be
responsible for something
▶ *nmf* ❶ person in charge ❷ person
responsible

ressembler *vb* [**28**] **ressembler à
(1)** to look like ▷ *Elle ne ressemble pas*

à sa sœur. She doesn't look like her sister. **(2)** to be like ▷ *Ça ressemble à un conte de fées.* It's like a fairy tale.; **se ressembler (1)** to look alike ▷ *Les deux frères ne se ressemblent pas.* The two brothers don't look alike. **(2)** to be alike ▷ *Ces deux pays ne se ressemblent pas.* These two countries aren't alike.

ressort *nm* (metal) spring

ressortir *vb* [**79**] to go out again

restaurant *nm* restaurant

reste *nm* rest; **un reste de poulet** some left-over chicken; **les restes** the left-overs

rester *vb* [**71**] ❶ to stay ▷ *Je reste à la maison ce week-end.* I'm staying at home this weekend. ❷ to be left ▷ *Il reste du pain.* There's some bread left.; **Il ne me reste plus qu'à ...** I've just got to ... ▷ *Il ne me reste plus qu'à ranger mes affaires.* I've just got to put my things away.; **Restons-en là.** Let's leave it at that.

résultat *nm* result

résumé *nm* summary

résumer *vb* [**28**] to summarize

▌ Be careful! **résumer** does not mean **to resume**.

se rétablir *vb* [**38**] to get well

retard *nm* delay; **avoir du retard** to be late; **être en retard de deux heures** to be two hours late; **prendre du retard** to be delayed

retarder *vb* [**28**] ❶ to be slow ▷ *Ma montre retarde.* My watch is slow. ❷ to put back ▷ *Je dois retarder la pendule d'une heure.* I've got to put the clock back an hour.; **être retardé** to be delayed

retenir *vb* [**83**] ❶ to remember ▷ *Tu as retenu leur adresse?* Do you remember their address? ❷ to book ▷ *J'ai retenu une chambre à l'hôtel.* I've booked a room at the hotel.; **retenir son souffle** to hold one's breath

retenu, e *adj* ❶ reserved ▷ *Cette place est retenue.* This seat is reserved. ❷ held up

retenue *nf* detention

retirer *vb* [**28**] ❶ to withdraw ▷ *Elle a retiré de l'argent.* She withdrew some money. ❷ to take off ▷ *Il a retiré son pull.* He took off his sweater.

retour *nm* return; **être de retour** to be back

retourner *vb* [**72**] ❶ to go back ▷ *Est-ce que tu es retourné à Londres?* Have you been back to London? ❷ to turn over ▷ *Elle a retourné la crêpe.* She turned the pancake over.; **se retourner (1)** to turn round ▷ *Janet s'est retournée.* Janet turned round. **(2)** to turn over ▷ *La voiture s'est retournée.* The car turned over.

retraite *nf* **être à la retraite** to be retired; **prendre sa retraite** to retire

retraité, e *adj* retired

retraité *nm* pensioner

retraitée *nf* pensioner

rétrécir *vb* [**38**] to shrink ▷ *Son pull a rétréci au lavage.* Her sweater shrank in the wash.; **se rétrécir** to get narrower ▷ *La rue se rétrécit.* The street gets narrower.

retrouver *vb* [28] ❶ to find ▷ *J'ai retrouvé mon portefeuille.* I've found my wallet. ❷ to meet up with ▷ *Je te retrouve au café à trois heures.* I'll meet you at the café at 3 o'clock.; **se retrouver (1)** to meet up ▷ *Ils se sont retrouvés devant le cinéma.* They met up in front of the cinema. **(2)** to find one's way around ▷ *Je n'arrive pas à me retrouver.* I can't find my way around.

rétroviseur *nm* rear-view mirror

réunion *nf* meeting

se **réunir** *vb* [38] to meet ▷ *Ils se sont réunis à cinq heures.* They met at 5 o'clock.

réussi, e *adj* successful; **être réussi** to be a success

réussir *vb* [38] to be successful ▷ *Tous ses enfants ont très bien réussi.* All her children are very successful.; **réussir à faire quelque chose** to succeed in doing something; **réussir à un examen** to pass an exam

réussite *nf* success

revanche *nf* return match; **prendre sa revanche** to get one's own back; **en revanche** on the other hand

rêve *nm* dream; **de rêve** fantastic

réveil *nm* alarm clock; **mettre le réveil à huit heures** to set the alarm for eight o'clock

réveille-matin (*pl* **réveille-matin**) *nm* alarm clock

réveiller *vb* [28] to wake up

▷ *réveiller quelqu'un* to wake somebody up; **se réveiller** to wake up

réveillon *nm* **le réveillon du Premier de l'an** New Year's Eve celebrations; **le réveillon de Noël** Christmas Eve celebrations

réveillonner *vb* [28] ❶ to celebrate New Year's Eve ❷ to celebrate Christmas Eve

revenir *vb* [73] to come back ▷ *Reviens vite!* Come back soon!; **Ça revient au même.** It comes to the same thing.; **Ça revient cher.** It costs a lot.; **Je n'en reviens pas!** I can't get over it!; **revenir sur ses pas** to retrace one's steps

revenu *nm* income

rêver *vb* [28] to dream; **rêver de quelque chose** to dream of something

réverbère *nm* street lamp

revers *nm* ❶ backhand ❷ (*of jacket*) lapel; **le revers de la médaille** the other side of the coin

revient *vb see* **revenir**

réviser *vb* [28] ❶ to revise ▷ *Je dois réviser mon anglais.* I've got to revise my English. ❷ to service ▷ *Je dois faire réviser ma voiture.* I must get my car serviced.

révision *nf* revision

revoir *vb* [92] ❶ to see again ▷ *J'ai revu Sophie hier soir.* I saw Sophie again last night. ❷ to revise ▷ *Il est en train de revoir sa géographie.* He's revising his geography.; **au revoir** goodbye

révolution *nf* revolution

revolver *nm* revolver
revue *nf* magazine
rez-de-chaussée *nm* ground floor
Rhin *nm* Rhine
rhinocéros *nm* rhinoceros
Rhône *nm* Rhone
rhubarbe *nf* rhubarb
rhum *nm* rum
rhume *nm* cold; **un rhume de cerveau** a head cold; **le rhume des foins** hay fever
ri *vb see* **rire**; **Nous avons bien ri.** We had a good laugh.
riche *adj* ❶ well-off ❷ rich
rideau (*pl* **rideaux**) *nm* curtain
ridicule *adj* ridiculous
rien *pron* ❶ nothing ▷ *Qu'est-ce que tu as acheté? — Rien.* What have you bought? — Nothing. ▷ *Ça n'a rien à voir.* It has nothing to do with it.; **rien d'intéressant** nothing interesting; **rien d'autre** nothing else; **rien du tout** nothing at all ❷ anything ▷ *Il n'a rien dit.* He didn't say anything.; **rien que (1)** just ▷ *rien que pour lui faire plaisir* just to please him ▷ *Rien que la voiture coûte un million.* The car alone costs a million. **(2)** nothing but ▷ *rien que la vérité* nothing but the truth; **De rien!** Not at all! ▷ *Merci beaucoup! — De rien!* Thank you very much! — Not at all!
▶ *nm* **pour un rien** at the slightest thing ▷ *Il se met en colère pour un rien.* He loses his temper over the slightest thing.; **en un rien de temps** in no time at all
rigoler *vb* [28] (informal) ❶ to laugh

▷ *Elle a rigolé en le voyant tomber.* She laughed when she saw him fall.
❷ to have fun ▷ *On a bien rigolé hier soir.* We had good fun last night.
❸ to be joking ▷ *Ne te fâche pas, je rigolais.* Don't get upset, I was only joking.; **pour rigoler** for a laugh
rigolo (*f* **rigolote**) *adj* (informal) funny
rincer *vb* [12] to rinse
rire *vb* [74] to laugh ▷ *Nous avons bien ri.* We had a good laugh.; **pour rire** for a laugh
▶ *nm* laughter
risque *nm* ❶ risk ❷ danger
risqué, e *adj* risky
risquer *vb* [28] to risk; **Ça ne risque rien.** It's quite safe.; **Il risque de se tuer.** He could get himself killed.; **C'est ce qui risque de se passer.** That's what might well happen.
rivage *nm* shore
rivière *nf* river
riz *nm* rice
RN *nf* (= route nationale) A road
robe *nf* dress; **une robe de soirée** an evening dress; **une robe de mariée** a wedding dress; **une robe de chambre** a dressing gown
robinet *nm* tap
robot *nm* robot
roche *nf* (stone) rock
rocher *nm* rock
rock *nm* (music) rock
rôder *vb* [28] to loiter ▷ *Il y a un homme louche qui rôde autour de l'école.* There's a suspicious man loitering around the school.

rognons *nmpl* (in cooking) kidneys
roi *nm* king; **le jour des Rois** Twelfth Night
rôle *nm* role
rollers *nmpl* Rollerblades®
romain, e *adj* Roman
roman *nm* novel; **un roman policier** a detective story; **un roman d'espionnage** a spy story
romancier *nm* novelist
romantique *adj* romantic
rompre *vb* [75] ❶ to split up ▷ *Paul et Justine ont rompu.* Paul and Justine have split up. ❷ to break off ▷ *Ils ont rompu leurs fiançailles.* They've broken off their engagement.
ronces *nfpl* brambles
ronchonner *vb* [28] (informal) to grouse
rond, e *adj* ❶ round ▷ *La Terre est ronde.* The earth is round.; **ouvrir des yeux ronds** to stare in amazement ❷ chubby ▷ *Il a les joues rondes.* He has chubby cheeks. ❸ drunk
▶ *nm* circle; **en rond** in a circle; **tourner en rond** to go round in circles; **Je n'ai plus un rond.** (informal) I haven't a penny left.
rondelle *nf* slice
rond-point (*pl* ronds-points) *nm* roundabout
ronfler *vb* [28] to snore
rosbif *nm* roast beef
rose *nf* rose
▶ *adj* pink
rosé *nm* rosé (wine)
rosier *nm* rosebush

rôti *nm* roast meat; **un rôti de bœuf** a joint of beef
rôtir *vb* [38] to roast ▷ *faire rôtir quelque chose* to roast something
roue *nf* wheel ▷ *une roue de secours* a spare wheel
rouge *adj* red
▶ *nm* ❶ red ▷ *Le rouge est ma couleur préférée.* Red is my favourite colour. ❷ red wine ▷ *un verre de rouge* a glass of red wine; **passer au rouge (1)** to change to red ▷ *Le feu est passé au rouge.* The light changed to red. **(2)** to go through a red light ▷ *Jean-Pierre est passé au rouge.* Jean-Pierre went through a red light.; **un rouge à lèvres** a lipstick
Word for word, this means 'red for lips'.
rougeole *nf* measles
rougir *vb* [38] ❶ to blush ▷ *Il a rougi en me voyant.* He blushed when he saw me. ❷ to flush ▷ *Il a rougi de colère.* He flushed with anger.
rouille *nf* rust
rouillé, e *adj* rusty
rouiller *vb* [28] to go rusty
roulant, e *adj* **un fauteuil roulant** a wheelchair; **une table roulante** a trolley
rouleau (*pl* rouleaux) *nm* roll; **un rouleau à pâtisserie** a rolling pin
rouler *vb* [28] ❶ to go ▷ *Le train roulait à 250 km/h.* The train was going at 250 km an hour. ❷ to drive ▷ *Il a roulé sans s'arrêter.* He drove without stopping. ❸ to roll ▷ *Gilles a roulé une cigarette.* Gilles rolled a cigarette. ❹ to roll up ▷ *Il a roulé le*

tapis. He rolled the carpet up. ❺ to
con ▷ *Ils se sont fait rouler.* (informal)
They were conned.; **Alors, ça
roule?** (informal) How's it going?

Roumanie *nf* Romania

rouquin *nm* (informal) redhead

rousse *adj f see* roux
  ▶ *nf* redhead

route *nf* ❶ road; **une route
nationale** an A road ❷ way ▷ *Je ne
connais pas la route.* I don't know
the way.; **Il y a trois heures de
route.** It's a 3-hour journey.; **en
route** on the way; **mettre en
route** to start up; **se mettre en
route** to set off

routier *nm* ❶ lorry driver
  ❷ transport café

routine *nf* routine

roux (*f* **rousse**) *adj* ❶ red
  ❷ red-haired
  ▶ *nm/f* redhead

royal, e (*mpl* **royaux**) *adj* royal

royaume *nm* kingdom; **le
Royaume-Uni** the United
Kingdom

ruban *nm* ribbon; **le ruban adhésif**
adhesive tape

rubéole *nf* German measles

ruche *nf* hive

rudement *adv* (informal) terribly

rue *nf* street

ruelle *nf* alley

rugby *nm* rugby

rugueux (*f* **rugueuse**) *adj* rough

ruine *nf* ruin

ruiner *vb* [28] to ruin

ruisseau (*pl* **ruisseaux**) *nm* stream

rumeur *nf* rumour

rupture *nf* break-up

ruse *nf* trickery

rusé, e *adj* cunning

russe *adj, nmf* Russian ▷ *Il parle
russe.* He speaks Russian.; **un
Russe** (*man*) a Russian; **une Russe**
(*woman*) a Russian; **les Russes** the
Russians

Russie *nf* Russia

rythme *nm* ❶ rhythm ❷ pace

S

s' *pron see* **se**

sa *adj f* ❶ his ▷ *Paul est allé voir sa grand-mère.* Paul's gone to see his grandmother. ❷ her ▷ *Elle a embrassé sa mère.* She kissed her mother.

sable *nm* sand; **des sables mouvants** quicksand

sablé *nm* shortbread biscuit

sabot *nm* ❶ clog ❷ (of horse) hoof

sac *nm* bag; **un sac de voyage** a travel bag; **un sac de couchage** a sleeping bag; **un sac à main** a handbag; **un sac à dos** a rucksack; **voyager sac au dos** to go backpacking

sachet *nm* (of sugar, coffee) sachet; **du potage en sachet** packet soup; **un sachet de thé** a tea bag

sacoche *nf* bag; **une sacoche de bicyclette** a saddlebag

sacré, e *adj* sacred

sage *adj* ❶ (well-behaved) good ❷ (sensible) wise

sagesse *nf* wisdom; **une dent de sagesse** a wisdom tooth

Sagittaire *nm* Sagittarius

saignant, e *adj* (meat) rare

saigner *vb* [28] to bleed; **saigner du nez** to have a nosebleed

sain, e *adj* healthy; **sain et sauf** safe and sound

saint, e *adj* holy; **la Sainte Vierge** the Blessed Virgin; **le vendredi saint** Good Friday; **la Saint-Sylvestre** New Year's Eve
▸ *nm* saint

sainte *nf* saint

sais *vb see* **savoir**; **Je ne sais pas.** I don't know.

saisir *vb* [38] to take hold of; **saisir l'occasion de faire quelque chose** to seize the opportunity to do something

saison *nf* season; **la saison des vendanges** harvest time

sait *vb see* **savoir**; **Il sait que ...** He knows that ...; **On ne sait jamais!** You never know!

salade *nf* ❶ lettuce ❷ salad

saladier *nm* salad bowl

salaire *nm* salary

salami *nm* salami

salarié *nm* salaried employee

salariée *nf* salaried employee

sale *adj* dirty

salé, e *adj* ❶ salty ❷ salted ❸ savoury

saler *vb* [28] to put salt in ▷ *J'ai*

oublié de saler la soupe. I forgot to put salt in the soup.

saleté *nf* dirt; **faire des saletés** to make a mess

salir *vb* [**38**] **salir quelque chose** to get something dirty; **se salir** to get oneself dirty

salle *nf* ❶ room ❷ audience ❸ *(in hospital)* ward; **la salle à manger** the dining room; **la salle de séjour** the living room; **la salle de bains** the bathroom; **la salle d'attente** the waiting room; **une salle de classe** a classroom; **la salle des professeurs** the staffroom; **une salle de concert** a concert hall; **la salle d'embarquement** the departure lounge

salon *nm* lounge; **un salon de thé** a tearoom; **un salon de coiffure** a hair salon; **un salon de beauté** a beauty salon

salopette *nf* ❶ dungarees ❷ overalls

saluer *vb* [**28**] **saluer quelqu'un** (1) to say hello to somebody ▷ *Je l'ai croisé dans la rue et il m'a salué.* I met him in the street and he said hello. (2) to say goodbye to somebody ▷ *Il nous a salués et il est parti.* He said goodbye and left.

salut *excl (informal)* hi!

salutation *nf* greeting

samedi *nm* ❶ Saturday ▷ *Aujourd'hui, nous sommes samedi.* It's Saturday today. ❷ on Saturday; **le samedi** on Saturdays; **tous les samedis** every Saturday; **samedi dernier** last Saturday; **samedi**

prochain next Saturday

SAMU *nm* ambulance service

sandale *nf* sandal

sandwich *nm* sandwich

sang *nm* blood; **en sang** covered in blood

sang-froid *nm* **garder son sang-froid** to keep calm; **perdre son sang-froid** to lose one's cool; **faire quelque chose de sang-froid** to do something in cold blood

sanglier *nm* wild boar

sanglot *nm* **éclater en sanglots** to burst into tears

sans *prep* without ▷ *Elle est venue sans son frère.* She came without her brother.; **un pull sans manches** a sleeveless sweater

sans-abri *(pl* **sans-abri***) nmf* homeless person

sans-gêne *adj* inconsiderate

santé *nf* health; **Santé!** Cheers!

saoudien *(f* **saoudienne***) adj, nm/f* Saudi Arabian; **un Saoudien** *(man)* a Saudi Arabian; **une Saoudienne** *(woman)* a Saudi Arabian

sapeur-pompier *(pl* **sapeurs-pompiers***) nm* firefighter; **les sapeurs-pompiers** the fire brigade

sapin *nm* fir tree; **un sapin de Noël** a Christmas tree

Sardaigne *nf* Sardinia

sardine *nf* sardine

satellite *nm* satellite

satisfaire *vb* [**36**] to satisfy

satisfaisant, e *adj* satisfactory

satisfait, e *adj* satisfied

sauce *nf* ❶ sauce ❷ gravy

a
b
c
d
e
f
g
h
i
j
k
l
m
n
o
p
q
r
s
t
u
v
w
x
y
z

saucisse nf sausage

saucisson nm salami

sauf prep except ▷ *Tout le monde est venu sauf lui.* Everyone came except him.; **sauf si** unless; **sauf que** except that

saumon nm salmon

saur adj m **un hareng saur** a kipper

saut nm jump; **le saut en longueur** the long jump; **le saut en hauteur** the high jump; **le saut à la perche** the pole vault; **le saut à l'élastique** bungee jumping; **un saut périlleux** a somersault

sauter vb [28] to jump ▷ *Nous avons sauté par-dessus la barrière.* We jumped over the gate.; **sauter à la corde** to skip *(with a rope)*; **faire sauter quelque chose** to blow something up

sauterelle nf grasshopper

sauvage adj ❶ wild ▷ *les animaux sauvages* wild animals; **une région sauvage** an unspoiled area ❷ shy ▷ *Il est sauvage.* He's shy.

sauvegarder vb [28] *(file on computer)* to save

sauver vb [28] to save; **se sauver** (1) to run away ▷ *Il s'est sauvé à toutes jambes.* He ran away as fast as he could. (2) *(informal)* to be off ▷ *Allez, je me sauve!* Right, I'm off.

sauvetage nm rescue

sauveur nm saviour

savais, savait vb see **savoir**; *Je ne savais pas qu'il devait venir.* I didn't know he was going to come.

savant nm scientist

savent vb see **savoir**; Ils ne savent pas ce qu'ils veulent. They don't know what they want.

saveur nf flavour

savez vb see **savoir**; Est-ce que vous savez où elle habite? Do you know where she lives?

savoir vb [76] to know ▷ *Je ne sais pas où il est allé.* I don't know where he's gone.; **Tu sais nager?** Can you swim?

savon nm soap

savonnette nf bar of soap

savons vb see **savoir**

savoureux (f **savoureuse**) adj tasty

saxo nm *(informal)* ❶ sax ❷ sax player ▶ nf *(informal)* sax player

scandale nm scandal; **faire scandale** to cause a scandal

scandaleux (f **scandaleuse**) adj outrageous

Scandinave nmf Scandinavian

scandinave adj Scandinavian

Scandinavie nf Scandinavia

scarabée nm beetle

scène nf scene ▷ *une scène d'amour* a love scene ▷ *la scène du crime* the scene of the crime ▷ *Il m'a fait une scène.* He made a scene.; **une scène de ménage** a domestic row

sceptique adj sceptical

schéma nm diagram

schématique adj l'explication schématique d'une théorie the broad outline of a theory; Cette interprétation est un peu trop schématique. This interpretation is a bit oversimplified.

scie nf saw; **une scie à métaux** a hacksaw

science *nf* science; **Elle est forte en sciences.** She is good at science.; **les sciences physiques** physics; **les sciences naturelles** biology; **les sciences économiques** economics; **les sciences po** (*informal*) politics

science-fiction *nf* science fiction

scientifique *adj* scientific
 ▶ *nmf* ❶ scientist ❷ science student

scier *vb* [**19**] to saw

scolaire *adj* school ▷ *l'année scolaire* the school year ▷ *les vacances scolaires* the school holidays

Scorpion *nm* Scorpio

Scotch® *nm* adhesive tape

scotché, e *adj* (*informal*) ❶ **Il reste des heures scotché devant la télévision.** He spends hours glued to the television. ❷ **je suis resté scotché** (*astounded*) I was flabbergasted

scrupule *nm* scruple

sculpter *vb* [**28**] to sculpt

sculpteur *nm* sculptor

sculpture *nf* sculpture

SDF *nmf* (= *sans domicile fixe*) homeless person; **les SDF** the homeless

se *pron*

> se forms part of reflexive constructions.

❶ himself ▷ *Il se regarde dans la glace.* He's looking at himself in the mirror. ❷ herself ▷ *Elle se regarde dans la glace.* She's looking at herself in the mirror. ❸ itself ▷ *Le chien s'est fait mal.* The dog hurt itself. ❹ oneself ▷ *se regarder dans une glace* to look at oneself in a mirror ❺ themselves ▷ *Ils se sont* regardés dans la glace. They looked at themselves in the mirror.

> se changes to **s'** before a vowel and most words beginning with 'h'.

▷ *Elle s'admire dans sa nouvelle robe.* She's admiring herself in her new dress. ❻ each other ▷ *Ils s'aiment.* They love each other.

séance *nf* ❶ session ❷ (*at the cinema*) showing

seau (*pl* **seaux**) *nm* bucket

sec (*f* **sèche**) *adj* ❶ dry ❷ dried

sèche-cheveux (*pl* **sèche-cheveux**) *nm* hair dryer

sèche-linge (*pl* **sèche-linge**) *nm* tumble dryer

sécher *vb* [**34**] ❶ to dry ❷ to be stumped ▷ *J'ai complètement séché à l'interrogation de maths.* (*informal*) I was completely stumped in the maths test.; **se sécher** to dry oneself ▷ *Sèche-toi avec cette serviette.* Dry yourself with this towel.

sécheresse *nf* drought

séchoir *nm* dryer

second, e *adj* second ▷ *Il est arrivé second.* He came second.

second *nm* second floor ▷ *Elle habite au second.* She lives on the second floor.

secondaire *adj* secondary; **des effets secondaires** side effects

seconde *nf* ❶ second ❷ year 11 ❸ second class

secouer *vb* [**28**] to shake ▷ *secouer la tête* to shake one's head

secourir *vb* [**16**] to rescue

secourisme *nm* first aid

secours nm help ▷ Au secours!
Help!; **les premiers secours** first
aid; **une sortie de secours** an
emergency exit; **la roue de
secours** the spare wheel

secret (f **secrète**) adj secret
▶ nm secret

secrétaire nm ❶ secretary
❷ writing desk
▶ nf secretary

secrétariat nm secretary's office

secteur nm sector

section nf (of school) department

sécu nf (informal) Social Security

sécurité nf ❶ safety; **être en
sécurité** to be safe; **la sécurité
routière** road safety; **une ceinture
de sécurité** a seatbelt ❷ security;
la sécurité sociale Social Security;
la sécurité de l'emploi job security

séduisant, e adj attractive

seigle nm rye

seigneur nm lord; **le Seigneur** the
Lord

sein nm breast; **au sein de** within

seize num sixteen ▷ Elle a seize ans.
She's sixteen.; **le seize février** the
sixteenth of February

seizième adj sixteenth

séjour nm stay ▷ J'ai fait un séjour
d'une semaine en Italie. I stayed in
Italy for a week.

sel nm salt

sélectionner vb [28] to select

self nm (informal) self-service
restaurant

selfie nm selfie

self-service nm self-service
restaurant

selle nf saddle

selon prep according to ▷ selon lui
according to him

semaine nf week; **en semaine** on
weekdays

semblable adj similar

semblant nm faire semblant de
faire quelque chose to pretend to
do something

sembler vb [28] to seem ▷ Le temps
semble s'améliorer. The weather
seems to be improving.

semelle nf ❶ sole ❷ insole

semoule nf semolina

sens nm ❶ sense ▷ avoir le sens de
l'humour to have a sense of
humour; **le bon sens** common
sense ❷ direction; **sens dessus
dessous** upside down; **un sens
interdit** a one-way street; **un sens
unique** a one-way street

sensation nf feeling

sensationnel (f **sensationnelle**)
adj sensational

sensé, e adj sensible

sensible adj ❶ sensitive ❷ visible

> Be careful! The French word
sensible does not mean
sensible.

sensiblement adv ❶ visibly
❷ approximately

sentence nf (judgement) sentence

sentier nm path

sentiment nm feeling

sentimental, e (mpl
sentimentaux) adj sentimental

sentir vb [77] ❶ to smell ▷ Ça sent
bon. That smells good. ▷ Ça sent
mauvais. It smells bad. ❷ to smell

of ▷ *Ça sent les frites ici.* It smells of chips in here. ❸ to taste ▷ *Tu sens l'ail dans le rôti?* Can you taste the garlic in the roast? ❹ to feel ▷ *Ça t'a fait mal? — Non, je n'ai rien senti.* Did it hurt? — No, I didn't feel a thing. ▷ *Je ne me sens pas bien.* I don't feel well.; **Il ne peut pas la sentir.** *(informal)* He can't stand her.

séparé, e *adj* separated

séparément *adv* separately

séparer *vb* [28] to separate; **se séparer** to separate

sept *num* seven ▷ *Elle a sept ans.* She's seven.; **le sept février** the seventh of February

septembre *nm* September; **en septembre** in September

septième *adj* seventh

sera, serai, seras, serez *vb see* **être**; **Je serai de retour à dix heures.** I'll be back at 10 o'clock.

série *nf* series

sérieusement *adv* seriously

sérieux (*f* **sérieuse**) *adj* ❶ serious ❷ responsible
  ▶ *nm* **garder son sérieux** to keep a straight face; **prendre quelque chose au sérieux** to take something seriously; **prendre quelqu'un au sérieux** to take somebody seriously; **Il manque un peu de sérieux.** He's not very responsible.

seringue *nf* syringe

séronégatif (*f* **séronégative**) *adj* HIV-negative

serons, seront *vb see* **être**

séropositif (*f* **séropositive**) *adj* HIV-positive

serpent *nm* snake

serre *nf* greenhouse; **l'effet de serre** the greenhouse effect

serré, e *adj* ❶ tight ▷ *Mon pantalon est trop serré.* My trousers are too tight. ❷ close-fought

serrer *vb* [28] *Ce pantalon me serre trop.* These trousers are too tight for me.; **serrer la main à quelqu'un** to shake hands with somebody; **se serrer** to squeeze up ▷ *Serrez-vous un peu pour que je puisse m'asseoir.* Squeeze up a bit so I can sit down.; **serrer quelqu'un dans ses bras** to hug somebody; **'Serrer à droite'** 'Keep right'

serrure *nf* lock

sers, sert *vb see* **servir**

serveur *nm* ❶ (*in café*) waiter ❷ (*computer*) server

serveuse *nf* waitress

serviable *adj* helpful

service *nm* ❶ (*in restaurant*) service ▷ *Le service est compris.* Service is included.; **être de service** to be on duty; **hors service** out of order; **faire le service** (*at table*) to serve ❷ favour ▷ *rendre service à quelqu'un* to do somebody a favour ❸ (*sport*) serve ▷ *Il a un bon service.* He's got a good serve.; **le service militaire** military service; **les services sociaux** the social services; **les services secrets** the secret service

serviette *nf* ❶ towel; **une serviette hygiénique** a sanitary towel ❷ (*napkin*) serviette ❸ briefcase

servir *vb* [78] to serve ▷ *On vous sert?*

a
b
c
d
e
f
g
h
i
j
k
l
m
n
o
p
q
r
s
t
u
v
w
x
y
z

Are you being served?; **À toi de servir.** *(tennis)* It's your serve.; **se servir** to help oneself ▷ *Servez-vous.* Help yourself.; **se servir de** to use ▷ *Tu te sers souvent de ton vélo?* Do you use your bike a lot?; **servir à quelqu'un** to be of use to somebody; **À quoi ça sert?** What's it for?; **Ça ne sert à rien.** It's no use.

ses *adj pl* **❶** his ▷ *Il est parti voir ses grands-parents.* He's gone to see his grandparents. **❷** her ▷ *Delphine a oublié ses baskets.* Delphine's forgotten her trainers. **❸** its ▷ *la ville et ses alentours* the town and its surroundings

set *nm* **❶** *(on table)* tablemat **❷** *(in tennis)* set

seuil *nm* doorstep

seul, e *adj, adv* **❶** alone **❷** by oneself; **faire quelque chose tout seul** to do something by oneself; **se sentir seul** to feel lonely; **un seul livre** one book only; **Il reste une seule nectarine.** There's only one nectarine left.; **le seul livre que ...** the only book that ...; **le seul** the only one

seulement *adv* only; **non seulement ... mais** not only ... but

sévère *adj* strict

sexe *nm* sex

sexuel *(f* **sexuelle)** *adj* sexual

shampo(o)ing *nm* shampoo; **se faire un shampo(o)ing** to wash one's hair

short *nm* shorts

si *conj, adv* **❶** if ▷ *si tu veux* if you like

▷ *Je me demande si elle va venir.* I wonder if she'll come. ▷ *si seulement* if only **❷** so ▷ *Elle est si gentille.* She's so kind. ▷ *Tout s'est passé si vite.* Everything happened so fast. **❸** yes ▷ *Tu n'es pas allé à l'école habillé comme ça? — Si.* You didn't go to school dressed like that? — Yes I did.

▶ *nm* **❶** B ▷ *en si bémol* in B flat **❷** ti ▷ *la, si, do* la, ti, do

Sicile *nf* Sicily

sida *nm* AIDS

siècle *nm* century

siège *nm* **❶** *(in vehicle)* seat **❷** head office

sien *pron m* **le sien** (1) his (2) hers

sienne *pron f* **la sienne** (1) his (2) hers

siennes *pron fpl* **les siennes** (1) his (2) hers

siens *pron mpl* **les siens** (1) his (2) hers

sieste *nf* nap

siffler *vb* **[28]** to whistle

sifflet *nm* whistle

sigle *nm* acronym

signal *(pl* **signaux)** *nm* signal

signature *nf* signature

signe *nm* sign; **faire un signe de la main** to wave; **faire signe à quelqu'un d'entrer** to beckon to somebody to come in; **les signes du zodiaque** the signs of the zodiac

signer *vb* **[28]** to sign

signet *nm* bookmark

signification *nf* meaning

signifier *vb* **[19]** to mean ▷ *Que*

signifie ce mot? What does this word mean?

silence *nm* silence; **Silence!** Be quiet!

silencieux (*f* **silencieuse**) *adj* ① silent ② quiet

silhouette *nf* figure

similaire *adj* similar

simple *nm* (*tennis*) singles
▶ *adj* simple

simplement *adv* simply

simuler *vb* [**28**] to simulate

simultané, e *adj* simultaneous

sincère *adj* sincere

sincèrement *adv* sincerely

sincérité *nf* sincerity

singe *nm* monkey

singulier *nm* singular

sinistre *adj* sinister

sinon *conj* otherwise

sinusite *nf* sinusitis

sirène *nf* mermaid; **la sirène d'alarme** the fire alarm

sirop *nm* syrup; **le sirop contre la toux** cough mixture

site *nm* setting; **un site pittoresque** a beauty spot; **un site touristique** a tourist attraction; **un site archéologique** an archaeological site; **un site Web** a website

sitôt *adv* **sitôt dit, sitôt fait** no sooner said than done; **pas de sitôt** not for a long time

situation *nf* ① situation; **la situation de famille** marital status ② job

se **situer** *vb* [**28**] to be situated
▷ *Versailles se situe à l'ouest de Paris.*

Versailles is situated to the west of Paris.; **bien situé** well situated

six *num* six ▷ *Il a six ans.* He's six.; **le six février** the sixth of February

sixième *adj* sixth ▷ *au sixième étage* on the sixth floor
▶ *nf* year 7 ▷ *Mon frère est en sixième.* My brother's in year 7.

⬤ In French secondary schools,
⬤ years are counted from the
⬤ **sixième** (youngest) to **première**
⬤ and **terminale** (oldest).

skate *nm* skateboarding; **faire du skate** to skateboard

ski *nm* ① ski ② skiing; **le ski de fond** cross-country skiing; **le ski nautique** water-skiing; **le ski de piste** downhill skiing; **le ski de randonnée** cross-country skiing

skier *vb* [**19**] to ski

skieur *nm* skier

slip *nm* pants; **un slip de bain** swimming trunks

Slovaquie *nf* Slovakia

Slovénie *nf* Slovenia

SMIC *nm* guaranteed minimum wage

smoking *nm* dinner suit

SNCF *nf* (= *Société nationale des chemins de fer français*) French railways

snob *adj* snobbish

sobre *adj* ① sober ② plain

social, e (*mpl* **sociaux**) *adj* social

socialiste *nmf* socialist

société *nf* ① society ② company

sociologie *nf* sociology

socquette *nf* ankle sock

sœur *nf* sister

soi *pron* oneself ▷ *avoir confiance en*

soi to have confidence in oneself;
rester chez soi to stay at home;
Ça va de soi. It goes without saying.

soi-disant (*f* **soi-disante**) *adv, adj* supposedly; **un soi-disant poète** a so-called poet

soie *nf* silk

soif *nf* thirst; **avoir soif** to be thirsty

soigner *vb* [**28**] (*ill person, animal*) to look after

soigneux (*f* **soigneuse**) *adj* careful

soi-même *pron* oneself ▷ *Il vaut mieux le faire soi-même.* It's better to do it oneself.

soin *nm* care; **prendre soin de quelque chose** to take care of something

soins *nmpl* treatment *sg*; **les premiers soins** first aid; **'aux bons soins de Madame Martin'** (*on letter*) 'c/o Mrs Martin'

soir *nm* evening; **à sept heures du soir** at 7 p.m.; **demain soir** tomorrow night; **hier soir** last night

soirée *nf* evening

sois *vb* see **être**; **Sois tranquille!** Don't worry!

soit *conj* **soit ..., soit ...** either ... or ... ▷ *soit lundi, soit mardi* either Monday or Tuesday

soixantaine *nf* about sixty; **Elle a la soixantaine.** She's in her sixties.

soixante *num* sixty; **soixante-dix** seventy; **soixante et onze** seventy-one; **soixante-quinze** seventy-five

soja *nm* soya; **des germes de soja** beansprouts

sol *nm* ❶ floor; **à même le sol** on the floor ❷ soil ❸ G ▷ *sol dièse* G sharp ❹ so ▷ *do, ré, mi, fa, sol ...* do, re, mi, fa, so ...

solaire *adj* solar; **la crème solaire** sun cream

soldat *nm* soldier

solde *nm* **être en solde** to be reduced; **les soldes** the sales ▷ *faire les soldes* to go round the sales

soldé, e *adj* **être soldé** to be reduced ▷ *un article soldé à dix euros* an item reduced to 10 euros

sole *nf* (*fish*) sole

soleil *nm* sun; **Il y a du soleil.** It's sunny.

solfège *nm* musical theory

solidaire *adj* **être solidaire de quelqu'un** to back somebody up

solide *adj* ❶ (*person*) strong ❷ (*object*) solid

solitaire *adj* solitary ▶ *nmf* loner

solitude *nf* loneliness

solution *nf* solution; **une solution de facilité** an easy way out

sombre *adj* dark

sommaire *nm* summary

somme *nf* sum ▶ *nm* nap

sommeil *nm* sleep; **avoir sommeil** to be sleepy

sommes *vb* see **être**; **Nous sommes en vacances.** We're on holiday.

sommet *nm* summit

somnifère *nm* sleeping pill

somptueux (*f* **somptueuse**) *adj*

sumptuous

son (*f* **sa**, *pl* **ses**) *adj* ❶ his ▷ *son père*
his father ▷ *Il a perdu son portefeuille.*
He's lost his wallet. ❷ her ▷ *son père*
her father ▷ *Elle a perdu son sac.*
She's lost her bag.
▶ *nm* ❶ sound ▷ *Le son n'est pas très
bon.* The sound's not very good.
▷ *baisser le son* to turn the sound
down ❷ bran; **le pain de son**
brown bread

sondage *nm* survey; **un sondage
d'opinion** an opinion poll

sonner *vb* [28] to ring ▷ *Le téléphone
a sonné.* The phone rang.

sonnerie *nf* ❶ (electric) bell ❷ (on
mobile phone) ringtone

sonnette *nf* bell

sono *nf* (informal) sound system

sont *vb see* **être**; **Ils sont en
vacances.** They're on holiday.

sophistiqué, e *adj* sophisticated

sorcière *nf* witch

sort *nm* ❶ spell; **un mauvais sort** a
curse ❷ fate; **tirer au sort** to draw
lots

sorte *nf* sort

sortie *nf* way out; **la sortie de
secours** the emergency exit;
**Attends-moi à la sortie de
l'école.** Meet me after school.

sortir *vb* [79] ❶ to go out ▷ *J'aime
sortir.* I like going out. ❷ to come
out ▷ *Elle sort de l'hôpital demain.*
She's coming out of hospital
tomorrow. ❸ to take out ▷ *Je vais
sortir la voiture du garage.* I'll get the
car out of the garage.; **sortir avec
quelqu'un** to be going out with

somebody ▷ *Tu sors avec lui?* Are you
going out with him?; **s'en sortir** to
manage ▷ *Ne t'en fais pas, tu t'en
sortiras.* Don't worry, you'll manage
OK.

sottise *nf* **Ne fais pas de sottises.**
Don't do anything silly.; **Ne dis pas
de sottises.** Don't talk nonsense.

sou *nm* **une machine à sous** a fruit
machine; **Je n'ai pas un sou sur
moi.** I haven't got a penny on me.;
être près de ses sous (informal) to
be tight-fisted

souci *nm* worry; **se faire du souci**
to worry

soucieux (*f* **soucieuse**) *adj* worried

soucoupe *nf* saucer; **une
soucoupe volante** a flying saucer

soudain, e *adj, adv* ❶ sudden
❷ suddenly

souffle *nm* breath; **à bout de
souffle** out of breath

soufflé *nm* soufflé

souffler *vb* [28] ❶ to blow ▷ *Le vent
soufflait fort.* The wind was blowing
hard. ❷ to blow out ▷ *Souffle les
bougies!* Blow out the candles!

souffrance *nf* suffering

souffrant, e *adj* unwell

souffrir *vb* [54] to be in pain

souhait *nm* wish ▷ *faire un souhait*
to make a wish ▷ *Tous nos souhaits
de réussite.* All our best wishes for
your success. ▷ *les souhaits de bonne
année* New Year's wishes;
Atchoum! — À tes souhaits!
Atchoo! — Bless you!

souhaiter *vb* [28] to wish

soûl, e *adj* (informal) drunk

a
b
c
d
e
f
g
h
i
j
k
l
m
n
o
p
q
r
s
t
u
v
w
x
y
z

soulager vb [**45**] to relieve
soulever vb [**43**] ❶ to lift ▷ Je n'arrive pas à soulever cette valise. I can't lift this suitcase. ❷ to raise
soulier nm shoe
souligner vb [**28**] to underline
soupçon nm suspicion; **un soupçon de** a dash of
soupçonner vb [**28**] to suspect
soupe nf soup
souper vb [**28**] to have supper
soupir nm sigh
soupirer vb [**28**] to sigh
souple adj ❶ (person) supple ❷ (system) flexible
source nf spring
sourcil nm eyebrow
sourd, e adj deaf
souriant, e adj cheerful
sourire nm smile
   ▶ vb [**74**] to smile ▷ sourire à quelqu'un to smile at somebody
souris nf mouse
sournois, e adj sly
sous prep under; **sous terre** underground; **sous la pluie** in the rain
sous-entendu, e adj implied
   ▶ nm insinuation
sous-marin, e adj underwater
   ▶ nm submarine
sous-sol nm basement
sous-titre nm subtitle
sous-titré, e adj with subtitles
soustraction nf subtraction
sous-vêtements nmpl underwear sg
soutenir vb [**83**] to support; **soutenir que** to maintain that

souterrain, e adj underground
   ▶ nm underground passage
soutien nm support
soutien-gorge (pl **soutiens-gorge**) nm bra
souvenir nm ❶ memory ❷ souvenir
se **souvenir** vb [**83**] se souvenir de quelque chose to remember something ▷ Je ne me souviens pas de son adresse. I can't remember his address.; **se souvenir que** to remember that ▷ Je me souviens qu'il neigeait. I remember it was snowing.
souvent adv often
soyez, soyons vb see **être**; **Soyons clairs!** Let's be clear about this!
SPA nf (= Société protectrice des animaux) RSPCA
spacieux (f spacieuse) adj spacious
spaghettis nmpl spaghetti sg
sparadrap nm sticking plaster
speaker nm announcer
spécial, e (mpl spéciaux) adj ❶ special; **les effets spéciaux** special effects ❷ peculiar
spécialement adv ❶ specially ❷ particularly
se **spécialiser** vb [**28**] se spécialiser dans quelque chose to specialize in something
spécialiste nmf specialist
spécialité nf speciality
spécifier vb [**19**] to specify
spectacle nm show
spectaculaire adj spectacular

spectateur nm ❶ member of the audience ❷ spectator

spéléologie nf potholing

spirituel (f **spirituelle**) adj ❶ spiritual ❷ witty

splendide adj magnificent

spontané, e adj spontaneous

sport nm sport; **les sports d'hiver** winter sports
  ▶ adj casual

sportif (f **sportive**) adj ❶ sporty
  ▷ Elle est très sportive. She's very sporty. ❷ sports ▷ un club sportif a sports club

sportif nm sportsman

sportive nf sportswoman

spot nm spotlight; **un spot publicitaire** a commercial break

square nm public gardens

squelette nm skeleton

stable adj stable; **un emploi stable** a steady job

stade nm stadium

stage nm ❶ training course ❷ work experience; **faire un stage en entreprise** to do a work placement
  ▌ Be careful! The French word **stage** does not mean **stage**.

stagiaire nmf trainee
  ▶ adj trainee ▷ un professeur stagiaire a trainee teacher

stand nm ❶ (at exhibition) stand ❷ (at fair) stall

standardiste nmf operator

station nf **une station de métro** an underground station; **une station de taxis** a taxi rank; **une station de ski** a ski resort

stationnement nm parking;

'stationnement interdit' 'no parking'

stationner vb [28] to park

station-service (pl **stations-service**) nf service station

statistique nf statistic

steak nm steak; **un steak frites** steak and chips; **un steak haché** a hamburger

sténo nf shorthand

sténodactylo nf shorthand typist

stérile adj sterile

stimulant, e adj stimulating

stimuler vb [28] to stimulate

stop nm stop sign; **faire du stop** to hitchhike

stopper vb [28] to stop

store nm ❶ (on window) blind ❷ awning

strapontin nm foldaway seat

stratégie nf strategy

stratégique adj strategic

stressant, e adj stressful

stressé, e adj stressed out

strict, e adj ❶ (person) strict ❷ (clothes) severe; **le strict minimum** the bare minimum

strophe nf stanza

studieux (f **studieuse**) adj studious

studio nm ❶ studio flat ❷ studio

stupéfait, e adj astonished

stupéfiants nmpl narcotics

stupéfier vb [19] to astonish ▷ Sa réponse m'a stupéfié. I was astonished by his answer.

stupide adj stupid

style nm style

styliste nmf designer

a b c d e f g h i j k l m n o p q r s t u v w x y z

stylo nm pen; **un stylo plume** a fountain pen; **un stylo bille** a ballpoint pen; **un stylo-feutre** a felt-tip pen

su vb see **savoir**; **Si j'avais su …** If I'd known …

subir vb [**38**] (defeat) to suffer; **subir une opération** to have an operation

subit, e adj sudden

subitement adv suddenly

subjectif (f **subjective**) adj subjective

subjonctif nm subjunctive

substituer vb [**28**] to substitute ▷ substituer un mot à un autre to substitute one word for another

subtil, e adj subtle

subvention nf subsidy

subventionner vb [**28**] to subsidize

succès nm success; **avoir du succès** to be successful

successeur nm successor

succursale nf (of company) branch

sucer vb [**12**] to suck

sucette nf lollipop

sucre nm sugar; **un sucre** a sugar lump; **du sucre en morceaux** lump sugar; **un sucre d'orge** a barley sugar; **du sucre en poudre** caster sugar; **du sucre glace** icing sugar

sucré, e adj ❶ sweet ❷ sweetened

sucreries nfpl sweet things

sucrier nm sugar bowl

sud nm south; **vers le sud** southwards; **au sud de Paris** south of Paris; **l'Amérique du Sud** South America; **le vent du sud** the south wind
▶ adj ❶ south; **le pôle Sud** the South Pole ❷ southern

sud-africain, e adj South African

sud-américain, e adj South American

sud-est nm south-east

sud-ouest nm south-west

Suède nf Sweden

suédois, e adj, n Swedish ▷ Ils parlent suédois. They speak Swedish.; **un Suédois** (man) a Swede; **une Suédoise** (woman) a Swede; **les Suédois** the Swedes

suer vb [**28**] to sweat

sueur nf sweat; **en sueur** sweating

suffire vb [**80**] to be enough ▷ Tiens, voilà dix euros. Ça te suffit? Here's 10 euros. Is that enough for you?; **Ça suffit!** That's enough!

suffisamment adv enough

suffisant, e adj ❶ sufficient ❷ smug

suffoquer vb [**28**] to suffocate

suggérer vb [**34**] to suggest

se **suicider** vb [**28**] to commit suicide

suis vb see **être**; **suivre**; **Je suis écossais.** I'm Scottish.; **Suis-moi.** Follow me.

Suisse nf Switzerland ▷ la Suisse allemande German-speaking Switzerland ▷ la Suisse romande French-speaking Switzerland

suisse adj, nmf Swiss ▷ le franc suisse the Swiss franc; **un Suisse** a Swiss man; **une Suisse** a Swiss woman

suite nf ❶ rest ❷ (to book, film)

sequel; **tout de suite**
straightaway; **de suite** in
succession; **par la suite**
subsequently

suivant, e *adj* following; **Au
suivant!** Next!

suivre *vb* [81] ❶ to follow ▷ *Il m'a
suivie jusque chez moi.* He followed
me home. ❷ to do ▷ *Je suis un cours
d'anglais à la fac.* I'm doing an
English course at college. ❸ to
keep up ▷ *Il n'arrive pas à suivre en
maths.* He can't keep up in maths.;
'à suivre' 'to be continued'; **suivre
un régime** to be on a diet

sujet *nm* subject; **au sujet de**
about; **un sujet de conversation**
a topic of conversation; **un sujet
d'examen** an examination
question; **un sujet de plaisanterie**
something to joke about

super *adj* great
▶ *nm* (petrol) super

superficiel (*f* **superficielle**) *adj*
superficial

superflu, e *adj* superfluous

supérieur, e *adj* ❶ upper ▷ *la lèvre
supérieure* the upper lip ❷ superior
▷ *qualité supérieure* superior quality;
supérieur à greater than
▶ *nm* superior

supermarché *nm* supermarket

superposé, e *adj* **des lits
superposés** bunk beds

superstitieux (*f* **superstitieuse**)
adj superstitious

suppléant *nm* supply teacher

supplément *nm* **payer un
supplément** to pay an additional

charge; **Le vin est en
supplément.** Wine is extra.; **un
supplément de travail** extra work

supplémentaire *adj* additional;
faire des heures supplémentaires
to do overtime

supplice *nm* torture

supplier *vb* [19] **supplier
quelqu'un de faire quelque chose**
to beg somebody to do something
▷ *Je t'en supplie!* I'm begging you!

supportable *adj* bearable

supporter *vb* [28] (*tolerate*) to
stand ▷ *Je ne peux pas la supporter.* I
can't stand her.

> Be careful! **supporter** does not
> mean **to support**.

supposer *vb* [28] to suppose

supprimer *vb* [28] ❶ to cut ▷ *Deux
mille emplois ont été supprimés.* Two
thousand jobs have been cut. ❷ to
cancel ▷ *Le train de Londres a été
supprimé.* The train to London has
been cancelled. ❸ to get rid of ▷ *Ils
ont supprimé les témoins gênants.*
They got rid of the awkward
witnesses.

sur *prep* ❶ on ▷ *Pose-le sur la table.*
Put it down on the table. ❷ in ▷ *une
personne sur dix* 1 person in 10 ❸ out
of ▷ *J'ai eu onze sur vingt en maths.* I
got 11 out of 20 in maths. ❹ by
▷ *quatre mètres sur deux* 4 metres by
2

sûr, e *adj* ❶ sure ▷ *Tu es sûr?* Are you
sure?; **sûr et certain** absolutely
certain ❷ reliable ❸ safe; **sûr de
soi** self-confident

sûrement *adv* certainly

a
b
c
d
e
f
g
h
i
j
k
l
m
n
o
p
q
r
s
t
u
v
w
x
y
z

sûreté *nf* mettre quelque chose
en sûreté to put something in a
safe place

surf *nm* surfing

surface *nf* surface; les grandes
surfaces the supermarkets

surfer *vb* [28] to go surfing; surfer
sur le Net to surf the Net

surgelé, e *adj* frozen

surgelés *nmpl* frozen food *sg*

surhumain, e *adj* superhuman

sur-le-champ *adv* immediately

surlendemain *nm* le
surlendemain de son arrivée two
days after he arrived; le
surlendemain dans la matinée
two days later, in the morning

se **surmener** *vb* [43] to work too
hard

surmonter *vb* [48] to overcome

surnaturel (*f* surnaturelle) *adj*
supernatural

surnom *nm* nickname

surnommer *vb* [28] to nickname

surpeuplé, e *adj* overpopulated

surprenant, e *adj* surprising

surprendre *vb* [65] to surprise;
surprendre quelqu'un en train de
faire quelque chose to catch
somebody doing something

surpris, e *adj* surprised

surprise *nf* surprise ▷ faire une
surprise à quelqu'un to give
somebody a surprise

sursauter *vb* [28] to jump ▷ J'ai
sursauté en entendant mon nom. I
jumped when I heard my name.

surtout *adv* ❶ especially
❷ crucially

surveillant *nm* (man) supervisor
● In French secondary schools, the
● teachers are not responsible for
● supervising the pupils outside
● class. This job is done by people
● called **surveillants** or **pions**.

surveiller *vb* [28] ❶ to keep an eye
on ❷ to keep a watch on ❸ to
supervise; surveiller un examen
to invigilate an exam; surveiller sa
ligne to watch one's figure

survêtement *nm* tracksuit

survie *nf* survival

survivant *nm* survivor

survivante *nf* survivor

survivre *vb* [91] to survive ▷ survivre
à un accident to survive an accident

survoler *vb* [28] to fly over

sus *adv* en sus in addition

susceptible *adj* touchy

suspect, e *adj* suspicious

suspecter *vb* [28] to suspect

suspense *nm* suspense; un film à
suspense a thriller

suture *nf* un point de suture a
stitch

svelte *adj* slender

SVP *abbr* (= s'il vous plaît) please

sweat *nm* sweatshirt

syllabe *nf* syllable

symbole *nm* symbol

symbolique *adj* symbolic

symboliser *vb* [28] to symbolize

symétrique *adj* symmetrical

sympa *adj* (informal) nice

sympathie *nf* J'ai beaucoup de
sympathie pour lui. I like him a
lot.

sympathique *adj* nice

▌Be careful! **sympathique** does
not mean **sympathetic**.

sympathiser vb [28] to get on well
▷ *Nous avons immédiatement
sympathisé avec nos voisins.* We got
on well with our neighbours
straight away.

symptôme nm symptom

synagogue nf synagogue

syndicat nm trade union; **le
syndicat d'initiative** the tourist
information office

synonyme adj synonymous
▶ nm synonym

synthétique adj synthetic

Syrie nf Syria

syrien (f **syrienne**) adj, nm/f Syrian

systématique adj systematic

système nm system

t' pron see **te**

ta adj f your ▷ *J'ai vu ta sœur hier.* I saw
your sister yesterday.

tabac nm ❶ tobacco ❷ smoking
▷ *Le tabac est mauvais pour la santé.*
Smoking is bad for you.

table nf table; **mettre la table** to
lay the table; **se mettre à table** to
sit down to eat; **À table!** Dinner's
ready!; **une table de nuit** a
bedside table; **'table des
matières'** 'contents'

tableau (pl **tableaux**) nm
painting; **le tableau d'affichage**
the notice board; **le tableau noir**
the blackboard

tablette nf **une tablette de
chocolat** a bar of chocolate

tableur nm spreadsheet

tablier nm apron

tabouret *nm* stool
tache *nf (stain)* mark; **des taches de rousseur** freckles
tâche *nf* task
tacher *vb* [28] to leave a stain
tâcher *vb* [28] **tâcher de faire quelque chose** to try to do something
tact *nm* tact
tactile *adj* **écran tactile** *(for computer)* touch-sensitive display
tactique *nf* tactics; **changer de tactique** to try something different
taie *nf* **une taie d'oreiller** a pillowcase
taille *nf* ❶ waist ❷ height ▷ *un homme de taille moyenne* a man of average height ❸ size ▷ *Avez-vous ma taille?* Have you got my size?
taille-crayon *nm* pencil sharpener
tailleur *nm* ❶ tailor ❷ *(lady's)* suit; **Il est assis en tailleur.** He's sitting cross-legged.
se taire *vb* [82] to stop talking; **Taisez-vous!** Be quiet!
talon *nm* heel
tambour *nm* drum
Tamise *nf* Thames
tampon *nm* pad; **un tampon hygiénique** a tampon
tamponneuse *adj f* **les autos tamponneuses** dodgems
tandis que *conj* while ▷ *Il a toujours de bonnes notes, tandis que les miennes sont mauvaises.* He always gets good marks, while mine are poor.
tant *adv* so much ▷ *Je l'aime tant!* I love him so much!; **tant de (1)** so much **(2)** so many; **tant que**

(1) until **(2)** while; **tant mieux** so much the better; **tant pis** never mind
tante *nf* aunt
tantôt *adv* sometimes
tapage *nm* ❶ racket ❷ fuss
taper *vb* [28] to beat down ▷ *Le soleil tape.* The sun's really beating down.; **taper quelqu'un** to hit somebody ▷ *Maman, il m'a tapé!* Mum, he hit me!; **taper sur quelque chose** to bang on something; **taper des pieds** to stamp one's feet; **taper des mains** to clap one's hands; **taper à la machine** to type
tapis *nm* carpet; **le tapis roulant (1)** *(for people)* the Travelator® **(2)** *(in factory)* the conveyor belt **(3)** *(at baggage reclaim)* the carousel; **un tapis de souris** a mouse mat
tapisser *vb* [28] to paper
tapisserie *nf* ❶ wallpaper ❷ tapestry
taquiner *vb* [28] to tease
tard *adv* late; **plus tard** later on; **au plus tard** at the latest
tardif *(f* **tardive**) *adj* late
tarif *nm* **le tarif des consommations** *(in café)* the price list; **une communication à tarif réduit** an off-peak phone call; **un billet de train à tarif réduit** a concessionary train ticket; **un billet de train à plein tarif** a full-price train ticket; **Est-ce que vous faites un tarif de groupe?** Is there a reduction for groups?

tarte *nf* tart

tartine *nf* slice of bread ▷ *une tartine de confiture* a slice of bread and jam

tartiner *vb* [28] to spread; **le fromage à tartiner** cheese spread

tas *nm* heap; **un tas de** (informal) loads of

tasse *nf* cup

taureau (*pl* **taureaux**) *nm* bull; **le Taureau** Taurus

taux *nm* rate

taxe *nf* tax; **la boutique hors taxes** the duty-free shop

taxi *nm* taxi

tchèque *adj, nmf* Czech; **la République tchèque** the Czech Republic

te *pron*

> **te** changes to **t'** before a vowel and most words beginning with 'h'.

❶ you ▷ *Je te vois.* I can see you. ▷ *Il t'a vu?* Did he see you? ❷ to you ▷ *Elle t'a parlé?* Did she speak to you? ❸ yourself ▷ *Tu vas te rendre malade.* You'll make yourself sick.

> With reflexive verbs, **te** is often not translated.

▷ *Comment tu t'appelles?* What's your name?

technicien *nm* technician

technicienne *nf* technician

technique *adj* technical

▶ *nf* technique

techno *nf* techno music

technologie *nf* technology

teint *nm* complexion

teinte *nf* (colour) shade

teinturier *nm* dry cleaner's

tel (*f* **telle**) *adj* **Il a un tel enthousiasme!** He's got such enthusiasm!; **rien de tel** nothing like; **J'ai tout laissé tel quel.** I left everything as it was.; **tel que** such as

télé *nf* telly ▷ *à la télé* on telly

télécarte *nf* phonecard

télécharger *vb* [45] ❶ (receive) to download ❷ (send) to upload

télécommande *nf* remote control

téléconférence *nf* video conference

télécopie *nf* fax

télégramme *nm* telegram

téléphérique *nm* cable car

téléphone *nm* telephone ▷ *Elle est au téléphone.* She's on the phone.

téléphoner *vb* [28] to phone ▷ *Je vais téléphoner à Claire.* I'll phone Claire.

téléréalité *nf* reality TV

télésiège *nm* chairlift

téléski *nm* ski-tow

téléspectateur *nm* (TV) viewer

téléviseur *nm* television set

télévision *nf* television ▷ *à la télévision* on television; **la télévision numérique** digital TV

telle *adj f* **Je n'ai jamais eu une telle peur.** I've never had such a fright.; **telle que** such as

tellement *adv* ❶ so ▷ *Andrew est tellement gentil.* Andrew's so nice. ❷ so much ❸ so many

telles *adj fpl* such

tels *adj mpl* such

témoignage *nm* testimony

a
b
c
d
e
f
g
h
i
j
k
l
m
n
o
p
q
r
s
t
u
v
w
x
y
z

témoigner vb [**28**] to testify
témoin nm witness
température nf temperature
tempête nf storm
temple nm ❶ (Protestant) church ❷ (Hindu, Sikh, Buddhist) temple
temporaire adj temporary
temps nm ❶ weather ▷ Quel temps fait-il? What's the weather like? ❷ time ▷ Je n'ai pas le temps. I haven't got time.; **juste à temps** just in time; **de temps en temps** from time to time; **en même temps** at the same time; **à temps** in time; **à plein temps** full time; **à temps complet** full time; **à temps partiel** part time; **dans le temps** at one time ❸ (of verb) tense
tenais, tenait vb see **tenir**
tendance nf avoir tendance à faire quelque chose to tend to do something
tendre adj tender
    ▶ vb [**88**] to stretch out ▷ Ils ont tendu une corde entre deux arbres. They stretched out a rope between two trees.; **tendre quelque chose à quelqu'un** to hold something out to somebody; **tendre la main** to hold out one's hand; **tendre le bras** to reach out; **tendre un piège à quelqu'un** to set a trap for someone
tendrement adv tenderly
tendresse nf tenderness
tendu, e adj tense
tenir vb [**83**] to hold ▷ Tu peux tenir la lampe, s'il te plaît? Can you hold the torch, please?; **Tenez votre chien**

en laisse. Keep your dog on the lead.; **tenir à quelqu'un** to be attached to somebody; **tenir à faire quelque chose** to be determined to do something ▷ Elle tient à y aller. She's determined to go.; **tenir de quelqu'un** to take after somebody ▷ Il tient de son père. He takes after his father.; **Tiens, voilà un stylo.** Here's a pen.; **Tiens, c'est Alain là-bas!** Look, that's Alain over there!; **Tiens?** Really?; **se tenir (1)** to stand ▷ Il se tenait près de la porte. He was standing by the door. **(2)** to be held ▷ La foire va se tenir place du marché. The fair will be held in the market place.; **se tenir droit (1)** to stand up straight ▷ Tiens-toi droit! Stand up straight! **(2)** to sit up straight ▷ Arrête de manger le nez dans ton assiette, tiens-toi droit. Don't slouch while you're eating, sit up straight.; **Tiens-toi bien!** Behave yourself!
tennis nm ❶ tennis; **le tennis de table** table tennis ❷ tennis court; **les tennis** trainers
tentant, e adj tempting
tentation nf temptation
tentative nf attempt
tente nf tent
tenter vb [**28**] to tempt ▷ J'ai été tenté de tout abandonner. I was tempted to give up. ▷ Ça ne me tente vraiment pas d'aller à la piscine. I don't really fancy going to the swimming pool.; **tenter de faire quelque chose** to try to do something

tenu vb see **tenir**

tenue nf clothes; **en tenue de soirée** in evening dress

terme nm **à court terme** short-term; **à long terme** long-term

terminale nf upper sixth ▷ Je suis en terminale. I'm in the upper sixth.
- In French secondary schools, years are counted from the **sixième** (youngest) to **première** and **terminale** (oldest).

terminer vb [28] to finish; **se terminer** to end ▷ Les vacances se terminent demain. The holidays end tomorrow.

terminus nm terminus

terrain nm land; **un terrain de camping** a campsite; **un terrain de football** a football pitch; **un terrain de golf** a golf course; **un terrain de jeu** a playground; **un terrain de sport** a sports ground; **un terrain vague** a piece of waste ground

terrasse nf terrace; Si on s'asseyait en terrasse? (at café) Shall we sit outside?

terre nf earth; **la Terre** the Earth; **Elle s'est assise par terre.** She sat on the floor.; **Il est tombé par terre.** He fell down.; **la terre cuite** terracotta; **la terre glaise** clay

terrible adj terrible; **pas terrible** (informal) nothing special

terrine nf pâté

territoire nm territory

terrorisé, e adj terrified

terrorisme nm terrorism

terroriste nmf terrorist

tes adj pl your ▷ J'aime bien tes baskets. I like your trainers.

test nm test

testament nm will

tester vb [28] to test

tétanos nm tetanus

têtard nm tadpole

tête nf head; **se laver la tête** to wash one's hair; **la tête la première** headfirst; **tenir tête à quelqu'un** to stand up to somebody; **faire la tête** to sulk; **en avoir par-dessus la tête** to be fed up

têtu, e adj stubborn

texte nm (written work) text

TGV nm (= train à grande vitesse) high-speed train

thé nm tea

théâtre nm theatre; **faire du théâtre** to act

théière nf teapot

thème nm ❶ subject ❷ prose (translation into the foreign language)

théorie nf theory

thermomètre nm thermometer

thon nm tuna

thune nf (informal) dosh

tibia nm ❶ shinbone ❷ shin

tic nm nervous twitch

ticket nm ticket; **le ticket de caisse** the till receipt

tiède adj ❶ (water, air) warm ❷ (food, drink) lukewarm

tien pron m **le tien** yours

tienne pron f **la tienne** yours

tiennes pron fpl **les tiennes** yours

tiens pron mpl **les tiens** yours

a b c d e f g h i j k l m n o p q r s t u v w x y z

▸ vb see **tenir**

tiers nm third; **le tiers-monde** the Third World

tige nf stem

tigre nm tiger

tilleul nm lime tea

timbre nm stamp

timbre-poste nm postage stamp

timide adj shy

timidement adv shyly

timidité nf shyness

tir nm shooting; **le tir à l'arc** archery

tirage nm **par tirage au sort** by drawing lots

tire-bouchon nm corkscrew

tirelire nf money box

tirer vb [28] ❶ to pull ▷ Elle a tiré un mouchoir de son sac. She pulled a handkerchief out of her bag. ▷ 'Tirer' 'Pull' ❷ to draw ▷ tirer les rideaux to draw the curtains ▷ tirer un trait to draw a line ▷ tirer des conclusions to draw conclusions; **tirer au sort** to draw lots ❸ to fire ▷ Il a tiré sur les policiers. He fired at the police.; **Tu t'en tires bien.** You're doing well.

tiret nm (hyphen) dash

tiroir nm drawer

tisane nf herbal tea

tisser vb [28] to weave

tissu nm material; **un sac en tissu** a cloth bag

titre nm title; **les gros titres** the headlines; **un titre de transport** a travel ticket

tituber vb [28] to stagger

TNT nf (= télévision numérique terrestre) digital television

toast nm ❶ piece of toast ❷ toast ▷ porter un toast à quelqu'un to drink a toast to somebody

toboggan nm slide

toi pron you ▷ Ça va? — Oui, et toi? How are you? — Fine, and you? ▷ J'ai faim, pas toi? I'm hungry, aren't you?; **Assieds-toi.** Sit down.; **C'est à toi de jouer.** It's your turn to play.; **Est-ce que ce stylo est à toi?** Is this pen yours?

toile nf **un pantalon de toile** cotton trousers; **un sac de toile** a canvas bag; **une toile cirée** an oilcloth; **une toile d'araignée** a cobweb

toilette nf ❶ wash ▷ faire sa toilette to have a wash ❷ outfit

toilettes nfpl toilet sg

toi-même pron yourself ▷ Tu as fait ça toi-même? Did you do it yourself?

toit nm roof; **un toit ouvrant** a sunroof

tolérant, e adj tolerant

tolérer vb [34] to tolerate

tomate nf tomato

tombe nf grave

tombeau (pl **tombeaux**) nm tomb

tombée nf **à la tombée de la nuit** at nightfall

tomber vb [84] to fall ▷ Attention, tu vas tomber! Be careful, you'll fall!; **laisser tomber (1)** to drop ▷ Elle a laissé tomber son stylo. She dropped her pen. **(2)** to give up ▷ Il a laissé tomber le piano. He gave up the piano. **(3)** to let down ▷ Il ne laisse jamais tomber ses amis. He never lets his friends down.; **tomber sur quelqu'un** to bump into somebody; **Ça tombe bien.** That's lucky.; **Il tombe de sommeil.** He's asleep on his feet.

ton (f **ta**, pl **tes**) adj your ▷ *C'est ton stylo?* Is this your pen?
▶ nm ❶ tone of voice ❷ colour

tonalité nf dialling tone

tondeuse nf lawnmower

tondre vb [69] to mow

tonique adj fortifying

tonne nf tonne

tonneau (pl **tonneaux**) nm barrel

tonnerre nm thunder

tonus nm **avoir du tonus** to be energetic

torchon nm tea towel

tordre vb [49] **se tordre la cheville** to twist one's ankle

tordu, e adj ❶ bent ❷ crazy ▷ *une histoire complètement tordue* a crazy story

torrent nm mountain stream

torse nm chest

tort nm **avoir tort** to be wrong; **donner tort à quelqu'un** to lay the blame on somebody

torticolis nm stiff neck

tortue nf tortoise

torture nf torture

torturer vb [28] to torture

tôt adv early; **au plus tôt** at the earliest; **tôt ou tard** sooner or later

total, e (mpl **totaux**) adj total
▶ nm total; **au total** in total

totalement adv totally

totalité nf **la totalité des profs** all the teachers; **la totalité du**

personnel the entire staff

touchant, e adj touching

touche nf key (keyboard, phone)

toucher vb [28] ❶ to touch ▷ *Ne touche pas à mes livres!* Don't touch my books!; **Nos deux jardins se touchent.** Our gardens are next to each other. ❷ to feel ▷ *Ce pull a l'air doux. Je peux toucher?* That sweater looks soft. Can I feel it? ❸ to hit ▷ *La balle l'a touché en pleine poitrine.* The bullet hit him right in the chest. ❹ to affect ▷ *Ces nouvelles réformes ne nous touchent pas.* The new reforms don't affect us. ❺ to receive ▷ *Il a touché une grosse somme d'argent.* He received a large sum of money.

toujours adv ❶ always ▷ *Il est toujours très gentil.* He's always very nice.; **pour toujours** forever ❷ still ▷ *Quand on est revenus, Pierre était toujours là.* When we got back Pierre was still there.

toupet nm (informal) **avoir du toupet** to have a nerve

tour nf ❶ tower ▷ *la Tour Eiffel* the Eiffel Tower ❷ tower block
▶ nm turn ▷ *C'est ton tour de jouer.* It's your turn to play.; **faire un tour** to go for a walk; **faire un tour en voiture** to go for a drive; **faire un tour à vélo** to go for a ride; **faire le tour du monde** to travel round the world; **à tour de rôle** alternately

tourbillon nm whirlpool

tourisme nm tourism

touriste nmf tourist

touristique adj tourist

a b c d e f g h i j k l m n o p q r s t u v w x y z

se **tourmenter** vb [**28**] to fret

tournant nm ❶ bend ❷ turning point

tournée nf ❶ round ▷ Le facteur commence sa tournée à sept heures du matin. The postman starts his round at 7 o'clock in the morning. ▷ Allez, qu'est-ce que vous voulez boire? C'est ma tournée. Right, what are you drinking? It's my round. ❷ tour ▷ Il est en tournée aux États-Unis. He's on tour in the United States.

tourner vb [**28**] ❶ to turn ▷ Tournez à droite au prochain feu. Turn right at the lights. ❷ to go sour ▷ Le lait a tourné. The milk's gone sour.; **mal tourner** to go wrong ▷ Ça a mal tourné. It all went wrong.; **tourner le dos à quelqu'un** to have one's back to somebody; **tourner un film** to make a film

tournesol nm sunflower

tournevis nm screwdriver

tournoi nm tournament

tourte nf pie

tous adj pl, pron pl see **tout**

Toussaint nf All Saints' Day

tousser vb [**28**] to cough

tout (f **toute**, mpl **tous**) adj, adv, pron ❶ all ▷ tout le lait all the milk ▷ toute la nuit all night ▷ tous les livres all the books ▷ toute la journée all day ▷ tout le temps all the time ▷ C'est tout. That's all.; **Il est tout seul.** He's all alone.; **pas du tout** not at all; **tout de même** all the same ❷ every ▷ tous les jours every day; **tout le monde** everybody;

tous les deux both; **tous les trois** all three ❸ everything ▷ Il a tout organisé. He organized everything. ❹ very ▷ Elle habite tout près. She lives very close.; **tout en haut** right at the top; **tout droit** straight ahead; **tout d'abord** first of all; **tout à coup** suddenly; **tout à fait** absolutely; **tout à l'heure (1)** just now **(2)** in a moment; **tout de suite** straight away; **Il a fait son travail tout en chantant.** He sang as he worked.

toutefois adv however

toutes adj fpl, pron fpl see **tout**

toux nf cough

toxicomane nmf drug addict

toxicomanie nf drug addiction

TP nm (= travaux pratiques) practical class

trac nm avoir le trac to be feeling nervous

tracasser vb [**28**] to worry ▷ La santé de mon père me tracasse. My dad's health worries me.; **se tracasser** to worry

trace nf ❶ trace ❷ mark ▷ des traces de doigts finger marks; **des traces de pas** footprints

tracer vb [**12**] to draw ▷ tracer un trait to draw a line

tracteur nm tractor

tradition nf tradition

traditionnel (f **traditionnelle**) adj traditional

traducteur nm translator

traduction nf translation

traductrice nf translator

traduire vb [**23**] to translate

trafic *nm* traffic; **le trafic de drogue** drug trafficking

trafiquant *nm* **un trafiquant de drogue** a drug trafficker

tragique *adj* tragic

trahir *vb* [**38**] to betray

trahison *nf* betrayal

train *nm* train; **un train électrique** a train set; **Il est en train de manger.** He's eating.

traîneau (*pl* **traîneaux**) *nm* sledge

traîner *vb* [**28**] ❶ to wander around ▷ *J'ai vu des jeunes qui traînaient en ville.* I saw some young people wandering around town. ❷ to hang about ▷ *Dépêche-toi, ne traîne pas!* Hurry up, don't hang about! ❸ to drag on ▷ *La réunion a traîné jusqu'à midi.* The meeting dragged on till 12 o'clock.; **traîner des pieds** to drag one's feet; **laisser traîner qch** to leave sth lying around

train-train *nm* humdrum routine

traire *vb* [**85**] to milk

trait *nm* ❶ line ▷ *Tracez un trait.* Draw a line. ❷ feature ▷ *Elle a les traits fins.* She has delicate features.; **boire quelque chose d'un trait** to drink something down in one gulp; **un trait d'union** a hyphen

traitement *nm* treatment; **le traitement de texte** word processing

traiter *vb* [**28**] to treat; **Il m'a traité d'imbécile.** He called me an idiot.; **traiter de** to be about ▷ *Cet article traite des sans-abri.* This article is about the homeless.

traiteur *nm* caterer

trajet *nm* ❶ journey ▷ *J'ai une heure de trajet pour aller au travail.* My journey to work takes an hour. ❷ route ▷ *C'est le trajet le plus court.* It's the shortest route.

tramway *nm* tram

tranchant, e *adj* (*knife*) sharp

tranche *nf* slice

tranquille *adj* quiet; **Sois tranquille, il ne va rien lui arriver.** Don't worry, nothing will happen to him.; **Tiens-toi tranquille!** Be quiet!; **Laisse-moi tranquille.** Leave me alone.; **Laisse ça tranquille.** Leave it alone.

tranquillement *adv* quietly; **Je peux travailler tranquillement cinq minutes?** Can I have five minutes to myself to work in peace?

tranquillité *nf* peace and quiet

transférer *vb* [**34**] to transfer

transformer *vb* [**28**] ❶ to transform ❷ to convert ▷ *Ils ont transformé la grange en garage.* They've converted the barn into a garage.; **se transformer en** to turn into

transfusion *nf* **une transfusion sanguine** a blood transfusion

transiger *vb* [**45**] to compromise

transmettre *vb* [**47**] **transmettre quelque chose à quelqu'un** to pass something on to somebody

transpercer *vb* [**12**] to go through ▷ *La pluie a transpercé mes vêtements.* The rain went through my clothes.

transpiration *nf* perspiration

a
b
c
d
e
f
g
h
i
j
k
l
m
n
o
p
q
r
s
t
u
v
w
x
y
z

transpirer vb [**28**] to perspire

transport nm transport; **les transports en commun** public transport

transporter vb [**28**] ❶ to carry ▷ *Le train transportait des marchandises.* The train was carrying freight. ❷ to move ▷ *Je ne sais pas comment je vais transporter mes affaires.* I don't know how I'm going to move my stuff.

traumatiser vb [**28**] to traumatize

travail (pl **travaux**) nm ❶ work ▷ *J'ai beaucoup de travail.* I've got a lot of work. ❷ job ▷ *Il a un travail intéressant.* He's got an interesting job.; **Il est sans travail depuis un an.** He has been out of work for a year.; **le travail au noir** moonlighting

travailler vb [**28**] to work

travailleur (f **travailleuse**) adj hard-working

travailleur nm worker

travailleuse nf worker

travaillistes nmpl the Labour Party sg

travaux nmpl ❶ work sg ▷ *des travaux de construction* building work ❷ roadworks; **être en travaux** to be undergoing alterations; **les travaux dirigés** supervised practical work; **les travaux manuels** handicrafts; **les travaux ménagers** housework; **les travaux pratiques** practical work

travers nm **en travers de** across; **de travers** crooked; **comprendre de travers** to misunderstand; **J'ai avalé de travers.** Something went down the wrong way.; **à travers** through

traversée nf crossing

traverser vb [**28**] ❶ to cross ▷ *Traversez la rue.* Cross the street. ❷ to go through ▷ *Nous avons traversé la France pour aller en Espagne.* We went through France on the way to Spain.

traversin nm bolster

trébucher vb [**28**] to trip up

trèfle nm ❶ clover ❷ (at cards) clubs

treize num thirteen ▷ *Il a treize ans.* He's thirteen.; **le treize février** the thirteenth of February

treizième adj thirteenth

tréma nm diaeresis

tremblement de terre nm earthquake

trembler vb [**28**] to shake ▷ *trembler de peur* to shake with fear; **trembler de froid** to shiver

trempé, e adj soaking wet; **trempé jusqu'aux os** soaked to the skin

tremper vb [**28**] to soak; **tremper sa main dans l'eau** to dip one's hand in the water

tremplin nm springboard

trentaine nf about thirty; **Il a la trentaine.** He's in his thirties.

trente num thirty; **le trente janvier** the thirtieth of January; **trente et un** thirty-one; **trente-deux** thirty-two

trentième adj thirtieth

très adv very

trésor *nm* treasure

tresse *nf* plait

triangle *nm* triangle

tribu *nf* tribe

tribunal (*pl* **tribunaux**) *nm* court

tricher *vb* [28] to cheat

tricolore *adj* three-coloured; **le drapeau tricolore** the French flag
  ● **le drapeau tricolore** is the
  ● French flag which is blue, white
  ● and red.

tricot *nm* ❶ knitting ❷ sweater

tricoter *vb* [28] to knit

trier *vb* [19] to sort out

trimestre *nm* term

trinquer *vb* [28] to clink glasses

triomphe *nm* triumph

triompher *vb* [28] to triumph

tripes *nfpl* tripe

triple *nm* **Ça m'a coûté le triple.** It cost me three times as much.; **Il gagne le triple de mon salaire.** He earns three times my salary.

tripler *vb* [28] to treble

triplés *nmpl* triplets

triste *adj* sad

tristesse *nf* sadness

trognon *nm* core

trois *num* three ▷ **Elle a trois ans.** She's three.; **le trois février** the third of February

troisième *adj* third
  ▶ *nf* year 10 ▷ **Mon frère est en troisième.** My brother's in year 10.
  ● In French secondary schools,
  ● years are counted from the
  ● **sixième** (youngest) to **première**
  ● and **terminale** (oldest).

trois-quarts *nmpl* three-quarters

trombone *nm* ❶ trombone
  ❷ paper clip

trompe *nf* trunk

tromper *vb* [28] to deceive; **se tromper** to make a mistake; **se tromper de jour** to get the wrong day; **Vous vous êtes trompé de numéro.** You've got the wrong number.

trompette *nf* trumpet; **Il a le nez en trompette.** He's got a turned-up nose.

tronc *nm* trunk

trop *adv* ❶ too ▷ *Il conduit trop vite.* He drives too fast. ❷ too much ▷ *J'ai trop mangé.* I've eaten too much.; **trop de (1)** too much **(2)** too many; **trois personnes de trop** 3 people too many

tropique *nm* tropic

trottoir *nm* pavement

trou *nm* hole; **J'ai eu un trou de mémoire.** My mind went blank.

trouble *adj, adv* cloudy; **Sans mes lunettes je vois trouble.** Without my glasses I can't see properly.

troubles *nmpl* **une période de troubles politiques** a period of political instability

trouer *vb* [28] to make a hole in

trouille *nf* **avoir la trouille** (*informal*) to be scared to death

troupe *nf* troop; **une troupe de théâtre** a theatre company

troupeau (*pl* **troupeaux**) *nm* **un troupeau de moutons** a flock of sheep; **un troupeau de vaches** a herd of cows

trousse *nf* pencil case; **une**

a b c d e f g h i j k l m n o p q r s **t** u v w x y z

trousse de secours a first-aid kit;
une trousse de toilette a toilet
bag

trouver vb [28] ❶ to find ▷ *Je ne
trouve pas mes lunettes.* I can't find
my glasses. ❷ to think ▷ *Je trouve
que c'est bête.* I think it's stupid.; **se
trouver** to be ▷ *Où se trouve la
poste?* Where is the post office?
▷ *Nice se trouve dans le sud de la
France.* Nice is in the South of
France.; **se trouver mal** to pass
out

truc nm (informal) ❶ thing ▷ *un truc
en plastique* a plastic thing ❷ trick

truite nf trout

T-shirt nm T-shirt

TSVP abbr (= *tournez s'il vous plaît*)
PTO (= *please turn over*)

tu pron you ▷ *Est-ce que tu as un
animal familier?* Have you got a pet?

tuba nm ❶ tuba ❷ snorkel

tube nm ❶ tube ▷ *un tube de
dentifrice* a tube of toothpaste; **un
tube de rouge à lèvres** a lipstick
❷ hit ▷ *Ça va être le tube de l'été.* It's
going to be this summer's hit.

tuer vb [28] to kill; **se tuer** to get
killed

tue-tête: **à tue-tête** adv at the top
of one's voice

tuile nf tile

tunique nf tunic

Tunisie nf Tunisia

tunisien (f **tunisienne**) adj, nm/f
Tunisian

tunnel nm tunnel; **le tunnel sous
la Manche** the Channel Tunnel

turbulent, e adj boisterous

turc (f **turque**) adj, nm/f Turkish
▷ *Il parle turc.* He speaks Turkish.;
un Turc (man) a Turk; **une Turque**
(woman) a Turk

Turquie nf Turkey

tutoyer vb [53] **tutoyer quelqu'un**
to address somebody as 'tu' ▷ *On se
tutoie?* Shall we use 'tu' to each
other?

* **tutoyer quelqu'un** means to
  use **tu** when speaking to
  someone, rather than **vous**. Use
  tu only when talking to one
  person and when that person is
  someone of your own age or
  whom you know well; use **vous**
  to everyone else. If in doubt use
  vous.

tuyau (pl **tuyaux**) nm ❶ pipe; **un
tuyau d'arrosage** a hosepipe ❷ tip

TVA nf (= *taxe sur la valeur ajoutée*)
VAT

tympan nm eardrum

type nm (informal) guy

typique adj typical

tyran nm tyrant

tzigane nmf gipsy

u

UE nf (= Union européenne) the EU
(= European Union)

un (f **une**) art, pron m, adj m **❶** a ▷ un
garçon a boy; an ▷ un œuf an egg
❷ one ▷ l'un des meilleurs one of the
best ▷ un citron et deux oranges one
lemon and two oranges; **l'un ...,
l'autre ...** one ..., the other ... ▷ L'un
est grand, l'autre est petit. One is tall,
the other is short.; **les uns ..., les
autres ...** some ..., others ... ▷ Les
uns marchaient, les autres couraient.
Some were walking, others were
running.; **l'un ou l'autre** either of
them ▷ Prends l'un ou l'autre, ça m'est
égal. Take either of them, I don't
mind.; **un par un** one by one
unanime adj unanimous
unanimité nf à l'unanimité
unanimously

une art, pron f, adj f **❶** a ▷ une fille a
girl; an ▷ une pomme an apple
❷ one ▷ une pomme et deux bananes
one apple and two bananas ▷ à une
heure du matin at one in the
morning ▷ l'une des meilleures one of
the best; **l'une ..., l'autre ...** one ...,
the other ... ▷ L'une est grande, l'autre
est petite. One is tall, the other is
short.; **les unes..., les autres...**
some ..., others ... ▷ Les unes
marchaient, les autres couraient.
Some were walking, others were
running.; **l'une ou l'autre** either of
them ▷ Prends l'une ou l'autre, ça
m'est égal. Take either of them, I
don't mind.; **une par une** one by
one
uni, e adj **❶** plain **❷** close-knit
uniforme nm uniform
union nf union; **l'Union
européenne** the European Union
unique adj unique; **Il est fils
unique.** He's an only child.; **Elle
est fille unique.** She's an only
child.
uniquement adv only
unité nf **❶** unity **❷** unit
univers nm universe
universitaire adj university; **faire
des études universitaires** to
study at university
université nf university
urgence nf **C'est une urgence.** It's
urgent.; **Il n'y a pas urgence.** It's
not urgent.; **le service des
urgences** the accident and
emergency department; **Il a été
transporté d'urgence à l'hôpital.**

He was rushed to hospital.;
Téléphonez d'urgence. Phone as
soon as possible.
urgent, e *adj* urgent
urine *nf* urine
USA *nmpl* USA; **aux USA (1)** in the
USA **(2)** to the USA
usage *nm* use; **hors d'usage** out of
action
usagé, e *adj* ❶ old ❷ used
usager *nm* user ▷ *les usagers de la
route* road users
usé, e *adj* worn
s'**user** *vb* [**28**] to wear out ▷ *Mes
baskets se sont usées en quinze jours.*
My trainers wore out in two
weeks.
usine *nf* factory
ustensile *nm* un ustensile de
cuisine a kitchen utensil
usuel (*f* **usuelle**) *adj* everyday
utile *adj* useful
utilisation *nf* use
utiliser *vb* [**28**] to use
utilité *nf* use

V

va *vb see* **aller**
vacances *nfpl* holidays ▷ *aller en
vacances* to go on holiday ▷ *être en
vacances* to be on holiday; **les
vacances de Noël** the Christmas
holidays; **les vacances de Pâques**
the Easter holidays; **les grandes
vacances** the summer holidays
vacancier *nm* holiday-maker
vacarme *nm* racket
vaccin *nm* vaccination
vaccination *nf* vaccination
vacciner *vb* [**28**] to vaccinate
vache *nf* cow
  ▷ *adj* (informal) mean ▷ *Il est vache.*
He's a mean sod.
vachement *adv* (informal) really
vagabond *nm* tramp
vagin *nm* vagina
vague *nf* (in sea) wave; **une vague**

de chaleur a heat wave
▶ *adj* vague
vain (*f* **vaine**) *adj* **en vain** in vain
vaincre *vb* [**86**] ❶ to defeat ❷ to overcome
vainqueur *nm* winner
vais *vb see* **aller**; **Je vais écrire à mes cousins.** I'm going to write to my cousins.
vaisseau (*pl* **vaisseaux**) *nm* **un vaisseau spatial** a spaceship; **un vaisseau sanguin** a blood vessel
vaisselle *nf* ❶ washing-up ▷ *Je vais faire la vaisselle.* I'll do the washing-up. ❷ dishes
valable *adj* valid
valet *nm* (*in card games*) jack
valeur *nf* value; **des objets de valeur** valuables
valider *vb* [**28**] to stamp ▷ *Vous devez faire valider votre billet avant votre départ.* You must get your ticket stamped before you leave.
valise *nf* suitcase; **faire sa valise** to pack
vallée *nf* valley
valoir *vb* [**87**] to be worth ▷ *Ça vaut combien?* How much is it worth?; **Ça vaut mieux.** That would be better. ▷ *Il vaut mieux ne rien dire.* It would be better to say nothing.; **valoir la peine** to be worth it ▷ *Ça vaudrait la peine d'essayer.* It would be worth a try.
vampire *nm* vampire
vandalisme *nm* vandalism
vanille *nf* vanilla
vanité *nf* vanity
vaniteux (*f* **vaniteuse**) *adj* conceited

se vanter *vb* [**28**] to boast
vapeur *nf* steam
varappe *nf* rock climbing
variable *adj* (*weather*) changeable
varicelle *nf* chickenpox
varié, e *adj* varied
varier *vb* [**19**] to vary; **Le menu varie tous les jours.** The menu changes every day.
variété *nf* variety; **une émission de variétés** a television variety show
vas *vb see* **aller**
vase *nm* vase
▶ *nf* mud
vaste *adj* vast
vaudrait, vaut *vb see* **valoir**
vautour *nm* vulture
veau (*pl* **veaux**) *nm* ❶ (*animal*) calf ❷ (*meat*) veal
vécu *vb see* **vivre**; **Il a vécu à Paris pendant dix ans.** He lived in Paris for ten years.
vedette *nf* ❶ star ▷ *une vedette de cinéma* a film star ❷ motor boat; **une vedette de police** a police launch
végétal, e (*mpl* **végétaux**) *adj* vegetable
végétalien (*f* **végétalienne**) *adj* vegan
végétarien (*f* **végétarienne**) *adj* vegetarian
végétation *nf* vegetation
véhicule *nm* vehicle
veille *nf* the day before ▷ *la veille au soir* the previous evening; **la veille de Noël** Christmas Eve; **la veille du jour de l'An** New Year's Eve
veiller *vb* [**28**] to stay up; **veiller**

sur quelqu'un to watch over somebody

veinard, e *adj (informal)* **Qu'est-ce qu'il est veinard!** He's such a lucky devil!

veine *nf* vein; **avoir de la veine** *(informal)* to be lucky

véliplanchiste *nmf* windsurfer

vélo *nm* bike; **un vélo tout-terrain** a mountain bike

vélomoteur *nm* moped

velours *nm* velvet; **le velours côtelé** corduroy

vendanges *nfpl* grape harvest *sg*

vendeur *nm* shop assistant

vendeuse *nf* shop assistant

vendre *vb* [88] to sell; **vendre quelque chose à quelqu'un** to sell somebody something; **'à vendre'** 'for sale'

vendredi *nm* ❶ Friday
▷ *Aujourd'hui, nous sommes vendredi.* It's Friday today. ❷ on Friday; **le vendredi** on Fridays; **tous les vendredis** every Friday; **vendredi dernier** last Friday; **vendredi prochain** next Friday; **le Vendredi saint** Good Friday

vénéneux *(f vénéneuse) adj (plant)* poisonous

vengeance *nf* revenge

se **venger** *vb* [45] to get revenge

venimeux *(f venimeuse) adj (animal)* poisonous

venin *nm* poison

venir *vb* [89] to come ▷ *Il viendra demain.* He'll come tomorrow. ▷ *Il est venu nous voir.* He came to see us.; **venir de** to have just ▷ *Je viens*

de le voir. I've just seen him.; **faire venir quelqu'un** to call somebody out

vent *nm* wind

vente *nf* sale; **en vente** on sale; **la vente par téléphone** telesales; **une vente aux enchères** an auction

ventilateur *nm (for cooling)* fan

ventre *nm* stomach

venu *vb see* **venir**

ver *nm* worm; **un ver de terre** an earthworm

verbe *nm* verb

verdict *nm* verdict

verger *nm* orchard

verglacé, e *adj* icy

verglas *nm* black ice

véridique *adj* truthful

vérification *nf* check

vérifier *vb* [19] to check

véritable *adj* real; **en cuir véritable** made of real leather

vérité *nf* truth

verni, e *adj* varnished; **des chaussures vernies** patent leather shoes

vernir *vb* [38] to varnish

vernis *nm* varnish

verra, verrai, verras *vb see* **voir**; **on verra ...** we'll see ...

verre *nm* ❶ glass ▷ *une table en verre* a glass table ▷ *un verre d'eau* a glass of water; **boire un verre** to have a drink ❷ *(of spectacles)* lens ▷ *des verres de contact* contact lenses

verrez, verrons, verront *vb see* **voir**

verrou *nm (on door)* bolt

verrouiller vb [28] to bolt
verrue nf wart
vers nm (of poetry) line
▶ prep ❶ towards ▷ Il allait vers la gare. He was going towards the station. ❷ at about ▷ Il est rentré chez lui vers cinq heures. He went home at about 5 o'clock.
verse: à verse adv ▷ Il pleut à verse. It's pouring with rain.
Verseau nm Aquarius
versement nm instalment
verser vb [28] to pour ▷ Est-ce que tu peux me verser un verre d'eau? Could you pour me a glass of water?
version nf ❶ version ❷ (from the foreign language) translation; un film en version originale a film in the original language
verso nm (of sheet of paper) back; voir au verso see overleaf
vert, e adj green; (ecological) green
▶ nm green; les Verts (in politics) the Greens
vertèbre nf vertebra
vertical, e (mpl verticaux) adj vertical
vertige nm vertigo
verveine nf verbena tea
vessie nf bladder
veste nf jacket
vestiaire nm ❶ (in theatre, museum) cloakroom ❷ (at sports ground) changing room
vestibule nm hall
vêtement nm garment; les vêtements clothes
vétérinaire nmf vet
veuf nm widower

veuille, veuillez, veuillons, veulent, veut vb see **vouloir**; **Veuillez fermer la porte en sortant.** Please shut the door when you go out.
veuve nf widow
veux vb see **vouloir**
vexer vb [28] vexer quelqu'un to hurt somebody's feelings; se vexer to be offended
viande nf meat; la viande hachée mince
vibrer vb [28] to vibrate
vice nm vice
vicieux (f vicieuse) adj lecherous
victime nf victim
victoire nf victory
vide adj empty
▶ nm vacuum; avoir peur du vide to be afraid of heights
vidéo nf video
▶ adj video ▷ un jeu vidéo a video game ▷ une caméra vidéo a video camera
vidéoclip nm music video
vidéoclub nm video shop
vider vb [28] to empty
vie nf life; être en vie to be alive
vieil adj m

> vieil is used in place of **vieux** when the noun begins with a vowel sound.

old ▷ un vieil arbre an old tree ▷ un vieil homme an old man
vieillard nm old man
vieille adj f see **vieux**
▶ nf old woman; Eh bien, ma vieille ... (informal) Well, my dear ...
vieillesse nf old age
vieillir vb [38] to age

a b c d e f g h i j k l m n o p q r s t u **v** w x y z

viendrai, vienne, viens vb see **venir**; **Je viendrai dès que possible.** I'll come as soon as possible.; **Je voudrais que tu viennes.** I'd like you to come.; **Viens ici!** Come here!

Vierge nf Virgo ▷ *Pascal est Vierge.* Pascal is Virgo.; **la Vierge** the Virgin Mary

vierge adj ❶ virgin ❷ blank

Viêt-Nam nm Vietnam

vietnamien (f **vietnamienne**) adj, nm/f Vietnamese; **un Vietnamien** (*man*) a Vietnamese; **une Vietnamienne** (*woman*) a Vietnamese; **les Vietnamiens** the Vietnamese

vieux (f **vieille**) adj old; **un vieux garçon** a bachelor ▶ nm old man; **les vieux** old people

vieux jeu adj old-fashioned

vif (f **vive**) adj ❶ (*mentally*) sharp ▷ *Il est très vif.* He's very sharp.; **avoir l'esprit vif** to be quick-witted ❷ crisp ▷ *L'air est plus vif à la campagne qu'en ville.* The air is crisper in the country than in the town. ❸ (*colour*) bright ▷ *un bleu vif* a bright blue; **à vive allure** at a brisk pace; **de vive voix** in person ▷ *Je te le dirai de vive voix.* I'll tell you about it when I see you.

vigne nf vine; **des champs de vigne** vineyards

vigneron nm wine grower

vignette nf tax disc

vignoble nm vineyard

vilain, e adj ❶ naughty ❷ ugly ▷ *Il n'est pas vilain.* He's not bad-looking.

villa nf villa

village nm village

villageois nm villager

ville nf town ▷ *Je vais en ville.* I'm going into town.; **une grande ville** a city

vin nm wine

vinaigre nm vinegar

vinaigrette nf French dressing

vingt num twenty; **le vingt février** the twentieth of February; **vingt et un** twenty-one; **vingt-deux** twenty-two

vingtaine nf about twenty; **Il a une vingtaine d'années.** He's about twenty.

vingtième adj twentieth

viol nm rape

violemment adv violently

violence nf violence; **violence conjugale** domestic violence

violent, e adj violent

violer vb [28] to rape

violet (f **violette**) adj purple

violette nf (*flower*) violet

violon nm violin

violoncelle nm cello

violoniste nmf violinist

vipère nf viper

virage nm bend

virgule nf ❶ comma ❷ decimal point

virus nm virus

vis vb see **vivre**; **Je vis en Écosse.** I live in Scotland. ▶ nf screw

visa nm visa

visage nm face

vis-à-vis de prep with regard to ▷ *Ce n'est pas très juste vis-à-vis de lui.*

It's not very fair to him.

viser vb [**28**] to aim at

visibilité nf visibility

visible adj visible

visière nf (of cap) peak

visite nf visit; **rendre visite à quelqu'un** to visit somebody; **avoir de la visite** to have visitors; **une visite guidée** a guided tour; **une visite médicale** a medical examination

visiter vb [**28**] to visit

visiteur nm visitor

vison nm (fur) mink

vit vb see **vivre**

vital, e (mpl **vitaux**) adj vital

vitamine nf vitamin

vite adv ① quick; **Le temps passe vite.** Time flies. ② fast ▷ Il roule trop vite. He drives too fast. ③ soon ▷ Il va vite oublier. He'll soon forget.; **Il a vite compris.** He understood immediately.

vitesse nf ① speed ② gear

viticulteur nm wine grower

vitrail (pl **vitraux**) nm stained-glass window

vitre nf window

vitrine nf shop window

vivant, e adj ① living ▷ les êtres vivants living creatures ② lively ▷ Elle est très vivante. She's very lively.

vive adj f see **vif**
▶ excl **Vive le roi!** Long live the king!

vivement excl **Vivement les vacances!** Roll on the holidays!

vivre vb [**91**] to live ▷ J'aimerais vivre à l'étranger. I'd like to live abroad.

vlan excl wham!

VO nf **un film en VO** a film in the original language

vocabulaire nm vocabulary

vocation nf vocation

vœu (pl **vœux**) nm wish ▷ Meilleurs vœux de bonne année! Best wishes for the New Year!

vogue nf fashion

voici prep ① this is ▷ Voici mon frère et voilà ma sœur. This is my brother and that's my sister. ② here is ▷ Tu as perdu ton stylo? Tiens, en voici un autre. Have you lost your pen? Here's another one.; **Le voici!** Here he is!

voie nf lane ▷ une route à trois voies a 3-lane road; **par voie orale** orally ▷ à prendre par voie orale to be taken orally; **la voie ferrée** the railway track

voilà prep ① there is ▷ Tiens! Voilà Paul. Look! There's Paul.; **Les voilà!** There they are! ② that is ▷ Voilà ma sœur. That's my sister.

voile nf ① sail ② sailing; **un bateau à voiles** a sailing boat
▶ nm veil

voilier nm sailing boat

voir vb [**92**] to see ▷ Venez me voir quand vous serez à Paris. Come and see me when you're in Paris.; **faire voir quelque chose à quelqu'un** to show somebody something; **se voir** to be obvious ▷ Est-ce que cette tache se voit? Does that stain show?; **avoir quelque chose à voir avec** to have something to do with; **Je ne peux vraiment pas la**

a b c d e f g h i j k l m n o p q r s t u v w x y z

voir. *(informal)* I really can't stand her.

voisin nm neighbour

voisinage nm **dans le voisinage** in the vicinity

voisine nf neighbour

voiture nf car

voix (pl **voix**) nf ❶ voice; **à haute voix** aloud ❷ vote

vol nm ❶ flight; **à vol d'oiseau** as the crow flies; **le vol à voile** gliding ❷ theft

volaille nf poultry

volant nm ❶ steering wheel ❷ shuttlecock

volcan nm volcano

volée nf *(in tennis)* volley; **rattraper une balle à la volée** to catch a ball in mid-air

voler vb [28] ❶ to fly ▷ J'aimerais savoir voler. I'd like to be able to fly. ❷ to steal ▷ On a volé mon appareil photo. My camera's been stolen.; **voler quelque chose à quelqu'un** to steal something from somebody; **voler quelqu'un** to rob somebody

volet nm shutter

voleur nm thief; **Au voleur !** Stop thief!

volley nm volleyball

volontaire nmf volunteer

volonté nf willpower; **la bonne volonté** goodwill; **la mauvaise volonté** lack of goodwill

volontiers adv ❶ gladly ❷ please

volume nm volume

volumineux (f **volumineuse**) adj bulky

vomir vb [38] to vomit

vont vb see **aller**

vos adj pl your ▷ Rangez vos jouets, les enfants! Children, put your toys away!

vote nm vote

voter vb [28] to vote

votre (pl **vos**) adj your

vôtre pron le vôtre yours; **À la vôtre!** Cheers!

vôtres pron pl les vôtres yours

voudra, voudrai, voudrais, voudras, voudrez, voudrons, voudront vb see **vouloir**; **Je voudrais ...** I'd like ... ▷ Je voudrais deux litres de lait, s'il vous plaît. I'd like two litres of milk, please.

vouloir vb [93] to want ▷ Elle veut un vélo pour Noël. She wants a bike for Christmas. ▷ Je ne veux pas de dessert. I don't want any pudding. ▷ Il ne veut pas venir. He doesn't want to come. ▷ On va au cinéma? — Si tu veux. Shall we go to the cinema? — If you want.; **Je veux bien.** I'll be happy to. ▷ Je veux bien le faire à ta place si ça t'arrange. I'd be happy to do it for you if you prefer.; **Voulez-vous une tasse de thé? — Je veux bien.** Would you like a cup of tea? — Yes, please.; **sans vouloir** without meaning to ▷ Je l'ai vexé sans le vouloir. I upset him without meaning to.; **en vouloir à quelqu'un** to be angry with somebody ▷ Il m'en veut de ne pas l'avoir invité. He's angry with me for not inviting him.; **vouloir dire** to mean ▷ Qu'est-ce que ça veut dire?

What does that mean?

voulu *vb see* **vouloir**

vous *sg, pron pl* ❶ you ▷ *Vous aimez la pizza?* Do you like pizza? ❷ to you ▷ *Je vous écrirai bientôt.* I'll write to you soon. ❸ yourself ▷ *Vous vous êtes fait mal?* Have you hurt yourself?; **vous-même** yourself ▷ *Vous l'avez fait vous-même?* Did you do it yourself?

vouvoyer *vb* [53] vouvoyer quelqu'un to address somebody as 'vous' ▷ *Est-ce que je dois vouvoyer ta sœur?* Should I use 'vous' to your sister?

  • **vouvoyer quelqu'un** means to
  • use **vous** when speaking to
  • someone, rather than **tu**. Use **tu**
  • only when talking to one person
  • and when that person is
  • someone of your own age or
  • whom you know well; use **vous**
  • to everyone else. If in doubt use
  • **vous**.

voyage *nm* journey ▷ *Avez-vous fait bon voyage?* Did you have a good journey?; **Bon voyage!** Have a good trip!

voyager *vb* [45] to travel

voyageur *nm* passenger

voyaient, voyais, voyait *vb see* **voir**

voyelle *nf* vowel

voyez, voyiez, voyions *vb see* **voir**

voyons *vb see* **voir** ❶ let's see ▷ *Voyons ce qu'on peut faire.* Let's see what we can do. ❷ come on ▷ *Voyons, sois raisonnable!* Come on,

be reasonable!

voyou *nm* hooligan

vrac: en vrac *adv* loose

vrai, e *adj* true ▷ *une histoire vraie* a true story ▷ *C'est vrai?* Is that true?; **à vrai dire** to tell the truth

vraiment *adv* really

vraisemblable *adj* likely

VTT *nm* (= vélo tout-terrain) mountain bike

vu *vb see* **voir** ▷ *J'ai vu ce film au cinéma.* I saw this film at the cinema.; **être bien vu** (person) to be popular ▷ *Est-ce qu'il est bien vu à l'école?* Is he popular at school?; **C'est mal vu de fumer ici.** They don't like people smoking here.

vue *nf* ❶ eyesight ▷ *J'ai une mauvaise vue.* I've got bad eyesight. ❷ view ▷ *Il y a une belle vue d'ici.* There's a lovely view from here.; **à vue d'œil** visibly

vulgaire *adj* vulgar

a
b
c
d
e
f
g
h
i
j
k
l
m
n
o
p
q
r
s
t
u
v
w
x
y
z

W X

wagon *nm* railway carriage
wagon-lit (*pl* **wagons-lits**) *nm*
(*on train*) sleeper
wagon-restaurant (*pl* **wagons-restaurants**) *nm* restaurant car
wallon (*f* **wallonne**) *adj*, *nm/f*
(*French-speaking Belgian*) Walloon;
les Wallons the French-speaking
Belgians
Wallonie *nf* French-speaking
Belgium
W.-C. *nmpl* toilet *sg*
Web *nm* Web
webcam *nf* webcam
webmaster *nm* webmaster
webzine *nm* webzine
week-end *nm* weekend
western *nm* (*film*) western
whisky (*pl* **whiskies**) *nm* whisky
wifi *nm* Wi-Fi

xénophobe *adj* prejudiced against
foreigners
xénophobie *nf* prejudice against
foreigners
xylophone *nm* xylophone

Yougoslavie *nf* Yugoslavia;
l'ex-Yougoslavie the former
Yugoslavia
youpi *excl* yippee!
yoyo *nm* yo-yo

y *pron* there ▷ *Nous y sommes allés
l'été dernier.* We went there last
summer. ▷ *Regarde dans le tiroir: je
pense que les clés y sont.* Look in the
drawer: I think the keys are in
there.

> **y** replaces phrases with **à** in
> constructions like the ones
> below:

**Je pensais à l'examen. — Mais
arrête d'y penser!** I was thinking
about the exam. — Well, stop
thinking about it!; **Je ne
m'attendais pas à ça. — Moi, je
m'y attendais.** I wasn't expecting
that. — I was expecting it.
yaourt *nm* yoghurt
yeux (*sg* œil) *nmpl* eyes
yoga *nm* yoga
yoghourt *nm* yoghurt

Z

zapper *vb* [28] to channel hop
zèbre *nm* zebra
zéro *nm* zero; **Ils ont gagné trois à zéro.** They won three-nil.
zézayer *vb* [59] to lisp ▷ *Il zézaie.* He's got a lisp.
zigzag *nm* **faire des zigzags** to zigzag
zone *nf* zone; **une zone industrielle** an industrial estate; **une zone piétonne** a pedestrian precinct
zoo *nm* zoo
zoologique *adj* zoological
zut *excl* oh heck!

a *art*

Use **un** for masculine nouns, **une** for feminine nouns.
un *m* ▷ *a book* un livre; une *f* ▷ *an apple* une pomme

You do not translate 'a' when you want to describe somebody's job in French.
▷ *She's a doctor.* Elle est médecin.; **once a week** une fois par semaine; **10 km an hour** dix kilomètres à l'heure; **30 pence a kilo** trente pence le kilo; **a hundred pounds** cent livres

abandon *vb* abandonner [28]
abbey *n* abbaye *f*
abbreviation *n* abréviation *f*
ability *n* to have the ability to do something être [35] capable de faire quelque chose

able *adj* to be able to do something être [35] capable de faire quelque chose
abolish *vb* abolir [38]
abortion *n* avortement *m*; **She had an abortion.** Elle s'est fait avorter.
about *prep, adv* ❶ *(concerning)* à propos de ▷ *I'm phoning you about tomorrow's meeting*. Je vous appelle à propos de la réunion de demain. ❷ *(approximately)* environ ▷ *It takes about 10 hours.* Ça prend dix heures environ.; **about a hundred pounds** une centaine de livres; **at about 11 o'clock** vers onze heures ❸ *(around)* dans ▷ *to walk about the town* se promener dans la ville ❹ sur ▷ *a book about London* un livre sur Londres; **to be about to do something** être [35] sur le point de faire quelque chose ▷ *I was about to go out.* J'étais sur le point de sortir.; **to talk about something** parler [28] de quelque chose; **What's it about?** De quoi s'agit-il?; **How about going to the cinema?** Et si nous allions au cinéma?
above *prep, adv* ❶ *(higher than)* au-dessus de ▷ *He put his hands above his head.* Il a mis ses mains au-dessus de sa tête.; **the flat above** l'appartement du dessus; **mentioned above** mentionné ci-dessus; **above all** par-dessus tout ❷ *(more than)* plus de ▷ *above 40 degrees* plus de quarante degrés
abroad *adv* à l'étranger ▷ *to go abroad* partir à l'étranger

absence n absence f
absent adj absent(e)
absent-minded adj distrait(e)
▷ She's a bit absent-minded. Elle est
un peu distraite.
absolutely adv ❶ (completely) tout
à fait ▷ Chantal's absolutely right.
Chantal a tout à fait raison.
❷ absolument ▷ Do you think it's a
good idea? — Absolutely! Tu trouves
que c'est une bonne idée? —
Absolument!
abuse n (misuse) abus m; **to shout
abuse at somebody** insulter [**28**]
quelqu'un; **the issue of child
abuse** la question des enfants
maltraités; **the problem of drug
abuse** le problème de la drogue
▶ vb ❶ maltraiter [**28**] ▷ abused
children les enfants maltraités mpl;
to be abused (child, woman) être
[**35**] maltraité ❷ (insult) injurier
[**19**]; **to abuse drugs** se droguer
[**28**]
academic adj universitaire ▷ the
academic year l'année universitaire f
academy n collège m ▷ a military
academy un collège militaire
accelerate vb accélérer [**34**]
accelerator n accélérateur m
accent n accent m ▷ He's got a
French accent. Il a l'accent français.
accept vb accepter [**28**]
acceptable adj acceptable
access n ❶ accès m ▷ He has access
to confidential information. Il a accès
à des renseignements
confidentiels. ❷ droit de visite m
▷ Her ex-husband has access to the
children. Son ex-mari a le droit de
visite.
accessory n accessoire m ▷ fashion
accessories les accessoires de mode
accident n accident m ▷ to have an
accident avoir un accident; **by
accident** (1) (by mistake)
accidentellement ▷ The burglar
killed him by accident. Le
cambrioleur l'a tué
accidentellement. (2) (by chance)
par hasard ▷ She met him by
accident. Elle l'a rencontré par
hasard.
accidental adj accidentel (f
accidentelle)
accommodation n logement m
accompany vb accompagner [**28**]
according to prep selon
▷ According to him, everyone had
gone. Selon lui, tout le monde était
parti.
account n ❶ compte m ▷ a bank
account un compte en banque; **to
do the accounts** tenir [**83**] la
comptabilité ❷ (report) compte
rendu m (pl comptes rendus) ▷ He
gave a detailed account of what
happened. Il a donné un compte
rendu détaillé des événements.; **to
take something into account**
tenir [**83**] compte de quelque
chose; **on account of** à cause de
▷ We couldn't go out on account of the
bad weather. Nous n'avons pas pu
sortir à cause du mauvais temps.
accountant n comptable mf
▷ She's an accountant. Elle est
comptable.

accuracy n exactitude f
accurate adj précis(e) ▷ accurate information les renseignements précis mpl
accurately adv avec précision
accuse vb to accuse somebody of something accuser [28] quelqu'un de quelque chose ▷ The police are accusing her of murder. La police l'accuse de meurtre.
ace n as m ▷ the ace of hearts l'as de cœur
ache n douleur f
  ▶ vb My leg's aching. J'ai mal à la jambe.
achieve vb ❶ (an aim) atteindre [60] ❷ (victory) remporter [28]
achievement n exploit m ▷ That was quite an achievement. C'était un véritable exploit.
acid n acide m
acid rain n pluies acides fpl
acne n acné f
acrobat n acrobate mf ▷ He's an acrobat. Il est acrobate.
across prep, adv de l'autre côté de ▷ the shop across the road la boutique de l'autre côté de la rue; **to walk across the road** traverser [28] la rue; **to run across the road** traverser [28] la rue en courant; **across from** (opposite) en face de ▷ He sat down across from her. Il s'est assis en face d'elle.
act vb ❶ (in play, film) jouer [28] ▷ He acts really well. Il joue vraiment bien. ❷ (take action) agir [38] ▷ The police acted quickly. La police a agi rapidement.; **She acts as his**

interpreter. Elle lui sert d'interprète.
  ▶ n (in play) acte m ▷ in the first act au premier acte
action n action f ▷ The film was full of action. Il y avait beaucoup d'action dans le film.; **to take firm action against** prendre [65] des mesures énergiques contre
active adj actif (f active) ▷ He's a very active person. Il est très actif.; **an active volcano** un volcan en activité
activity n activité f ▷ outdoor activities les activités de plein air
actor n acteur m ▷ Brad Pitt is a well-known actor. Brad Pitt est un acteur connu.
actress n actrice f ▷ Julia Roberts is a well-known actress. Julia Roberts est une actrice connue.
actual adj réel (f réelle) ▷ The film is based on actual events. Le film repose sur des faits réels.; **What's the actual amount?** Quel est le montant exact?
  ▌ Be careful not to translate **actual** by **actuel**.
actually adv ❶ (really) vraiment ▷ Did it actually happen? Est-ce que c'est vraiment arrivé? ❷ (in fact) en fait ▷ Actually, I don't know him at all. En fait, je ne le connais pas du tout.
  ▌ Be careful not to translate **actually** by **actuellement**.
AD abbr ap. J.-C. (= après Jésus-Christ) ▷ in 800 AD en huit cents après Jésus-Christ
ad n ❶ (in paper) annonce f ❷ (on TV, radio) pub f

adapt vb adapter [28] ▷ *His novel was adapted for television.* Son roman a été adapté pour la télévision.; **to adapt to something** (*get used to*) s'adapter [28] à quelque chose ▷ *He adapted to his new school very quickly.* Il s'est adapté très vite à sa nouvelle école.

adaptor n adaptateur m

add vb ajouter [28] ▷ *Add two eggs to the mixture.* Ajoutez deux œufs au mélange.

add up vb additionner [28] ▷ *Add the figures up.* Additionnez les chiffres.

addict n (*drug addict*) drogué m, droguée f; **Jean-Pierre's a football addict.** Jean-Pierre est un mordu de football.

addicted adj **to be addicted to** être [35] dépendant de ▷ *She's addicted to heroin.* Elle est héroïnomane.; **She's addicted to YouTube.** Elle est fan de YouTube.

addition n **in addition** en plus ▷ *He's broken his leg and, in addition, he's caught a cold.* Il s'est cassé la jambe et en plus, il a attrapé un rhume.; **in addition to** en plus de ▷ *There's a postage fee in addition to the repair charge.* Il y a des frais de port en plus du prix de la réparation.

address n adresse f ▷ *What's your address?* Quelle est votre adresse?

adjective n adjectif m

adjust vb régler [34] ▷ *You can adjust the height of the chair.* Tu peux régler la hauteur de la chaise.; **to adjust to something** (*get used to*) s'adapter [28] à quelque chose ▷ *He adjusted to his new school very quickly.* Il s'est adapté très vite à sa nouvelle école.

adjustable adj réglable

administration n administration f

admiral n amiral m

admire vb admirer [28]

admission n entrée f; **'admission free'** 'entrée gratuite'

admit vb ❶ (*agree*) admettre [47] ▷ *I must admit that …* Je dois admettre que …　❷ (*confess*) reconnaître [14] ▷ *He admitted that he'd done it.* Il a reconnu qu'il l'avait fait.

adolescent n adolescent m, adolescente f

adopt vb adopter [28] ▷ *Phil was adopted.* Phil a été adopté.

adopted adj adoptif (f adoptive) ▷ *an adopted son* un fils adoptif

adoption n adoption f

adore vb adorer [28]

Adriatic Sea n mer Adriatique f

adult n adulte mf; **adult education** l'enseignement pour adultes m

advance vb ❶ (*move forward*) avancer [12] ▷ *The troops are advancing.* Les troupes avancent. ❷ (*progress*) progresser [28] ▷ *Technology has advanced a lot.* La technologie a beaucoup progressé.
▶ n **in advance** à l'avance ▷ *They*

bought the tickets in advance. Ils ont acheté les billets à l'avance.

advanced *adj* avancé(e)

advantage *n* avantage *m* ▷ *Going to university has many advantages.* Aller à l'université présente de nombreux avantages.; **to take advantage of something** profiter [28] de quelque chose ▷ *He took advantage of the good weather to go for a walk.* Il a profité du beau temps pour faire une promenade.; **to take advantage of somebody** exploiter [28] quelqu'un ▷ *The company was taking advantage of its employees.* La société exploitait ses employés.

adventure *n* aventure *f*

adverb *n* adverbe *m*

advert, advertisement *n* ❶ *(on TV)* publicité *f* ❷ *(in newspaper)* annonce *f*

advertise *vb* faire [36] de la publicité pour ▷ *They're advertising the new model.* Ils font de la publicité pour leur nouveau modèle.; **Jobs are advertised in the paper.** Le journal publie des annonces d'emplois.

advertising *n* publicité *f*

advice *n* conseils *mpl* ▷ *to give somebody advice* donner des conseils à quelqu'un; **a piece of advice** un conseil ▷ *He gave me a good piece of advice.* Il m'a donné un bon conseil.

advise *vb* conseiller [28] ▷ *He advised me to wait.* Il m'a conseillé d'attendre. ▷ *He advised me not to go there.* Il m'a

conseillé de ne pas y aller.

aerial *n* antenne *f*

aerobics *n* aérobic *f* ▷ *I'm going to aerobics tonight.* Je vais au cours d'aérobic ce soir.

aeroplane *n* avion *m*

aerosol *n* bombe *f*

affair *n* ❶ *(romantic)* aventure *f* ▷ *to have an affair with somebody* avoir une aventure avec quelqu'un ❷ *(event)* affaire *f*

affect *vb* affecter [1]

affectionate *adj* affectueux (*f* affectueuse)

afford *vb* avoir [8] les moyens d'acheter ▷ *I can't afford a new pair of jeans.* Je n'ai pas les moyens d'acheter un nouveau jean.; **We can't afford to go on holiday.** Nous n'avons pas les moyens de partir en vacances.

afraid *adj* **to be afraid of something** avoir [8] peur de quelque chose ▷ *I'm afraid of spiders.* J'ai peur des araignées.; **I'm afraid I can't come.** Je crains de ne pouvoir venir.; **I'm afraid so.** Hélas oui.; **I'm afraid not.** Hélas non.

Africa *n* Afrique *f*; **in Africa** en Afrique

African *n* Africain *m*, Africaine *f* ▶ *adj* africain(e)

after *prep, adv, conj* après ▷ *after dinner* après le dîner ▷ *He ran after me.* Il a couru après moi. ▷ *soon after* peu après; **after I'd had a rest** après m'être reposé; **after having asked** après avoir demandé; **after all** après tout

afternoon n après-midi mf ▷ 3
o'clock in the afternoon trois heures
de l'après-midi ▷ this afternoon cet
après-midi ▷ on Saturday afternoon
samedi après-midi

afters n dessert m

aftershave n après-rasage m

afterwards adv après ▷ She left not
long afterwards. Elle est partie peu
de temps après.

again adv ❶ (once more) de nouveau
▷ They're friends again. Ils sont de
nouveau amis. ❷ (one more time)
encore une fois ▷ Can you tell me
again? Tu peux me le dire encore
une fois?; **not ... again** ne ... plus
▷ I won't go there again. Je n'y
retournerai plus.; **Do it again!**
Refais-le!; **again and again** à
plusieurs reprises

against prep contre ▷ He leant
against the wall. Il s'est appuyé
contre le mur. ▷ I'm against nuclear
testing. Je suis contre les essais
nucléaires.

age n âge m ▷ at the age of 16 à l'âge
de seize ans; **I haven't been to the
cinema for ages.** Ça fait une
éternité que je ne suis pas allé au
cinéma.

agenda n ordre du jour m ▷ on the
agenda à l'ordre du jour

Be careful not to translate
agenda by the French word
agenda.

agent n agent m ▷ an estate agent
un agent immobilier

aggressive adj agressif (f
agressive)

ago adv two days ago il y a deux
jours; **two years ago** il y a deux
ans; **not long ago** il n'y a pas
longtemps; **How long ago did it
happen?** Il y a combien de temps
que c'est arrivé?

agony n to be in agony souffrir
[54] le martyre ▷ He was in agony. Il
souffrait le martyre.

agree vb to agree with être [35]
d'accord avec ▷ I agree with Carol. Je
suis d'accord avec Carol.; **to agree
to do something** accepter [28] de
faire quelque chose ▷ He agreed to
go and pick her up. Il a accepté d'aller
la chercher.; **to agree that ...**
admettre [47] que ... ▷ I agree that
it's difficult. J'admets que c'est
difficile.; **Garlic doesn't agree
with me.** Je ne supporte pas l'ail.

agreement n accord m; **to be in
agreement** être [35] d'accord
▷ Everybody was in agreement with
Ray. Tout le monde était d'accord
avec Ray.

agricultural adj agricole

agriculture n agriculture f

ahead adv devant ▷ She looked
straight ahead. Elle regardait droit
devant elle.; **ahead of time** en
avance; **to plan ahead** organiser
[28] à l'avance; **The French are 5
points ahead.** Les Français ont
cinq points d'avance.; **Go ahead!**
Allez-y!

aid n in aid of charity au profit
d'associations caritatives

AIDS n sida m

aim vb to aim at braquer [28] sur

▷ *He aimed a gun at me.* Il a braqué un revolver sur moi.; **The film is aimed at children.** Le film est destiné aux enfants.; **to aim to do something** avoir [8] l'intention de faire quelque chose ▷ *Janice aimed to leave at 5 o'clock.* Janice avait l'intention de partir à cinq heures.
▶ n objectif m ▷ *The aim of the festival is to raise money.* L'objectif du festival est de collecter des fonds.

air n air m ▷ *to get some fresh air* prendre l'air; **by air** en avion ▷ *I prefer to travel by air.* Je préfère voyager en avion.

air-conditioned adj climatisé(e)
air conditioning n climatisation f
Air Force n armée de l'air f
air hostess n hôtesse de l'air f ▷ *She's an air hostess.* Elle est hôtesse de l'air f
airline n compagnie aérienne f
airmail n by airmail par avion
airplane n (US) avion m
airport n aéroport m
aisle n allée centrale f
alarm n (warning) alarme f; **a fire alarm** une alarme à incendie
alarm clock n réveil m
album n album m
alcohol n alcool m
alcoholic n alcoolique mf ▷ *He's an alcoholic.* C'est un alcoolique.
▶ adj alcoolisé(e) ▷ *alcoholic drinks* des boissons alcoolisées
alert adj ❶ (bright) vif (f vive) ▷ *a very alert baby* un bébé très vif ❷ (paying attention) vigilant(e) ▷ *We must stay alert.* Nous devons rester vigilants.

A levels npl baccalauréat msg
The **baccalauréat** (or **bac** for short) is taken at the age of 17 or 18. Students have to sit one of a variety of set subject combinations, rather than being able to choose any combination of subjects they want. If you pass you have the right to a place at university.
Algeria n Algérie f; **in Algeria** en Algérie
alien n (from outer space) extra-terrestre mf
alike adv to look alike se ressembler [28] ▷ *The two sisters look alike.* Les deux sœurs se ressemblent.
alive adj vivant(e)
all adj, pron, adv tout(e) (mpl tous) ▷ *all the time* tout le temps ▷ *I ate all of it.* J'ai tout mangé. ▷ *all day* toute la journée ▷ *all the books* tous les livres ▷ *all the girls* toutes les filles; **All of us went.** Nous y sommes tous allés.; **after all** après tout ▷ *After all, nobody can make us go.* Après tout, personne ne peut nous obliger à y aller.; **all alone** tout seul ▷ *She's all alone.* Elle est toute seule.; **not at all** pas du tout ▷ *I'm not tired at all.* Je ne suis pas du tout fatigué.; **The score is 5 all.** Le score est de cinq partout.
allergic adj allergique; **to be allergic to something** être [35] allergique à quelque chose ▷ *I'm allergic to cats' hair.* Je suis allergique aux poils de chat.

allergy n allergie f
allow vb **to be allowed to do something** être [35] autorisé à faire quelque chose ▷ He's not allowed to go out at night. Il n'est pas autorisé à sortir le soir.; **to allow somebody to do something** permettre [47] à quelqu'un de faire quelque chose ▷ His mum allowed him to go out. Sa mère lui a permis de sortir.

all right adv ❶ (okay) bien ▷ Everything turned out all right. Tout s'est bien terminé.; **Are you all right?** Ça va? ❷ (not bad) pas mal ▷ The film was all right. Le film n'était pas mal. ❸ (when agreeing) d'accord ▷ We'll talk about it later. —All right. On en reparlera plus tard. — D'accord.; **Is that all right with you?** Tu es d'accord?

almond n amande f
almost adv presque ▷ I've almost finished. J'ai presque fini.

alone adj, adv seul(e) ▷ She lives alone. Elle habite seule.; **to leave somebody alone** laisser [28] quelqu'un tranquille ▷ Leave her alone! Laisse-la tranquille!; **to leave something alone** ne pas toucher [28] à quelque chose ▷ Leave my things alone! Ne touche pas à mes affaires!

along prep, adv le long de ▷ Chris was walking along the beach. Chris se promenait le long de la plage.; **all along** depuis le début ▷ He was lying to me all along. Il m'a menti depuis le début.

aloud adv à haute voix ▷ He read the poem aloud. Il a lu le poème à haute voix.

alphabet n alphabet m
Alps npl Alpes fpl
already adv déjà ▷ Liz had already gone. Liz était déjà partie.
also adv aussi
alter vb changer [45]
alternate adj **on alternate days** tous les deux jours
alternative n choix m ▷ You have no alternative. Tu n'as pas le choix.; **Fruit is a healthy alternative to chocolate.** Les fruits sont plus sains que le chocolat.; **There are several alternatives.** Il y a plusieurs possibilités.
▶ adj autre ▷ They made alternative plans. Ils ont pris d'autres dispositions.; **an alternative solution** une solution de rechange; **alternative medicine** la médecine douce

alternatively adv **Alternatively, we could just stay at home.** On pourrait aussi rester à la maison.

although conj bien que

▌ bien que has to be followed by a verb in the subjunctive.

▷ Although she was tired, she stayed up late. Bien qu'elle soit fatiguée, elle s'est couchée tard.

altogether adv ❶ (in total) en tout ▷ You owe me £20 altogether. Tu me dois vingt livres en tout. ❷ (completely) tout à fait ▷ I'm not altogether happy with your work. Je ne suis pas tout à fait satisfait de votre travail.

aluminium (US **aluminum**) *n*
aluminium *m*

always *adv* toujours ▷ *He's always
moaning.* Il est toujours en train de
ronchonner.

am *vb see* **be**

a.m. *abbr* du matin ▷ *at 4 a.m.* à
quatre heures du matin

amateur *n* amateur *m*

amaze *vb* **to be amazed** être [**35**]
stupéfait ▷ *I was amazed that I
managed to do it.* J'étais stupéfait
d'avoir réussi.

amazing *adj* ❶ (*surprising*)
stupéfiant(e) ▷ *That's amazing
news!* C'est une nouvelle
stupéfiante! ❷ (*excellent*)
exceptionnel (*f* exceptionnelle)
▷ *Vivian's an amazing cook.* Vivian
est une cuisinière exceptionnelle.

ambassador *n* ambassadeur *m*,
ambassadrice *f*

ambition *n* ambition *f*

ambitious *adj* ambitieux (*f*
ambitieuse) ▷ *She's very ambitious.*
Elle est très ambitieuse.

ambulance *n* ambulance *f*

amenities *npl* aménagements
mpl; **The hotel has very good
amenities.** L'hôtel est très bien
aménagé.

America *n* Amérique *f*; **in America**
en Amérique; **to America** en
Amérique

American *n* Américain *m*,
Américaine *f*; **the Americans** les
Américains

▶ *adj* américain(e) ▷ *She's American.*
Elle est américaine.

among *prep* parmi ▷ *There were six
children among them.* Il y avait six
enfants parmi eux.; **We were
among friends.** Nous étions entre
amis.; **among other things** entre
autres

amount *n* ❶ somme *f* ▷ *a large
amount of money* une grosse somme
d'argent ❷ quantité *f* ▷ *a huge
amount of rice* une énorme quantité
de riz

amp *n* ❶ (*of electricity*) ampère *m*
❷ (*for hi-fi*) ampli *m*

amplifier *n* (*for hi-fi*)
amplificateur *m*

amuse *vb* amuser [**28**] ▷ *He was
most amused by the story.* L'histoire
l'a beaucoup amusé.

amusement arcade *n* salle de
jeux électroniques *f*

an *art see* **a**

analyse *vb* analyser [**28**]

analysis *n* analyse *f*

ancestor *n* ancêtre *mf*

anchor *n* ancre *f*

ancient *adj* ❶ (*civilization*) antique
▷ *ancient Greece* la Grèce antique
❷ (*custom, building*) ancien (*f*
ancienne) ▷ *an ancient monument*
un monument ancien

and *conj* et ▷ *you and me* toi et moi;
Please try and come! Essaie de
venir!; **He talked and talked.** Il n'a
pas arrêté de parler.; **better and
better** de mieux en mieux

angel *n* ange *m*

anger *n* colère *f*

angle *n* angle *m*

angry adj en colère ▷ *Dad looks very angry.* Papa a l'air très en colère.; **to be angry with somebody** être [**35**] furieux contre quelqu'un ▷ *Mum's really angry with you.* Maman est vraiment furieuse contre toi.; **to get angry** se fâcher [**28**]

animal n animal m (pl animaux) .

ankle n cheville f

anniversary n anniversaire m ▷ *a wedding anniversary* un anniversaire de mariage

announce vb annoncer [**12**]

announcement n annonce f

annoy vb agacer [**12**] ▷ *He's really annoying me.* Il m'agace vraiment.; **to get annoyed** se fâcher [**28**] ▷ *Don't get so annoyed!* Ne vous fâchez pas!

annoying adj agaçant(e) ▷ *It's really annoying.* C'est vraiment agaçant.

annual adj annuel (f annuelle) ▷ *an annual meeting* une réunion annuelle

anorak n anorak m

another adj un autre (f une autre) ▷ *Would you like another piece of cake?* Tu veux un autre morceau de gâteau?

answer vb répondre [**69**] à ▷ *Can you answer my question?* Peux-tu répondre à ma question? ▷ *to answer the phone* répondre au téléphone; **to answer the door** aller [**3**] ouvrir ▷ *Can you answer the door please?* Tu peux aller ouvrir s'il te plaît?
▶ n ❶ (to question) réponse f

❷ (to problem) solution f

answering machine n répondeur m

ant n fourmi f

Antarctic n Antarctique f

anthem n **the national anthem** l'hymne national m

antibiotic n antibiotique m

antique n (furniture) meuble ancien m

antique shop n magasin d'antiquités m

antiseptic n antiseptique m

any adj, pron, adv

Use **du**, **de la** or **des** to translate 'any' according to the gender of the French noun that follows it. **du** and **de la** become **de l'** when they're followed by a noun starting with a vowel.

❶ du ▷ *Would you like any bread?* Voulez-vous du pain?; de la ▷ *Would you like any beer?* Voulez-vous de la bière?; de l' ▷ *Have you got any mineral water?* Avez-vous de l'eau minérale?; des ▷ *Have you got any Madonna CDs?* Avez-vous des CD de Madonna?

If you want to say you haven't got any of something, use **de** whatever the gender of the following noun is. **de** becomes **d'** when it comes before a noun starting with a vowel.

❷ de ▷ *I haven't got any books.* Je n'ai pas de livres.; d' ▷ *I haven't got any money.* Je n'ai pas d'argent. ❸ en

Use **en** where there is no noun after 'any'.

▷ *Sorry, I haven't got any.* Désolé, je n'en ai pas.; **any more**
(1) *(additional)* encore de ▷ *Would you like any more coffee?* Est-ce que tu veux encore du café? **(2)** *(no longer)* ne ... plus ▷ *I don't love him any more.* Je ne l'aime plus.

anybody *pron* ❶ *(in question)* quelqu'un ▷ *Has anybody got a pen?* Est-ce que quelqu'un a un stylo? ❷ *(no matter who)* n'importe qui ▷ *Anybody can learn to swim.* N'importe qui peut apprendre à nager. ❸ ne ... personne

Use **ne ... personne** in a negative sentence. **ne** comes before the verb, **personne** after it.

▷ *I can't see anybody.* Je ne vois personne.

anyhow *adv* de toute façon
anyone *pron* ❶ *(in question)* quelqu'un ❷ *(no matter who)* n'importe qui ❸ ne ... personne
anything *pron* ❶ *(in question)* quelque chose ▷ *Would you like anything to eat?* Tu veux manger quelque chose? ❷ *(no matter what)* n'importe quoi ▷ *Anything could happen.* Il pourrait arriver n'importe quoi. ❸ ne ... rien

Use **ne ... rien** in a negative sentence. **ne** comes before the verb, **rien** after it.

▷ *I can't hear anything.* Je n'entends rien.

anyway *adv* de toute façon ▷ *He*

doesn't want to go out and anyway he's not allowed. Il ne veut pas sortir et de toute façon il n'y est pas autorisé.

anywhere *adv* ❶ *(in question)* quelque part ▷ *Have you seen my coat anywhere?* Est-ce que tu as vu mon manteau quelque part? ❷ n'importe où ▷ *You can buy stamps almost anywhere.* On peut acheter des timbres presque n'importe où. ❸ ne ... nulle part

Use **ne ... nulle part** in a negative sentence. **ne** comes before the verb, **nulle part** after it.

▷ *I can't find it anywhere.* Je ne le trouve nulle part.

apart *adv* The two towns are 10 kilometres apart. Les deux villes sont à dix kilomètres l'une de l'autre.; **apart from** à part ▷ *Apart from that, everything's fine.* À part ça, tout va bien.

apartment *n* appartement *m*
apologize *vb* s'excuser **[28]** ▷ *He apologized for being late.* Il s'est excusé de son retard.; **I apologize!** Je vous prie de m'excuser.
apology *n* excuses *fpl*
apostrophe *n* apostrophe *f*
app *n* (= application) appli *f*
apparent *adj* apparent(e)
apparently *adv* apparemment
appeal *vb* lancer **[12]** un appel ▷ *They appealed for help.* Ils ont lancé un appel au secours.; **Greece doesn't appeal to me.** Ça ne me tente pas d'aller en Grèce.; **Does**

that appeal to you? Ça te tente?
▶ *n* appel *m* ▷ *They have launched an appeal.* Ils ont lancé un appel.

appear *vb* ❶ *(come into view)* apparaître [**56**] ▷ *The bus appeared around the corner.* Le bus est apparu au coin de la rue.; **to appear on TV** passer [**58**] à la télé ❷ *(seem)* paraître [**56**] ▷ *She appeared to be asleep.* Elle paraissait dormir.

appendicitis *n* appendicite *f*

appetite *n* appétit *m*

applaud *vb* applaudir [**38**]

applause *n* applaudissements *mpl*

apple *n* pomme *f*; **an apple tree** un pommier

applicant *n* candidat *m*, candidate *f* ▷ *There were a hundred applicants for the job.* Il y avait cent candidats pour ce poste.

application *n* **a job application** une candidature

application form *n* ❶ *(for job)* dossier de candidature *m* ❷ *(for university)* dossier d'inscription *m*

apply *vb* **to apply for a job** poser [**28**] sa candidature à un poste; **to apply to** *(be relevant)* s'appliquer [**28**] à ▷ *This rule doesn't apply to us.* Ce règlement ne s'applique pas à nous.

appointment *n* rendez-vous *m* ▷ *I've got a dental appointment.* J'ai rendez-vous chez le dentiste.

appreciate *vb* être [**35**] reconnaissant de ▷ *I really appreciate your help.* Je vous suis extrêmement reconnaissant de votre aide.

apprentice *n* apprenti *m*, apprentie *f*

approach *vb* ❶ *(get nearer to)* s'approcher [**28**] de ▷ *He approached the house.* Il s'est approché de la maison. ❷ *(tackle)* aborder [**28**] ▷ *to approach a problem* aborder un problème

appropriate *adj* approprié(e) ▷ *That dress isn't very appropriate for an interview.* Cette robe n'est pas très appropriée pour un entretien.

approval *n* approbation *f*

approve *vb* **to approve of** approuver [**28**] ▷ *I don't approve of his choice.* Je n'approuve pas son choix.; **They didn't approve of his girlfriend.** Sa copine ne leur a pas plu.

approximate *adj* approximatif (*f* approximative)

apricot *n* abricot *m*

April *n* avril *m*; **in April** en avril; **April Fools' Day** le premier avril

 ● Pinning a paper fish to
 ● somebody's back is a traditional
 ● April Fool joke in France.

apron *n* tablier *m*

Aquarius *n* Verseau *m* ▷ *I'm Aquarius.* Je suis Verseau.

Arab *n* Arabe *mf*
▶ *adj* arabe ▷ *the Arab countries* les pays arabes

Arabic *n* arabe *m*

arch *n* arc *m*

archaeologist *n* archéologue *mf* ▷ *He's an archaeologist.* Il est archéologue.

archaeology *n* archéologie *f*

archbishop n archevêque m
archeologist n (US) archéologue mf
archeology n (US) archéologie f
architect n architecte mf ▷ She's an architect. Elle est architecte.
architecture n architecture f
Arctic n Arctique m
are vb see **be**
area n ① région f ▷ She lives in the Paris area. Elle habite dans la région parisienne. ② quartier m ▷ My favourite area of Paris is Montmartre. Montmartre est le quartier de Paris que je préfère. ③ superficie f ▷ The field has an area of 1500m². Le champ a une superficie de mille cinq cents mètres carrés.
Argentina n Argentine f; **in Argentina** en Argentine
Argentinian adj argentin(e)
argue vb se disputer [28] ▷ They never stop arguing. Ils n'arrêtent pas de se disputer.
argument n to have an argument se disputer [28] ▷ They had an argument. Ils se sont disputés.
Aries n Bélier m ▷ I'm Aries. Je suis Bélier.
arm n bras m
armchair n fauteuil m
army n armée f
around prep, adv ① autour de ▷ She wore a scarf around her neck. Elle portait une écharpe autour du cou. ② (approximately) environ ▷ It costs around £100. Cela coûte environ cent livres. ③ (date, time) vers ▷ Let's meet at around 8 p.m.

Retrouvons-nous vers vingt heures.; **around here (1)** (nearby) près d'ici ▷ Is there a chemist's around here? Est-ce qu'il y a une pharmacie près d'ici? **(2)** (in this area) dans les parages ▷ He lives around here. Il habite dans les parages.
arrange vb to arrange to do something prévoir [92] de faire quelque chose ▷ They arranged to go out together on Friday. Ils ont prévu de sortir ensemble vendredi.; **to arrange a meeting** convenir [89] d'un rendez-vous ▷ Can we arrange a meeting? Pouvons-nous convenir d'un rendez-vous?; **to arrange a party** organiser [28] une fête
arrangement n (plan) arrangement m; **They made arrangements to go out on Friday night.** Ils ont organisé une sortie vendredi soir.
arrest vb arrêter [28] ▷ The police have arrested 5 people. La police a arrêté cinq personnes.
▶ n arrestation f; **to be under arrest** être [35] en état d'arrestation ▷ You're under arrest! Vous êtes en état d'arrestation!
arrival n arrivée f
arrive vb arriver [5] ▷ I arrived at 5 o'clock. Je suis arrivé à cinq heures.
arrow n flèche f
art n art m
artery n artère f
art gallery n musée m
article n article m ▷ a newspaper article un article de journal
artificial adj artificiel (f artificielle)

a b c d e f g h i j k l m n o p q r s t u v w x y z

artist n artiste mf ▷ She's an artist.
C'est une artiste.

artistic adj artistique

as conj, adv ❶ (while) au moment où
▷ He came in as I was leaving. Il est
arrivé au moment où je partais.
❷ (since) puisque ▷ As it's Sunday,
you can have a lie-in. Tu peux faire la
grasse matinée, puisque c'est
dimanche.; **as ... as** aussi ... que
▷ Pierre's as tall as Michel. Pierre est
aussi grand que Michel.; **twice
as ... as** deux fois plus ... que ▷ Her
coat cost twice as much as mine. Son
manteau a coûté deux fois plus
cher que le mien.; **as much ... as**
autant ... que ▷ I haven't got as much
money as you. Je n'ai pas autant
d'argent que toi.; **as soon as
possible** dès que possible ▷ I'll do it
as soon as possible. Je le ferai dès que
possible.; **as from tomorrow** à
partir de demain ▷ As from
tomorrow, the shop will be closed on
Sundays. À partir de demain, le
magasin sera fermé le dimanche.;
as though comme si ▷ She acted as
though she hadn't seen me. Elle a fait
comme si elle ne m'avait pas vu.;
as if comme si; **He works as a
waiter in the holidays.** Il travaille
comme serveur pendant les
vacances.

ashamed adj **to be ashamed** avoir
[8] honte ▷ You should be ashamed of
yourself! Tu devrais avoir honte!

ashtray n cendrier m

Asia n Asie f; **in Asia** en Asie

Asian n Asiatique mf

▶ adj asiatique; **He's Asian.** C'est
un Asiatique.

ask vb ❶ (inquire, request) demander
[28] ▷ 'Have you finished?' she asked.
'Tu as fini?' a-t-elle demandé.;
to ask somebody something
demander [28] quelque chose à
quelqu'un ▷ He asked her how old she
was. Il lui a demandé quel âge elle
avait.; **to ask for something**
demander [28] quelque chose ▷ He
asked for a cup of tea. Il a demandé
une tasse de thé.; **to ask somebody
to do something** demander [28] à
quelqu'un de faire quelque chose
▷ She asked him to do the shopping.
Elle lui a demandé de faire les
courses.; **to ask about something**
se renseigner [28] sur quelque
chose ▷ I asked about train times to
Leeds. Je me suis renseigné sur les
horaires des trains pour Leeds.; **to
ask somebody a question** poser
[28] une question à quelqu'un
❷ inviter [28] ▷ Have you asked
Nadiya to the party? Est-ce que tu as
invité Nadiya à la fête?; **He asked
her out.** (on a date) Il lui a demandé
de sortir avec lui.

asleep adj **to be asleep** dormir [29]
▷ He's asleep. Il dort.; **to fall asleep**
s'endormir [29] ▷ I fell asleep in front
of the TV. Je me suis endormi devant
la télé.

asparagus n asperges fpl

aspirin n aspirine f

assembly n
There is no assembly in French
schools.

assignment n (in school) devoir m

assistance n aide f

assistant n ❶ (in shop) vendeur m, vendeuse f ❷ (helper) assistant m, assistante f

association n association f

assortment n assortiment m

assume vb supposer [28] ▷ I assume she won't be coming. Je suppose qu'elle ne viendra pas.

assure vb assurer [28] ▷ He assured me he was coming. Il m'a assuré qu'il viendrait.

asthma n asthme m ▷ I've got asthma. J'ai de l'asthme.

astonished adj étonné(e)

astonishing adj étonnant(e)

astrology n astrologie f

astronaut n astronaute mf

astronomy n astronomie f

at prep

à + le becomes au, à + les becomes aux.

à ▷ at 4 o'clock à quatre heures ▷ at Christmas à Noël ▷ at home à la maison ▷ at school à l'école au ▷ at the office au bureau aux ▷ at the races aux courses; **at night** la nuit; **What are you doing at the weekend?** Qu'est-ce que tu fais ce week-end?

▶ n (@ symbol) arobase f

ate vb see **eat**

Athens n Athènes; **in Athens** à Athènes

athlete n athlète mf

athletic adj athlétique

athletics n athlétisme m ▷ I love athletics. J'aime l'athlétisme.

Atlantic n océan Atlantique m

atlas n atlas m

atmosphere n atmosphère f

atom n atome m

atomic adj atomique

attach vb fixer [28] ▷ He attached a rope to the car. Il a fixé une corde à la voiture.; **Please find attached ...** Veuillez trouver ci-joint ...

attached adj **to be attached to** être [35] attaché à ▷ He's very attached to his family. Il est très attaché à sa famille.

attachment n (email) pièce jointe f

attack vb attaquer [28] ▷ The dog attacked her. Le chien l'a attaquée. ▶ n attaque f

attempt n tentative f ▷ She gave up after several attempts. Elle y a renoncé après plusieurs tentatives. ▶ vb **to attempt to do something** essayer [59] de faire quelque chose ▷ I attempted to write a song. J'ai essayé d'écrire une chanson.

attend vb assister [28] à ▷ to attend a meeting assister à une réunion

Be careful not to translate **to attend** by **attendre**.

attention n **to pay attention to** faire [36] attention à ▷ He didn't pay attention to what I was saying. Il ne faisait pas attention à ce que je disais.

attic n grenier m

attitude n (way of thinking) attitude f ▷ I really don't like your attitude! Je n'aime pas du tout ton attitude!

attorney n (US) avocat m, avocate f

attract vb attirer [28] ▷ The Lake

District attracts lots of tourists. La région des lacs attire de nombreux touristes.

attraction *n* attraction *f* ▷ *a tourist attraction* une attraction touristique

attractive *adj* séduisant(e) ▷ *She's very attractive.* Elle est très séduisante.

aubergine *n* aubergine *f*

auction *n* vente aux enchères *f*

audience *n* (*in theatre*) spectateurs *mpl*

August *n* août *m*; **in August** en août

aunt, aunty *n* tante *f* ▷ *my aunt* ma tante

au pair *n* jeune fille au pair *f* ▷ *She's an au pair.* Elle est jeune fille au pair.

Australia *n* Australie *f*; **in Australia** en Australie; **to Australia** en Australie

Australian *n* Australien *m*, Australienne *f*; **the Australians** les Australiens
▶ *adj* australien (*f* australienne)
▷ *He's Australian.* Il est australien.

Austria *n* Autriche *f*; **in Austria** en Autriche

Austrian *n* Autrichien *m*, Autrichienne *f*; **the Austrians** les Autrichiens
▶ *adj* autrichien (*f* autrichienne)
▷ *She's Austrian.* Elle est autrichienne.

author *n* auteur *m* ▷ *She's a famous author.* C'est un auteur connu.

autobiography *n* autobiographie *f*

autograph *n* autographe *m*

automatic *adj* automatique ▷ *an automatic door* une porte automatique

automatically *adv* automatiquement

autumn *n* automne *m*; **in autumn** en automne

availability *n* disponibilité *f*

available *adj* disponible ▷ *Free brochures are available on request.* Des brochures gratuites sont disponibles sur demande. ▷ *Is Mr Cooke available today?* Est-ce que Monsieur Cooke est disponible aujourd'hui?

avalanche *n* avalanche *f*

avatar *n* avatar *m*

avenue *n* avenue *f*

average *n* moyenne *f* ▷ *on average* en moyenne
▶ *adj* moyen (*f* moyenne) ▷ *the average price* le prix moyen

avocado *n* avocat *m*

avoid *vb* éviter [**28**] ▷ *He avoids her when she's in a bad mood.* Il l'évite lorsqu'elle est de mauvaise humeur.; **to avoid doing something** éviter [**28**] de faire quelque chose ▷ *Avoid going out on your own at night.* Évite de sortir seul le soir.

awake *adj* **to be awake** être [**35**] réveillé ▷ *Is she awake?* Elle est réveillée?; **He was still awake.** Il ne dormait pas encore.

award *n* prix *m* ▷ *He's won an award.* Il a remporté un prix.

aware *adj* **to be aware of something** être [**35**] conscient de

quelque chose

away adj, adv (not here) <u>absent(e)</u>
▷ André's away today. André est
absent aujourd'hui.; **He's away for
a week.** Il est parti pour une
semaine.; **The town's 2
kilometres away.** La ville est à
deux kilomètres d'ici.; **The coast is
2 hours away by car.** La côte est à
deux heures de route.; **Go away!**
Va-t'en!; **to put something away**
ranger [**45**] quelque chose ▷ He put
the books away in the cupboard. Il a
rangé les livres dans le placard.

away match n <u>match à
l'extérieur</u> m

awful adj <u>affreux</u> (f affreuse)
▷ That's awful! C'est affreux!; **an
awful lot of ...** énormément de ...

awkward adj ❶ (difficult to deal
with) <u>délicat(e)</u> ▷ an awkward
situation une situation délicate
❷ (embarrassing) <u>gênant(e)</u> ▷ an
awkward question une question
gênante; **It's a bit awkward for
me to come and see you.** Ce n'est
pas très pratique pour moi de venir
vous voir.

axe n <u>hache</u> f

baby n <u>bébé</u> m
babysit vb <u>faire</u> [**36**] <u>du
baby-sitting</u>
babysitter n <u>baby-sitter</u> mf
babysitting n <u>baby-sitting</u> m
back n ❶ (of person, horse, book) <u>dos</u>
m ❷ (of car, house) <u>arrière</u> m ▷ in the
back à l'arrière ❸ (of page) <u>verso</u> m
▷ on the back au verso ❹ (of room,
garden) <u>fond</u> m ▷ at the back au fond
▶ adj, adv <u>arrière</u> ▷ the back seat le
siège arrière ▷ the back wheel of my
bike la roue arrière de mon vélo;
the back door la porte de
derrière; **to get back** rentrer [**68**]
▷ What time did you get back? À
quelle heure est-ce que tu es
rentré?; **We went there by bus
and walked back.** Nous y sommes
allés en bus et nous sommes

rentrés à pied.; **He's not back yet.**
Il n'est pas encore rentré.; **to call**
somebody back rappeler [**4**]
quelqu'un ▷ *I'll call back later.* Je
rappellerai plus tard.
▶ *vb (support)* soutenir [**83**] ▷ *I'm*
backing Nicola Sturgeon. Je soutiens
Nicola Sturgeon.; **to back a horse**
parier [**19**] sur un cheval

back out *vb* se désister [**28**] ▷ *They*
backed out at the last minute. Ils se
sont désistés au dernier moment.

back up *vb* to back somebody up
soutenir [**83**] quelqu'un

backache *n* mal au dos *m* ▷ *to have*
backache avoir mal au dos

backbone *n (spine)* colonne
vertébrale *f*

backfire *vb (go wrong)* échouer [**28**]

background *n* ❶ *(of picture)*
arrière-plan *m* ▷ *a house in the*
background une maison à
l'arrière-plan; **background noise**
les bruits de fond *mpl* ❷ milieu *m (pl*
milieux) ▷ *his family background* son
milieu familial

backhand *n* revers *m*

backing *n (support)* soutien *m*

backpack *n* sac à dos *m*

backpacker *n* ❶ *(globe-trotter)*
routard *m*, routarde *f* ❷ *(hill-walker)*
randonneur *m*, randonneuse *f*

backside *n* derrière *m*

backstroke *n* dos crawlé *m*

backup *n (support)* soutien *m*; **a**
backup file une sauvegarde

backwards *adv* en arrière ▷ *to take*
a step backwards faire un pas en
arrière; **to fall backwards** tomber

[**84**] à la renverse

bacon *n* ❶ *(French type)* lard *m*
❷ *(British type)* bacon *m* ▷ *bacon and*
eggs des œufs au bacon

bad *adj* ❶ mauvais(e) ▷ *to be in a bad*
mood être de mauvaise humeur; **to**
be bad at something être [**35**]
mauvais en quelque chose ▷ *I'm*
really bad at maths. Je suis vraiment
mauvais en maths. ❷ *(serious)*
grave ▷ *a bad accident* un accident
grave ❸ *(naughty)* vilain(e) ▷ *You*
bad boy! Vilain!; **to go bad** *(food)* se
gâter [**28**]; **I feel bad about it.** Ça
m'ennuie.; **not bad** pas mal
▷ *That's not bad at all.* Ce n'est pas
mal du tout.

badge *n* badge *m*

badly *adv* mal ▷ *badly paid* mal payé;
badly wounded grièvement
blessé; **He badly needs a rest.**
Il a sérieusement besoin de se
reposer.

badminton *n* badminton *m* ▷ *to*
play badminton jouer au badminton

bad-tempered *adj* to be
bad-tempered **(1)** *(by nature)* avoir
[**8**] mauvais caractère ▷ *He's a really*
bad-tempered person. Il a vraiment
mauvais caractère. **(2)** *(temporarily)*
être [**35**] de mauvaise humeur ▷ *He*
was really bad-tempered yesterday. Il
était vraiment de mauvaise
humeur hier.

bag *n* sac *m*

baggage *n* bagages *mpl*

baggage reclaim *n* livraison des
bagages *f*

bagpipes *npl* cornemuse *fsg* ▷ *Ed*

plays the bagpipes. Ed joue de la cornemuse.

bake *vb* **to bake a cake** faire [**36**] un gâteau

baked *adj* cuit au four (*f* cuite au four) ▷ *baked potatoes* les pommes de terre cuites au four *fpl*; **baked beans** les haricots blancs en sauce *mpl*

baker *n* boulanger *m*, boulangère *f* ▷ *He's a baker.* Il est boulanger.

bakery *n* boulangerie *f*

balance *n* équilibre *m* ▷ *to lose one's balance* perdre l'équilibre

balanced *adj* équilibré(e)

balcony *n* balcon *m*

bald *adj* chauve

ball *n* ❶ (*tennis, golf, cricket*) balle *f* ❷ (*football, rugby*) ballon *m*

ballet *n* ballet *m* ▷ *We went to a ballet.* Nous sommes allés voir un ballet.; **ballet lessons** les cours de danse *mpl*

ballet dancer *n* danseur classique *m*, danseuse classique *f*

ballet shoes *npl* chaussons de danse *mpl*

balloon *n* (*for parties*) ballon *m*; **a hot-air balloon** une montgolfière

ballpoint pen *n* stylo à bille *m*

ban *n* interdiction *f*
▶ *vb* interdire [**27**]

banana *n* banane *f* ▷ *a banana skin* une peau de banane

band *n* ❶ (*rock band*) groupe *m* ❷ (*brass band*) fanfare *f*

bandage *n* bandage *m*
▶ *vb* mettre [**47**] un bandage à ▷ *The nurse bandaged his arm.* L'infirmière

lui a mis un bandage au bras.

Band-Aid® *n* (*US*) pansement adhésif *m*

bang *n* ❶ détonation *f* ▷ *I heard a loud bang.* J'ai entendu une forte détonation. ❷ coup *m* ▷ *a bang on the head* un coup sur la tête; **Bang!** Pan!
▶ *vb* (*part of body*) se cogner [**28**] ▷ *I banged my head.* Je me suis cogné la tête.; **to bang the door** claquer [**28**] la porte; **to bang on the door** cogner [**28**] à la porte

Bangladesh *n* Bangladesh *m*; **from Bangladesh** du Bangladesh

bank *n* ❶ (*financial*) banque *f* ❷ (*of river, lake*) bord *m*

bank account *n* compte en banque *m*

banker *n* banquier *m*

bank holiday *n* jour férié *m*

banknote *n* billet de banque *m*

bar *n* ❶ (*pub*) bar *m* ❷ (*counter*) comptoir *m*; **a bar of chocolate** une tablette de chocolat; **a bar of soap** une savonnette

barbecue *n* barbecue *m*

bare *adj* nu(e)

barefoot *adj, adv* nu-pieds ▷ *The children go around barefoot.* Les enfants se promènent nu-pieds.; **to be barefoot** avoir [**8**] les pieds nus ▷ *She was barefoot.* Elle avait les pieds nus.

barely *adv* à peine ▷ *I could barely hear what she was saying.* J'entendais à peine ce qu'elle disait.

bargain *n* affaire *f* ▷ *It was a bargain!* C'était une affaire!

barge n péniche f
bark vb aboyer [53]
barmaid n barmaid f ▷ She's a barmaid. Elle est barmaid.
barman n barman m ▷ He's a barman. Il est barman.
barn n grange f
barrel n tonneau m (pl tonneaux)
barrier n barrière f
base n base f
baseball n base-ball m; **a baseball cap** une casquette de base-ball
based adj **based on** fondé sur
basement n sous-sol m
bash vb **to bash something** taper [28] sur quelque chose
▷ n **I'll have a bash.** Je vais essayer.
basic adj ❶ de base ▷ It's a basic model. C'est un modèle de base.
❷ rudimentaire ▷ The accommodation is pretty basic. Le logement est plutôt rudimentaire.
basically adv tout simplement
▷ Basically, I just don't like him. Tout simplement, je ne l'aime pas.
basics npl rudiments mpl
basin n (washbasin) lavabo m
basis n **on a daily basis** quotidiennement; **on a regular basis** régulièrement
basket n panier m
basketball n basket m
bass n ❶ (guitar, singer) basse f ▷ He plays the bass. Il joue de la basse.; **a bass guitar** une guitare basse ❷ (on hi-fi) graves mpl
bass drum n grosse caisse f
bassoon n basson m ▷ I play the bassoon. Je joue du basson.

bat n ❶ (for cricket, rounders) batte f ❷ (for table tennis) raquette f ❸ (animal) chauve-souris f (pl chauves-souris)
bath n ❶ bain m ▷ to have a bath prendre un bain; **a hot bath** un bain chaud ❷ (bathtub) baignoire f ▷ There's a spider in the bath. Il y a une araignée dans la baignoire.
bathe vb se baigner [28]
bathroom n salle de bains f
bath towel n serviette de bain f
batter n pâte à frire f
battery n ❶ (for torch, toy) pile f ❷ (of car) batterie f
battle n bataille f ▷ the Battle of Hastings la bataille de Hastings; **It was a battle, but we managed in the end.** Il a fallu se battre, mais on a fini par y arriver.
bay n baie f
BC abbr (= before Christ) av. J.-C. (= avant Jésus-Christ) ▷ in 200 BC en deux cents avant Jésus-Christ
be vb être [35] ▷ I'm tired. Je suis fatigué. ▷ I've been ill. J'ai été malade.; **It's the 28th of October today.** Nous sommes le vingt-huit octobre.; **Have you been to Greece before?** Est-ce que tu es déjà allé en Grèce?; **I've never been to Paris.** Je ne suis jamais allé à Paris.; **to be killed** être [35] tué

When you are saying what somebody's occupation is, you leave out the 'a' in French.
▷ He's a student. Il est étudiant.

With certain adjectives, such as 'cold', 'hot', 'hungry' and 'thirsty', use **avoir** instead of **être**.

I'm cold. J'ai froid.; **I'm hungry.** J'ai faim.

When saying how old somebody is, use **avoir** not **être**.

I'm fourteen. J'ai quatorze ans.; **How old are you?** Quel âge as-tu?

When referring to the weather, use **faire**.

It's cold. Il fait froid.; **It's a nice day.** Il fait beau.; **It's too hot.** Il fait trop chaud.

beach n plage f

bead n perle f

beak n bec m

beam n rayon m

beans n ❶ haricots mpl ❷ (baked beans) haricots blancs à la sauce tomate mpl; **broad beans** les fèves fpl; **green beans** les haricots verts mpl; **kidney beans** les haricots rouges mpl

bear n ours m
▶ vb **I can't bear it!** C'est insupportable!

bear up vb tenir [83] le coup; **Bear up!** Tiens bon!

beard n barbe f; **He's got a beard.** Il est barbu.; **a man with a beard** un barbu

bearded adj barbu(e)

beat n rythme m
▶ vb battre [9] ▷ We beat them 3-0. On les a battus trois à zéro.; **Beat it!** Fiche le camp! (informal); **to**

beat somebody up (informal) tabasser [28] quelqu'un

beautiful adj beau (f belle, mpl beaux)

beautifully adv admirablement

beauty n beauté f

became vb see **become**

because conj parce que ▷ I did it because … Je l'ai fait parce que …; **because of** à cause de ▷ because of the weather à cause du temps

become vb devenir [25] ▷ He became a famous writer. Il est devenu un grand écrivain.

bed n lit m ▷ in bed au lit; **to go to bed** aller [3] se coucher; **to go to bed with somebody** coucher [28] avec quelqu'un

bed and breakfast n chambre d'hôte f ▷ We stayed in a bed and breakfast. Nous avons logé dans une chambre d'hôte.

bedclothes npl draps et les couvertures mpl

bedding n literie f

bedroom n chambre f

bedsit n chambre meublée f

bedspread n dessus-de-lit m (pl dessus-de-lit)

bedtime n Ten o'clock is my usual bedtime. Je me couche généralement à dix heures.; **Bedtime!** Au lit!

bee n abeille f

beef n bœuf m; **roast beef** le rosbif

beefburger n hamburger m

been vb see **be**

beer n bière f

beetle n scarabée m

a
b
c
d
e
f
g
h
i
j
k
l
m
n
o
p
q
r
s
t
u
v
w
x
y
z

beetroot n betterave rouge f
before prep, conj, adv ❶ avant
▷ before Tuesday avant mardi
❷ avant de ▷ I'll phone before I leave.
J'appellerai avant de partir.
❸ (already) déjà ▷ I've seen this film
before. J'ai déjà vu ce film.; **the day
before** la veille; **the week before**
la semaine précédente
beforehand adv à l'avance
beg vb ❶ (for money) mendier [**19**]
❷ supplier [**19**] ▷ He begged me to
stop. Il m'a supplié d'arrêter.
began vb see **begin**
beggar n mendiant m, mendiante f
begin vb commencer [**12**]; **to begin
doing something** commencer [**12**]
à faire quelque chose
beginner n débutant m, débutante
f ▷ I'm just a beginner. Je ne suis
qu'un débutant.
beginning n début m ▷ in the
beginning au début
begun vb see **begin**
behalf n **on behalf of somebody**
pour quelqu'un
behave vb se comporter [**28**] ▷ He
behaved like an idiot. Il s'est comporté
comme un idiot. ▷ She behaved very
badly. Elle s'est très mal comportée.;
to behave oneself être [**35**] sage
▷ Did the children behave themselves?
Est-ce que les enfants ont été
sages?; **Behave!** Sois sage!
behaviour (US **behavior**) n
comportement m
behind prep, adv derrière ▷ behind
the television derrière la télévision;
to be behind (late) avoir [**8**] du

retard ▷ I'm behind with my revision.
J'ai du retard dans mes révisions.
▶ n derrière m
beige adj beige
Belgian n Belge mf; **the Belgians**
les Belges
▶ adj belge ▷ She's Belgian. Elle est
belge.
Belgium n Belgique f; **in Belgium**
en Belgique
believe vb croire [**20**] ▷ I don't
believe you. Je ne te crois pas.; **to
believe in something** croire [**20**] à
quelque chose ▷ Do you believe in
ghosts? Tu crois aux fantômes?; **to
believe in God** croire [**20**] en Dieu
bell n ❶ (doorbell) sonnette f; **to
ring the bell** sonner [**28**] à la porte
❷ (in church) cloche f ❸ (in school)
sonnerie f ❹ clochette f ▷ Our cat
has a bell on its collar. Notre chat a
une clochette sur son collier.
belong vb **to belong to somebody**
être [**35**] à quelqu'un ▷ Who does it
belong to? C'est à qui? ▷ That belongs
to me. C'est à moi.; **Do you belong
to any clubs?** Est-ce que tu es
membre d'un club?; **Where does
this belong?** Où est-ce que ça va?
belongings npl affaires fpl
below prep, adv ❶ au-dessous de
▷ below the castle au-dessous du
château ❷ en dessous ▷ on the floor
below à l'étage en dessous; **10
degrees below freezing** moins dix
belt n ceinture f
bench n ❶ (seat) banc m ❷ (for
woodwork) établi m
benchmark n référence f

bend n ❶ (in road) virage m ❷ (in river) coude m
▶ vb ❶ (back) courber [28] ❷ (leg, arm) plier [19] ▷ I can't bend my arm. Je n'arrive pas à plier le bras.; 'do not bend' ne pas plier' ❸ (object) tordre [49] ▷ You've bent it. Tu l'as tordu. ❹ se tordre [49] ▷ It bends easily. Ça se tord facilement.
bend down vb se baisser [28]
bend over vb se pencher [28]
beneath prep sous
benefit n (advantage) avantage m; **unemployment benefit** les allocations chômage
▶ vb **He'll benefit from the change.** Le changement lui fera du bien.
bent vb see **bend**
▶ adj tordu(e) ▷ a bent fork une fourchette tordue
beret n béret m
berth n couchette f
beside prep à côté de ▷ beside the television à côté de la télévision; **He was beside himself.** Il était hors de lui.; **That's beside the point.** Cela n'a rien à voir.
besides adv en plus ▷ Besides, it's too expensive. En plus, c'est trop cher.
best adj, adv ❶ meilleur(e) ▷ He's the best player in the team. Il est le meilleur joueur de l'équipe. ▷ Janet's the best at maths. Janet est la meilleure en maths. ❷ le mieux ▷ Emma sings best. C'est Emma qui chante le mieux. ▷ That's the best I can do. Je ne peux pas faire mieux.; **to do one's best** faire [36] de son

mieux ▷ It's not perfect, but I did my best. Ça n'est pas parfait, mais j'ai fait de mon mieux.; **to make the best of it** s'en contenter [28] ▷ We'll have to make the best of it. Il va falloir nous en contenter.
best man n garçon d'honneur m
bet n pari m ▷ to make a bet faire un pari
▶ vb parier [19] ▷ I bet he forgot. Je parie qu'il a oublié.
better adj, adv ❶ meilleur(e) ▷ This one's better than that one. Celui-ci est meilleur que celui-là. ▷ a better way to do it une meilleure façon de le faire ❷ mieux ▷ That's better! C'est mieux comme ça.; **better still** encore mieux ▷ Go and see her tomorrow, or better still, go today. Va la voir demain, ou encore mieux, vas-y aujourd'hui.; **to get better** (1) (improve) s'améliorer [28] ▷ My French is getting better. Mon français s'améliore. (2) (from illness) se remettre [47] ▷ I hope you get better soon. J'espère que tu vas vite te remettre.; **to feel better** se sentir [77] mieux ▷ Are you feeling better now? Tu te sens mieux maintenant?; **You'd better do it straight away.** Vous feriez mieux de le faire immédiatement.; **I'd better go home.** Je ferais mieux de rentrer.
between prep entre ▷ Stroud is between Oxford and Bristol. Stroud est entre Oxford et Bristol. ▷ between 15 and 20 minutes entre quinze et vingt minutes

a
b
c
d
e
f
g
h
i
j
k
l
m
n
o
p
q
r
s
t
u
v
w
x
y
z

beyond prep au-delà de ▷ There was a lake beyond the mountain. Il y avait un lac au-delà de la montagne.; **beyond belief** incroyable; **beyond repair** irréparable

Bible n Bible f

bicycle n vélo m

big adj ❶ grand(e) ▷ a big house une grande maison ▷ my big brother mon grand frère; **He's a big guy.** C'est un grand gaillard. ❷ (car, animal, book, parcel) gros (f grosse) ▷ a big car une grosse voiture

bigheaded adj to be bigheaded avoir [8] la grosse tête

bike n vélo m ▷ by bike en vélo

bikini n bikini m

bilingual adj bilingue

bill n ❶ (in restaurant) addition f ▷ Can we have the bill, please? L'addition, s'il vous plaît. ❷ (for gas, electricity) facture f ❸ (US) billet m ▷ a five-dollar bill un billet de cinq dollars

billiards n billard m ▷ to play billiards jouer au billard

billion n milliard m

bin n poubelle f

binoculars npl jumelles fpl; **a pair of binoculars** des jumelles

biochemistry n biochimie f

biography n biographie f

biology n biologie f

bird n oiseau m (pl oiseaux)

birdwatching n My hobby's birdwatching. Mon passe-temps favori est d'observer les oiseaux.; **to go birdwatching** aller [3] observer les oiseaux

Biro® n bic® m

birth n naissance f ▷ date of birth la date de naissance

birth certificate n acte de naissance m

birth control n contraception f

birthday n anniversaire m ▷ When's your birthday? Quelle est la date de ton anniversaire?; **a birthday cake** un gâteau d'anniversaire; **a birthday card** une carte d'anniversaire; **I'm going to have a birthday party.** Je vais faire une fête pour mon anniversaire.

biscuit n gâteau sec m (pl gâteaux secs)

bishop n évêque m

bit vb see bite
▶ n morceau m (pl morceaux) ▷ Would you like another bit? Est-ce que tu en veux un autre morceau?; **a bit of (1)** (piece of) un morceau de ▷ a bit of cake un morceau de gâteau **(2)** (a little) un peu de ▷ a bit of music un peu de musique; **It's a bit of a nuisance.** C'est ennuyeux.; **a bit** un peu ▷ a bit too hot un peu trop chaud; **to fall to bits** se désintégrer [34]; **to take something to bits** démonter [28] quelque chose; **bit by bit** petit à petit

bite vb ❶ (person, dog) mordre [49] ❷ (insect) piquer [28] ▷ I got bitten by mosquitoes. Je me suis fait piquer par des moustiques.; **to bite one's nails** se ronger [45] les ongles
▶ n ❶ (insect bite) piqûre f ❷ (animal bite) morsure f; **to have a bite to**

eat manger [**45**] un morceau
bitten vb see **bite**
bitter adj ❶ amer (f amère)
❷ (weather, wind) glacial(e) (mpl
glaciaux) ▷ It's bitter today. Il fait un
froid glacial aujourd'hui.
  ▶ n bière brune f
black adj noir(e) ▷ a black jacket une
veste noire
blackberry n mûre f
blackbird n merle m
blackboard n tableau noir m (pl
tableaux noirs)
blackcurrant n cassis m
blackmail n chantage m ▷ That's
blackmail! C'est du chantage!
  ▶ vb to blackmail somebody faire
[**36**] chanter quelqu'un ▷ He
blackmailed her. Il l'a fait chanter.
black pudding n boudin m
blade n lame f
blame vb Don't blame me! Ça n'est
pas ma faute!; **I blame the police.**
À mon avis, c'est la faute de la
police.; **He blamed it on my
sister.** Il a dit que c'était la faute de
ma sœur.
blank adj ❶ (paper) blanc (f blanche)
❷ (video, page) vierge; **My mind
went blank.** J'ai eu un trou.
  ▶ n blanc m ▷ Fill in the blanks.
Remplissez les blancs.
blanket n couverture f
blast n a bomb blast une explosion
blaze n incendie m
blazer n blazer m
bleach n eau de Javel f
bleed vb saigner [**28**] ▷ My nose is
bleeding. Je saigne du nez.

blender n mixer m
bless vb (religiously) bénir [**38**];
  Bless you! (after sneezing) À tes
souhaits!
blew vb see **blow**
blind adj aveugle
  ▶ n (for window) store m
blink vb cligner [**28**] des yeux
blister n ampoule f
blizzard n tempête de neige f
block n immeuble m ▷ He lives in our
block. Il habite dans notre immeuble.;
  a block of flats un immeuble
  ▶ vb bloquer [**28**]
blog n blog m
  ▶ vb bloquer [**28**]
blogger n bloggeur m, bloggeuse f
blogpost n post m de blog
blonde adj blond(e) ▷ She's got
blonde hair. Elle a les cheveux blonds.
blood n sang m
blood pressure n to have high
  blood pressure faire [**36**] de la
  tension
blood test n prise de sang f
blouse n chemisier m
blow n coup m
  ▶ vb (wind, person) souffler [**28**]; to
  blow one's nose se moucher [**28**];
  to blow a whistle siffler [**28**]; to
  blow out a candle éteindre [**60**]
  une bougie
blow up vb ❶ faire [**36**] sauter ▷ The
terrorists blew up a police station. Les
terroristes ont fait sauter un
commissariat de police. ❷ gonfler
[**28**] ▷ to blow up a balloon gonfler
un ballon; **The house blew up.** La
maison a sauté.

a
b
c
d
e
f
g
h
i
j
k
l
m
n
o
p
q
r
s
t
u
v
w
x
y
z

blow-dry n brushing m; **A cut and blow-dry, please.** Une coupe brushing, s'il vous plaît.

blown vb see **blow**

blue adj bleu(e) ▷ a blue dress une robe bleue; **It came out of the blue.** C'était complètement inattendu.

blues npl blues msg

blunder n gaffe f

blunt adj ❶ (person) brusque ❷ (knife) émoussé(e)

blush vb rougir [38]

board n ❶ (wooden) planche f ❷ (blackboard) tableau m (pl tableaux) ▷ on the board au tableau ❸ (noticeboard) panneau m (pl panneaux) ❹ (for board games) jeu m (pl jeux) ❺ (for chess) échiquier m; **on board** à bord; **'full board'** pension complète'

boarder n interne mf

board game n jeu de société m (pl jeux de société)

boarding card n carte d'embarquement f

boarding school n pensionnat m; **I go to boarding school.** Je suis interne.

boast vb se vanter [28] ▷ Stop boasting! Arrête de te vanter!; **to boast about something** se vanter [28] de quelque chose

boat n bateau m (pl bateaux)

body n corps m

bodybuilding n culturisme m

bodyguard n garde du corps m

boil n furoncle m

▶ vb ❶ faire [36] bouillir ▷ to boil some water faire bouillir de l'eau; **to boil an egg** faire [36] cuire un œuf ❷ bouillir [11] ▷ The water's boiling. L'eau bout. ▷ The water's boiled. L'eau a bouilli.

boil over vb déborder [28]

boiled adj à l'eau ▷ boiled potatoes des pommes de terre à l'eau; **a boiled egg** un œuf à la coque

boiling adj **It's boiling in here!** Il fait une chaleur torride ici!; **boiling hot** torride ▷ a boiling hot day une journée torride

bolt n ❶ (on door) verrou m ❷ (with nut) boulon m

bomb n bombe f
▶ vb bombarder [28]

bomber n bombardier m

bombing n attentat à la bombe m

bone n ❶ (of human, animal) os m ❷ (of fish) arête f

bonfire n feu m (pl feux)

bonnet n (of car) capot m

bonus n ❶ (extra payment) prime f ❷ (added advantage) plus m

book n livre m
▶ vb réserver [28] ▷ We haven't booked. Nous n'avons pas réservé.

bookcase n bibliothèque f

booklet n brochure f

bookshelf n étagère à livres f

bookshop n librairie f

boot n ❶ (of car) coffre m ❷ (fashion boot) botte f ❸ (for hiking) chaussure de marche f; **football boots** des chaussures de foot

border n frontière f

bore vb see **bear**

bored adj **to be bored** s'ennuyer
[53] ▷ I was bored. Je m'ennuyais.;
to get bored s'ennuyer [53]
boring adj ennuyeux (f ennuyeuse)
born adj **to be born** naître [52]
▷ I was born in 1990. Je suis né en
mille neuf cent quatre-vingt-dix.
borrow vb emprunter [28] ▷ Can I
borrow your pen? Je peux emprunter
ton stylo?; **to borrow something
from somebody** emprunter [28]
quelque chose à quelqu'un
▷ I borrowed some money from a
friend. J'ai emprunté de l'argent à
un ami.
Bosnia n Bosnie f
Bosnian adj bosniaque
boss n patron m, patronne f
boss around vb **to boss
somebody around** donner [28]
des ordres à quelqu'un
bossy adj autoritaire
both adj, pron tous les deux mpl,
toutes les deux fpl ▷ We both went.
Nous y sommes allés tous les deux.
▷ Both of your answers are wrong. Vos
réponses sont toutes les deux
mauvaises. ▷ Both of them have left.
Ils sont partis tous les deux. ▷ Both
of us went. Nous y sommes allés
tous les deux. ▷ Both Maggie and
John are against it. Maggie et John
sont tous les deux contre.; **He
speaks both German and Italian.**
Il parle allemand et italien.
bother vb ❶ (worry) tracasser [28]
▷ What's bothering you? Qu'est-ce
qui te tracasse? ❷ (disturb)
déranger [45] ▷ I'm sorry to bother

you. Je suis désolé de vous
déranger.; **no bother** aucun
problème; **Don't bother!** Ça n'est
pas la peine!; **to bother to do
something** prendre [65] la peine
de faire quelque chose ▷ He didn't
bother to tell me about it. Il n'a pas
pris la peine de m'en parler.
bottle n bouteille f
bottle bank n conteneur à verre m
bottle-opener n ouvre-
bouteille m
bottom n ❶ (of container, bag, sea)
fond m ❷ (buttocks) derrière m ❸ (of
page, list) bas m
▶ adj inférieur(e) ▷ the bottom shelf
l'étagère inférieure; **the bottom
sheet** le drap de dessous
bought vb see **buy**
bounce vb rebondir [38]
bouncer n videur m
bound adj **He's bound to fail.** Il va
sûrement échouer.
boundary n frontière f
bow n ❶ (knot) nœud m ▷ to tie a
bow faire un nœud ❷ arc m ▷ a bow
and arrows un arc et des flèches
▶ vb faire [36] une révérence
bowl n (for soup, cereal) bol m
▶ vb (in cricket) lancer [12] la balle
bowling n bowling m; **to go
bowling** jouer [28] au bowling; **a
bowling alley** un bowling
bow tie n nœud papillon m
box n boîte f ▷ a box of matches une
boîte d'allumettes; **a cardboard
box** un carton
boxer n boxeur m
boxer shorts npl caleçon msg

a
b
c
d
e
f
g
h
i
j
k
l
m
n
o
p
q
r
s
t
u
v
w
x
y
z

boxing n boxe f
Boxing Day n lendemain de Noël m ▷ on Boxing Day le lendemain de Noël

> Word for word, this means 'the day after Christmas'.

boy n garçon m
boyfriend n copain m ▷ Have you got a boyfriend? Est-ce que tu as un copain?
bra n soutien-gorge m (pl soutiens-gorge)
brace n (on teeth) appareil m ▷ She wears a brace. Elle a un appareil.
bracelet n bracelet m
brackets npl in brackets entre parenthèses
brain n cerveau m (pl cerveaux)
brainy adj intelligent(e)
brake n frein m
> vb freiner [28]
branch n ❶ (of tree) branche f ❷ (of bank) agence f
brand n marque f ▷ a well-known brand of coffee une marque de café bien connue
brand-new adj tout neuf (f toute neuve)
brandy n cognac m
brass n cuivre m; the brass section les cuivres
brass band n fanfare f
brave adj courageux (f courageuse)
Brazil n Brésil m; in Brazil au Brésil
bread n pain m ▷ brown bread le pain complet ▷ white bread le pain blanc; **bread and butter** les tartines de pain beurrées fpl

break n ❶ (rest) pause f ▷ to take a break faire une pause ❷ (at school) récréation f ▷ during morning break pendant la récréation du matin; **the Christmas break** les vacances de Noël; **Give me a break!** Laisse-moi tranquille!
> vb ❶ casser [28] ▷ Careful, you'll break something! Attention, tu vas casser quelque chose! ❷ (get broken) se casser [28] ▷ Careful, it'll break! Attention, ça va se casser!; **to break one's leg** se casser [28] la jambe ▷ I broke my leg. Je me suis cassé la jambe. ▷ He broke his arm. Il s'est cassé le bras.; **to break a promise** rompre [75] une promesse; **to break a record** battre [9] un record; **to break the law** violer [28] la loi
break down vb tomber [84] en panne ▷ The car broke down. La voiture est tombée en panne.
break in vb entrer [32] par effraction
break off vb ❶ casser [28] ❷ se casser [28]
break open vb (door, cupboard) forcer [12]
break out vb ❶ (fire) se déclarer [28] ❷ (war) éclater [28] ❸ (prisoner) s'évader [28]; **to break out in a rash** être [35] couvert de boutons
break up vb ❶ (crowd) se disperser [28] ❷ (meeting, party) se terminer [28] ❸ (couple) se séparer [28]; **to break up a fight** mettre [47] fin à une bagarre; **We break up next**

Wednesday. Nos vacances commencent mercredi.

breakdown n ❶ (in vehicle) panne f ▷ to have a breakdown tomber en panne ❷ (mental) dépression f ▷ to have a breakdown faire une dépression

breakfast n petit déjeuner m ▷ What would you like for breakfast? Qu'est-ce vous voulez pour le petit déjeuner?

break-in n cambriolage m

breast n (of woman) sein m; **chicken breast** le blanc de poulet

breaststroke n brasse f

breath n haleine f ▷ to have bad breath avoir mauvaise haleine; **to be out of breath** être [35] essoufflé; **to get one's breath back** reprendre [65] son souffle

breathe vb respirer [28]

breathe in vb inspirer [28]

breathe out vb expirer [28]

breed vb (reproduce) se reproduire [23]; **to breed dogs** faire [36] de l'élevage de chiens
▷ n race f

breeze n brise f

brewery n brasserie f

bribe vb soudoyer [53]

brick n brique f ▷ a brick wall un mur en brique

bride n mariée f

bridegroom n marié m

bridesmaid n demoiselle d'honneur f

bridge n ❶ pont m ▷ a suspension bridge un pont suspendu ❷ bridge m ▷ to play bridge jouer au bridge

brief adj bref (f brève)

briefcase n serviette f

briefly adv brièvement

briefs npl slip msg; **a pair of briefs** un slip

bright adj ❶ (colour, light) vif (f vive) ▷ a bright colour une couleur vive; **bright blue** bleu vif ▷ a bright blue car une voiture bleu vif ❷ intelligent(e) ▷ He's not very bright. Il n'est pas très intelligent.

brilliant adj ❶ (wonderful) génial(e) (mpl géniaux) ▷ Brilliant! Génial! ❷ (clever) brillant(e) ▷ a brilliant scientist un savant brillant

bring vb ❶ apporter [28] ▷ Bring warm clothes. Apportez des vêtements chauds. ❷ (person) amener [43] ▷ Can I bring a friend? Est-ce que je peux amener un ami?

bring back vb rapporter [28]

bring forward vb avancer [12]

bring up vb élever [43] ▷ She brought up 5 children on her own. Elle a élevé cinq enfants toute seule.

Britain n Grande-Bretagne f; **in Britain** en Grande-Bretagne; **to Britain** en Grande-Bretagne; **I'm from Britain.** Je suis britannique.; **Great Britain** la Grande-Bretagne

British adj britannique; **the British** les Britanniques mpl; **the British Isles** les îles Britanniques fpl

Brittany n Bretagne f; **in Brittany** en Bretagne; **to Brittany** en Bretagne; **She's from Brittany.** Elle est bretonne.

broad adj (wide) large; **in broad daylight** en plein jour

a
b
c
d
e
f
g
h
i
j
k
l
m
n
o
p
q
r
s
t
u
v
w
x
y
z

broadband n ADSL m ▷ Do you have fast broadband? Tu as une connexion haut débit?

broadcast n émission f ▶ vb diffuser [**28**] ▷ The interview was broadcast yesterday. L'interview a été diffusée hier.; **to broadcast live** retransmettre [**47**] en direct

broccoli n brocolis mpl

brochure n brochure f

broke vb see **break** ▶ adj **to be broke** (without money) être [**35**] fauché

broken adj cassé(e) ▷ It's broken. C'est cassé. ▷ He's got a broken arm. Il a le bras cassé.

bronchitis n bronchite f

bronze n bronze m ▷ the bronze medal la médaille de bronze

brooch n broche f

broom n balai m

brother n frère m ▷ my brother mon frère ▷ my big brother mon grand frère

brother-in-law n beau-frère m (pl beaux-frères)

brought vb see **bring**

brown adj ❶ (clothes) marron ❷ (hair) brun(e) ❸ (tanned) bronzé(e); **brown bread** le pain complet

browse vb (on internet) parcourir [**16**] le Net

bruise n bleu m

brush n ❶ brosse f ❷ (paintbrush) pinceau m (pl pinceaux) ▶ vb brosser [**28**]; **to brush one's hair** se brosser [**28**] les cheveux ▷ I brushed my hair. Je me suis brossé les cheveux.; **to brush one's teeth**

se brosser [**28**] les dents ▷ I brush my teeth every night. Je me brosse les dents tous les soirs.

Brussels n Bruxelles; **in Brussels** à Bruxelles; **to Brussels** à Bruxelles

Brussels sprouts npl choux de Bruxelles mpl

bubble n bulle f

bubble bath n bain moussant m

bubble gum n chewing-gum m

bucket n seau m (pl seaux)

buckle n (on belt, watch, shoe) boucle f

Buddhism n bouddhisme m

Buddhist adj bouddhiste

budgie n perruche f

buffet n buffet m

buffet car n voiture-bar f

bug n ❶ (insect) insecte m ❷ (infection) microbe m ▷ There's a bug going round. Il y a un microbe qui traîne.; **a stomach bug** une gastroentérite ❸ (in computer) bug m

build vb construire [**23**] ▷ He's building a garage. Il construit un garage.

build up vb (increase) s'accumuler [**28**]

builder n ❶ (owner of firm) entrepreneur m ❷ (worker) maçon m

building n bâtiment m

built vb see **build**

bulb n (electric) ampoule f

Bulgaria n Bulgarie f

bull n taureau m (pl taureaux)

bullet n balle f

bullfighting n tauromachie f

bully n brute f ▷ He's a big bully. C'est une brute.
▶ vb tyranniser [28]

bum n (bottom) derrière m

bum bag n banane f

bump n ❶ (lump) bosse f ❷ (minor accident) accrochage m ▷ We had a bump. Nous avons eu un accrochage.

bump into vb to bump into **something** rentrer [68] dans quelque chose ▷ I bumped into the table in the dark. Je suis rentrée dans la table dans le noir.; **to bump into somebody (1)** (literally) rentrer [68] dans quelqu'un ▷ He stopped suddenly and I bumped into him. Il s'est arrêté subitement et je lui suis rentré dedans. **(2)** (meet by chance) rencontrer [28] par hasard ▷ I bumped into Jane in the supermarket. J'ai rencontré Jane par hasard au supermarché.

bumper n pare-chocs m (pl pare-chocs)

bumpy adj cahoteux (f cahoteuse)

bun n petit pain au lait m

bunch n a bunch of flowers un bouquet de fleurs; **a bunch of grapes** une grappe de raisin; **a bunch of keys** un trousseau de clés

bunches npl couettes fpl ▷ She has her hair in bunches. Elle a des couettes.

bungalow n bungalow m

bunk n couchette f; **bunk beds** les lits superposés mpl

burger n hamburger m

burglar n cambrioleur m, cambrioleuse f

burglary n cambriolage m

burgle vb cambrioler [28] ▷ Her house was burgled. Sa maison a été cambriolée.

burn n brûlure f
▶ vb ❶ (rubbish, documents) brûler [28] ❷ (food) faire [36] brûler ▷ I burned the cake. J'ai fait brûler le gâteau. ❸ (CD, DVD) graver [28]; **to burn oneself** se brûler [28] ▷ I burned myself on the oven door. Je me suis brûlé sur la porte du four.; **I've burned my hand.** Je me suis brûlé la main.

burn down vb brûler [28] ▷ The factory burned down. L'usine a brûlé.

burst vb éclater [28] ▷ The balloon burst. Le ballon a éclaté.; **to burst a balloon** faire [36] éclater un ballon; **to burst out laughing** éclater [28] de rire; **to burst into flames** prendre [65] feu; **to burst into tears** fondre [69] en larmes

bury vb enterrer [28]

bus n autobus m ▷ a bus stop un arrêt d'autobus; **the school bus** le car scolaire; **a bus pass** une carte d'abonnement pour le bus; **a bus station** une gare routière; **a bus ticket** un ticket de bus

bush n buisson m

business n ❶ (firm) entreprise f ▷ He's got his own business. Il a sa propre entreprise. ❷ (commerce) affaires fpl ▷ He's away on business. Il est en voyage d'affaires.; **a business trip** un voyage d'affaires; **It's none of my business.** Ça ne me regarde pas.

a
b
c
d
e
f
g
h
i
j
k
l
m
n
o
p
q
r
s
t
u
v
w
x
y
z

businessman n homme
d'affaires m
businesswoman n femme
d'affaires f
bust n (chest) poitrine f
busy adj ❶ (person, phone line)
occupé(e) ❷ (day, schedule)
chargé(e) ❸ (shop, street) très
fréquenté(e)
but conj mais ▷ I'd like to come, but I'm
busy. J'aimerais venir mais je suis
occupé.
butcher n boucher m ▷ He's a
butcher. Il est boucher.
butcher's n boucherie f
butter n beurre m
butterfly n papillon m
button n bouton m
buy vb acheter [1] ▷ I bought him an
ice cream. Je lui ai acheté une glace.;
**to buy something from
somebody** acheter [1] quelque
chose à quelqu'un ▷ I bought a
watch from him. Je lui ai acheté une
montre.
▶ n **It was a good buy.** C'était une
bonne affaire.
by prep ❶ par ▷ The thieves were
caught by the police. Les voleurs ont
été arrêtés par la police. ❷ de
▷ a painting by Picasso un tableau de
Picasso ▷ a book by Balzac un livre
de Balzac ❸ en ▷ by car en voiture
▷ by train en train ▷ by bus en
autobus ❹ (close to) à côté de
▷ Where's the bank? — It's by the post
office. Où est la banque? — Elle est à
côté de la poste. ❺ (not later than)
avant ▷ We have to be there by 4

o'clock. Nous devons y être avant
quatre heures.; **by the time ...**
quand ... ▷ By the time I got there it
was too late. Quand je suis arrivé il
était déjà trop tard. ▷ It'll be ready by
the time you get back. Ça sera prêt
quand vous reviendrez.; **That's
fine by me.** Ça me va.; **all by
himself** tout seul.; **all by herself**
toute seule; **I did it all by myself.**
Je l'ai fait tout seul.; **by the way** au
fait
bye excl salut!
bypass n route de contournement f

C

cab n taxi m
cabbage n chou m (pl choux)
cabin n (on ship) cabine f
cable n câble m
cable car n téléphérique m
cable television n télévision par câble f
cactus n cactus m
café n café m
* Cafés in France sell both alcoholic and non-alcoholic drinks.
cafeteria n cafétéria f
cage n cage f
cagoule n K-way® m
cake n gâteau m (pl gâteaux)
calculate vb calculer [28]
calculation n calcul m
calculator n machine à calculer f
calendar n calendrier m

calf n ❶ (of cow) veau m (pl veaux) ❷ (of leg) mollet m
call n (by phone) appel m ▷ Thanks for your call. Merci de votre appel.; **a phone call** un coup de téléphone; **to be on call** (doctor) être [35] de permanence ▷ He's on call this evening. Il est de permanence ce soir.
▶ vb appeler [4] ▷ I'll tell him you called. Je lui dirai que vous avez appelé. ▷ We called the police. Nous avons appelé la police. ▷ Everyone calls him Jimmy. Tout le monde l'appelle Jimmy.; **to be called** s'appeler [4] ▷ What's she called? Elle s'appelle comment?; **to call somebody names** insulter [28] quelqu'un; **He called me an idiot.** Il m'a traité d'idiot.
call back vb (phone again) rappeler [4] ▷ I'll call back at 6 o'clock. Je rappellerai à six heures.
call for vb passer [58] prendre ▷ I'll call for you at 2.30. Je passerai te prendre à deux heures et demie.
call off vb annuler [28] ▷ The match was called off. Le match a été annulé.
call box n cabine téléphonique f
call centre n centre d'appels m
calm adj calme
calm down vb se calmer [28] ▷ Calm down! Calme-toi!
calorie n calorie f
calves npl see calf
Cambodia n Cambodge m; **in Cambodia** au Cambodge
camcorder n caméscope m

came vb see **come**

camel n chameau m (pl chameaux)

camera n ❶ (for photos) appareil photo m (pl appareils photo) ❷ (for filming, TV) caméra f

cameraman n caméraman m

camp vb camper [28]
▶ n camp m; **a camp bed** un lit de camp

campaign n campagne f

camper n ❶ (person) campeur m, campeuse f ❷ (van) camping-car m

camping n camping m; **to go camping** faire [36] du camping ▷ We went camping in Cornwall. Nous avons fait du camping en Cornouailles.

campsite n terrain de camping m

can vb ❶ (be able to, be allowed to) pouvoir [64] ▷ I can't come. Je ne peux pas venir. ▷ Can I help you? Est-ce que je peux vous aider? ▷ You could hire a bike. Tu pourrais louer un vélo. ▷ I couldn't sleep because of the noise. Je ne pouvais pas dormir à cause du bruit.

▌ 'can' is sometimes not translated.

▷ I can't hear you. Je ne t'entends pas. ▷ Can you speak French? Parlez-vous français? ❷ (have learnt how to) savoir [76] ▷ I can swim. Je sais nager.; **That can't be true!** Ce n'est pas possible!; **You could be right.** Vous avez peut-être raison.
▶ n ❶ (tin) boîte f; **a can of beer** une cannette de bière ❷ (container) bidon m ▷ a can of petrol un bidon d'essence

Canada n Canada m; **in Canada** au Canada; **to Canada** au Canada

Canadian n Canadien m, Canadienne f
▶ adj canadien (f canadienne)

canal n canal m (pl canaux)

Canaries npl **the Canaries** les îles Canaries fpl

canary n canari m

cancel vb annuler [28] ▷ The match was cancelled. Le match a été annulé.

cancer n ❶ cancer m ▷ He's got cancer. Il a le cancer. ❷ Cancer m ▷ I'm Cancer. Je suis Cancer.

candidate n candidat m, candidate f

candle n bougie f

candy n (US) bonbons mpl; **a candy** un bonbon

candyfloss n barbe à papa f

canned adj (food) en conserve

cannot vb see **can**

canoe n canoë m

canoeing n **to go canoeing** faire [36] du canoë ▷ We went canoeing. Nous avons fait du canoë.

can-opener n ouvre-boîte m

can't vb see **can**

canteen n cantine f

canter vb aller [3] au petit galop

canvas n toile f

cap n ❶ (hat) casquette f ❷ (of bottle, tube) bouchon m

capable adj capable

capacity n capacité f

capital n ❶ capitale f ▷ Cardiff is the capital of Wales. Cardiff est la capitale du pays de Galles.

❷ (letter) majuscule f ▷ Write your address in capitals. Écris ton adresse en majuscules.

capitalism n capitalisme m

Capricorn n Capricorne m ▷ I'm Capricorn. Je suis Capricorne.

captain n capitaine m ▷ She's captain of the hockey team. Elle est capitaine de l'équipe de hockey.

capture vb capturer [**28**]

car n voiture f; **to go by car** aller [**3**] en voiture ▷ We went by car. Nous y sommes allés en voiture.; **a car crash** un accident de voiture

caramel n caramel m

caravan n caravane f ▷ a caravan site un camping pour caravanes

carbon footprint n empreinte carbone f

card n carte f; **a card game** un jeu de cartes

cardboard n carton m

cardigan n cardigan m

cardphone n téléphone à carte m

care n soin m ▷ with care avec soin; **to take care of** s'occuper [**28**] de ▷ I take care of the children on Saturdays. Le samedi, je m'occupe des enfants.; **Take care! (1)** (Be careful!) Fais attention! **(2)** (Look after yourself!) Prends bien soin de toi!

▶ vb **to care about** se soucier [**19**] de ▷ They don't really care about their image. Ils ne se soucient pas trop de leur image.; **I don't care!** Ça m'est égal! ▷ She doesn't care. Ça lui est égal.; **to care for somebody** (patients, old people) s'occuper [**28**]

de quelqu'un

career n carrière f; **a careers adviser** un conseiller d'orientation

careful adj **Be careful!** Fais attention!

carefully adv **❶** soigneusement ▷ She carefully avoided talking about it. Elle évitait soigneusement d'en parler. **❷** (safely) prudemment ▷ Drive carefully! Conduisez prudemment!; **Think carefully!** Réfléchis bien!

careless adj **❶** (work) peu soigné(e); **a careless mistake** une faute d'inattention **❷** (person) peu soigneux (f peu soigneuse) ▷ She's very careless. Elle est bien peu soigneuse. **❸** imprudent(e) ▷ a careless driver un conducteur imprudent

caretaker n gardien m, gardienne f

car-ferry n ferry m

cargo n cargaison f

car hire n location de voitures f

Caribbean n **❶** (islands) Caraïbes fpl ▷ We're going to the Caribbean. Nous allons aux Caraïbes.; **He's from the Caribbean.** Il est antillais. **❷** (sea) mer des Caraïbes f ▶ adj antillais(e) ▷ Caribbean food la cuisine antillaise

carnation n œillet m

carnival n carnaval m

carol n **a Christmas carol** un chant de Noël

car park n parking m

carpenter n charpentier m ▷ He's a carpenter. Il est charpentier.

carpentry n menuiserie f

a b c d e f g h i j k l m n o p q r s t u v w x y z

carpet n ❶ tapis m ▷ a Persian carpet un tapis persan ❷ (fitted) moquette f

car rental n (US) location de voitures f

carriage n voiture f

carrier bag n sac en plastique m

carrot n carotte f

carry vb ❶ porter [**28**] ▷ I'll carry your bag. Je vais porter ton sac. ❷ transporter [**28**] ▷ a plane carrying 100 passengers un avion transportant cent passagers

carry on vb continuer [**28**] ▷ She carried on talking. Elle a continué à parler.

carry out vb (orders) exécuter [**28**]

carrycot n nacelle f

cart n charrette f

carton n (of milk, juice) brique f

cartoon n ❶ (film) dessin animé m ❷ (in newspaper) dessin humoristique m; **a strip cartoon** une bande dessinée

cartridge n cartouche f

carve vb (meat) découper [**28**]

case n ❶ valise f ▷ I've packed my case. J'ai fait ma valise. ❷ cas m (pl cas) ▷ in some cases dans certains cas; **in that case** dans ce cas ▷ I don't want it. — In that case, I'll take it. Je n'en veux pas. — Dans ce cas, je le prends.; **in case** au cas où ▷ in case it rains au cas où il pleuvrait; **just in case** à tout hasard ▷ Take some money, just in case. Prends de l'argent à tout hasard.

cash n argent m ▷ I'm a bit short of cash. Je suis un peu à court d'argent.; **in cash** en liquide ▷ £2000 in cash deux mille livres en liquide; **to pay cash** payer [**59**] comptant; **a cash card** une carte de retrait; **the cash desk** la caisse; **a cash machine** un distributeur de billets; **a cash register** une caisse

cashew n noix de cajou f (pl noix de cajou)

cashier n caissier m, caissière f

cashmere n cachemire m ▷ a cashmere sweater un pull en cachemire

casino n casino m

cassette n cassette f; **a cassette player** un lecteur de cassettes; **a cassette recorder** un magnétophone

cast n acteurs mpl ▷ the cast of Eastenders les acteurs de la série Eastenders

castle n château m (pl châteaux)

casual adj ❶ décontracté(e) ▷ casual clothes les vêtements décontractés ❷ désinvolte ▷ a casual attitude une attitude désinvolte ❸ en passant ▷ It was just a casual remark. C'était juste une remarque en passant.

casualty n (in hospital) urgences fpl

cat n (female) chat m, chatte f ▷ Have you got a cat? Est-ce que tu as un chat?

catalogue n catalogue m

catastrophe n catastrophe f

catch vb ❶ attraper [**28**] ▷ to catch a thief attraper un voleur ▷ My cat catches birds. Mon chat attrape des oiseaux.; **to catch somebody doing something** attraper [28] quelqu'un en train de faire quelque chose ▷ *If they catch you smoking ...* S'ils t'attrapent en train de fumer ...; **to catch a cold** attraper [28] un rhume ❷ *(bus, train)* prendre [65] ▷ *We caught the last bus.* On a pris le dernier bus. ❸ *(hear)* saisir [38] ▷ *I didn't catch his name.* Je n'ai pas saisi son nom.

catch up *vb* rattraper [28] son retard ▷ *I've got to catch up: I was off yesterday.* Je dois rattraper mon retard: j'étais absent hier.

catering *n* restauration *f*

cathedral *n* cathédrale *f*

Catholic *adj* catholique
▶ *n* catholique *mf* ▷ *I'm a Catholic.* Je suis catholique.

cattle *npl* bétail *msg*

caught *vb* see **catch**

cauliflower *n* chou-fleur *m* (*pl* choux-fleurs)

cause *n* cause *f*
▶ *vb* provoquer [28] ▷ *to cause an accident* provoquer un accident

cautious *adj* prudent(e)

cave *n* grotte *f*

CD *n* CD *m* (*pl* CD)

CD burner *n* graveur de CD *m*

CD player *n* platine laser *f*

CD-ROM *n* CD-ROM *m* (*pl* CD-ROM)

ceiling *n* plafond *m*

celebrate *vb* (*birthday*) fêter [28]

celebrity *n* célébrité *f*

celery *n* céleri *m*

cell *n* cellule *f*

cellar *n* cave *f* ▷ *a wine cellar* une cave à vins

cello *n* violoncelle *m* ▷ *I play the cello.* Je joue du violoncelle.

cell phone *n* (*US*) téléphone portable *m*

cement *n* ciment *m*

cemetery *n* cimetière *m*

cent *n* cent *m* ▷ *twenty cents* vingt cents

centenary *n* centenaire *m*

center *n* (*US*) centre *m*

centigrade *adj* centigrade ▷ *20 degrees centigrade* vingt degrés centigrade

centimetre (*US* **centimeter**) *n* centimètre *m*

central *adj* central(e) (*mpl* centraux)

central heating *n* chauffage central *m*

centre *n* centre *m* ▷ *a sports centre* un centre sportif

century *n* siècle *m* ▷ *the 21st century* le vingt et unième siècle

cereal *n* céréales *fpl* ▷ *I have cereal for breakfast.* Je prends des céréales au petit déjeuner.

ceremony *n* cérémonie *f*

certain *adj* certain(e) ▷ *a certain person* une certaine personne ▷ *I'm absolutely certain it was him.* Je suis absolument certain que c'était lui.; **I don't know for certain.** Je n'en suis pas certain.; **to make certain** s'assurer [28] ▷ *I made certain the door was locked.* Je me suis assuré que la porte était fermée à clé.

certainly *adv* vraiment ▷ *I certainly*

expected something better. Je m'attendais vraiment à quelque chose de mieux.; **Certainly not!** Certainement pas!; **So it was a surprise? — It certainly was!** C'était donc une surprise? — Ça oui alors!

certificate *n* certificat *m*

chain *n* chaîne *f*

chair *n* ❶ chaise *f* ▷ *a table and 4 chairs* une table et quatre chaises ❷ *(armchair)* fauteuil *m*

chairman *n* président *m*

chairperson *n* président *m*, présidente *f*

chairwoman *n* présidente *f*

chalet *n* chalet *m*

challenge *n* défi *m*
▶ *vb* **She challenged me to a race.** Elle m'a proposé de faire la course avec elle.

champagne *n* champagne *m*

champion *n* champion *m*, championne *f*

championship *n* championnat *m*

chance *n* ❶ chance *f* ▷ *Do you think I've got any chance?* Tu crois que j'ai une chance?; **No chance!** Pas question! ❷ occasion *f* ▷ *I'd like to have a chance to travel.* J'aimerais avoir l'occasion de voyager.; **I'll write when I get the chance.** J'écrirai quand j'aurai un moment.; **by chance** par hasard ▷ *We met by chance.* Nous nous sommes rencontrés par hasard.; **to take a chance** prendre [65] un risque ▷ *I'm taking no chances!* Je ne veux prendre aucun risque!

change *vb* ❶ changer [45] ▷ *The town has changed a lot.* La ville a beaucoup changé. ▷ *I'd like to change £50.* Je voudrais changer cinquante livres. ❷ changer [45] de
  ▎ Use **changer de** when you change one thing for another.
▷ *You have to change trains in Paris.* Il faut changer de train à Paris. ▷ *I'm going to change my shoes.* Je vais changer de chaussures. ▷ *He wants to change his job.* Il veut changer d'emploi.; **to change one's mind** changer [45] d'avis ▷ *I've changed my mind.* J'ai changé d'avis.; **to change gear** changer [45] de vitesse ❸ se changer [45] ▷ *She changed to go to the party.* Elle s'est changée pour aller à la fête.; **to get changed** se changer [45] ▷ *I'm going to get changed.* Je vais me changer. ❹ *(swap)* échanger [45] ▷ *Can I change this sweater? It's too small.* Est-ce que je peux échanger ce pull? Il est trop petit.
▶ *n* ❶ changement *m* ▷ *There's been a change of plan.* Il y a eu un changement de programme. ❷ *(money)* monnaie *f* ▷ *I haven't got any change.* Je n'ai pas de monnaie.; **a change of clothes** des vêtements de rechange; **for a change** pour changer ▷ *Let's play tennis for a change.* Si on jouait au tennis pour changer?

changing room *n* ❶ *(in shop)* salon d'essayage *m* ❷ *(for sport)* vestiaire *m*

channel *n* *(TV)* chaîne *f* ▷ *There's*

football on the other channel. Il y a du football sur l'autre chaîne.; **the Channel** la Manche; **the Channel Islands** les îles Anglo-Normandes *fpl*; **the Channel Tunnel** le tunnel sous la Manche

chaos *n* chaos *m*

chapel *n* (*part of church*) chapelle *f*

chapter *n* chapitre *m*

character *n* ❶ caractère *m*; **She's quite a character.** C'est un drôle de numéro. ❷ (*in play, film*) personnage *m* ▷ *The character played by Depardieu …* Le personnage joué par Depardieu …

characteristic *n* caractéristique *f*

charcoal *n* charbon de bois *m*

charge *n* frais *mpl* ▷ *Is there a charge for delivery?* Est-ce qu'il y a des frais de livraison?; **an extra charge** un supplément; **free of charge** gratuit; **to reverse the charges** appeler [4] en PCV. ▷ *I'd like to reverse the charges.* Je voudrais appeler en PCV.; **to be in charge** être [35] responsable ▷ *Mrs Munday was in charge of the group.* Madame Munday était responsable du groupe.

▶ *vb* ❶ (*money*) prendre [65] ▷ *How much did he charge you?* Combien est-ce qu'il vous a pris? ▷ *They charge £10 an hour.* Ils prennent dix livres de l'heure. ❷ (*with crime*) inculper [28] ▷ *The police have charged him with murder.* La police l'a inculpé de meurtre.

charity *n* association caritative *f* ▷ *He gave the money to charity.* Il a

donné l'argent à une association caritative.

charm *n* charme *m* ▷ *He's got a lot of charm.* Il a beaucoup de charme.

charming *adj* charmant(e)

chart *n* tableau *m* (*pl* tableaux) ▷ *The chart shows the rise of unemployment.* Le tableau indique la progression du chômage.; **the charts** le hit-parade ▷ *This album is number one in the charts.* Cet album est numéro un au hit-parade.

charter flight *n* charter *m*

chase *vb* pourchasser [28] ▶ *n* poursuite *f* ▷ *a car chase* une poursuite en voiture

chat *n* **to have a chat** bavarder [28] ▶ *vb* bavarder [28]; **to chat somebody up** draguer [28] quelqu'un (*informal*) ▷ *He likes to chat up the girls.* Il aime bien draguer les filles.; **She likes chatting online.** Elle aime chatter sur internet.

chatroom *n* forum de discussion *m*

chat show *n* talk-show *m*

chauvinist *n* **a male chauvinist** un machiste

cheap *adj* bon marché ▷ *a cheap T-shirt* un T-shirt bon marché

cheaper *adj* moins cher (*f* moins chère) ▷ *It's cheaper by bus.* C'est moins cher en bus.

cheat *vb* tricher [28] ▷ *You're cheating!* Tu triches! ▶ *n* tricheur *m*, tricheuse *f*

check *n* ❶ contrôle *m* ▷ *a security check* un contrôle de sécurité ❷ (*US*) chèque *m* ▷ *to write a check*

a b c d e f g h i j k l m n o p q r s t u v w x y z

faire un chèque ❸ (US) addition f
▷ Can we have the check, please?
L'addition, s'il vous plaît.
▶ vb vérifier [**19**] ▷ I'll check the time
of the train. Je vais vérifier l'heure du
train. ▷ Could you check the oil,
please? Pourriez-vous vérifier le
niveau d'huile, s'il vous plaît?

check in vb ❶ (at airport) se
présenter [**28**] à l'enregistrement
▷ Where do we check in? Où est-ce
qu'on doit se présenter à
l'enregistrement? ❷ (in hotel) se
présenter [**28**] à la réception; **I'd
like to check in.** Je voudrais
prendre ma chambre.

check out vb (from hotel) régler [**34**]
la note ▷ Can I check out, please? Je
peux régler la note, s'il vous plaît?

checked adj (fabric) à carreaux

checkers n (US) dames fpl ▷ to play
checkers jouer aux dames

check-in n enregistrement m

checkout n caisse f

check-up n examen de routine m

cheek n ❶ joue f ▷ He kissed her on
the cheek. Il l'a embrassée sur la
joue. ❷ culot m ▷ What a cheek!
Quel culot!

cheeky adj effronté(e) ▷ Don't be
cheeky! Ne sois pas effronté!; **a
cheeky smile** un sourire malicieux

cheer n hourras mpl; **to give a
cheer** pousser [**28**] des hourras;
Cheers! (1) (good health) À la vôtre!
(2) (thanks) Merci!
▶ vb applaudir [**38**]; **to cheer
somebody up** remonter [**48**] le
moral à quelqu'un ▷ I was trying to

cheer him up. J'essayais de lui
remonter le moral.; **Cheer up!** Ne
te laisse pas abattre!

cheerful adj gai(e)

cheese n fromage m

chef n chef m

chemical n produit chimique m

chemist n ❶ (dispenser)
pharmacien m, pharmacienne f
❷ (shop) pharmacie f ▷ You get it
from the chemist. C'est vendu en
pharmacie.
　● Chemists' shops in France are
　● identified by a special green
　● cross outside the shop.
❸ (scientist) chimiste mf

chemistry n chimie f ▷ the
chemistry lab le laboratoire de
chimie

cheque n chèque m ▷ to write a
cheque faire un chèque

chequebook n carnet de
chèques m

cherry n cerise f

chess n échecs mpl ▷ to play chess
jouer aux échecs

chessboard n échiquier m

chest n (of person) poitrine f ▷ his
chest measurement son tour de
poitrine; **a chest of drawers** une
commode

chestnut n marron m ▷ We have
turkey with chestnuts. Nous
mangeons de la dinde aux
marrons.

chew vb mâcher [**28**]

chewing gum n chewing-gum m

chick n poussin m ▷ a hen and her
chicks une poule et ses poussins

chicken n poulet m

chickenpox n varicelle f

chickpeas npl pois chiches mpl

chief n chef m ▷ the chief of security le chef de la sécurité

▶ adj principal(e) ▷ His chief reason for resigning was stress. La principale raison de sa démission était le stress.

child n enfant mf ▷ all the children tous les enfants

childish adj puéril(e)

child minder n nourrice f

children npl see **child**

Chile n Chili m; **in Chile** au Chili

chill vb mettre [47] au frais ▷ Put the wine in the fridge to chill. Mets le vin au frais dans le réfrigérateur.

chilli n piment m

chilly adj froid(e)

chimney n cheminée f

chin n menton m

China n Chine f; **in China** en Chine

china n porcelaine f ▷ a china plate une assiette en porcelaine

Chinese n (language) chinois m; **the Chinese** les Chinois

▶ adj chinois(e) ▷ a Chinese restaurant un restaurant chinois; **a Chinese man** un Chinois; **a Chinese woman** une Chinoise

chip n ❶ (food) frite f ▷ We bought some chips. Nous avons acheté des frites. ❷ (in computer) puce f

chiropodist n pédicure mf ▷ He's a chiropodist. Il est pédicure.

chives npl ciboulette fsg

chocolate n chocolat m
▷ a chocolate cake un gâteau au chocolat; **hot chocolate** le chocolat chaud

choice n choix m ▷ I had no choice. Je n'avais pas le choix.

choir n chorale f ▷ I sing in the school choir. Je chante dans la chorale de l'école.

choke vb s'étrangler [28]; **He choked on a fishbone.** Il s'est étranglé avec une arête de poisson.

choose vb choisir [38] ▷ It's difficult to choose. C'est difficile de choisir.

chop vb émincer [12] ▷ Chop the onions. Émincez les oignons.
▶ n côte f ▷ a pork chop une côte de porc

chopsticks npl baguettes fpl

chose, chosen vb see **choose**

Christ n Christ m ▷ the birth of Christ la naissance du Christ

christening n baptême m

Christian n chrétien m, chrétienne f

▶ adj chrétien (f chrétienne)

Christian name n prénom m

Christmas n Noël m ▷ Happy Christmas! Joyeux Noël!; **Christmas Day** le jour de Noël; **Christmas Eve** la veille de Noël; **a Christmas tree** un arbre de Noël; **a Christmas card** une carte de Noël

- The French more often send greetings cards (**une carte de vœux**) in January rather than at Christmas, with best wishes for the New Year.

Christmas dinner le repas de Noël

a b c d e f g h i j k l m n o p q r s t u v w x y z

● Most French people have their
● Christmas meal (**réveillon de**
● **Noël**) on the evening of
● Christmas Eve, though some
● have a **repas de Noël** on
● Christmas Day. The French
● usually have a Yule log (**une**
● **bûche de Noël**) for pudding at
● the Christmas meal.

chunk n gros morceau m (pl gros
morceaux) ▷ Cut the meat into
chunks. Coupez la viande en gros
morceaux.

church n église f ▷ I don't go to
church every Sunday. Je ne vais pas à
l'église tous les dimanches.; **the
Church of England** l'Église
anglicane

cider n cidre m

cigar n cigare m

cigarette n cigarette f

cigarette lighter n briquet m

cinema n cinéma m ▷ I'm going to
the cinema this evening. Je vais au
cinéma ce soir.

cinnamon n cannelle f

circle n cercle m

circular adj circulaire

circumflex n accent circonflexe m

circumstances npl circonstances
fpl

circus n cirque m

citizen n citoyen m, citoyenne f
▷ a French citizen un citoyen français

citizenship n citoyenneté f

city n ville f; **the city centre** le
centre-ville ▷ It's in the city centre.
C'est au centre-ville.

civilization n civilisation f

civil servant n fonctionnaire mf

civil war n guerre civile f

claim vb ❶ prétendre [88] ▷ He
claims to have found the money. Il
prétend avoir trouvé l'argent.
❷ (receive) percevoir [28] ▷ She's
claiming unemployment benefit. Elle
perçoit des allocations chômage.;
**She can't claim unemployment
benefit.** Elle n'a pas droit aux
allocations chômage.; **to claim on
one's insurance** se faire [36]
rembourser par son assurance
▷ We claimed on our insurance. On
s'est fait rembourser par notre
assurance.
▶ n (on insurance policy) demande
d'indemnité f ▷ to make a claim faire
une demande d'indemnité

clap vb (applaud) applaudir [38]; **to
clap one's hands** frapper [28] ▷ to
clap one's hands frapper [28] ses
mains ▷ My dog sits when I clap
my hands. Mon chien s'assoit quand
je frappe dans mes mains.

clarinet n clarinette f ▷ I play the
clarinet. Je joue de la clarinette.

clash vb ❶ (colours) jurer [28]
▷ These two colours clash. Ces deux
couleurs jurent. ❷ (events) tomber
[84] en même temps ▷ The concert
clashes with Ann's party. Le concert
tombe en même temps que la
soirée d'Ann.

clasp n (of necklace) fermoir m

class n ❶ (group) classe f ▷ We're in
the same class. Nous sommes dans
la même classe. ❷ (lesson) cours m
▷ I go to dancing classes. Je vais à des
cours de danse.

classic adj classique ▷ a classic example un cas classique
▶ n (book, film) classique m

classical adj classique ▷ I like classical music. J'aime la musique classique.

classmate n camarade de classe m, camarade de classe f

classroom n classe f

classroom assistant n aide-éducateur m, aide-éducatrice f

claw n ❶ (of cat, dog) griffe f ❷ (of bird) serre f ❸ (of crab, lobster) pince f

clean adj propre ▷ a clean shirt une chemise propre
▶ vb nettoyer [53]

cleaner n (woman, man) femme de ménage f, agent d'entretien m

cleaner's n teinturerie f

cleansing lotion n lotion démaquillante f

clear adj ❶ clair(e) ▷ a clear explanation une explication claire ▷ It's clear you don't believe me. Il est clair que tu ne me crois pas. ❷ (road, way) libre ▷ The road's clear now. La route est libre maintenant.
▶ vb ❶ dégager [45] ▷ The police are clearing the road after the accident. La police dégage la route après l'accident. ❷ (fog, mist) se dissiper [28] ▷ The mist cleared. La brume s'est dissipée.; **to be cleared of a crime** être [35] reconnu non coupable d'un crime ▷ She was cleared of murder. Elle a été reconnue non coupable du

meurtre.; **to clear the table** débarrasser [28] la table ▷ I'll clear the table. Je vais débarrasser la table.

clear off vb filer [28] ▷ Clear off and leave me alone! File et laisse-moi tranquille!

clear up vb ranger [45] ▷ Who's going to clear all this up? Qui va ranger tout ça?; **I think it's going to clear up.** (weather) Je pense que le temps va se lever.

clearly adv ❶ clairement ▷ She explained it very clearly. Elle l'a expliqué très clairement. ❷ nettement ▷ You could clearly make out the French coast. On distinguait nettement la côte française. ❸ distinctement ▷ to speak clearly parler distinctement

clementine n clémentine f

clever adj ❶ intelligent(e) ▷ She's very clever. Elle est très intelligente. ❷ (ingenious) astucieux (f astucieuse) ▷ a clever system un système astucieux; **What a clever idea!** Quelle bonne idée!

click n (of door, camera) petit bruit m
▶ vb (with mouse) cliquer [28] ▷ to click on an icon cliquer sur une icône

client n client m, cliente f

cliff n falaise f

climate n climat m

climate change n changement climatique m

climb vb ❶ escalader [28] ▷ We're going to climb Snowdon. Nous allons escalader le Snowdon. ❷ (stairs) monter [48]

a
b
c
d
e
f
g
h
i
j
k
l
m
n
o
p
q
r
s
t
u
v
w
x
y
z

climber n grimpeur m, grimpeuse f

climbing n escalade f; **to go climbing** faire [36] de l'escalade ▷ We're going climbing in Scotland. Nous allons faire de l'escalade en Écosse.

Clingfilm® n film alimentaire m

clinic n centre médical m (pl centres médicaux)

clip n ❶ (for hair) barrette f ❷ (film) court extrait m ▷ some clips from Disney's latest film quelques courts extraits du dernier film Disney

cloakroom n ❶ (for coats) vestiaire m ❷ (toilet) toilettes fpl

clock n ❶ horloge f ▷ the church clock l'horloge de l'église ❷ (smaller) pendule f; **an alarm clock** un réveil; **a clock-radio** un radio-réveil

close adj, adv ❶ (near) près ▷ The shops are very close. Les magasins sont tout près.; **close to** près de ▷ The youth hostel is close to the station. L'auberge de jeunesse est près de la gare.; **Come closer.** Rapproche-toi. ❷ (in relationship) proche ▷ We're just inviting close relations. Nous n'invitons que les parents proches. ▷ She's a close friend of mine. C'est une proche amie. ❸ (contest) très serré(e) ▷ It's going to be very close. Ça va être très très serré. ❹ (weather) lourd(e) ▷ It's close this afternoon. Il fait lourd cet après-midi.

▶ vb ❶ fermer [28] ▷ The shops close at 5.30. Les magasins ferment à cinq heures et demie. ❷ se fermer

[28] ▷ The doors close automatically. Les portes se ferment automatiquement.

closed adj fermé(e) ▷ The bank's closed. La banque est fermée.

closely adv (look, examine) de près

cloth n (material) tissu m; **a cloth** un chiffon ▷ Wipe it with a damp cloth. Nettoyez-le avec un chiffon humide.

clothes npl vêtements mpl ▷ new clothes des vêtements neufs; **a clothes line** un fil à linge; **a clothes peg** une pince à linge

cloud n nuage m
▶ adj **cloud computing** l'informatique dans le cloud

cloudy adj nuageux (f nuageuse)

clove n **a clove of garlic** une gousse d'ail

clown n clown m

club n club m ▷ a golf club un club de golf; **the youth club** la maison des jeunes; **clubs** (in cards) le trèfle ▷ the ace of clubs l'as de trèfle

club together vb se cotiser [28]

clubbing n **to go clubbing** sortir [79] en boîte

clue n indice m ▷ an important clue un indice important; **I haven't a clue.** Je n'en ai pas la moindre idée.

clumsy adj maladroit(e)

clutch n (of car) pédale d'embrayage f

clutter n désordre m ▷ There's too much clutter in here. Il y a trop de désordre ici.

coach n ❶ car m ▷ We went there by coach. Nous y sommes allés en car.;

the coach station la gare routière;
a coach trip une excursion en car
❷ (*trainer*) entraîneur *m* ▷ *the
French coach* l'entraîneur de l'équipe
de France

coal *n* charbon *m*; **a coal mine** une
mine de charbon; **a coal miner** un
mineur

coarse *adj* ❶ (*surface, fabric*)
rugueux (*f* rugueuse) ▷ *The bag was
made of coarse cloth.* Le sac était fait
d'un tissu rugueux. ❷ (*vulgar*)
grossier (*f* grossière) ▷ *coarse
language* un langage grossier

coast *n* côte *f* ▷ *It's on the west coast
of Scotland.* C'est sur la côte ouest
de l'Écosse.

coastguard *n* garde-côte *m* (*pl*
garde-côtes)

coat *n* manteau *m* (*pl* manteaux)
▷ *a warm coat* un manteau chaud;
a coat of paint une couche de
peinture

coat hanger *n* cintre *m*

cobweb *n* toile d'araignée *f*

cocaine *n* cocaïne *f*

cockerel *n* coq *m*

cocoa *n* cacao *m* ▷ *a cup of cocoa* une
tasse de cacao

coconut *n* noix de coco *f*

code *n* code *m*
▶ *vb* coder [**28**]

coffee *n* café *m*; **A cup of coffee,
please.** Un café, s'il vous plaît.

coffee table *n* table basse *f*

coffin *n* cercueil *m*

coin *n* pièce de monnaie *f*; **a 2 euro
coin** une pièce de deux euros

coincidence *n* coïncidence *f*

Coke® *n* coca *m* ▷ *a can of Coke*®
une cannette de coca

colander *n* passoire *f*

cold *adj* froid(e) ▷ *The water's cold.*
L'eau est froide.; **It's cold today.** Il
fait froid aujourd'hui.; **to be cold**
(*person*) avoir [**8**] froid ▷ *I'm cold.* J'ai
froid.
▶ *n* ❶ froid *m* ▷ *I can't stand the cold.*
Je ne supporte pas le froid.
❷ rhume *m* ▷ *to catch a cold*
attraper un rhume; **to have a cold**
avoir [**8**] un rhume ▷ *I've got a bad
cold.* J'ai un gros rhume.; **a cold
sore** un bouton de fièvre

coleslaw *n* salade de chou cru à la
mayonnaise *f*

collapse *vb* s'effondrer [**28**] ▷ *He
collapsed.* Il s'est effondré.

collar *n* ❶ (*of coat, shirt*) col *m* ❷ (*for
animal*) collier *m*

collarbone *n* clavicule *f* ▷ *I broke my
collarbone.* Je me suis cassé la clavicule.

colleague *n* collègue *mf*

collect *vb* ❶ ramasser [**28**] ▷ *The
teacher collected the exercise books.*
Le professeur a ramassé les
cahiers. ▷ *They collect the rubbish on
Fridays.* Ils ramassent les ordures le
vendredi. ❷ faire [**36**] collection de
▷ *I collect stamps.* Je fais collection
de timbres. ❸ aller [**3**] chercher
▷ *Their mother collects them from
school.* Leur mère va les chercher à
l'école. ❹ faire [**36**] une collecte
▷ *They're collecting for charity.* Ils font
une collecte pour une association
caritative.

collection *n* ❶ collection *f* ▷ *my*

a b c d e f g h i j k l m n o p q r s t u v w x y z

DVD collection ma collection de DVD ❷ collecte *f* ▷ *a collection for charity* une collecte pour une association caritative ❸ *(of mail)* levée *f* ▷ *Next collection: 5pm* Prochaine levée: 17 heures

collector *n* collectionneur *m*, collectionneuse *f*

college *n* collège *m* ▷ *a technical college* un collège d'enseignement technique

collide *vb* entrer [**32**] en collision

collie *n* colley *m*

collision *n* collision *f*

colon *n* *(punctuation mark)* deux-points *mpl*

colonel *n* colonel *m*

colour *(US* **color***) n* couleur *f* ▷ *What colour is it?* C'est de quelle couleur?; **a colour film** *(for camera)* une pellicule en couleur

colourful *(US* **colorful***) adj* coloré(e)

comb *n* peigne *m*
▷ *vb* **to comb one's hair** se peigner [**28**] ▷ *You haven't combed your hair.* Tu ne t'es pas peigné.

combination *n* combinaison *f*

combine *vb* ❶ allier [**19**] ▷ *The film combines humour with suspense.* Le film allie l'humour au suspense. ❷ concilier [**19**] ▷ *It's difficult to combine a career with a family.* Il est difficile de concilier carrière et vie de famille.

come *vb* ❶ venir [**89**] ▷ *Can I come too?* Est-ce que je peux venir aussi? ▷ *Some friends came to see us.* Quelques amis sont venus nous voir. ▷ *I'll come with you.* Je viens

avec toi. ❷ *(arrive)* arriver [**5**] ▷ *I'm coming!* J'arrive! ▷ *They came late.* Ils sont arrivés en retard. ▷ *The letter came this morning.* La lettre est arrivée ce matin.; **Where do you come from?** Tu viens d'où?; **Come on!** Allez!

come back *vb* revenir [**73**] ▷ *Come back!* Reviens!

come down *vb* ❶ *(person, lift)* descendre [**24**] ❷ *(prices)* baisser [**28**]

come in *vb* entrer [**32**] ▷ *Come in!* Entrez!

come out *vb* sortir [**79**] ▷ *I tripped as we came out of the cinema.* J'ai trébuché quand nous sommes sortis du cinéma. ▷ *It's just come out on DVD.* Ça vient de sortir en DVD.; **None of my photos came out.** Mes photos n'ont rien donné.

come round *vb* *(after faint, operation)* reprendre [**65**] connaissance

come up *vb* monter [**48**] ▷ *Come up here!* Monte!; **to come up to somebody (1)** s'approcher [**28**] de quelqu'un ▷ *She came up to me and kissed me.* Elle s'est approchée de moi et m'a embrassé. **(2)** *(to speak to them)* aborder [**28**] quelqu'un ▷ *A man came up to me and said ...* Un homme m'a abordé et m'a dit ...

comedian *n* comique *m*

comedy *n* comédie *f*

comfortable *adj* ❶ *(bed, chair)* confortable ❷ *(person)* à l'aise ▷ *I'm very comfortable, thanks.* Je suis parfaitement à l'aise, merci.

comic n (magazine) illustré m
comic strip n bande dessinée f
comma n virgule f
command n ordre m
comment n commentaire m ▷ He made no comment. Il n'a fait aucun commentaire.; **No comment!** Je n'ai rien à dire!
▷ vb **to comment on something** faire [36] des commentaires sur quelque chose
commentary n (on TV, radio) reportage en direct m
commentator n commentateur sportif m, commentatrice sportive f
commercial n spot publicitaire m
commit vb **to commit a crime** commettre [47] un crime; **to commit oneself** s'engager [45] ▷ I don't want to commit myself. Je ne veux pas m'engager.; **to commit suicide** se suicider [28] ▷ He committed suicide. Il s'est suicidé.
committee n comité m
common adj courant(e) ▷ 'Smith' is a very common surname. 'Smith' est un nom de famille très courant.; **in common** en commun ▷ We've got a lot in common. Nous avons beaucoup de choses en commun.
Commons npl **the House of Commons** la Chambre des communes
common sense n bon sens m ▷ Use your common sense! Sers-toi de ton bon sens!
communicate vb communiquer [28]

communication n communication f
communion n communion f ▷ my First Communion ma première communion
communism n communisme m
community n communauté f
commute vb faire [36] la navette ▷ She commutes between Liss and London. Elle fait la navette entre Liss et Londres.
compact disc n disque compact m; **a compact disc player** une platine laser
company n ❶ société f ▷ He works for a big company. Il travaille pour une grosse société. ❷ compagnie f ▷ an insurance company une compagnie d'assurance; **to keep somebody company** tenir [83] compagnie à quelqu'un ▷ I'll keep you company. Je vais te tenir compagnie.
comparatively adv relativement
compare vb comparer [28] ▷ People always compare him with his brother. On le compare toujours à son frère.; **compared with** en comparaison de ▷ Oxford is small compared with London. Oxford est une petite ville en comparaison de Londres.
comparison n comparaison f
compartment n compartiment m
compass n boussole f
compensation n indemnité f ▷ They got £2000 compensation. Ils ont reçu une indemnité de deux mille livres.

compete *vb* participer [**28**] ▷ *I'm competing in the marathon.* Je participe au marathon.; **to compete for something** se disputer [**28**] quelque chose ▷ *There are 50 students competing for 6 places.* Ils sont cinquante étudiants à se disputer six places.

competent *adj* compétent(e)

competition *n* concours *m* ▷ *a singing competition* un concours de chant

competitive *adj* compétitif (*f* compétitive) ▷ *a very competitive price* un prix très compétitif; **to be competitive** (*person*) avoir [**8**] l'esprit de compétition ▷ *He's a very competitive person.* Il a vraiment l'esprit de compétition.

competitor *n* concurrent *m*, concurrente *f*

complain *vb* se plaindre [**17**] ▷ *I'm going to complain to the manager.* Je vais me plaindre au directeur.

complaint *n* plainte *f* ▷ *There were lots of complaints about the food.* Il y a eu beaucoup de plaintes à propos de la nourriture.

complete *adj* complet (*f* complète)

completely *adv* complètement

complexion *n* teint *m*

complicated *adj* compliqué(e)

compliment *n* compliment *m*
▶ *vb* complimenter [**28**] ▷ *They complimented me on my French.* Ils m'ont complimenté sur mon français.

composer *n* compositeur *m*, compositrice *f*

comprehension *n*
❶ (*understanding*) compréhension *f*
❷ (*school exercise*) exercice de compréhension *m*

comprehensive *adj* complet (*f* complète) ▷ *a comprehensive guide* un guide complet

> Be careful not to translate **comprehensive** by **compréhensif**.

comprehensive school *n*
❶ collège *m* ❷ lycée *m*
> In France pupils go to a **collège** between the ages of 11 and 15, and then to a **lycée** until the age of 18.

compulsory *adj* obligatoire

computer *n* ordinateur *m*

computer game *n* jeu vidéo *m* (*pl* jeux vidéo)

computer programmer *n* programmeur *m*, programmeuse *f* ▷ *She's a computer programmer.* Elle est programmeuse.

computer science *n* informatique *f*

computing *n* informatique *f*

concentrate *vb* se concentrer [**28**] ▷ *I couldn't concentrate.* Je n'arrivais pas à me concentrer.

concentration *n* concentration *f*

concern *n* (*preoccupation*) inquiétude *f* ▷ *They expressed concern about her health.* Ils ont exprimé leur inquiétude concernant sa santé.

concerned *adj* **to be concerned** s'inquiéter [**34**] ▷ *His mother is concerned about him.* Sa mère s'inquiète à son sujet.; **as far as I'm concerned** en ce qui me concerne

concerning prep concernant ▷ For further information concerning the job, contact ... Pour plus d'informations concernant cet emploi, contacter ...

concert n concert m

concrete n béton m

condemn vb condamner [28] ▷ The government has condemned the decision. Le gouvernement a condamné cette décision.

condition n ❶ condition f ▷ I'll do it, on one condition ... Je veux bien le faire, à une condition ... ❷ état m ▷ in bad condition en mauvais état

conditional n conditionnel m

conditioner n (for hair) baume démêlant m

condom n préservatif m

conduct vb (orchestra) diriger [45]

conductor n chef d'orchestre m

cone n cornet m ▷ an ice-cream cone un cornet de glace

conference n conférence f

confess vb avouer [28] ▷ He confessed to the murder. Il a avoué avoir commis le meurtre.

confession n confession f

confidence n ❶ confiance f ▷ I've got confidence in you. J'ai confiance en toi. ❷ assurance f ▷ She lacks confidence. Elle manque d'assurance.

confident adj sûr(e) ▷ I'm confident everything will be okay. Je suis sûr que tout ira bien.; **She's seems**

quite confident. Elle a l'air sûre d'elle.

confidential adj confidentiel (f confidentielle)

confirm vb (booking) confirmer [28]

confuse vb to confuse somebody embrouiller [28] les idées de quelqu'un ▷ Don't confuse me! Ne m'embrouille pas les idées!

confused adj désorienté(e)

confusing adj The traffic signs are confusing. Les panneaux de signalisation ne sont pas clairs.

confusion n confusion f

congratulate vb féliciter [28] ▷ My aunt congratulated me on my results. Ma tante m'a félicité pour mes résultats.

congratulations npl félicitations fpl ▷ Congratulations on your new job! Félicitations pour votre nouveau poste!

conjunction n conjonction f

conjurer n prestidigitateur m

connection n ❶ rapport m ▷ There's no connection between the two events. Il n'y a aucun rapport entre les deux événements. ❷ (electrical) contact m ▷ There's a loose connection. Il y a un mauvais contact. ❸ (of trains, planes) correspondance f ▷ We missed our connection. Nous avons raté la correspondance.

conscience n conscience f

conscious adj conscient(e)

consciousness n connaissance f; **to lose consciousness** perdre [61] connaissance ▷ I lost consciousness.

J'ai perdu connaissance.
consequence n conséquence f
▷ What are the consequences for the environment? Quelles sont les conséquences pour l'environnement?; **as a consequence** en conséquence
consequently adv par conséquent
conservation n protection f
conservative adj conservateur (f conservatrice); **the Conservative Party** le Parti conservateur
conservatory n jardin d'hiver m
consider vb ❶ considérer [34] ▷ He considers it a waste of time. Il considère que c'est une perte de temps. ❷ envisager [45] ▷ We considered cancelling our holiday. Nous avons envisagé d'annuler nos vacances.; **I'm considering the idea.** J'y songe.
considerate adj délicat(e)
considering prep ❶ étant donné ▷ Considering we were there for a month ... Étant donné que nous étions là pour un mois ... ❷ tout compte fait ▷ I got a good mark, considering. J'ai eu une bonne note, tout compte fait.
consist vb **to consist of** être [35] composé de ▷ The band consists of a singer and a guitarist. Le groupe est composé d'un chanteur et d'un guitariste.
consonant n consonne f
constant adj constant(e)
constantly adv constamment
constipated adj constipé(e)
construct vb construire [23]

construction n construction f
consult vb consulter [28]
consumer n consommateur m, consommatrice f
contact n contact m ▷ I'm in contact with her. Je suis en contact avec elle. ▷ vb joindre [42] ▷ Where can we contact you? Où pouvons-nous vous joindre?
contact lenses npl verres de contact mpl
contactless adj sans contact
contain vb contenir [83]
container n récipient m
contents npl ❶ (of container) contenu msg ❷ (of book) table des matières fsg
contest n concours m
contestant n concurrent m, concurrente f
context n contexte m
continent n continent m ▷ How many continents are there? Combien y a-t-il de continents?; **the Continent** l'Europe f ▷ I've never been to the Continent. Je ne suis jamais allé en Europe.
continental breakfast n petit déjeuner à la française m
continue vb ❶ continuer [28] ▷ She continued talking to her friend. Elle a continué à parler à son amie. ❷ (after interruption) reprendre [65] ▷ We continued working after lunch. Nous avons repris le travail après le déjeuner.
continuous adj continu(e); **continuous assessment** le contrôle continu

contraceptive n contraceptif m

contract n contrat m

contradict vb contredire [**27**]

contrary n contraire m; **on the contrary** au contraire

contrast n contraste m

contribute vb ❶ (to success, achievement) contribuer [**28**] ▷ The treaty will contribute to world peace. Le traité va contribuer à la paix dans le monde. ❷ (share in) participer [**28**] ▷ He didn't contribute to the discussion. Il n'a pas participé à la discussion. ❸ (give) donner [**28**] ▷ She contributed £10. Elle a donné dix livres.

contribution n ❶ contribution f ❷ (to pension, national insurance) cotisation f

control n contrôle m; **to lose control** (of vehicle) perdre [**61**] le contrôle ▷ He lost control of the car. Il a perdu le contrôle de son véhicule.; **the controls** (of machine) les commandes fpl; **to be in control** être [**35**] maître de la situation; **to keep control** (of people) se faire [**36**] obéir ▷ He can't keep control of the class. Il ne se fait pas obéir de sa classe.; **out of control** (child, class) déchaîné ▶ vb ❶ (country, organization) diriger [**45**] ❷ se faire [**36**] obéir de ▷ He can't control the class. Il ne se fait pas obéir de sa classe. ❸ maîtriser [**28**] ▷ I couldn't control the horse. Je ne suis pas arrivé à maîtriser le cheval.; **to control oneself** se contrôler [**28**]

controversial adj controversé(e) ▷ a controversial book un livre controversé

convenient adj (place) bien situé(e) ▷ The hotel's convenient for the airport. L'hôtel est bien situé par rapport à l'aéroport.; **It's not a convenient time for me.** C'est une heure qui ne m'arrange pas.; **Would Monday be convenient for you?** Est-ce que lundi vous conviendrait?

conventional adj conventionnel (f conventionnelle)

conversation n conversation f ▷ a French conversation class un cours de conversation française

convert vb transformer [**28**] ▷ We've converted the loft into a spare room. Nous avons transformé le grenier en chambre d'amis.

convince vb persuader [**28**] ▷ I'm not convinced. Je n'en suis pas persuadé.

cook vb ❶ faire [**36**] la cuisine ▷ I can't cook. Je ne sais pas faire la cuisine. ❷ préparer [**28**] ▷ She's cooking lunch. Elle est en train de préparer le déjeuner. ❸ faire [**36**] cuire ▷ Cook the pasta for 10 minutes. Faites cuire les pâtes pendant dix minutes.; **to be cooked** être [**35**] cuit ▷ When the potatoes are cooked ... Lorsque les pommes de terre sont cuites ... ▶ n cuisinier m, cuisinière f ▷ Matthew's an excellent cook. Matthew est un excellent cuisinier.

cooker n cuisinière f ▷ a gas cooker

a
b
c
d
e
f
g
h
i
j
k
l
m
n
o
p
q
r
s
t
u
v
w
x
y
z

une cuisinière à gaz

cookery n cuisine f

cookie n (US) gâteau sec m (pl gâteaux secs)

cooking n cuisine f ▷ I like cooking. J'aime bien faire la cuisine.

cool adj ① frais (f fraîche) ▷ a cool place un endroit frais ② (great) cool ▷ That's really cool! C'est vraiment cool!

cooperation n coopération f

cop n (informal) flic m

co-parent vb élever [48] en coparentalité

cope vb se débrouiller [28] ▷ It was hard, but we coped. C'était dur, mais nous nous sommes débrouillés.; **to cope with** faire [36] face à ▷ She's got a lot of problems to cope with. Elle doit faire face à de nombreux problèmes.

copper n ① cuivre m ▷ a copper bracelet un bracelet en cuivre ② (informal: police officer) flic m

copy n ① (of letter, document) copie f ② (of book) exemplaire m
▶ vb copier [19] ▷ The teacher accused him of copying. Le professeur l'a accusé d'avoir copié.; **to copy and paste** copier-coller [28]

core n (of fruit) trognon m ▷ an apple core un trognon de pomme

cork n ① (of bottle) bouchon m ② (material) liège m ▷ a cork table mat un set de table en liège

corkscrew n tire-bouchon m

corn n ① (wheat) blé m ② (sweetcorn) maïs m; **corn on the cob** l'épi de maïs m

corner n ① coin m ▷ in a corner of the room dans un coin de la pièce; **the shop on the corner** la boutique au coin de la rue; **He lives just round the corner.** Il habite tout près d'ici. ② (in football) corner m

cornflakes npl corn-flakes mpl

Cornwall n Cornouailles f; **in Cornwall** en Cornouailles

corpse n cadavre m

correct adj exact(e) ▷ That's correct. C'est exact.; **the correct choice** le bon choix; **the correct answer** la bonne réponse
▶ vb corriger [45]

correction n correction f

correctly adv correctement

corridor n couloir m

corruption n corruption f

Corsica n Corse f; **in Corsica** en Corse

cosmetics npl produits de beauté mpl

cosmetic surgery n chirurgie esthétique f

cost vb coûter [28] ▷ It costs too much. Ça coûte trop cher.
▶ n coût m; **the cost of living** le coût de la vie; **at all costs** à tout prix

costume n costume m

cosy adj douillet (f douillette)

cot n lit d'enfant m

cottage n cottage m; **a thatched cottage** une chaumière

cotton n coton m ▷ a cotton shirt une chemise en coton; **cotton wool** le coton hydrophile

couch n canapé m

cough vb tousser [28]
▶ n toux f ▷ a bad cough une

mauvaise toux; **I've got a cough.**
Je tousse.; **a cough sweet** une
pastille
could vb see **can**
council n conseil m
- The nearest French equivalent
  of a local council would be a
- **conseil municipal**, which
- administers a **commune**.
He's on the council. Il fait partie
du conseil municipal.; **a council
estate** une cité HLM; **a council
house** une HLM
- **HLM** stands for **habitation à
  loyer modéré** which means
- 'low-rent home'.
councillor n **She's a local
councillor.** Elle fait partie du
conseil municipal.
count vb compter [28]
count on vb compter [28] sur ▷ You
can count on me. Tu peux compter
sur moi.
counter n ❶ (in shop) comptoir m
❷ (in post office, bank) guichet m
❸ (in game) jeton m
country n ❶ pays m ▷ the border
between the two countries la
frontière entre les deux pays
❷ campagne f ▷ I live in the
country. J'habite à la campagne.;
country dancing la danse
folklorique
countryside n campagne f
county n comté m
- The nearest French equivalent
  of a county would be a
- **département**.
the county council

The nearest French equivalent of
a county council would be a
conseil général, which
administers a **département**.
couple n couple m ▷ the couple who
live next door le couple qui habite à
côté; **a couple** deux ▷ a couple of
hours deux heures; **Could you wait
a couple of minutes?**
Pourriez-vous attendre quelques
minutes?
courage n courage m
courgette n courgette f
courier n ❶ (for tourists)
accompagnateur m,
accompagnatrice f ❷ (delivery
service) coursier m ▷ They sent it by
courier. Ils l'ont envoyé par coursier.
> Be careful not to translate
courier by **courrier**.
course n ❶ cours m ▷ a French course
un cours de français ▷ to go on a
course suivre un cours ❷ plat m
▷ the main course le plat principal;
the first course l'entrée f ❸ terrain
m ▷ a golf course un terrain de golf;
of course bien sûr ▷ Do you love me?
— Of course I do! Tu m'aimes? — Bien
sûr que oui!
court n ❶ (of law) tribunal m (pl
tribunaux) ▷ He was in court
yesterday. Il est passé devant le
tribunal hier. ❷ (tennis) court m
▷ There are tennis and squash courts.
Il y a des courts de tennis et de
squash.
courtyard n cour f
cousin n cousin m, cousine f
cover n ❶ (of book) couverture f

❷ *(of duvet)* housse f
▸ *vb* **❶** couvrir [**55**] ▷ *My face was covered with mosquito bites.* J'avais le visage couvert de piqûres de moustique. **❷** prendre [**65**] en charge ▷ *Our insurance didn't cover it.* Notre assurance ne l'a pas pris en charge.; **to cover up a scandal** étouffer [**28**] un scandale

cow *n* vache f

coward *n* lâche m ▷ *She's a coward.* Elle est lâche.

cowboy *n* cow-boy m

crab *n* crabe m

crack *n* **❶** *(in wall)* fissure f **❷** *(in cup, window)* fêlure f **❸** *(drug)* crack m; **I'll have a crack at it.** Je vais tenter le coup.
▸ *vb* *(nut, egg)* casser [**28**]; **to crack a joke** sortir [**79**] une blague

crack down on *vb* être [**35**] ferme avec

cracked *adj* *(cup, window)* fêlé(e)

cracker *n* **❶** *(biscuit)* cracker m **❷** *(Christmas cracker)* papillote f

craft *n* travaux manuels mpl ▷ *We do craft at school.* Nous avons des cours de travaux manuels à l'école.; **a craft centre** un centre artisanal

crammed *adj* **crammed with** bourré de ▷ *Her bag was crammed with books.* Son sac était bourré de livres.

crane *n* *(machine)* grue f

crash *vb* avoir [**8**] un accident ▷ *He's crashed his car.* Il a eu un accident de voiture.; **The plane crashed.** L'avion s'est écrasé.

▸ *n* **❶** *(of car)* collision f **❷** *(of plane)* accident m; **a crash helmet** un casque; **a crash course** un cours intensif

crawl *vb* *(baby)* marcher [**28**] à quatre pattes
▸ *n* crawl m ▷ *to do the crawl* nager le crawl

crazy *adj* fou *(f* folle)

cream *adj* *(colour)* crème
▸ *n* crème f ▷ *strawberries and cream* les fraises à la crème; **a cream cake** un gâteau à la crème; **cream cheese** le fromage à la crème; **sun cream** la crème solaire

crease *n* pli m

creased *adj* froissé(e)

create *vb* créer [**18**]

creative *adj* créatif *(f* créative)

creature *n* créature f

crèche *n* crèche f

credit *n* crédit m ▷ *on credit* à crédit

credit card *n* carte de crédit f

creeps *npl* **It gives me the creeps.** Ça me donne la chair de poule.

creep up *vb* **to creep up on somebody** s'approcher [**28**] de quelqu'un à pas de loup

crept *vb see* **creep up**

crew *n* **❶** *(of ship, plane)* équipage m **❷** équipe f ▷ *a film crew* une équipe de tournage

crew cut *n* cheveux en brosse mpl

cricket *n* **❶** cricket m ▷ *I play cricket.* Je joue au cricket.; **a cricket bat** une batte de cricket **❷** *(insect)* grillon m

crime *n* **❶** délit m ▷ *Murder is a crime.* Le meurtre est un délit.

❷ *(lawlessness)* criminalité f; ▷ *Crime is rising.* La criminalité augmente.

criminal n criminel m, criminelle f
▶ *adj* criminel *(f* criminelle) ▷ *It's criminal!* C'est criminel!; **It's a criminal offence.** C'est un crime puni par la loi.; **to have a criminal record** avoir **[8]** un casier judiciaire

crisis n crise f

crisp *adj (food)* croquant(e)

crisps npl chips fpl ▷ *a bag of crisps* un paquet de chips

critical *adj* critique; **a critical remark** une critique

criticism n critique f

criticize vb critiquer **[28]**

Croatia n Croatie f; **in Croatia** en Croatie

crochet vb crocheter **[1]**

crocodile n crocodile m

crook n *(criminal)* escroc m

crop n récolte f ▷ *a good crop of apples* une bonne récolte de pommes

cross n croix f
▶ *adj* fâché(e) ▷ *to be cross about something* être fâché à propos de quelque chose
▶ *vb (street, bridge)* traverser **[28]**

cross out vb barrer **[28]**

cross over vb traverser **[28]**

cross-country n *(race)* cross m; **cross-country skiing** le ski de fond

crossing n ❶ *(by boat)* traversée f
▷ *the crossing from Dover to Calais* la traversée de Douvres à Calais
❷ *(for pedestrians)* passage clouté m

crossroads n carrefour m

crossword n mots croisés mpl
▷ *I like doing crosswords.* J'aime faire les mots croisés.

crouch down vb s'accroupir **[38]**

crow n corbeau m *(pl* corbeaux)

crowd n foule f; **the crowd** *(at sports match)* les spectateurs

crowded *adj* bondé(e)

crowdfunding n crowdfunding m

crown n couronne f

crude *adj (vulgar)* grossier *(f* grossière)

cruel *adj* cruel *(f* cruelle)

cruise n croisière f ▷ *to go on a cruise* faire une croisière

crumb n miette f

crush vb écraser **[28]**

crutch n béquille f

cry n cri m ▷ *He gave a cry of surprise.* Il a poussé un cri de surprise.; **Go on, have a good cry!** Vas-y, pleure un bon coup!
▶ *vb* pleurer **[28]** ▷ *The baby's crying.* Le bébé pleure.

crystal n cristal m *(pl* cristaux)

cub n ❶ *(animal)* petit m ❷ *(scout)* louveteau m *(pl* louveteaux)

cube n cube m

cubic *adj* **a cubic metre** un mètre cube

cucumber n concombre m

cuddle n câlin m ▷ *Come and give me a cuddle.* Viens me faire un câlin.

cue n *(for snooker, pool)* queue de billard f

culture n culture f

cunning *adj* ❶ *(person)* rusé(e) ❷ *(plan, idea)* astucieux *(f* astucieuse)

cup n ❶ tasse f ▷ *a china cup* une tasse en porcelaine; **a cup of coffee** un café ❷ *(trophy)* coupe f

a
b
c
d
e
f
g
h
i
j
k
l
m
n
o
p
q
r
s
t
u
v
w
x
y
z

cupboard n placard m
cure vb guérir [38]
　▶ n remède m
curious adj curieux (f curieuse)
curl n (in hair) boucle f
curly adj ❶ (loosely curled) bouclé(e)
　❷ (tightly curled) frisé(e)
currant n (dried fruit) raisin de
　Corinthe m
currency n devise f ▷ foreign
　currency les devises étrangères
current n courant m ▷ The current is
　very strong. Le courant est très fort.
　▶ adj actuel (f actuelle) ▷ the current
　situation la situation actuelle
current affairs npl actualité f
curriculum n programme m
curriculum vitae n curriculum
　vitae m
curry n curry m
curtain n rideau m (pl rideaux) ▷ to
　draw the curtains tirer les rideaux
cushion n coussin m
custard n (for pouring) crème
　anglaise f
custody n (of child) garde f
custom n coutume f, m ▷ It's an old
　custom. C'est une ancienne
　coutume.
customer n client m, cliente f
customs npl douane fsg
customs officer n douanier m,
　douanière f
cut n ❶ coupure f ▷ He's got a cut on
　his forehead. Il a une coupure au
　front. ❷ coupe f ▷ a cut and blow-dry
　une coupe brushing ❸ (in price,
　spending) réduction f
　▶ vb ❶ couper [28] ▷ I'll cut some

bread. Je vais couper du pain.; **to
cut oneself** se couper [28] ▷ I cut
my foot on a piece of glass. Je me suis
coupé au pied avec un morceau de
verre. ❷ (price, spending) réduire [23]
cut down vb (tree) abattre [9]
cut off vb couper [28] ▷ The
electricity was cut off. L'électricité a
été coupée.
cut up vb (vegetables, meat) hacher
[28]
cute adj mignon (f mignonne)
cutlery n couverts mpl
CV n C.V. m
cyberbully n personne f coupable
de cyberharcèlement
cyberbullying n
cyberharcèlement m
cybercafé n cybercafé m
cycle vb faire [36] de la bicyclette
▷ I like cycling. J'aime faire de la
bicyclette.; **I cycle to school.** Je
vais à l'école à bicyclette.
　▶ n bicyclette f; **a cycle ride** une
promenade à bicyclette; **a cycle
lane** une piste cyclable
cycling n cyclisme m
cyclist n cycliste mf
cylinder n cylindre m
Cyprus n Chypre; **in Cyprus** à
Chypre; **We went to Cyprus.** Nous
sommes allés à Chypre.
Czech n ❶ (person) Tchèque mf
❷ (language) tchèque m
　▶ adj tchèque; **the Czech Republic**
la République tchèque

dad n ❶ père m ▷ *my dad* mon père
❷ papa m

> Use **papa** only when you are
> talking to your father or using
> it as his name; otherwise use
> **père**.

Dad! Papa! ▷ *I'll ask Dad.* Je vais
demander à papa.

daffodil n jonquille f

daft adj idiot(e)

daily adj, adv ❶ quotidien (f
quotidienne) ▷ *It's part of my daily
routine.* Ça fait partie de mes
occupations quotidiennes. ❷ tous
les jours ▷ *The pool is open daily.* La
piscine est ouverte tous les jours.

dairy products npl produits
laitiers mpl

daisy n pâquerette f

dam n barrage m

damage n dégâts mpl ▷ *The storm
did a lot of damage.* La tempête a fait
beaucoup de dégâts.
> ▶ vb endommager [**45**]

damp adj humide

dance n ❶ danse f ▷ *The last dance
was a waltz.* La dernière danse était
une valse. ❷ bal m ▷ *Are you going to
the dance tonight?* Tu vas au bal ce
soir?
> ▶ vb danser [**28**]; **to go dancing**
> aller [**3**] danser ▷ *Let's go dancing!* Si
> on allait danser?

dancer n danseur m, danseuse f

dandruff n pellicules fpl

Dane n Danois m, Danoise f

danger n danger m; **in danger** en
danger ▷ *His life is in danger.* Sa vie
est en danger.; **to be in danger of**
risquer [**28**] de ▷ *We were in danger
of missing the plane.* Nous risquions
de rater l'avion.

dangerous adj dangereux (f
dangereuse)

Danish adj danois(e)
> ▶ n (language) danois m

dare vb oser [**28**]; **to dare to do
something** oser [**28**] faire quelque
chose ▷ *I didn't dare to tell my
parents.* Je n'ai pas osé le dire à mes
parents.; **I dare say it'll be okay.** Je
suppose que ça va aller.

daring adj audacieux (f audacieuse)

dark adj ❶ (room) sombre ▷ *It's dark.
(inside)* Il fait sombre.; **It's dark
outside.** Il fait nuit dehors.; **It's
getting dark.** La nuit tombe.
❷ (colour) foncé(e) ▷ *She's got dark
hair.* Elle a les cheveux foncés.

▷ *a dark green sweater* un pull vert foncé

▶ *n* noir *m* ▷ *I'm afraid of the dark.* J'ai peur du noir.; **after dark** après la tombée de la nuit

darkness *n* obscurité *f* ▷ *The room was in darkness.* La chambre était dans l'obscurité.

darling *n* chéri *m*, chérie *f* ▷ *Thank you, darling!* Merci, chéri!

dart *n* fléchette *f* ▷ *to play darts* jouer aux fléchettes

data *npl* données *fpl*

database *n* (on computer) base de données *f*

date *n* ❶ date *f* ▷ *my date of birth* ma date de naissance; **What's the date today?** Quel jour sommes-nous?; **to have a date with somebody** sortir [**79**] avec quelqu'un ▷ *She's got a date with Ian tonight.* Elle sort avec Ian ce soir.; **out of date (1)** (passport) périmé **(2)** (technology) dépassé **(3)** (clothes) démodé ❷ (fruit) datte *f*

daughter *n* fille *f*

daughter-in-law *n* belle-fille *f* (pl belles-filles)

dawn *n* aube *f* ▷ *at dawn* à l'aube

day *n*

> Use **jour** to refer to the whole 24-hour period. **journée** only refers to the time when you are awake.

❶ jour *m* ▷ *We stayed in Nice for three days.* Nous sommes restés trois jours à Nice.; **every day** tous les jours ❷ journée *f* ▷ *I stayed at home all day.* Je suis resté à la maison

toute la journée.; **the day before** la veille ▷ *the day before my birthday* la veille de mon anniversaire; **the day after** le lendemain; **the day after tomorrow** après-demain ▷ *We're leaving the day after tomorrow.* Nous partons après-demain.; **the day before yesterday** avant-hier ▷ *He arrived the day before yesterday.* Il est arrivé avant-hier.

dead *adj, adv* ❶ mort(e) ▷ *He was already dead when the doctor came.* Il était déjà mort quand le docteur est arrivé.; **He was shot dead.** Il a été abattu. ❷ (totally) absolument ▷ *You're dead right!* Tu as absolument raison!; **dead on time** à l'heure pile ▷ *The train arrived dead on time.* Le train est arrivé à l'heure pile.

dead end *n* impasse *f*

deadline *n* date limite *f* ▷ *The deadline for entries is May 2nd.* La date limite d'inscription est le deux mai.

deaf *adj* sourd(e)

deafening *adj* assourdissant(e)

deal *n* marché *m*; **It's a deal!** Marché conclu!; **a great deal** beaucoup ▷ *a great deal of money* beaucoup d'argent

▶ *vb* (cards) donner [**28**] ▷ *It's your turn to deal.* C'est à toi de donner.; **to deal with something** s'occuper [**28**] de quelque chose ▷ *He promised to deal with it immediately.* Il a promis de s'en occuper immédiatement.

dealer n ❶ marchand m, marchande f ❷ (of drugs) dealer m

dealt vb see **deal**

dear adj ❶ cher (f chère) ▷ Dear Mrs Duval Chère Madame Duval; **Dear Sir/Madam** (in a letter) Madame, Monsieur ❷ (expensive) coûteux (f coûteuse)

death n mort f ▷ after his death après sa mort; **I was bored to death.** Je me suis ennuyé à mourir.

debate n débat m
▶ vb débattre [9]

debt n dette f ▷ He's got a lot of debts. Il a beaucoup de dettes.; **to be in debt** avoir [8] des dettes

decade n décennie f

decaffeinated adj décaféiné(e)

deceive vb tromper [28]

December n décembre m; **in December** en décembre

decent adj convenable ▷ a decent education une éducation convenable

decide vb ❶ décider [28] ▷ I decided to write to her. J'ai décidé de lui écrire. ▷ I decided not to go. J'ai décidé de ne pas y aller. ❷ se décider [28] ▷ I can't decide. Je n'arrive pas à me décider.; **to decide on something** se mettre [47] d'accord sur quelque chose ▷ They haven't decided on a name yet. Ils ne se sont pas encore mis d'accord sur un nom.

decimal adj décimal(e) ▷ the decimal system le système décimal

decision n décision f; **to make a decision** prendre [65] une décision

deck n ❶ (of ship) pont m; **on deck** sur le pont ❷ (of cards) jeu m (pl jeux)

deckchair n chaise longue f

declare vb déclarer [28]

decorate vb ❶ décorer [28] ▷ I decorated the cake with glacé cherries. J'ai décoré le gâteau avec des cerises confites. ❷ (paint) peindre [60] ❸ (wallpaper) tapisser [28]

decrease n diminution f ▷ a decrease in the number of unemployed une diminution du nombre de chômeurs
▶ vb diminuer [28]

dedication n ❶ (commitment) dévouement m ❷ (in book, on radio) dédicace f

deduct vb déduire [23]

deep adj ❶ (water, hole, cut) profond(e) ▷ Is it deep? Est-ce que c'est profond?; **How deep is the lake?** Quelle est la profondeur du lac?; **a hole 4 metres deep** un trou de quatre mètres de profondeur ❷ (layer) épais (f épaisse) ▷ The snow was really deep. Il y avait une épaisse couche de neige.; **He's got a deep voice.** Il a la voix grave.; **to take a deep breath** respirer [28] à fond

deeply adv (depressed) profondément

deer n ❶ (red deer) cerf m ❷ (fallow deer) daim m ❸ (roe deer) chevreuil m

defeat n défaite f
▶ vb battre [9]

defect n défaut m

defence n défense f

defend vb défendre [88]

defender n défenseur m

define vb définir [38]

definite adj ❶ précis(e) ▷ I haven't got any definite plans. Je n'ai pas de projets précis. ❷ net (f nette) ▷ It's a definite improvement. Cela constitue une nette amélioration. ❸ sûr(e) ▷ We might go to Spain, but it's not definite. Nous irons peut-être en Espagne, mais ce n'est pas sûr.; **He was definite about it.** Il a été catégorique.

definitely adv vraiment ▷ He's definitely the best player. C'est vraiment lui le meilleur joueur.; **He's the best player. — Definitely!** C'est le meilleur joueur. — C'est sûr!; **I definitely think he'll come.** Je suis sûr qu'il va venir.

definition n définition f

degree n ❶ degré m ▷ a temperature of 30 degrees une température de trente degrés ❷ licence f ▷ a degree in English une licence d'anglais

delay vb ❶ retarder [28] ▷ We decided to delay our departure. Nous avons décidé de retarder notre départ. ❷ tarder [28] ▷ Don't delay! Ne tarde pas!; **to be delayed** être [35] retardé ▷ Our flight was delayed. Notre vol a été retardé.
▶ n retard m ▷ There will be delays to trains on the London-Brighton line. Il y aura des retards sur la ligne Londres-Brighton.

Be careful not to translate **delay** by **délai**.

delete vb (on computer, tape) effacer [12]

deliberate adj délibéré(e)

deliberately adv exprès ▷ She did it deliberately. Elle l'a fait exprès.

delicate adj délicat(e)

delicatessen n épicerie fine f

delicious adj délicieux (f délicieuse)

delight n to her delight à sa plus grande joie

delighted adj ravi(e) ▷ He'll be delighted to see you. Il sera ravi de vous voir.

deliver vb ❶ livrer [28] ▷ I deliver newspapers. Je livre les journaux. ❷ (mail) distribuer [28]

delivery n livraison f

demand vb exiger [45]

Be careful not to translate **to demand** by **demander**.

▶ n (for product) demande f

democracy n démocratie f

democratic adj démocratique

demolish vb démolir [38]

demonstrate vb ❶ (show) faire [36] une démonstration de ▷ She demonstrated the technique. Elle a fait une démonstration de la technique. ❷ (protest) manifester [28] ▷ to demonstrate against something manifester contre quelque chose

demonstration n ❶ (of method, technique) démonstration f ❷ (protest) manifestation f

demonstrator n (protester) manifestant m, manifestante f

denim n jean m ▷ a denim jacket une veste en jean

Denmark n Danemark m; **in Denmark** au Danemark; **to Denmark** au Danemark

dense adj ❶ (crowd, fog) dense ❷ (smoke) épais (fépaisse); **He's so dense!** Il est vraiment bouché!

dent n bosse f
▶ vb cabosser [**28**]

dental adj dentaire; **dental floss** le fil dentaire

dentist n dentiste mf ▷ Catherine is a dentist. Catherine est dentiste.

deny vb nier [**19**] ▷ She denied everything. Elle a tout nié.

deodorant n déodorant m

depart vb partir [**57**]

department n ❶ (in shop) rayon m ▷ the shoe department le rayon chaussures ❷ (in university, school) département m ▷ the English department le département d'anglais

department store n grand magasin m

departure n départ m

departure lounge n hall des départs m

depend vb to depend on dépendre [**88**] de ▷ The price depends on the quality. Le prix dépend de la qualité.; **depending on the weather** selon le temps; **It depends.** Ça dépend.

deposit n ❶ (part payment) arrhes fpl ▷ You have to pay a deposit when you book. Il faut verser des arrhes lors de la réservation. ❷ (when hiring something) caution f ▷ You get the deposit back when you return the bike. On vous remboursera la caution quand vous ramènerez le vélo. ❸ (on bottle) consigne f

depressed adj déprimé(e) ▷ I'm feeling depressed. Je suis déprimé.

depressing adj déprimant(e)

depth n profondeur f

deputy head n directeur adjoint m, directrice adjointe f

descend vb descendre [**24**]

describe vb décrire [**30**]

description n description f

desert n désert m

desert island n île déserte f

deserve vb mériter [**28**]

design n ❶ conception f ▷ It's a completely new design. C'est une conception entièrement nouvelle. ❷ motif m ▷ a geometric design un motif géométrique; **fashion design** le stylisme
▶ vb (clothes, furniture) dessiner [**28**]

designer n (of clothes) styliste mf; **designer clothes** les vêtements griffés

desire n désir m
▶ vb désirer [**28**]

desk n ❶ (in office) bureau m (pl bureaux) ❷ (for pupil) pupitre m ❸ (in hotel) réception f ❹ (at airport) comptoir m

desktop n (computer) ordinateur de bureau m (pl ordinateurs de bureau)

despair n désespoir m; **I was in despair.** J'étais désespéré.

desperate adj désespéré(e)

▷ *a desperate situation* une situation désespérée; **to get desperate** désespérer [**34**] ▷ *I was getting desperate.* Je commençais à désespérer.

desperately *adv* ❶ terriblement ▷ *We're desperately worried.* Nous sommes terriblement inquiets. ❷ désespérément ▷ *He was desperately trying to persuade her.* Il essayait désespérément de la persuader.

despise *vb* mépriser [**28**]

despite *prep* malgré

dessert *n* dessert *m* ▷ *for dessert* comme dessert

destination *n* destination *f*

destroy *vb* détruire [**23**]

destruction *n* destruction *f*

detached house *n* pavillon *m*

detail *n* détail *m* ▷ *in detail* en détail

detailed *adj* détaillé(e)

detective *n* inspecteur de police *m*; **a private detective** un détective privé; **a detective story** un roman policier

detention *n* **to get a detention** être [**35**] consigné

detergent *n* ❶ détergent *m* ❷ *(US)* lessive *f*

determined *adj* déterminé(e); **to be determined to do something** être [**35**] déterminé à faire quelque chose ▷ *She's determined to succeed.* Elle est déterminée à réussir.

detour *n* détour *m*

devastated *adj* anéanti(e) ▷ *I was devastated.* J'étais anéanti.

develop *vb* ❶ développer [**28**] ▷ *to get a film developed* faire développer un film ❷ se développer [**28**] ▷ *Girls develop faster than boys.* Les filles se développent plus vite que les garçons.; **to develop into** se transformer [**28**] en ▷ *The argument developed into a fight.* La dispute s'est transformée en bagarre.; **a developing country** un pays en voie de développement

development *n* développement *m* ▷ *the latest developments* les derniers développements

devil *n* diable *m* ▷ *Poor devil!* Pauvre diable!

devoted *adj* dévoué(e) ▷ *He's completely devoted to her.* Il lui est très dévoué.

diabetes *n* diabète *m*

diabetic *n* diabétique *mf* ▷ *I'm a diabetic.* Je suis diabétique.

diagonal *adj* diagonal(e) *(mpl* diagonaux)

diagram *n* diagramme *m*

dial *vb (number)* composer [**28**]

dialling tone *n* tonalité *f*

dialogue *n* dialogue *m*

diamond *n* diamant *m* ▷ *a diamond ring* une bague en diamant; **diamonds** *(at cards)* le carreau *sg*

diaper *n (US)* couche *f*

diarrhoea *n* diarrhée *f* ▷ *I've got diarrhoea.* J'ai la diarrhée.

diary *n* ❶ agenda *m* ▷ *I've got her phone number in my diary.* J'ai son numéro de téléphone dans mon agenda. ❷ journal *m (pl* journaux) ▷ *I keep a diary.* Je tiens un journal.

dice n dé m

dictation n dictée f

dictionary n dictionnaire m

did vb see do

die vb mourir [51] ▷ He died last year. Il est mort l'année dernière.; **to be dying to do something** mourir [51] d'envie de faire quelque chose ▷ I'm dying to see you. Je meurs d'envie de te voir.

diesel n ❶ (fuel) gazole m ▷ 30 litres of diesel trente litres de gazole ❷ (car) voiture diesel f ▷ My car's a diesel. J'ai une voiture diesel.

diet n ❶ alimentation f ❷ (for slimming) régime m ▷ I'm on a diet. Je suis au régime.
▶ vb faire [36] un régime ▷ I've been dieting for two months. Je fais un régime depuis deux mois.

difference n différence f ▷ There's not much difference in age between us. Il n'y a pas une grande différence d'âge entre nous.; **It makes no difference.** Ça revient au même.

different adj différent(e) ▷ Paris is different from London. Paris est différent de Londres.

difficult adj difficile ▷ It's difficult to choose. C'est difficile de choisir.

difficulty n difficulté f ▷ without difficulty sans difficulté; **to have difficulty doing something** avoir [8] du mal à faire quelque chose

dig vb ❶ (hole) creuser [28] ❷ (garden) bêcher [28]; **to dig something up** déterrer [28] quelque chose

digestion n digestion f

digital camera n appareil photo numérique m

digital radio n radio numérique f

digital television n télévision numérique f

digital watch n montre à affichage numérique f

dim adj ❶ (light) faible ❷ (stupid) limité(e)

dimension n dimension f

din n vacarme m

diner n (US) snack m

dinghy n **a rubber dinghy** un canot pneumatique; **a sailing dinghy** un dériveur

dining room n salle à manger f

dinner n ❶ (at midday) déjeuner m ❷ (in the evening) dîner m

dinner lady n la dame de service f

dinner party n dîner m

dinner time n ❶ (midday) heure du déjeuner f ❷ (in the evening) heure du dîner f

dinosaur n dinosaure m

diploma n diplôme m

direct adj, adv direct(e) ▷ the most direct route le chemin le plus direct ▷ You can't fly to Nice direct from Cork. Il n'y a pas de vols directs de Cork à Nice.
▶ vb ❶ (film, programme) réaliser [28] ❷ (play, show) mettre [47] en scène

direction n direction f ▷ We're going in the wrong direction. Nous allons dans la mauvaise direction.; **to ask somebody for directions** demander [28] son chemin à quelqu'un

a
b
c
d
e
f
g
h
i
j
k
l
m
n
o
p
q
r
s
t
u
v
w
x
y
z

director n ❶ (of company) directeur
m, directrice f ❷ (of play) metteur
en scène m ❸ (of film, programme)
réalisateur m, réalisatrice f

directory n ❶ (phone book)
annuaire m ❷ (computing)
répertoire m

dirt n saleté f

dirty adj sale; **to get dirty** se salir
[**38**]; **to get something dirty** salir
[**38**] quelque chose

disabled adj handicapé(e)

disadvantage n désavantage m

disagree vb We always disagree.
Nous ne sommes jamais d'accord.;
I disagree! Je ne suis pas d'accord!;
He disagrees with me. Il n'est pas
d'accord avec moi.

disagreement n désaccord m

disappear vb disparaître [**56**]

disappearance n disparition f

disappointed adj déçu(e)

disappointment n déception f

disaster n désastre m

disastrous adj désastreux (f
désastreuse)

disc n disque m

discipline n discipline f

disc jockey n disc-jockey m

disco n soirée disco f ▷ There's a disco
at the school tonight. Il y a une soirée
disco à l'école ce soir.

disconnect vb ❶ (electrical
equipment) débrancher [**28**]
❷ (telephone, water supply) couper
[**28**]

discount n réduction f ▷ a discount
for students une réduction pour
les étudiants

discourage vb décourager [**45**];
to get discouraged se décourager
[**45**] ▷ Don't get discouraged! Ne te
décourage pas!

discover vb découvrir [**55**]

discrimination n discrimination f
▷ racial discrimination la
discrimination raciale

discuss vb ❶ discuter [**28**] de ▷ I'll
discuss it with my parents. Je vais en
discuter avec mes parents.
❷ (topic) discuter [**28**] sur ▷ We
discussed the problem of pollution.
Nous avons discuté du problème
de la pollution.

discussion n discussion f

disease n maladie f

disgraceful adj scandaleux
(f scandaleuse)

disguise vb déguiser [**28**] ▷ He was
disguised as a police officer. Il était
déguisé en policier.

disgusted adj dégoûté(e)
▷ I was absolutely disgusted.
J'étais complètement
dégoûté.

disgusting adj ❶ (food, smell)
dégoûtant(e) ▷ It looks disgusting.
Ça a l'air dégoûtant. ❷ (disgraceful)
honteux (f honteuse) ▷ That's
disgusting! C'est honteux!

dish n plat m ▷ a vegetarian dish un
plat végétarien; **to do the dishes**
faire [**36**] la vaisselle ▷ He never does
the dishes. Il ne fait jamais la
vaisselle.

dishonest adj malhonnête

dishwasher n lave-vaisselle m
(pl lave-vaisselle)

disinfectant n désinfectant m

disk n disque m; **the hard disk** le disque dur

dismal adj lugubre

dismiss vb (employee) renvoyer [**33**]

disobedient adj désobéissant(e)

display n étalage m ▷ There was a lovely display of fruit in the window. Il y avait un superbe étalage de fruits en vitrine.; **to be on display** être [**35**] exposé ▷ Her best paintings were on display. Ses meilleurs tableaux étaient exposés.; **a firework display** un feu d'artifice
▶vb ❶ montrer [**28**] ▷ She proudly displayed her medal. Elle a montré sa médaille avec fierté. ❷ (in shop window) exposer [**28**]

disposable adj jetable

disqualify vb disqualifier [**19**]; **to be disqualified** être [**35**] disqualifié ▷ He was disqualified. Il a été disqualifié.

disrupt vb perturber [**28**]
▷ Protesters disrupted the meeting. Des manifestants ont perturbé la réunion.

dissolve vb dissoudre [**70**]

distance n distance f ▷ a distance of 40 kilometres une distance de quarante kilomètres; **It's within walking distance.** On peut y aller à pied.; **in the distance** au loin

distant adj lointain(e) ▷ in the distant future dans un avenir lointain

distract vb distraire [**85**]

distribute vb distribuer [**28**]

district n ❶ (of town) quartier m

❷ (of country) région f

disturb vb déranger [**45**] ▷ I'm sorry to disturb you. Je suis désolé de vous déranger.

ditch n fossé m
▶vb (informal) plaquer [**28**] ▷ She's just ditched her boyfriend. Elle vient de plaquer son copain.

dive n plongeon m
▶vb plonger [**45**]

diver n plongeur m, plongeuse f

diversion n (for traffic) déviation f

divide vb ❶ diviser [**28**] ▷ Divide the pastry in half. Divisez la pâte en deux. ▷ 12 divided by 3 is 4. Douze divisé par trois égale quatre. ❷ se diviser [**28**] ▷ We divided into two groups. Nous nous sommes divisés en deux groupes.

diving n plongée f; **a diving board** un plongeoir

division n division f

divorce n divorce m

divorced adj divorcé(e) ▷ My parents are divorced. Mes parents sont divorcés.

DIY n bricolage m ▷ to do DIY faire du bricolage

dizzy adj **to feel dizzy** avoir [**8**] la tête qui tourne ▷ I feel dizzy. J'ai la tête qui tourne.

DJ n disc-jockey m

do vb ❶ faire [**36**] ▷ What are you doing this evening? Qu'est-ce que tu fais ce soir? ▷ I do a lot of cycling. Je fais beaucoup de vélo. ▷ I haven't done my homework. Je n'ai pas fait mes devoirs. ▷ She did it by herself. Elle l'a fait toute seule. ▷ I'll do my best. Je ferai de mon mieux.; **to do well** marcher [**28**] bien ▷ *The firm is doing well.* L'entreprise marche bien. ▷ *She's doing well at school.* Ses études marchent bien. ❷ *(be enough)* aller [**3**] ▷ *It's not very good, but it'll do.* Ce n'est pas très bon, mais ça ira.; **That'll do, thanks.** Ça ira, merci.

> In English 'do' is used to make questions. In French questions are made either with **est-ce que** or by reversing the order of verb and subject.

▷ *Do you like French food?* Est-ce que vous aimez la cuisine française? ▷ *Where does he live?* Où est-ce qu'il habite? ▷ *Do you speak English?* Parlez-vous anglais? ▷ *What do you do in your free time?* Qu'est-ce que vous faites pendant vos loisirs? ▷ *Where did you go for your holidays?* Où es-tu allé pendant tes vacances?

> Use **ne ... pas** in negative sentences for 'don't'.

▷ *I don't understand.* Je ne comprends pas. ▷ *Why didn't you come?* Pourquoi n'êtes-vous pas venus?

> 'do' is not translated when it is used in place of another verb.

▷ *I hate maths. — So do I.* Je déteste les maths. — Moi aussi. ▷ *I didn't like the film. — Neither did I.* Je n'ai pas aimé le film. — Moi non plus. ▷ *Do you like horses? — No I don't.* Est-ce que tu aimes les chevaux? — Non.

> Use **n'est-ce pas** to check information.

▷ *You go swimming on Fridays, don't you?* Tu fais de la natation le vendredi, n'est-ce pas? ▷ *The bus stops at the youth hostel, doesn't it?* Le bus s'arrête à l'auberge de jeunesse, n'est-ce pas?; **How do you do?** Enchanté?

do up *vb* ❶ *(shoes)* lacer [**12**] ▷ *Do up your shoes!* Lace tes chaussures! ❷ *(renovate)* retaper [**28**] ▷ *They're doing up an old cottage.* Ils retapent une vieille maison. ❸ *(shirt, cardigan)* boutonner [**28**]; **Do up your zip!** *(on trousers)* Ferme ta braguette!

do without *vb* se passer [**58**] de ▷ *I couldn't do without my computer.* Je ne pourrais pas me passer de mon ordinateur.

doctor *n* médecin *m* ▷ *She's a doctor.* Elle est médecin.

document *n* document *m*

documentary *n* documentaire *m*

dodge *vb (attacker)* échapper [**28**] à

dodgems *npl* autos tamponneuses *fpl* ▷ *to go on the dodgems* aller faire un tour d'autos tamponneuses

does *vb see* **do**

doesn't = **does not**

dog *n* chien *m*, chienne *f* ▷ *Have you got a dog?* Est-ce que tu as un chien?

do-it-yourself *n* bricolage *m*

dole *n* allocations chômage *fpl*; **to be on the dole** toucher [**28**] le chômage ▷ *A lot of people are on the dole.* Beaucoup de gens touchent le chômage.; **to go on the dole**

s'inscrire [**30**] au chômage
doll n poupée f
dollar n dollar m
dolphin n dauphin m
dominoes npl **to have a game of
dominoes** faire [**36**] une partie de
dominos
donate vb donner [**28**]
done vb see **do**
donkey n âne m
don't = **do not**
door n ❶ porte f ▷ the first door on
the right la première porte à droite
❷ (of car, train) portière f
doorbell n sonnette f; **to ring the
doorbell** sonner [**28**]; **Suddenly
the doorbell rang.** Soudain, on a
sonné.
doorstep n pas de la porte m
dormitory n dortoir m
dot n (on letter 'i', in email address)
point m; **on the dot** à l'heure pile
▷ He arrived at 9 o'clock on the dot. Il
est arrivé à neuf heures pile.
double adj, adv double ▷ a double
helping une double portion; **to
cost double** coûter [**28**] le double
▷ First-class tickets cost double. Les
billets de première classe coûtent
le double.; **a double bed** un grand
lit; **a double room** une chambre
pour deux personnes; **a
double-decker bus** un autobus à
impériale
▶ vb doubler [**28**] ▷ The number of
attacks has doubled. Le nombre
d'agressions a doublé.
double bass n contrebasse f
▷ I play the double bass. Je joue de

la contrebasse.
double-click vb double-cliquer
[**28**] ▷ to double-click on an icon
double-cliquer sur une icône
double glazing n double vitrage m
doubles npl (in tennis) double msg
▷ to play mixed doubles jouer en
double mixte
doubt n doute m ▷ I have my doubts.
J'ai des doutes.
▶ vb douter [**28**] de; **I doubt it.** J'en
doute.; **to doubt that** douter [**28**]
que

> douter que has to be followed
by a verb in the subjunctive.
▷ I doubt he'll agree. Je doute qu'il
soit d'accord.
doubtful adj **to be doubtful about
doing something** hésiter [**28**] à
faire quelque chose ▷ I'm doubtful
about going by myself. J'hésite à y
aller tout seul.; **It's doubtful.** Ce
n'est pas sûr.; **You sound
doubtful.** Tu n'as pas l'air sûr.
dough n pâte f
doughnut n beignet m ▷ a jam
doughnut un beignet à la confiture
Dover n Douvres ▷ We went from
Dover to Boulogne. Nous sommes
allés de Douvres à Boulogne.; **in
Dover** à Douvres
down adv, adj, prep ❶ (below) en bas
▷ His office is down on the first floor.
Son bureau est en bas, au premier
étage. ▷ It's down there. C'est là-bas.
❷ (to the ground) à terre ▷ He threw
down his racket. Il a jeté sa raquette
à terre.; **They live just down
the road.** Ils habitent tout à côté.;

a
b
c
d
e
f
g
h
i
j
k
l
m
n
o
p
q
r
s
t
u
v
w
x
y
z

to come down descendre [**24**] ▷ *Come down here!* Descends!; **to go down** descendre [**24**] ▷ *The rabbit went down the hole.* Le lapin est descendu dans le terrier.; **to sit down** s'asseoir [**6**] ▷ *Sit down!* Asseyez-vous!; **to feel down** avoir [**8**] le cafard ▷ *I'm feeling a bit down.* J'ai un peu le cafard.; **The computer's down.** L'ordinateur est en panne.

download *vb* télécharger [**45**] ▷ *to download a file* télécharger un fichier
▶ *n* téléchargement *m* ▷ *a free download* un téléchargement gratuit

downstairs *adv, adj* ❶ au rez-de-chaussée ▷ *The bathroom's downstairs.* La salle de bain est au rez-de-chaussée. ❷ du rez-de-chaussée ▷ *the downstairs bathroom* la salle de bain du rez-de-chaussée; **the people downstairs** les voisins du dessous

downtown *adj (US)* dans le centre

doze *vb* sommeiller [**28**]

doze off *vb* s'assoupir [**38**]

dozen *n* douzaine *f* ▷ *two dozen* deux douzaines ▷ *a dozen eggs* une douzaine d'œufs; **I've told you that dozens of times.** Je t'ai dit ça des centaines de fois.

draft *n (US)* courant d'air *m*

drag *vb (thing, person)* traîner [**28**]
▶ *n* **It's a real drag!** *(informal)* C'est la barbe!; **in drag** travesti ▷ *He was in drag.* Il était travesti.

dragon *n* dragon *m*

drain *n* égout *m* ▷ *The drains are blocked.* Les égouts sont bouchés.
▶ *vb (vegetables, pasta)* égoutter [**28**]

drama *n* art dramatique *m* ▷ *Drama is my favourite subject.* L'art dramatique est ma matière préférée.; **drama school** l'école d'art dramatique ▷ *I'd like to go to drama school.* J'aimerais entrer dans une école d'art dramatique.; **Greek drama** le théâtre grec

dramatic *adj* spectaculaire ▷ *a dramatic improvement* une amélioration spectaculaire; **dramatic news** une nouvelle extraordinaire

drank *vb see* **drink**

drapes *npl (US)* rideaux *mpl*

draught *n* courant d'air *m*

draughts *n* dames *fpl* ▷ *to play draughts* jouer aux dames

draw *vb* ❶ dessiner [**28**] ▷ *He's good at drawing.* Il dessine bien.; **to draw a picture** faire [**36**] un dessin; **to draw a picture of somebody** faire [**36**] le portrait de quelqu'un; **to draw a line** tirer [**28**] un trait ❷ *(sport)* faire [**36**] match nul ▷ *We drew 2-2.* Nous avons fait match nul deux à deux.; **to draw the curtains** tirer [**28**] les rideaux; **to draw lots** tirer [**28**] au sort
▶ *n* ❶ *(sport)* match nul *m* ▷ *The game ended in a draw.* La partie s'est soldée par un match nul. ❷ *(in lottery)* tirage au sort *m* ▷ *The draw takes place on Saturday.* Le tirage au sort a lieu samedi.

drawback n inconvénient m

drawer n tiroir m

drawing n dessin m

drawing pin n punaise f

drawn vb see **draw**

dreadful adj ❶ terrible ▷ a dreadful mistake une terrible erreur ❷ affreux (f affreuse) ▷ The weather was dreadful. Il a fait un temps affreux.; **I feel dreadful.** Je ne me sens vraiment pas bien.; **You look dreadful.** (ill) Tu as une mine affreuse.

dream vb rêver [28] ▷ I dreamed I was in Belgium. J'ai rêvé que j'étais en Belgique.
▷ n rêve m ▷ It was just a dream. Ce n'était qu'un rêve.; **a bad dream** un cauchemar

drench vb to get drenched se faire [36] tremper ▷ We got drenched. Nous nous sommes fait tremper.

dress n robe f
▷ vb s'habiller [28] ▷ I got up, dressed, and went downstairs. Je me suis levé, je me suis habillé et je suis descendu.; **to dress somebody** habiller [28] quelqu'un ▷ She dressed the children. Elle a habillé les enfants.; **to get dressed** s'habiller [28] ▷ I got dressed quickly. Je me suis habillé rapidement.

dress up vb se déguiser [28] ▷ I dressed up as a ghost. Je me suis déguisé en fantôme.

dressed adj habillé(e) ▷ I'm not dressed yet. Je ne suis pas encore habillé.; **She was dressed in a green sweater and jeans.** Elle portait un pull vert et un jean.

dresser n (furniture) vaisselier m

dressing gown n robe de chambre f

dressing table n coiffeuse f

drew vb see **draw**

dried vb see **dry**

drier n séchoir m

drift n a snow drift une congère
▷ vb ❶ (boat) aller [3] à la dérive ❷ (snow) s'amonceler [4]

drill n perceuse f
▷ vb percer [12]

drink vb boire [10] ▷ What would you like to drink? Qu'est-ce que vous voulez boire?; **I don't drink.** Je ne bois pas d'alcool.
▷ n ❶ boisson f ▷ a cold drink une boisson fraîche ❷ (alcoholic) verre m ▷ They've gone out for a drink. Ils sont allés prendre un verre.; **to have a drink** prendre [65] un verre

drive n ❶ tour en voiture m; **to go for a drive** aller [3] faire un tour en voiture ▷ We went for a drive in the country. Nous sommes allés faire un tour à la campagne.; **We've got a long drive tomorrow.** Nous avons une longue route à faire demain. ❷ (of house) allée f ▷ He parked his car in the drive. Il a garé sa voiture dans l'allée.
▷ vb ❶ (a car) conduire [23] ▷ She's learning to drive. Elle apprend à conduire. ▷ Can you drive? Tu sais conduire? ❷ (go by car) aller [3] en voiture ▷ I'd rather drive than take the train. Je préfère conduire que de prendre le train. ❸ emmener [43]

a
b
c
d
e
f
g
h
i
j
k
l
m
n
o
p
q
r
s
t
u
v
w
x
y
z

en voiture ▷ *My mother drives me to school.* Ma mère m'emmène à l'école en voiture.; **to drive somebody home** raccompagner [**28**] quelqu'un ▷ *He offered to drive me home.* Il m'a proposé de me raccompagner.; **to drive somebody mad** rendre [**7**] quelqu'un fou ▷ *He drives her mad.* Il la rend folle.

driver n ❶ conducteur m, conductrice f ▷ *She's an excellent driver.* C'est une excellente conductrice. ❷ (*of taxi, bus*) chauffeur m ▷ *He's a bus driver.* Il est chauffeur d'autobus.

driver's license n (US) permis de conduire m

driving instructor n moniteur d'auto-école m ▷ *He's a driving instructor.* Il est moniteur d'auto-école.

driving lesson n leçon de conduite f

driving licence n permis de conduire m

driving test n **to take one's driving test** passer [**58**] son permis de conduire ▷ *He's taking his driving test tomorrow.* Il passe son permis de conduire demain.; **She's just passed her driving test.** Elle vient d'avoir son permis.

drop n goutte f ▷ *a drop of water* une goutte d'eau
▷ vb ❶ laisser [**28**] tomber ▷ *I dropped the glass and it broke.* J'ai laissé tomber le verre et il s'est

cassé. ▷ *I'm going to drop chemistry.* Je vais laisser tomber la chimie. ❷ déposer [**28**] ▷ *Could you drop me at the station?* Pouvez-vous me déposer à la gare?

drought n sécheresse f

drove vb see **drive**

drown vb se noyer [**53**] ▷ *A boy drowned here yesterday.* Un jeune garçon s'est noyé ici hier.

drug n ❶ (*medicine*) médicament m ▷ *They need food and drugs.* Ils ont besoin de nourriture et de médicaments. ❷ (*illegal*) drogue f ▷ *hard drugs* les drogues dures; **to take drugs** se droguer [**28**]; **a drug addict** un drogué ▷ *She's a drug addict.* C'est une droguée.; **a drug dealer** un dealer

drugstore n (US) drugstore m

drum n tambour m ▷ *an African drum* un tambour africain; **a drum kit** une batterie; **drums** la batterie sg ▷ *I play drums.* Je joue de la batterie.

drummer n (*in rock group*) batteur m, batteuse f

drunk adj ivre ▷ *He was drunk.* Il était ivre.
▷ n ivrogne mf ▷ *The streets were full of drunks.* Les rues étaient pleines d'ivrognes.

dry adj ❶ sec (f sèche) ▷ *The paint isn't dry yet.* La peinture n'est pas encore sèche. ❷ (*weather*) sans pluie ▷ *a long dry period* une longue période sans pluie
▷ vb ❶ sécher [**34**] ▷ *The washing will dry quickly in the sun.* Le linge va

sécher vite au soleil.; **to dry one's hair** se sécher [**34**] les cheveux ▷ *I haven't dried my hair yet.* Je ne me suis pas encore séché les cheveux ❷ *(clothes)* faire [**36**] sécher ▷ *There's nowhere to dry clothes here.* Il n'y a pas d'endroit où faire sécher les vêtements ici.; **to dry the dishes** essuyer [**53**] la vaisselle

dry-cleaner's *n* teinturerie *f*

dryer *n (for clothes)* séchoir *m*; **a tumble dryer** un séchoir à linge; **a hair dryer** un sèche-cheveux

dubbed *adj* doublé(e) ▷ *The film was dubbed into French.* Le film était doublé en français.

duck *n* canard *m*

due *adj, adv* **to be due to do something** devoir [**26**] faire quelque chose ▷ *He's due to arrive tomorrow.* Il doit arriver demain.; **The plane's due in half an hour.** L'avion doit arriver dans une demi-heure.; **When's the baby due?** Le bébé est prévu pour quand?; **due to** à cause de ▷ *The trip was cancelled due to bad weather.* Le voyage a été annulé à cause du mauvais temps.

dug *vb see* **dig**

dull *adj* ❶ ennuyeux (*f* ennuyeuse) ▷ *He's nice, but a bit dull.* Il est sympathique, mais un peu ennuyeux. ❷ *(weather, day)* maussade

dumb *adj (stupid)* bête ▷ *That was a really dumb thing I did!* C'était vraiment bête de ma part!

dummy *n (for baby)* tétine *f*

dump *n* **It's a real dump!** C'est un endroit minable!; **a rubbish dump** une décharge
▶ *vb* ❶ *(waste)* déposer [**28**] ▷ *'no dumping'* 'défense de déposer des ordures' ❷ *(informal)* plaquer [**28**] ▷ *He's just dumped his girlfriend.* Il vient de plaquer sa copine.

dungarees *npl* salopette *fsg*

dungeon *n* cachot *m*

during *prep* pendant ▷ *during the day* pendant la journée

dusk *n* crépuscule *m* ▷ *at dusk* au crépuscule

dust *n* poussière *f*
▶ *vb* épousseter [**41**] ▷ *I dusted the shelves.* J'ai épousseté les étagères.; **I hate dusting!** Je déteste faire les poussières!

dustbin *n* poubelle *f*

dustman *n* éboueur *m* ▷ *He's a dustman.* Il est éboueur.

dusty *adj* poussiéreux (*f* poussiéreuse)

Dutch *n (language)* hollandais *m*; **the Dutch** les Hollandais
▶ *adj* hollandais(e) ▷ *She's Dutch.* Elle est hollandaise.

Dutchman *n* Hollandais *m*

Dutchwoman *n* Hollandaise *f*

duty *n* devoir *m* ▷ *It was his duty to tell the police.* C'était son devoir de prévenir la police.; **to be on duty** **(1)** *(police officer)* être [**35**] de service **(2)** *(doctor, nurse)* être [**35**] de garde

duty-free *adj* hors taxes; **the duty-free shop** la boutique hors taxes

duvet *n* couette *f*

DVD *n* DVD *m* (*pl* DVD) ▷ *I've got that film on DVD.* J'ai ce film en DVD.
DVD player *n* lecteur de DVD *m*
dying *vb see* **die**
dynamic *adj* dynamique
dyslexia *n* dyslexie *f*
dyspraxia *n* dyspraxie *f*
dyspraxic *adj* dyspraxique

each *adj, pron* ❶ chaque ▷ *each day* chaque jour ❷ chacun(e) ▷ *The girls each have their own bedroom.* Les filles ont chacune leur chambre. ▷ *They have 10 points each.* Ils ont dix points chacun. ▷ *He gave each of us £10.* Il nous a donné dix livres à chacun.

> Use a reflexive verb to translate 'each other'.

They hate each other. Ils se détestent.; **We wrote to each other.** Nous nous sommes écrit.; **They don't know each other.** Ils ne se connaissent pas.
ear *n* oreille *f*
earache *n* **to have earache** avoir [8] mal aux oreilles
earlier *adv* ❶ tout à l'heure ▷ *I saw him earlier.* Je l'ai vu tout à l'heure.

② (in the morning) plus tôt ▷ I ought to get up earlier. Je devrais me lever plus tôt.

early adv, adj **①** (early in the day) tôt ▷ I have to get up early. Je dois me lever tôt.; **to have an early night** se coucher [28] tôt **②** (ahead of time) en avance ▷ I came early to get a good seat. Je suis venu en avance pour avoir une bonne place.

earn vb gagner [28] ▷ She earns £5 an hour. Elle gagne cinq livres de l'heure.

earnings npl salaire msg

earphones npl écouteurs mpl

earring n boucle d'oreille f

earth n terre f

earthquake n tremblement de terre m

easily adv facilement

east adj, adv **①** est ▷ the east coast la côte est; **an east wind** un vent d'est; **east of** à l'est de ▷ It's east of London. C'est à l'est de Londres. **②** vers l'est ▷ We were travelling east. Nous allions vers l'est.
▶ n est m ▷ in the east dans l'est

Easter n Pâques f ▷ at Easter à Pâques ▷ We went to my grandparents' for Easter. Nous sommes allés chez mes grands-parents à Pâques.

Easter egg n œuf de Pâques m

eastern adj **the eastern part of the island** la partie est de l'île; **Eastern Europe** l'Europe de l'Est

easy adj facile

eat vb manger [45]; **Would you like something to eat?** Est-ce que tu veux manger quelque chose?

e-book n livre numérique m

echo n écho m

eco-friendly adj respectueux de l'environnement (f respectueuse de l'environnement)

ecological adj écologique

ecology n écologie f

economic adj (profitable) rentable

economical adj **①** (person) économe **②** (method, car) économique

economics n économie f ▷ He's studying economics. Il étudie les sciences économiques.

economy n économie f

ecstasy n (drug) ecstasy f; **to be in ecstasy** s'extasier [19]

eczema n eczéma m

edge n bord m

Edinburgh n Édimbourg

editor n (of newspaper) rédacteur en chef m, rédactrice en chef f

education n **①** éducation f ▷ There should be more investment in education. On devrait investir plus dans l'éducation. **②** (teaching) enseignement m ▷ She works in education. Elle travaille dans l'enseignement.

educational adj (experience, toy) éducatif (f éducative) ▷ It was very educational. C'était très éducatif.

effect n effet m ▷ special effects les effets spéciaux

effective adj efficace

effectively adv efficacement

Be careful not to translate **effectively** by **effectivement**.

efficient adj efficace

effort n effort m

e.g. abbr p. ex. (= par exemple)

egg n œuf m ▷ a hard-boiled egg un œuf dur ▷ a fried egg un œuf sur le plat; **scrambled eggs** les œufs brouillés

egg cup n coquetier m

eggplant n (US) aubergine f

Egypt n Égypte f; **in Egypt** en Égypte

Eiffel Tower n tour Eiffel f

eight num huit ▷ She's eight. Elle a huit ans.

eighteen num dix-huit ▷ She's eighteen. Elle a dix-huit ans.

eighteenth adj dix-huitième ▷ her eighteenth birthday son dix-huitième anniversaire ▷ the eighteenth floor le dix-huitième étage; **the eighteenth of August** le dix-huit août

eighth adj huitième ▷ the eighth floor le huitième étage; **the eighth of August** le huit août

eighty num quatre-vingts

Eire n République d'Irlande f; **in Eire** en République d'Irlande

either adv, conj, pron non plus ▷ I don't like milk, and I don't like eggs either. Je n'aime pas le lait, et je n'aime pas les œufs non plus. ▷ I've never been to Spain. — I haven't either. Je ne suis jamais allé en Espagne. — Moi non plus.; **either ... or ...** soit ... soit ... ▷ You can have either ice cream or yoghurt. Tu peux prendre soit une glace soit un yaourt.; **either of them** l'un ou l'autre ▷ Take either of them. Prends l'un ou

l'autre.; **I don't like either of them.** Je n'aime ni l'un ni l'autre.

elastic n élastique m

elastic band n élastique m

elbow n coude m

elder adj aîné(e) ▷ my elder sister ma sœur aînée

elderly adj âgé(e)

eldest adj aîné(e) ▷ my eldest sister ma sœur aînée ▷ He's the eldest. C'est l'aîné.

elect vb élire [44]

election n élection f

electric adj électrique ▷ an electric fire un radiateur électrique ▷ an electric guitar une guitare électrique; **an electric blanket** une couverture chauffante

electrical adj électrique; **an electrical engineer** un ingénieur électricien

electrician n électricien m ▷ He's an electrician. Il est électricien.

electricity n électricité f

electronic adj électronique

electronics n électronique f ▷ My hobby is electronics. Ma passion, c'est l'électronique.

elegant adj élégant(e)

elementary school n (US) école primaire f

elephant n éléphant m

elevator n (US) ascenseur m

eleven num onze ▷ She's eleven. Elle a onze ans.

eleventh adj onzième ▷ the eleventh floor le onzième étage ▷ the eleventh of August le onze août

else adv d'autre ▷ somebody else quelqu'un d'autre ▷ nobody else personne d'autre ▷ nothing else rien d'autre; **something else** autre chose; **anything else** autre chose ▷ Would you like anything else? Désirez-vous autre chose?; **I don't want anything else.** Je ne veux rien d'autre.; **somewhere else** ailleurs; **anywhere else** autre part

email n courrier électronique m; **email address** adresse e-mail f ▷ My email address is: ... Mon adresse e-mail, c'est: ...
▶ vb **to email somebody** envoyer [33] un e-mail à quelqu'un

embankment n talus m

embarrassed adj gêné(e) ▷ I was really embarrassed. J'étais vraiment gêné.

embarrassing adj gênant(e) ▷ It was so embarrassing. C'était tellement gênant.

embassy n ambassade f ▷ the British Embassy l'ambassade de Grande-Bretagne ▷ the French Embassy l'ambassade de France

embroider vb broder [28]

embroidery n broderie f ▷ I do embroidery. Je fais de la broderie.

emergency n urgence f ▷ This is an emergency! C'est une urgence!; **in an emergency** en cas d'urgence; **an emergency exit** une sortie de secours; **an emergency landing** un atterrissage forcé; **the emergency services** les services d'urgence mpl

emigrate vb émigrer [28]

emoji n emoji m

emotion n émotion f

emotional adj (person) émotif (f émotive)

emperor n empereur m

emphasize vb **to emphasize something** insister [28] sur quelque chose; **to emphasize that ...** souligner [28] que ...

empire n empire m

employ vb employer [53] ▷ The factory employs 600 people. L'usine emploie six cents personnes.

employee n employé m, employée f

employer n employeur m

employment n emploi m

empty adj vide
▶ vb vider [28]; **to empty something out** vider [28] quelque chose

encourage vb encourager [45]; **to encourage somebody to do something** encourager [45] quelqu'un à faire quelque chose

encouragement n encouragement m

encyclopedia n encyclopédie f

end n ❶ fin f ▷ the end of the film la fin du film; **in the end** en fin de compte ▷ In the end I decided to stay at home. En fin de compte j'ai décidé de rester à la maison.; **It turned out all right in the end.** Ça s'est bien terminé. ❷ bout m ▷ at the end of the street au bout de la rue; **for hours on end** des heures entières
▶ vb finir [38] ▷ What time does the film end? À quelle heure est-ce que

le film finit?; **to end up doing something** finir [**38**] par faire quelque chose ▷ *I ended up walking home.* J'ai fini par rentrer chez moi à pied.

ending *n* fin *f* ▷ *It was an exciting film, especially the ending.* C'était un film passionnant, surtout la fin.

endless *adj* interminable ▷ *The journey seemed endless.* Le voyage a paru interminable.

enemy *n* ennemi *m*, ennemie *f*

energetic *adj* (person) énergique

energy *n* énergie *f*

engaged *adj* ❶ (busy, in use) occupé(e) ▷ *I phoned, but it was engaged.* J'ai téléphoné, mais c'était occupé. ❷ (to be married) fiancé(e) ▷ *She's engaged to Brian.* Elle est fiancée à Brian.; **to get engaged** se fiancer [**12**]

engagement *n* fiançailles *fpl* ▷ *an engagement ring* une bague de fiançailles

engine *n* moteur *m*

Be careful not to translate **engine** by **engin**.

engineer *n* ingénieur *m* ▷ *He's an engineer.* Il est ingénieur.

engineering *n* ingénierie *f*

England *n* Angleterre *f*; **in England** en Angleterre; **to England** en Angleterre; **I'm from England.** Je suis anglais.

English *n* (language) anglais *m* ▷ *Do you speak English?* Est-ce que vous parlez anglais?; **the English** les Anglais

▶ *adj* anglais(e) ▷ *I'm English.* Je suis

anglais.; **English people** les Anglais

Englishman *n* Anglais *m*

Englishwoman *n* Anglaise *f*

enjoy *vb* aimer [**28**] ▷ *Did you enjoy the film?* Est-ce que vous avez aimé le film?; **to enjoy oneself** s'amuser [**28**] ▷ *I really enjoyed myself.* Je me suis vraiment bien amusé.

enjoyable *adj* agréable

enlargement *n* (of photo) agrandissement *m*

enormous *adj* énorme

enough *pron, adj* assez de ▷ *enough time* assez de temps ▷ *I didn't have enough money.* Je n'avais pas assez d'argent. ▷ *I've had enough!* J'en ai assez!; **big enough** suffisamment grand; **warm enough** suffisamment chaud; **That's enough.** Ça suffit.

enquire *vb* **to enquire about something** se renseigner [**28**] sur quelque chose ▷ *I am going to enquire about train times.* Je vais me renseigner sur les horaires de trains.

enquiry *n* **to make enquiries (about something)** se renseigner [**28**] (sur quelque chose) ▷ *'enquiries'* 'renseignements'

enter *vb* entrer [**32**]; **to enter a room** entrer [**32**] dans une pièce; **to enter a competition** s'inscrire [**30**] à une compétition

entertain *vb* (guests) recevoir [**67**]

entertaining *adj* amusant(e)

enthusiasm *n* enthousiasme *m*

enthusiast *n* a railway

enthusiast un passionné des trains; **She's a DIY enthusiast.** C'est une passionnée de bricolage.

enthusiastic *adj* enthousiaste

entire *adj* entier (f entière) ▷ *the entire world* le monde entier

entirely *adv* entièrement

entrance *n* entrée f; **an entrance exam** un concours d'entrée; **entrance fee** le prix d'entrée

entry *n* entrée f; **'no entry' (1)** *(on door)* 'défense d'entrer' **(2)** *(on road sign)* 'sens interdit'; **an entry form** une feuille d'inscription

entry phone *n* interphone *m*

envelope *n* enveloppe f

envious *adj* envieux (f envieuse)

environment *n* environnement *m*

environmental *adj* écologique

environment-friendly *adj* écologique

envy *n* envie f
　▶ *vb* envier [**19**] ▷ *I don't envy you!* Je ne t'envie pas!

epileptic *adj* épileptique

episode *n* *(of TV programme, story)* épisode *m*

equal *adj* égal(e) *(mpl* égaux)
　▶ *vb* égaler [**28**]

equality *n* égalité f

equalize *vb* *(in sport)* égaliser [**28**]

equator *n* équateur *m*

equipment *n* équipement *m*
　▷ *fishing equipment* l'équipement de pêche ▷ *skiing equipment* l'équipement de ski

equipped *adj* **equipped with** équipé de; **to be well equipped** être [**35**] bien équipé

error *n* erreur f

escalator *n* escalier roulant *m*

escape *n* *(from prison)* évasion f
　▶ *vb* s'échapper [**28**] ▷ *A lion has escaped.* Un lion s'est échappé.; **to escape from prison** s'évader [**28**] de prison

escort *n* escorte f ▷ *a police escort* une escorte de police

especially *adv* surtout ▷ *It's very hot there, especially in the summer.* Il fait très chaud là-bas, surtout en été.

essay *n* dissertation f ▷ *a history essay* une dissertation d'histoire

essential *adj* essentiel (f essentielle) ▷ *It's essential to bring warm clothes.* Il est essentiel d'apporter des vêtements chauds.

estate *n* *(housing estate)* cité f ▷ *I live on an estate.* J'habite dans une cité.

estate agent *n* agent immobilier *m*

estate car *n* break *m*

estimate *vb* estimer [**28**] ▷ *They estimated it would take three weeks.* Ils ont estimé que cela prendrait trois semaines.

etc *abbr* (= et cetera) etc.

Ethiopia *n* Éthiopie f; **in Ethiopia** en Éthiopie

ethnic *adj* ❶ *(racial)* ethnique ▷ *an ethnic minority* une minorité ethnique ❷ *(clothes, music)* folklorique

EU *n* (= European Union) Union européenne f

euro *n* euro *m* ▷ *50 euros* 50 euros

Europe *n* Europe f; **in Europe** en

a
b
c
d
e
f
g
h
i
j
k
l
m
n
o
p
q
r
s
t
u
v
w
x
y
z

Europe; **to Europe** en Europe
European n (person) Européen m,
Européenne f
▶ adj européen (f européenne)
eve n **Christmas Eve** la veille de
Noël; **New Year's Eve** la
Saint-Sylvestre
even adv même ▷ *I like all animals,
even snakes.* J'aime tous les
animaux, même les serpents.;
even if même si ▷ *I'd never do that,
even if you asked me.* Je ne ferais
jamais ça, même si tu me le
demandais.; **not even** même pas
▷ *He never stops working, not even at
the weekend.* Il n'arrête jamais de
travailler, même pas le week-end.;
even though bien que

> bien que has to be followed by
a verb in the subjunctive.

▷ *He wants to go out, even though it's
raining.* Il veut sortir bien qu'il
pleuve.; **even more** encore plus
▷ *I liked Boulogne even more than
Paris.* J'ai encore plus aimé
Boulogne que Paris.
▶ adj régulier (f régulière) ▷ *an even
layer of snow* une couche régulière
de neige; **an even number** un
nombre pair; **to get even with
somebody** prendre [65] sa
revanche sur quelqu'un ▷ *He
wanted to get even with her.* Il voulait
prendre sa revanche sur elle.
evening n soir m ▷ *in the evening* le
soir ▷ *yesterday evening* hier soir
▷ *tomorrow evening* demain soir; **all
evening** toute la soirée; **Good
evening!** Bonsoir!

evening class n cours du soir m (pl
cours du soir)
event n événement m; **a sporting
event** une épreuve sportive
eventful adj mouvementé(e)
eventual adj final(e)

> Be careful not to translate
eventual by **éventuel**.

eventually adv finalement

> Be careful not to translate
eventually by
éventuellement.

ever adv **Have you ever been to
Germany?** Est-ce que tu es déjà
allé en Allemagne?; **Have you ever
seen her?** Vous l'avez déjà vue?; **I
haven't ever done that.** Je ne l'ai
jamais fait.; **the best I've ever
seen** le meilleur que j'aie jamais vu;
for the first time ever pour la
première fois; **ever since** depuis
que ▷ *ever since I met him* depuis que
je l'ai rencontré; **ever since then**
depuis ce moment-là
every adj chaque ▷ *every pupil*
chaque élève; **every time** chaque
fois ▷ *Every time I see him he's
depressed.* Chaque fois que je le vois
il est déprimé.; **every day** tous les
jours; **every week** toutes les
semaines; **every now and then** de
temps en temps
everybody pron tout le monde
▷ *Everybody had a good time.* Tout le
monde s'est bien amusé.
everyone pron tout le monde
everything pron tout ▷ *You've
thought of everything!* Tu as pensé à
tout!; **Have you remembered**

everything? Est-ce que tu n'as rien oublié?; **Money isn't everything.** L'argent ne fait pas le bonheur.

everywhere adv partout ▷ I looked everywhere, but I couldn't find it. J'ai regardé partout, mais je n'ai pas pu le trouver.

evil adj mauvais(e)

exact adj exact(e)

exactly adv exactement ▷ exactly the same exactement le même ▷ Not exactly. Pas exactement.; **It's exactly 10 o'clock.** Il est dix heures précises.

exaggerate vb exagérer [**34**]

exaggeration n exagération f

exam n examen m ▷ a French exam un examen de français ▷ the exam results les résultats des examens mpl

examination n examen m

examine vb examiner [**28**] ▷ He examined her passport. Il a examiné son passeport.

examiner n examinateur m, examinatrice f

example n exemple m; **for example** par exemple

excellent adj excellent(e) ▷ Her results were excellent. Elle a eu d'excellents résultats.; **It was excellent fun.** C'était vraiment super.

except prep sauf ▷ everyone except me tout le monde sauf moi; **except for** sauf; **except that** sauf que ▷ The holiday was great, except that it rained. Les vacances étaient super, sauf qu'il a plu.

exception n exception f; **to make an exception** faire [**36**] une exception

exchange vb échanger [**45**] ▷ I exchanged the book for a video. J'ai échangé le livre contre une vidéo.

exchange rate n taux de change m

excited adj excité(e)

exciting adj passionnant(e)

exclamation mark n point d'exclamation m

excuse n excuse f ▶ vb **Excuse me!** Pardon!

exercise n exercice m; **an exercise bike** un vélo d'appartement; **an exercise book** un cahier

exhausted adj épuisé(e)

exhaust fumes npl gaz d'échappement mpl

exhaust pipe n tuyau d'échappement m

exhibition n exposition f

exist vb exister [**28**]

exit n sortie f

expect vb ❶ attendre [**7**] ▷ I'm expecting him for dinner. Je l'attends pour dîner. ▷ She's expecting a baby. Elle attend un enfant. ❷ s'attendre [**7**] à ▷ I was expecting the worst. Je m'attendais au pire. ❸ supposer [**28**] ▷ I expect it's a mistake. Je suppose qu'il s'agit d'une erreur.

expedition n expédition f

expel vb **to get expelled** (from school) se faire [**36**] renvoyer

expenses npl frais mpl

expensive adj cher (f chère)

experience n expérience f

experienced adj expérimenté(e)
experiment n expérience f
expert n spécialiste m, spécialiste f
▷ *He's a computer expert.* C'est un
spécialiste en informatique.; **He's
an expert cook.** Il cuisine très
bien.
expire vb expirer [**28**]
explain vb expliquer [**28**]
explanation n explication f
explode vb exploser [**28**]
explore vb (place) explorer [**28**]
explosion n explosion f
express vb exprimer [**28**]; **to
express oneself** s'exprimer [**28**]
▷ *It's hard to express oneself in French.*
C'est dur de s'exprimer en français.
expression n expression f ▷ *It's an
English expression.* C'est une
expression anglaise.
expressway n (US) autoroute
urbaine f
extension n ❶ (of building) annexe
f ❷ (telephone) poste m; **Extension
3137, please.** Poste trente et un
trente-sept, s'il vous plaît.

> In France phone numbers are
> broken into groups of two
> digits where possible.

extent n **to some extent** dans une
certaine mesure
exterior adj extérieur(e)
extinct adj **to become extinct**
disparaître [**56**]; **to be extinct**
avoir [**8**] disparu ▷ *The species is
almost extinct.* Cette espèce a
presque disparu.
extinguisher n (fire extinguisher)
extincteur m

extra adj, adv supplémentaire ▷ *an
extra blanket* une couverture
supplémentaire; **to pay extra**
payer [**59**] un supplément;
Breakfast is extra. Il y a un
supplément pour le petit
déjeuner.; **It costs extra.** Il y a un
supplément.
extraordinary adj extraordinaire
extravagant adj (person)
dépensier (f dépensière)
extreme adj extrême
extremely adv extrêmement
extremist n extrémiste mf
eye n œil m (pl yeux) ▷ *I've got green
eyes.* J'ai les yeux verts.; **to keep an
eye on something** surveiller [**28**]
quelque chose
eyebrow n sourcil m
eyelash n cil m
eyelid n paupière f
eyeliner n eye-liner m
eye shadow n ombre à paupières f
eyesight n vue f

f

fabric n tissu m
fabulous adj formidable ▷ The show was fabulous. Le spectacle était formidable.
face n ❶ (of person) visage m ❷ (of clock) cadran m ❸ (of cliff) paroi f; **on the face of it** à première vue; **in the face of these difficulties** face à ces difficultés; **face to face** face à face
▶ vb (place, problem) faire [36] face à; **to face up to something** faire [36] face à quelque chose ▷ You must face up to your responsibilities. Vous devez faire face à vos responsabilités.
Facebook® n Facebook® m
▶ vb facebooker [28]
face cloth n gant de toilette m

The French traditionally wash with a towelling glove rather than a flannel.

facilities npl équipement msg ▷ This school has excellent facilities. Cette école dispose d'un excellent équipement.; **toilet facilities** les toilettes fpl; **cooking facilities** la cuisine équipée sg
fact n fait m; **in fact** en fait
factory n usine f
fail vb ❶ rater [28] ▷ I failed the history exam. J'ai raté l'examen d'histoire. ❷ échouer [28] ▷ In our class, no one failed. Dans notre classe, personne n'a échoué. ❸ lâcher [28] ▷ My brakes failed. Mes freins ont lâché.; **to fail to do something** ne pas faire [36] quelque chose ▷ She failed to return her library books. Elle n'a pas rendu ses livres à la bibliothèque.
▶ n **without fail** sans faute
failure n ❶ échec m ▷ feelings of failure un sentiment d'échec sg ❷ raté m, ratée f ▷ He's a failure. C'est un raté. ❸ défaillance f ▷ a mechanical failure une défaillance mécanique
faint adj faible ▷ His voice was very faint. Sa voix était très faible.; **to feel faint** se trouver [28] mal
▶ vb s'évanouir [38] ▷ All of a sudden she fainted. Tout à coup elle s'est évanouie.
fair adj ❶ juste ▷ That's not fair. Ce n'est pas juste. ❷ (hair) blond(e) ▷ He's got fair hair. Il a les cheveux blonds. ❸ (skin) clair(e) ▷ people

with *fair skin* les gens qui ont la peau claire ❹ (*weather*) beau (f belle) ▷ *The weather was fair.* Il faisait beau. ❺ (*good enough*) assez bon (f assez bonne) ▷ *I have a fair chance of winning.* J'ai d'assez bonnes chances de gagner. ❻ (*sizeable*) considérable ▷ *That's a fair distance.* Ça représente une distance considérable.
▶ n foire f ▷ *They went to the fair.* Ils sont allés à la foire.; **a trade fair** une foire commerciale

fairground n champ de foire m

fairly adv ❶ équitablement ▷ *The cake was divided fairly.* Le gâteau a été partagé équitablement. ❷ (*quite*) assez ▷ *That's fairly good.* C'est assez bien.

fairy n fée f

fairy tale n conte de fées m

faith n ❶ foi f ▷ *the Catholic faith* la foi catholique ❷ confiance f ▷ *People have lost faith in the government.* Les gens ont perdu confiance dans le gouvernement.

faithful adj fidèle

faithfully adv **Yours faithfully ...** (*in letter*) Veuillez agréer mes salutations distinguées ...

fake n faux m ▷ *The painting was a fake.* Le tableau était un faux.
▶ adj faux (f fausse) ▷ *She wore fake fur.* Elle portait une fausse fourrure.

fall n ❶ chute f ▷ *a fall of snow* une chute de neige ▷ *She had a nasty fall.* Elle a fait une mauvaise chute.;

the Niagara Falls les chutes du Niagara ❷ (*US: autumn*) automne m
▶ vb ❶ tomber [84] ▷ *He tripped and fell.* Il a trébuché et il est tombé. ❷ baisser [28] ▷ *Prices are falling.* Les prix baissent.

fall down vb ❶ (*person*) tomber [84] ▷ *She's fallen down.* Elle est tombée. ❷ (*building*) s'écrouler [28] ▷ *The house is slowly falling down.* La maison se met à s'écrouler.

fall for vb ❶ se laisser [28] prendre à ▷ *They fell for it.* Ils s'y sont laissé prendre. ❷ tomber [84] amoureux de ▷ *She's falling for him.* Elle est en train de tomber amoureuse de lui.

fall off vb tomber [84] de ▷ *The book fell off the shelf.* Le livre est tombé de l'étagère.

fall out vb **to fall out with somebody** se fâcher [28] avec quelqu'un ▷ *Sarah's fallen out with her boyfriend.* Sarah s'est fâchée avec son copain.

fall through vb tomber [84] à l'eau ▷ *Our plans have fallen through.* Nos projets sont tombés à l'eau.

fallen vb *see* **fall**

false adj faux (f fausse); **a false alarm** une fausse alerte; **false teeth** les fausses dents

fame n renommée f

familiar adj familier (f familière) ▷ *a familiar face* un visage familier; **to be familiar with something** bien connaître [14] quelque chose ▷ *I'm familiar with his work.* Je connais bien ses œuvres.

family n famille f; **the Cooke**

family la famille Cooke
famine n famine f
famous adj célèbre
fan n ❶ (hand-held) éventail m
❷ (electric) ventilateur m ❸ (of
person, band) fan mf ▷ I'm a fan of
Coldplay. Je suis une fan de
Coldplay. ❹ (of sport) supporter mf
▷ football fans les supporters de
football
fanatic n fanatique mf
fancy vb to fancy something avoir
[8] envie de quelque chose ▷ I fancy
an ice cream. J'ai envie d'une glace.;
to fancy doing something avoir
[8] envie de faire quelque chose;
He fancies her. Elle lui plaît.
fancy dress n déguisement m ▷ He
was wearing fancy dress. Il portait un
déguisement.; a fancy-dress ball
un bal costumé
fantastic adj fantastique
far adj, adv loin ▷ Is it far? Est-ce que
c'est loin?; far from loin de ▷ It's not
far from London. Ce n'est pas loin de
Londres.; How far is it? C'est à
quelle distance?; How far is it to
Geneva? Combien y a-t-il jusqu'à
Genève?; How far have you got?
(with a task) Où en êtes-vous?; at
the far end à l'autre bout ▷ at the
far end of the room à l'autre bout de
la pièce; far better beaucoup
mieux; as far as I know pour
autant que je sache
fare n ❶ (on trains, buses) prix du
billet m ❷ (in taxi) prix de la course
m; half fare le demi-tarif; full fare
le plein tarif

Far East n Extrême-Orient m; in
the Far East en Extrême-Orient
farm n ferme f
farmer n agriculteur m, agricultrice
f ▷ He's a farmer. Il est agriculteur.
farmhouse n ferme f
farming n agriculture f
fascinating adj fascinant(e)
fashion n mode f ▷ a fashion show
un défilé de mode; in fashion à la
mode
fashionable adj à la mode ▷ Jane
wears very fashionable clothes. Jane
porte des vêtements très à la
mode. ▷ a fashionable restaurant un
restaurant à la mode
fast adj, adv ❶ vite ▷ He can run fast.
Il sait courir vite. ❷ rapide ▷ a fast
car une voiture rapide; That
clock's fast. Cette pendule
avance.; He's fast asleep. Il est
profondément endormi.
fat adj gros (f grosse)
▶ n ❶ (on meat, in food) gras m ▷ It's
very high in fat. C'est très gras. ❷ (for
cooking) matière grasse f
fatal adj ❶ (causing death) mortel
(f mortelle) ▷ a fatal accident un
accident mortel ❷ (disastrous)
fatal(e) ▷ He made a fatal mistake.
Il a fait une erreur fatale.
father n père m ▷ my father mon père
father-in-law n beau-père m (pl
beaux-pères)
faucet n (US) robinet m
fault n ❶ (mistake) faute f ▷ It's my
fault. C'est de ma faute. ❷ (defect)
défaut m ▷ There's a fault in this
material. Ce tissu a un défaut.;

a mechanical fault une
défaillance mécanique
favour (US **favor**) n <u>service</u> m; **to
do somebody a favour** rendre [**7**]
service à quelqu'un ▷ *Could you do
me a favour?* Tu peux me rendre
service?; **to be in favour of
something** être [**35**] pour quelque
chose ▷ *I'm in favour of nuclear
disarmament.* Je suis pour le
désarmement nucléaire.
favourite (US **favorite**) adj <u>favori</u> (f
favorite) ▷ *Blue's my favourite colour.*
Le bleu est ma couleur favorite.
▸ n <u>favori</u> m, <u>favorite</u> f ▷ *Liverpool
are favourites to win the Cup.* L'équipe
de Liverpool est favorite pour la
coupe.
fax n <u>fax</u> m; **to send somebody a
fax** envoyer [**33**] un fax à quelqu'un
▸ vb **to fax somebody** envoyer [**33**]
un fax à quelqu'un
fear n <u>peur</u> f
▸ vb <u>craindre</u> [**17**] ▷ *You have nothing
to fear.* Vous n'avez rien à craindre.
feather n <u>plume</u> f
feature n (of person, object)
<u>caractéristique</u> f ▷ *an important
feature* une caractéristique
essentielle
February n <u>février</u> m; **in February**
en février
fed vb see **feed**
fed up adj **to be fed up of
something** en avoir [**8**] marre de
quelque chose ▷ *I'm fed up of waiting
for him.* J'en ai marre de l'attendre.
feed vb <u>donner</u> [**28**] à manger à
▷ *Have you fed the cat?* Est-ce que tu

as donné à manger au chat?; **He
worked hard to feed his family.** Il
travaillait dur pour nourrir sa
famille.
feel vb ❶ <u>se sentir</u> [**77**] ▷ *I don't feel
well.* Je ne me sens pas bien. ▷ *I feel
a bit lonely.* Je me sens un peu seul.
❷ <u>sentir</u> [**77**] ▷ *I didn't feel much pain.*
Je n'ai presque rien senti. ❸ <u>toucher</u> [**28**] ▷ *The doctor felt his
forehead.* Le docteur lui a touché le
front.; **I was feeling hungry.**
J'avais faim.; **I was feeling cold, so
I went inside.** J'avais froid, alors je
suis rentré.; **I feel like ...** (want) J'ai
envie de ... ▷ *Do you feel like an ice
cream?* Tu as envie d'une glace?
feeling n ❶ (physical) <u>sensation</u> f
▷ *a burning feeling* une sensation de
brûlure ❷ (emotional) <u>sentiment</u> m
▷ *a feeling of satisfaction* un
sentiment de satisfaction
feet npl see **foot**
fell vb see **fall**
felt vb see **feel**
felt-tip pen n <u>stylo-feutre</u> m
female adj ❶ <u>femelle</u> ▷ *a female
animal* un animal femelle
❷ <u>féminin(e)</u> ▷ *the female sex* le sexe
féminin
▸ n (animal) <u>femelle</u> f
feminine adj <u>féminin(e)</u>
feminist n <u>féministe</u> mf
fence n <u>barrière</u> f
fern n <u>fougère</u> f
ferry n <u>ferry</u> m
festival n <u>festival</u> m ▷ *a jazz festival*
un festival de jazz
fetch vb ❶ <u>aller</u> [**3**] <u>chercher</u> ▷ *Fetch*

the bucket. Va chercher le seau.
❷ (sell for) se vendre [**88**] ▷ His
painting fetched £5000. Son tableau
s'est vendu cinq mille livres.
fever n (temperature) fièvre f
few adj, pron (not many) peu de ▷ few
books peu de livres; **a few**
(1) quelques ▷ a few hours quelques
heures **(2)** quelques-uns ▷ How
many apples do you want? — A few. Tu
veux combien de pommes? —
Quelques-unes.; **quite a few**
people pas mal de monde
fewer adj moins de ▷ There are fewer
pupils in this class. Il y a moins
d'élèves dans cette classe.
fiancé n fiancé m ▷ He's my fiancé.
C'est mon fiancé.
fiancée n fiancée f ▷ She's my
fiancée. C'est ma fiancée.
fiction n (novels) romans mpl
field n ❶ (in countryside) champ m
▷ a field of wheat un champ de blé
❷ (for sport) terrain m ▷ a football
field un terrain de football
❸ (subject) domaine m ▷ He's an
expert in his field. C'est un expert
dans son domaine.
fierce adj ❶ féroce ▷ The dog looked
very fierce. Le chien avait l'air très
féroce. ❷ violent(e) ▷ a fierce attack
une attaque violente
fifteen num quinze ▷ I'm fifteen. J'ai
quinze ans.
fifteenth adj quinzième ▷ the
fifteenth floor le quinzième étage;
the fifteenth of August le quinze
août
fifth adj cinquième ▷ the fifth floor le

cinquième étage; **the fifth of**
August le cinq août
fifty num cinquante ▷ He's fifty. Il a
cinquante ans.
fight n ❶ bagarre f ▷ There was a
fight in the pub. Il y a eu une bagarre
au pub. ❷ lutte f ▷ the fight against
cancer la lutte contre le cancer
▶ vb ❶ se battre [**9**] ▷ They were
fighting. Ils se battaient. ❷ lutter
[**28**] contre ▷ The doctors tried to
fight the disease. Les médecins ont
essayé de lutter contre la maladie.
figure n ❶ (number) chiffre m ▷ Can
you give me the exact figures?
Pouvez-vous me donner les
chiffres exacts? ❷ (outline of person)
silhouette f ▷ Hélène saw the figure
of a man on the bridge. Hélène a vu la
silhouette d'un homme sur le
pont.; **She's got a good figure.**
Elle est bien faite.; **I have to watch**
my figure. Je dois faire attention à
ma ligne. ❸ (personality)
personnage m ▷ She's an important
political figure. C'est un personnage
politique important.
figure out vb ❶ calculer [**28**] ▷ I'll
try to figure out how much it'll cost. Je
vais essayer de calculer combien ça
va coûter. ❷ voir [**92**] ▷ I couldn't
figure out what it meant. Je n'arrivais
pas à voir ce que ça voulait dire.
❸ cerner [**28**] ▷ I can't figure him out
at all. Je n'arrive pas du tout à le
cerner.
file n ❶ (document) dossier m ▷ Have
we got a file on the suspect? Est-ce
que nous avons un dossier sur le

a
b
c
d
e
f
g
h
i
j
k
l
m
n
o
p
q
r
s
t
u
v
w
x
y
z

suspect? ❷ *(folder)* chemise *f* ▷ *She keeps all her letters in a cardboard file.* Elle garde toutes ses lettres dans une chemise en carton. ❸ *(ring binder)* classeur *m* ❹ *(on computer)* fichier *m* ❺ *(for nails, metal)* lime *f*
▶ *vb* ❶ *(papers)* classer [**28**] ❷ *(nails, metal)* limer [**28**] ▷ *to file one's nails* se limer les ongles

fill *vb* remplir [**38**] ▷ *She filled the glass with water.* Elle a rempli le verre d'eau.

fill in *vb* ❶ remplir [**38**] ▷ *Can you fill this form in please?* Est-ce que vous pouvez remplir ce formulaire s'il vous plaît? ❷ boucher [**28**] ▷ *He filled the hole in with soil.* Il a bouché le trou avec de la terre.

fill up *vb* remplir [**38**] ▷ *He filled the cup up to the brim.* Il a rempli la tasse à ras bords.; **Fill it up, please.** *(at petrol station)* Le plein, s'il vous plaît.

film *n* ❶ *(movie)* film *m* ❷ *(for camera)* pellicule *f*

film star *n* vedette de cinéma *f* ▷ *He's a film star.* C'est une vedette de cinéma.

filthy *adj* dégoûtant(e)

final *adj* ❶ *(last)* dernier *(f* dernière*)* ▷ *our final farewells* nos derniers adieux ❷ *(definite)* définitif *(f* définitive*)* ▷ *a final decision* une décision définitive; **I'm not going and that's final.** Je n'y vais pas, un point c'est tout.
▶ *n* finale *f* ▷ *Andy Murray is in the final.* Andy Murray va disputer la finale.

finally *adv* ❶ *(lastly)* enfin ▷ *Finally, I would like to say …* Enfin, je voudrais dire … ❷ *(eventually)* finalement ▷ *She finally chose the red shoes.* Elle a finalement choisi les chaussures rouges.

find *vb* ❶ trouver [**28**] ▷ *I can't find the exit.* Je ne trouve pas la sortie. ❷ *(something lost)* retrouver [**28**] ▷ *Did you find your pen?* Est-ce que tu as retrouvé ton crayon?

find out *vb* découvrir [**55**] ▷ *I'm determined to find out the truth.* Je suis décidé à découvrir la vérité.; **to find out about (1)** *(make enquiries)* se renseigner [**28**] sur ▷ *Try to find out about the cost of a hotel.* Essaye de te renseigner sur le prix d'un hôtel. **(2)** *(by chance)* apprendre [**65**] ▷ *I found out about their affair.* J'ai appris leur liaison.

fine *adj, adv* ❶ *(very good)* excellent(e) ▷ *He's a fine musician.* C'est un excellent musicien.; **to be fine** aller [**3**] bien ▷ *How are you? — I'm fine.* Comment ça va? — Ça va bien.; **I feel fine.** Je me sens bien.; **The weather is fine today.** Il fait beau aujourd'hui. ❷ *(not coarse)* fin(e) ▷ *She's got very fine hair.* Elle a les cheveux très fins.
▶ *n* ❶ amende *f* ▷ *She got a £50 fine.* Elle a eu une amende de cinquante livres. ❷ *(for traffic offence)* contravention *f* ▷ *I got a fine for speeding.* J'ai eu une contravention pour excès de vitesse.

finger *n* doigt *m*; **my little finger** mon petit doigt

fingernail n ongle m

finish n (of race) arrivée f ▷ We saw the finish of the London Marathon. Nous avons vu l'arrivée du marathon de Londres.
▶ vb ❶ finir [38] ▷ I've finished! J'ai fini!; **to finish doing something** finir [38] de faire quelque chose ❷ terminer [28] ▷ I've finished the book. J'ai terminé ce livre. ▷ The film has finished. Le film est terminé.

Finland n Finlande f; **in Finland** en Finlande; **to Finland** en Finlande

Finn n Finlandais m, Finlandaise f

Finnish n (language) finnois m
▶ adj finlandais(e)

fire n ❶ feu m (pl feux) ▷ He made a fire in the woods. Il a fait du feu dans les bois.; **to be on fire** être [35] en feu ❷ (accidental) incendie m ▷ The house was destroyed by fire. La maison a été détruite par un incendie. ❸ (heater) radiateur m ▷ Turn the fire on. Allume le radiateur.; **the fire brigade** les pompiers mpl; **a fire alarm** une alarme à incendie; **a fire engine** une voiture de pompiers; **a fire escape** un escalier de secours; **a fire extinguisher** un extincteur; **a fire station** une caserne de pompiers
▶ vb (shoot) tirer [28] ▷ She fired twice. Elle a tiré deux fois.; **to fire at somebody** tirer [28] sur quelqu'un ▷ The terrorist fired at the crowd. Le terroriste a tiré sur la foule.; **to fire a gun** tirer [28] un coup de feu; **to fire somebody**

mettre [47] quelqu'un à la porte ▷ He was fired from his job. Il a été mis à la porte.

firefighter n pompier m ▷ She's a firefighter. Elle est pompier.

fireplace n cheminée f

fireworks npl feu d'artifice msg ▷ Are you going to see the fireworks? Est-ce que tu vas voir le feu d'artifice?

firm adj ferme ▷ to be firm with somebody se montrer ferme avec quelqu'un
▶ n entreprise f ▷ He works for a large firm in London. Il travaille pour une grande entreprise à Londres.

first adj, adv ❶ premier (f première) ▷ the first of September le premier septembre ▷ the first time la première fois; **to come first** (in exam, race) arriver [5] premier ▷ Rachel came first. Rachel est arrivée première. ❷ d'abord ▷ I want to get a job, but first I have to graduate. Je veux trouver du travail, mais d'abord je dois finir mes études.; **first of all** tout d'abord
▶ n premier m, première f ▷ She was the first to arrive. Elle est arrivée la première.; **at first** au début

first aid n premiers secours mpl; **a first aid kit** une trousse de secours

first-class adj, adv ❶ de première classe ▷ She has booked a first-class ticket. Elle a réservé un billet de première classe. ❷ excellent(e) ▷ a first-class meal un excellent repas; **a first-class stamp**

In France there is no first-class or second-class postage. However letters cost more to send than postcards, so you have to remember to say what you are sending when buying stamps.

firstly adv premièrement ▷ *Firstly, let's see what the book is about.* Premièrement, voyons de quoi parle ce livre.

fir tree n sapin m

fish n poisson m ▷ *I caught three fish.* J'ai pêché trois poissons. ▷ *I don't like fish.* Je n'aime pas le poisson.
▶ vb pêcher [28]; **to go fishing** aller [3] à la pêche ▷ *We went fishing in the River Dee.* Nous sommes allés à la pêche sur la Dee.

fisherman n pêcheur m ▷ *He's a fisherman.* Il est pêcheur.

fishing n pêche f ▷ *My hobby is fishing.* La pêche est mon passe-temps favori.

fishing boat n bateau de pêche m
fishing rod n canne à pêche f
fishing tackle n matériel de pêche m

fist n poing m

fit adj (in condition) en forme ▷ *He likes to stay fit.* Il aime se maintenir en forme.; **to keep fit** se maintenir [83] en forme ▷ *She does aerobics to keep fit.* Elle fait de l'aérobic pour se maintenir en forme.
▶ n **to have a fit (1)** (epileptic) avoir [8] une crise d'épilepsie **(2)** (be angry) piquer [28] une crise de nerfs ▷ *My Mum will have a fit when she sees the carpet!* Ma mère va piquer

une crise de nerfs quand elle va voir la moquette!
▶ vb ❶ (be the right size) être [35] la bonne taille ▷ *Does it fit?* Est-ce que c'est la bonne taille?

In French you usually specify whether something is too big, small, tight etc.

These trousers don't fit me.
(1) (too big) Ce pantalon est trop grand pour moi. **(2)** (too small) Ce pantalon est trop petit pour moi.
❷ (fix up) installer [28] ▷ *He fitted an alarm in his car.* Il a installé une alarme dans sa voiture. ❸ (attach) adapter [28] ▷ *She fitted a plug to the hair dryer.* Elle a adapté une prise au sèche-cheveux.

fit in vb ❶ (match up) correspondre [69] ▷ *That story doesn't fit in with the facts.* Cette histoire ne correspond pas aux faits.
❷ (person) s'adapter [28] ▷ *She fitted in well at her new school.* Elle s'est bien adaptée à sa nouvelle école.

fitted carpet n moquette f

five num cinq ▷ *He's five.* Il a cinq ans.

fix vb ❶ (mend) réparer [28] ▷ *Can you fix my bike?* Est-ce que tu peux réparer mon vélo? ❷ (decide) fixer [28] ▷ *Let's fix a date for the party.* Fixons une date pour la soirée.
❸ préparer [28] ▷ *Janice fixed some food for us.* Janice nous a préparé à manger.

fizzy adj gazeux (f gazeuse) ▷ *I don't like fizzy drinks.* Je n'aime pas les boissons gazeuses.

flag n drapeau m (pl drapeaux)
flame n flamme f
flan n ❶ (sweet) tarte f ▷ a raspberry flan une tarte aux framboises ❷ (savoury) quiche f ▷ a cheese and onion flan une quiche au fromage et aux oignons
flap vb battre [9] de ▷ The bird flapped its wings. L'oiseau battait des ailes.
flash n flash m (pl flashes) ▷ Has your camera got a flash? Est-ce que ton appareil photo a un flash?; **a flash of lightning** un éclair; **in a flash** en un clin d'œil
▶ vb ❶ clignoter [28] ▷ The police car's blue light was flashing. Le gyrophare de la voiture de police clignotait. ❷ projeter [41] ▷ They flashed a torch in his face. Ils lui ont projeté la lumière d'une torche en plein visage.; **She flashed her headlights.** Elle a fait un appel de phares.
flask n (vacuum flask) thermos m
flat adj ❶ plat(e) ▷ flat shoes des chaussures plates ❷ (tyre) crevé(e) ▷ I've got a flat tyre. J'ai un pneu crevé.
▶ n appartement m ▷ She lives in a flat. Elle habite un appartement.
flatter vb flatter [28]
flavour (US **flavor**) n ❶ (taste) goût m ▷ It has a very strong flavour. Ça a un goût très fort. ❷ (variety) parfum m ▷ Which flavour of ice cream would you like? Quel parfum de glace est-ce que tu veux?
flew vb see **fly**

flexible adj flexible ▷ flexible working hours les horaires flexibles
flick vb appuyer [53] sur; **to flick through a book** feuilleter [41] un livre
flight n vol m ▷ What time is the flight to Paris? À quelle heure est le vol pour Paris?; **a flight of stairs** un escalier
flight attendant n ❶ (woman) hôtesse de l'air f ❷ (man) steward m
fling vb jeter [41] ▷ He flung the book onto the floor. Il a jeté le livre par terre.
flippers n palmes fpl
float vb flotter [28] ▷ A leaf was floating on the water. Une feuille flottait sur l'eau.
flood n ❶ inondation f ▷ We had a flood in the kitchen. On a eu une inondation dans la cuisine. ❷ flot m ▷ He received a flood of letters. Il a reçu un flot de lettres.
▶ vb inonder [28] ▷ The river has flooded the village. La rivière a inondé le village.
floor n ❶ sol m ▷ a tiled floor un sol carrelé; **on the floor** par terre ❷ (storey) étage m ▷ the first floor le premier étage; **the ground floor** le rez-de-chaussée; **on the third floor** au troisième étage
floppy disk n disquette f
florist n fleuriste mf
flour n farine f
flow vb ❶ (river) couler [28] ❷ (flow out) s'écouler [28]
flower n fleur f
▶ vb fleurir [38]

flown vb see **fly**

flu n grippe f ▷ She's got flu. Elle a la grippe.

fluent adj He speaks fluent French. Il parle couramment le français.

flung vb see **fling**

flush n (of toilet) chasse d'eau f ▷ vb to flush the toilet tirer [28] la chasse

flute n flûte f ▷ I play the flute. Je joue de la flûte.

fly n (insect) mouche f ▷ vb ❶ voler [28] ▷ The plane flew through the night. L'avion a volé toute la nuit. ❷ (passenger) aller [3] en avion ▷ He flew from Paris to New York. Il est allé de Paris à New York en avion.

fly away vb s'envoler [28] ▷ The bird flew away. L'oiseau s'est envolé.

focus n to be out of focus être [35] flou ▷ The house is out of focus in this photo. La maison est floue sur cette photo.
▷ vb mettre [47] au point ▷ Try to focus the binoculars. Essaye de mettre les jumelles au point.; to focus on something (1) (with camera, telescope) régler [34] la mise au point sur quelque chose ▷ The cameraman focused on the bird. Le caméraman a réglé la mise au point sur l'oiseau. (2) (concentrate) se concentrer [28] sur quelque chose ▷ Let's focus on the plot of the play. Concentrons-nous sur l'intrigue de la pièce.

fog n brouillard m

foggy adj It's foggy. Il y a du brouillard.; a foggy day un jour de brouillard

foil n (kitchen foil) papier d'aluminium m ▷ She wrapped the meat in foil. Elle a enveloppé la viande dans du papier d'aluminium.

fold n pli m
▷ vb plier [19] ▷ He folded the newspaper in half. Il a plié le journal en deux.; to fold something up plier [19] quelque chose; to fold one's arms croiser [28] ses bras ▷ She folded her arms. Elle a croisé les bras.

folder n ❶ chemise f ▷ She kept all her letters in a folder. Elle gardait toutes ses lettres dans une chemise. ❷ (ring binder) classeur m

follow vb suivre [81] ▷ She followed him. Elle l'a suivi.

following adj suivant(e) ▷ the following day le jour suivant

fond adj to be fond of somebody aimer [28] beaucoup quelqu'un ▷ I'm very fond of her. Je l'aime beaucoup.

food n nourriture f; We need to buy some food. Nous devons acheter à manger.; cat food la nourriture pour chat; dog food la nourriture pour chien

fool n idiot m, idiote f

foot n ❶ (of person) pied m ▷ My feet are aching. J'ai mal aux pieds. ❷ (of animal) patte f ▷ The dog's foot was injured. Le chien était blessé à la patte.; on foot à pied ❸ (12 inches) pied m

In France measurements are in metres and centimetres rather than feet and inches. A foot is about 30 centimetres.

Dave is 6 foot tall. Dave mesure un mètre quatre-vingts.; **That mountain is 5000 feet high.** Cette montagne fait mille six cents mètres de haut.

football n ❶ (game) football m ▷ I like playing football. J'aime jouer au football. ❷ (ball) ballon m ▷ Paul threw the football over the fence. Paul a envoyé le ballon par dessus la clôture.

footballer n footballeur m, footballeuse f

footie n (informal) foot m

footpath n sentier m ▷ Jane followed the footpath through the forest. Jane a suivi le sentier à travers la forêt.

for prep

There are several ways of translating 'for'. Scan the examples to find one that is similar to what you want to say.

❶ pour ▷ a present for me un cadeau pour moi ▷ the train for London le train pour Londres ▷ He works for the government. Il travaille pour le gouvernement. ▷ I'll do it for you. Je vais le faire pour toi. ▷ Can you do it for tomorrow? Est-ce que vous pouvez le faire pour demain? ▷ Are you for or against the idea? Êtes-vous pour ou contre cette idée? ▷ Oxford is famous for its university. Oxford est célèbre pour son université.

When referring to periods of time, use **pendant** for the future and completed actions in the past, and **depuis** (with the French verb in the present tense) for something that started in the past and is still going on.

❷ pendant ▷ He worked in France for two years. Il a travaillé en France pendant deux ans. ▷ She will be away for a month. Elle sera absente pendant un mois. ▷ There are roadworks for three kilometres. Il y a des travaux pendant trois kilomètres. ❸ depuis ▷ He's been learning French for two years. Il apprend le français depuis deux ans. ▷ She's been away for a month. Elle est absente depuis un mois.

When talking about amounts of money, you do not translate 'for'.

▷ I sold it for £5. Je l'ai vendu cinq livres. ▷ He paid fifty pence for his ticket. Il a payé son billet cinquante pence.; **What's the French for 'lion'?** Comment dit-on 'lion' en français?; **It's time for lunch.** C'est l'heure du déjeuner.; **What for?** Pour quoi faire? ▷ Give me some money! —What for? Donne-moi de l'argent! — Pour quoi faire?; **What's it for?** Ça sert à quoi?; **for sale** à vendre ▷ The factory's for sale. L'usine est en vente.

forbid vb défendre [88]; **to forbid somebody to do something** défendre [88] à quelqu'un de faire quelque chose ▷ *I forbid you to go out tonight!* Je te défends de sortir ce soir.

forbidden *adj* défendu(e)
▷ *Smoking is strictly forbidden.* Il est strictement défendu de fumer.

force *n* force f ▷ *the force of the explosion* la force de l'explosion; **in force** en vigueur ▷ *No-smoking rules are now in force.* Un règlement qui interdit de fumer est maintenant en vigueur.
▶ *vb* forcer [12] ▷ *They forced him to open the safe.* Ils l'ont obligé à ouvrir le coffre-fort.

forecast *n* **the weather forecast** la météo

forehead *n* front *m*

foreign *adj* étranger (*f* étrangère)

foreigner *n* étranger *m*, étrangère *f*

forest *n* forêt f

forever *adv* ❶ pour toujours ▷ *He's gone forever.* Il est parti pour toujours. ❷ (*always*) toujours ▷ *She's forever complaining.* Elle est toujours en train de se plaindre.

forgave *vb see* **forgive**

forge *vb* contrefaire [36] ▷ *She tried to forge his signature.* Elle a essayé de contrefaire sa signature.

forged *adj* faux (*f* fausse) ▷ *forged banknotes* des faux billets

forget *vb* oublier [19] ▷ *I've forgotten his name.* J'ai oublié son nom.

forgive *vb* **to forgive somebody** pardonner [28] à quelqu'un ▷ *I forgive you.* Je te pardonne.; **to forgive somebody for doing something** pardonner [28] à

quelqu'un d'avoir fait quelque chose ▷ *She forgave him for forgetting her birthday.* Elle lui a pardonné d'avoir oublié son anniversaire.

forgot, forgotten *vb see* **forget**

fork *n* ❶ (*for eating*) fourchette f ❷ (*for gardening*) fourche f ❸ (*in road*) bifurcation f

form *n* ❶ (*paper*) formulaire *m* ▷ *to fill in a form* remplir un formulaire ❷ (*type*) forme f ▷ *I'm against hunting in any form.* Je suis contre la chasse sous toutes ses formes.; **in top form** en pleine forme; **She's in the fourth form.** Elle est en troisième.

formal *adj* ❶ (*occasion*) officiel (*f* officielle) ▷ *a formal dinner* un dîner officiel ❷ (*person*) guindé(e) ❸ (*language*) soutenu(e) ▷ *In English, 'residence' is a formal term.* En anglais, 'residence' est un terme soutenu.; **formal clothes** une tenue habillée; **He's got no formal education.** Il n'a pas fait beaucoup d'études.

former *adj* ancien (*f* ancienne) ▷ *a former pupil* un ancien élève

fortnight *n* **a fortnight** quinze jours ▷ *I'm going on holiday for a fortnight.* Je pars en vacances pendant quinze jours.

fortunate *adj* **to be fortunate** avoir [8] de la chance ▷ *He was extremely fortunate to survive.* Il a eu énormément de chance de survivre.; **It's fortunate that I remembered the map.** C'est une chance que j'aie pris la carte.

fortunately *adv* heureusement
▷ *Fortunately, it didn't rain.*
Heureusement, il n'a pas plu.

fortune *n* fortune *f* ▷ *Kate earns a fortune!* Kate gagne une fortune!;
to tell somebody's fortune dire
[27] la bonne aventure à quelqu'un

forty *num* quarante ▷ *He's forty.* Il a quarante ans.

forward *adv* **to move forward**
avancer [12]
▶ *vb* faire [36] suivre ▷ *He forwarded all Janette's letters.* Il a fait suivre toutes les lettres de Janette.

forward slash *n* barre oblique *f*

foster child *n* enfant adoptif *m*,
enfant adoptive *f*

fought *vb see* **fight**

foul *adj* infect(e) ▷ *The weather was foul.* Le temps était infect.
▶ *n* faute *f* ▷ *Ferguson committed a foul.* Ferguson a fait une faute.

fountain *n* fontaine *f*

fountain pen *n* stylo à encre *m*

four *num* quatre ▷ *She's four.* Elle a quatre ans.

fourteen *num* quatorze ▷ *I'm fourteen.* J'ai quatorze ans.

fourteenth *adj* quatorzième ▷ *the fourteenth floor* le quatorzième étage; **the fourteenth of August**
le quatorze août

fourth *adj* quatrième ▷ *the fourth floor* le quatrième étage; **the fourth of July** le quatre juillet

fox *n* renard *m*

fragile *adj* fragile

frame *n* (*for picture*) cadre *m*

France *n* France *f*; **in France** en
France; **to France** en France; **He's from France.** Il est français.

frantic *adj* **I was going frantic.**
J'étais dans tous mes états.; **to be frantic with worry** être [35] fou
d'inquiétude

fraud *n* ❶ (*crime*) fraude *f* ▷ *He was jailed for fraud.* On l'a mis en prison pour fraude. ❷ (*person*) imposteur
m ▷ *He's not a real doctor, he's a fraud.*
Ce n'est pas un vrai médecin, c'est
un imposteur.

freckles *npl* taches de rousseur *fpl*

free *adj* ❶ (*free of charge*) gratuit(e)
▷ *a free brochure* une brochure
gratuite ❷ (*not busy, not taken*) libre
▷ *Is this seat free?* Est-ce que cette
place est libre? ▷ *Are you free after school?* Tu es libre après l'école?
▶ *vb* libérer [34]

freedom *n* liberté *f*

freeway *n* (*US*) autoroute *f*

freeze *vb* ❶ geler [43] ▷ *The water had frozen.* L'eau avait gelé. ❷ (*food*)
congeler [1] ▷ *She froze the rest of the raspberries.* Elle a congelé le reste
des framboises.

freezer *n* congélateur *m*

freezing *adj* **It's freezing!** (*informal*)
Il fait un froid de canard!; **I'm freezing!** (*informal*) Je suis gelé!; **3 degrees below freezing** moins
trois

French *n* (*language*) français *m* ▷ *Do you speak French?* Est-ce que tu
parles français?; **the French**
(*people*) les Français
▶ *adj* français(e) ▷ *She's French.* Elle
est française.

a
b
c
d
e
f
g
h
i
j
k
l
m
n
o
p
q
r
s
t
u
v
w
x
y
z

French beans npl haricots verts mpl

French fries npl frites fpl

French kiss n baiser profond m

Frenchman n Français m

French windows npl porte-fenêtre fsg (pl portes-fenêtres)

Frenchwoman n Française f

frequent adj fréquent(e) ▷ frequent showers des averses fréquentes; **There are frequent buses to the town centre.** Il y a beaucoup de bus pour le centre ville.

fresh adj frais (f fraîche); **I need some fresh air.** J'ai besoin de prendre l'air.

Friday n vendredi m ▷ on Friday vendredi ▷ on Fridays le vendredi ▷ every Friday tous les vendredis

fridge n frigo m

fried adj frit(e) ▷ fried vegetables des légumes frits; **a fried egg** un œuf sur le plat

friend n ami m, amie f
▶ vb ajouter [28] comme ami(e) ▷ I've friended her on Facebook. Elle est devenue mon amie sur Facebook.

friendly adj ❶ gentil (f gentille) ▷ She's really friendly. Elle est vraiment gentille. ❷ accueillant(e) ▷ Liverpool is a very friendly city. Liverpool est une ville très accueillante.

friendship n amitié f

fright n peur f ▷ I got a terrible fright! Ça m'a fait une peur terrible!

frighten vb faire [36] peur à

▷ Horror films frighten him. Les films d'horreur lui font peur.

frightened adj to be frightened avoir [8] peur ▷ I'm frightened! J'ai peur!; **to be frightened of something** avoir [8] peur de quelque chose ▷ Anna's frightened of spiders. Anna a peur des araignées.

frightening adj effrayant(e)

fringe n (of hair) frange f ▷ She's got a fringe. Elle a une frange.

frog n grenouille f; **frogs' legs** les cuisses de grenouille

from prep de ▷ Where do you come from? D'où venez-vous? ▷ I come from Perth. Je viens de Perth.; **from ... to** de ... à ... ▷ He flew from London to Paris. Il a pris l'avion de Londres à Paris.; **from ... onwards** à partir de ... ▷ We'll be at home from 7 o'clock onwards. Nous serons chez nous à partir de sept heures.

front n devant m ▷ the front of the house le devant de la maison; **in front** devant ▷ the car in front la voiture de devant; **in front of** devant ▷ in front of the house devant la maison ▷ the car in front of us la voiture devant nous; **in the front** (of car) à l'avant ▷ I was sitting in the front. J'étais assis à l'avant.; **at the front of the train** à l'avant du train ▶ adj ❶ de devant ▷ the front row la rangée de devant ❷ avant ▷ the front seats of the car les sièges avant de la voiture; **the front door** la porte d'entrée

frontier n frontière f

frost n gel m

frosty adj It's frosty today. Il gèle aujourd'hui.

frown vb froncer [12] les sourcils ▷ He frowned. Il a froncé les sourcils.

froze vb see **freeze**

frozen adj (food) surgelé(e) ▷ frozen chips des frites surgelées

fruit n fruit m; **fruit juice** le jus de fruits; **a fruit salad** une salade de fruits

fruit machine n machine à sous f

frustrated adj frustré(e)

fry vb faire [36] frire ▷ Fry the onions for 5 minutes. Faites frire les oignons pendant cinq minutes.

frying pan n poêle f

fuel n (for car, aeroplane) carburant m ▷ to run out of fuel avoir une panne de carburant

full adj, adv ❶ plein(e) ▷ The tank's full. Le réservoir est plein. ❷ complet (f complète) ▷ He asked for full details about the job. Il a demandé des renseignements complets sur le poste.; **your full name** vos nom et prénoms ▷ My full name is Ian John Marr. Je m'appelle Ian John Marr.; **I'm full.** (after meal) J'ai bien mangé.; **at full speed** à toute vitesse ▷ He drove at full speed. Il conduisait à toute vitesse.; **There was a full moon.** C'était la pleine lune.

full stop n point m

full-time adj, adv à plein temps ▷ She's got a full-time job. Elle a un travail à plein temps. ▷ She works full-time. Elle travaille à plein temps.

fully adv complètement ▷ He hasn't fully recovered from his illness. Il n'est pas complètement remis de sa maladie.

fumes npl fumées fpl; **exhaust fumes** les gaz d'échappement mpl

fun adj marrant(e) ▷ She's a fun person. Elle est marrante.
▶ n to have fun s'amuser [28] ▷ We had great fun playing in the snow. Nous nous sommes bien amusés à jouer dans la neige.; **for fun** pour rire ▷ He entered the competition just for fun. Il a participé à la compétition juste pour rire.; **to make fun of somebody** se moquer [28] de quelqu'un ▷ They made fun of him. Ils se sont moqués de lui.; **It's fun!** C'est chouette!; **Have fun!** Amuse-toi bien!

funds npl fonds mpl ▷ to raise funds collecter des fonds

funeral n enterrement m

funfair n fête foraine f

funny adj ❶ (amusing) drôle ▷ It was really funny. C'était vraiment drôle. ❷ (strange) bizarre ▷ There's something funny about him. Il est un peu bizarre.

fur n ❶ fourrure f ▷ a fur coat un manteau de fourrure ❷ poil m ▷ the dog's fur le poil du chien

furious adj furieux (f furieuse) ▷ Dad was furious with me. Papa était furieux contre moi.

furniture n meubles mpl ▷ a piece of furniture un meuble

further adv, adj plus loin ▷ London is further from Manchester than Leeds is.

a b c d e f g h i j k l m n o p q r s t u v w x y z

Londres est plus loin de
Manchester que Leeds.; **How
much further is it?** C'est encore
loin?

further education *n*
enseignement postscolaire *m*

fuse *n* fusible *m* ▷ *The fuse has blown.*
Le fusible a sauté.

fuss *n* agitation *f* ▷ *What's all the fuss
about?* Qu'est-ce que c'est que
toute cette agitation?; **to make a
fuss** faire [**36**] des histoires ▷ *He's
always making a fuss about nothing.* Il
fait toujours des histoires pour
rien.

fussy *adj* difficile ▷ *She is very fussy
about her food.* Elle est très difficile
sur la nourriture.

future *n* ❶ avenir *m* ▷ *What are your
plans for the future?* Quels sont vos
projets pour l'avenir?; **in future** à
l'avenir ▷ *Be more careful in future.*
Sois plus prudent à l'avenir. ❷ *(in
grammar)* futur *m* ▷ *Put this sentence
into the future.* Mettez cette phrase
au futur.

g

gain *vb* **to gain weight** prendre [**65**]
du poids; **to gain speed** prendre
[**65**] de la vitesse

gallery *n* musée *m* ▷ *an art gallery*
un musée d'art

gamble *vb* jouer [**28**] ▷ *He gambled
£100 at the casino.* Il a joué cent
livres au casino.

gambling *n* jeu *m* ▷ *He likes
gambling.* Il aime le jeu.

game *n* ❶ jeu *m* (*pl* jeux) ▷ *The
children were playing a game.* Les
enfants jouaient à un jeu. ❷ *(sport)*
match *m* ▷ *a game of football* un
match de football; **a game of
cards** une partie de cartes

gamer *n* ❶ *(on computer)* joueur sur
ordinateur *m*, joueuse sur
ordinateur *f* ❷ *(on mobile phone)*
joueur sur téléphone portable *m*,

joueuse sur téléphone portable f
gaming n ❶ (on computer) jeux sur ordinateur mpl ❷ (on mobile phone) jeux sur téléphone portable mpl
gang n bande f
gangster n gangster m
gap n ❶ trou m ▷ There's a gap in the hedge. Il y a un trou dans la haie. ❷ intervalle m ▷ a gap of four years un intervalle de quatre ans
gap year n année sabbatique avant d'aller à l'université
garage n garage m
garbage n ordures fpl
garden n jardin m
gardener n jardinier m ▷ He's a gardener. Il est jardinier.
gardening n jardinage m ▷ Margaret loves gardening. Margaret aime le jardinage.
garlic n ail m
garment n vêtement m
gas n ❶ gaz m; **a gas cooker** une cuisinière à gaz; **a gas cylinder** une bouteille de gaz; **a gas fire** un radiateur à gaz; **a gas leak** une fuite de gaz ❷ (US: petrol) essence f
gasoline n (US) essence f
gate n ❶ (of garden) portail m ❷ (of field) barrière f ❸ (at airport) porte f
gather vb (assemble) se rassembler [28] ▷ People gathered in front of Buckingham Palace. Les gens se sont rassemblés devant Buckingham Palace.; **to gather speed** prendre [65] de la vitesse ▷ The train gathered speed. Le train a pris de la vitesse.
gave vb see **give**
gay adj homosexuel (f homosexuelle)

GCSE n brevet des collèges m
gear n ❶ (in car) vitesse f ▷ in first gear en première vitesse ▷ to change gear changer de vitesse ❷ matériel m ▷ camping gear le matériel de camping; **your sports gear** (clothes) tes affaires de sport
gear lever n levier de vitesse m
gearshift n (US) levier de vitesse m
geese npl see **goose**
gel n gel m; **hair gel** le gel pour les cheveux
Gemini n Gémeaux mpl ▷ I'm Gemini. Je suis Gémeaux.
gender n ❶ (of person) sexe m ❷ (of noun) genre m
general n général m (pl généraux) ▶ adj général(e) (mpl généraux); **in general** en général
general election n élections législatives fpl
general knowledge n connaissances générales fpl
generally adv généralement ▷ I generally go shopping on Saturday. Généralement, je fais mes courses le samedi.
generation n génération f ▷ the younger generation la nouvelle génération
generous adj généreux (f généreuse) ▷ That's very generous of you. C'est très généreux de votre part.
genetically-modified adj génétiquement modifié(e)
genetics n génétique f
Geneva n Genève; **in Geneva** à Genève; **to Geneva** à Genève; **Lake Geneva** le lac Léman

genius n génie m ▷ *She's a genius!* C'est un génie!

gentle adj doux (f douce)

gentleman n monsieur m (pl messieurs)

gently adv doucement

gents n toilettes pour hommes fpl ▷ *Can you tell me where the gents is, please?* Pouvez-vous me dire où sont les toilettes, s'il vous plaît?; **'gents'** (on sign) 'messieurs'

genuine adj ❶ (real) véritable ▷ *These are genuine diamonds.* Ce sont de véritables diamants. ❷ (sincere) sincère ▷ *She's a very genuine person.* C'est quelqu'un de très sincère.

geography n géographie f

gerbil n gerbille f

germ n microbe m

German n ❶ (person) Allemand m, Allemande f ❷ (language) allemand ▷ *Do you speak German?* Parlez-vous allemand? ▸ adj allemand(e)

Germany n Allemagne f; **in Germany** en Allemagne; **to Germany** en Allemagne

get vb

> There are several ways of translating 'get'. Scan the examples to find one that is similar to what you want to say.

❶ (have, receive) avoir [8] ▷ *I got lots of presents.* J'ai eu beaucoup de cadeaux. ▷ *He got first prize.* Il a eu le premier prix. ▷ *He got good exam results.* Il a eu de bons résultats aux

examens. ▷ *How many have you got?* Combien en avez-vous? ❷ (fetch) aller [3] chercher ▷ *Quick, get help!* Allez vite chercher de l'aide! ❸ (catch) attraper [28] ▷ *They've got the thief.* Ils ont attrapé le voleur. ❹ (train, bus) prendre [65] ▷ *I'm getting the bus into town.* Je prends le bus pour aller en ville. ❺ (understand) comprendre [65] ▷ *I don't get it.* Je ne comprends pas. ❻ (go) aller [3] ▷ *How do you get to the castle?* Comment est-ce qu'on va au château? ❼ (arrive) arriver [5] ▷ *He should get here soon.* Il devrait arriver bientôt. ❽ (become) devenir [25] ▷ *to get old* devenir vieux; **to get something done** faire [36] faire quelque chose ▷ *to get one's hair cut* se faire couper les cheveux; **to get something for somebody** trouver [28] quelque chose pour quelqu'un ▷ *The librarian got the book for me.* Le bibliothécaire m'a trouvé le livre.; **to have got to do something** devoir [26] faire quelque chose ▷ *I've got to tell him.* Je dois le lui dire.

get away vb s'échapper [28] ▷ *One of the burglars got away.* L'un des cambrioleurs s'est échappé.

get back vb ❶ rentrer [68] ▷ *What time did you get back?* Tu es rentré à quelle heure? ❷ récupérer [34] ▷ *He got his money back.* Il a récupéré son argent.

get in vb rentrer [68] ▷ *What time did you get in last night?* Tu es rentré à quelle heure hier soir?

get into vb monter [48] dans
▷ *Sharon got into the car.* Sharon est
montée dans la voiture.

get off vb (vehicle, bike) descendre
[24] de ▷ *Isobel got off the train.*
Isobel est descendue du train.

get on vb ❶ (vehicle) monter [48]
dans ▷ *Phyllis got on the bus.* Phyllis
est montée dans le bus. ❷ (bike)
enfourcher [28] ▷ *Carol got on her
bike.* Carol a enfourché son vélo.;
to get on with somebody
s'entendre [88] avec quelqu'un
▷ *He doesn't get on with his parents.* Il
ne s'entend pas avec ses parents.
▷ *We got on really well.* Nous nous
sommes très bien entendus.

get out vb sortir [79] ▷ *Hélène got
out of the car.* Hélène est sortie de la
voiture. ▷ *Get out!* Sortez!; **to get
something out** sortir [79] quelque
chose ▷ *She got the map out.* Elle a
sorti la carte.

get over vb se remettre [47] ▷ *She
never got over his death.* Elle ne s'est
jamais remise de sa mort.

get together vb se retrouver [28]
▷ *Could we get together this evening?*
Pourrait-on se retrouver ce soir?

get up vb se lever [43] ▷ *What time
do you get up?* Tu te lèves à quelle
heure?

ghost n fantôme m

giant adj énorme ▷ *They ate a giant
meal.* Ils ont mangé un énorme
repas.
▶n géant m, géante f

gift n ❶ (present) cadeau m (pl
cadeaux) ❷ (talent) don m; **to have**

a gift for something être [35] doué
pour quelque chose ▷ *Dave has a
gift for painting.* Dave est doué pour
la peinture.

gin n gin m

ginger n gingembre m ▷ *Add a
teaspoon of ginger.* Ajoutez une
cuillère à café de gingembre.
▶adj roux (f rousse) ▷ *Chris has
ginger hair.* Chris a les cheveux roux.

giraffe n girafe f

girl n ❶ fille f ▷ *They've got a girl and
two boys.* Ils ont une fille et deux
garçons. ❷ (young) petite fille f
▷ *a five-year-old girl* une petite fille
de cinq ans ❸ (older) jeune fille f
▷ *a sixteen-year-old girl* une jeune
fille de seize ans ▷ *an English girl*
une jeune Anglaise

girlfriend n ❶ (lover) copine f
▷ *Damon's girlfriend is called Justine.*
La copine de Damon s'appelle
Justine. ❷ (friend) amie f ▷ *She often
went out with her girlfriends.* Elle
sortait souvent avec ses amies.

give vb donner [28]; **to give
something to somebody** donner
[28] quelque chose à quelqu'un
▷ *He gave me £10.* Il m'a donné dix
livres.; **to give something back to
somebody** rendre [7] quelque
chose à quelqu'un ▷ *I gave the book
back to him.* Je lui ai rendu le livre.;
to give way (in traffic) céder [34] la
priorité

give in vb céder [34] ▷ *His mum gave
in and let him go out.* Sa mère a cédé
et l'a laissé sortir.

give out vb distribuer [28] ▷ *He*

gave out the exam papers. Il a distribué les sujets d'examen.

give up *vb* laisser [28] tomber ▷ *I couldn't do it, so I gave up.* Je n'arrivais pas à le faire, alors j'ai laissé tomber.; **to give up doing something** arrêter [28] de faire quelque chose ▷ *He gave up smoking.* Il a arrêté de fumer.; **to give oneself up** se rendre [7] ▷ *The thief gave himself up.* Le voleur s'est rendu.

glad *adj* content(e) ▷ *She's glad she's done it.* Elle est contente de l'avoir fait.

glamorous *adj* ❶ (*person*) glamour ▷ *She's very glamourous.* Elle est très glamour. ❷ (*job*) prestigieux (*f* prestigieuse); **to have a glamorous lifestyle** vivre [91] comme une star

glass *n* verre *m* ▷ *a glass of milk* un verre de lait

glasses *npl* lunettes *fpl* ▷ *Jean-Pierre wears glasses.* Jean-Pierre porte des lunettes.

glider *n* planeur *m*

global *adj* mondial(e) (*mpl* mondiaux); **on a global scale** à l'échelle mondiale

global warming *n* réchauffement de la planète *m*

globe *n* globe *m*

gloomy *adj* ❶ morose ▷ *She looked gloomy when she heard the news.* Elle avait l'air morose quand elle a entendu les nouvelles. ❷ lugubre ▷ *He lives in a small gloomy flat.* Il habite un petit appartement lugubre.

glorious *adj* magnifique

glove *n* gant *m*

glue *n* colle *f*
▶ *vb* coller [28]

GM *adj* (= *genetically modified*) génétiquement modifié(e) ▷ *GM foods* les aliments génétiquement modifiés *mpl*

go *n* **to have a go at doing something** essayer [59] de faire quelque chose ▷ *He had a go at making a cake.* Il a essayé de faire un gâteau.; **Whose go is it?** À qui le tour?
▶ *vb* ❶ aller [3] ▷ *I'm going to the cinema tonight.* Je vais au cinéma ce soir. ❷ (*leave*) partir [57] ▷ *Where's Pierre? — He's gone.* Où est Pierre? — Il est parti. ❸ (*go away*) s'en aller [3] ▷ *I'm going now.* Je m'en vais. ❹ (*vehicle*) marcher [28] ▷ *My car won't go.* Ma voiture ne marche pas.; **to go home** rentrer [68] à la maison ▷ *I go home at about 4 o'clock.* Je rentre à la maison vers quatre heures.; **to go for a walk** aller [3] se promener ▷ *Shall we go for a walk?* Si on allait se promener?; **How did it go?** Comment est-ce que ça s'est passé?; **I'm going to do it tomorrow.** Je vais le faire demain.; **It's going to be difficult.** Ça va être difficile.

go after *vb* suivre [81] ▷ *Quick, go after them!* Vite, suivez-les!

go ahead *vb* **The meeting will go ahead as planned.** La réunion aura bien lieu comme prévu.; **We'll go ahead with your plan.** Nous allons mettre votre projet à exécution.; **Go ahead!** Vas-y!

go away vb s'en aller [3] ▷ *Go away!* Allez-vous-en!

go back vb

> Use **retourner** in most cases, unless you are entering a building (usually your home) when you would use **rentrer**.

❶ retourner [72] ▷ *We went back to the same place.* Nous sommes retournés au même endroit. ❷ rentrer [68] ▷ *After the film he went back home.* Il est rentré chez lui après le film.

go by vb passer [58] ▷ *Two police officers went by.* Deux policiers sont passés.

go down vb ❶ (*person*) descendre [24] ▷ *to go down the stairs* descendre l'escalier ❷ (*decrease*) baisser [28] ▷ *The price of computers has gone down.* Le prix des ordinateurs a baissé. ❸ (*deflate*) se dégonfler [28] ▷ *My airbed kept going down.* Mon matelas pneumatique se dégonflait constamment.; **My brother's gone down with flu.** Mon frère a attrapé la grippe.

go for vb (*attack*) attaquer [28] ▷ *Suddenly the dog went for me.* Soudain, le chien m'a attaqué.; **Go for it!** (*go on!*) Vas-y, fonce!

go in vb entrer [32] ▷ *He knocked on the door and went in.* Il a frappé à la porte et il est entré.

go off vb ❶ (*bomb*) exploser [28] ▷ *The bomb went off.* La bombe a explosé. ❷ (*alarm, gun*) se

déclencher [28] ▷ *The fire alarm went off.* L'alarme à incendie s'est déclenchée. ❸ (*alarm clock*) sonner [28] ▷ *My alarm clock goes off at seven every morning.* Mon réveil sonne à sept heures tous les matins. ❹ (*food*) tourner [28] ▷ *The milk's gone off.* Le lait a tourné. ❻ (*go away*) partir [57] ▷ *He went off in a huff.* Il est parti de mauvaise humeur.

go on vb ❶ (*happen*) se passer [58] ▷ *What's going on?* Qu'est-ce qui se passe? ❷ (*carry on*) continuer [28] ▷ *The concert went on until 11 o'clock at night.* Le concert a continué jusqu'à onze heures du soir.; **to go on doing something** continuer [28] à faire quelque chose ▷ *He went on reading.* Il a continué à lire.; **to go on at somebody** être [35] sur le dos de quelqu'un ▷ *My parents always go on at me.* Mes parents sont toujours sur mon dos.; **Go on!** Allez! ▷ *Go on, tell me what the problem is!* Allez, dis-moi quel est le problème!

go out vb ❶ (*person*) sortir [79] ▷ *Are you going out tonight?* Tu sors ce soir?; **to go out with somebody** sortir [79] avec quelqu'un ▷ *Are you going out with him?* Est-ce que tu sors avec lui? ❷ (*light, fire, candle*) s'éteindre [60] ▷ *Suddenly the lights went out.* Soudain, les lumières se sont éteintes.

go past vb **to go past something** passer [58] devant quelque chose ▷ *He went past the shop.* Il est passé devant la boutique.

a
b
c
d
e
f
g
h
i
j
k
l
m
n
o
p
q
r
s
t
u
v
w
x
y
z

go round vb to go round a corner
prendre [**65**] un tournant; **to go
round to somebody's house** aller
[**3**] chez quelqu'un; **to go round a
museum** visiter [**28**] un musée; **to
go round the shops** faire [**36**] les
boutiques; **There's a bug going
round.** Il y a un microbe qui circule.

go through vb traverser [**28**] ▷ We
went through Paris to get to Rennes.
Nous avons traversé Paris pour
aller à Rennes.

go up vb ❶ (person) monter [**48**] ▷ to
go up the stairs monter l'escalier
❷ (increase) augmenter [**28**] ▷ The
price has gone up. Le prix a
augmenté.; **to go up in flames**
s'embraser [**28**] ▷ The whole factory
went up in flames. L'usine toute
entière s'est embrasée.

go with vb aller [**3**] avec ▷ Does this
blouse go with that skirt? Est-ce que
ce chemisier va avec cette jupe?

goal n but m ▷ to score a goal
marquer un but

goalkeeper n gardien de but m

goat n chèvre f; **goat's cheese** le
fromage de chèvre

god n dieu m (pl dieux) ▷ I believe in
God. Je crois en Dieu.

goddaughter n filleule f

godfather n parrain m

godmother n marraine f

godson n filleul m

goggles npl ❶ (of welder, mechanic
etc) lunettes de protection fpl ❷ (of
swimmer) lunettes de plongée fpl

gold n or m ▷ a gold necklace un
collier en or

goldfish n poisson rouge m ▷ I've
got five goldfish. J'ai cinq poissons
rouges.

golf n golf m ▷ My dad plays golf. Mon
père joue au golf.; **a golf club** un
club de golf

golf course n terrain de golf m

gone vb see go

good adj ❶ bon (f bonne) ▷ It's a very
good film. C'est un très bon film.
▷ Vegetables are good for you. Les
légumes sont bons pour la santé.;
to be good at something être [**35**]
bon en quelque chose ▷ Jane's very
good at maths. Jane est très bonne
en maths. ❷ (kind) gentil (f
gentille) ▷ That's very good of you.
C'est très gentil de votre part.
❸ (not naughty) sage ▷ Be good! Sois
sage!; **for good** pour de bon ▷ One
day he left for good. Un jour il est
parti pour de bon.; **Good
morning!** Bonjour!; **Good
afternoon!** Bonjour!; **Good
evening!** Bonsoir!; **Good night!**
Bonne nuit!; **It's no good
complaining.** Cela ne sert à rien de
se plaindre.

goodbye excl au revoir!

Good Friday n Vendredi saint m

good-looking adj beau (f belle,
mpl beaux) ▷ He's very good-looking.
Il est très beau.

goods npl (in shop) marchandises
fpl; **a goods train** un train de
marchandises

google vb googler [**28**]

goose n oie f

gorgeous adj ❶ superbe ▷ She's

gorgeous! Elle est superbe!
② splendide ▷ *The weather was gorgeous.* Il a fait un temps splendide.
gorilla n gorille m
gossip n **①** *(rumours)* cancans mpl ▷ *Tell me the gossip!* Raconte-moi les cancans! **②** *(woman)* commère f ▷ *She's such a gossip!* C'est une vraie commère! **③** *(man)* bavard m ▷ *What a gossip!* Quel bavard!
▶ vb **①** *(chat)* bavarder [28] ▷ *They were always gossiping.* Elles étaient tout le temps en train de bavarder. **②** *(about somebody)* faire [36] des commérages ▷ *They gossiped about her.* Elles faisaient des commérages à son sujet.
got vb see **get**
gotten vb *(US)* see **get**
government n gouvernement m
GP n médecin généraliste m
grab vb saisir [38]
graceful adj élégant(e)
grade n *(at school)* note f ▷ *He got good grades in his exams.* Il a eu de bonnes notes à ses examens.
grade school n *(US)* école primaire f
gradual adj progressif *(f* progressive)
gradually adv peu à peu ▷ *We gradually got used to it.* Nous nous y sommes habitués peu à peu.
graffiti npl graffiti mpl
grain n grain m
gram n gramme m
grammar n grammaire f
grammar school n **①** collège m **②** lycée m

In France pupils go to a **collège** between the ages of 11 and 15, and then to a **lycée** until the age of 18. French schools are mostly non-selective.

grammatical adj grammatical(e) *(mpl* grammaticaux)
gramme n gramme m ▷ *500 grammes of cheese* cinq cents grammes de fromage
grand adj somptueux *(f* somptueuse) ▷ *Samantha lives in a very grand house.* Samantha habite une maison somptueuse.
grandchild n petit-fils m, petite-fille f; **my grandchildren** mes petits-enfants mpl
granddad n papi m ▷ *my granddad* mon papi
granddaughter n petite-fille f *(pl* petites-filles)
grandfather n grand-père m *(pl* grands-pères) ▷ *my grandfather* mon grand-père
grandma n mamie f ▷ *my grandma* ma mamie
grandmother n grand-mère f *(pl* grands-mères) ▷ *my grandmother* ma grand-mère
grandpa n papi m ▷ *my grandpa* mon papi
grandparents npl grands-parents mpl ▷ *my grandparents* mes grands-parents
grandson n petit-fils m *(pl* petits-fils)
granny n mamie f ▷ *my granny* ma mamie
grape n raisin m

a b c d e f g h i j k l m n o p q r s t u v w x y z

grapefruit n pamplemousse m
graph n graphique m
graphics npl ❶ (computer generated) images de synthèse fpl ❷ (graphic design) graphisme mpl ▷ I designed the graphics, she wrote the text. J'ai fait le graphisme, elle a écrit le texte.; **He works in computer graphics.** Il fait de l'infographie.
grass n herbe f ▷ The grass is long. L'herbe est haute.; **to cut the grass** tondre [69] le gazon
grasshopper n sauterelle f
grate vb râper [28] ▷ to grate some cheese râper du fromage
grateful adj reconnaissant(e)
grave n tombe f
gravel n gravier m
graveyard n cimetière m
gravy n sauce au jus de viande f
grease n lubrifiant m
greasy adj gras (f grasse) ▷ He has greasy hair. Il a les cheveux gras.
great adj ❶ génial(e) (mpl géniaux) ▷ That's great! C'est génial! ❷ grand(e) ▷ a great mansion un grand manoir
Great Britain n Grande-Bretagne f; **in Great Britain** en Grande-Bretagne; **to Great Britain** en Grande-Bretagne; **I'm from Great Britain.** Je suis britannique.
great-grandfather n arrière-grand-père m (pl arrière-grands-pères)
great-grandmother n arrière-grand-mère f (pl arrière-grands-mères)

Greece n Grèce f; **in Greece** en Grèce; **to Greece** en Grèce
greedy adj ❶ (for food) gourmand(e) ▷ I want some more cake. — Don't be so greedy! Je veux encore du gâteau. — Ne sois pas si gourmand! ❷ (for money) avide
Greek n ❶ (person) Grec m, Grecque f ❷ (language) grec m ▶ adj grec (f grecque) ▷ She's Greek. Elle est grecque.
green adj ❶ vert(e) ▷ a green light un feu vert ▷ a green salad une salade verte ❷ (movement, candidate) écologiste ▷ the Green Party le parti écologiste ▶ n vert m ▷ a dark green un vert foncé; **greens** (vegetables) les légumes verts mpl; **the Greens** (party) les Verts mpl
greengrocer's n marchand de fruits et légumes m
greenhouse n serre f; **the greenhouse effect** l'effet de serre m
Greenland n Groenland m
greetings card n carte de vœux f
grew vb see **grow**
grey adj gris(e) ▷ She's got grey hair. Elle a les cheveux gris.; **He's going grey.** Il grisonne.
grey-haired adj grisonnant(e)
grid n ❶ (in road) grille f ❷ (of electricity) réseau m (pl réseaux)
grief n chagrin m
grill n (of cooker) gril m; **a mixed grill** un assortiment de grillades ▶ vb **to grill something** faire [36] griller quelque chose

339 | **guess**

grin vb sourire [74] ▷ *Dave grinned at me.* Dave m'a souri.
▶ n large sourire m
grip vb saisir [38]
grit n gravillon m
groan vb gémir [38] ▷ *He groaned with pain.* Il a gémi sous l'effet de la douleur.
▶ n (of pain) gémissement m
grocer n épicier m ▷ *He's a grocer.* Il est épicier.
groceries npl provisions fpl
grocer's n épicerie f
grocery store n (US) épicerie f
groom n (bridegroom) marié m ▷ *the groom and his best man* le marié et son témoin
gross adj (revolting) dégoûtant(e) ▷ *It was really gross!* C'était vraiment dégoûtant!
ground n ❶ (earth) sol m ▷ *The ground's wet.* Le sol est mouillé. ❷ (for sport) terrain m ▷ *a football ground* un terrain de football ❸ (reason) raison f ▷ *We've got grounds for complaint.* Nous avons des raisons de nous plaindre.; **on the ground** par terre ▷ *We sat on the ground.* Nous nous sommes assis par terre.
ground floor n rez-de-chaussée m; **on the ground floor** au rez-de-chaussée
group n groupe m
grow vb ❶ (plant) pousser [28] ▷ *Grass grows quickly.* L'herbe pousse vite. ❷ (person, animal) grandir [38] ▷ *Haven't you grown!* Comme tu as grandi! ❸ (increase)

augmenter [28] ▷ *The number of unemployed people has grown.* Le nombre de chômeurs a augmenté. ❹ (cultivate) faire [36] pousser ▷ *My Dad grows potatoes.* Mon père fait pousser des pommes de terre.; **to grow a beard** se laisser [28] pousser la barbe; **He's grown out of his jacket.** Sa veste est devenue trop petite pour lui.
grow up vb grandir [38] ▷ *Oh, grow up!* Ne fais pas l'enfant!
growl vb grogner [28]
grown vb see **grow**
growth n croissance f ▷ *economic growth* la croissance économique
grudge n rancune f; **to bear a grudge against somebody** garder [28] rancune à quelqu'un
gruesome adj horrible
guarantee n garantie f; **a five-year guarantee** une garantie de cinq ans
▶ vb garantir [38] ▷ *I can't guarantee he'll come.* Je ne peux pas garantir qu'il viendra.
guard vb garder [28] ▷ *They guarded the palace.* Ils gardaient le palais.; **to guard against something** protéger [66] contre quelque chose
▶ n (of train) chef de train m; **a security guard** un vigile; **a guard dog** un chien de garde
guess vb deviner [28] ▷ *Guess what this is?* Devine ce que c'est!; **to guess wrong** se tromper [28] ▷ *Janice guessed wrong.* Janice s'est trompée.

▶ *n* supposition *f* ▷ *It's just a guess.* C'est une simple supposition.; **Have a guess!** Devine!

guest *n* ❶ invité *m*, invitée *f* ▷ *We have guests staying with us.* Nous avons des invités. ❷ *(of hotel)* client *m*, cliente *f*

guesthouse *n* petit hôtel *m*

guide *n* ❶ *(book, person)* guide *m* ▷ *We bought a guide to Paris.* Nous avons acheté un guide sur Paris. ▷ *The guide showed us round the castle.* Le guide nous a fait visiter le château. ❷ *(girl guide)* éclaireuse *f*; **the Guides** les Éclaireuses

guidebook *n* guide *m*

guide dog *n* chien d'aveugle *m*

guilty *adj* coupable ▷ *to feel guilty* se sentir coupable ▷ *She was found guilty.* Elle a été reconnue coupable.

guinea pig *n* cobaye *m*

guitar *n* guitare *f* ▷ *I play the guitar.* Je joue de la guitare.

gum *n* *(sweet)* chewing-gum *m*; **gums** *(in mouth)* les gencives *fpl*

gun *n* ❶ *(small)* revolver *m* ❷ *(rifle)* fusil *m*

gunpoint *n* **at gunpoint** sous la menace d'une arme

guy *n* type *m* ▷ *He's a nice guy.* C'est un type sympa.

gym *n* gym *f* ▷ *I go to the gym every day.* Je vais tous les jours à la gym.; **gym classes** les cours de gym *mpl*

gymnast *n* gymnaste *mf* ▷ *She's a gymnast.* Elle est gymnaste.

gymnastics *n* gymnastique *f*

▷ **to do gymnastics** faire de la gymnastique

gypsy *n* Tzigane *m*, Tzigane *f*

h

habit n habitude f ▷ a bad habit une mauvaise habitude

had vb see **have**

hadn't = had not

hail n grêle f
▶ vb grêler [**28**] ▷ It's hailing. Il grêle.

hair n ❶ cheveux mpl ▷ She's got long hair. Elle a les cheveux longs.; **to brush one's hair** se brosser [**28**] les cheveux ▷ I'm brushing my hair. Je me brosse les cheveux.; **to wash one's hair** se laver [**28**] les cheveux ▷ I need to wash my hair. Il faut que je me lave les cheveux.; **to have one's hair cut** se faire [**36**] couper les cheveux ▷ I've just had my hair cut. Je viens de me faire couper les cheveux.; **a hair (1)** (from head) un cheveu **(2)** (from body) un poil ❷ (fur of animal) pelage m

hairbrush n brosse à cheveux f

haircut n coupe f; **to have a haircut** se faire [**36**] couper les cheveux ▷ I've just had a haircut. Je viens de me faire couper les cheveux.

hairdresser n coiffeur m, coiffeuse f ▷ He's a hairdresser. Il est coiffeur.

hairdresser's n coiffeur m ▷ at the hairdresser's chez le coiffeur

hair dryer n sèche-cheveux m (pl sèche-cheveux)

hair gel n gel pour les cheveux m

hairgrip n pince à cheveux f

hair spray n laque f

hairstyle n coiffure f

half n ❶ moitié f ▷ half of the cake la moitié du gâteau ❷ (ticket) billet demi-tarif m ▷ A half to York, please. Un billet demi-tarif pour York, s'il vous plaît.; **two and a half** deux et demi; **half an hour** une demi-heure; **half past ten** dix heures et demie; **half a kilo** cinq cents grammes; **to cut something in half** couper [**28**] quelque chose en deux
▶ adj, adv ❶ demi(e) ▷ a half chicken un demi-poulet ❷ à moitié ▷ He was half asleep. Il était à moitié endormi.

half-brother n demi-frère m (pl demi-frères)

half-hour n demi-heure f

half-price adj, adv **at half-price** à moitié prix

half-sister n demi-sœur f (pl demi-sœurs)

half-term n petites vacances fpl

There are two half-term holidays in France: **les vacances de la Toussaint** (in October/November) and **les vacances de février** (in February).

half-time n mi-temps f
halfway adv ❶ à mi-chemin ▷ halfway between Oxford and London à mi-chemin entre Oxford et Londres ❷ à la moitié ▷ halfway through the chapter à la moitié du chapitre

hall n ❶ (in house) entrée f ❷ salle f ▷ the village hall la salle des fêtes

Hallowe'en n veille de la Toussaint f

hallway n vestibule m

ham n jambon m ▷ a ham sandwich un sandwich au jambon

hamburger n hamburger m

hammer n marteau m (pl marteaux)

hamster n hamster m

hand n ❶ (of person) main f; **to give somebody a hand** donner [28] un coup de main à quelqu'un ▷ Can you give me a hand? Tu peux me donner un coup de main?; **on the one hand ..., on the other hand ...** d'une part ..., d'autre part ... ❷ (of clock) aiguille f
▶ vb passer [58] ▷ He handed me the book. Il m'a passé le livre.; **to hand something in** rendre [7] quelque chose ▷ He handed his exam paper in. Il a rendu sa copie d'examen.; **to hand something out** distribuer [28] quelque chose ▷ The teacher handed out the books. Le professeur

a distribué les livres.; **to hand something over** remettre [47] quelque chose ▷ She handed the keys over to me. Elle m'a remis les clés.

handbag n sac à main m
handcuffs npl menottes fpl
handkerchief n mouchoir m
handle n ❶ (of door) poignée f ❷ (of cup) anse f ❸ (of knife) manche m ❹ (of saucepan) queue f
▶ vb He handled it well. Il s'en est bien tiré.; **Kath handled the travel arrangements.** Kath s'est occupée de l'organisation du voyage.; **She's good at handling children.** Elle sait bien s'y prendre avec les enfants.

handlebars npl guidon msg
handmade adj fait à la main (f faite à la main)
hands-free kit n (phone) kit mains libres m
handsome adj beau (f belle, mpl beaux) ▷ He's handsome. Il est beau.
handwriting n écriture f
handy adj ❶ pratique ▷ This knife's very handy. Ce couteau est très pratique. ❷ sous la main ▷ Have you got a pen handy? Est-ce que tu as un stylo sous la main?
hang vb ❶ accrocher [28] ▷ Mike hung the painting on the wall. Mike a accroché le tableau au mur. ❷ pendre [88] ▷ They hanged the criminal. Ils ont pendu le criminel.
hang around vb traîner [28] ▷ On Saturdays we hang around in the park. Le samedi nous traînons dans le parc.

hang on vb patienter [28] ▷ Hang on a minute please. Patientez une minute s'il vous plaît.

hang up vb ❶ (clothes) accrocher [28] ▷ Hang your jacket up on the hook. Accrochez votre veste au portemanteau. ❷ (phone) raccrocher [28] ▷ Don't hang up! Ne raccroche pas!; **to hang up on someone** raccrocher [28] au nez de quelqu'un ▷ He always hangs up on me. Il me raccroche toujours au nez.

hanger n (coat hanger) cintre m

hangover n gueule de bois f ▷ I've got a terrible hangover. J'ai une gueule de bois terrible.

happen vb se passer [58] ▷ What's happened? Qu'est-ce qui s'est passé?; **as it happens** justement ▷ As it happens, I don't want to go. Justement, je ne veux pas y aller.

happily adv ❶ joyeusement ▷ 'Don't worry!' he said happily. 'Ne te fais pas de souci!' dit-il joyeusement. ❷ (fortunately) heureusement ▷ Happily, everything went well. Heureusement, tout s'est bien passé.

happiness n bonheur m

happy adj heureux (f heureuse) ▷ Janet looks happy. Janet a l'air heureuse.; **I'm very happy with your work.** Je suis très satisfait de ton travail.; **Happy birthday!** Bon anniversaire!

harassment n harcèlement m ▷ police harassment le harcèlement policier

harbour (US **harbor**) n port m

hard adj, adv ❶ dur(e) ▷ This cheese is very hard. Ce fromage est très dur. ▷ He's worked very hard. Il a travaillé très dur. ❷ difficile ▷ This question's too hard for me. Cette question est trop difficile pour moi.

hard disk n (of computer) disque dur m

hardly adv I've hardly got any money. Je n'ai presque pas d'argent.; **I hardly know you.** Je te connais à peine.; **hardly ever** presque jamais

hard up adj fauché(e)

harm vb to harm somebody faire [36] du mal à quelqu'un ▷ I didn't mean to harm you. Je ne voulais pas te faire de mal.; **to harm something** nuire [23] à quelque chose ▷ Chemicals harm the environment. Les produits chimiques nuisent à l'environnement.

harmful adj nocif (f nocive) ▷ harmful chemicals des produits chimiques nocifs

harmless adj inoffensif (f inoffensive) ▷ Most spiders are harmless. La plupart des araignées sont inoffensives.

has vb see **have**

hasn't = has not

hat n chapeau m (pl chapeaux)

hate vb détester [28] ▷ I hate maths. Je déteste les maths.

hatred n haine f

haunted adj hanté(e) ▷ a haunted house une maison hantée

have vb ❶ avoir [**8**] ▷ Have you got a sister? Tu as une sœur? ▷ He's got blue eyes. Il a les yeux bleus. ▷ I've got a cold. J'ai un rhume. ▷ He's done it, hasn't he? Il l'a fait, non? ❷ être [**35**]

The perfect tense of some verbs is formed with **être**.
▷ They have arrived. Ils sont arrivés.
❸ prendre [**65**] ▷ He had his breakfast. Il a pris son petit déjeuner.; **to have got to do something** devoir [**26**] faire quelque chose ▷ She's got to do it. Elle doit le faire.; **to have a party** faire [**36**] une fête; **to have one's hair cut** se faire [**36**] couper les cheveux

haven't = **have not**

hay n foin m

hay fever n rhume des foins m ▷ Do you get hay fever? Est-ce que vous êtes sujet au rhume des foins?

hazelnut n noisette f

he pron il ▷ He loves dogs. Il aime les chiens.

head n ❶ (of person) tête f ▷ The wine went to my head. Le vin m'est monté à la tête. ❷ (of private or primary school) directeur m, directrice f ❸ (of state secondary school) proviseur m ❹ (leader) chef m ▷ a head of state un chef d'État; **to have a head for figures** être [**35**] doué pour les chiffres; **Heads or tails? — Heads.** Pile ou face? — Face.

▶ vb **to head for something** se diriger [**45**] vers quelque chose

▷ They headed for the church. Ils se sont dirigés vers l'église.

headache n I've got a headache. J'ai mal à la tête.

headlight n phare m

headline n titre m

headmaster n ❶ (of private or primary school) directeur m ❷ (of state secondary school) proviseur m

headmistress n ❶ (of private or primary school) directrice f ❷ (of state secondary school) proviseur m

headphones npl écouteurs mpl

headquarters npl (of organization) siège msg

headteacher n ❶ (of private or primary school) directeur m, directrice f ❷ (of state secondary school) proviseur m ▷ She's a headteacher. Elle est proviseur.

heal vb cicatriser [**28**] ▷ The wound soon healed. La blessure a vite cicatrisé.

health n santé f

healthy adj ❶ (person) en bonne santé ▷ Lesley's a healthy person. Lesley est en bonne santé. ❷ (climate, food) sain(e) ▷ a healthy diet une alimentation saine

heap n tas m ▷ a rubbish heap un tas d'ordures

hear vb ❶ entendre [**88**] ▷ He heard the dog bark. Il a entendu le chien aboyer.; **to hear about something** entendre [**88**] parler de quelque chose ❷ (news) apprendre [**65**] ▷ Did you hear the good news? Est-ce que tu as appris la bonne nouvelle?; **to hear from**

somebody avoir [**8**] des nouvelles de quelqu'un ▷ *I haven't heard from him recently.* Je n'ai pas eu de ses nouvelles récemment.

heart n cœur m; **to learn something by heart** apprendre [**65**] quelque chose par cœur; **the ace of hearts** l'as de cœur

heart attack n crise cardiaque f

heartbroken adj **to be heartbroken** avoir [**8**] le cœur brisé

heat n chaleur f
▶ vb faire [**36**] chauffer ▷ *Heat gently for 5 minutes.* Faire chauffer à feu doux pendant cinq minutes.

heat up vb ❶ (cooked food) faire [**36**] réchauffer ▷ *He heated the soup up.* Il a fait réchauffer la soupe. ❷ (water, oven) chauffer [**28**] ▷ *The water is heating up.* L'eau chauffe.

heater n radiateur m ▷ *an electric heater* un radiateur électrique

heather n bruyère f

heating n chauffage m

heaven n paradis m

heavy adj ❶ lourd(e) ▷ *This bag's very heavy.* Ce sac est très lourd.; **heavy rain** une grosse averse ❷ (busy) chargé(e) ▷ *I've got a very heavy week ahead.* Je vais avoir une semaine très chargée.; **to be a heavy drinker** être [**35**] un gros buveur

he'd = he would; he had

hedge n haie f

hedgehog n hérisson m

heel n talon m

height n ❶ (of person) taille f ❷ (of

object) hauteur f ❸ (of mountain) altitude f

held vb see **hold**

helicopter n hélicoptère m

hell n enfer m

he'll = he will; he shall

hello excl bonjour!

helmet n casque m

help vb aider [**28**] ▷ *Can you help me?* Est-ce que vous pouvez m'aider?; **Help!** Au secours!; **Help yourself!** Servez-vous!; **He can't help it.** Il n'y peut rien.
▶ n aide f ▷ *Do you need any help?* Vous avez besoin d'aide?

helpful adj serviable ▷ *He was very helpful.* Il a été très serviable.

hen n poule f

her adj son m ▷ *her father* son père sa f ▷ *her mother* sa mère; ses pl ▷ *her parents* ses parents

> sa becomes **son** before a vowel sound.

her friend (1) (male) son ami (2) (female) son amie

> Do not use **son/sa/ses** with parts of the body.

▷ *She's going to wash her hair.* Elle va se laver les cheveux. ▷ *She's cleaning her teeth.* Elle se brosse les dents. ▷ *She's hurt her foot.* Elle s'est fait mal au pied.
▶ pron ❶ la ▷ *I can see her.* Je la vois.

> la becomes **l'** before a vowel sound.

▷ *I saw her.* Je l'ai vue. ❷ lui

> Use **lui** when 'her' means 'to her'.

▷ *I gave her a book.* Je lui ai donné un livre. ▷ *I told her the truth.* Je lui ai dit la vérité. ❸ <u>elle</u>

Use **elle** after prepositions.

▷ *I'm going with her.* Je vais avec elle.

elle is also used in comparisons.

▷ *I'm older than her.* Je suis plus âgé qu'elle.

herb n <u>herbe</u> f; **herbs** les fines herbes fpl ▷ *What herbs do you use in this sauce?* Quelles fines herbes utilise-t-on pour cette sauce?

here adv <u>ici</u> ▷ *I live here.* J'habite ici.; **here is ...** voici ... ▷ *Here's Helen.* Voici Helen. ▷ *Here he is!* Le voici!; **here are ...** voici ... ▷ *Here are the books.* Voici les livres.

hero n <u>héros</u> m ▷ *He's a real hero!* C'est un véritable héros!

heroin n <u>héroïne</u> f ▷ *Heroin is a hard drug.* L'héroïne est une drogue dure.; **a heroin addict** un héroïnomane ▷ *She's a heroin addict.* C'est une héroïnomane.

heroine n <u>héroïne</u> f ▷ *the heroine of the novel* l'héroïne du roman

hers pron <u>le sien</u> ▷ *Is this her coat? — No, hers is black.* C'est son manteau? — Non, le sien est noir.

<u>la sienne</u> ▷ *Is this her car? — No, hers is white.* C'est sa voiture? — Non, la sienne est blanche.

<u>les siens</u> ▷ *my parents and hers* mes parents et les siens

<u>les siennes</u> ▷ *my reasons and hers* mes raisons et les siennes; **Is this hers?** C'est à elle? ▷ *This book is hers.* Ce livre est à elle. ▷ *Whose is this?*

— *It's hers.* C'est à qui? — À elle.

herself pron ❶ <u>se</u> ▷ *She's hurt herself.* Elle s'est blessée. ❷ *(after preposition)* <u>elle</u> ▷ *She talked mainly about herself.* Elle a surtout parlé d'elle. ❸ <u>elle-même</u> ▷ *She did it herself.* Elle l'a fait elle-même.; **by herself** toute seule ▷ *She doesn't like travelling by herself.* Elle n'aime pas voyager toute seule.

he's = **he is**; **he has**

hesitate vb <u>hésiter</u> [**28**]

heterosexual adj <u>hétérosexuel</u> (f hétérosexuelle)

hi excl <u>salut!</u>

hiccups npl **to have hiccups** avoir [**8**] le hoquet

hide vb <u>se cacher</u> [**28**] ▷ *He hid behind a bush.* Il s'est caché derrière un buisson.; **to hide something** cacher [**28**] quelque chose ▷ *Paula hid the present.* Paula a caché le cadeau.

hide-and-seek n **to play hide-and-seek** jouer [**28**] à cache-cache

hi-fi n <u>chaîne hi-fi</u> f (pl chaînes hi-fi)

high adj, adv ❶ <u>haut(e)</u> ▷ *It's too high.* C'est trop haut.; **How high is the wall?** Quelle est la hauteur du mur?; **The wall's 2 metres high.** Le mur fait deux mètres de haut. ❷ <u>élevé(e)</u> ▷ *a high price* un prix élevé; **at high speed** à grande vitesse; **It's very high in fat.** C'est très gras.; **She's got a very high voice.** Elle a la voix très aiguë.; **to be high** *(on drugs) (informal)* être [**35**] défoncé; **to get high** *(informal)* se défoncer [12] ▷ *to get high on crack* se défoncer au crack

higher education n enseignement supérieur m

high-heeled adj à hauts talons ▷ *high-heeled shoes* des chaussures à hauts talons

high jump n (sport) saut en hauteur m

high-rise n tour f ▷ *I live in a high-rise.* J'habite dans une tour.

high school n ❶ collège m ❷ lycée m

hijack vb détourner [28]

hijacker n pirate de l'air m

hiking n to go hiking faire [36] une randonnée

hilarious adj hilarant(e) ▷ *It was hilarious!* C'était hilarant!

hill n colline f ▷ *She walked up the hill.* Elle a gravi la colline.

hill-walking n randonnée de basse montagne f ▷ *to go hill-walking* faire de la randonnée de basse montagne

him pron ❶ le ▷ *I can see him.* Je le vois.

l'

le becomes l' before a vowel sound.

▷ *I saw him.* Je l'ai vu. ❷ lui

Use lui when 'him' means 'to him', and after prepositions.

▷ *I gave him a book.* Je lui ai donné un livre. ▷ *I'm going with him.* Je vais avec lui.

lui is also used in comparisons.

▷ *I'm older than him.* Je suis plus âgé que lui.

himself pron ❶ se ▷ *He's hurt himself.* Il s'est blessé. ❷ lui ▷ *He talked mainly about himself.* Il a surtout parlé de lui. ❸ lui-même ▷ *He did it himself.* Il l'a fait lui-même.; **by himself** tout seul ▷ *He was travelling by himself.* Il voyageait tout seul.

Hindu adj hindou(e) ▷ *a Hindu temple* un temple hindou

hip n hanche f

hippie n hippie m, hippie f

hippo n hippopotame m

hire vb ❶ louer [28] ▷ *to hire a car* louer une voiture ❷ (person) engager [45] ▷ *They hired a cleaner.* Ils ont engagé une femme de ménage.

▶ n location f; **car hire** location de voitures; **for hire** à louer

his adj son m ▷ *his father* son père; sa f ▷ *his mother* sa mère; ses pl ▷ *his parents* ses parents

sa becomes son before a vowel sound.

his friend (1) (male) son ami (2) (female) son amie

Do not use son/sa/ses with parts of the body.

▷ *He's going to wash his hair.* Il va se laver les cheveux. ▷ *He's cleaning his teeth.* Il se brosse les dents. ▷ *He's hurt his foot.* Il s'est fait mal au pied.

▶ pron le sien m ▷ *Is this his coat?* — *No, his is black.* C'est son manteau? — Non, le sien est noir.; la sienne f ▷ *Is this his car?* — *No, his is white.* C'est sa voiture? — Non, la sienne est blanche.

a
b
c
d
e
f
g
h
i
j
k
l
m
n
o
p
q
r
s
t
u
v
w
x
y
z

les siens *mpl* ▷ *my parents and his* mes parents et les siens
les siennes *fpl* ▷ *my reasons and his* mes raisons et les siennes; **Is this his?** C'est à lui? ▷ *This book is his.* Ce livre est à lui. ▷ *Whose is this? — It's his.* C'est à qui? — À lui.

history *n* histoire *f*

hit *vb* ❶ frapper [**28**] ▷ *Andrew hit him.* Andrew l'a frappé. ❷ renverser [**28**] ▷ *He was hit by a car.* Il a été renversé par une voiture. ❸ toucher [**28**] ▷ *The arrow hit the target.* La flèche a touché la cible.; **to hit it off with somebody** bien s'entendre [**88**] avec quelqu'un ▷ *She hit it off with his parents.* Elle s'est bien entendue avec ses parents.
▶ *n* ❶ *(song)* tube *m* ▷ *Madonna's latest hit* le dernier tube de Madonna ❷ *(success)* succès *m* ▷ *The film was a massive hit.* Le film a eu un immense succès.

hitch *n* contretemps *m* ▷ *There's been a slight hitch.* Il y a eu un léger contretemps.

hitchhike *vb* faire [**36**] de l'auto-stop

hitchhiker *n* auto-stoppeur *m*, auto-stoppeuse *f*

hitchhiking *n* auto-stop *m* ▷ *Hitchhiking can be dangerous.* Il peut être dangereux de faire de l'auto-stop.

HIV-negative *adj* séronégatif (*f* séronégative)

HIV-positive *adj* séropositif (*f* séropositive)

hobby *n* passe-temps favori *m* ▷ *What are your hobbies?* Quels sont tes passe-temps favoris?

hockey *n* hockey *m* ▷ *I play hockey.* Je joue au hockey.

hold *vb* ❶ *(hold on to)* tenir [**83**] ▷ *She held the baby.* Elle tenait le bébé. ❷ *(contain)* contenir [**83**] ▷ *This bottle holds one litre.* Cette bouteille contient un litre.; **to hold a meeting** avoir [**8**] une réunion; **Hold the line!** *(on telephone)* Ne quittez pas!; **Hold it!** *(wait)* Attends!; **to get hold of something** *(obtain)* trouver [**28**] quelque chose ▷ *I couldn't get hold of it.* Je n'ai pas réussi à en trouver.

hold on *vb* ❶ *(keep hold)* tenir [**83**] bon ▷ *Hold on! I'll help you get down.* Tiens bon! Je vais t'aider à descendre.; **to hold on to something** se cramponner [**28**] à quelque chose ▷ *He held on to the chair.* Il se cramponnait à la chaise. ❷ *(wait)* attendre [**7**] ▷ *Hold on, I'm coming!* Attends, je viens!; **Hold on!** *(on telephone)* Ne quittez pas!

hold up *vb* **to hold up one's hand** lever [**43**] la main ▷ *Pierre held up his hand.* Pierre a levé la main.; **to hold somebody up** *(delay)* retenir [**83**] quelqu'un ▷ *I was held up at the office.* J'ai été retenu au bureau.; **to hold up a bank** *(rob)* braquer [**28**] une banque *(informal)*

hold-up *n* ❶ *(at bank)* hold-up *m* ❷ *(delay)* retard *m* ❸ *(traffic jam)* bouchon *m*

hole *n* trou *m*

holiday n ❶ vacances fpl ▷ our holidays in France nos vacances en France; **on holiday** en vacances ▷ to go on holiday partir en vacances; **the school holidays** les vacances scolaires ❷ (public holiday) jour férié m ▷ Next Wednesday is a holiday. Mercredi prochain est un jour férié. ❸ (day off) jour de congé m ▷ He took a day's holiday. Il a pris un jour de congé.; **a holiday camp** un camp de vacances

Holland n Hollande f; **in Holland** en Hollande; **to Holland** en Hollande

hollow adj creux (f creuse)

holly n houx m ▷ a sprig of holly un brin de houx

holy adj saint(e)

home n maison f; **at home** à la maison; **Make yourself at home.** Faites comme chez vous.
▶ adv à la maison ▷ I'll be home at 5 o'clock. Je serai à la maison à cinq heures.; **to get home** rentrer [68] ▷ What time did he get home? Il est rentré à quelle heure?

homeland n patrie f

homeless adj sans abri; **the homeless** les sans-abri

home match n match à domicile m

home page n page d'accueil f

homesick adj **to be homesick** avoir [8] le mal du pays

homework n devoirs mpl ▷ Have you done your homework? Est-ce que tu as fait tes devoirs? ▷ my geography homework mes devoirs de géographie

homosexual adj homosexuel (f homosexuelle)
▶ n homosexuel m, homosexuelle f

honest adj ❶ (trustworthy) honnête ▷ She's a very honest person. Elle est très honnête. ❷ (sincere) franc (f franche) ▷ He was very honest with her. Il a été très franc avec elle.

honestly adv franchement ▷ I honestly don't know. Franchement, je n'en sais rien.

honesty n honnêteté f

honey n miel m

honeymoon n lune de miel f

honour (US **honor**) n honneur m

hood n ❶ (on coat) capuche f ❷ (US: of car) capot m

hook n crochet m ▷ He hung the painting on the hook. Il a suspendu le tableau au crochet.; **to take the phone off the hook** décrocher [28] le téléphone; **a fish-hook** un hameçon

hooligan n voyou m (pl voyoux)

hooray excl hourra!

Hoover® n aspirateur m

hoover vb passer [58] l'aspirateur ▷ to hoover the lounge passer l'aspirateur dans le salon

hope vb espérer [34] ▷ I hope he comes. J'espère qu'il va venir. ▷ I'm hoping for good results. J'espère avoir de bons résultats.; **I hope so.** Je l'espère.; **I hope not.** J'espère que non.
▶ n espoir m; **to give up hope** perdre [61] espoir ▷ Don't give up

hope! Ne perds pas espoir!

hopefully adv avec un peu de chance ▷ *Hopefully he'll make it in time.* Avec un peu de chance, il arrivera à temps.

hopeless adj nul (f nulle) ▷ *I'm hopeless at maths.* Je suis nul en maths.

horizon n horizon m

horizontal adj horizontal(e) (mpl horizontaux)

horn n ❶ klaxon m ▷ *He sounded his horn.* Il a klaxonné. ❷ cor m ▷ *I play the horn.* Je joue du cor.

horoscope n horoscope m

horrible adj horrible ▷ *What a horrible dress!* Quelle robe horrible!

horrifying adj effrayant(e)

horror n horreur f

horror film n film d'horreur m

horse n cheval m (pl chevaux)

horse-racing n courses de chevaux fpl

hose n tuyau m (pl tuyaux) ▷ *a garden hose* un tuyau d'arrosage

hospital n hôpital m (pl hôpitaux) ▷ *in hospital* à l'hôpital

hospitality n hospitalité f

host n hôte m, hôtesse f ▷ *Don't forget to write and thank your hosts.* N'oublie pas d'écrire à tes hôtes pour les remercier.

hostage n otage m; **to take somebody hostage** prendre [**65**] quelqu'un en otage

hostel n (*for refugees, homeless people*) foyer m; **a youth hostel** une auberge de jeunesse

hot adj ❶ (*warm*) chaud(e) ▷ *a hot* bath un bain chaud ▷ *a hot country* un pays chaud

When you are talking about a person being hot, you use **avoir chaud**.
▷ *I'm hot.* J'ai chaud.

When you mean that the weather is hot, you use **faire chaud**.
▷ *It's hot.* Il fait chaud. ❷ (*spicy*) épicé(e) ▷ *a very hot curry* un curry très épicé

hot dog n hot-dog m

hotel n hôtel m ▷ *We stayed in a hotel.* Nous avons logé à l'hôtel.

hour n heure f ▷ *She always takes hours to get ready.* Elle passe toujours des heures à se préparer.; **a quarter of an hour** un quart d'heure; **half an hour** une demi-heure; **two and a half hours** deux heures et demie

hourly adj, adv toutes les heures ▷ *There are hourly buses.* Il y a des bus toutes les heures.; **to be paid hourly** être [**35**] payé à l'heure

house n maison f; **at his house** chez lui; **We stayed at their house.** Nous avons séjourné chez eux.

housewife n femme au foyer f ▷ *She's a housewife.* Elle est femme au foyer.

housework n ménage m; **to do the housework** faire [**36**] le ménage

hovercraft n aéroglisseur m

how adv comment ▷ *How are you?* Comment allez-vous?; **How**

many? Combien?; **How many ...?** Combien de ...? ▷ *How many pupils are there in the class?* Combien d'élèves y a-t-il dans la classe?; **How much?** Combien?; **How much ...?** Combien de ...? ▷ *How much sugar do you want?* Combien de sucres voulez-vous?; **How old are you?** Quel âge as-tu?; **How far is it to Edinburgh?** Combien y a-t-il de kilomètres d'ici à Édimbourg?; **How long have you been here?** Depuis combien de temps êtes-vous là?; **How do you say 'apple' in French?** Comment dit-on 'apple' en français?

however *conj* pourtant ▷ *This, however, isn't true.* Pourtant, ce n'est pas vrai.

hug *vb* serrer [28] dans ses bras ▷ *He hugged her.* Il l'a serrée dans ses bras.

▶ *n* **to give somebody a hug** serrer [28] quelqu'un dans ses bras ▷ *She gave them a hug.* Elle les a serrés dans ses bras.

huge *adj* immense

hum *vb* fredonner [28]

human *adj* humain(e) ▷ *the human body* le corps humain

human being *n* être humain *m*

humour (US **humor**) *n* humour *m*; **to have a sense of humour** avoir [8] le sens de l'humour

hundred *num* **a hundred** cent ▷ *a hundred euros* cent euros; **five hundred** cinq cents; **five hundred and one** cinq cent un; **hundreds of people** des centaines de personnes

hung *vb see* **hang**

Hungarian *n* ❶ (person) Hongrois *m*, Hongroise *f* ❷ (language) hongrois *m*
▶ *adj* hongrois(e) ▷ *She's Hungarian.* Elle est hongroise.

Hungary *n* Hongrie *f*; **in Hungary** en Hongrie; **to Hungary** en Hongrie

hunger *n* faim *f*

hungry *adj* **to be hungry** avoir [8] faim ▷ *I'm hungry.* J'ai faim.

hunt *vb* ❶ (animal) chasser [28] ▷ *People used to hunt wild boar.* On chassait le sanglier autrefois.; **to go hunting** aller [3] à la chasse ❷ (criminal) pourchasser [28] ▷ *The police are hunting the killer.* La police pourchasse le meurtrier.; **to hunt for something** (search) chercher [28] quelque chose partout ▷ *I hunted everywhere for that book.* J'ai cherché ce livre partout.

hunting *n* chasse *f* ▷ *I'm against hunting.* Je suis contre la chasse.; **fox-hunting** la chasse au renard

hurdle *n* obstacle *m*

hurricane *n* ouragan *m*

hurry *vb* se dépêcher [28] ▷ *Sharon hurried back home.* Sharon s'est dépêchée de rentrer chez elle.; **Hurry up!** Dépêche-toi!
▶ *n* **to be in a hurry** être [35] pressé; **to do something in a hurry** faire [36] quelque chose en vitesse; **There's no hurry.** Rien ne presse.

hurt *vb* **to hurt somebody** (1) (physically) faire [36] mal à

a
b
c
d
e
f
g
h
i
j
k
l
m
n
o
p
q
r
s
t
u
v
w
x
y
z

quelqu'un ▷ *You're hurting me!* Tu me fais mal! **(2)** *(emotionally)* blesser [**28**] quelqu'un ▷ *His remarks really hurt me.* Ses remarques m'ont vraiment blessé.; **to hurt oneself** se faire [**36**] mal ▷ *I fell over and hurt myself.* Je me suis fait mal en tombant.; **That hurts.** Ça fait mal. ▷ *It hurts to have a tooth out.* Ça fait mal de se faire arracher une dent.; **My leg hurts.** J'ai mal à la jambe. ▶ *adj* blessé(e) ▷ *Is he badly hurt?* Est-ce qu'il est grièvement blessé? ▷ *I was hurt by what he said.* J'ai été blessé par ce qu'il a dit.; **Luckily, nobody got hurt.** Heureusement, il n'y a pas eu de blessés.

husband *n* mari *m*

hut *n* hutte *f*

hymn *n* cantique *m*

hypermarket *n* hypermarché *m*

hyphen *n* trait d'union *m*

I *pron* ❶ je ▷ *I speak French.* Je parle français.

> je changes to **j'** before a vowel and most words beginning with 'h'.

j' ▷ *I love cats.* J'aime les chats.
❷ moi ▷ *Ann and I* Ann et moi

ice *n* ❶ glace *f* ▷ *There was ice on the lake.* Il y avait de la glace sur le lac. ❷ *(on road)* verglas *m*

iceberg *n* iceberg *m*

ice cream *n* glace *f* ▷ *vanilla ice cream* la glace à la vanille

ice cube *n* glaçon *m*

ice hockey *n* hockey sur glace *m*

Iceland *n* Islande *f*; **in Iceland** en Islande; **to Iceland** en Islande

ice rink *n* patinoire *f*

ice-skating *n* patinage sur glace *m*;

to go ice-skating faire [**36**] du
patin à glace
icing n (on cake) glaçage m; **icing
sugar** le sucre glace
icon n icône f
ICT n informatique f
icy adj glacial(e) (mpl glaciaux)
▷ There was an icy wind. Il y avait un
vent glacial.; **The roads are icy.** Il y
a du verglas sur les routes.
I'd = **I had**; **I would**
idea n idée f ▷ Good idea! Bonne idée!
ideal adj idéal(e) (mpl idéaux)
identical adj identique
identification n identification f
identify vb identifier [**19**]
identity card n carte d'identité f
idiot n idiot m, idiote f
idiotic adj stupide
i.e. abbr c.-à-d. (= c'est-à-dire)
if conj si ▷ You can have it if you like. Tu
peux le prendre si tu veux.
s'

⬛ si changes to **s'** before **il** and **ils.**
▷ Do you know if he's there?
Savez-vous s'il est là?; **if only** si
seulement ▷ If only I had more
money! Si seulement j'avais plus
d'argent!; **if not** sinon ▷ Are you
coming? If not, I'll go with Mark.
Est-ce que tu viens? Sinon, j'irai
avec Mark.
ignore vb **to ignore something** ne
tenir [**83**] aucun compte de
quelque chose ▷ She ignored my
advice. Elle n'a tenu aucun compte
de mes conseils.; **to ignore
somebody** ignorer [**28**] quelqu'un
▷ She saw me, but she ignored me. Elle

m'a vu, mais elle m'a ignoré.; **Just
ignore him!** Ne fais pas attention à
lui!
ill adj (sick) malade; **to be taken ill**
tomber [**84**] malade ▷ She was
taken ill while on holiday. Elle est
tombée malade pendant qu'elle
était en vacances.
I'll = **I will**
illegal adj illégal(e) (mpl illégaux)
illness n maladie f
illusion n illusion f
illustration n illustration f
image n image f ▷ The company has
changed its image. La société a
changé d'image.
imagination n imagination f
imagine vb imaginer [**28**] ▷ You can
imagine how I felt! Tu peux imaginer
ce que j'ai ressenti! ▷ Is he angry? — I
imagine so. Est-ce qu'il est en
colère? — J'imagine que oui.
imitate vb imiter [**28**]
imitation n imitation f
immediate adj immédiat(e)
immediately adv immédiatement
▷ I'll do it immediately. Je vais le faire
immédiatement.
immigrant n immigré m,
immigrée f
immigration n immigration f
impatience n impatience f
impatient adj impatient(e); **to get
impatient** s'impatienter [**28**]
▷ People are getting impatient. Les
gens commencent à s'impatienter.
impatiently adv avec impatience
▷ We waited impatiently. Nous avons
attendu avec impatience.

a
b
c
d
e
f
g
h
i
j
k
l
m
n
o
p
q
r
s
t
u
v
w
x
y
z

importance n importance f
important adj important(e)
impossible adj impossible
impress vb impressionner [**28**]
▷ *She's trying to impress you.* Elle
essaie de t'impressionner.

impressed adj impressionné(e)
▷ *I'm very impressed!* Je suis très
impressionné!

impression n impression f ▷ *I was
under the impression that ...* J'avais
l'impression que ...

impressive adj impressionnant(e)

improve vb ❶ (make better)
améliorer [**28**] ▷ *They have improved
the service.* Ils ont amélioré le
service. ❷ (get better) s'améliorer
[**28**] ▷ *My French has improved.* Mon
français s'est amélioré.

improvement n ❶ (of condition)
amélioration f ▷ *It's a great
improvement.* C'est une nette
amélioration. ❷ (of learner) progrès
m ▷ *There's been an improvement in
his French.* Il a fait des progrès en
français.

in prep, adv

> There are several ways of
> translating 'in'. Scan the
> examples to find one that is
> similar to what you want to
> say. For other expressions with
> 'in', see the verbs 'go', 'come',
> 'get', 'give' etc.

❶ dans ▷ *in the house* dans la
maison ▷ *in the sixties* dans les
années soixante ▷ *I'll see you in
three weeks.* Je te verrai dans trois
semaines. ❷ à ▷ *in the country* à la

campagne ▷ *in school* à l'école ▷ *in
London* à Londres ▷ *in spring* au
printemps ▷ *in a loud voice* à voix
haute ▷ *the boy in the blue shirt* le
garçon à la chemise bleue ▷ *It was
written in pencil.* C'était écrit au
crayon. ❸ en ▷ *in French* en français
▷ *in summer* en été ▷ *in town* en ville
▷ *in good condition* en bon état

> When 'in' refers to a country
> which is feminine, use **en**;
> when the country is masculine,
> use **au**; when the country is
> plural, use **aux**.

▷ *in France* en France ▷ *in Portugal*
au Portugal ▷ *in the United States*
aux États-Unis ❹ de ▷ *the best pupil
in the class* le meilleur élève de la
classe ▷ *at 6 in the morning* à six
heures du matin; **in the afternoon**
l'après-midi; **You look good in
that dress.** Tu es jolie avec cette
robe.; **in time** à temps ▷ *We arrived
in time for dinner.* Nous sommes
arrivés à temps pour le dîner.; **in
here** ici ▷ *It's hot in here.* Il fait chaud
ici.; **in the rain** sous la pluie; **one
person in ten** une personne sur
dix; **to be in** (at home, work) être
[**35**] là ▷ *He wasn't in.* Il n'était pas
là.; **to ask somebody in** inviter
[**28**] quelqu'un à entrer

inbox n boîte de réception f
include vb comprendre [**65**]
▷ *Service is not included.* Le service
n'est pas compris.

including prep compris ▷ *It will be
200 euros, including tax.* Ça coûtera
deux cents euros, toutes taxes

comprises.

income n revenu m

income tax n impôt sur le revenu m

inconsistent adj incohérent(e)

inconvenient adj That's very inconvenient for me. Ça ne m'arrange pas du tout.

incorrect adj incorrect(e)

increase n augmentation f ▷ an increase in road accidents une augmentation des accidents de la route

▶ vb augmenter [**28**]

incredible adj incroyable

indeed adv vraiment ▷ It's very hard indeed. C'est vraiment très difficile.; **Know what I mean? — Indeed I do.** Tu vois ce que je veux dire? — Oui, tout à fait.; **Thank you very much indeed!** Merci beaucoup!

independence n indépendance f

independent adj indépendant(e); **an independent school** une école privée

index n (in book) index m

index finger n index m

India n Inde f; **in India** en Inde; **to India** en Inde

Indian n (person) Indien m, Indienne f; **an American Indian** un Indien d'Amérique

▶ adj indien (f indienne)

indicate vb indiquer [**28**]

indicator n (on car) clignotant m

indigestion n indigestion f; **I've got indigestion.** J'ai une indigestion.

individual adj individuel (f individuelle)

indoor adj an indoor swimming pool une piscine couverte

indoors adv à l'intérieur ▷ They're indoors. Ils sont à l'intérieur.; **to go indoors** rentrer [**68**] ▷ We'd better go indoors. Nous ferions mieux de rentrer.

industrial adj industriel (f industrielle)

industrial estate n zone industrielle f

industry n industrie f ▷ the tourist industry l'industrie du tourisme

inevitable adj inévitable

inexperienced adj inexpérimenté(e)

infant school n He's just started at infant school. Il vient d'entrer au cours préparatoire.

   CP (cours préparatoire) is the equivalent of first-year infants, and **CE1 (cours élémentaire première année)** the equivalent of second-year infants.

infection n infection f ▷ an ear infection une infection de l'oreille; **a throat infection** une angine

infectious adj contagieux (f contagieuse) ▷ It's not infectious. Ce n'est pas contagieux.

infinitive n infinitif m

inflation n inflation f

inform vb informer [**28**]; **to inform somebody of something** informer [**28**] quelqu'un de quelque chose ▷ Nobody informed me of the new plan. Personne ne m'a informé de ce nouveau projet.

informal adj ❶ (person, party) décontracté(e) ▷ 'informal dress' 'tenue décontractée' ❷ (colloquial) familier (f familière) ▷ informal language le langage familier; **an informal visit** une visite non officielle

information n renseignements mpl ▷ important information les renseignements importants; **a piece of information** un renseignement; **Could you give me some information about trains to Paris?** Pourriez-vous me renseigner sur les trains pour Paris?

information office n bureau des renseignements m (pl bureaux des renseignements)

information technology n informatique f

infuriating adj exaspérant(e)

ingredient n ingrédient m

inherit vb hériter [28] de ▷ She inherited her father's house. Elle a hérité de la maison de son père.

initials npl initiales fpl ▷ Her initials are CDT. Ses initiales sont CDT.

injection n piqûre f

injure vb blesser [28]

injured adj blessé(e)

injury n blessure f

ink n encre f

in-laws npl beaux-parents mpl

innocent adj innocent(e)

insane adj fou (f folle)

inscription n inscription f

insect n insecte m

insect repellent n insectifuge m

inside n intérieur m

▶ adv, prep à l'intérieur ▷ inside the house à l'intérieur de la maison; **to go inside** rentrer [68]; **Come inside!** Rentrez!

insist vb insister [28] ▷ I didn't want to, but he insisted. Je ne voulais pas, mais il a insisté.; **to insist on doing something** insister [28] pour faire quelque chose ▷ She insisted on paying. Elle a insisté pour payer.; **He insisted he was innocent.** Il affirmait qu'il était innocent.

inspector n (police) inspecteur m ▷ Inspector Jill Brown l'inspecteur Jill Brown; **ticket inspector** (on buses) le contrôleur

instalment n ❶ (payment) versement m ▷ to pay in instalments payer en plusieurs versements ❷ (episode) épisode m

instance n for instance par exemple

instant adj immédiat(e) ▷ It was an instant success. Ça a été un succès immédiat.; **instant coffee** le café instantané

instantly adv tout de suite

instead adv instead of (1) (followed by noun) à la place de ▷ He went instead of Peter. Il y est allé à la place de Peter. (2) (followed by verb) au lieu de ▷ We played tennis instead of going swimming. Nous avons joué au tennis au lieu d'aller nager.; **The pool was closed, so we played tennis instead.** La piscine était fermée, alors nous avons joué au tennis.

instinct n instinct m
instruct vb to instruct somebody
to do something donner [**28**]
l'ordre à quelqu'un de faire quelque
chose ▷ She instructed us to wait
outside. Elle nous a donné l'ordre
d'attendre dehors.
instructions npl ❶ instructions fpl
▷ Follow the instructions carefully.
Suivez soigneusement les
instructions. ❷ (booklet) mode
d'emploi msg ▷ Where are the
instructions? Où est le mode
d'emploi?
instructor n moniteur m,
monitrice f ▷ a driving instructor un
moniteur d'auto-école
instrument n instrument m ▷ Do
you play an instrument? Est-ce que
tu joues d'un instrument?
insulin n insuline f
insult n insulte f
  ▶ vb insulter [**28**]
insurance n assurance f ▷ his car
insurance son assurance
automobile; **an insurance policy**
une police d'assurance
intelligent adj intelligent(e)
intend vb to intend to do
something avoir [**8**] l'intention de
faire quelque chose ▷ I intend to do
French at university. J'ai l'intention
d'étudier le français à l'université.
intensive adj intensif (f intensive)
intention n intention f
interest n intérêt m ▷ to show an
interest in something manifester de
l'intérêt pour quelque chose;
What interests do you have?

Quels sont tes centres d'intérêt?;
My main interest is music. Ce qui
m'intéresse le plus c'est la
musique.
  ▶ vb intéresser [**28**] ▷ It doesn't
interest me. Ça ne m'intéresse pas.;
to be interested in something
s'intéresser [**28**] à quelque chose
▷ I'm not interested in politics. Je ne
m'intéresse pas à la politique.
interesting adj intéressant(e)
interior n intérieur m
interior designer n architecte
d'intérieur mf
international adj international(e)
(mpl internationaux)
internet n Internet m ▷ on the
internet sur Internet
internet café n cybercafé m
internet user n internaute mf
interpreter n interprète mf
interrupt vb interrompre [**75**]
interruption n interruption f
interval n (in play, concert)
entracte m
interview n ❶ (on TV, radio)
interview f ❷ (for job) entretien m
  ▶ vb (on TV, radio) interviewer [**28**]
▷ I was interviewed on the radio. J'ai
été interviewé à la radio.
interviewer n (on TV, radio)
interviewer m
into prep ❶ dans ▷ He got into the
car. Il est monté dans la voiture.
❷ en ▷ I'm going into town. Je vais en
ville. ▷ Translate it into French.
Traduisez ça en français.
introduce vb présenter [**28**] ▷ He
introduced me to his parents. Il m'a

présenté à ses parents.
introduction n (in book)
introduction f
invade vb envahir [**38**]
invalid n malade mf
invent vb inventer [**28**]
invention n invention f
investigation n (police) enquête f
invisible adj invisible
invitation n invitation f
invite vb inviter [**28**] ▷ He's not
invited. Il n'est pas invité.; **to invite
somebody to a party** inviter [**28**]
quelqu'un à une fête
involve vb nécessiter [**28**] ▷ His job
involves a lot of travelling. Son travail
nécessite de nombreux
déplacements.; **to be involved in
something** (crime, drugs) être [**35**]
impliqué dans quelque chose; **to
be involved with somebody** (in
relationship) avoir [**8**] une relation
avec quelqu'un
iPad® n iPad® m
iPhone® n iPhone® m
iPod® n iPod® m
Iran n Iran m; **in Iran** en Iran
Iraq n Irak m; **in Iraq** en Irak
Iraqi n Irakien m, Irakienne f
▶ adj irakien (f irakienne) ▷ the Iraqi
government le gouvernement
irakien
Ireland n Irlande f; **in Ireland** en
Irlande; **to Ireland** en Irlande; **I'm
from Ireland.** Je suis irlandais.
Irish n (language) irlandais m; **the
Irish** (people) les Irlandais
▶ adj irlandais(e) ▷ Irish music la
musique irlandaise

Irishman n Irlandais m
Irishwoman n Irlandaise f
iron n ❶ (metal) fer m ❷ (for clothes)
fer à repasser m
▶ vb repasser [**28**]
ironing n repassage m ▷ to do the
ironing faire le repassage
ironing board n planche à
repasser f
irresponsible adj (person)
irresponsable ▷ That was
irresponsible of him. C'était
irresponsable de sa part.
irritating adj irritant(e)
is vb see be
Islam n Islam m
Islamic adj islamique ▷ Islamic law
la loi islamique; **Islamic
fundamentalists** les intégristes
musulmans
island n île f
isle n the Isle of Man l'île de Man f;
the Isle of Wight l'île de Wight f
isolated adj isolé(e)
Israel n Israël m; **in Israel** en Israël
Israeli adj israélien (f israélienne)
▶ n Israélien m, Israélienne f
issue n ❶ (matter) question f
▷ a controversial issue une question
controversée ❷ (of magazine)
numéro m
▶ vb (equipment, supplies) distribuer
[**28**]
it pron

> Remember to check if 'it'
> stands for a masculine or
> feminine noun.
❶ il ▷ Where's my book? — It's on
the table. Où est mon livre? — Il est

sur la table.; elle ▷ *When does the pool close? — It closes at 8.* La piscine ferme à quelle heure? — Elle ferme à vingt heures.

> Use **le** or **la** when 'it' is the object of the sentence. **le** and **la** change to **l'** before a vowel and most words beginning with 'h'.

❷ le ▷ *There's a croissant left. Do you want it?* Il reste un croissant. Tu le veux?; la ▷ *I don't want this apple. Take it.* Je ne veux pas de cette pomme. Prends-la.; l' ▷ *It's a good film. Did you see it?* C'est un bon film. L'as-tu vu? ▷ *He's got a new car. — Yes, I saw it.* Il a une nouvelle voiture. — Oui, je l'ai vue.; **It's raining.** Il pleut.; **It's 6 o'clock.** Il est six heures.; **It's Friday tomorrow.** Demain c'est vendredi.; **Who is it? — It's me.** Qui est-ce? — C'est moi.; **It's expensive.** C'est cher.

Italian n ❶ (person) Italien m, Italienne f ❷ (language) italien m ▶ adj italien (f italienne)

Italy n Italie f; **in Italy** en Italie; **to Italy** en Italie

itch vb **It itches.** Ça me démange.; **My head's itching.** J'ai des démangeaisons à la tête.

itchy adj **My arm is itchy.** J'ai des fourmis dans le bras.

it'd = it had; it would

item n (object) article m

it'll = it will

its adj

> Remember to check if 'its' refers to a masculine, feminine or plural noun.

son m ▷ *What's its name?* Quel est son nom?; sa f; ses pl

it's = it is; it has

itself pron se

> **se** changes to **s'** before a vowel and most words beginning with 'h'.

s' ▷ *The heating switches itself off.* Le chauffage s'arrête automatiquement.

I've = I have

jack n ❶ (for car) cric m ❷ (playing card) valet m

jacket n veste f; **jacket potatoes** les pommes de terre en robe des champs

jail n prison f; **to go to jail** aller [3] en prison
▶ vb emprisonner [28]

jam n confiture f ▷ strawberry jam la confiture de fraises; **a traffic jam** un embouteillage

jammed adj coincé(e) ▷ The window's jammed. La fenêtre est coincée.

janitor n concierge m ▷ He's a janitor. Il est concierge.

January n janvier m; **in January** en janvier

Japan n Japon m; **in Japan** au Japon; **from Japan** du Japon

Japanese n ❶ (person) Japonais m, Japonaise f; **the Japanese** les Japonais ❷ (language) japonais m
▶ adj japonais(e)

jar n bocal m (pl bocaux) ▷ an empty jar un bocal vide; **a jar of honey** un pot de miel

javelin n javelot m

jaw n mâchoire f

jazz n jazz m

jealous adj jaloux (f jalouse)

jeans npl jean msg

Jello® n (US) gelée f

jelly n gelée f

jellyfish n méduse f

jersey n (pullover) pull-over m

Jesus n Jésus m

jet n (plane) jet m

jetlag n **to be suffering from jetlag** être [35] sous le coup du décalage horaire

Jew n Juif m, Juive f

jewel n bijou m (pl bijoux)

jeweller (US **jeweler**) n bijoutier m, bijoutière f ▷ He's a jeweller. Il est bijoutier.

jeweller's shop (US **jeweler's shop**) n bijouterie f

jewellery (US **jewelry**) n bijoux mpl

Jewish adj juif (f juive)

jigsaw n puzzle m

job n ❶ emploi m ▷ He's lost his job. Il a perdu son emploi.; **I've got a Saturday job.** Je travaille le samedi. ❷ (chore, task) travail m (pl travaux) ▷ That was a difficult job. C'était un travail difficile.

jobless adj sans emploi

jockey n jockey m

jog vb faire [36] du jogging

jogging n jogging m; **to go jogging** faire [36] du jogging

join vb ❶ (become member of) s'inscrire [30] à ▷ I'm going to join the ski club. Je vais m'inscrire au club de ski. ❷ se joindre [42] à ▷ Do you mind if I join you? Puis-je me joindre à vous?

joiner n menuisier m ▷ He's a joiner. Il est menuisier.

joint n ❶ (in body) articulation f ❷ (of meat) rôti m ❸ (drugs) joint m

joke n plaisanterie f ▷ to tell a joke raconter une plaisanterie ▶ vb plaisanter [28] ▷ I'm only joking. Je plaisante.

Jordan n (country) Jordanie f; **in Jordan** en Jordanie

jotter n (pad) bloc-notes m (pl blocs-notes)

journalism n journalisme m

journalist n journaliste mf ▷ She's a journalist. Elle est journaliste.

journey n ❶ voyage m ▷ I don't like long journeys. Je n'aime pas les longs voyages.; **to go on a journey** faire [36] un voyage ❷ (to school, work) trajet m ▷ The journey to school takes about half an hour. Il y a une demi-heure de trajet pour aller à l'école.; **a bus journey** un trajet en autobus

joy n joie f

joystick n (for computer game) manette de jeu f

judge n juge m ▷ She's a judge. Elle est juge.
▶ vb juger [45]

judo n judo m ▷ My hobby is judo. Je fais du judo.

jug n pot m

juggler n jongleur m, jongleuse f

juice n jus m ▷ orange juice le jus d'orange

July n juillet m; **in July** en juillet

jumble sale n vente de charité f

jump vb sauter [28] ▷ to jump over something sauter par-dessus quelque chose ▷ to jump out of the window sauter par la fenêtre ▷ to jump off the roof sauter du toit

jumper n (pullover) pull-over m

junction n (of roads) carrefour m

June n juin m; **in June** en juin

jungle n jungle f

junior n **the juniors** (in school) les élèves des petites classes

junior school n école primaire f

junk n (old things) bric-à-brac m ▷ The attic's full of junk. Le grenier est rempli de bric-à-brac.; **to eat junk food** manger [45] n'importe comment; **a junk shop** un magasin de brocante

jury n jury m

just adv juste ▷ just after Christmas juste après Noël ▷ just in time juste à temps; **just here** ici; **I'm rather busy just now.** Je suis assez occupé en ce moment.; **I did it just now.** Je viens de le faire.; **He's just arrived.** Il vient d'arriver.; **I'm just coming!** J'arrive!; **It's just a suggestion.** Ce n'est qu'une suggestion.

justice n justice f

k

kangaroo n kangourou m
karaoke n karaoké m
karate n karaté m
kebab n ❶ (shish kebab) brochette f
❷ (doner kebab) doner kebab m
keen adj enthousiaste ▷ He doesn't
seem very keen. Il n'a pas l'air très
enthousiaste.; **She's a keen
student.** C'est une étudiante
assidue.; **to be keen on
something** aimer [**28**] quelque
chose ▷ I'm keen on maths. J'aime les
maths.; **to be keen on somebody**
(fancy them) être [**35**] très attiré par
quelqu'un ▷ He's keen on her. Il est
très attiré par elle.; **to be keen on
doing something** avoir [**8**] très
envie de faire quelque chose ▷ I'm
not very keen on going. Je n'ai pas très
envie d'y aller.

keep vb ❶ (retain) garder [**28**] ▷ You
can keep it. Tu peux le garder.
❷ (remain) rester [**71**] ▷ Keep still!
Reste tranquille!; **Keep quiet!**
Tais-toi!; **I keep forgetting my
keys.** J'oublie tout le temps mes
clés.
keep on vb to keep on doing
something (1) (continue) continuer
[**28**] à faire quelque chose ▷ He kept
on reading. Il a continué à lire.
(2) (repeatedly) ne pas arrêter [**28**]
de faire quelque chose ▷ The car
keeps on breaking down. La voiture
n'arrête pas de tomber en panne.
keep out vb 'keep out' 'défense
d'entrer'
keep up vb se maintenir [**83**] à la
hauteur de quelqu'un ▷ Matthew
walks so fast I can't keep up.
Matthew marche tellement vite
que je n'arrive pas à me maintenir à
sa hauteur.; **I can't keep up with
the rest of the class.** Je n'arrive
pas à suivre le reste de la classe.
keep-fit n gymnastique d'entretien
f; **I go to keep-fit classes.** Je vais à
des cours de gymnastique.
kept vb see keep
kettle n bouilloire f
key n clé f
keyboard n clavier m ▷ ... with Matt
Bellamy on keyboards ... avec Matt
Bellamy aux claviers
kick n coup de pied m
  ▶ vb to kick somebody donner [**28**]
un coup de pied à quelqu'un ▷ He
kicked me. Il m'a donné un coup de
pied. ▷ He kicked the ball hard. Il a

donné un bon coup de pied dans le ballon.

kick off *vb (in football)* donner [**28**] le coup d'envoi

kick-off *n* coup d'envoi *m* ▷ *The kick-off is at 10 o'clock.* Le coup d'envoi sera donné à dix heures.

kid *n (child)* gosse *mf*
▶ *vb* plaisanter [**28**] ▷ *I'm just kidding.* Je plaisante.

kidnap *vb* kidnapper [**28**]

kidney *n* ❶ *(human)* rein *m* ▷ *He's got kidney trouble.* Il a des problèmes de reins. ❷ *(to eat)* rognon *m* ▷ *I don't like kidneys.* Je n'aime pas les rognons.

kill *vb* tuer [**28**] ▷ *He was killed in a car accident.* Il a été tué dans un accident de voiture.; **Luckily, nobody was killed.** Il n'y a heureusement pas eu de victimes.; **Six people were killed in the accident.** L'accident a fait six morts.; **to kill oneself** se suicider [**28**] ▷ *He killed himself.* Il s'est suicidé.

killer *n* ❶ *(murderer)* meurtrier *m*, meurtrière *f* ▷ *The police are searching for the killer.* La police recherche le meurtrier. ❷ *(assassin)* tueur *m*, tueuse *f* ▷ *a hired killer* un tueur à gages; **Meningitis can be a killer.** La méningite peut être mortelle.

kilo *n* kilo *m* ▷ *10 euros a kilo* dix euros le kilo

kilometre *(US* **kilometer)** *n* kilomètre *m*

kilt *n* kilt *m*

kind *adj* gentil (*f* gentille); **to be kind to somebody** être [**35**] gentil avec quelqu'un; **Thank you for being so kind.** Merci pour votre gentillesse.
▶ *n* sorte *f* ▷ *It's a kind of sausage.* C'est une sorte de saucisse.

kindness *n* gentillesse *f*

king *n* roi *m*

kingdom *n* royaume *m*

kiosk *n (phone box)* cabine téléphonique *f*

kiss *n* baiser *m* ▷ *a passionate kiss* un baiser passionné
▶ *vb* ❶ embrasser [**28**] ▷ *He kissed her passionately.* Il l'a embrassée passionnément. ❷ s'embrasser [**28**] ▷ *They kissed.* Ils se sont embrassés.

kit *n* ❶ *(clothes for sport)* affaires *fpl* ▷ *I've forgotten my gym kit.* J'ai oublié mes affaires de gym. ❷ trousse *f* ▷ *a first aid kit* une trousse de secours; **a drum kit** une batterie; **a sewing kit** un nécessaire à couture

kitchen *n* cuisine *f* ▷ *a fitted kitchen* une cuisine aménagée; **the kitchen units** les éléments de cuisine; **a kitchen knife** un couteau de cuisine

kite *n* cerf-volant *m* (*pl* cerfs-volants)

kitten *n* chaton *m*

knee *n* genou *m* (*pl* genoux) ▷ *He was on his knees.* Il était à genoux.

kneel *vb* s'agenouiller [**28**]

kneel down *vb* s'agenouiller [**28**]

knew *vb see* **know**

a
b
c
d
e
f
g
h
i
j
k
l
m
n
o
p
q
r
s
t
u
v
w
x
y
z

knickers npl culotte fsg; **a pair of knickers** une culotte

knife n couteau m (pl couteaux); **a kitchen knife** un couteau de cuisine; **a sheath knife** un couteau à gaine; **a penknife** un canif

knit vb tricoter [**28**]

knitting n tricot m ▷ I like knitting. J'aime faire du tricot.

knives npl see **knife**

knob n (on door, radio, TV, radiator) bouton m

knock vb frapper [**28**] ▷ Someone's knocking at the door. Quelqu'un frappe à la porte.
▶ n coup m

knock down vb renverser [**28**] ▷ She was knocked down by a car. Elle a été renversée par une voiture.

knock out vb ❶ (defeat) éliminer [**28**] ▷ They were knocked out early in the tournament. Ils ont été éliminés au début du tournoi. ❷ (stun) assommer [**28**] ▷ They knocked out the security guard. Ils ont assommé le vigile.

knot n nœud m; **to tie a knot in something** faire [**36**] un nœud à quelque chose

know vb

> Use **savoir** for knowing facts, **connaître** for knowing people and places.

❶ savoir [**76**] ▷ It's a long way. — Yes, I know. C'est loin. — Oui, je sais. ▷ I don't know. Je ne sais pas. ▷ I don't know what to do. Je ne sais pas quoi faire. ▷ I don't know how to do it. Je

ne sais pas comment faire.
❷ connaître [**14**] ▷ I know her. Je la connais. ▷ I know Paris well. Je connais bien Paris.; **I don't know any German.** Je ne parle pas du tout allemand.; **to know that ...** savoir [**76**] que ... ▷ I know that you like chocolate. Je sais que tu aimes le chocolat. ▷ I didn't know that your dad was a police officer. Je ne savais pas que ton père était policier.; **to know about something (1)** (be aware of) être [**35**] au courant de quelque chose ▷ Do you know about the meeting this afternoon? Tu es au courant de la réunion de cet après-midi? **(2)** (be knowledgeable about) s'y connaître [**14**] en quelque chose ▷ He knows a lot about cars. Il s'y connaît en voitures. ▷ I don't know much about computers. Je ne m'y connais pas bien en informatique.; **to get to know somebody** apprendre [**65**] à connaître quelqu'un; **How should I know?** (I don't know!) Comment veux-tu que je le sache?; **You never know!** On ne sait jamais!

knowledge n connaissance f

known vb see **know**

Koran n Coran m

Korea n Corée f; **in Korea** en Corée

kosher adj kascher

lab n (= laboratory) labo m; **a lab technician** un laborantin

label n étiquette f

laboratory n laboratoire m

labour n **to be in labour** être [35] en train d'accoucher; **the labour market** le marché du travail

lace n ❶ (of shoe) lacet m ❷ dentelle f ▷ a lace collar un col en dentelle

lad n gars m

ladder n échelle f

lady n dame f; **a young lady** une jeune fille; **Ladies and gentlemen ...** Mesdames, Messieurs ...; **the ladies** les toilettes pour dames fpl

ladybird n coccinelle f

lager n bière blonde f

laid vb see **lay**

laid-back adj relaxe

lain vb see **lie**

lake n lac m; **Lake Geneva** le lac Léman

lamb n agneau m (pl agneaux); **a lamb chop** une côtelette d'agneau

lamp n lampe f

lamppost n réverbère m

lampshade n abat-jour m (pl abat-jour)

land n terre f; **a piece of land** un terrain

▶ vb (plane, passenger) atterrir [38]

landing n ❶ (of plane) atterrissage m ❷ (of staircase) palier m

landlady n propriétaire f

landlord n propriétaire m

landscape n paysage m

lane n ❶ (in country) chemin m ❷ (on motorway) voie f

language n langue f ▷ French isn't a difficult language. Le français n'est pas une langue difficile.; **to use bad language** dire [27] des grossièretés

language laboratory n laboratoire de langues m

lap n (sport) tour de piste m ▷ I ran ten laps. J'ai fait dix tours de piste en courant.; **on my lap** sur mes genoux

laptop n (computer) portable m

large adj ❶ grand(e) ▷ a large house une grande maison ❷ (person, animal) gros (f grosse) ▷ a large dog un gros chien

laser n laser m

last adj, adv ❶ dernier (f dernière) ▷ last Friday vendredi dernier ▷ last week la semaine dernière ▷ last *summer* l'été dernier ❷ en dernier ▷ *He arrived last.* Il est arrivé en dernier. ❸ pour la dernière fois ▷ *I've lost my bag. —When did you see it last?* J'ai perdu mon sac. — Quand est-ce que tu l'as vu pour la dernière fois? ▷ *When I last saw him, he was wearing a blue shirt.* La dernière fois que je l'ai vu, il portait une chemise bleue.; **the last time** la dernière fois ▷ *the last time I saw her* la dernière fois que je l'ai vue ▷ *That's the last time I take your advice!* C'est la dernière fois que je suis tes conseils!; **last night** **(1)** *(evening)* hier soir ▷ *I got home at midnight last night.* Je suis rentré à minuit hier soir. **(2)** *(sleeping hours)* la nuit dernière ▷ *I couldn't sleep last night.* J'ai eu du mal à dormir la nuit dernière.; **at last** enfin

▶ *vb* durer [**28**] ▷ *The concert lasts two hours.* Le concert dure deux heures.

lastly *adv* finalement ▷ *Lastly, what time do you arrive?* Finalement, à quelle heure arrives-tu?

late *adj, adv* ❶ en retard ▷ *Hurry up or you'll be late!* Dépêche-toi, sinon tu vas être en retard! ▷ *I'm often late for school.* J'arrive souvent en retard à l'école.; **to arrive late** arriver [**5**] en retard ▷ *She arrived late.* Elle est arrivée en retard. ❷ tard ▷ *I went to bed late.* Je me suis couché tard.; **in the late afternoon** en fin d'après-midi; **in late May** fin mai

lately *adv* ces derniers temps ▷ *I haven't seen him lately.* Je ne l'ai

pas vu ces derniers temps.

later *adv* plus tard ▷ *I'll do it later.* Je ferai ça plus tard.; **See you later!** À tout à l'heure!

latest *adj* dernier (*f* dernière) ▷ *their latest album* leur dernier album; **at the latest** au plus tard ▷ *by 10 o'clock at the latest* à dix heures au plus tard

Latin *n* latin *m* ▷ *I do Latin.* Je fais du latin.

Latin America *n* Amérique latine *f*; **in Latin America** en Amérique latine

Latin American *adj* latino-américain(e)

latter *n* second *m*, seconde *f*; **the former …, the latter …** le premier …, le second … ▷ *The former lives in the US, the latter in Australia.* Le premier habite aux États-Unis, le second en Australie.

laugh *n* rire *m*; **It was a good laugh.** *(it was fun)* On s'est bien amusés.

▶ *vb* rire [**74**]; **to laugh at something** se moquer [**28**] de quelque chose ▷ *They laughed at her.* Ils se sont moqués d'elle.

launch *vb* *(product, rocket, boat)* lancer [**12**] ▷ *They're going to launch a new model.* Ils vont lancer un nouveau modèle.

Launderette® *n* laverie *f*
Laundromat® *n* (US) laverie *f*
laundry *n* (clothes) linge *m*
lavatory *n* toilettes *fpl*
lavender *n* lavande *f*
law *n* ❶ loi *f* ▷ *The laws are very strict.*

Les lois sont très sévères.; **It's against the law.** C'est illégal. ❷ (subject) droit m ▷ My sister's studying law. Ma sœur fait des études de droit.

lawn n pelouse f

lawnmower n tondeuse à gazon f

lawyer n avocat m, avocate f ▷ My mother's a lawyer. Ma mère est avocate.

lay vb

'lay' is also a form of the verb 'lie'.

mettre [47] ▷ She laid the baby in her cot. Elle a mis le bébé dans son lit.; **to lay the table** mettre [47] la table; **to lay something on (1)** (provide) organiser [28] quelque chose ▷ They laid on extra buses. Ils ont organisé un service de bus supplémentaire. **(2)** (prepare) préparer [28] quelque chose ▷ They laid on a special meal. Ils ont préparé un repas soigné.

lay off vb licencier [19]

lay-by n aire de stationnement f

layer n couche f ▷ the ozone layer la couche d'ozone

layout n ❶ (of newspaper article) mise en page f ❷ (of house, buildings) disposition f ▷ No one likes the new office layout. Personne n'aime la nouvelle disposition des bureaux.

lazy adj paresseux (f paresseuse)

lead n

This word has two pronunciations. Make sure you choose the right translation.

❶ (cable) fil m ❷ (for dog) laisse f; **to be in the lead** être [35] en tête ▷ Our team is in the lead. Notre équipe est en tête. ❸ (metal) plomb m

▶ vb mener [43] ▷ the street that leads to the station la rue qui mène à la gare; **to lead the way** montrer [28] le chemin; **to lead somebody away** emmener [43] quelqu'un ▷ The police led the man away. La police a emmené l'homme.

leader n ❶ (of expedition, gang) chef m ❷ (of political party) dirigeant m, dirigeante f

lead-free adj lead-free petrol de l'essence sans plomb

lead singer n chanteur principal m, chanteuse principale f

leaf n feuille f

leaflet n brochure f

league n championnat m ▷ They are at the top of the league. Ils sont en tête du championnat.; **the Premier League** la première division

leak n fuite f ▷ a gas leak une fuite de gaz

▶ vb (pipe, water, gas) fuir [39]

lean vb se pencher [28]; **to be leaning against something** être [35] appuyé contre quelque chose ▷ The ladder was leaning against the wall. L'échelle était appuyée contre le mur.; **to lean something against a wall** appuyer [53] quelque chose contre un mur ▷ He leant his bike against the wall. Il a appuyé son vélo contre le mur.

lean forward vb se pencher [**28**] en avant

lean on vb to lean on something s'appuyer [**53**] contre quelque chose ▷ He leant on the wall. Il s'est appuyé contre le mur.

lean out vb se pencher [**28**] au dehors; **She leant out of the window.** Elle s'est penchée par la fenêtre.

lean over vb se pencher [**28**] ▷ Don't lean over too far. Ne te penche pas trop loin.

leap vb sauter [**28**] ▷ They leapt over the stream. Ils ont sauté pour traverser la rivière.; **He leapt out of his chair when his team scored.** Il s'est levé d'un bond lorsque son équipe a marqué.

leap year n année bissextile f

learn vb apprendre [**65**] ▷ I'm learning to ski. J'apprends à skier.

learner n She's a quick learner. Elle apprend vite.; **French learners** (people learning French) ceux qui apprennent le français

learner driver n conducteur débutant m, conductrice débutante f

learnt vb see **learn**

least adv, adj, pron the least (1) (followed by noun) le moins de ▷ It takes the least time. C'est ce qui prend le moins de temps. (2) (after a verb) le moins ▷ Maths is the subject I like the least. Les maths sont la matière que j'aime le moins.

> When 'least' is followed by an adjective, the translation depends on whether the noun referred to is masculine, feminine or plural.

the least ... (1) le moins ... ▷ the least expensive hotel l'hôtel le moins cher **(2)** la moins ... ▷ the least expensive seat la place la moins chère **(3)** les moins ... ▷ the least expensive hotels les hôtels les moins chers; **It's the least I can do.** C'est le moins que je puisse faire.; **at least (1)** au moins ▷ It'll cost at least £200. Ça va coûter au moins deux cents livres. **(2)** du moins ▷ ... but at least nobody was hurt. ... mais du moins personne n'a été blessé.

leather n cuir m ▷ a black leather jacket un blouson en cuir noir

leave n ❶ (from job) congé m ❷ (from army) permission f ▷ My brother is on leave for a week. Mon frère est en permission pendant une semaine.

▶ vb ❶ (deliberately) laisser [**28**] ▷ Don't leave your camera in the car. Ne laisse pas ton appareil photo dans la voiture. ❷ (by mistake) oublier [**19**] ▷ I've left my book at home. J'ai oublié mon livre à la maison. ▷ Make sure you haven't left anything behind. Vérifiez bien que vous n'avez rien oublié. ❸ (go) partir [**57**] ▷ The bus leaves at 8. Le car part à huit heures. ▷ She's just left. Elle vient de partir. ❹ (go away from) quitter [**28**] ▷ We leave London at six o'clock. Nous quittons Londres à six heures. ▷ *My sister left home last year.* Ma sœur a quitté la maison l'an dernier.; **to leave somebody alone** laisser [**28**] quelqu'un tranquille ▷ *Leave me alone!* Laisse-moi tranquille!

leave out *vb* mettre [**47**] à l'écart ▷ *As the new girl, I felt really left out.* En tant que nouvelle, je me suis vraiment sentie à l'écart.

leaves *npl see* **leaf**

Lebanon *n* Liban *m*; **in Lebanon** au Liban

lecture *n* ❶ *(public)* conférence *f* ❷ *(at university)* cours magistral *m* *(pl* cours magistraux)

> Be careful not to translate **lecture** by the French word **lecture**.

▶ *vb* ❶ enseigner [**28**] ▷ *She lectures at the technical college.* Elle enseigne au collège technique. ❷ faire [**36**] la morale ▷ *He's always lecturing us.* Il n'arrête pas de nous faire la morale.

lecturer *n* professeur d'université *m* ▷ *She's a lecturer.* Elle est professeur d'université.

led *vb see* **lead**

leek *n* poireau *m* *(pl* poireaux)

left *vb see* **leave**

▶ *adj, adv* ❶ *(not right)* gauche ▷ *my left hand* ma main gauche ❷ à gauche ▷ *Turn left at the traffic lights.* Tournez à gauche aux prochains feux.; **I haven't got any money left.** Il ne me reste plus d'argent.

▶ *n* gauche *f*; **on the left** à gauche

▷ *Remember to drive on the left.* N'oubliez pas de conduire à gauche.

left-hand *adj* **the left-hand side** la gauche ▷ *It's on the left-hand side.* C'est à gauche.

left-handed *adj* gaucher *(f* gauchère)

left-luggage office *n* consigne *f*

leg *n* jambe *f* ▷ *She's broken her leg.* Elle s'est cassé la jambe.; **a chicken leg** une cuisse de poulet; **a leg of lamb** un gigot d'agneau

legal *adj* légal(e) *(mpl* légaux)

leggings *npl* leggings *mpl*

leisure *n* loisirs *mpl* ▷ *What do you do in your leisure time?* Qu'est-ce que tu fais pendant tes loisirs?

leisure centre *n* centre de loisirs *m*

lemon *n* citron *m*

lemonade *n* limonade *f*

lend *vb* prêter [**28**] ▷ *I can lend you some money.* Je peux te prêter de l'argent.

length *n* longueur *f*; **It's about a metre in length.** Ça fait environ un mètre de long.

lens *n* ❶ *(contact lens)* lentille *f* ❷ *(of spectacles)* verre *m* ❸ *(of camera)* objectif *m*

Lent *n* carême *m*

lent *vb see* **lend**

lentil *n* lentille *f*

Leo *n* Lion *m* ▷ *I'm Leo.* Je suis Lion.

leotard *n* justaucorps *m*

lesbian *n* lesbienne *f*

less *pron, adv, adj* ❶ moins ▷ *He's less intelligent than her.* Il est moins intelligent qu'elle. ❷ moins de ▷ *I've*

a b c d e f g h i j k l m n o p q r s t u v w x y z

got less time for hobbies now. J'ai moins de temps pour les loisirs maintenant.; **less than (1)** (with amounts) moins de ▷ It's less than a kilometre from here. C'est à moins d'un kilomètre d'ici. ▷ less than half moins de la moitié **(2)** (in comparisons) moins que ▷ He spent less than me. Il a dépensé moins que moi.

lesson n ❶ leçon f ▷ a French lesson une leçon de français ❷ (class) cours m ▷ The lessons last forty minutes each. Chaque cours dure quarante minutes.

let vb ❶ (allow) laisser [**28**]; **to let somebody do something** laisser [**28**] quelqu'un faire quelque chose ▷ Let me have a look. Laisse-moi voir. ▷ My parents won't let me stay out that late. Mes parents ne me laissent pas sortir aussi tard.; **to let somebody know** faire [**36**] savoir à quelqu'un ▷ I'll let you know as soon as possible. Je vous le ferai savoir dès que possible.; **to let somebody go** lâcher [**28**] quelqu'un ▷ Let me go! Lâche-moi!

To make suggestions using 'let's', you can ask questions beginning with **si on**.

▷ Let's go to the cinema! Si on allait au cinéma? **Let's go!** Allons-y! ❷ (hire out) louer [**28**]; **'to let'** 'à louer'

let down vb décevoir [**67**] ▷ I won't let you down. Je ne vous décevrai pas.

let in vb laisser [**28**] entrer ▷ They wouldn't let me in because I was under 18. Ils ne m'ont pas laissé entrer parce que j'avais moins de dix-huit ans.

letter n lettre f

letterbox n boîte à lettres f

lettuce n salade f

leukaemia n leucémie f

level adj plan(e) ▷ A snooker table must be perfectly level. Un billard doit être parfaitement plan.

▶ n niveau m (pl niveaux) ▷ The level of the river is rising. Le niveau de la rivière monte.; **A levels** le baccalauréat

The French **baccalauréat** (or **bac** for short) is taken at the age of 17 or 18. Students have to sit one of a variety of set subject combinations, rather than being able to choose any combination of subjects they want. If you pass you have the right to a place at university.

level crossing n passage à niveau m

lever n levier m

liar n menteur m, menteuse f

liberal adj (opinions) libéral(e) (mpl libéraux); **the Liberal Democrats** le parti libéral-démocrate

Libra n Balance f ▷ I'm Libra. Je suis Balance.

librarian n bibliothécaire mf ▷ She's a librarian. Elle est bibliothécaire.

library n bibliothèque f

Be careful not to translate **library** by **librairie**.

licence (US **license**) n permis m; **a**

driving licence un permis de conduire

lick vb lécher [**34**]

lid n couvercle m

lie vb (not tell the truth) mentir [**77**] ▷ I know she's lying. Je sais qu'elle ment.; **to lie down** s'allonger [**45**]; **to be lying down** être [**35**] allongé ▷ He was lying down on the sofa. Il était allongé sur le canapé.; **to lie on the beach** être [**35**] allongé sur la plage
▶ n mensonge m; **to tell a lie** mentir [**77**]; **That's a lie!** Ce n'est pas vrai!

lie-in n **to have a lie-in** faire [**36**] la grasse matinée ▷ I have a lie-in on Sundays. Je fais la grasse matinée le dimanche.

lieutenant n lieutenant m

life n vie f

lifebelt n bouée de sauvetage f

lifeboat n canot de sauvetage m

lifeguard n maître nageur m

life jacket n gilet de sauvetage m

lifestyle n style de vie m

lift vb soulever [**43**] ▷ It's too heavy, I can't lift it. C'est trop lourd, je ne peux pas le soulever.
▶ n ascenseur m ▷ The lift isn't working. L'ascenseur est en panne.; **He gave me a lift to the cinema.** Il m'a emmené au cinéma en voiture.; **Would you like a lift?** Est-ce que je peux vous déposer quelque part?

light adj ❶ (not heavy) léger (f légère) ▷ a light jacket une veste légère ▷ a light meal un repas léger ❷ (colour) clair(e) ▷ a light blue sweater un pull bleu clair
▶ n ❶ lumière f ▷ to switch on the light allumer la lumière ❷ lampe f ▷ There's a light by my bed. Il y a une lampe près de mon lit.; **the traffic lights** les feux mpl; **Have you got a light?** (for cigarette) Avez-vous du feu?
▶ vb (candle, cigarette, fire) allumer [**28**]

light bulb n ampoule f

lighter n (for cigarettes) briquet m

lighthouse n phare m

lightning n éclairs mpl; **a flash of lightning** un éclair

like vb ❶ aimer [**28**] ▷ I don't like mustard. Je n'aime pas la moutarde. ▷ I like riding. J'aime monter à cheval.

> Note that **aimer** also means to love, so make sure you use **aimer bien** for just liking somebody.

❷ aimer [**28**] bien ▷ I like Paul, but I don't want to go out with him. J'aime bien Paul, mais je ne veux pas sortir avec lui.; **I'd like ...** Je voudrais ... ▷ I'd like an orange juice, please. Je voudrais un jus d'orange, s'il vous plaît. ▷ Would you like some coffee? Voulez-vous du café?; **I'd like to ...** J'aimerais ... ▷ I'd like to wash my hands. J'aimerais me laver les mains.; **Would you like to go for a walk?** Tu veux aller faire une promenade?; **... if you like** ... si tu veux
▶ prep comme ▷ It's fine like that.

a b c d e f g h i j k l m n o p q r s t u v w x y z

C'est bien comme ça. ▷ *Do it like this.* Fais-le comme ça. ▷ *a city like Paris* une ville comme Paris; **What's the weather like?** Quel temps fait-il?; **to look like somebody** ressembler [28] à quelqu'un ▷ *You look like my brother.* Tu ressembles à mon frère.

likely *adj* probable ▷ *That's not very likely.* C'est peu probable.; **She's likely to come.** Elle viendra probablement.; **She's not likely to come.** Elle ne viendra probablement pas.

lily of the valley *n* muguet *m*

lime *n* (*fruit*) citron vert *m*

limit *n* limite *f* ▷ *The speed limit is 70 mph.* La vitesse est limitée à cent dix kilomètres à l'heure.

limp *vb* boiter [28]

line *n* ❶ ligne *f* ▷ *a straight line* une ligne droite ❷ (*to divide, cancel*) trait *m* ▷ *Draw a line under each answer.* Tirez un trait après chaque réponse. ❸ (*railway track*) voie *f*; **Hold the line, please.** Ne quittez pas.; **It's a very bad line.** La ligne est très mauvaise.

linen *n* lin *m* ▷ *a linen jacket* une veste en lin

lining *n* (*of jacket, skirt etc*) doublure *f*

link *n* ❶ rapport *m* ▷ *the link between smoking and cancer* le rapport entre le tabagisme et le cancer ❷ (*computing*) lien *m* ▶ *vb* relier [19]

lion *n* lion *m*

lip *n* lèvre *f*

lip-read *vb* lire [44] sur les lèvres

lipstick *n* rouge à lèvres *m*

Word for word, this means 'red for lips'.

liquid *n* liquide *m*

liquidizer *n* mixer *m*

list *n* liste *f* ▶ *vb* faire [36] une liste de ▷ *List your hobbies!* Fais une liste de tes hobbies!

listen *vb* écouter [28] ▷ *Listen to me!* Écoutez-moi!

lit *vb see* **light**

liter *n* (*US*) litre *m*

literature *n* littérature *f* ▷ *I'm studying English Literature.* J'étudie la littérature anglaise.

litre *n* litre *m*

litter *n* ordures *fpl*

litter bin *n* poubelle *f*

little *adj* petit(e) ▷ *a little girl* une petite fille; **a little** un peu ▷ *How much would you like? — Just a little.* Combien en voulez-vous? — Juste un peu.; **very little** très peu ▷ *We've got very little time.* Nous avons très peu de temps.; **little by little** petit à petit

live *adj* ❶ (*animal*) vivant(e) ❷ (*broadcast*) en direct; **There's live music on Fridays.** Il y a des musiciens qui jouent le vendredi. ▶ *vb* ❶ vivre [91] ▷ *I live with my grandmother.* Je vis avec ma grand-mère. ❷ (*reside*) habiter [28] ▷ *Where do you live?* Où est-ce que tu habites? ▷ *I live in Edinburgh.* J'habite à Édimbourg.

live on *vb* to live on something

vivre [**91**] de quelque chose
▷ *He lives on benefit.* Il vit de ses
indemnités.

live together *vb* ❶ *(as flatmates)*
partager [**45**] un appartement
▷ *She's living with two Greek students.*
Elle partage un appartement avec
deux étudiants grecs. ❷ vivre [**91**]
ensemble ▷ *My parents aren't living
together any more.* Mes parents ne
vivent plus ensemble.; **They're
not married, they're living
together.** Ils ne sont pas mariés, ils
vivent en concubinage.

lively *adj* animé(e) ▷ *It was a lively
party.* C'était une soirée animée.;
She's got a lively personality. Elle
est pleine de vitalité.

liver *n* foie *m*

lives *npl see* **life**

livestream *n* diffusion *f* en direct
sur Internet
▶ *vb* diffuser en direct sur Internet

living *n* to make a living gagner
[**28**] sa vie; **What does she do for
a living?** Qu'est-ce qu'elle fait dans
la vie?

living room *n* salle de séjour *f*

lizard *n* lézard *m*

load *n* loads of un tas de ▷ *loads of
people* un tas de gens; **You're
talking a load of rubbish!** Tu ne dis
que des bêtises!
▶ *vb* charger [**45**] ▷ *a trolley loaded with
luggage* un chariot chargé de bagages

loaf *n* pain *m*; **a loaf of bread** un pain

loan *n* prêt *m*
▶ *vb* prêter [**28**]

loaves *npl see* **loaf**

lobster *n* homard *m*

local *adj* local(e) (*mpl* locaux) ▷ *the
local paper* le journal local; **a local
call** une communication urbaine

location *n* endroit *m*; ▷ *a hotel set in
a beautiful location* un hôtel situé
dans un endroit magnifique

> Be careful not to translate
> **location** by the French word
> **location**.

loch *n* loch *m*

lock *n* serrure *f* ▷ *The lock is broken.*
La serrure est cassée.
▶ *vb* fermer [**28**] à clé ▷ *Make sure
you lock your door.* N'oubliez pas de
fermer votre porte à clé.

lock out *vb* **The door slammed
and I was locked out.** La porte a
claqué et je me suis retrouvé à la
porte.

locker *n* casier *m*; **the locker room**
le vestiaire; **the left-luggage
lockers** la consigne automatique *sg*

lodger *n* locataire *mf*

loft *n* grenier *m*

log *n* (*of wood*) bûche *f*

log in *vb* se connecter [**28**]

log off *vb* se déconnecter [**28**]

log on *vb* se connecter [**28**]

log out *vb* se déconnecter [**28**]

logical *adj* logique

lollipop *n* sucette *f*

London *n* Londres; **in London** à
Londres; **to London** à Londres; **I'm
from London.** Je suis de Londres.

Londoner *n* Londonien *m*,
Londonienne *f*

loneliness *n* solitude *f*

lonely *adj* seul(e); **to feel lonely** se

a
b
c
d
e
f
g
h
i
j
k
l
m
n
o
p
q
r
s
t
u
v
w
x
y
z

sentir [**77**] seul ▷ *She feels a bit lonely.* Elle se sent un peu seule.

long *adj, adv* long (*f* longue) ▷ *She's got long hair.* Elle a les cheveux longs.; **The room is 6 metres long.** La pièce fait six mètres de long.; **how long?** (*time*) combien de temps? ▷ *How long did you stay there?* Combien de temps êtes-vous resté là-bas?; **I've been waiting a long time.** J'attends depuis longtemps.; **It takes a long time.** Ça prend du temps.; **as long as** si ▷ *I'll come as long as it's not too expensive.* Je viendrai si ce n'est pas trop cher.

▶ *vb* **to long to do something** attendre [**7**] avec impatience de faire quelque chose ▷ *I'm longing to see my boyfriend again.* J'attends avec impatience de revoir mon copain.

longer *adv* **They're no longer going out together.** Ils ne sortent plus ensemble.; **I can't stand it any longer.** Je ne peux plus le supporter.

long jump *n* saut en longueur *m*

loo *n* toilettes *fpl* ▷ *Where's the loo?* Où sont les toilettes?

look *n* **to have a look** regarder [**28**] ▷ *Have a look at this!* Regardez ceci!; **I don't like the look of it.** Ça ne me dit rien.

▶ *vb* ❶ regarder [**28**] ▷ *Look!* Regardez!; **to look at something** regarder [**28**] quelque chose ▷ *Look at the picture.* Regardez cette image. ❷ (*seem*) avoir [**8**] l'air ▷ *She*

looks surprised. Elle a l'air surprise. ▷ *That cake looks nice.* Ce gâteau a l'air bon. ▷ *It looks fine.* Ça a l'air bien.; **to look like somebody** ressembler [**28**] à quelqu'un ▷ *He looks like his brother.* Il ressemble à son frère.; **What does she look like?** Comment est-elle physiquement?; **to look forward to something** attendre [**7**] quelque chose avec impatience ▷ *I'm looking forward to the holidays.* J'attends les vacances avec impatience.; **Looking forward to hearing from you …** J'espère avoir bientôt de tes nouvelles …; **Look out!** Attention!

look after *vb* s'occuper [**28**] de ▷ *I look after my little sister.* Je m'occupe de ma petite sœur.

look for *vb* chercher [**28**] ▷ *I'm looking for my passport.* Je cherche mon passeport.

look round *vb* ❶ (*look behind*) se retourner [**72**] ▷ *I shouted and he looked round.* J'ai crié et il s'est retourné. ❷ (*have a look*) jeter [**41**] un coup d'œil ▷ *I'm just looking round.* Je jette simplement un coup d'œil.; **to look round a museum** visiter [**28**] un musée; **I like looking round the shops.** J'aime faire les boutiques.

look up *vb* (*word, name*) chercher [**28**] ▷ *Look the word up in the dictionary.* Cherchez le mot dans le dictionnaire.

loose *adj* (*clothes*) ample; **loose change** la petite monnaie

lord n (feudal) seigneur m; **the House of Lords** la Chambre des lords; **good Lord!** mon Dieu!

lorry n camion m

lorry driver n routier m ▷ He's a lorry driver. Il est routier.

lose vb perdre [**61**] ▷ I've lost my purse. J'ai perdu mon porte-monnaie.; **to get lost** se perdre [**61**] ▷ I was afraid of getting lost. J'avais peur de me perdre.

loser n ❶ perdant m, perdante f; **to be a bad loser** être [**35**] mauvais perdant ❷ (pathetic person) loser m ▷ He's such a loser! C'est un vrai loser!

loss n perte f

lost vb see **lose**
▶ adj perdu(e)

lost-and-found n (US) objets trouvés mpl

lost property office n objets trouvés mpl

Word for word, this means 'things that have been found'.

lot n a lot beaucoup; **a lot of** beaucoup de ▷ We saw a lot of interesting things. Nous avons vu beaucoup de choses intéressantes.; **lots of** un tas de ▷ She's got lots of money. Elle a un tas d'argent. ▷ He's got lots of friends. Il a un tas d'amis.; **What did you do at the weekend? — Not a lot.** Qu'as-tu fait ce week-end? — Pas grand-chose.; **Do you like football? — Not a lot.** Tu aimes le football? — Pas tellement.; **That's the lot.** C'est tout.

lottery n loterie f ▷ to win the lottery gagner à la loterie

loud adj fort(e) ▷ The television is too loud. La télévision est trop forte.

loudly adv fort

loudspeaker n haut-parleur m

lounge n salon m

love n amour m; **to be in love** être [**35**] amoureux ▷ She's in love with Paul. Elle est amoureuse de Paul.; **to make love** faire [**36**] l'amour; **Give Delphine my love.** Embrasse Delphine pour moi.; **Love, Rosemary.** Amitiés, Rosemary.
▶ vb ❶ (be in love with) aimer [**28**] ▷ I love you. Je t'aime. ❷ (like a lot) aimer [**28**] beaucoup ▷ Everybody loves her. Tout le monde l'aime beaucoup. ▷ I'd love to come. J'aimerais beaucoup venir. ❸ (things) adorer [**28**] ▷ I love chocolate. J'adore le chocolat.

lovely adj charmant(e) ▷ What a lovely surprise! Quelle charmante surprise! ▷ She's a lovely person. Elle est charmante.; **It's a lovely day.** Il fait très beau aujourd'hui.; **Is your meal OK? — Yes, it's lovely.** Est-ce que c'est bon? — Oui, c'est délicieux.; **They've got a lovely house.** Ils ont une très belle maison.; **Have a lovely time!** Amusez-vous bien!

lover n ❶ (in relationship) amant m, maîtresse f ❷ (of hobby, wine) amateur m ▷ an art lover un amateur d'art

low adj, adv (price, level) bas (f basse) ▷ That plane is flying very low. Cet avion vole très bas.; **the low season** la basse saison ▷ *in the low season* en basse saison

lower sixth n première f ▷ *He's in the lower sixth*. Il est en première.

loyalty n fidélité f

loyalty card n carte de fidélité f

luck n chance f ▷ *She hasn't had much luck*. Elle n'a pas eu beaucoup de chance.; **Good luck!** Bonne chance!; **Bad luck!** Pas de chance!

luckily adv heureusement

lucky adj **to be lucky (1)** (be fortunate) avoir [8] de la chance ▷ *He's lucky, he's got a job*. Il a de la chance, il a un emploi. **(2)** (bring luck) porter [28] bonheur ▷ *Black cats are lucky in Britain*. Les chats noirs portent bonheur en Grande-Bretagne.; **a lucky horseshoe** un fer à cheval porte-bonheur

luggage n bagages mpl

lump n ❶ morceau m (pl morceaux) ▷ *a lump of butter* un morceau de beurre ❷ (swelling) bosse f ▷ *He's got a lump on his forehead*. Il a une bosse sur le front.

lunch n déjeuner m; **to have lunch** déjeuner [28] ▷ *We have lunch at 12.30*. Nous déjeunons à midi et demi.

lung n poumon m ▷ *lung cancer* le cancer du poumon

Luxembourg n ❶ (country) Luxembourg m; **in Luxembourg** au Luxembourg; **to Luxembourg** au Luxembourg ❷ (city)

Luxembourg; **in Luxembourg** à Luxembourg

luxurious adj luxueux (fluxueuse)

luxury n luxe m ▷ *It was luxury!* C'était le luxe!; **a luxury hotel** un hôtel de luxe

lying vb see **lie**

lyrics npl (of song) paroles fpl

m

macaroni n macaronis mpl
machine n machine f
machine gun n mitrailleuse f
machinery n machines fpl
mad adj ❶ (insane) fou (f folle)
▷ You're mad! Tu es fou! ❷ (angry)
furieux (f furieuse) ▷ She'll be mad
when she finds out. Elle sera furieuse
quand elle va s'en apercevoir.; **to
be mad about (1)** (sport, activity)
être [**35**] enragé de ▷ He's mad about
football. Il est enragé de foot.
(2) (person, animal) adorer [**28**]
▷ She's mad about horses. Elle adore
les chevaux.
madam n madame f ▷ Would you
like to order, Madam? Désirez-vous
commander, Madame?
made vb see **make**
madness n folie f ▷ It's absolute

madness. C'est de la pure folie.
magazine n magazine m
maggot n asticot m
magic adj ❶ (magical) magique
▷ a magic wand une baguette
magique ❷ (brilliant) super ▷ It was
magic! C'était super!
▶ n magie f; **a magic trick** un tour
de magie; **My hobby is magic.** Je
fais des tours de magie.
magician n (conjurer)
prestidigitateur m
magnet n aimant m
magnifying glass n loupe f
maid n (servant) domestique f
maiden name n nom de jeune
fille m
mail n ❶ courrier m ▷ Here's your
mail. Voici ton courrier. ❷ (email)
courrier électronique m ▷ Can I
check my mail on your PC? Je peux
consulter mon courrier électronique
sur ton PC?; **by mail** par la poste
▶ vb **to mail something** (email)
envoyer [**33**] quelque chose par
courrier électronique
mailbox n (US) boîte à lettres f
mailman n (US) facteur m
main adj principal(e) (mpl
principaux) ▷ the main problem le
principal problème; **the main
thing is to ...** l'essentiel est de ...
mainly adv principalement
main road n grande route f ▷ I don't
like cycling on main roads. Je n'aime
pas faire du vélo sur les grandes
routes.
majesty n majesté f; **Your Majesty**
Votre Majesté

major adj majeur(e) ▷ *a major problem* un problème majeur; **in C major** en do majeur

Majorca n Majorque f ▷ *We went to Majorca in August.* Nous sommes allés à Majorque en août.

majority n majorité f

make n marque f ▷ *What make is that car?* De quelle marque est cette voiture?
▶ vb ❶ faire [36] ▷ *I'm going to make a cake.* Je vais faire un gâteau.
▷ *I make my bed every morning.* Je fais mon lit tous les matins.
❷ (manufacture) fabriquer [28]
▷ *made in France* fabriqué en France
❸ (earn) gagner [28] ▷ *He makes a lot of money.* Il gagne beaucoup d'argent.; **to make somebody do something** obliger [45] quelqu'un à faire quelque chose ▷ *My mother makes me do my homework.* Ma mère m'oblige à faire mes devoirs.; **to make lunch** préparer [28] le repas ▷ *She's making lunch.* Elle prépare le repas.; **to make a phone call** donner [28] un coup de téléphone ▷ *I'd like to make a phone call.* J'aimerais donner un coup de téléphone.; **to make fun of somebody** se moquer [28] de quelqu'un ▷ *They made fun of him.* Ils se sont moqués de lui.; **What time do you make it?** Quelle heure avez-vous?

make out vb ❶ (read) déchiffrer [28] ❷ (understand) comprendre [65] ❸ (claim, pretend) prétendre [88]

make up vb ❶ (invent) inventer [28] ▷ *He made up the whole story.* Il a inventé cette histoire de toutes pièces. ❷ (after argument) se réconcilier [19] ▷ *They had a quarrel, but soon made up.* Ils se sont disputés, mais se sont vite réconciliés.; **to make oneself up** se maquiller [28] ▷ *She spends hours making herself up.* Elle passe des heures à se maquiller.

make-up n maquillage m

Malaysia n Malaisie f; **in Malaysia** en Malaisie

male adj ❶ (animals, plants) mâle ▷ *a male kitten* un chaton mâle ❷ (person, on official forms) masculin(e) ▷ *Sex: male.* Sexe : masculin.; **Most football players are male.** La plupart des joueurs de football sont des hommes.; **a male chauvinist** un macho; **a male nurse** un infirmier

malicious adj malveillant(e) ▷ *a malicious rumour* une rumeur malveillante

> Be careful not to translate **malicious** by **malicieux**.

mall n centre commercial m

Malta n Malte; **in Malta** à Malte; **to Malta** à Malte

man n homme m ▷ *an old man* un vieil homme

manage vb ❶ (be in charge of) diriger [45] ▷ *She manages a big store.* Elle dirige un grand magasin. ❷ (get by) se débrouiller [28] ▷ *It's okay, I can manage.* Ça va, je me débrouille.; **Can you manage**

okay? Tu y arrives?; **to manage to do something** réussir [**38**] à faire quelque chose ▷ *Luckily I managed to pass the exam.* J'ai heureusement réussi à avoir mon examen.; **I can't manage all that.** *(food)* C'est trop pour moi.

management n ❶ *(organization)* gestion f ▷ *He's responsible for the management of the company.* Il est responsable de la gestion de la société. ❷ *(people in charge)* direction f; **'under new management'** 'changement de direction'

manager n ❶ *(of company)* directeur m, directrice f ❷ *(of shop, restaurant)* gérant m, gérante f ❸ *(of team, performer)* manager m

manageress n gérante f

mandarin n *(fruit)* mandarine f

mango n mangue f

mania n manie f

maniac n fou m, folle f ▷ *He drives like a maniac.* Il conduit comme un fou.; **a religious maniac** un fanatique religieux

mankind n humanité f

manner n façon f ▷ *She behaves in an odd manner.* Elle se comporte de façon étrange.; **He has a confident manner.** Il a de l'assurance.

manners npl manières fpl ▷ *good manners* les bonnes manières; **It's bad manners to speak with your mouth full.** Ce n'est pas poli de parler la bouche pleine.

mansion n manoir m

mantelpiece n cheminée f

manual n manuel m

manufacture vb fabriquer [**28**]

manufacturer n fabricant m

many adj, pron beaucoup de ▷ *He hasn't got many friends.* Il n'a pas beaucoup d'amis. ▷ *Were there many people at the concert?* Est-ce qu'il y avait beaucoup de gens au concert?; **very many** beaucoup de ▷ *I haven't got very many CDs.* Je n'ai pas beaucoup de CD.; **Not many.** Pas beaucoup.; **How many?** Combien? ▷ *How many do you want?* Combien en veux-tu?; **how many ...?** combien de ...? ▷ *How many euros do you get for £1?* Combien d'euros a-t-on pour une livre?; **too many** trop ▷ *That's too many.* C'est trop.; **so many** autant ▷ *I didn't know there would be so many.* Je ne pensais pas qu'il y en aurait autant.

map n ❶ *(of country, area)* carte f ❷ *(of town)* plan m

marathon n marathon m ▷ *the London marathon* le marathon de Londres

marble n marbre m ▷ *a marble statue* une statue en marbre; **to play marbles** jouer [**28**] aux billes

March n mars m; **in March** en mars

march n *(demonstration)* manifestation f ▶ vb ❶ *(soldiers)* marcher [**28**] au pas ❷ *(protesters)* défiler [**28**]

mare n jument f

margarine n margarine f

margin n marge f ▷ *Write notes in*

the margin. Écrivez vos notes dans la marge.

marijuana *n* marijuana *f*

mark *n* ❶ *(in school)* note *f* ▷ *I get good marks for French.* J'ai de bonnes notes en français. ❷ *(stain)* tache *f* ▷ *You've got a mark on your skirt.* Tu as une tache sur ta jupe. ❸ *(former German currency)* mark *m* ▶ *vb* corriger [**45**] ▷ *The teacher hasn't marked my homework yet.* Le professeur n'a pas encore corrigé mon devoir.

market *n* marché *m*

marketing *n* marketing *m*

marmalade *n* confiture d'oranges *f*

marriage *n* mariage *m*

married *adj* marié(e) ▷ *They are not married.* Ils ne sont pas mariés. ▷ *They have been married for 15 years.* Ils sont mariés depuis quinze ans.

marry *vb* épouser [**28**] ▷ *He wants to marry her.* Il veut l'épouser.; **to get married** se marier [**19**] ▷ *My sister's getting married in June.* Ma sœur se marie en juin.

marvellous (*US* **marvelous**) *adj* ❶ excellent(e) ▷ *She's a marvellous cook.* C'est une excellente cuisinière. ❷ superbe ▷ *The weather was marvellous.* Il a fait un temps superbe.

marzipan *n* pâte d'amandes *f*

mascara *n* mascara *m*

masculine *adj* masculin(e)

mashed potatoes *npl* purée *fsg* ▷ *sausages and mashed potatoes* des saucisses avec de la purée

mask *n* masque *m*

mass *n* ❶ multitude *f* ▷ *a mass of books and papers* une multitude de livres et de papiers ❷ *(in church)* messe *f* ▷ *We go to mass on Sunday.* Nous allons à la messe le dimanche.; **the mass media** les médias

massage *n* massage *m*

massive *adj* énorme

master *vb* maîtriser [**28**]

masterpiece *n* chef-d'œuvre *m* (*pl* chefs-d'œuvre)

mat *n* *(doormat)* paillasson *m*; **a table mat** un set de table; **a beach mat** un tapis de plage

match *n* ❶ allumette *f* ▷ *a box of matches* une boîte d'allumettes ❷ *(sport)* match *m* ▷ *a football match* un match de foot ▶ *vb* être [**35**] assorti à ▷ *The jacket matches the trousers.* La veste est assortie au pantalon.; **These colours don't match.** Ces couleurs ne vont pas ensemble.

mate *n* *(informal)* pote *m* ▷ *On Friday night I go out with my mates.* Vendredi soir, je sors avec mes potes.

material *n* ❶ *(cloth)* tissu *m* ❷ *(information, data)* documentation *f* ▷ *I'm collecting material for my project.* Je rassemble une documentation pour mon dossier.; **raw materials** les matières premières *fpl*

mathematics *n* mathématiques *fpl*

maths *n* maths *fpl*

matter n question f ▷ It's a matter of life and death. C'est une question de vie ou de mort.; **What's the matter?** Qu'est-ce qui ne va pas?; **as a matter of fact** en fait
▷ vb **it doesn't matter (1)** (I don't mind) ça ne fait rien ▷ I can't give you the money today. — It doesn't matter. Je ne peux pas te donner l'argent aujourd'hui. — Ça ne fait rien. **(2)** (it makes no difference) ça n'a pas d'importance ▷ It doesn't matter if you're late. Ça n'a pas d'importance si tu es en retard.; **It matters a lot to me.** C'est très important pour moi.

mattress n matelas m

mature adj mûr(e) ▷ She's quite mature for her age. Elle est très mûre pour son âge.

maximum n maximum m
▷ adj maximum ▷ The maximum speed is 100 km/h. La vitesse maximum autorisée est de cent kilomètres à l'heure.; **the maximum amount** le maximum

May n mai m; **in May** en mai; **May Day** le Premier Mai

may vb **He may come.** Il va peut-être venir. ▷ It may rain. Il va peut-être pleuvoir.; **May I smoke?** Est-ce que je peux fumer?

maybe adv peut-être ▷ maybe not peut-être pas ▷ Maybe she's at home. Elle est peut-être chez elle. ▷ Maybe he'll change his mind. Il va peut-être changer d'avis.

mayonnaise n mayonnaise f

mayor n maire m

me pron ❶ me ▷ Could you lend me your pen? Est-ce que tu peux me prêter ton stylo?
m'

> **me** becomes **m'** before a vowel sound.

▷ Can you help me? Est-ce que tu peux m'aider? ❷ moi

> **moi** is used in exclamations.

▷ Me too! Moi aussi! ▷ Excuse me! Excusez-moi! ▷ Wait for me! Attends-moi!

> **moi** is also used after prepositions and in comparisons.

▷ You're after me. Tu es après moi.
▷ She's older than me. Elle est plus âgée que moi.

meal n repas m

mean vb vouloir [93] dire ▷ I don't know what it means. Je ne sais pas ce que ça veut dire. ▷ What do you mean? Qu'est-ce que vous voulez dire? ▷ That's not what I meant. Ce n'est pas ce que je voulais dire.; **Which one do you mean?** Duquel veux-tu parler?; **Do you really mean it?** Tu es sérieux?; **to mean to do something** avoir [8] l'intention de faire quelque chose ▷ I didn't mean to offend you. Je n'avais pas l'intention de vous blesser.
▷ adj ❶ (with money) radin(e) ▷ He's too mean to buy Christmas presents. Il est trop radin pour acheter des cadeaux de Noël. ❷ (unkind) méchant(e) ▷ You're being mean to me. Tu es méchant avec moi.; **That's a really mean thing to say!**

Ce n'est vraiment pas gentil de dire ça!

meaning n sens m

meant vb see **mean**

meanwhile adv pendant ce temps

measles n rougeole f

measure vb ❶ mesurer [28] ▷ I measured the page. J'ai mesuré la page. ❷ faire [36] ▷ The room measures 3 metres by 4. La pièce fait trois mètres sur quatre.

measurements npl ❶ (of object) dimensions fpl ▷ What are the measurements of the room? Quelles sont les dimensions de la pièce? ❷ (of body) mensurations fpl ▷ What are your measurements? Quelles sont tes mensurations?; **my waist measurement** mon tour de taille; **What's your neck measurement?** Quel est votre tour de cou?

meat n viande f ▷ I don't eat meat. Je ne mange pas de viande.

Mecca n La Mecque

mechanic n mécanicien m ▷ He's a mechanic. Il est mécanicien.

medal n médaille f; **the gold medal** la médaille d'or

media npl médias mpl

medical adj médical(e) (mpl médicaux) ▷ medical treatment les soins médicaux; **medical insurance** l'assurance maladie; **to have medical problems** avoir [8] des problèmes de santé; **She's a medical student.** Elle est étudiante en médecine.
▶ n **to have a medical** passer [58] une visite médicale

medicine n ❶ (subject) médecine f ▷ I want to study medicine. Je veux faire médecine.; **alternative medicine** la médecine douce ❷ (medication) médicament m ▷ I need some medicine. J'ai besoin d'un médicament.

Mediterranean adj méditerranéen (f méditerranéenne); **the Mediterranean** la Méditerranée

medium adj moyen (f moyenne) ▷ a man of medium height un homme de taille moyenne

medium-sized adj de taille moyenne ▷ a medium-sized town une ville de taille moyenne

meet vb ❶ (by chance) rencontrer [28] ▷ I met Paul in the street. J'ai rencontré Paul dans la rue. ▷ Have you met him before? Tu l'as déjà rencontré? ❷ se rencontrer [28] ▷ We met by chance in the shopping centre. Nous nous sommes rencontrés par hasard dans le centre commercial. ❸ (by arrangement) retrouver [28] ▷ I'm going to meet my friends. Je vais retrouver mes amis. ❹ se retrouver [28] ▷ Let's meet in front of the tourist office. Retrouvons-nous devant l'office de tourisme.; **I like meeting new people.** J'aime faire de nouvelles connaissances. ❺ (pick up) aller [3] chercher ▷ I'll meet you at the station. J'irai te chercher à la gare.

meet up vb se retrouver [28] ▷ What time shall we meet up? On se retrouve à quelle heure?

meeting n ❶ (for work) réunion f
▷ a business meeting une réunion
d'affaires ❷ (socially) rencontre f
▷ their first meeting leur première
rencontre

mega adj He's mega rich. (informal)
Il est hyper-riche.

melon n melon m

melt vb fondre [69] ▷ The snow is
melting. La neige est en train de
fondre.

member n membre m; **a Member
of Parliament** un député

meme n mème m

memorial n monument m ▷ a war
memorial un monument aux morts

memorize vb apprendre [65] par
cœur

memory n ❶ (also for computer)
mémoire f ▷ I haven't got a good
memory. Je n'ai pas une bonne
mémoire. ❷ (recollection) souvenir
m ▷ to bring back memories rappeler
des souvenirs

men npl see **man**

mend vb réparer [28]

mental adj mental(e) (mpl
mentaux) ▷ a mental illness une
maladie mentale

mention vb mentionner [28];
Thank you! — Don't mention it!
Merci! — Il n'y a pas de quoi!

mentor n mentor m
▶ vb servir [78] de mentor à

menu n menu m ▷ Could I have the
menu please? Est-ce que je pourrais
avoir le menu s'il vous plaît?

meringue n meringue f

merry adj Merry Christmas!
Joyeux Noël!

merry-go-round n manège m

mess n fouillis m ▷ My bedroom's
usually in a mess. Il y a
généralement du fouillis dans
ma chambre.

mess about vb to mess about
with something (interfere with)
tripoter [28] quelque chose ▷ Stop
messing about with my computer!
Arrête de tripoter mon ordinateur!;
**Don't mess about with my
things!** Ne touche pas à mes
affaires!

mess up vb to mess something up
mettre [47] la pagaille dans
quelque chose ▷ My little brother
has messed up my DVDs. Mon petit
frère a mis la pagaille dans mes
DVDs.

message n message m
▶ vb envoyer [33] un message ▷ She
messaged me on Facebook. Elle m'a
envoyé un message sur Facebook.

messenger n messager m

messy adj ❶ (dirty) salissant(e)
▷ a messy job un travail salissant
❷ (untidy) en désordre ▷ Your desk is
really messy. Ton bureau est
vraiment en désordre. ❸ (person)
désordonné(e) ▷ She's so messy! Elle
est tellement désordonnée!; **My
writing is terribly messy.** J'ai une
écriture de cochon.

met vb see **meet**

metal n métal m (pl métaux)

meter n ❶ (for gas, electricity, taxi)
compteur m ❷ (parking meter)

a b c d e f g h i j k l **m** n o p q r s t u v w x y z

parcmètre m ❸ (US: unit of
measurement) mètre m
method n méthode f
Methodist n méthodiste mf ▷ I'm a
Methodist. Je suis méthodiste.
metre n mètre m
metric adj métrique
Mexico n Mexique m; in Mexico au
Mexique; to Mexico au Mexique
mice npl see mouse
microchip n puce f
microphone n microphone m
microscope n microscope m
microwave oven n four à
micro-ondes m
midday n midi m; at midday à midi
middle n milieu m ▷ in the middle of
the road au milieu de la route ▷ in
the middle of the night au milieu de la
nuit
middle-aged adj d'un certain âge
▷ a middle-aged man un homme
d'un certain âge; to be
middle-aged avoir [8] la
cinquantaine; She's middle-aged.
Elle a la cinquantaine.
middle-class adj de la classe
moyenne ▷ a middle-class family
une famille de la classe moyenne
Middle East n Moyen-Orient m; in
the Middle East au Moyen-Orient
middle name n deuxième nom m
midge n moucheron m
midnight n minuit m; at midnight
à minuit
midwife n sage-femme f (pl
sages-femmes) ▷ She's a midwife.
Elle est sage-femme.
might vb ▷ He might come later. Il va

peut-être venir plus tard. ▷ She
might not have understood. Elle n'a
peut-être pas compris.
migraine n migraine f ▷ I've got a
migraine. J'ai la migraine.
mike n micro m
mild adj doux (f douce) ▷ The winters
are quite mild. Les hivers sont assez
doux.
mile n mille m ▷ It's 5 miles from here.
C'est à huit kilomètres d'ici.
  ● In France distances are
  ● expressed in kilometres. A mile is
  ● about 1.6 kilometres.
We walked miles! Nous avons fait
des kilomètres à pied!
military adj militaire
milk n lait m ▷ tea with milk du thé
au lait
  ▶ vb traire [85]
milk chocolate n chocolat au
lait m
milkman n He's a milkman. Il livre
le lait à domicile.
  ● In France milk is not delivered to
  ● people's homes.
milk shake n milk-shake m
millennium n millénaire m ▷ the
third millennium le troisième
millénaire
millimetre (US **millimeter**) n
millimètre m
million n million m
millionaire n millionnaire m
mince n viande hachée f
mind vb ❶ garder [28] ▷ Could you
mind the baby this afternoon? Est-ce
que tu pourrais garder le bébé cet
après-midi? ❷ (keep an eye on)

surveiller [**28**] ▷ *Could you mind my
bags for a few minutes?* Est-ce que
vous pourriez surveiller mes
bagages pendant quelques
minutes?; **Do you mind if I open
the window?** Est-ce que je
pourrais ouvrir la fenêtre?; **I don't
mind.** Ça ne me dérange pas.
▷ *I don't mind the noise.* Le bruit ne
me dérange pas.; **Never mind!** Ça
ne fait rien!; **Mind that bike!**
Attention au vélo!; **Mind the step!**
Attention à la marche!
  ▶ *n* **to make up one's mind** se
décider [**28**] ▷ *I haven't made up my
mind yet.* Je ne me suis pas encore
décidé.; **to change one's mind**
changer [**45**] d'avis ▷ *He's changed
his mind.* Il a changé d'avis.; **Are
you out of your mind?** Tu as perdu
la tête?
mindfulness *n* pleine conscience *f*
mine *pron* le mien ▷ *Is this your coat?
— No, mine's black.* C'est ton
manteau? — Non, le mien est noir.
la mienne ▷ *Is this your car? — No,
mine's green.* C'est ta voiture? —
Non, la mienne est verte.
les miens ▷ *her parents and mine* ses
parents et les miens
les miennes ▷ *Your hands are dirty,
mine are clean.* Tes mains sont sales,
les miennes sont propres.; **It's
mine.** C'est à moi. ▷ *This book is
mine.* Ce livre est à moi. ▷ *Whose is
this? — It's mine.* C'est à qui? — À moi.
  ▶ *n* mine *f* ▷ *a coal mine* une mine de
charbon ▷ *a land mine* une mine
terrestre

miner *n* mineur *m*
mineral water *n* eau minérale *f*
miniature *adj* miniature
  ▷ *a miniature version* une version
miniature
  ▶ *n* miniature *f*
minibus *n* minibus *m*
minimum *n* minimum *m*
  ▶ *adj* minimum ▷ *The minimum age
for driving is 17.* L'âge minimum pour
conduire est dix-sept ans.; **the
minimum amount** le minimum
miniskirt *n* mini-jupe *f*
minister *n* ❶ (*in government*)
ministre *m* ❷ (*of church*) pasteur *m*
minor *adj* mineur(e) ▷ *a minor
problem* un problème mineur; **in D
minor** en ré mineur; **a minor
operation** une opération bénigne
minority *n* minorité *f*
mint *n* ❶ (*plant*) menthe *f* ▷ *mint
sauce* la sauce à la menthe
❷ (*sweet*) bonbon à la menthe *m*
minus *prep* moins ▷ *16 minus 3 is 13.*
Seize moins trois égale treize. ▷ *It's
minus two degrees outside.* Il fait
moins deux dehors.
minute *n* minute *f* ▷ *Wait a minute!*
Attends une minute!
  ▶ *adj* minuscule ▷ *Her flat is minute.*
Son appartement est minuscule.
miracle *n* miracle *m*
mirror *n* ❶ (*on wall*) glace *f* ❷ (*in car*)
rétroviseur *m*
misbehave *vb* se conduire [**23**]
mal
miscellaneous *adj* divers(e)
mischief *n* bêtises *fpl* ▷ *My little
sister's always up to mischief.* Ma

a b c d e f g h i j k l **m** n o p q r s t u v w x y z

petite sœur fait constamment des bêtises.

mischievous adj coquin(e)

miser n avare mf

miserable adj ❶ (person) malheureux (f malheureuse) ▷ You're looking miserable. Tu as l'air malheureux. ❷ (weather) épouvantable ▷ The weather was miserable. Il faisait un temps épouvantable.; **to feel miserable** ne pas avoir [8] le moral ▷ I'm feeling miserable. Je n'ai pas le moral.

misery n ❶ (unhappiness) tristesse f ▷ All that money brought nothing but misery. Tout cet argent n'a apporté que de la tristesse. ❷ (unhappy person) pleurnicheur m, pleurnicheuse f ▷ She's a real misery. C'est une vraie pleurnicheuse.

Miss n ❶ Mademoiselle (pl Mesdemoiselles) ❷ (in address) Mlle (pl Mlles)

miss vb ❶ rater [28] ▷ Hurry or you'll miss the bus. Dépêche-toi ou tu vas rater le bus. ❷ manquer [28] ▷ to miss an opportunity manquer une occasion; **I miss you.** Tu me manques. ▷ I'm missing my family. Ma famille me manque. ▷ I miss them. Ils me manquent.

missing adj manquant(e) ▷ the missing part la pièce manquante; **to be missing** avoir [8] disparu ▷ Two members of the group are missing. Deux membres du groupe ont disparu.

mist n brume f

mistake n ❶ (slip) faute f ▷ a spelling mistake une faute d'orthographe; **to make a mistake** (1) (in writing, speaking) faire [36] une faute (2) (get mixed up) se tromper [28] ▷ I'm sorry, I made a mistake. Je suis désolé, je me suis trompé. ❷ (misjudgement) erreur f ▷ It was a mistake to come. J'ai fait une erreur en venant.; **by mistake** par erreur ▷ I took his bag by mistake. J'ai pris son sac par erreur.

▶ vb **He mistook me for my sister.** Il m'a prise pour ma sœur.

mistaken adj **to be mistaken** se tromper [28] ▷ If you think I'm coming with you, you're mistaken. Si tu penses que je vais venir avec toi, tu te trompes.

mistletoe n gui m

mistook vb see **mistake**

misty adj brumeux (f brumeuse) ▷ a misty morning un matin brumeux

misunderstand vb mal comprendre [65] ▷ Sorry, I misunderstood you. Je suis désolé, je t'avais mal compris.

misunderstanding n malentendu m

misunderstood vb see **misunderstand**

mix n mélange m ▷ It's a mix of science fiction and comedy. C'est un mélange de science-fiction et de comédie.; **a cake mix** une préparation pour gâteau

▶ vb ❶ mélanger [45] ▷ Mix the flour with the sugar. Mélangez la farine au sucre. ❷ combiner [**28**] ▷ *He's mixing business with pleasure.* Il combine les affaires et le plaisir.; **to mix with somebody** *(associate)* fréquenter [**28**] quelqu'un; **He doesn't mix much.** Il se tient à l'écart.

mix up *vb (people)* confondre [**69**] ▷ *He always mixes me up with my sister.* Il me confond toujours avec ma sœur.; **The travel agent mixed up the bookings.** L'agence de voyage s'est embrouillée dans les réservations.; **I'm getting mixed up.** Je ne m'y retrouve plus.

mixed *adj* **a mixed salad** une salade composée; **a mixed school** une école mixte; **a mixed grill** un assortiment de grillades

mixer *n* **She's a good mixer.** Elle est très sociable.

mixture *n* mélange *m* ▷ *a mixture of spices* un mélange d'épices; **cough mixture** le sirop pour la toux

mix-up *n* confusion *f*

moan *vb* râler [**28**] ▷ *She's always moaning.* Elle est toujours en train de râler.

mobile *n (phone)* portable *m*

mobile home *n* mobile home *m*

mobile phone *n* portable *m*

mock *vb* ridiculiser [**28**]
▶ *adj* **a mock exam** un examen blanc

model *n* ❶ *(type)* modèle *m* ▷ *His car is the latest model.* Sa voiture est le tout dernier modèle. ❷ *(mock-up)* maquette *f* ▷ *a model of the castle* une maquette du château

❸ *(fashion)* mannequin *m* ▷ *She's a famous model.* C'est un mannequin célèbre.
▶ *adj* **a model plane** un modèle réduit d'avion; **a model railway** un modèle réduit de voie ferrée; **He's a model pupil.** C'est un élève modèle.
▶ *vb* **She was modelling a Lorna Bailey outfit.** Elle présentait une tenue de la collection Lorna Bailey.

modem *n* modem *m*

moderate *adj* modéré(e) ▷ *His views are quite moderate.* Ses opinions sont assez modérées.; **a moderate amount of** un peu de; **a moderate price** un prix raisonnable

modern *adj* moderne

modernize *vb* moderniser [**28**]

modest *adj* modeste

moisturizer *n* ❶ *(cream)* crème hydratante *f* ❷ *(lotion)* lait hydratant *m*

moldy *adj (US)* moisi(e)

mole *n* ❶ *(animal)* taupe *f* ❷ *(on skin)* grain de beauté *m*

moment *n* instant *m* ▷ *Could you wait a moment?* Pouvez-vous attendre un instant? ▷ *in a moment* dans un instant; **at the moment** en ce moment; **any moment now** d'un moment à l'autre ▷ *They'll be arriving any moment now.* Ils vont arriver d'un moment à l'autre.

Monaco *n* Monaco; **in Monaco** à Monaco

monarchy *n* monarchie *f*

Monday *n* lundi *m* ▷ *on Monday*

a
b
c
d
e
f
g
h
i
j
k
l
m
n
o
p
q
r
s
t
u
v
w
x
y
z

lundi ▷ *on Mondays* le lundi ▷ *every Monday* tous les lundis

monetize *vb* monétiser [**28**]

money *n* argent *m* ▷ *I need to change some money.* J'ai besoin de changer de l'argent.; **to make money** gagner [**28**] de l'argent

mongrel *n* bâtard *m* ▷ *My dog's a mongrel.* Mon chien est un bâtard.

monitor *n* (*of computer*) moniteur *m*

monkey *n* singe *m*

monotonous *adj* monotone

monster *n* monstre *m*

month *n* mois *m* ▷ *this month* ce mois-ci ▷ *next month* le mois prochain ▷ *last month* le mois dernier ▷ *every month* tous les mois

monthly *adj* mensuel (*f* mensuelle)

monument *n* monument *m*

mood *n* humeur *f*; **to be in a bad mood** être [**35**] de mauvaise humeur; **to be in a good mood** être [**35**] de bonne humeur

moody *adj* ❶ (*temperamental*) lunatique ❷ (*in a bad mood*) maussade

moon *n* lune *f* ▷ *There's a full moon tonight.* Il y a pleine lune ce soir.

moped *n* cyclomoteur *m*

moral *adj* moral(e) (*mpl* moraux)
▶ *n* morale *f* ▷ *the moral of the story* la morale de l'histoire; **morals** la moralité

more *adj, pron, adv*

> When comparing one amount with another, you usually use **plus**.

❶ plus ▷ *Could you speak more slowly?* Est-ce que vous pourriez parler plus lentement? ▷ *a bit more* un peu plus ▷ *There isn't any more.* Il n'y en a plus.; **more ... than** plus ... que ▷ *He's more intelligent than me.* Il est plus intelligent que moi.

❷ (*followed by noun*) plus de ▷ *I get more homework than you do.* J'ai plus de devoirs que toi. ▷ *I spent more than 500 euros.* J'ai dépensé plus de cinq cents euros.

> When referring to an additional amount, more than there is already, you usually use **encore**.

❸ encore ▷ *Is there any more?* Est-ce qu'il y en a encore? ▷ *Would you like some more?* Vous en voulez encore?

❹ (*followed by noun*) encore de ▷ *Do you want some more tea?* Voulez-vous encore du thé?; **more or less** plus ou moins; **more than ever** plus que jamais

morning *n* matin *m* ▷ *this morning* ce matin ▷ *tomorrow morning* demain matin ▷ *every morning* tous les matins; **in the morning** le matin ▷ *at 7 o'clock in the morning* à sept heures du matin; **a morning paper** un journal du matin

Morocco *n* Maroc *m*; **in Morocco** au Maroc

Moscow *n* Moscou; **in Moscow** à Moscou

Moslem *n* musulman *m*, musulmane *f* ▷ *He's a Moslem.* Il est musulman.

mosque *n* mosquée *f*

mosquito *n* moustique *m*; **a mosquito bite** une piqûre de moustique

most *adv, adj, pron*

> Use **la plupart de** when 'most (of)' is followed by a plural noun and **la majeure partie (de)** when 'most (of)' is followed by a singular noun.

❶ la plupart de ▷ *most of my friends* la plupart de mes amis ▷ *most people* la plupart des gens; **most of them** la plupart d'entre eux; **most of the time** la plupart du temps ❷ la majeure partie de ▷ *most of the work* la majeure partie du travail ▷ *most of the night* la majeure partie de la nuit; **the most** le plus ▷ *He's the one who talks the most.* C'est lui qui parle le plus.

> When 'most' is followed by an adjective, the translation depends on whether the noun referred to is masculine, feminine or plural.

the most ... (1) les plus ... **(2)** le plus ... ▷ *the most expensive restaurant* le restaurant le plus cher **(3)** la plus ... ▷ *the most expensive seat* la place la plus chère; **to make the most of something** profiter [28] au maximum de quelque chose; **at the most** au maximum ▷ *Two hours at the most.* Deux heures au maximum.

moth *n* papillon de nuit *m*

> Word for word, this means 'butterfly of the night'.

mother *n* mère *f* ▷ *my mother* ma mère; **mother tongue** la langue maternelle

mother-in-law *n* belle-mère *f*

(*pl* belles-mères)

Mother's Day *n* fête des Mères *f*

> Mother's Day is usually on the last Sunday of May in France.

motivated *adj* motivé(e) ▷ *He is highly motivated.* Il est très motivé.

motivation *n* motivation *f*

motor *n* moteur *m* ▷ *The boat has a motor.* Le bateau a un moteur.

motorbike *n* moto *f*

motorboat *n* bateau à moteur *m* (*pl* bateaux à moteur)

motorcycle *n* vélomoteur *m*

motorcyclist *n* motard *m*

motorist *n* automobiliste *mf*

motor racing *n* course automobile *f*

motorway *n* autoroute *f* ▷ *on the motorway* sur l'autoroute

mouldy *adj* moisi(e)

mount *vb* ❶ monter [48] ▷ *They're mounting a publicity campaign.* Ils montent une campagne publicitaire. ❷ augmenter [28] ▷ *Tension is mounting.* La tension augmente.

mount up *vb* ❶ s'accumuler [28] ❷ augmenter [28]

mountain *n* montagne *f*; **a mountain bike** un VTT (= *vélo tout-terrain*)

mountaineer *n* alpiniste *mf*

mountaineering *n* alpinisme *m* ▷ *I go mountaineering.* Je fais de l'alpinisme.

mountainous *adj* montagneux (*f* montagneuse)

mouse *n* (*also for computer*) souris *f* ▷ *white mice* des souris blanches

a b c d e f g h i j k l m n o p q r s t u v w x y z

mouse mat n tapis de souris m

mousse n ❶ (food) mousse f
▷ chocolate mousse la mousse au chocolat ❷ (for hair) mousse coiffante f

moustache n moustache f ▷ He's got a moustache. Il a une moustache.; **a man with a moustache** un moustachu

mouth n bouche f

mouthful n bouchée f

mouth organ n harmonica m
▷ I play the mouth organ. Je joue de l'harmonica.

move n ❶ tour m ▷ It's your move. C'est ton tour. ❷ déménagement m ▷ Our move from Oxford to Luton ... Notre déménagement d'Oxford à Luton ...; **to get a move on** se remuer [28] ▷ Get a move on! Remue-toi!
▶ vb ❶ bouger [45] ▷ Don't move! Ne bouge pas! ▷ Could you move your stuff please? Est-ce que tu peux bouger tes affaires s'il te plaît? ❷ avancer [12] ▷ The car was moving very slowly. La voiture avançait très lentement. ❸ émouvoir [31] ▷ I was very moved by the film. J'ai été très émue par ce film.; **to move house** déménager [45] ▷ We're moving in July. Nous allons déménager en juillet.

move forward vb avancer [12]

move in vb emménager [45]
▷ They're moving in next week. Ils emménagent la semaine prochaine.

move over vb se pousser [28]

▷ Could you move over a bit? Est-ce que vous pouvez vous pousser un peu?

movement n mouvement m

movie n film m; **the movies** le cinéma ▷ Let's go to the movies! Si on allait au cinéma!

moving adj ❶ (not stationary) en marche ▷ a moving bus un bus en marche ❷ (touching) touchant(e)
▷ a moving story une histoire touchante

MP n député m ▷ She's an MP. Elle est député.

mph abbr (= miles per hour) km/h (= kilomètres-heure) ▷ to drive at 50 mph rouler à 80 km/h
  In France, speed is expressed in kilometres per hour. 50 mph is about 80 km/h.

Mr n ❶ Monsieur (pl Messieurs) ❷ (in address) M. (pl MM.)

Mrs n ❶ Madame (pl Mesdames) ❷ (in address) Mme (pl Mmes)

MS n (= multiple sclerosis) sclérose en plaques f ▷ She's got MS. Elle a la sclérose en plaques.

Ms n ❶ Madame (pl Mesdames) ❷ (in address) Mme (pl Mmes)
  There isn't a direct equivalent of 'Ms' in French. If you are writing to somebody and don't know whether she is married, use **Madame**.

much adj, adv, pron ❶ (with verb) beaucoup ▷ Do you go out much? Tu sors beaucoup? ▷ I don't like sport much. Je n'aime pas beaucoup le sport. ▷ I feel much better now. Je me

sens beaucoup mieux maintenant.
❷ (with noun) <u>beaucoup de</u>
▷ *I haven't got much money.* Je n'ai
pas beaucoup d'argent. ▷ *I don't
want much rice.* Je ne veux pas
beaucoup de riz.; **very much**
(1) (with verb) beaucoup ▷ *I enjoyed
the film very much.* J'ai beaucoup
apprécié le film. ▷ *Thank you very
much.* Merci beaucoup. **(2)** (followed
by noun) beaucoup de ▷ *I haven't got
very much money.* Je n'ai pas
beaucoup d'argent.; **not much**
(1) pas beaucoup ▷ *Have you got a
lot of luggage? — No, not much.* As-tu
beaucoup de bagages? — Non, pas
beaucoup. **(2)** pas grand-chose
▷ *What's on TV? — Not much.*
Qu'est-ce qu'il y a à la télé? — Pas
grand-chose. ▷ *What did you think of
it? — Not much.* Qu'est-ce que tu en
as pensé? — Pas grand-chose.;
How much? Combien? ▷ *How much
do you want?* Tu en veux combien?
▷ *How much time have you got?* Tu as
combien de temps? ▷ *How much is
it?* (cost) Combien est-ce que ça
coûte?; **too much** trop ▷ *That's too
much!* C'est trop! ▷ *It costs too much.*
Ça coûte trop cher. ▷ *They give us
too much homework.* Ils nous
donnent trop de devoirs.; **so much**
autant ▷ *I didn't think it would cost so
much.* Je ne pensais pas que ça
coûterait autant. ▷ *I've never seen so
much traffic.* Je n'ai jamais vu autant
de circulation.

mud n <u>boue</u> f

muddle n <u>désordre</u> m ▷ *The photos*

are in a muddle. Les photos sont en
désordre.

muddle up vb (people) <u>confondre</u>
[69] ▷ *He muddles me up with my
sister.* Il me confond avec ma sœur.;
to get muddled up s'embrouiller
[28] ▷ *I'm getting muddled up.* Je
m'embrouille.

muddy adj <u>boueux</u> (f boueuse)

muesli n <u>muesli</u> m

mug n <u>grande tasse</u> f ▷ *Do you want
a cup or a mug?* Est-ce que vous
voulez une tasse normale ou une
grande tasse?
▶ vb <u>agresser</u> **[28]** ▷ *He was mugged
in the city centre.* Il s'est fait agresser
au centre-ville.

mugging n <u>agression</u> f

multiple choice test n <u>QCM</u> m
(= *le questionnaire à choix multiples*)

multiplication n <u>multiplication</u> f

multiply vb <u>multiplier</u> **[19]** ▷ *to
multiply 6 by 3* multiplier six par
trois

mum n

> You use **mère** in most cases,
> except when you are talking to
> your mother or using it as her
> name, then you would use
> **maman**.

❶ <u>mère</u> f ▷ *my mum* ma mère ▷ *her
mum* sa mère ❷ <u>maman</u> f ▷ *Mum!*
Maman! ▷ *I'll ask Mum.* Je vais
demander à maman.

mummy n ❶ (mum) <u>maman</u> f
▷ *Mummy says I can go.* Maman dit
que je peux y aller. ❷ (Egyptian)
<u>momie</u> f

mumps n <u>oreillons</u> mpl

a b c d e f g h i j k l m n o p q r s t u v w x y z

murder n meurtre m
  ▶ vb assassiner [28] ▷ He was
murdered. Il a été assassiné.
murderer n assassin m
muscle n muscle m
museum n musée m
mushroom n champignon m ▷ a
mushroom omelette une omelette
aux champignons
music n musique f
musical adj doué pour la musique
(f douée pour la musique) ▷ I'm not
musical. Je ne suis pas doué pour la
musique.; **a musical instrument**
un instrument de musique
  ▶ n comédie musicale f
musician n musicien m,
musicienne f
Muslim n musulman m,
musulmane f ▷ He's a Muslim. Il est
musulman.
mussel n moule f
must vb

> When 'must' means that you
> assume or suppose something,
> use **devoir**; when it means it's
> necessary to do something, eg
> 'I must buy some presents', use
> **il faut que ...**, which comes
> from the verb **falloir** and is
> followed by a verb in the
> subjunctive.

  ❶ (I suppose) devoir [26] ▷ You must
be tired. Tu dois être fatigué. ▷ They
must have plenty of money. Ils
doivent avoir beaucoup d'argent.
▷ There must be some problem. Il doit
y avoir un problème. ❷ il faut que
▷ I must buy some presents. Il faut

que j'achète des cadeaux. ▷ I really
must go now. Il faut que j'y aille.;
**You mustn't forget to send her a
card.** N'oublie surtout pas de lui
envoyer une carte.; **You must
come and see us.** (invitation)
Venez donc nous voir.
mustard n moutarde f
mustn't vb = **must not**
my adj mon m ▷ my father mon père
ma f ▷ my aunt ma tante
mes pl ▷ my parents mes parents

> **ma** becomes **mon** before a
> vowel sound.

  my friend (1) (male) mon ami
(2) (female) mon amie

> Do not use **mon/ma/mes** with
> parts of the body.

▷ I want to wash my hair. Je voudrais
me laver les cheveux. ▷ I'm going to
clean my teeth. Je vais me brosser les
dents. ▷ I've hurt my foot. Je me suis
fait mal au pied.
myself pron ❶ me ▷ I've hurt myself.
Je me suis fait mal. ▷ I really enjoyed
myself. Je me suis vraiment bien
amusé. ▷ ... when I look at myself in
the mirror. ... quand je me regarde
dans la glace. ❷ moi ▷ I don't like
talking about myself. Je n'aime pas
parler de moi. ❸ moi-même
▷ I made it myself. Je l'ai fait
moi-même.; **by myself** tout seul
▷ I don't like travelling by myself. Je
n'aime pas voyager tout seul.
mysterious adj mystérieux (f
mystérieuse)
mystery n mystère m; **a murder
mystery** (novel) un roman policier

myth n ❶ (legend) <u>mythe</u> m ▷ a Greek myth un mythe grec ❷ (untrue idea) <u>idée reçue</u> f ▷ That's a myth. C'est une idée reçue.

nag vb (scold) <u>harceler</u> [**43**] ▷ She's always nagging me. Elle me harcèle constamment.

nail n ❶ (on finger, toe) <u>ongle</u> m ▷ Don't bite your nails! Ne te ronge pas les ongles! ❷ (made of metal) <u>clou</u> m

nailbrush n <u>brosse à ongles</u> f

nailfile n <u>lime à ongles</u> f

nail scissors npl <u>ciseaux à ongles</u> mpl

nail varnish n <u>vernis à ongles</u> m; **nail varnish remover** le dissolvant

naked adj <u>nu(e)</u>

name n <u>nom</u> m; **What's your name?** Comment vous appelez-vous?

nanny n <u>garde d'enfants</u> f ▷ She's a nanny. C'est une garde d'enfants.

napkin n <u>serviette</u> f

nappy n couche f
narrow adj étroit(e)
nasty adj ❶ (bad) mauvais(e)
▷ a nasty cold un mauvais rhume
❷ (unfriendly) méchant(e) ▷ He gave
me a nasty look. Il m'a regardé d'un
air méchant.
nation n nation f
national adj national(e) (mpl
nationaux) ▷ He's the national
champion. C'est le champion
national.; **the national elections**
les élections législatives
national anthem n hymne
national m
nationality n nationalité f
National Lottery n Loterie
nationale f
national park n parc national m
(pl parcs nationaux)
natural adj naturel (f naturelle)
naturally adv naturellement
▷ Naturally, we were very
disappointed. Nous avons
naturellement été très déçus.
nature n nature f
naughty adj vilain(e) ▷ Don't be
naughty! Ne fais pas le vilain!
navy n marine f ▷ He's in the navy. Il
est dans la marine.
navy-blue adj bleu marine
▷ a navy-blue skirt une jupe bleu
marine
near adj proche ▷ It's fairly near.
C'est assez proche.; **It's near
enough to walk.** On peut
facilement y aller à pied.; **the
nearest** le plus proche ▷ The nearest
shops were three kilometres away. Les

magasins les plus proches étaient
à trois kilomètres.
▶ prep, adv près de ▷ near my house
près de chez moi; **near here** près
d'ici ▷ Is there a bank near here?
Est-ce qu'il y a une banque près
d'ici?; **near to** près de ▷ It's very near
to the school. C'est tout près de
l'école.
nearby adv à proximité ▷ There's a
supermarket nearby. Il y a un
supermarché à proximité.
▶ adj ❶ (close) proche ▷ a nearby
garage un garage proche
❷ (neighbouring) voisin(e) ▷ We
went to the nearby village of Torrance.
Nous sommes allés à Torrance, le
village voisin.
nearly adv presque ▷ Dinner's nearly
ready. Le dîner est presque prêt.
▷ I'm nearly 15. J'ai presque quinze
ans.; **I nearly missed the train.** J'ai
failli rater le train.
neat adj soigné(e) ▷ She has very neat
writing. Elle a une écriture très
soignée.; **a neat whisky** un
whisky sec
neatly adv soigneusement
necessarily adv not necessarily
pas forcément
necessary adj nécessaire
neck n ❶ (of body) cou m; **a stiff
neck** un torticolis ❷ (of garment)
encolure f ▷ a V-neck sweater un pull
avec une encolure en V
necklace n collier m
need vb avoir [8] besoin de ▷ I need a
bigger size. J'ai besoin d'une plus
grande taille.; **to need to do**

something avoir [8] besoin de faire quelque chose ▷ *I need to change some money.* J'ai besoin de changer de l'argent.
▶ *n* **There's no need to book.** Il n'est pas nécessaire de réserver.

needle *n* aiguille *f*

negative *n* (photo) négatif *m*
▶ *adj* négatif (*f* négative) ▷ *He's got a very negative attitude.* Il a une attitude très négative.

neglected *adj* (untidy) mal tenu(e) ▷ *The garden is neglected.* Le jardin est mal tenu.

negotiate *vb* négocier [19]

neighbour (US **neighbor**) *n* voisin *m*, voisine *f* ▷ *the neighbours' garden* le jardin des voisins

neighbourhood (US **neighborhood**) *n* quartier *m*

neither *pron, conj, adv* aucun des deux ▷ *Neither of them is coming.* Aucun des deux ne vient. ▷ *Carrots or peas? — Neither, thanks.* Des carottes ou des petits pois? — Aucun des deux merci.; aucune des deux ▷ *neither team* aucune des deux équipes; **neither ... nor ...** ni ... ni ... ▷ *Neither Sarah nor Tamsin is coming to the party.* Ni Sarah ni Tamsin ne viennent à la soirée.; **Neither do I.** Moi non plus. ▷ *I don't like him. — Neither do I!* Je ne l'aime pas. — Moi non plus!; **Neither have I.** Moi non plus. ▷ *I've never been to Spain. — Neither have I.* Je ne suis jamais allé en Espagne. — Moi non plus.

nephew *n* neveu *m* (*pl* neveux)

▷ *my nephew* mon neveu

nerve *n* ❶ nerf *m* ▷ *She sometimes gets on my nerves.* Elle me tape quelquefois sur les nerfs. ❷ (cheek) toupet *m* ▷ *He's got a nerve!* Il a du toupet!

nervous *adj* (tense) tendu(e) ▷ *I bite my nails when I'm nervous.* Je me ronge les ongles quand je suis tendu.; **to be nervous about something** appréhender [28] de faire quelque chose ▷ *I'm a bit nervous about flying to Paris by myself.* J'appréhende un peu d'aller toute seule en avion à Paris.

nest *n* nid *m*

Net *n* Net *m* ▷ *to surf the Net* surfer sur le Net

net *n* filet *m* ▷ *a fishing net* un filet de pêche

netball *n*
● Netball is not played in France.
● Both sexes play basketball or volleyball instead.

Netherlands *npl* Pays-Bas *m*; **in the Netherlands** aux Pays-Bas

network *n* ❶ réseau *m* (*pl* réseaux) ❷ (for mobile phone) opérateur *m*

never *adv* ❶ jamais ▷ *Have you ever been to Germany? — No, never.* Est-ce que tu es déjà allé en Allemagne? — Non, jamais. ▷ *When are you going to phone him? — Never!* Quand est-ce que tu vas l'appeler? — Jamais! ❷ ne ... jamais
▐ Add **ne** if the sentence contains a verb.
▷ *I never write letters.* Je n'écris jamais. ▷ *I have never been camping.*

Je n'ai jamais fait de camping.
▷ *Never leave valuables in your car.* Ne
laissez jamais d'objets de valeur
dans votre voiture.; **Never again!**
Plus jamais!; **Never mind.** Ça ne
fait rien.

new adj ❶ nouveau (f nouvelle, mpl
nouveaux) ▷ *her new boyfriend* son
nouveau copain ❷ *(brand new)*
neuf (f neuve) ▷ *They've got a new
car.* Ils ont une voiture neuve.

news n ❶ nouvelles fpl ▷ *I've had
some bad news.* J'ai reçu de
mauvaises nouvelles. ❷ *(single
piece of news)* nouvelle f ▷ *That's
wonderful news!* Quelle bonne
nouvelle! ❸ *(on TV)* journal télévisé
m ▷ *I watch the news every evening.* Je
regarde le journal télévisé tous les
soirs. ❹ *(on radio)* informations fpl
▷ *I listen to the news every morning.*
J'écoute les informations tous les
matins.

newsagent n marchand de
journaux m

newspaper n journal m (pl
journaux) ▷ *I deliver newspapers.* Je
distribue des journaux.

newsreader n présentateur m,
présentatrice f

New Year n Nouvel An m ▷ *to
celebrate New Year* fêter le Nouvel
An; **Happy New Year!** Bonne
Année!; **New Year's Day** le Premier
de l'an; **New Year's Eve** la
Saint-Sylvestre

New Zealand n Nouvelle-Zélande
f; **in New Zealand** en
Nouvelle-Zélande

New Zealander n Néo-Zélandais
m, Néo-Zélandaise f

next adj, adv, prep ❶ *(in time)*
prochain(e) ▷ *next Saturday* samedi
prochain ▷ *next year* l'année
prochaine ▷ *next summer* l'été
prochain ❷ *(in sequence)* suivant(e)
▷ *the next train* le train suivant
▷ *Next please!* Au suivant!
❸ *(afterwards)* ensuite ▷ *What shall I
do next?* Qu'est-ce que je fais
ensuite?; **next to** à côté de ▷ *next to
the bank* à côté de la banque; **the
next day** le lendemain ▷ *The next
day we visited Versailles.* Le
lendemain nous avons visité
Versailles.; **the next time** la
prochaine fois ▷ *the next time you see
her* la prochaine fois que tu la
verras; **next door** à côté ▷ *They live
next door.* Ils habitent à côté.; **the
next room** la pièce d'à côté

NHS n Sécurité sociale f
● In France you have to pay for
● medical treatment when you
● receive it, and then claim it back
● from the **Sécurité sociale**.

nice adj ❶ *(kind)* gentil (f gentille)
▷ *Your parents are very nice.* Tes
parents sont très gentils.; **to be
nice to somebody** être [35] gentil
avec quelqu'un ❷ *(pretty)* joli(e)
▷ *That's a nice dress!* Qu'est-ce
qu'elle est jolie, cette robe! ❸ *(food)*
bon (f bonne) ▷ *a nice cup of coffee*
une bonne tasse de café; **Have a
nice time!** Amuse-toi bien!; **nice
weather** le beau temps; **It's a nice
day.** Il fait beau.

nickname n surnom m

niece n nièce f ▷ my niece ma nièce

Nigeria n Nigéria m; **in Nigeria** au Nigéria

night n ❶ nuit f ▷ I want a single room for two nights. Je veux une chambre à un lit pour deux nuits.; **My mother works nights.** Ma mère travaille de nuit.; **at night** la nuit; **Goodnight!** Bonne nuit! ❷ (evening) soir m ▷ last night hier soir

nightie n chemise de nuit f

nightmare n cauchemar m ▷ It was a real nightmare! Ça a été un vrai cauchemar!; **to have a nightmare** faire [36] un cauchemar

nil n zéro m ▷ We won one-nil. Nous avons gagné un à zéro.

nine num neuf ▷ She's nine. Elle a neuf ans.

nineteen num dix-neuf ▷ She's nineteen. Elle a dix-neuf ans.

nineteenth adj dix-neuvième ▷ the nineteenth floor le dix-neuvième étage; **the nineteenth of August** le dix-neuf août

ninety num quatre-vingt-dix

ninth adj neuvième ▷ the ninth floor le neuvième étage; **the ninth of August** le neuf août

no adv, adj ❶ non ▷ Are you coming? — No. Est-ce que vous venez? — Non. ▷ Would you like some more? — No thank you. Vous en voulez encore? — Non merci. ❷ (not any) pas de ▷ There's no hot water. Il n'y a pas d'eau chaude. ▷ There are no trains on Sundays. Il n'y a pas de trains le dimanche. ▷ No problem. Pas de problème.; **I've got no idea.** Je n'en ai aucune idée.; **No way!** Pas question!; **'no smoking'** 'défense de fumer'

nobody pron ❶ personne ▷ Who's going with you? — Nobody. Qui t'accompagne? — Personne. ❷ ne ... personne

⬛ Add **ne** if the sentence contains a verb.

▷ There was nobody in the office. Il n'y avait personne au bureau.; **Nobody likes him.** Personne ne l'aime.

nod vb (in agreement) acquiescer [12] d'un signe de tête; **to nod at somebody** (as greeting) saluer [28] quelqu'un d'un signe de tête

noise n bruit m ▷ Please make less noise. Faites moins de bruit s'il vous plaît.

noisy adj bruyant(e)

nominate vb ❶ (appoint) nommer [28] ▷ She was nominated as director. Elle a été nommée directrice. ❷ (propose) proposer [28] ▷ I nominate Ian Alexander as president of the society. Je propose Ian Alexander comme président de la société.; **He was nominated for an Oscar.** Il a été nominé pour un Oscar.

none pron ❶ aucun ▷ What sports do you do? — None. Qu'est-ce que tu fais comme sport? — Je n'en fais aucun. aucune ▷ How many sisters have you got? — None. Tu as combien de

sœurs? —Aucune. **❷** aucun ... ne
▌ Add **ne** if the sentence contains a verb.
▷ *None of my friends wanted to come.* Aucun de mes amis n'a voulu venir.; **There's none left.** Il n'y en a plus.; **There are none left.** Il n'y en a plus.

nonsense *n* bêtises *fpl* ▷ *She talks a lot of nonsense.* Elle dit beaucoup de bêtises.

non-smoking *adj* non-fumeurs
▷ *a non-smoking carriage* une voiture non-fumeurs

non-stop *adj, adv* **❶** direct(e)
▷ *a non-stop flight* un vol direct
❷ sans arrêt ▷ *He talks non-stop.* Il parle sans arrêt.

noodles *npl* nouilles *fpl*

noon *n* midi *m* ▷ *at noon* à midi

no one *pron* **❶** personne ▷ *Who's going with you? —No one.* Qui t'accompagne? —Personne.
❷ ne ... personne
▌ Add **ne** if the sentence contains a verb.
▷ *There was no one in the office.* Il n'y avait personne au bureau.; **No one likes Christopher.** Personne n'aime Christopher.

nor *conj* **neither ... nor** ni ... ni
▷ *neither the cinema nor the swimming pool* ni le cinéma, ni la piscine; **Nor do I.** Moi non plus.
▷ *I didn't like the film. —Nor did I.* Je n'ai pas aimé le film. —Moi non plus.; **Nor have I.** Moi non plus.
▷ *I haven't seen him. —Nor have I.* Je ne l'ai pas vu. —Moi non plus.

normal *adj* **❶** (*usual*) habituel (*f* habituelle) ▷ *at the normal time* à l'heure habituelle **❷** (*standard*) normal(e) (*mpl* normaux)
▷ *a normal car* une voiture normale

normally *adv* **❶** (*usually*) généralement ▷ *I normally arrive at nine o'clock.* J'arrive généralement à neuf heures. **❷** (*as normal*) normalement ▷ *In spite of the strike, the airports are working normally.* Malgré la grève, les aéroports fonctionnent normalement.

Normandy *n* Normandie *f*; **in Normandy** en Normandie; **to Normandy** en Normandie

north *adj, adv* **❶** nord ▷ *the north coast* la côte nord; **a north wind** un vent du nord **❷** vers le nord ▷ *We were travelling north.* Nous allions vers le nord.; **north of** au nord de ▷ *It's north of London.* C'est au nord de Londres.
▶ *n* nord *m* ▷ *in the north* dans le nord

North America *n* Amérique du Nord *f*

northeast *n* nord-est *m* ▷ *in the northeast* au nord-est

northern *adj* **the northern part of the island** la partie nord de l'île; **Northern Europe** l'Europe du Nord

Northern Ireland *n* Irlande du Nord *f*; **in Northern Ireland** en Irlande du Nord; **to Northern Ireland** en Irlande du Nord; **I'm from Northern Ireland.** Je viens d'Irlande du Nord.

North Pole *n* pôle Nord *m*

North Sea n mer du Nord f

northwest n nord-ouest m ▷ in the northwest au nord-ouest

Norway n Norvège f; **in Norway** en Norvège

Norwegian n ❶ (person) Norvégien m, Norvégienne f ❷ (language) norvégien m
▶ adj norvégien (f norvégienne)

nose n nez m (pl nez)

nosebleed n **to have a nosebleed** saigner [28] du nez ▷ I often get nosebleeds. Je saigne souvent du nez.

nosy adj fouineur (f fouineuse)

not adv ❶ pas ▷ Are you coming or not? Est-ce que tu viens ou pas?; **not really** pas vraiment; **not at all** pas du tout; **not yet** pas encore ▷ Have you finished? — Not yet. As-tu fini? — Pas encore. ❷ ne ... pas

Add **ne** if the sentence contains a verb.

▷ I'm not sure. Je ne suis pas sûr.
▷ It's not raining. Il ne pleut pas.
▷ You shouldn't do that. Tu ne devrais pas faire ça. ▷ They haven't arrived yet. Ils ne sont pas encore arrivés.
❸ non ▷ I hope not. J'espère que non. ▷ Can you lend me £10? — I'm afraid not. Est-ce que tu peux me prêter dix livres? — Non, désolé.

note n ❶ note f ▷ to take notes prendre des notes ❷ (letter) mot m ▷ I'll write her a note. Je vais lui écrire un mot. ❸ (banknote) billet m ▷ a £5 note un billet de cinq livres

note down vb noter [28]

notebook n carnet m

notepad n bloc-notes m (pl blocs-notes)

nothing n ❶ rien ▷ What's wrong? — Nothing. Qu'est-ce qui ne va pas? — Rien. ▷ nothing special rien de particulier ❷ ne ... rien

Add **ne** if the sentence contains a verb.

▷ He does nothing. Il ne fait rien.
▷ He ate nothing for breakfast. Il n'a rien mangé au petit déjeuner.;
Nothing is open on Sundays. Rien n'est ouvert le dimanche.

notice n (sign) panneau m (pl panneaux); **to put up a notice** mettre [47] un panneau; **a warning notice** un avertissement; **Don't take any notice of him!** Ne fais pas attention à lui!
▶ vb remarquer [28]

notice board n panneau d'affichage m (pl panneaux d'affichage)

nought n zéro m

noun n nom m

novel n roman m

novelist n romancier m, romancière f

November n novembre m; **in November** en novembre

now adv, conj maintenant ▷ What are you doing now? Qu'est-ce que tu fais maintenant?; **just now** en ce moment ▷ I'm rather busy just now. Je suis très occupé en ce moment.;
I did it just now. Je viens de le faire.; **He should be there by now.** Il doit être arrivé à l'heure qu'il est.;
It should be ready by now. Ça

a
b
c
d
e
f
g
h
i
j
k
l
m
n
o
p
q
r
s
t
u
v
w
x
y
z

devrait être déjà prêt.; **now and then** de temps en temps

nowhere adv nulle part ▷ nowhere else nulle part ailleurs

nuclear adj nucléaire ▷ nuclear power l'énergie nucléaire ▷ a nuclear power station une centrale nucléaire

nuisance n It's a nuisance. C'est très embêtant.; **Sorry to be a nuisance.** Désolé de vous déranger.

numb adj engourdi(e) ▷ My leg's gone numb. J'ai la jambe engourdie.; **numb with cold** engourdi par le froid

number n ① (total amount) nombre m ▷ a large number of people un grand nombre de gens ② (of house, telephone, bank account) numéro m ▷ They live at number 5. Ils habitent au numéro cinq. ▷ What's your phone number? Quel est votre numéro de téléphone? ▷ You've got the wrong number. Vous vous êtes trompé de numéro. ③ (figure, digit) chiffre m ▷ I can't read the second number. Je n'arrive pas à lire le deuxième chiffre.

number plate n plaque d'immatriculation f

nun n religieuse f ▷ She's a nun. Elle est religieuse.

nurse n infirmier m, infirmière f ▷ She's a nurse. Elle est infirmière.

nursery n ① (for children) crèche f ② (for plants) pépinière f

nursery school n école maternelle f

The **école maternelle** is a state school for 2-6 year-olds.

nut n ① (peanut) cacahuète f ② (hazelnut) noisette f ③ (walnut) noix f (pl noix) ④ (made of metal) écrou m

nuts adj He's nuts. Il est dingue.

nylon n nylon m

oak *n* chêne *m* ▷ *an oak table* une table en chêne

oar *n* aviron *m*

oats *n* avoine *f*

obedient *adj* obéissant(e)

obey *vb* **to obey the rules** respecter [**28**] le règlement

object *n* objet *m* ▷ *a familiar object* un objet familier

objection *n* objection *f*

oboe *n* hautbois *m* ▷ *I play the oboe.* Je joue du hautbois.

obsessed *adj* obsédé(e) ▷ *He's obsessed with trains.* Il est obsédé par les trains.

obsession *n* obsession *f* ▷ *It's getting to be an obsession with you.* Ça devient une obsession chez toi.; **Football's an obsession of mine.** Le football est une de mes passions.

obtain *vb* obtenir [**83**]

obvious *adj* évident(e)

obviously *adv* ❶ *(of course)* évidemment ▷ *Do you want to pass the exam? — Obviously!* Tu veux être reçu à l'examen? — Évidemment!; **Obviously not!** Bien sûr que non! ❷ *(visibly)* manifestement ▷ *She was obviously exhausted.* Elle était manifestement épuisée.

occasion *n* occasion *f* ▷ *a special occasion* une occasion spéciale; **on several occasions** à plusieurs reprises

occasionally *adv* de temps en temps

occupation *n* profession *f*

occupy *vb* occuper [**28**] ▷ *That seat is occupied.* Cette place est occupée.

occur *vb* *(happen)* avoir [**8**] lieu ▷ *The accident occurred yesterday.* L'accident a eu lieu hier.; **It suddenly occurred to me that …** Il m'est soudain venu à l'esprit que …

OCD *n* (= *obsessive compulsive disorder*) TOC *m*

ocean *n* océan *m*

o'clock *adv* **at four o'clock** à quatre heures; **It's five o'clock.** Il est cinq heures.

October *n* octobre *m*; **in October** en octobre

octopus *n* pieuvre *f*

odd *adj* ❶ bizarre ▷ *That's odd!* C'est bizarre! ❷ impair(e) ▷ *an odd number* un chiffre impair

of *prep* ❶ de ▷ *a boy of ten* un garçon de dix ans

de changes to **d'** before a vowel and most words beginning with 'h'.

d' ▷ *a kilo of oranges* un kilo d'oranges

de + le changes to **du**, and **de + les** changes to **des**.

du ▷ *the end of the film* la fin du film des ▷ *the end of the holidays* la fin des vacances ❷ *(with quantity, amount)* en ▷ *Can I have half of that?* Je peux en avoir la moitié?; **three of us** trois d'entre nous; **a friend of mine** un de mes amis; **the 14th of September** le quatorze septembre; **That's very kind of you.** C'est très gentil de votre part.; **It's made of wood.** C'est en bois.

off adv, prep, adj

For other expressions with 'off', see the verbs 'get', 'take', 'turn' etc.

❶ *(heater, light, TV)* éteint(e) ▷ *All the lights are off.* Toutes les lumières sont éteintes. ❷ *(tap, gas)* fermé(e) ▷ *Are you sure the tap is off?* Tu es sûr que le robinet est fermé? ❸ *(cancelled)* annulé(e) ▷ *The match is off.* Le match est annulé.; **to be off sick** être [35] malade; **a day off** un jour de congé ▷ *to take a day off work* prendre un jour de congé; **She's off school today.** Elle n'est pas à l'école aujourd'hui.; **I must be off now.** Je dois m'en aller maintenant.; **I'm off.** Je m'en vais.

offence (US **offense**) n *(crime)* délit m

offer n proposition f ▷ *a good offer* une proposition intéressante; **'on special offer'** 'en promotion'
▶ vb proposer [28] ▷ *He offered to help me.* Il m'a proposé de m'aider.

office n bureau m (pl bureaux) ▷ *She works in an office.* Elle travaille dans un bureau.

officer n officier m

official adj officiel (f officielle)

off-licence n marchand de vins et spiritueux m

offside adj *(in football)* hors jeu

often adv souvent ▷ *It often rains.* Il pleut souvent. ▷ *How often do you go to the gym?* Tu vas souvent à la gym?

oil n ❶ *(for lubrication, cooking)* huile f; **an oil painting** une peinture à l'huile ❷ *(crude oil)* pétrole m ▷ *North Sea oil* le pétrole de la mer du Nord
▶ vb graisser [28]

oil rig n plateforme pétrolière f ▷ *He works on an oil rig.* Il travaille sur une plateforme pétrolière.

ointment n pommade f

okay excl, adj *(agreed)* d'accord ▷ *Could you call back later? — Okay!* Tu peux rappeler plus tard? — D'accord! ▷ *I'll meet you at six o'clock, okay?* Je te retrouve à six heures, d'accord? ▷ *Is that okay?* C'est d'accord? ▷ *I'll do it tomorrow, if that's okay with you.* Je le ferai demain, si tu es d'accord.; **Are you okay?** Ça va?; **How was your holiday? — It was okay.** C'était comment tes vacances? — Pas

mal.; **What's your teacher like?**
— He's okay. Il est comment ton
prof? — Il est sympa. *(informal)*
old *adj* ❶ vieux (*f* vieille, *mpl* vieux)
▷ *an old dog* un vieux chien ▷ *an old*
house une vieille maison

> vieux changes to **vieil** before a
> vowel and most words
> beginning with 'h'.

vieil ▷ *an old man* un vieil homme;
âgé(e)

> When talking about people it is
> more polite to use **âgé** instead
> of **vieux**.

▷ *old people* les personnes âgées
❷ *(former)* ancien (*f* ancienne) ▷ *my*
old English teacher mon ancien
professeur d'anglais; **How old are**
you? Quel âge as-tu?; **He's ten**
years old. Il a dix ans.; **my older**
brother mon frère aîné ▷ *my older*
sister ma sœur aînée; **She's two**
years older than me. Elle a deux
ans de plus que moi.; **I'm the**
oldest in the family. Je suis l'aîné
de la famille.
old age pensioner *n* retraité *m*,
retraitée *f* ▷ *She's an old age*
pensioner. Elle est retraitée.
old-fashioned *adj* ❶ démodé(e)
▷ *She wears old-fashioned clothes.*
Elle porte des vêtements démodés.
❷ *(person)* vieux jeu ▷ *My parents are*
rather old-fashioned. Mes parents
sont plutôt vieux jeu.
olive *n* olive *f*
olive oil *n* huile d'olive *f*
Olympic® *adj* olympique; **the**
Olympics® les Jeux olympiques *mpl*

omelette *n* omelette *f*
on *prep, adv*

> There are several ways of
> translating 'on'. Scan the
> examples to find one that is
> similar to what you want to
> say. For other expressions with
> 'on', see the verbs 'go', 'put',
> 'turn' etc.

❶ sur ▷ *on the table* sur la table ❷ à
▷ *on the left* à gauche ▷ *on the 2nd*
floor au deuxième étage ▷ *I go to*
school on my bike. Je vais à l'école à
vélo.

> With days and dates 'on' is not
> translated.

▷ *on Friday* vendredi ▷ *on Fridays* le
vendredi ▷ *on Christmas Day* le jour
de Noël ▷ *on my birthday* le jour de
mon anniversaire; **on TV** à la télé
▷ *What's on TV?* Qu'est-ce qu'il y a à
la télé?; **on the radio** à la radio
▷ *I heard it on the radio.* Je l'ai
entendu à la radio.; **on the bus**
(1) *(by bus)* en bus ▷ *I go into town on*
the bus. Je vais en ville en bus.
(2) *(inside bus)* dans le bus ▷ *There*
were no empty seats on the bus. Il n'y
avait pas de places libres dans le
bus.; **on holiday** en vacances
▷ *They're on holiday.* Ils sont en
vacances.; **on strike** en grève
▶ *adj* ❶ *(heater, light, TV)* allumé(e)
▷ *I think I left the light on.* Je crois que
j'ai laissé la lumière allumée.
❷ *(tap, gas)* ouvert(e) ▷ *Leave the*
tap on. Laisse le robinet ouvert.
❸ *(machine)* en marche ▷ *Is the*
dishwasher on? Est-ce que le

a
b
c
d
e
f
g
h
i
j
k
l
m
n
o
p
q
r
s
t
u
v
w
x
y
z

lave-vaisselle est en marche?;
What's on at the cinema?
Qu'est-ce qui passe au cinéma?
once *adv* une fois ▷ *once a week* une
fois par semaine ▷ *once more* encore
une fois; **Once upon a time …** Il était
une fois …; **at once** tout de suite;
once in a while de temps en temps
one *num, pron*

> Use **un** for masculine nouns
> and **une** for feminine nouns.

❶ un ▷ *one day* un jour ▷ *Do you need
a stamp? — No thanks, I've got one.*
Est-ce que tu as besoin d'un
timbre? — Non merci, j'en ai un.
une ▷ *one minute* une minute ▷ *I've
got one brother and one sister.* J'ai un
frère et une sœur. ❷ *(impersonal)* on
▷ *One never knows.* On ne sait
jamais.; **this one (1)** celui-ci *m*
▷ *Which foot is hurting? — This one.*
Quel pied te fait mal? — Celui-ci.
(2) celle-ci *f* ▷ *Which is the best
photo? — This one.* Quelle est la
meilleure photo? — Celle-ci; **that
one (1)** celui-là *m* ▷ *Which bag is
yours? — That one.* Lequel est ton
sac? — Celui-là. **(2)** celle-là *f*
▷ *Which seat do you want? — That
one.* Quelle place voulez-vous? —
Celle-là.
oneself *pron* ❶ se ▷ *to hurt oneself* se
faire mal ❷ soi-même ▷ *It's quicker
to do it oneself.* C'est plus rapide de
le faire soi-même.
one-way *adj* **a one-way street**
une impasse
onion *n* oignon *m* ▷ *onion soup* la
soupe à l'oignon

online *adj* en ligne
▶ *adv* en ligne; **to go online** se
connecter [**28**] à Internet
only *adv, adj, conj* ❶ seul(e)
▷ *Monday is the only day I'm free.* Le
lundi est le seul jour où je suis libre.
▷ *French is the only subject I like.* Le
français est la seule matière que
j'aime. ❷ seulement ▷ *How much
was it? — Only 10 euros.* Combien
c'était? — Seulement dix euros.
❸ ne … que ▷ *We only want to stay
for one night.* Nous ne voulons rester
qu'une nuit. ▷ *These books are only
3 euros.* Ces livres ne coûtent que
trois euros. ❹ mais ▷ *I'd like the same
sweater, only in black.* Je voudrais le
même pull, mais en noir.; **an only
child** un enfant unique
onwards *adv* à partir de ▷ *from July
onwards* à partir de juillet
open *adj* ouvert(e) ▷ *The baker's is
open on Sunday morning.* La
boulangerie est ouverte le
dimanche matin.; **in the open air**
en plein air
▶ *vb* ❶ ouvrir [**55**] ▷ *Can I open the
window?* Est-ce que je peux ouvrir la
fenêtre? ▷ *What time do the shops
open?* Les magasins ouvrent à
quelle heure? ❷ s'ouvrir [**55**] ▷ *The
door opens automatically.* La porte
s'ouvre automatiquement.
opening hours *npl* heures
d'ouverture *fpl*
opera *n* opéra *m*
operate *vb* ❶ fonctionner [**28**]
▷ *The lights operate on a timer.* Les
lumières fonctionnent avec une

minuterie. ❷ faire [**36**] fonctionner ▷ *How do you operate the camcorder?* Comment fait-on fonctionner le caméscope? ❸ *(perform surgery)* opérer [**34**]; **to operate on someone** opérer [**34**] quelqu'un

operation n opération f ▷ *a major operation* une grave opération; **to have an operation** se faire [**36**] opérer ▷ *I have never had an operation.* Je ne me suis jamais fait opérer.

opinion n avis m ▷ *in my opinion* à mon avis ▷ *He asked me my opinion.* Il m'a demandé mon avis.; **What's your opinion?** Qu'est-ce que vous en pensez?

opinion poll n sondage m

opponent n adversaire mf

opportunity n occasion f; **to have the opportunity to do something** avoir [**8**] l'occasion de faire quelque chose ▷ *I've never had the opportunity to go to France.* Je n'ai jamais eu l'occasion d'aller en France.

opposed adj **I've always been opposed to violence.** J'ai toujours été contre la violence.; **as opposed to** par opposition à

opposite adj, adv, prep ❶ opposé(e) ▷ *It's in the opposite direction.* C'est dans la direction opposée. ❷ en face ▷ *They live opposite.* Ils habitent en face. ❸ en face de ▷ *the girl sitting opposite me* la fille assise en face de moi; **the opposite sex** l'autre sexe

opposition n opposition f

optician n opticien m, opticienne f

▷ *She's an optician.* Elle est opticienne.

optimistic adj optimiste

option n ❶ *(choice)* choix m ▷ *I've got no option.* Je n'ai pas le choix. ❷ *(optional subject)* matière à option f ▷ *I'm doing geology as my option.* La géologie est ma matière à option.

or conj ❶ ou ▷ *Would you like tea or coffee?* Est-ce que tu veux du thé ou du café?

> Use **ni ... ni** in negative sentences.

▷ *I don't eat meat or fish.* Je ne mange ni viande, ni poisson. ❷ *(otherwise)* sinon ▷ *Hurry up or you'll miss the bus.* Dépêche-toi, sinon tu vas rater le bus.; **Give me the money, or else!** Donne-moi l'argent, sinon tu vas le regretter!

oral adj oral(e) *(mpl* oraux*)*; **an oral exam** un oral

▶ n oral m *(pl* oraux*)* ▷ *I've got my French oral soon.* Je vais bientôt passer mon oral de français.

orange n orange f; **an orange juice** un jus d'orange

▶ adj orange

orchard n verger m

orchestra n orchestre m ▷ *I play in the school orchestra.* Je joue dans l'orchestre de l'école.

order n ❶ *(sequence)* ordre m ▷ *in alphabetical order* dans l'ordre alphabétique ❷ *(instruction)* commande f ▷ *The waiter took our order.* Le garçon a pris notre commande.; **in order to** pour ▷ *He* *does it in order to earn money.* Il le fait pour gagner de l'argent.; **'out of order'** 'en panne'

▶ *vb* commander [**28**] ▷ *We ordered steak and chips.* Nous avons commandé un steak frites. ▷ *Are you ready to order?* Vous êtes prêt à commander?; **to order somebody about** donner [**28**] des ordres à quelqu'un ▷ *She liked to order him about.* Elle aimait lui donner des ordres.

ordinary *adj* ❶ ordinaire ▷ *an ordinary day* une journée ordinaire ❷ *(people)* comme les autres ▷ *an ordinary family* une famille comme les autres

organ *n (instrument)* orgue *m* ▷ *I play the organ.* Je joue de l'orgue.

organic *adj (vegetables, fruit)* biologique

organization *n* organisation *f*

organize *vb* organiser [**28**]

original *adj* original(e) *(mpl originaux)* ▷ *It's a very original idea.* C'est une idée très originale.; **Our original plan was to go camping.** À l'origine nous avions l'intention de faire du camping.

originally *adv* à l'origine

ornament *n* bibelot *m*

orphan *n* orphelin *m*, orpheline *f*

other *adj, pron* autre ▷ *Have you got these jeans in other colours?* Est-ce que vous avez ce jean dans d'autres couleurs? ▷ *on the other side of the street* de l'autre côté de la rue ▷ *the other day* l'autre jour; **the other one** l'autre ▷ *This one? — No, the*

other one. Celui-ci? — Non, l'autre.; **the others** les autres ▷ *The others are going but I'm not.* Les autres y vont mais pas moi.

otherwise *adv, conj* ❶ *(if not)* sinon ▷ *Note down the number, otherwise you'll forget it.* Note le numéro, sinon tu vas l'oublier. ❷ *(in other ways)* à part ça ▷ *I'm tired, but otherwise I'm fine.* Je suis fatigué, mais à part ça, ça va.

ought *vb*

> To translate 'ought to' use the conditional tense of **devoir**.

▷ *I ought to phone my parents.* Je devrais appeler mes parents.

our *adj* notre *(pl* nos) ▷ *Our house is quite big.* Notre maison est plutôt grande.

ours *pron* le nôtre ▷ *Your garden is very big, ours is much smaller.* Votre jardin est très grand, le nôtre est beaucoup plus petit.
la nôtre ▷ *Your school is very different from ours.* Votre école est très différente de la nôtre.
les nôtres ▷ *Our teachers are strict. — Ours are too.* Nos professeurs sont sévères. — Les nôtres aussi.; **Is this ours?** C'est à nous? ▷ *This car is ours.* Cette voiture est à nous. ▷ *Whose is this? — It's ours.* C'est à qui? — À nous.

ourselves *pron* ❶ nous ▷ *We really enjoyed ourselves.* Nous nous sommes vraiment bien amusés. ❷ nous-mêmes ▷ *We built our garage ourselves.* Nous avons construit notre garage nous-mêmes.

out adv, adj

There are several ways of translating 'out'. Scan the examples to find one that is similar to what you want to say. For other expressions with 'out', see the verbs 'go', 'put', 'turn' etc.

❶ (outside) <u>dehors</u> ▷ It's cold out. Il fait froid dehors. ❷ (light, fire) <u>éteint(e)</u> ▷ All the lights are out. Toutes les lumières sont éteintes.; **She's out.** Elle est sortie.; **She's out shopping.** Elle est sortie faire des courses.; **She's out for the afternoon.** Elle ne sera pas là de tout l'après-midi.; **out there** dehors ▷ It's cold out there. Il fait froid dehors.; **to go out** sortir [79] ▷ I'm going out tonight. Je sors ce soir.; **to go out with somebody** sortir [79] avec quelqu'un ▷ I've been going out with him for two months. Je sors avec lui depuis deux mois.; **out of (1)** dans ▷ to drink out of a glass boire dans un verre **(2)** sur ▷ in 9 cases out of 10 dans neuf cas sur dix **(3)** en dehors de ▷ He lives out of town. Il habite en dehors de la ville.; **3 km out of town** à trois kilomètres de la ville; **out of curiosity** par curiosité; **out of work** sans emploi; **That is out of the question.** C'est hors de question.; **You're out!** (in game) Tu es éliminé!; **'way out'** 'sortie'

outdoor adj <u>en plein air</u> ▷ an outdoor swimming pool une piscine en plein air; **outdoor activities** les activités de plein air

outdoors adv <u>au grand air</u>

outfit n <u>tenue</u> f ▷ She bought a new outfit for the wedding. Elle a acheté une nouvelle tenue pour le mariage.; **a cowboy outfit** une panoplie de cowboy

outing n <u>sortie</u> f ▷ to go on an outing faire une sortie

outline n ❶ (summary) <u>grandes lignes</u> fpl ▷ This is an outline of the plan. Voici les grandes lignes du projet. ❷ (shape) <u>contours</u> mpl ▷ We could see the outline of the mountain in the mist. Nous distinguions les contours de la montagne dans la brume.

outside n <u>extérieur</u> m ▷ adj, adv, prep ❶ <u>extérieur(e)</u> ▷ the outside walls les murs extérieurs ❷ <u>dehors</u> ▷ It's very cold outside. Il fait très froid dehors. ❸ <u>en dehors de</u> ▷ outside the school en dehors de l'école ▷ outside school hours en dehors des heures de cours

outskirts npl <u>banlieue</u> f ▷ on the outskirts of the town dans les banlieues de la ville

outstanding adj <u>remarquable</u>

oval adj <u>ovale</u>

oven n <u>four</u> m

over prep, adv, adj

When there is movement over something, use **par-dessus**; when something is located above something, use **au-dessus de**.

❶ <u>par-dessus</u> ▷ The ball went over the wall. Le ballon est passé

a b c d e f g h i j k l m n o p q r s t u v w x y z

par-dessus le mur. ❷ au-dessus de
▷ There's a mirror over the washbasin.
Il y a une glace au-dessus du
lavabo. ❸ (more than) plus de ▷ It's
over twenty kilos. Ça pèse plus de
vingt kilos. ▷ The temperature was
over thirty degrees. Il faisait une
température de plus de trente
degrés. ❹ (during) pendant ▷ over
the holidays pendant les vacances
❺ (finished) terminé(e) ▷ I'll be
happy when the exams are over. Je
serai content quand les examens
seront terminés.; **over here** ici;
over there là-bas; **all over
Scotland** dans toute l'Écosse; **The
baker's is over the road.** La
boulangerie est de l'autre côté de
la rue.; **I spilled coffee over my
shirt.** J'ai renversé du café sur ma
chemise.

overcast adj couvert(e) ▷ The sky
was overcast. Le ciel était couvert.

overdose n (of drugs) overdose f
▷ to take an overdose faire une
overdose

overdraft n découvert m; **to have
an overdraft** être [**35**] à découvert

overseas adv à l'étranger ▷ I'd like to
work overseas. J'aimerais travailler à
l'étranger.

overtake vb dépasser [**58**]

overtime n heures
supplémentaires fpl ▷ to work
overtime faire des heures
supplémentaires

overtook vb see **overtake**

overweight adj trop gros (f trop
grosse)

owe vb devoir [**26**]; **to owe
somebody something** devoir [**26**]
quelque chose à quelqu'un ▷ I owe
you 50 euros. Je te dois cinquante
euros.

owing to prep en raison de ▷ owing
to bad weather en raison du
mauvais temps

owl n hibou m (pl hiboux)

own adj propre ▷ I've got my own
bathroom. J'ai ma propre salle de
bain.; **I'd like a room of my own.**
J'aimerais avoir une chambre à
moi.; **on his own** tout seul ▷ on her
own toute seule
▸ vb posséder [**34**]

own up vb avouer [**28**]; **to own up
to something** admettre [**47**]
quelque chose

owner n propriétaire mf

oxygen n oxygène m

oyster n huître f

ozone layer n couche d'ozone f

p

Pacific n Pacifique m

pack vb faire [**36**] ses bagages ▷ I'll help you pack. Je vais t'aider à faire tes bagages.; **I've already packed my case.** J'ai déjà fait ma valise.; **Pack it in!** (stop it) Laisse tomber! ▶ n ❶ (packet) paquet m ▷ a pack of cigarettes un paquet de cigarettes ❷ (of yoghurts, cans) pack m ▷ a six-pack un pack de six; **a pack of cards** un jeu de cartes

package n paquet m; **a package holiday** un voyage organisé

packed adj bondé(e) ▷ The cinema was packed. Le cinéma était bondé.

packed lunch n repas froid m ▷ I take a packed lunch to school. J'apporte un repas froid à l'école.

packet n paquet m ▷ a packet of cigarettes un paquet de cigarettes

pad n (notepad) bloc-notes m (pl blocs-notes)

paddle vb ❶ (canoe) pagayer [**59**] ❷ (in water) faire [**36**] trempette ▶ n (for canoe) pagaie f; **to go for a paddle** faire [**36**] trempette

padlock n cadenas m

page n (of book) page f ▶ vb **to page somebody** faire [**36**] appeler quelqu'un

pain n douleur f ▷ a terrible pain une douleur insupportable; **I've got a pain in my stomach.** J'ai mal à l'estomac.; **to be in pain** souffrir [**54**] ▷ She's in a lot of pain. Elle souffre beaucoup.; **He's a real pain.** Il est vraiment pénible.

painful adj douloureux (f douloureuse) ▷ to suffer from painful periods souffrir de règles douloureuses; **Is it painful?** Ça te fait mal?

painkiller n analgésique m

paint n peinture f ▶ vb peindre [**60**] ▷ to paint something green peindre quelque chose en vert

paintbrush n pinceau m (pl pinceaux)

painter n peintre m

painting n ❶ peinture f ▷ My hobby is painting. Je fais de la peinture. ❷ (picture) tableau m (pl tableaux) ▷ a painting by Picasso un tableau de Picasso

pair n paire f ▷ a pair of shoes une paire de chaussures; **a pair of trousers** un pantalon; **a pair of jeans** un jean; **a pair of pants**

(1) *(briefs)* un slip **(2)** *(boxer shorts)* un caleçon **(3)** *(US: trousers)* un pantalon; **in pairs** deux par deux ▷ *We work in pairs.* On travaille deux par deux.

Pakistan n Pakistan m; **in Pakistan** au Pakistan; **to Pakistan** au Pakistan; **He's from Pakistan.** Il est pakistanais.

Pakistani n Pakistanais m, Pakistanaise f
▶ *adj* pakistanais(e)

palace n palais m

pale *adj* pâle ▷ *a pale blue shirt* une chemise bleu pâle

Palestine n Palestine f; **in Palestine** en Palestine

Palestinian n Palestinien m, Palestinienne f
▶ *adj* palestinien (f palestinienne)

palm n *(of hand)* paume f; **a palm tree** un palmier

pan n ❶ *(saucepan)* casserole f ❷ *(frying pan)* poêle f

pancake n crêpe f; **Pancake Day** mardi gras
● Pancake Day is celebrated in
● France as well. Children dress up
● and eat **crêpes**.

panic n panique f
▶ *vb* s'affoler [28] **Don't panic!** Pas de panique!

panther n panthère f

pantomime n spectacle de Noël pour enfants m

pants npl ❶ *(briefs)* slip msg ▷ *a pair of pants* un slip ❷ *(boxer shorts)* caleçon msg ▷ *a pair of pants* un caleçon ❸ *(trousers: US)* pantalon

msg ▷ *a pair of pants* un pantalon

pantyhose npl *(US)* collant msg

paper n ❶ papier m ▷ *a piece of paper* un morceau de papier; **a paper towel** une serviette en papier; **an exam paper** une épreuve écrite ❷ *(newspaper)* journal m *(pl journaux)* ▷ *I saw an advert in the paper.* J'ai vu une annonce dans le journal.

paperback n livre de poche m

paper clip n trombone m

paper round n tournée de distribution de journaux f

parachute n parachute m

parade n défilé m

paradise n paradis m

paragraph n paragraphe m

parallel *adj* parallèle

paralysed *adj* paralysé(e)

paramedic n auxiliaire médical m, auxiliaire médicale f

parcel n colis m

pardon n **Pardon?** Pardon?

parent n ❶ *(father)* père m ❷ *(mother)* mère f; **my parents** mes parents mpl

Paris n Paris f; **in Paris** à Paris; **to Paris** à Paris; **She's from Paris.** Elle est parisienne.

Parisian n Parisien m, Parisienne f
▶ *adj* parisien (f parisienne)

park n parc m; **a national park** un parc national; **a theme park** un parc à thème; **a car park** un parking
▶ *vb* ❶ garer [28] ▷ *Where can I park my car?* Où est-ce que je peux garer ma voiture? ❷ se garer [28] ▷ *We*

couldn't find anywhere to park. Nous avons eu du mal à nous garer.

parking n stationnement m ▷ 'no parking' 'stationnement interdit'

| Be careful not to translate **parking** by the French word **parking**.

parking lot n (US) parking m

parking meter n parcmètre m

parking ticket n p.-v. m (informal)

parliament n parlement m

parole n on parole en liberté conditionnelle

parrot n perroquet m

parsley n persil m

part n ❶ (section) partie f ▷ The first part of the film was boring. La première partie du film était ennuyeuse. ❷ (component) pièce f ▷ spare parts les pièces de rechange ❸ (in play, film) rôle m; **to take part in something** participer [28] à quelque chose ▷ A lot of people took part in the demonstration. Beaucoup de gens ont participé à la manifestation.

particular adj particulier (f particulière) ▷ Are you looking for anything particular? Est-ce que vous voulez quelque chose de particulier?; **nothing in particular** rien de particulier

particularly adv particulièrement

partly adv en partie

partner n ❶ (in game) partenaire mf ❷ (in business) associé m, associée f ❸ (in dance) cavalier m, cavalière f ❹ (in relationship) compagnon m, compagne f

part-time adj, adv à temps partiel ▷ a part-time job un travail à temps partiel ▷ She works part-time. Elle travaille à temps partiel.

party n ❶ fête f ▷ a birthday party une fête d'anniversaire ❷ (more formal) soirée f ▷ I'm going to a party on Saturday. Je vais à une soirée samedi. ❸ (political) parti m ▷ the Conservative Party le Parti conservateur ❹ (group) groupe m ▷ a party of tourists un groupe de touristes

pass n ❶ (in mountains) col m ▷ The pass was blocked with snow. Le col était enneigé. ❷ (in football) passe f; **to get a pass** (in exam) être [35] reçu ▷ I got six passes. J'ai été reçu dans six matières.; **a bus pass** une carte de bus

▶ vb ❶ (exam) être [35] reçu ▷ Did you pass? Tu as été reçu?; **to pass an exam** être [35] reçu à un examen

| Be careful not to translate **to pass an exam** by **passer un examen**.

❷ passer [58] ▷ Could you pass me the salt, please? Est-ce que vous pourriez me passer le sel, s'il vous plaît? ▷ The time has passed quickly. Le temps a passé rapidement. ❸ passer [58] devant ▷ I pass his house on my way to school. Je passe devant chez lui en allant à l'école.

pass out vb (faint) s'évanouir [38]

passage n ❶ (piece of writing) passage m ▷ Read the passage carefully. Lisez attentivement le

a
b
c
d
e
f
g
h
i
j
k
l
m
n
o
p
q
r
s
t
u
v
w
x
y
z

passage. ❷ *(corridor)* couloir m
passenger n passager m,
   passagère f
passion n passion f
passive adj passif *(f* passive*)*;
   passive smoking le tabagisme
   passif
Passover n Pâque juive f ▷ *at
   Passover* à la Pâque juive
passport n passeport m ▷ *passport
   control* le contrôle des passeports
password n mot de passe m
past adv, prep *(beyond)* après ▷ *It's on
   the right, just past the station.* C'est
   sur la droite, juste après la gare.;
   to go past (1) passer [**58**] ▷ *The bus
   went past without stopping.* Le bus
   est passé sans s'arrêter. **(2)** passer
   [**58**] devant ▷ *The bus goes past our
   house.* Le bus passe devant notre
   maison.; **It's half past ten.** Il est
   dix heures et demie.; **It's quarter
   past nine.** Il est neuf heures et
   quart.; **It's ten past eight.** Il est
   huit heures dix.; **It's past
   midnight.** Il est minuit passé.
   ▶ n passé m ▷ *She lives in the past.*
   Elle vit dans le passé.; **in the past**
   (previously) autrefois ▷ *This was
   common in the past.* C'était courant
   autrefois.
pasta n pâtes fpl ▷ *Pasta is easy to
   cook.* Les pâtes sont faciles à
   préparer.
pasteurized adj pasteurisé(e)
pastry n pâte f; **pastries** les
   pâtisseries fpl
patch n ❶ pièce f ▷ *a patch of
   material* une pièce de tissu ❷ *(for*

flat tyre) rustine f; **He's got a bald
   patch.** Il a le crâne dégarni.
path n ❶ *(footpath)* chemin m ❷ *(in
   garden, park)* allée f
pathetic adj lamentable ▷ *Our
   team was pathetic.* Notre équipe a
   été lamentable.
patience n ❶ patience f ▷ *He hasn't
   got much patience.* Il n'a pas
   beaucoup de patience. ❷ *(card
   game)* réussite f ▷ *to play patience*
   faire une réussite
patient n patient m, patiente f
   ▶ adj patient(e)
patio n patio m
patrol n patrouille f
patrol car n voiture de police f
pattern n motif m ▷ *a geometric
   pattern* un motif géométrique; **a
   sewing pattern** un patron
pause n pause f
pavement n trottoir m
paw n patte f
pay n salaire m
   ▶ vb ❶ payer [**59**] ▷ *They pay me
   more on Sundays.* Je suis payé
   davantage le dimanche. ❷ régler
   [**34**] ▷ *to pay by cheque* régler par
   chèque ▷ *to pay by credit card* régler
   par carte de crédit; **to pay for
   something** payer [**59**] quelque
   chose ▷ *I paid for my ticket.* J'ai payé
   mon billet. ▷ *I paid 50 euros for it.* Je
   l'ai payé cinquante euros.; **to pay
   extra for something** payer [**59**] un
   supplément pour quelque chose
   ▷ *You have to pay extra for breakfast.* Il
   faut payer un supplément pour le
   petit déjeuner.; **to pay attention**

faire [**36**] attention ▷ *Don't pay any attention to him!* Ne fais pas attention à lui!; **to pay somebody a visit** rendre [**7**] visite à quelqu'un ▷ *Paul paid us a visit last night.* Paul nous a rendu visite hier soir.; **to pay somebody back** rembourser [**28**] quelqu'un ▷ *I'll pay you back tomorrow.* Je te rembourserai demain.

payment n paiement m

payphone n téléphone public m

PC n (= *personal computer*) PC m ▷ *She typed the report on her PC.* Elle a tapé le rapport sur son PC.

PE n EPS f ▷ *We do PE twice a week.* Nous avons EPS deux fois par semaine.

pea n petit pois m

peace n ① (*after war*) paix f ② (*quietness*) calme m

peaceful adj ① (*calm*) paisible ▷ *a peaceful afternoon* un après-midi paisible ② (*not violent*) pacifique ▷ *a peaceful protest* une manifestation pacifique

peach n pêche f

peacock n paon m

peak n (*of mountain*) cime f; **the peak rate** le plein tarif ▷ *You pay the peak rate for calls at this time of day.* On paie le plein tarif quand on appelle à cette heure-ci.; **in peak season** en haute saison

peanut n cacahuète f ▷ *a packet of peanuts* un paquet de cacahuètes

peanut butter n beurre de cacahuètes m ▷ *a peanut-butter sandwich* un sandwich au beurre de cacahuètes

pear n poire f

pearl n perle f

pebble n galet m ▷ *a pebble beach* une plage de galets

peculiar adj bizarre ▷ *He's a peculiar person.* Il est bizarre. ▷ *It tastes peculiar.* Ça a un goût bizarre.

pedal n pédale f

pedestrian n piéton m

pedestrian crossing n passage pour piétons m

pee n **to have a pee** faire [**36**] pipi

peel n (*of orange*) écorce f ▶ vb ① éplucher [**28**] ▷ *Shall I peel the potatoes?* J'épluche les pommes de terre? ② peler [**43**] ▷ *My nose is peeling.* Mon nez pèle.

peg n ① (*for coats*) portemanteau m (pl portemanteaux) ② (*clothes peg*) pince à linge f ③ (*tent peg*) piquet m

pelvis n bassin m

pen n stylo m

penalty n ① (*punishment*) peine f; **the death penalty** la peine de mort ② (*in football*) penalty m ③ (*in rugby*) pénalité f; **a penalty shoot-out** les tirs au but

pence npl pence mpl

pencil n crayon m; **in pencil** au crayon

pencil case n trousse f

pencil sharpener n taille-crayon m (pl taille-crayons)

pendant n pendentif m

penfriend n correspondant m, correspondante f

penguin n pingouin m

penicillin n pénicilline f

penis n pénis m
penknife n canif m
penny n penny m (pl pence)
pension n retraite f
pensioner n retraité m, retraitée f
people npl ❶ gens mpl ▷ a lot of
people beaucoup de gens
❷ (individuals) personnes fpl ▷ six
people six personnes; **How many
people are there in your family?**
Vous êtes combien dans votre
famille?; **French people** les
Français; **People say that ...** On
dit que ...
pepper n ❶ (spice) poivre m ▷ Pass
the pepper, please. Passez-moi le
poivre, s'il vous plaît. ❷ (vegetable)
poivron m ▷ a green pepper un
poivron vert
peppermill n moulin à poivre m
peppermint n (sweet) pastille de
menthe f; **peppermint chewing
gum** le chewing-gum à la menthe
per prep par ▷ per day par jour ▷ per
week par semaine; **30 miles per
hour** trente miles à l'heure
per cent adv pour cent ▷ fifty per
cent cinquante pour cent
percentage n pourcentage m
percussion n percussion f ▷ I play
percussion. Je joue des percussions.
perfect adj parfait(e) ▷ Chantal
speaks perfect English. Chantal parle
un anglais parfait.
perfectly adv parfaitement
perform vb (act, play) jouer [28]
performance n ❶ (show)
spectacle m ▷ The performance lasts
two hours. Le spectacle dure deux

heures. ❷ (acting) interprétation f
▷ his performance as Hamlet son
interprétation d'Hamlet ❸ (results)
performance f ▷ the team's poor
performance la médiocre
performance de l'équipe
perfume n parfum m
perhaps adv peut-être ▷ Perhaps
he's ill. Il est peut-être malade.;
perhaps not peut-être pas
period n ❶ période f ▷ for a limited
period pour une période limitée
❷ (in history) époque f ▷ the
Victorian period l'époque
victorienne ❸ (menstruation) règles
fpl ▷ I'm having my period. J'ai mes
règles. ❹ (lesson time) cours m
▷ Each period lasts forty minutes.
Chaque cours dure quarante
minutes.
perm n permanente f ▷ She's got a
perm. Elle a une permanente.; **to
have a perm** se faire [36] faire une
permanente
permanent adj permanent(e)
permission n permission f ▷ Could I
have permission to leave early?
Pourrais-je avoir la permission de
partir plus tôt?
permit n permis m ▷ a fishing permit
un permis de pêche
persecute vb persécuter [28]
person n personne f ▷ She's a very
nice person. C'est une personne très
sympathique.; **in person** en
personne
personal adj personnel (f
personnelle); **personal column** les
annonces personnelles fpl

personality n personnalité f

personally adv personnellement
▷ I don't know him personally. Je ne le connais pas personnellement.

personal stereo n Walkman® m

perspiration n transpiration f

persuade vb persuader [**28**]; **to persuade somebody to do something** persuader [**28**] quelqu'un de faire quelque chose ▷ She persuaded me to go with her. Elle m'a persuadé de l'accompagner.

pessimistic adj pessimiste

pest n (person) casse-pieds mf ▷ He's a real pest! C'est un vrai casse-pieds!

pester vb importuner [**28**]

pet n animal familier m ▷ Have you got a pet? Est-ce que tu as un animal familier?; **She's the teacher's pet.** C'est la chouchoute de la maîtresse.

petrol n essence f; **unleaded petrol** l'essence sans plomb

▌ Be careful not to translate **petrol** by **pétrole**.

petrol station n station-service f (pl stations-service)

pharmacy n pharmacie f
● Pharmacies in France are
● identified by a special green
● cross outside the shop.

pheasant n faisan m

philosophy n philosophie f

phobia n phobie f

phone n téléphone m ▷ Where's the phone? Où est le téléphone?; **by phone** par téléphone; **to be on the phone** être [**35**] au téléphone ▷ She's on the phone at the moment. Elle est au téléphone en ce moment.; **Can I use the phone, please?** Est-ce que je peux téléphoner, s'il vous plaît?
▶ vb appeler [**4**] ▷ I'll phone the station. Je vais appeler la gare.

phone bill n facture de téléphone f

phone book n annuaire m

phone box n cabine téléphonique f

phone call n appel m ▷ There's a phone call for you. Il y a un appel pour vous.; **to make a phone call** téléphoner [**28**] ▷ Can I make a phone call? Est-ce que peux téléphoner?

phonecard n carte de téléphone f

phone number n numéro de téléphone m

photo n photo f; **to take a photo** prendre [**65**] une photo; **to take a photo of somebody** prendre [**65**] quelqu'un en photo

photocopier n photocopieuse f

photocopy n photocopie f
▶ vb photocopier [**19**]

photograph n photo f; **to take a photograph** prendre [**65**] une photo; **to take a photograph of somebody** prendre [**65**] quelqu'un en photo
▶ vb photographier [**19**]

photographer n photographe mf ▷ She's a photographer. Elle est photographe.

photography n photo f ▷ My hobby is photography. Je fais de la photo.

phrase n expression f

a b c d e f g h i j k l m n o p q r s t u v w x y z

phrase book n guide de conversation m

physical adj physique
▶ n (US) examen médical m

physicist n physicien m, physicienne f ▷ He's a physicist. Il est physicien.

physics n physique f ▷ She teaches physics. Elle enseigne la physique.

physiotherapist n kinésithérapeute mf

physiotherapy n kinésithérapie f

pianist n pianiste mf

piano n piano m ▷ I play the piano. Je joue du piano. ▷ I have piano lessons. Je prends des leçons de piano.

pick n Take your pick! Faites votre choix!
▶ vb ❶ (choose) choisir [38] ▷ I picked the biggest piece. J'ai choisi le plus gros morceau. ❷ (for team) sélectionner [28] ▷ I've been picked for the team. J'ai été sélectionné pour faire partie de l'équipe. ❸ (fruit, flowers) cueillir [22]

pick on vb harceler [43] ▷ She's always picking on me. Elle me harcèle constamment.

pick out vb choisir [38] ▷ I like them all — it's difficult to pick one out. Ils me plaisent tous — c'est difficile d'en choisir un.

pick up vb ❶ (collect) venir [89] chercher ▷ We'll come to the airport to pick you up. Nous viendrons vous chercher à l'aéroport. ❷ (from floor) ramasser [28] ▷ Could you help me pick up the toys? Tu peux m'aider à ramasser les jouets? ❸ (learn)

apprendre [65] ▷ I picked up some Spanish during my holiday. J'ai appris quelques mots d'espagnol pendant mes vacances.

pickpocket n pickpocket m

picnic n pique-nique m; **to have a picnic** pique-niquer [28] ▷ We had a picnic on the beach. Nous avons pique-niqué sur la plage.

picture n ❶ illustration f ▷ Children's books have lots of pictures. Il y a beaucoup d'illustrations dans les livres pour enfants. ❷ photo f ▷ My picture was in the paper. Ma photo était dans le journal. ❸ (painting) tableau m (pl tableaux) ▷ a famous picture un tableau célèbre; **to paint a picture of something** peindre [60] quelque chose ❹ (drawing) dessin m; **to draw a picture of something** dessiner [28] quelque chose; **the pictures** (cinema) le cinéma ▷ Shall we go to the pictures? On va au cinéma?

picture messaging n envoi de photos par MMS m

pie n tourte f ▷ an apple pie une tourte aux pommes

piece n morceau m (pl morceaux) ▷ A small piece, please. Un petit morceau, s'il vous plaît.; **a piece of furniture** un meuble; **a piece of advice** un conseil

pier n jetée f

pierce vb percer [12] ▷ She's going to have her ears pierced. Elle va se faire percer les oreilles.

pierced adj percé(e) ▷ I've got pierced

ears. J'ai les oreilles percées.

piercing n piercing m ▷ *She has several piercings.* Elle a plusieurs piercings.

pig n cochon m

pigeon n pigeon m

piggy bank n tirelire f

pigtail n natte f

pile n ❶ (*untidy heap*) tas m ❷ (*tidy stack*) pile f

pill n pilule f; **to be on the pill** prendre [**65**] la pilule

pillow n oreiller m

pilot n pilote m ▷ *He's a pilot.* Il est pilote.

pimple n bouton m

PIN n (= *personal identification number*) code confidentiel m

pin n épingle f; **I've got pins and needles.** J'ai des fourmis dans les jambes.

pinball n flipper m ▷ *to play pinball* jouer au flipper; **a pinball machine** un flipper

pinch vb ❶ pincer [**12**] ▷ *He pinched me!* Il m'a pincé! ❷ (*informal: steal*) piquer [**28**] ▷ *Who's pinched my pen?* Qui est-ce qui m'a piqué mon stylo?

pine n pin m ▷ *a pine table* une table en pin

pineapple n ananas m

pink adj rose

pint n pinte f

● In France measurements are in litres and centilitres. A pint is about 0.6 litres.

a pint of milk un demi-litre de lait; **to have a pint** boire [**10**] une bière

▷ *He's gone out for a pint.* Il est parti boire une bière.

pipe n ❶ (*for water, gas*) conduite f ▷ *The pipes froze.* Les conduites d'eau ont gelé. ❷ (*for smoking*) pipe f ▷ *He smokes a pipe.* Il fume la pipe.; **the pipes** (*bagpipes*) la cornemuse ▷ *He plays the pipes.* Il joue de la cornemuse.

pirate n pirate m

pirated adj pirate ▷ *a pirated DVD* un DVD pirate

Pisces n Poissons m ▷ *I'm Pisces.* Je suis Poissons.

pistol n pistolet m

pitch n terrain m ▷ *a football pitch* un terrain de football

▶ vb (*tent*) dresser [**28**] ▷ *We pitched our tent near the beach.* Nous avons dressé notre tente près de la plage.

pity n pitié f; **What a pity!** Quel dommage!

▶ vb plaindre [**17**]

pizza n pizza f

place n ❶ (*location*) endroit m ▷ *It's a quiet place.* C'est un endroit tranquille. ❷ (*space*) place f ▷ *a parking place* une place de parking ▷ *a university place* une place à l'université; **to change places** changer [**45**] de place ▷ *Tamsin, change places with Delphine!* Tamsin, change de place avec Delphine!; **to take place** avoir [**8**] lieu; **at your place** chez toi ▷ *Shall we meet at your place?* On se retrouve chez toi?; **to my place** chez moi ▷ *Do you want to come round to my place?* Tu veux venir chez moi?

▶ vb ❶ poser [**28**] ▷ *He placed his hand on hers.* Il a posé la main sur la sienne. ❷ *(in competition, contest)* classer [**28**]

placement n stage m; **to do a work placement** faire [**36**] un stage en entreprise

plain n plaine f
　▶ adj, adv ❶ *(not patterned)* uni(e) ▷ *a plain carpet* un tapis uni ❷ *(not fancy)* simple ▷ *a plain white blouse* un chemisier blanc simple

plain chocolate n chocolat à croquer m

plait n natte f ▷ *She wears her hair in a plait.* Elle a une natte.

plan n ❶ projet m ▷ *What are your plans for the holidays?* Quels sont tes projets pour les vacances? ▷ *to make plans* faire des projets; **Everything went according to plan.** Tout s'est passé comme prévu. ❷ *(map)* plan m ▷ *a plan of the campsite* un plan du terrain de camping; **my essay plan** le plan de ma dissertation
　▶ vb ❶ *(make plans for)* préparer [**28**] ▷ *We're planning a trip to France.* Nous préparons un voyage en France. ❷ *(make schedule for)* planifier [**19**] ▷ *Plan your revision carefully.* Planifiez vos révisions avec soin.; **to plan to do something** avoir [**8**] l'intention de faire quelque chose ▷ *I'm planning to get a job in the holidays.* J'ai l'intention de trouver un job pour les vacances.

plane n avion m ▷ *by plane* en avion

planet n planète f

plant n ❶ plante f ▷ *to water the plants* arroser les plantes ❷ *(factory)* usine f
　▶ vb planter [**28**]

plaster n ❶ *(sticking plaster)* pansement adhésif m ▷ *Have you got a plaster, by any chance?* Vous n'auriez pas un pansement adhésif, par hasard? ❷ *(for fracture)* plâtre m ▷ *Her leg's in plaster.* Elle a la jambe dans le plâtre.

plastic n plastique m ▷ *It's made of plastic.* C'est en plastique.
　▶ adj en plastique ▷ *a plastic bag* un sac en plastique

plate n *(for food)* assiette f

platform n ❶ *(at station)* quai m ▷ *on platform 7* sur le quai numéro sept ❷ *(for performers)* estrade f

play n pièce f ▷ *a play by Shakespeare* une pièce de Shakespeare; **to put on a play** monter [**48**] une pièce
　▶ vb ❶ jouer [**28**] ▷ *He's playing with his friends.* Il joue avec ses amis. ▷ *What sort of music do they play?* Quel genre de musique jouent-ils? ❷ *(against person, team)* jouer [**28**] contre ▷ *France will play Scotland next month.* La France jouera contre l'Écosse le mois prochain. ❸ *(sport, game)* jouer [**28**] à ▷ *I play hockey.* Je joue au hockey. ▷ *Can you play pool?* Tu sais jouer au billard américain? ❹ *(instrument)* jouer [**28**] de ▷ *I play the guitar.* Je joue de la guitare. ❺ *(CD, music)* écouter [**28**] ▷ *She's always playing that song.* Elle écoute tout le temps cette chanson.

play down vb dédramatiser [28]
▷ *He tried to play down his illness.* Il a essayé de dédramatiser sa maladie.

player n ❶ *(of sport)* joueur m, joueuse f ▷ *a football player* un joueur de football ❷ *(of instrument)* musicien m, musicienne f; **a piano player** un pianiste; **a saxophone player** un saxophoniste

playground n ❶ *(at school)* cour de récréation f ❷ *(in park)* aire de jeux f

playgroup n garderie f

playing card n carte à jouer f

playing field n terrain de sport m

playtime n récréation f

pleasant adj agréable

please excl ❶ *(polite form)* s'il vous plaît ▷ *Two coffees, please.* Deux cafés, s'il vous plaît. ❷ *(familiar form)* s'il te plaît ▷ *Please write back soon.* Réponds vite, s'il te plaît.

pleased adj content(e) ▷ *My mother's not going to be very pleased.* Ma mère ne va pas être contente du tout.; **Pleased to meet you!** Enchanté!

pleasure n plaisir m ▷ *I read for pleasure.* Je lis pour le plaisir.

plenty n largement assez ▷ *I've got plenty.* J'en ai largement assez. ▷ *That's plenty, thanks.* Ça suffit largement, merci.; **plenty of (1)** *(a lot)* beaucoup de ▷ *I've got plenty of things to do.* J'ai beaucoup de choses à faire. **(2)** *(enough)* largement assez de ▷ *I've got plenty of money.* J'ai largement assez d'argent. ▷ *We've got plenty of time.*

Nous avons largement le temps.

pliers npl pince fsg; **a pair of pliers** une pince

plot n ❶ *(of story, play)* intrigue f ❷ *(against somebody)* conspiration f ▷ *a plot against the president* une conspiration contre le président ❸ *(of land)* carré m ▷ *a vegetable plot* un carré de légumes
▶ vb comploter [28] ▷ *They were plotting to kill him.* Ils complotaient de le tuer.

plough n charrue f
▶ vb labourer [28]

plug n ❶ *(electrical)* prise de courant f ▷ *The plug is faulty.* La prise est défectueuse. ❷ *(for sink)* bouchon m

plug in vb brancher [28] ▷ *Is it plugged in?* Est-ce que c'est branché?

plum n prune f ▷ *plum jam* la confiture de prunes

plumber n plombier m ▷ *He's a plumber.* Il est plombier.

plump adj dodu(e)

plural n pluriel m

plus prep, adj plus ▷ *4 plus 3 equals 7.* Quatre plus trois égalent sept. ▷ *three children plus a dog* trois enfants plus un chien; **I got a B plus.** J'ai eu un Bien.

p.m. abbr **at 8 p.m.** à huit heures du soir; **at 2 p.m.** à quatorze heures
  • In France times are often given
  • using the 24-hour clock.

pneumonia n pneumonie f

poached adj **a poached egg** un œuf poché

a
b
c
d
e
f
g
h
i
j
k
l
m
n
o
p
q
r
s
t
u
v
w
x
y
z

pocket n poche f; **pocket money**
l'argent de poche m ▷ *£8 a week
pocket money* huit livres d'argent de
poche par semaine
podcast n podcast m; **to
download a podcast** télécharger
[**45**] un podcast
poem n poème m
poet n poète m
poetry n poésie f
point n ❶ (*spot, score*) point m
▷ *a point on the horizon* un point à
l'horizon ▷ *They scored 5 points.* Ils
ont marqué cinq points.
❷ (*comment*) remarque f ▷ *He made
some interesting points.* Il a fait
quelque remarques intéressantes.
❸ (*tip*) pointe f ▷ *a pencil with a
sharp point* un crayon à la pointe
aiguisée ❹ (*in time*) moment m ▷ *At
that point, we decided to leave.* À ce
moment-là, nous avons décidé de
partir.; **a point of view** un point de
vue; **to get the point** comprendre
[**65**] ▷ *Sorry, I don't get the point.*
Désolé, je ne comprends pas.;
That's a good point! C'est vrai!;
There's no point. Cela ne sert à
rien. ▷ *There's no point in waiting.*
Cela ne sert à rien d'attendre.;
What's the point? À quoi bon?
▷ *What's the point of leaving so early?*
À quoi bon partir si tôt?;
**Punctuality isn't my strong
point.** La ponctualité n'est pas
mon fort.; **two point five (2.5)**
deux virgule cinq (2,5)
▶ vb montrer [**28**] du doigt ▷ *Don't
point!* Ne montre pas du doigt!; **to**

point at somebody montrer [**28**]
quelqu'un du doigt ▷ *She pointed at
Anne.* Elle a montré Anne du doigt.;
to point a gun at somebody
braquer [**28**] un revolver sur
quelqu'un
point out vb ❶ (*show*) montrer [**28**]
▷ *The guide pointed out Notre-Dame
to us.* Le guide nous a montré
Notre-Dame. ❷ (*mention*) signaler
[**28**] ▷ *I should point out that ...* Je
dois vous signaler que ...
pointless adj inutile ▷ *It's pointless
to argue.* Il est inutile de discuter.
poison n poison m
▶ vb empoisonner [**28**]
poisonous adj ❶ (*snake*) venimeux
(f venimeuse) ❷ (*plant, mushroom*)
vénéneux (f vénéneuse) ❸ (*gas*)
toxique
poke vb **He poked the ground with
his stick.** Il tapotait le sol avec sa
canne.; **She poked me in the ribs.**
Elle m'a enfoncé le doigt dans les
côtes.
poker n poker m ▷ *I play poker.* Je
joue au poker.
Poland n Pologne f; **in Poland** en
Pologne; **to Poland** en Pologne
polar bear n ours blanc m
Pole n Polonais m, Polonaise f
pole n poteau m (pl poteaux)
▷ *a telegraph pole* un poteau
télégraphique; **a tent pole** un
montant de tente; **a ski pole** un
bâton de ski; **the North Pole** le
pôle Nord; **the South Pole** le pôle
Sud
police npl police f ▷ *We called the*

police. Nous avons appelé la police.; **a police car** une voiture de police; **a police station** un commissariat de police

policeman n policier m ▷ *He's a policeman.* Il est policier.

police officer n policier m, policière f

policewoman n policière f ▷ *She's a policewoman.* Elle est policière.

Polish (language) polonais m ▷ adj polonais(e)

polish n ❶ (for shoes) cirage m ❷ (for furniture) cire f ▷ vb ❶ (shoes, furniture) cirer [28] ❷ (glass) faire [36] briller

polite adj poli(e)

politely adv poliment

political adj politique

politician n ❶ homme politique m ❷ femme politique f

politics npl politique fsg ▷ *I'm not interested in politics.* La politique ne m'intéresse pas.

pollute vb polluer [28]

polluted adj pollué(e)

pollution n pollution f

polo-necked sweater n pull à col roulé m

polythene bag n sac en plastique m

pond n ❶ (big) étang m ❷ (smaller) mare f ❸ (in garden) bassin m ▷ *We've got a pond in our garden.* Nous avons un bassin dans notre jardin.

pony n poney m

ponytail n queue de cheval f ▷ *He's got a ponytail.* Il a une queue de cheval.

pony trekking n **to go pony trekking** faire [36] une randonnée à dos de poney

poodle n caniche m

pool n ❶ (puddle) flaque f ❷ (pond) étang m ❸ (for swimming) piscine f ❹ (game) billard américain m ▷ *Shall we have a game of pool?* Si on jouait au billard américain?; **the pools** (football) le loto sportif ▷ **to do the pools** jouer au loto sportif

poor adj ❶ pauvre ▷ *a poor family* une famille pauvre ▷ *Poor David, he's very unlucky!* Le pauvre David, il n'a vraiment pas de chance!; **the poor** les pauvres m ❷ (bad) médiocre ▷ *a poor mark* une note médiocre

pop adj pop ▷ *pop music* la musique pop ▷ *a pop star* une pop star

pop in vb passer [58] ▷ *I just popped in to say hello.* Je suis juste passé dire bonjour.

pop out vb sortir [79]

pop round vb passer [58]

popcorn n pop-corn m

pope n pape m

poppy n coquelicot m

popular adj populaire ▷ *She's a very popular girl.* C'est une fille très populaire.

population n population f

porch n porche m

pork n porc m ▷ *a pork chop* une côtelette de porc

porridge n porridge m

port n ❶ (harbour) port m ❷ (wine) porto m ▷ *a glass of port* un verre de porto

a
b
c
d
e
f
g
h
i
j
k
l
m
n
o
p
q
r
s
t
u
v
w
x
y
z

portable adj portable ▷ a portable TV un téléviseur portable

porter n ❶ (in hotel) portier m ❷ (at station) porteur m

portion n portion f ▷ a large portion of chips une grosse portion de frites

portrait n portrait m

Portugal n Portugal m; **in Portugal** au Portugal; **We went to Portugal.** Nous sommes allés au Portugal.

Portuguese n ❶ (person) Portugais m, Portugaise f ❷ (language) portugais m ▶ adj portugais(e)

posh adj chic ▷ a posh hotel un hôtel chic

position n position f ▷ an uncomfortable position une position inconfortable

positive adj ❶ (good) positif (f positive) ▷ a positive attitude une attitude positive ❷ (sure) certain(e) ▷ I'm positive. J'en suis certain.

possession n Have you got all your possessions? Est-ce tu as toutes tes affaires?

possibility n It's a possibility. C'est possible.

possible adj possible ▷ as soon as possible aussitôt que possible

possibly adv (perhaps) peut-être ▷ Are you coming to the party? — Possibly. Est-ce que tu viens à la soirée? — Peut-être.; **... if you possibly can.** ... si cela vous est possible.; **I can't possibly come.** Je ne peux vraiment pas venir.

post n ❶ (letters) courrier m ▷ Is there any post for me? Est-ce qu'il y a du courrier pour moi? ❷ (pole) poteau m (pl poteaux) ▷ The ball hit the post. Le ballon a heurté le poteau. ❸ (on forum, blog) post m ▶ vb (also online) poster [28] ▷ I've got some cards to post. J'ai quelques cartes à poster.

postbox n boîte aux lettres f

postcard n carte postale f

postcode n code postal m

poster n ❶ poster m ▷ I've got posters on my bedroom walls. J'ai des posters sur les murs de ma chambre. ❷ (advertising) affiche f ▷ There are posters all over town. Il y a des affiches dans toute la ville.

postman n facteur m ▷ He's a postman. Il est facteur.

post office n poste f ▷ Where's the post office, please? Où est la poste, s'il vous plaît?

postpone vb remettre [47] à plus tard ▷ The match has been postponed. Le match a été remis à plus tard.

postwoman n factrice f ▷ She's a postwoman. Elle est factrice.

pot n ❶ pot m ▷ a pot of jam un pot de confiture; **the pots and pans** les casseroles ❷ (teapot) théière f ❸ (coffeepot) cafetière f ❹ (marijuana) herbe f ▷ to smoke pot fumer de l'herbe

potato n pomme de terre f ▷ potato salad la salade de pommes de terre; **mashed potatoes** la purée; **boiled potatoes** les pommes vapeur; **a baked potato** une pomme de terre en robe des champs

pottery n poterie f

pound n (weight, money) livre f
▷ How many euros do you get for a pound? Combien d'euros a-t-on pour une livre?

● In France measurements are in
● grams and kilograms. One
● pound is about 450 grams.
▷ a pound of carrots un demi-kilo de carottes

pour vb ❶ (liquid) verser [28] ▷ She poured some water into the pan. Elle a versé de l'eau dans la casserole.; **She poured him a drink.** Elle lui a servi à boire.; **Shall I pour you a cup of tea?** Je vous sers une tasse de thé? ❷ (rain) pleuvoir [63] à verse ▷ It's pouring. Il pleut à verse.; **in the pouring rain** sous une pluie torrentielle

poverty n pauvreté f

powder n poudre f

power n ❶ (electricity) courant m ▷ The power's off. Le courant est coupé.; **a power cut** une coupure de courant; **a power point** une prise de courant; **a power station** une centrale électrique ❷ (energy) énergie f ▷ nuclear power l'énergie nucléaire ❸ (authority) pouvoir m ▷ to be in power être au pouvoir

powerful adj puissant(e)

practical adj pratique ▷ a practical suggestion un conseil pratique; **She's very practical.** Elle a l'esprit pratique.

practically adv pratiquement ▷ It's practically impossible. C'est

pratiquement impossible.

practice n (for sport) entraînement m ▷ football practice l'entraînement de foot; **I've got to do my piano practice.** Je dois travailler mon piano.; **It's normal practice in our school.** C'est ce qui se fait dans notre école.; **in practice** en pratique; **a medical practice** un cabinet médical

practise (US **practice**) vb ❶ (music, hobby) s'exercer [12] ▷ I ought to practise more. Je devrais m'exercer davantage. ❷ (instrument) travailler [28] ▷ I practise the flute every evening. Je travaille ma flûte tous les soirs. ❸ (language) pratiquer [28] ▷ I practised my French when we were on holiday. J'ai pratiqué mon français pendant les vacances. ❹ (sport) s'entraîner [28] ▷ I don't practise enough. Je ne m'entraîne pas assez.

praise vb faire [36] l'éloge de ▷ The teachers praised our work. Les professeurs ont fait l'éloge de notre travail.

pram n landau m

prawn n crevette f

pray vb prier [19] ▷ to pray for something prier pour quelque chose

prayer n prière f

precious adj précieux (f précieuse)

precise adj précis(e) ▷ at that precise moment à cet instant précis

precisely adv précisément ▷ Precisely! Précisément!; **at 10 a.m. precisely** à dix heures précises

a
b
c
d
e
f
g
h
i
j
k
l
m
n
o
P
q
r
s
t
u
v
w
x
y
z

predict vb prédire [**27**]
prefect n
 ● French schools do not have
 ● prefects. You could explain what
 ● a prefect is using the example
 ● given.
 My sister's a prefect. Ma sœur est
 en dernière année et est chargée
 de maintenir la discipline.
prefer vb préférer [**34**] ▷ Which
 would you prefer? Lequel
 préfères-tu? ▷ I prefer French to
 chemistry. Je préfère le français à la
 chimie.
pregnant adj enceinte ▷ She's six
 months pregnant. Elle est enceinte
 de six mois.
prejudice n ❶ préjugé m ▷ That's
 just a prejudice. C'est un préjugé.
 ❷ préjugés mpl ▷ There's a lot of
 racial prejudice. Il y a beaucoup de
 préjugés raciaux.
prejudiced adj to be prejudiced
 against somebody avoir [**8**] des
 préjugés contre quelqu'un
premature adj prématuré(e); a
 premature baby un prématuré
Premier League n première
 division f ▷ in the Premier League en
 première division
premises npl locaux mpl ▷ They're
 moving to new premises. Ils vont
 occuper de nouveaux locaux.
prep n (homework) devoirs mpl
 ▷ history prep les devoirs d'histoire
preparation n préparation f
prepare vb préparer [**28**] ▷ She has
 to prepare lessons in the evening. Elle
 doit préparer ses cours le soir.; **to**

prepare for something se
 préparer [**28**] pour quelque chose
 ▷ We're preparing for our skiing
 holiday. Nous nous préparons pour
 nos vacances à la neige.
prepared adj to be prepared to do
 something être [**35**] prêt à faire
 quelque chose ▷ I'm prepared to help
 you. Je suis prêt à t'aider.
prep school n école primaire
 privée f
prescribe vb prescrire [**30**]
prescription n ordonnance f ▷ You
 can't get it without a prescription. On
 ne peut pas se le procurer sans
 ordonnance.
present adj ❶ (in attendance)
 présent(e) ▷ He wasn't present at the
 meeting. Il n'était pas présent à la
 réunion. ❷ (current) actuel (f
 actuelle) ▷ the present situation la
 situation actuelle; **the present
 tense** le présent
 ▶ n ❶ (gift) cadeau m (pl cadeaux)
 ▷ I'm going to buy presents. Je vais
 acheter des cadeaux.; **to give
 somebody a present** offrir [**54**] un
 cadeau à quelqu'un ❷ (time)
 présent m ▷ up to the present jusqu'à
 présent; **for the present** pour
 l'instant; **at present** en ce
 moment
 ▶ vb to present somebody with
 something (prize, medal) remettre
 [**47**] quelque chose à quelqu'un
presenter n (on TV) présentateur
 m, présentatrice f
president n président m,
 présidente f

press n presse f; **a press conference** une conférence de presse
▶ vb ❶ appuyer [53] ▷ *Don't press too hard!* N'appuie pas trop fort! ❷ appuyer [53] sur ▷ *He pressed the accelerator.* Il a appuyé sur l'accélérateur.

press-up n **to do press-ups** faire [36] des pompes ▷ *I do twenty press-ups every morning.* Je fais vingt pompes tous les matins.

pressure n pression f ▷ *He's under a lot of pressure at work.* Il est sous pression au travail.; **a pressure group** un groupe de pression
▶ vb faire [36] pression sur ▷ *My parents are pressuring me.* Mes parents font pression sur moi.

presume vb supposer [28]
▷ *I presume so.* Je suppose que oui.

pretend vb **to pretend to do something** faire [36] semblant de faire quelque chose ▷ *He pretended to be asleep.* Il faisait semblant de dormir.

> Be careful not to translate **to pretend** by **prétendre**.

pretty adj, adv ❶ joli(e) ▷ *She's very pretty.* Elle est très jolie. ❷ (*rather*) plutôt ▷ *That film was pretty bad.* Ce film était plutôt mauvais.; **The weather was pretty awful.** Il faisait un temps minable.; **It's pretty much the same.** C'est pratiquement la même chose.

prevent vb empêcher [28]; **to prevent somebody from doing something** empêcher [28]

quelqu'un de faire quelque chose
▷ *They try to prevent us from smoking.* Ils essaient de nous empêcher de fumer.

previous adj précédent(e)

previously adv auparavant

price n prix m

price list n liste des prix f

prick vb piquer [28] ▷ *I've pricked my finger.* Je me suis piqué le doigt.

pride n fierté f

priest n prêtre m ▷ *He's a priest.* Il est prêtre.

primarily adv principalement

primary adj principal(e) (mpl principaux)

primary school n école primaire f ▷ *She's still at primary school.* Elle est encore à l'école primaire.

prime minister n Premier ministre m

prince n prince m ▷ *the Prince of Wales* le prince de Galles

princess n princesse f ▷ *Princess Anne* la princesse Anne

principal adj principal(e) (mpl principaux)
▶ n (*of college*) principal m (pl principaux)

principle n principe m; **on principle** par principe

print n ❶ (*photo*) tirage m ▷ *colour prints* des tirages en couleur ❷ (*letters*) caractères mpl ▷ *in small print* en petits caractères ❸ (*fingerprint*) empreinte digitale f ❹ (*picture*) gravure f ▷ *a framed print* une gravure encadrée

printer n (*machine*) imprimante f

a
b
c
d
e
f
g
h
i
j
k
l
m
n
o
p
q
r
s
t
u
v
w
x
y
z

printout n tirage m
priority n priorité f
prison n prison f; **in prison** en prison
prisoner n prisonnier m, prisonnière f
private adj privé(e) ▷ a private school une école privée; **'private property'** 'propriété privée'; **'private'** (on envelope) 'personnel'; **a private bathroom** une salle de bain individuelle; **I have private lessons.** Je prends des cours particuliers.
prize n prix m ▷ to win a prize gagner un prix
prize-giving n distribution des prix f
prizewinner n gagnant m, gagnante f
pro n **the pros and cons** le pour et le contre ▷ We weighed up the pros and cons. Nous avons pesé le pour et le contre.
probability n probabilité f
probable adj probable
probably adv probablement ▷ probably not probablement pas
problem n problème m ▷ No problem! Pas de problème!
process n processus m ▷ the peace process le processus de paix; **to be in the process of doing something** être [35] en train de faire quelque chose ▷ We're in the process of painting the kitchen. Nous sommes en train de peindre la cuisine.
procession n (religious) procession f

produce vb ❶ (manufacture) produire [23] ❷ (play, show) monter [48]
producer n (of play, show) metteur en scène m
product n produit m
production n ❶ production f ▷ They're increasing production of luxury models. Ils augmentent la production des modèles de luxe. ❷ (play, show) mise en scène f ▷ a production of 'Hamlet' une mise en scène de 'Hamlet'
profession n profession f
professional n professionnel m, professionnelle f
▶ adj (player) professionnel (f professionnelle) ▷ a professional musician un musicien professionnel; **a very professional piece of work** un vrai travail de professionnel
professor n professeur d'université m; **He's the French professor.** Il est titulaire de la chaire de français.
profit n bénéfice m
profitable adj rentable
program n programme m ▷ a computer program un programme informatique; **a TV program** (US) une émission de télévision
▶ vb (computer) programmer [28]
programme n ❶ (on TV, radio) émission f ❷ (of events) programme m
programmer n programmeur m, programmeuse f ▷ She's a programmer. Elle est programmeuse.

progress n progrès m ▷ You're making progress! Vous faites des progrès!

prohibit vb interdire [27] ▷ Smoking is prohibited. Il est interdit de fumer.

project n ❶ (plan) projet m ▷ a development project un projet de développement ❷ (research) dossier m ▷ I'm doing a project on education in France. Je prépare un dossier sur l'éducation en France.

projector n projecteur m

promise n promesse f ▷ He made me a promise. Il m'a fait une promesse.; **That's a promise!** C'est promis! ▶ vb promettre [47] ▷ She promised to write. Elle a promis d'écrire.

promote vb to be promoted être [35] promu ▷ She was promoted after six months. Elle a été promue au bout de six mois.

promotion n promotion f

prompt adj, adv rapide ▷ a prompt reply une réponse rapide; **at eight o'clock prompt** à huit heures précises

pronoun n pronom m

pronounce vb prononcer [12] ▷ How do you pronounce that word? Comment est-ce qu'on prononce ce mot?

pronunciation n prononciation f

proof n preuve f

proper adj ❶ (genuine) vrai(e) ▷ proper French bread du vrai pain français; **It's difficult to get a proper job.** Il est difficile de trouver un travail correct. ❷ adéquat(e) ▷ You have to have the proper

equipment. Il faut avoir l'équipement adéquat. ▷ We need proper training. Il nous faut une formation adéquate.; **If you had come at the proper time ...** Si tu étais venu à l'heure dite ...

properly adv ❶ (correctly) comme il faut ▷ You're not doing it properly. Tu ne t'y prends pas comme il faut. ❷ (appropriately) convenablement ▷ Dress properly for your interview. Habille-toi convenablement pour ton entretien.

property n propriété f; 'private property' 'propriété privée'; **stolen property** les objets volés

propose vb proposer [28] ▷ I propose a new plan. Je propose un changement de programme.; **to propose to do something** avoir [8] l'intention de faire quelque chose ▷ What do you propose to do? Qu'est-ce que tu as l'intention de faire?; **to propose to somebody** (for marriage) demander [28] quelqu'un en mariage ▷ He proposed to her at the restaurant. Il l'a demandée en mariage au restaurant.

prosecute vb poursuivre [81] en justice ▷ They were prosecuted for murder. Ils ont été poursuivis en justice pour meurtre.; **'Trespassers will be prosecuted'** 'Défense d'entrer sous peine de poursuites'

prostitute n prostituée f; **a male prostitute** un prostitué

protect vb protéger [66]

protection n protection f
protein n protéine f
protest n protestation f ▷ He
ignored their protests. Il a ignoré
leurs protestations.; **a protest
march** une manifestation
▶ vb protester [**28**]
Protestant n protestant m,
protestante f ▷ I'm a Protestant.
Je suis protestant.
▶ adj protestant(e) ▷ a Protestant
church une église protestante
protester n manifestant m,
manifestante f
proud adj fier (f fière) ▷ Her parents
are proud of her. Ses parents sont
fiers d'elle.
prove vb prouver [**28**] ▷ The police
couldn't prove it. La police n'a pas pu
le prouver.
proverb n proverbe m
provide vb fournir [**38**]; **to provide
somebody with something**
fournir [**38**] quelque chose à
quelqu'un ▷ They provided us with
maps. Ils nous ont fourni des cartes.
provide for vb subvenir [**89**] aux
besoins de
provided conj à condition que
▌ à condition que has to be
followed by the subjunctive.
▷ He'll play in the next match provided
he's fit. Il jouera dans le prochain
match, à condition qu'il soit en
forme.
prune n pruneau m (pl pruneaux)
psychiatrist n psychiatre mf
▷ She's a psychiatrist. Elle est
psychiatre.

psychological adj psychologique
psychologist n psychologue mf
▷ He's a psychologist. Il est
psychologue.
psychology n psychologie f
PTO abbr (= please turn over) T.S.V.P.
(= tournez, s'il vous plaît)
pub n pub m
public n public m ▷ open to the public
ouvert au public; **in public** en
public
▶ adj public (f publique); **a public
holiday** un jour férié; **public
opinion** l'opinion publique f; **the
public address system** les
haut-parleurs
publicity n publicité f
public school n école privée f
public transport n transports en
commun mpl
publish vb publier [**19**]
publisher n éditeur m
pudding n dessert m ▷ What's for
pudding? Qu'est-ce qu'il y a comme
dessert?; **rice pudding** le riz au
lait; **black pudding** le boudin noir
puddle n flaque f
puff pastry n pâte feuilletée f
pull vb tirer [**28**] ▷ Pull! Tirez!; **He
pulled the trigger.** Il a appuyé sur
la gâchette.; **to pull a muscle** se
froisser [**28**] un muscle ▷ I pulled a
muscle when I was training. Je me
suis froissé un muscle à
l'entraînement.; **You're pulling
my leg!** Tu me fais marcher!
pull down vb démolir [**38**]
pull out vb ❶ (tooth, weed) arracher
[**28**] ❷ (car) déboîter [**28**] ▷ The car

pulled out to overtake. La voiture a déboîté pour doubler. ❸ *(withdraw)* se retirer [**28**] ▷ *She pulled out of the tournament.* Elle s'est retirée du tournoi.

pull through *vb* s'en sortir [**79**] ▷ *They think he'll pull through.* Ils pensent qu'il va s'en sortir.

pull up *vb (car)* s'arrêter [**28**] ▷ *A black car pulled up beside me.* Une voiture noire s'est arrêtée à côté de moi.

pullover *n* pull-over *m*

pulse *n* pouls *m* ▷ *The nurse felt his pulse.* L'infirmière a pris son pouls.

pump *n* ❶ pompe *f* ▷ *a bicycle pump* une pompe à vélo ▷ *a petrol pump* une pompe à essence ❷ *(shoe)* chausson de gym *m*
  ▶ *vb* pomper [**28**]

pump up *vb (tyre)* gonfler [**28**]

pumpkin *n* potiron *m*

punch *n* ❶ *(blow)* coup de poing *m* ▷ *He gave me a punch.* Il m'a donné un coup de poing. ❷ *(drink)* punch *m*
  ▶ *vb* ❶ *(hit)* donner [**28**] un coup de poing à ▷ *He punched me!* Il m'a donné un coup de poing! ❷ *(in ticket machine)* composter [**28**] ▷ *Punch your ticket before you get on the train.* Compostez votre billet avant de monter dans le train. ❸ *(by hand)* poinçonner [**28**] ▷ *He forgot to punch my ticket.* Il a oublié de poinçonner mon billet.

punctual *adj* ponctuel *(f* ponctuelle)

punctuation *n* ponctuation *f*

puncture *n* crevaison *f* ▷ *I had to mend a puncture.* J'ai dû réparer une crevaison.; **to have a puncture** crever [**43**] ▷ *I had a puncture on the motorway.* J'ai crevé sur l'autoroute.

punish *vb* punir [**38**]; **to punish somebody for something** punir [**38**] quelqu'un de quelque chose; **to punish somebody for doing something** punir [**38**] quelqu'un d'avoir fait quelque chose

punishment *n* punition *f*

punk *n (person)* punk *mf*; **a punk rock band** un groupe de punk rock

pupil *n* élève *mf*

puppet *n* marionnette *f*

puppy *n* chiot *m*

purchase *vb* acheter [**1**]

pure *adj* pur(e) ▷ *pure orange juice* du pur jus d'orange

purple *adj* violet *(f* violette)

purpose *n* but *m* ▷ *What is the purpose of these changes?* Quel est le but de ces changements?; **on purpose** exprès ▷ *He did it on purpose.* Il l'a fait exprès.

purr *vb* ronronner [**28**]

purse *n* ❶ porte-monnaie *m (pl* porte-monnaie) ❷ *(US: handbag)* sac à main *m*

pursue *vb* poursuivre [**81**]

push *n* to give somebody a push pousser [**28**] quelqu'un ▷ *He gave me a push.* Il m'a poussé.
  ▶ *vb* ❶ pousser [**28**] ▷ *Don't push!* Arrêtez de pousser! ❷ *(button)* appuyer [**53**] sur; **to push somebody to do something** pousser [**28**] quelqu'un à faire

a
b
c
d
e
f
g
h
i
j
k
l
m
n
o
p
q
r
s
t
u
v
w
x
y
z

quelque chose ▷ *My parents are pushing me to go to university.* Mes parents me poussent à entrer à l'université.; **to push drugs** revendre [**88**] de la drogue; **Push off!** Dégage!

push around vb bousculer [**28**] ▷ *He likes pushing people around.* Il aime bien bousculer les gens.

push through vb se frayer [**59**] un passage

pushchair n poussette f

push-up n to do push-ups faire [**36**] des pompes

put vb ❶ (place) mettre [**47**] ▷ *Where shall I put my things?* Où est-ce que je peux mettre mes affaires? ▷ *She's putting the baby to bed.* Elle met le bébé au lit. ❷ (write) écrire [**30**] ▷ *Don't forget to put your name on the paper.* N'oubliez pas d'écrire votre nom sur la feuille.

put aside vb mettre [**47**] de côté ▷ *Can you put this aside for me till tomorrow?* Est-ce que vous pouvez mettre ça de côté pour moi jusqu'à demain?

put away vb ranger [**45**] ▷ *Can you put away the dishes, please?* Tu peux ranger la vaisselle, s'il te plaît?

put back vb (replace) remettre [**47**] en place ▷ *Put it back when you've finished with it.* Remets-le en place une fois que tu auras fini.

put down vb ❶ poser [**28**] ▷ *I'll put these bags down for a minute.* Je vais poser ces sacs une minute. ❷ (in writing) noter [**28**] ▷ *I've put down a few ideas.* J'ai noté quelques idées.;

to have an animal put down faire [**36**] piquer un animal ▷ *We had to have our old dog put down.* Nous avons dû faire piquer notre vieux chien.

put forward vb ❶ (clock) avancer [**12**] ▷ *Don't forget to put the clocks forward.* N'oubliez pas d'avancer les pendules d'une heure. ❷ (idea, argument) proposer [**28**] ▷ *to put forward a suggestion* proposer une suggestion

put in vb (install) installer [**28**] ▷ *We're going to get central heating put in.* Nous allons faire installer le chauffage central.; **He has put in a lot of work on this project.** Il a fourni beaucoup de travail pour ce projet.

put off vb ❶ (switch off) éteindre [**60**] ▷ *Shall I put the light off?* Est-ce que j'éteins la lumière? ❷ (postpone) remettre [**47**] à plus tard ▷ *I keep putting it off.* Je n'arrête pas de remettre ça à plus tard. ❸ (distract) déranger [**45**] ▷ *Stop putting me off!* Arrête de me déranger! ❹ (discourage) décourager [**45**] ▷ *He's not easily put off.* Il ne se laisse pas facilement décourager.

put on vb ❶ (clothes, lipstick, CD) mettre [**47**] ▷ *I'll put my coat on.* Je vais mettre mon manteau. ❷ (light, heater, TV) allumer [**28**] ▷ *Shall I put the heater on?* J'allume le chauffage? ❸ (play, show) monter [**48**] ▷ *We're putting on 'Bugsy Malone'.* Nous sommes en train de monter 'Bugsy Malone'. ❹ mettre

[47] à cuire ▷ *I'll put the potatoes on.* Je vais mettre les pommes de terre à cuire.; **to put on weight** grossir [38] ▷ *He's put on a lot of weight.* Il a beaucoup grossi.

put out *vb* (light, cigarette, fire) éteindre [60] ▷ *It took them five hours to put out the fire.* Ils ont mis cinq heures à éteindre l'incendie.

put through *vb* passer [58] ▷ *Can you put me through to the manager?* Est-ce que vous pouvez me passer le directeur?; **I'm putting you through.** Je vous passe la communication.

put up *vb* ❶ (pin up) mettre [47] ▷ *I'll put the poster up on my wall.* Je vais mettre le poster sur mon mur. ❷ (tent) monter [48] ▷ *We put up our tent in a field.* Nous avons monté la tente dans un champ. ❸ (price) augmenter [28] ▷ *They've put up the price.* Ils ont augmenté le prix. ❹ (accommodate) héberger [45] ▷ *My friend will put me up for the night.* Mon ami va m'héberger pour la nuit.; **to put one's hand up** lever [43] la main ▷ *If you have any questions, put up your hand.* Si vous avez une question, levez la main.; **to put up with something** supporter [28] quelque chose ▷ *I'm not going to put up with it any longer.* Je ne vais pas supporter ça plus longtemps.

puzzle *n* (jigsaw) puzzle *m*

puzzled *adj* perplexe ▷ *You look puzzled!* Tu as l'air perplexe!

pyjamas *npl* pyjama *msg* ▷ *my pyjamas* mon pyjama ▷ *a pair of pyjamas* un pyjama; **a pyjama top** un haut de pyjama

pyramid *n* pyramide *f*

Pyrenees *npl* Pyrénées *fpl*; **in the Pyrenees** dans les Pyrénées; **We went to the Pyrenees.** Nous sommes allés dans les Pyrénées.

a
b
c
d
e
f
g
h
i
j
k
l
m
n
o
p
q
r
s
t
u
v
w
x
y
z

q

qualification n diplôme m ▷ *to leave school without any qualifications* quitter l'école sans aucun diplôme; **vocational qualifications** des qualifications professionnelles

qualified adj ❶ (trained) qualifié(e) ▷ *a qualified driving instructor* un moniteur d'auto-école qualifié ❷ (nurse, teacher) diplômé(e) ▷ *a qualified nurse* une infirmière diplômée

qualify vb ❶ (for job) obtenir [**83**] son diplôme ▷ *She qualified as a teacher last year.* Elle a obtenu son diplôme de professeur l'année dernière. ❷ (in competition) se qualifier [**19**] ▷ *Our team didn't qualify.* Notre équipe ne s'est pas qualifiée.

quality n qualité f ▷ *a good quality of life* une bonne qualité de vie ▷ *She's got lots of good qualities.* Elle a beaucoup de qualités.

quantity n quantité f

quarantine n quarantaine f ▷ *in quarantine* en quarantaine

quarrel n dispute f
▶ vb se disputer [**28**]

quarry n (for stone) carrière f

quarter n quart m; **three quarters** trois quarts; **a quarter of an hour** un quart d'heure ▷ *three quarters of an hour* trois quarts d'heure; **a quarter past ten** dix heures et quart; **a quarter to eleven** onze heures moins le quart

quarter final n quart de finale m

quartet n quatuor m ▷ *a string quartet* un quatuor à cordes

quay n quai m

queen n ❶ reine f ▷ *Queen Elizabeth* la reine Élisabeth ❷ (playing card) dame f ▷ *the queen of hearts* la dame de cœur; **the Queen Mother** la reine mère

query n question f
▶ vb mettre [**47**] en question ▷ *No one queried my decision.* Personne n'a mis en question ma décision.

question n question f ▷ *Can I ask a question?* Est-ce que je peux poser une question? ▷ *That's a difficult question.* C'est une question difficile.; **It's out of the question.** C'est hors de question.
▶ vb interroger [**45**] ▷ *He was questioned by the police.* Il a été interrogé par la police.

question mark n point d'interrogation m

questionnaire n questionnaire m

queue n queue f
▸ vb faire [**36**] la queue; **to queue for something** faire [**36**] la queue pour avoir quelque chose ▷ *We had to queue for tickets.* Nous avons dû faire la queue pour avoir les billets.

quick adj, adv rapide ▷ *a quick lunch* un déjeuner rapide ▷ *It's quicker by train.* C'est plus rapide en train.; **Be quick!** Dépêche-toi!; **She's a quick learner.** Elle apprend vite.; **Quick, phone the police!** Téléphonez vite à la police!

quickly adv vite ▷ *It was all over very quickly.* Ça s'est passé très vite.

quiet adj ❶ (not talkative or noisy) silencieux (f silencieuse) ▷ *You're very quiet today.* Tu es bien silencieux aujourd'hui. ▷ *The engine's very quiet.* Le moteur est très silencieux. ❷ (peaceful) tranquille ▷ *a quiet weekend* un week-end tranquille; **Be quiet!** Tais-toi!; **Quiet!** Silence!

quietly adv ❶ (speak) doucement ▷ *'She's dead,' he said quietly.* 'Elle est morte' dit-il doucement. ❷ (move) silencieusement; **He quietly opened the door.** Il a ouvert la porte sans faire de bruit.

quilt n (duvet) couette f

quit vb (place, premises, job) quitter [**28**] ▷ *She's decided to quit her job.* Elle a décidé de quitter son emploi.; **I quit!** J'abandonne!

quite adv ❶ (rather) assez ▷ *It's quite warm today.* Il fait assez bon aujourd'hui. ❷ (entirely) tout à fait ▷ *I'm not quite sure.* Je n'en suis pas tout à fait sûr.; **quite good** pas mal; **I've been there quite a lot.** J'y suis allé pas mal de fois.; **quite a lot of money** pas mal d'argent; **It costs quite a lot to go abroad.** Ça coûte assez cher d'aller à l'étranger.; **It's quite a long way.** C'est assez loin.; **It was quite a shock.** Ça a été un sacré choc.; **There were quite a few people there.** Il y avait pas mal de gens.

quiz n jeu-concours m

quotation n citation f ▷ *a quotation from Shakespeare* une citation de Shakespeare

quote n citation f ▷ *a Shakespeare quote* une citation de Shakespeare; **quotes** (quotation marks) les guillemets mpl ▷ *in quotes* entre guillemets
▸ vb citer [**28**] ▷ *He's always quoting Shakespeare.* Il n'arrête pas de citer Shakespeare.

a b c d e f g h i j k l m n o p q r s t u v w x y z

r

rabbi n rabbin m
rabbit n lapin m; **a rabbit hutch** un clapier
race n ❶ (sport) course f ▷ a cycle race une course cycliste ❷ (species) race f ▷ the human race la race humaine; **race relations** les relations interraciales fpl
▶ vb ❶ courir [16] ▷ We raced to catch the bus. Nous avons couru pour attraper le bus. ❷ (have a race) faire [36] la course; **I'll race you!** On fait la course!
racecourse n champ de courses m
racer n (bike) vélo de course m
racetrack n piste f
racial adj racial(e) (mpl raciaux)
▷ racial discrimination la discrimination raciale
racing car n voiture de course f

racing driver n pilote de course m
racism n racisme m
racist adj raciste
▶ n raciste mf
rack n (for luggage) porte-bagages m (pl porte-bagages)
racket n ❶ (for sport) raquette f ▷ my tennis racket ma raquette de tennis ❷ (noise) boucan m ▷ They're making a terrible racket. (informal) Ils font un boucan de tous les diables.
racquet n raquette f
radar n radar m
radiation n radiation f
radiator n radiateur m
radio n radio f; **on the radio** à la radio; **a radio station** une station de radio
radioactive adj radioactif (f radioactive)
radish n radis m
RAF n (= Royal Air Force) R.A.F. f ▷ He's in the RAF. Il est dans la R.A.F.
raffle n tombola f ▷ a raffle ticket un billet de tombola
raft n radeau m (pl radeaux)
rag n chiffon m ▷ a piece of rag un chiffon; **dressed in rags** en haillons
rage n rage f ▷ mad with rage fou de rage; **to be in a rage** être [35] furieux ▷ She was in a rage. Elle était furieuse.; **It's all the rage.** Ça fait fureur.
rail n ❶ (on stairs) rampe f ❷ (on bridge, balcony) balustrade f ▷ Don't lean over the rail! Ne vous penchez pas sur la balustrade! ❸ (on railway line) rail m; **by rail** en train

railcard n carte de chemin de fer f
▷ *a young person's railcard* une carte de chemin de fer tarif jeune

railroad n (US) chemin de fer m

railway n chemin de fer m ▷ *the privatization of the railways* la privatisation des chemins de fer; **a railway line** une ligne de chemin de fer; **a railway station** une gare

rain n pluie f ▷ *in the rain* sous la pluie ▶ vb pleuvoir [63] ▷ *It rains a lot here.* Il pleut beaucoup par ici.; **It's raining.** Il pleut.

rainbow n arc-en-ciel m (pl arcs-en-ciel)

raincoat n imperméable m

rainforest n forêt tropicale humide f

rainy adj pluvieux (f pluvieuse)

raise vb ❶ (lift) lever [43] ▷ *He raised his hand.* Il a levé la main.
❷ (improve) améliorer [28] ▷ *They want to raise standards in schools.* Ils veulent améliorer le niveau dans les écoles.; **to raise money** collecter [28] des fonds ▷ *The school is raising money for a new gym.* L'école collecte des fonds pour un nouveau gymnase.

raisin n raisin sec m

rake n râteau m (pl râteaux)

rally n ❶ (of people) rassemblement m ❷ (sport) rallye m ▷ *a rally driver* un pilote de rallye ❸ (in tennis) échange m

rambler n randonneur m, randonneuse f

ramp n (for wheelchairs) rampe d'accès f

ran vb see **run**

rang vb see **ring**

range n choix m ▷ *a wide range of colours* un grand choix de coloris; **a range of subjects** diverses matières ▷ *We study a range of subjects.* Nous étudions diverses matières.; **a mountain range** une chaîne de montagnes
▶ vb **to range from ... to** se situer [28] entre ... et ▷ *Temperatures in summer range from 20 to 35 degrees.* Les températures estivales se situent entre vingt et trente-cinq degrés.; **Tickets range from £2 to £20.** Les billets coûtent entre deux et vingt livres.

rap n (music) rap m

rape n viol m
▶ vb violer [28]

rapids npl rapides mpl

rare adj ❶ (unusual) rare ▷ *a rare plant* une plante rare ❷ (steak) saignant(e)

raspberry n framboise f ▷ *raspberry jam* la confiture de framboises

rat n rat m

rather adv plutôt ▷ *I was rather disappointed.* J'étais plutôt déçu. ▷ *£20! That's rather a lot!* Vingt livres! C'est plutôt cher!; **rather a lot of** pas mal de ▷ *I've got rather a lot of homework to do.* J'ai pas mal de devoirs à faire.; **rather than** plutôt que ▷ *We decided to camp, rather than stay at a hotel.* Nous avons décidé de camper plutôt que d'aller à l'hôtel.; **I'd rather ...** J'aimerais mieux ... ▷ *I'd rather stay in tonight.*

J'aimerais mieux rester à la maison ce soir. ▷ *I'd rather have an apple than a banana.* J'aimerais mieux une pomme qu'une banane.

rattlesnake n serpent à sonnette m

rave vb s'extasier [**19**]
▶ n (party) rave f

ravenous adj **to be ravenous** avoir [**8**] une faim de loup ▷ *I'm ravenous!* J'ai une faim de loup!

raw adj (food) cru(e); **raw materials** les matières premières fpl

razor n rasoir m ▷ *some disposable razors* des rasoirs jetables; **a razor blade** une lame de rasoir

RE n éducation religieuse f

reach n **out of reach** hors de portée ▷ *The light switch was out of reach.* L'interrupteur était hors de portée.; **within easy reach of** à proximité de ▷ *The hotel is within easy reach of the town centre.* L'hôtel se trouve à proximité du centre-ville.
▶ vb ❶ arriver [**5**] à ▷ *We reached the hotel at 7 p.m.* Nous sommes arrivés à l'hôtel à sept heures du soir.; **We hope to reach the final.** Nous espérons aller en finale.
❷ (decision) parvenir [**89**] à ▷ *Eventually they reached a decision.* Ils sont finalement parvenus à une décision.; **He reached for his gun.** Il a tendu la main pour prendre son revolver.

reaction n réaction f

reactor n réacteur m ▷ *a nuclear reactor* un réacteur nucléaire

read vb lire [**44**] ▷ *I don't read much.* Je ne lis pas beaucoup. ▷ *Read the text out loud.* Lis le texte à haute voix.

read out vb lire [**44**] ▷ *He read out the article to me.* Il m'a lu l'article.; **to read out the results** annoncer [**12**] les résultats

reading n lecture f ▷ *Reading is one of my hobbies.* La lecture est l'une de mes activités favorites.

ready adj prêt(e) ▷ *She's nearly ready.* Elle est presque prête. ▷ *He's always ready to help.* Il est toujours prêt à rendre service.; **a ready meal** un plat cuisiné; **to get ready** se préparer [**28**] ▷ *She's getting ready to go out.* Elle est en train de se préparer pour sortir.; **to get something ready** préparer [**28**] quelque chose ▷ *He's getting the dinner ready.* Il est en train de préparer le dîner.

real adj ❶ vrai(e) ▷ *He wasn't a real police officer.* Ce n'était pas un vrai policier. ▷ *Her real name is Cordelia.* Son vrai nom est Cordelia.
❷ véritable ▷ *It's real leather.* C'est du cuir véritable. ▷ *It was a real nightmare.* C'était un véritable cauchemar.; **in real life** dans la réalité

realistic adj réaliste

reality n réalité f

realize vb **to realize that ...** se rendre [**7**] compte que ... ▷ *We realized that something was wrong.* Nous nous sommes rendu compte que quelque chose n'allait pas.

really adv vraiment ▷ She's really nice. Elle est vraiment sympathique. ▷ Do you want to go? — Not really. Tu veux y aller? — Pas vraiment.; **I'm learning German. — Really?** J'apprends l'allemand. —Ah bon?; **Do you really think so?** Tu es sûr?

realtor n (US) agent immobilier m

reason n raison f ▷ There's no reason to think that ... Il n'y a aucune raison de penser que ... ▷ for security reasons pour des raisons de sécurité; **That was the main reason I went.** C'est surtout pour ça que j'y suis allé.

reasonable adj ❶ (sensible) raisonnable ▷ Be reasonable! Sois raisonnable! ❷ (not bad) correct(e) ▷ He wrote a reasonable essay. Sa dissertation était correcte.

reasonably adv raisonnablement ▷ The team played reasonably well. L'équipe a joué raisonnablement bien.; **reasonably priced accommodation** un logement à un prix raisonnable

reassure vb rassurer [28]

reassuring adj rassurant(e)

rebellious adj rebelle

receipt n reçu m

receive vb recevoir [67]

receiver n (of phone) combiné m; **to pick up the receiver** décrocher [28]

recent adj récent(e)

recently adv ces derniers temps ▷ I've been doing a lot of training recently. Je me suis beaucoup entraîné ces derniers temps.

reception n réception f ▷ Please leave your key at reception. Merci de laisser votre clé à la réception. ▷ The reception will be at a big hotel. La réception aura lieu dans un grand hôtel.

receptionist n réceptionniste mf

recipe n recette f

reckon vb penser [28] ▷ What do you reckon? Qu'est-ce que tu en penses?

recognize vb reconnaître [14] ▷ You'll recognize me by my red hair. Vous me reconnaîtrez à mes cheveux roux.

recommend vb conseiller [28] ▷ What do you recommend? Qu'est-ce que vous me conseillez?

reconsider vb reconsidérer [34]

record n ❶ (sport) record m ▷ the world record le record du monde; **in record time** en un temps record ▷ She finished the job in record time. Elle a terminé le travail en un temps record. ❷ (recording) disque m ▷ my favourite record mon disque préféré; **a criminal record** un casier judiciaire ▷ He's got a criminal record. Il a un casier judiciaire.; **records** (of police, hospital) les archives fpl ▷ I'll check in the records. Je vais vérifier dans les archives.; **There is no record of your booking.** Il n'y a aucune trace de votre réservation.
▶ vb (on film) enregistrer [28] ▷ They've just recorded their new album. Ils viennent d'enregistrer leur nouveau disque.

recorded delivery *n* to send something recorded delivery envoyer [**33**] quelque chose en recommandé

recorder *n (instrument)* flûte à bec *f* ▷ *She plays the recorder.* Elle joue de la flûte à bec.; **a video recorder** un magnétoscope

recording *n* enregistrement *m*

record player *n* tourne-disque *m*

recover *vb* se remettre [**47**] ▷ *He's recovering from a knee injury.* Il se remet d'une blessure au genou.

recovery *n* rétablissement *m*; **Best wishes for a speedy recovery!** Meilleurs vœux de prompt rétablissement!

rectangle *n* rectangle *m*

rectangular *adj* rectangulaire

recycle *vb* recycler [**28**]

recycling *n* recyclage *m*

red *adj* ❶ rouge ▷ *a red rose* une rose rouge ▷ *red meat* la viande rouge; **a red light** *(traffic light)* un feu rouge ▷ *to go through a red light* brûler un feu rouge ❷ *(hair)* roux (*f* rousse) ▷ *Sam's got red hair.* Sam a les cheveux roux.

Red Cross *n* Croix-Rouge *f*

redcurrant *n* groseille *f*

redecorate *vb* ❶ *(with wallpaper)* retapisser [**28**] ❷ *(with paint)* refaire [**36**] les peintures

redo *vb* refaire [**36**]

reduce *vb* réduire [**23**] ▷ *at a reduced price* à prix réduit; **'reduce speed now'** 'ralentir'

reduction *n* réduction *f* ▷ *a 5% reduction* une réduction de cinq

pour cent; **'huge reductions!'** 'prix sacrifiés!'

redundant *adj* **to be made redundant** être [**35**] licencié ▷ *He was made redundant yesterday.* Il a été licencié hier.

refer *vb* **to refer to** faire [**36**] allusion à ▷ *What are you referring to?* À quoi faites-vous allusion?

referee *n* arbitre *m*

reference *n* ❶ allusion *f* ▷ *He made no reference to the murder.* Il n'a fait aucune allusion au meurtre. ❷ *(for job application)* références *fpl* ▷ *Would you please give me a reference?* Pouvez-vous me fournir des références?; **a reference book** un ouvrage de référence

refill *vb* remplir [**38**] à nouveau ▷ *He refilled my glass.* Il a rempli mon verre à nouveau.

reflect *vb (light, image)* refléter [**34**]

reflection *n (in mirror)* reflet *m*

reflex *n* réflexe *m*

reflexive *adj* réfléchi(e) ▷ *a reflexive verb* un verbe réfléchi

refreshing *adj* rafraîchissant(e)

refreshments *npl* rafraîchissements *mpl*

refrigerator *n* réfrigérateur *m*

refuge *n* refuge *m*

refugee *n* réfugié *m*, réfugiée *f*

refund *n* remboursement *m* ▶ *vb* rembourser [**28**]

refuse *vb* refuser [**28**] ▶ *n* ordures *fpl*; **refuse collection** le ramassage des ordures

regain *vb* **to regain consciousness** reprendre [**65**] connaissance

regard n Give my regards to Alice. Transmettez mon bon souvenir à Alice.; **Louis sends his regards.** Vous avez le bonjour de Louis.; **'with kind regards'** 'bien cordialement'
▶ vb **to regard something as** considérer [34] quelque chose comme; **as regards ...** concernant ...

regiment n régiment m
region n région f
regional adj régional(e) (mpl régionaux)
register n (in school) registre d'absences m
▶ vb (at school, college) s'inscrire [30]
registered adj **a registered letter** une lettre recommandée
registration n ❶ (roll call) appel m ❷ (of car) numéro d'immatriculation m
regret n regret m; **I've got no regrets.** Je ne regrette rien.
▶ vb regretter [28] ▷ Give me the money or you'll regret it! Donne-moi l'argent, sinon tu vas le regretter!
regular adj ❶ régulier (f régulière) ▷ at regular intervals à intervalles réguliers ▷ a regular verb un verbe régulier; **to take regular exercise** faire [36] régulièrement de l'exercice ❷ (average) normal(e) (mpl normaux) ▷ a regular portion of fries une portion de frites normale
regularly adv régulièrement
regulation n règlement m
rehearsal n répétition f
rehearse vb répéter [34]

rein n rêne f ▷ the reins les rênes
reindeer n renne m
reject vb (idea, suggestion) rejeter [41] ▷ We rejected that idea straight away. Nous avons immédiatement rejeté cette idée.; **I applied but they rejected me.** J'ai posé ma candidature mais ils l'ont rejetée.
related adj (people) apparenté(e) ▷ We're related. Nous sommes apparentés.; **The two events were not related.** Il n'y avait aucun rapport entre les deux événements.
relation n ❶ (person) parent m, parente f ▷ He's a distant relation. C'est un parent éloigné. ▷ my close relations mes parents proches; **my relations** ma famille; **I've got relations in London.** J'ai de la famille à Londres. ❷ (connection) rapport m ▷ It has no relation to reality. Cela n'a aucun rapport avec la réalité.; **in relation to** par rapport à
relationship n relations fpl ▷ We have a good relationship. Nous avons de bonnes relations.; **I'm not in a relationship at the moment.** Je ne sors avec personne en ce moment.
relative n parent m, parente f ▷ my close relatives mes proches parents; **all her relatives** toute sa famille
relatively adv relativement
relax vb se détendre [88] ▷ I relax listening to music. Je me détends en écoutant de la musique.; **Relax! Everything's fine.** Ne t'en fais pas! Tout va bien.

a
b
c
d
e
f
g
h
i
j
k
l
m
n
o
p
q
r
s
t
u
v
w
x
y
z

relaxation n détente f ▷ I don't have much time for relaxation. Je n'ai pas beaucoup de moments de détente.
relaxed adj détendu(e)
relaxing adj reposant(e); **I find cooking relaxing.** Cela me détend de faire la cuisine.
relay n a relay race une course de relais
release vb ❶ (prisoner) libérer [34] ❷ (report, news) divulguer [28] ❸ (CD, DVD) sortir [79] ▶ n (from prison) libération f ▷ the release of the prisoners la libération des prisonniers; **the band's latest release** le dernier disque du groupe
relevant adj (documents) approprié(e); **That's not relevant.** Ça n'a aucun rapport.; **to be relevant to something** être [35] en rapport avec quelque chose ▷ Education should be relevant to real life. L'enseignement devrait être en rapport avec la réalité.
reliable adj fiable ▷ a reliable car une voiture fiable ▷ He's not very reliable. Il n'est pas très fiable.
relief n soulagement m ▷ That's a relief! Quel soulagement!
relieved adj soulagé(e) ▷ I was relieved to hear ... J'ai été soulagé d'apprendre ...
religion n religion f ▷ What religion are you? Quelle est votre religion?
religious adj ❶ religieux (f religieuse) ▷ my religious beliefs mes croyances religieuses ❷ croyant(e) ▷ I'm not religious. Je ne suis pas croyant.

reluctant adj to be reluctant to do something être [35] peu disposé à faire quelque chose ▷ They were reluctant to help us. Ils étaient peu disposés à nous aider.
reluctantly adv à contrecœur
rely on vb compter [28] sur ▷ I'm relying on you. Je compte sur toi.
remain vb rester [71]; to remain silent garder [28] le silence
remaining adj le reste de ▷ the remaining ingredients le reste des ingrédients
remark n remarque f
remarkable adj remarquable
remarkably adv remarquablement
remember vb se souvenir [83] de ▷ I can't remember his name. Je ne me souviens pas de son nom. ▷ I don't remember. Je ne m'en souviens pas.
In French you often say 'don't forget' instead of 'remember'. ▷ Remember your passport! N'oublie pas ton passeport!
remind vb rappeler [4] ▷ It reminds me of Scotland. Cela me rappelle l'Écosse. ▷ I'll remind you tomorrow. Je te le rappellerai demain.
remote adj isolé(e) ▷ a remote village un village isolé
remote control n télécommande f
remotely adv I'm not remotely interested. Je ne suis absolument pas intéressé.; Do you think it would be remotely possible? Pensez-vous que cela serait éventuellement possible?

remove vb ❶ enlever [**43**] ▷ *Please remove your bag from my seat.* Est-ce que vous pouvez enlever votre sac de mon siège? ❷ *(stain)* faire [**36**] partir ▷ *Did you remove the stain?* Est-ce que tu as fait partir la tache?

renew vb *(passport, licence)* renouveler [**4**]

renewable adj *(energy, resource)* renouvelable

renovate vb rénover [**28**] ▷ *The building's been renovated.* Le bâtiment a été rénové.

rent n loyer m
▶ vb louer [**28**] ▷ *We rented a car.* Nous avons loué une voiture.

reorganize vb réorganiser [**28**]

rep n *(= representative)* représentant m, représentante f

repaid vb see **repay**

repair vb réparer [**28**]; **to get something repaired** faire [**36**] réparer quelque chose ▷ *I got the washing machine repaired.* J'ai fait réparer la machine à laver.
▶ n réparation f

repay vb *(money)* rembourser [**28**]

repeat vb répéter [**34**]
▶ n reprise f ▷ *There are too many repeats on TV.* Il y a trop de reprises à la télé.

repeatedly adv à plusieurs reprises

repetitive adj *(movement, work)* répétitif (f répétitive)

replace vb remplacer [**12**]

replay n **There will be a replay on Friday.** Le match sera rejoué vendredi.
▶ vb *(match)* rejouer [**28**]

reply n réponse f
▶ vb répondre [**69**]

report n ❶ *(of event)* compte rendu m (pl comptes rendus) ❷ *(news report)* reportage m ▷ *a report in the paper* un reportage dans le journal ❸ *(at school)* bulletin scolaire m ▷ *I got a good report this term.* J'ai un bon bulletin scolaire ce trimestre.
▶ vb ❶ signaler [**28**] ▷ *I reported the theft to the police.* J'ai signalé le vol au commissariat. ❷ se présenter [**28**] ▷ *Report to reception when you arrive.* Présentez-vous à la réception à votre arrivée.

reporter n reporter m ▷ *I'd like to be a reporter.* J'aimerais être reporter.

represent vb représenter [**28**]

representative adj représentatif (f représentative)

reptile n reptile m

republic n république f

reputation n réputation f

request n demande f
▶ vb demander [**28**]

require vb exiger [**45**] ▷ *The job requires good computational skills.* Cet emploi exige une bonne connaissance de l'informatique.; **What qualifications are required?** Quelles sont les diplômes requis?

rescue vb sauver [**28**]
▶ n ❶ sauvetage m ▷ *a rescue operation* une opération de sauvetage; **a mountain rescue team** une équipe de sauvetage en montagne ❷ secours m ▷ *the rescue services* les services de secours;

a
b
c
d
e
f
g
h
i
j
k
l
m
n
o
p
q
r
s
t
u
v
w
x
y
z

to come to somebody's rescue
venir [**89**] au secours de quelqu'un
▷ *He came to my rescue.* Il est venu à
mon secours.

research n ❶ (*experimental*)
recherche f ▷ *He's doing research.* Il
fait de la recherche. ❷ (*theoretical*)
recherches fpl ▷ *She's doing some
research in the library.* Elle fait des
recherches à la bibliothèque.

resemblance n ressemblance f

resent vb être [**35**] contrarié par
▷ *I really resented your criticism.* J'ai
été vraiment contrarié par tes
critiques.

resentful adj plein de ressentiment
(f pleine de ressentiment); **to feel
resentful towards somebody** en
vouloir [**93**] à quelqu'un

reservation n (*booking*)
réservation f ▷ *I'd like to make a
reservation for this evening.*
J'aimerais faire une réservation
pour ce soir.

reserve n ❶ (*place*) réserve f
▷ *a nature reserve* une réserve
naturelle ❷ (*person*) remplaçant m,
remplaçante f ▷ *I was reserve in the
game last Saturday.* J'étais
remplaçant dans le match de
samedi dernier.
▶ vb réserver [**28**] ▷ *I'd like to reserve
a table for tomorrow evening.*
J'aimerais réserver une table pour
demain soir.

reserved adj réservé(e) ▷ *a reserved
seat* une place réservée ▷ *He's quite
reserved.* Il est assez réservé.

resident n résident m, résidente f

residential adj résidentiel (f
résidentielle) ▷ *a residential area* un
quartier résidentiel

resign vb donner [**28**] sa démission

resit vb repasser [**28**] ▷ *I'm resitting
the exam in December.* Je vais
repasser l'examen en décembre.

resolution n résolution f; **Have
you made any New Year's
resolutions?** Tu as pris de bonnes
résolutions pour la nouvelle année?

resort n (*at seaside*) station
balnéaire f ▷ *It's a resort on the Costa
del Sol.* C'est une station balnéaire
sur la Costa del Sol.; **a ski resort**
une station de ski; **as a last resort**
en dernier recours

resource n ressource f

respect n respect m
▶ vb respecter [**28**]

respectable adj ❶ respectable
❷ (*standard, marks*) correct(e)

responsibility n responsabilité f

responsible adj ❶ (*in charge*)
responsable; **to be responsible
for something** être [**35**]
responsable de quelque chose
▷ *He's responsible for booking the
tickets.* Il est responsable de la
réservation des billets.; **It's a
responsible job.** C'est un poste à
responsabilités. ❷ (*mature*) sérieux
(f sérieuse) ▷ *You should be more
responsible.* Tu devrais être un peu
plus sérieux.

rest n ❶ (*relaxation*) repos m ▷ *five
minutes' rest* cinq minutes de repos;
to have a rest se reposer [**28**] ▷ *We
stopped to have a rest.* Nous nous

ENGLISH > FRENCH

sommes arrêtés pour nous reposer. ❷ (remainder) reste m ▷ I'll do the rest. Je ferai le reste. ▷ the rest of the money le reste de l'argent; **the rest of them** les autres ▷ The rest of them went swimming. Les autres sont allés nager.

▶ vb ❶ (relax) se reposer [28] ▷ She's resting in her room. Elle se repose dans sa chambre. ❷ (not overstrain) ménager [45] ▷ He has to rest his knee. Il doit ménager son genou. ❸ (lean) appuyer [53] ▷ I rested my bike against the window. J'ai appuyé mon vélo contre la fenêtre.

restaurant n restaurant m ▷ We don't often go to restaurants. Nous n'allons pas souvent au restaurant.; **a restaurant car** un wagon-restaurant

restless adj agité(e)

restore vb (building, picture) restaurer [28]

restrict vb limiter [28]

rest room n (US) toilettes fpl

result n résultat m ▷ my exam results mes résultats d'examen

▶ vb **to result in** occasionner [28]

resume vb reprendre [65] ▷ They've resumed work. Ils ont repris le travail.

> Be careful not to translate **to resume** by résumer.

résumé n (US) curriculum vitae m

retire vb prendre [65] sa retraite ▷ He retired last year. Il a pris sa retraite l'an dernier.

retired adj retraité(e) ▷ She's retired. Elle est retraitée.; **a retired**

teacher un professeur à la retraite

retirement n retraite f

return n ❶ retour m ▷ after our return à notre retour; **the return journey** le voyage de retour; **a return match** un match retour ❷ (ticket) aller retour m ▷ A return to Avignon, please. Un aller retour pour Avignon, s'il vous plaît.; **in return** en échange ▷ ... and I help her in return ... et je l'aide en échange; **in return for** en échange de; **Many happy returns!** Bon anniversaire!

▶ vb ❶ (come back) revenir [73] ▷ I've just returned from holiday. Je viens de revenir de vacances.; **to return home** rentrer [68] à la maison ❷ (go back) retourner [72] ▷ He returned to France the following year. Il est retourné en France l'année suivante. ❸ (give back) rendre [7] ▷ She borrows my things and doesn't return them. Elle m'emprunte mes affaires et ne me les rend pas.

reunion n réunion f

reveal vb révéler [34]

revenge n vengeance f ▷ in revenge par vengeance; **to take revenge** se venger [45] ▷ They planned to take revenge on him. Ils voulaient se venger de lui.

reverse vb (car) faire [36] marche arrière ▷ He reversed without looking. Il a fait marche arrière sans regarder.; **to reverse the charges** (telephone) appeler [4] en PCV ▷ I'd like to reverse the charges to Britain. Je voudrais appeler la Grande-Bretagne en PCV.

▶ adj inverse ▷ in reverse order dans l'ordre inverse; **in reverse gear** en marche arrière

review n (of book, film, programme) critique f ▷ The book had good reviews. Ce livre a eu de bonnes critiques.

revise vb réviser [**28**] ▷ I haven't started revising yet. Je n'ai pas encore commencé à réviser.; **I've revised my opinion.** J'ai changé d'opinion.

revision n révisions fpl ▷ Have you done a lot of revision? Est-ce que tu as fait beaucoup de révisions?

revolting adj dégoûtant(e)

revolution n révolution f; **the French Revolution** la Révolution française

reward n récompense f

rewarding adj gratifiant(e) ▷ a rewarding job un travail gratifiant

rewind vb rembobiner [**28**] ▷ to rewind a cassette rembobiner une cassette

Rhine n Rhin m

rhinoceros n rhinocéros m

Rhone n Rhône m

rhubarb n rhubarbe f ▷ a rhubarb tart une tarte à la rhubarbe

rhythm n rythme m

rib n côte f

ribbon n ruban m

rice n riz m; **rice pudding** le riz au lait

rich adj riche; **the rich** les riches mpl

rid vb **to get rid of** se débarrasser [**28**] de ▷ I want to get rid of some old clothes. Je veux me débarrasser de vieux vêtements.

ridden vb see **ride**

ride n **to go for a ride (1)** (on horse) monter [**48**] à cheval **(2)** (on bike) faire [**36**] un tour en vélo ▷ We went for a bike ride. Nous sommes allés faire un tour en vélo.; **It's a short bus ride to the town centre.** Ce n'est pas loin du centre-ville en bus.

▶ vb (on horse) monter [**48**] à cheval ▷ I'm learning to ride. J'apprends à monter à cheval.; **to ride a bike** faire [**36**] du vélo ▷ Can you ride a bike? Tu sais faire du vélo?

rider n ❶ (on horse) cavalier m, cavalière f ▷ She's a good rider. C'est une bonne cavalière. ❷ (on bike) cycliste mf

ridiculous adj ridicule ▷ Don't be ridiculous! Ne sois pas ridicule!

riding n équitation f; **to go riding** faire [**36**] de l'équitation; **a riding school** une école d'équitation

rifle n fusil m ▷ a hunting rifle un fusil de chasse

right adj, adv

> There are several ways of translating 'right'. Scan the examples to find one that is similar to what you want to say.

❶ (factually correct, suitable) bon (f bonne) ▷ the right answer la bonne réponse ▷ It isn't the right size. Ce n'est pas la bonne taille. ▷ We're on the right train. Nous sommes dans le bon train.; **Is this the right road**

for Arles? Est-ce que c'est bien la route pour aller à Arles? ❷ *(correctly)* correctement ▷ *Am I pronouncing it right?* Est-ce que je prononce ça correctement?; **to be right (1)** *(person)* avoir [**8**] raison ▷ *You were right!* Tu avais raison! **(2)** *(statement, opinion)* être [**35**] vrai ▷ *That's right!* C'est vrai! ❸ *(accurate)* juste ▷ *Do you have the right time?* Est-ce que vous avez l'heure juste? ❹ *(morally correct)* bien ▷ *It's not right to behave like that.* Ce n'est pas bien d'agir comme ça.; **I think you did the right thing.** Je pense que tu as bien fait. ❺ *(not left)* droit(e) ▷ *my right hand* ma main droite ❻ *(turn, look)* à droite ▷ *Turn right at the traffic lights.* Tournez à droite aux prochains feux.; **Right! Let's get started.** Bon! On commence.; **right away** tout de suite ▷ *I'll do it right away.* Je vais le faire tout de suite.
▶ *n* ❶ droit *m*; **You've got no right to do that.** Vous n'avez pas le droit de faire ça. ❷ *(not left)* droite *f*; **on the right** à droite ▷ *Remember to drive on the right.* N'oubliez pas de conduire à droite.; **right of way** la priorité ▷ *It was our right of way.* Nous avions la priorité.
right-hand *adj* **the right-hand side** la droite ▷ *It's on the right-hand side.* C'est à droite.
right-handed *adj* droitier (*f* droitière)
rightly *adv* avec raison ▷ *She rightly*

decided not to go. Elle a décidé, avec raison, de ne pas y aller.; **if I remember rightly** si je me souviens bien
ring *n* ❶ anneau *m* (*pl* anneaux) ▷ *a gold ring* un anneau en or ❷ *(with stones)* bague *f* ▷ *a diamond ring* une bague de diamants; **a wedding ring** une alliance ❸ *(circle)* cercle *m* ▷ *to stand in a ring* se mettre en cercle ❹ *(of bell)* coup de sonnette *m* ▷ *I was woken by a ring at the door.* J'ai été réveillé par un coup de sonnette.; **to give somebody a ring** appeler [**4**] quelqu'un ▷ *I'll give you a ring this evening.* Je t'appellerai ce soir.
▶ *vb* ❶ téléphoner [**28**] ▷ *Your mother rang this morning.* Ta mère a téléphoné ce matin.; **to ring somebody** appeler [**4**] quelqu'un ▷ *I'll ring you tomorrow morning.* Je t'appellerai demain matin. ❷ sonner [**28**] ▷ *The phone's ringing.* Le téléphone sonne.; **to ring the bell** *(doorbell)* sonner [**28**] à la porte ▷ *I rang the bell three times.* J'ai sonné trois fois à la porte.
ring back *vb* rappeler [**4**] ▷ *I'll ring back later.* Je rappellerai plus tard.
ring up *vb* **to ring somebody up** donner [**28**] un coup de fil à quelqu'un
ring binder *n* classeur *m*
rinse *vb* rincer [**12**]
riot *n* émeute *f*
▶ *vb* faire [**36**] une émeute
rip *vb* ❶ déchirer [**28**] ▷ *I've ripped my jeans.* J'ai déchiré mon jean. ❷ se

a
b
c
d
e
f
g
h
i
j
k
l
m
n
o
p
q
r
s
t
u
v
w
x
y
z

déchirer **[28]** ▷ *My skirt's ripped.* Ma jupe s'est déchirée.

rip off *vb* arnaquer **[28]** ▷ *The hotel ripped us off.* L'hôtel nous a arnaqués.

rip up *vb* déchirer **[28]** ▷ *He read the note and then ripped it up.* Il a lu le mot, puis l'a déchiré.

ripe *adj* mûr(e)

rip-off *n* It's a rip-off! (*informal*) C'est de l'arnaque!

rise *n* ❶ (*in prices, temperature*) hausse *f* ▷ *a sudden rise in temperature* une hausse subite de température ❷ (*pay rise*) augmentation *f*
▶ *vb* ❶ (*increase*) augmenter **[28]** ▷ *Prices are rising.* Les prix augmentent. ❷ se lever **[43]** ▷ *The sun rises early in June.* Le soleil se lève tôt en juin.

risk *n* risque *m*; **to take risks** prendre **[65]** des risques; **It's at your own risk.** C'est à vos risques et périls.
▶ *vb* risquer **[28]** ▷ *You risk getting a fine.* Vous risquez de recevoir une amende.; **I wouldn't risk it if I were you.** À votre place, je ne prendrais pas ce risque.

rival *n* rival *m* (*pl* rivaux), rivale *f*
▶ *adj* ❶ rival(e) (*mpl* rivaux) ▷ *a rival gang* une bande rivale
❷ concurrent(e) ▷ *a rival company* une société concurrente

river *n* ❶ rivière *f* ▷ *The river runs alongside the canal.* La rivière longe le canal. ❷ (*major*) fleuve *m* ▷ *the rivers of France* les fleuves de France;

the river Seine la Seine

road *n* ❶ route *f* ▷ *There's a lot of traffic on the roads.* Il y a beaucoup de circulation sur les routes.
❷ (*street*) rue *f* ▷ *They live across the road.* Ils habitent de l'autre côté de la rue.

road map *n* carte routière *f*

road rage *n* agressivité au volant *f*

road sign *n* panneau de signalisation *m* (*pl* panneaux de signalisation)

roadworks *npl* travaux *mpl*

roast *adj* rôti(e) ▷ *roast chicken* le poulet rôti; **roast pork** le rôti de porc; **roast beef** le rôti de bœuf

rob *vb* **to rob somebody** voler **[28]** quelqu'un ▷ *I've been robbed.* On m'a volé.; **to rob somebody of something** voler **[28]** quelque chose à quelqu'un ▷ *He was robbed of his wallet.* On lui a volé son portefeuille.; **to rob a bank** dévaliser **[28]** une banque

robber *n* voleur *m*; **a bank-robber** un cambrioleur de banques

robbery *n* vol *m*; **a bank robbery** un hold-up; **armed robbery** le vol à main armée

robin *n* rouge-gorge *m*

robot *n* robot *m*

rock *n* ❶ (*substance*) roche *f* ▷ *They tunnelled through the rock.* Ils ont creusé un tunnel dans la roche.
❷ (*boulder*) rocher *m* ▷ *I sat on a rock.* Je me suis assis sur un rocher.
❸ (*stone*) pierre *f* ❹ (*music*) rock *m* ▷ *a rock concert* un concert de rock
❺ (*sweet*) sucre d'orge *m*

▶ vb ébranler [28] ▷ *The explosion rocked the building.* L'explosion a ébranlé le bâtiment.

rocket n *(firework, spacecraft)* fusée f

rocking horse n cheval à bascule m *(pl* chevaux à bascule*)*

rod n *(for fishing)* canne à pêche f

rode vb *see* **ride**

role n rôle m

role play n jeu de rôle m *(pl* jeux de rôles*)* ▷ *to do a role play* faire un jeu de rôle

roll n ❶ rouleau m *(pl* rouleaux*)* ▷ *a roll of tape* un rouleau de ruban adhésif ▷ *a toilet roll* un rouleau de papier hygiénique ❷ *(bread)* petit pain m

▶ vb rouler [28]; **to roll out the pastry** abaisser [28] la pâte

Rollerblade® n roller m ▷ *a pair of Rollerblades* une paire de rollers

rollercoaster n montagnes russes fpl

roller skates npl patins à roulettes mpl

roller-skating n patin à roulettes m; **to go roller-skating** faire [36] du patin à roulettes

Roman adj, n *(ancient)* romain(e) ▷ *a Roman villa* une villa romaine ▷ *the Roman empire* l'empire romain

Roman Catholic n catholique mf ▷ *He's a Roman Catholic.* Il est catholique.

romance n ❶ *(novels)* romans d'amour mpl ▷ *I read a lot of romance.* Je lis beaucoup de romans d'amour. ❷ *(glamour)* charme m ▷ *the romance of Paris* le charme de Paris;

a holiday romance une idylle de vacances

Romania n Roumanie f; **in Romania** en Roumanie

Romanian adj roumain(e)

romantic adj romantique

roof n toit m

roof rack n galerie f

room n ❶ pièce f ▷ *the biggest room in the house* la plus grande pièce de la maison ❷ *(bedroom)* chambre f ▷ *She's in her room.* Elle est dans sa chambre.; **a single room** une chambre pour une personne; **a double room** une chambre pour deux personnes ❸ *(in school)* salle f ▷ *the music room* la salle de musique ❹ *(space)* place f ▷ *There's no room for that box.* Il n'y a pas de place pour cette boîte.

root n racine f

root around vb fouiller [28] ▷ *She started rooting around in her handbag.* Elle a commencé à fouiller dans son sac à main.

root out vb traquer [28] ▷ *They are determined to root out corruption.* Ils sont déterminés à traquer la corruption.

rope n corde f

rope in vb enrôler [28] ▷ *I was roped in to help with the refreshments.* J'ai été enrôlé pour servir les rafraîchissements.

rose vb *see* **rise**

▶ n *(flower)* rose f

rot vb pourrir [38]

rotten adj *(decayed)* pourri(e) ▷ *a rotten apple* une pomme

a
b
c
d
e
f
g
h
i
j
k
l
m
n
o
p
q
r
s
t
u
v
w
x
y
z

pourrie; **rotten weather** un temps pourri; **That's a rotten thing to do.** Ce n'est vraiment pas gentil.; **to feel rotten** être [**35**] mal fichu (informal)

rough adj ❶ (surface) rêche ▷ My hands are rough. J'ai les mains rêches. ❷ (game) violent(e) ▷ Rugby's a rough sport. Le rugby est un sport violent. ❸ (place) difficile ▷ It's a rough area. C'est un quartier difficile. ❹ (water) houleux (f houleuse) ▷ The sea was rough. La mer était houleuse.
❺ approximatif (f approximative) ▷ I've got a rough idea. J'en ai une idée approximative.; **to feel rough** ne pas être [**35**] dans son assiette ▷ I feel rough. Je ne suis pas dans mon assiette.

roughly adv à peu près ▷ It weighs roughly 20 kilos. Ça pèse à peu près vingt kilos.

round adj, adv, prep ❶ rond(e) ▷ a round table une table ronde ❷ (around) autour de ▷ We were sitting round the table. Nous étions assis autour de la table.; **It's just round the corner.** (very near) C'est tout près.; **to go round to somebody's house** aller [**3**] chez quelqu'un ▷ I went round to my friend's house. Je suis allé chez mon ami.; **to have a look round** faire [**36**] un tour; **to go round a museum** visiter [**28**] un musée; **round here** près d'ici ▷ Is there a chemist's round here? Est-ce qu'il y a une pharmacie près d'ici?; **He lives**

round here. Il habite dans les parages.; **all round** partout; **all year round** toute l'année; **round about** (roughly) environ ▷ It costs round about £100. Cela coûte environ cent livres. ▷ round about 8 o'clock à huit heures environ ▶ n ❶ (of tournament) manche f ❷ (of boxing match) round m; **a round of golf** une partie de golf; **a round of drinks** une tournée ▷ He bought a round of drinks. Il a offert une tournée.

round off vb terminer [**28**] ▷ They rounded off the meal with liqueurs. Ils ont terminé le repas par des liqueurs.

round up vb ❶ (sheep, cattle, suspects) rassembler [**28**] ❷ (figure) arrondir [**38**]

roundabout n ❶ (at junction) rond-point m (pl ronds-points) ❷ (at funfair) manège m

rounders n Rounders is a bit like baseball. Le 'rounders' ressemble un peu au base-ball.
● Rounders is not played in
● France.

round trip n (US) aller et retour m

route n ❶ itinéraire m ▷ We're planning our route. Nous établissons notre itinéraire. ❷ (of bus) parcours m

routine n my daily routine mes occupations quotidiennes

row n

This word has two pronunciations. Make sure you choose the right translation.

❶ rangée f ▷ a row of houses une rangée de maisons ❷ (of seats) rang m ▷ Our seats are in the front row. Nos places se trouvent au premier rang.; **five times in a row** cinq fois d'affilée ❸ (noise) vacarme m ▷ What's that terrible row? Qu'est-ce que c'est que ce vacarme? ❹ (quarrel) dispute f; **to have a row** se disputer [28] ▷ They've had a row. Ils se sont disputés.
▶ vb ❶ ramer [28] ▷ We took turns to row. Nous avons ramé à tour de rôle. ❷ (as sport) faire [36] de l'aviron

rowboat n (US) bateau à rames m

rowing n (sport) aviron m ▷ My hobby is rowing. Je fais de l'aviron.; **a rowing boat** un bateau à rames

royal adj royal(e) (mpl royaux); **the royal family** la famille royale

rub vb ❶ (stain) frotter [28] ❷ (part of body) se frotter [28] ▷ Don't rub your eyes! Ne te frotte pas les yeux!; **to rub something out** effacer [12] quelque chose

rubber n ❶ caoutchouc m ▷ rubber soles des semelles en caoutchouc ❷ (eraser) gomme f ▷ Can I borrow your rubber? Je peux emprunter ta gomme?; **a rubber band** un élastique

rubbish n ❶ (refuse) ordures fpl ▷ When do they collect the rubbish? Quand est-ce qu'ils ramassent les ordures? ❷ (junk) camelote f ▷ They sell a lot of rubbish at the market. Ils vendent beaucoup de camelote au marché. ❸ (nonsense) bêtises fpl

▷ Don't talk rubbish! Ne dis pas de bêtises!; **That's a load of rubbish!** (informal) C'est vraiment n'importe quoi!; **a rubbish bin** une poubelle; **a rubbish dump** une décharge
▶ adj nul (f nulle) ▷ They're a rubbish team! Cette équipe est nulle!

rucksack n sac à dos m

rude adj ❶ (impolite) impoli(e) ▷ It's rude to interrupt. C'est impoli de couper la parole aux gens. ❷ (offensive) grossier (f grossière) ▷ He was very rude to me. Il a été très grossier avec moi.; **a rude word** un gros mot

rug n ❶ tapis m ▷ a Persian rug un tapis persan ❷ (blanket) couverture f ▷ a tartan rug une couverture écossaise

rugby n rugby m ▷ I play rugby. Je joue au rugby.

ruin n ruine f ▷ the ruins of the castle les ruines du château; **in ruins** en ruine
▶ vb ❶ abîmer [28] ▷ You'll ruin your shoes. Tu vas abîmer tes chaussures. ❷ gâcher [28] ▷ It ruined our holiday. Ça a gâché nos vacances. ❸ (financially) ruiner [28]

rule n ❶ règle f ▷ the rules of grammar les règles de grammaire; **as a rule** en règle générale ❷ (regulation) règlement m ▷ It's against the rules. C'est contre le règlement.

rule out vb (possibility) écarter [28]

ruler n règle f ▷ Can I borrow your ruler? Je peux emprunter ta règle?

rum n rhum m

rumour (US rumor) n rumeur f

a b c d e f g h i j k l m n o p q r s t u v w x y z

▷ *It's just a rumour.* Ce n'est qu'une rumeur.

run n (in cricket) point m ▷ *to score a run* marquer un point; **to go for a run** courir [16] ▷ *I go for a run every morning.* Je cours tous les matins.; **I did a ten-kilometre run.** J'ai couru dix kilomètres.; **on the run** en fuite ▷ *The criminals are still on the run.* Les criminels sont toujours en fuite.; **in the long run** à long terme

▶ vb ❶ courir [16] ▷ *I ran five kilometres.* J'ai couru cinq kilomètres.; **to run a marathon** participer [28] à un marathon ❷ (manage) diriger [45] ▷ *He runs a large company.* Il dirige une grosse société. ❸ (organize) organiser [28] ▷ *They run music courses in the holidays.* Ils organisent des cours de musique pendant les vacances. ❹ (water) couler [28] ▷ *Don't leave the tap running.* Ne laisse pas couler le robinet.; **to run a bath** faire [36] couler un bain ❺ (by car) conduire [23] ▷ *I can run you to the station.* Je peux te conduire à la gare.

run away vb s'enfuir [39] ▷ *They ran away before the police came.* Ils se sont enfuis avant l'arrivée de la police.

run out vb **Time is running out.** Il ne reste plus beaucoup de temps.; **to run out of something** se trouver [28] à court de quelque chose ▷ *We ran out of money.* Nous nous sommes trouvés à court d'argent.

run over vb **to run somebody over** écraser [28] quelqu'un; **to get run over** se faire [36] écraser ▷ *Be careful, or you'll get run over!* Fais attention, sinon tu vas te faire écraser!

rung vb see **ring**

runner n coureur m, coureuse f

runner-up n second m, seconde f

running n course f ▷ *Running is my favourite sport.* La course est mon sport préféré.

run-up n **in the run-up to Christmas** pendant la période de préparation de Noël

runway n piste f

rush n hâte f; **in a rush** à la hâte
▶ vb ❶ (run) se précipiter [28] ▷ *Everyone rushed outside.* Tout le monde s'est précipité dehors. ❷ (hurry) se dépêcher [28] ▷ *There's no need to rush.* Ce n'est pas la peine de se dépêcher.

rush hour n heures de pointe fpl ▷ *in the rush hour* aux heures de pointe

Russia n Russie f; **in Russia** en Russie; **to Russia** en Russie

Russian n ❶ (person) Russe mf ❷ (language) russe m
▶ adj russe

rust n rouille f

rusty adj rouillé(e) ▷ *a rusty bike* un vélo rouillé ▷ *My French is very rusty.* Mon français est très rouillé.

rye n seigle m; **rye bread** le pain de seigle

S

Sabbath n ❶ (Christian) dimanche
m ❷ (Jewish) sabbat m
sack n sac m; **to get the sack** être
[**35**] mis à la porte
▶ vb **to sack somebody** mettre
[**47**] quelqu'un à la porte ▷ He was
sacked. On l'a mis à la porte.
sacred adj sacré(e)
sacrifice n sacrifice m
sad adj triste
saddle n selle f
saddlebag n sacoche f
safe n coffre-fort m (pl coffres-forts)
▷ She put the money in the safe. Elle a
mis l'argent dans le coffre-fort.
▶ adj ❶ sans danger ▷ Don't worry,
it's perfectly safe. Ne vous inquiétez
pas, c'est absolument sans
danger.; **Is it safe?** Ça n'est pas
dangereux? ❷ (machine, ladder)

sûr(e) ▷ This car isn't safe. Cette
voiture n'est pas sûre. ❸ (out of
danger) hors de danger ▷ You're safe
now. Vous êtes hors de danger
maintenant.; **to feel safe** se sentir
[**77**] en sécurité; **safe sex** le sexe
sans risques
safety n sécurité f; **a safety belt**
une ceinture de sécurité; **a safety
pin** une épingle de nourrice
Sagittarius n Sagittaire mf ▷ I'm
Sagittarius. Je suis Sagittaire.
said vb see **say**
sail n voile f
▶ vb ❶ (travel) naviguer [**28**] ❷ (set
off) prendre [**65**] la mer ▷ The boat
sails at eight o'clock. Le bateau
prend la mer à huit heures.
sailing n voile f ▷ His hobby is sailing.
Son passe-temps, c'est la voile.; **to
go sailing** faire [**36**] de la voile; **a
sailing boat** un voilier; **a sailing
ship** un grand voilier
sailor n marin m ▷ He's a sailor. Il est
marin.
saint n saint m, sainte f
sake n **for the sake of** dans l'intérêt
de
salad n salade f; **salad dressing** la
vinaigrette
salami n salami m
salary n salaire m
sale n (reductions) soldes mpl
▷ There's a sale on at Harrods. Ce sont
les soldes chez Harrods.; **on sale**
en vente; **The factory's for sale.**
L'usine est en vente.; **'for sale'** 'à
vendre'
sales assistant n vendeur m,

vendeuse f ▷ *She's a sales assistant.* Elle est vendeuse.

salesman n ❶ (*sales rep*) représentant m ▷ *He's a salesman.* Il est représentant.; **a double-glazing salesman** un représentant en doubles vitrages ❷ (*sales assistant*) vendeur m

saleswoman n ❶ (*sales rep*) représentante f ▷ *She's a saleswoman.* Elle est représentante. ❷ (*sales assistant*) vendeuse f

salmon n saumon m

salon n salon m ▷ *a hair salon* un salon de coiffure

salt n sel m

salty adj salé(e)

Salvation Army n armée du Salut f

same adj même ▷ *at the same time* en même temps; **They're exactly the same.** Ils sont exactement pareils.; **It's not the same.** Ça n'est pas pareil.

sample n échantillon m

sand n sable m

sandal n sandale f ▷ *a pair of sandals* une paire de sandales

sand castle n château de sable m (*pl* châteaux de sable)

sandwich n sandwich m ▷ *a cheese sandwich* un sandwich au fromage

sang vb see **sing**

sanitary towel n serviette hygiénique f

sank vb see **sink**

Santa Claus n père Noël m

sarcastic adj sarcastique

sardine n sardine f

sat vb see **sit**

satchel n cartable m

satellite n satellite m ▷ *satellite television* la télévision par satellite; **a satellite dish** une antenne parabolique

satisfactory adj satisfaisant(e)

satisfied adj satisfait(e)

sat nav n GPS m

Saturday n samedi m ▷ *on Saturday* samedi ▷ *on Saturdays* le samedi ▷ *every Saturday* tous les samedis ▷ *last Saturday* samedi dernier ▷ *next Saturday* samedi prochain; **I've got a Saturday job.** Je travaille le samedi.

sauce n sauce f

saucepan n casserole f

saucer n soucoupe f

Saudi Arabia n Arabie Saoudite f; **in Saudi Arabia** en Arabie Saoudite

sausage n ❶ saucisse f ❷ (*salami*) saucisson m; **a sausage roll** un friand à la saucisse

save vb ❶ (*save up money*) mettre [47] de côté ▷ *I've saved £50 already.* J'ai déjà mis cinquante livres de côté. ❷ (*spend less*) économiser [28] ▷ *I saved £20 by waiting for the sales.* J'ai économisé vingt livres en attendant les soldes.; **to save time** gagner [28] du temps ▷ *We took a taxi to save time.* Nous avons pris un taxi pour gagner du temps. ▷ *It saved us time.* Ça nous a fait gagner du temps. ❸ (*rescue*) sauver [28] ▷ *Luckily, all the passengers were saved.* Heureusement, tous les passagers ont été sauvés. ❹ (*on

computer) <u>sauvegarder</u> [**28**] ▷ *Don't forget to save your work regularly.* N'oublie pas de sauvegarder ton travail régulièrement.
save up *vb* <u>mettre</u> [**47**] <u>de l'argent de côté</u> ▷ *I'm saving up for a new bike.* Je mets de l'argent de côté pour un nouveau vélo.
savings *npl* <u>économies</u> *fpl* ▷ *She spent all her savings on a computer.* Elle a dépensé toutes ses économies en achetant un ordinateur.
savoury *adj* <u>salé(e)</u> ▷ *Is it sweet or savoury?* C'est sucré ou salé?
saw *vb see* **see**
  ▶ *n* <u>scie</u> *f*
saxophone *n* <u>saxophone</u> *m* ▷ *I play the saxophone.* Je joue du saxophone.
say *vb* <u>dire</u> [**27**] ▷ *What did he say?* Qu'est-ce qu'il a dit? ▷ *Did you hear what she said?* Tu as entendu ce qu'elle a dit?; **Could you say that again?** Pourriez-vous répéter s'il vous plaît?; **That goes without saying.** Cela va sans dire.
saying *n* <u>dicton</u> *m* ▷ *It's just a saying.* C'est juste un dicton.
scale *n* ❶ (*of map*) <u>échelle</u> *f* ▷ *a large-scale map* une carte à grande échelle ❷ (*size, extent*) <u>ampleur</u> *f* ▷ *a disaster on a massive scale* un désastre d'une ampleur incroyable ❸ (*in music*) <u>gamme</u> *f*
scales *npl* (*in kitchen, shop*) <u>balance</u> *fsg*; **bathroom scales** le pèse-personne *sg*
scampi *npl* <u>scampi</u> *mpl*

scandal *n* ❶ (*outrage*) <u>scandale</u> *m* ▷ *It caused a scandal.* Ça a fait scandale. ❷ (*gossip*) <u>ragots</u> *mpl* ▷ *It's just scandal.* Ce ne sont que des ragots.
Scandinavia *n* <u>Scandinavie</u> *f*; **in Scandinavia** en Scandinavie
Scandinavian *adj* <u>scandinave</u>
scar *n* <u>cicatrice</u> *f*
scarce *adj* <u>limité(e)</u> ▷ *scarce resources* des ressources limitées; **Jobs are scarce these days.** Il y a peu de travail ces temps-ci.
scarcely *adv* <u>à peine</u> ▷ *I scarcely knew him.* Je le connaissais à peine.
scare *n* <u>panique</u> *f*; **a bomb scare** une alerte à la bombe
  ▶ *vb* **to scare somebody** <u>faire</u> [**36**] <u>peur à quelqu'un</u> ▷ *He scares me.* Il me fait peur.
scarecrow *n* <u>épouvantail</u> *m*
scared *adj* **to be scared** <u>avoir</u> [**8**] <u>peur</u> ▷ *I was scared stiff.* J'avais terriblement peur.; **to be scared of** <u>avoir</u> [**8**] <u>peur de</u> ▷ *Are you scared of him?* Est-ce que tu as peur de lui?
scarf *n* ❶ (*long*) <u>écharpe</u> *f* ❷ (*square*) <u>foulard</u> *m*
scary *adj* <u>effrayant(e)</u> ▷ *It was really scary.* C'était vraiment effrayant.
scene *n* ❶ (*place*) <u>lieux</u> *mpl* ▷ *the scene of the crime* les lieux du crime ❷ (*event, sight*) <u>spectacle</u> *m* ▷ *It was an amazing scene.* C'était un spectacle étonnant.; **to make a scene** <u>faire</u> [**36**] <u>une scène</u>
scenery *n* (*landscape*) <u>paysage</u> *m*
schedule *n* <u>programme</u> *m* ▷ *a busy schedule* un programme chargé; **on**

a
b
c
d
e
f
g
h
i
j
k
l
m
n
o
p
q
r
s
t
u
v
w
x
y
z

schedule comme prévu; **to be behind schedule** avoir [8] du retard

scheduled flight n vol régulier m

scheme n ❶ (idea) truc m ▷ a crazy scheme he dreamed up un truc farfelu qu'il a inventé ❷ (project) projet m ▷ a council road-widening scheme un projet municipal d'élargissement des routes

scholarship n bourse f

school n école f; **to go to school** aller [3] à l'école

schoolbag n cartable m

schoolbook n livre scolaire m

schoolboy n écolier m

schoolchildren n écoliers mpl

schoolgirl n écolière f

school uniform n uniforme scolaire m

science n science f

science fiction n science-fiction f

scientific adj scientifique

scientist n chercheur m, chercheuse f; **He trained as a scientist.** Il a une formation scientifique.

scissors npl ciseaux mpl ▷ a pair of scissors une paire de ciseaux

scooter n ❶ scooter m ❷ (child's toy) trottinette f

score n score m ▷ The score was three nil. Le score était trois à zéro.
▶ vb ❶ (goal, point) marquer [28]
▷ to score a goal marquer un but; **to score 6 out of 10** obtenir [83] un score de six sur dix ❷ (keep score) compter [28] les points ▷ Who's going to score? Qui va compter les points?

Scorpio n Scorpion m ▷ I'm Scorpio. Je suis Scorpion.

Scot n Écossais m, Écossaise f

Scotch tape® n (US) scotch® m

Scotland n Écosse f; **in Scotland** en Écosse; **to Scotland** en Écosse; **I'm from Scotland.** Je suis écossais.

Scots adj écossais(e) ▷ a Scots accent un accent écossais

Scotsman n Écossais m

Scotswoman n Écossaise f

Scottish adj écossais(e) ▷ a Scottish accent un accent écossais

scout n scout m ▷ I'm in the Scouts. Je suis scout.

scrambled eggs npl œufs brouillés mpl

scrap n ❶ bout m ▷ a scrap of paper un bout de papier ❷ (fight) bagarre f
▶ vb (plan) abandonner [28] ▷ The idea was scrapped. L'idée a été abandonnée.

scrapbook n album m

scratch vb se gratter [28] ▷ Stop scratching! Arrête de te gratter!
▶ n (on skin) égratignure f; **to start from scratch** partir [57] de zéro

scream n hurlement m
▶ vb hurler [28]

screen n écran m

screen-saver n économiseur d'écran m

screw n vis f

screwdriver n tournevis m

scribble vb griffonner [28]

scrub vb récurer [28] ▷ to scrub a pan récurer une casserole

sculpture n sculpture f
sea n mer f
seafood n fruits de mer mpl ▷ I don't
like seafood. Je n'aime pas les fruits
de mer.
seagull n mouette f
seal n ❶ (animal) phoque m ❷ (on
letter) cachet m
  ▶ vb ❶ (document) sceller [28]
  ❷ (letter) coller [28]
seaman n marin m
search vb fouiller [28] ▷ They
searched the woods for her. Ils ont
fouillé les bois pour la trouver.; **to
search for something** chercher
[28] quelque chose ▷ He searched for
evidence. Il cherchait des preuves.
  ▶ n fouille f
search party n expédition de
secours f
seashore n bord de la mer m ▷ on
the seashore au bord de la mer
seasick adj **to be seasick** avoir [8]
le mal de mer
seaside n bord de la mer m ▷ at the
seaside au bord de la mer
season n saison f ▷ What's your
favourite season? Quelle est ta
saison préférée?; **out of season**
hors saison ▷ It's cheaper to go there
out of season. C'est moins cher d'y
aller hors saison.; **during the
holiday season** en période de
vacances; **a season ticket** une
carte d'abonnement
seat n siège m
seat belt n ceinture de sécurité f
seaweed n algues fpl
second adj deuxième ▷ on the

second page à la deuxième page; **to
come second** (in race) arriver [5]
deuxième; **the second of March** le
deux mars
  ▶ n seconde f ▷ It'll only take a
second. Ça va prendre juste une
seconde.
secondary school n ❶ collège m
  ❷ lycée m
  ● In France pupils go to a **collège**
  ● between the ages of 11 and 15,
  ● and then to a **lycée** until the age
  ● of 18.
second-class adj, adv ❶ (ticket,
compartment) de seconde classe;
to travel second class voyager
[45] en seconde ❷ (stamp, letter) à
tarif réduit ▷ to send something
second class envoyer quelque chose
à tarif réduit
secondhand adj d'occasion
  ▷ a secondhand car une voiture
d'occasion
secondly adv deuxièmement;
firstly ... secondly ... d'abord ...
ensuite ... ▷ Firstly, it's too expensive.
Secondly, it wouldn't work anyway.
D'abord, c'est trop cher. Ensuite, ça
ne marcherait pas de toute façon.
secret adj secret (f secrète)
  ▷ a secret mission une mission
secrète
  ▶ n secret m ▷ It's a secret. C'est un
secret. ▷ Can you keep a secret? Tu
sais garder un secret?; **in secret** en
secret
secretary n secrétaire mf ▷ She's a
secretary. Elle est secrétaire.
secretly n secrètement

section n section f

security n sécurité f ▷ a feeling of security un sentiment de sécurité; **airport security** la sécurité dans les aéroports; **job security** la sécurité de l'emploi

security guard n ❶ (on guard) garde chargé de la sécurité m ❷ (transporting money) un convoyeur de fonds

see vb voir [**92**] ▷ I can't see. Je n'y vois rien. ▷ I saw him yesterday. Je l'ai vu hier. ▷ Have you seen him? Est-ce que tu l'as vu?; **See you!** Salut!; **See you soon!** À bientôt!; **to see to something** s'occuper [**28**] de quelque chose ▷ Can you see to the kids, please? Tu peux t'occuper des enfants, s'il te plaît?

seed n graine f ▷ sunflower seeds des graines de tournesol

seek vb chercher [**28**]; **to seek help** chercher [**28**] de l'aide

seem vb avoir [**8**] l'air ▷ She seems tired. Elle a l'air fatiguée. ▷ The shop seemed to be closed. Le magasin avait l'air d'être fermé.; **That seems like a good idea.** Ce n'est pas une mauvaise idée.; **It seems that ...** Il paraît que ... ▷ It seems she's getting married. Il paraît qu'elle va se marier.; **There seems to be a problem.** Il semble y avoir un problème.

seen vb see **see**

seesaw n tapecul m

seldom adv rarement

select vb sélectionner [**28**]

selection n sélection f

self-catering adj **a self-catering apartment** un appartement de vacances

self-confidence n confiance en soi f ▷ He hasn't got much self-confidence. Il n'a pas très confiance en lui.

self-conscious adj **to be self-conscious (1)** (embarrassed) être [**35**] mal à l'aise ▷ She was really self-conscious at first. Elle était vraiment mal à l'aise au début. **(2)** (shy) manquer [**28**] d'assurance ▷ He's always been rather self-conscious. Il a toujours manqué un peu d'assurance.

self-defence (US **self-defense**) n autodéfense f ▷ self-defence classes les cours d'autodéfense; **She killed him in self-defence.** Elle l'a tué en légitime défense.

self-employed adj **to be self-employed** travailler [**28**] à son compte ▷ He's self-employed. Il travaille à son compte.; **the self-employed** les travailleurs indépendants

selfie n selfie m

selfie stick n perche f à selfie

selfish adj égoïste ▷ Don't be so selfish. Ne sois pas si égoïste.

self-service adj **It's self-service.** (café, shop) C'est un self-service.; **a self-service restaurant** un restaurant self-service

sell vb vendre [**88**] ▷ He sold it to me. Il me l'a vendu.

sell off vb liquider [**28**]

sell out vb se vendre [**88**] ▷ The

tickets sold out in three hours.
Les billets se sont tous vendus en
trois heures. ▷ *The show didn't quite
sell out.* Ce spectacle ne s'est pas
très bien vendu.; **The tickets are
all sold out.** Il ne reste plus de
billets.
sell-by date *n* date limite de
vente *f*
Sellotape® *n* scotch® *m*
semi *n* maison jumelée *f* ▷ *We live in
a semi.* Nous habitons dans une
maison jumelée.
semicircle *n* demi-cercle *m*
semicolon *n* point-virgule *m*
semi-detached house *n* maison
jumelée *f* ▷ *We live in a semi-detached
house.* Nous habitons dans une
maison jumelée.
semi-final *n* demi-finale *f*
semi-skimmed milk *n* lait
demi-écrémé *m*
send *vb* envoyer [33] ▷ *She sent me a
birthday card.* Elle m'a envoyé une
carte d'anniversaire.
send back *vb* renvoyer [33]
send off *vb* ❶ (goods, letter) envoyer
[33] ❷ (in sports match) renvoyer
[33] du terrain ▷ *He was sent off.* On
l'a renvoyé du terrain.; **to send off
for something (1)** (free) se faire [36]
envoyer quelque chose ▷ *I've sent
off for a brochure.* Je me suis fait
envoyer une brochure. **(2)** (paid for)
commander [28] quelque chose
▷ *She sent off for a book.* Elle a commandé un livre
par correspondance.
send out *vb* envoyer [33]; **to send**

out for commander [28] par
téléphone ▷ *Shall we send out for a
pizza?* Et si on commandait une
pizza par téléphone?
senior *adj* haut placé(e); **senior
management** les cadres
supérieurs; **senior school** le lycée;
senior pupils les grandes classes
senior citizen *n* personne du
troisième âge *f*
sensational *adj* sensationnel (*f*
sensationnelle)
sense *n* ❶ (wisdom) bon sens *m*
▷ *Use your common sense!* Un peu de
bon sens, voyons!; **It makes
sense.** C'est logique.; **It doesn't
make sense.** Ça n'a pas de sens.
❷ (faculty) sens *m* ▷ *the five senses*
les cinq sens; **the sense of touch**
le toucher; **the sense of smell**
l'odorat *m*; **the sixth sense** le
sixième sens; **sense of humour** le
sens de l'humour ▷ *He's got no sense
of humour.* Il n'a aucun sens de
l'humour.
sensible *adj* raisonnable ▷ *Be
sensible!* Sois raisonnable!

Be careful not to translate
sensible by the French word
sensible.

sensitive *adj* sensible ▷ *She's very
sensitive.* Elle est très sensible.
sent *vb see* **send**
sentence *n* ❶ phrase *f* ▷ *What does
this sentence mean?* Que veut dire
cette phrase? ❷ (judgment)
condamnation *f* ❸ (punishment)
peine *f* ▷ *the death sentence* la peine
de mort; **He got a life sentence.**

Il a été condamné à la réclusion à perpétuité.
▸ *vb* condamner [**28**]; **to sentence somebody to life imprisonment** condamner [**28**] quelqu'un à la réclusion à perpétuité; **to sentence somebody to death** condamner [**28**] quelqu'un à mort

sentimental *adj* sentimental(e) (*mpl* sentimentaux)

separate *adj* séparé(e) ▷ *I wrote it on a separate sheet.* Je l'ai écrit sur une feuille séparée.; **The children have separate rooms.** Les enfants ont chacun leur chambre.; **on separate occasions** à différentes reprises
▸ *vb* ❶ séparer [**28**] ❷ (*married couple*) se séparer [**28**]

separately *adv* séparément

separation *n* séparation *f*

September *n* septembre *m*; **in September** en septembre

sequel *n* (*book, film*) suite *f*

sergeant *n* ❶ (*army*) sergent *m* ❷ (*police*) brigadier *m*

serial *n* feuilleton *m*

series *n* ❶ série *f* ▷ *a TV series* une série télévisée ❷ (*of numbers*) suite *f*

serious *adj* ❶ sérieux (*f* sérieuse) ▷ *You look very serious.* Tu as l'air sérieux.; **Are you serious?** Sérieusement? ❷ (*illness, mistake*) grave

seriously *adv* sérieusement ▷ *No, but seriously ...* Non, mais sérieusement ...; **to take somebody seriously** prendre [**65**] quelqu'un au sérieux; **seriously**

injured gravement blessé; **Seriously?** Vraiment?

servant *n* domestique *mf*

serve *vb* ❶ servir [**78**] ▷ *Dinner is served.* Le dîner est servi. ▷ *It's Murray's turn to serve.* C'est à Murray de servir. ❷ (*prison sentence*) purger [**45**]; **to serve time** être [**35**] en prison; **It serves you right.** C'est bien fait pour toi.
▸ *n* (*tennis*) service *m*; **It's your serve.** C'est à toi de servir.

service *vb* (*car, washing machine*) réviser [**28**]
▸ *n* ❶ service *m* ▷ *Service is included.* Le service est compris. ❷ (*of car*) révision *f* ❸ (*church service*) office *m*; **the Fire Service** les sapeurs-pompiers; **the armed services** les forces armées

service charge *n* service *m* ▷ *There's no service charge.* Le service est compris.

service station *n* station-service *f* (*pl* stations-service)

serviette *n* serviette *f*

session *n* séance *f*

set *n* ❶ jeu *m* (*pl* jeux) ▷ *a set of keys* un jeu de clés ▷ *a chess set* un jeu d'échecs; **a train set** un train électrique ❷ (*in tennis*) set *m*
▸ *vb* ❶ (*alarm clock*) mettre [**47**] à sonner ▷ *I set the alarm for 7 o'clock.* J'ai mis le réveil à sonner pour sept heures. ❷ (*record*) établir [**38**] ▷ *The world record was set last year.* Le record du monde a été établi l'année dernière. ❸ (*sun*) se coucher [**28**] ▷ *The sun was setting.*

Le soleil se couchait.; **The film is set in Morocco.** L'action du film se déroule au Maroc.; **to set sail** prendre [**65**] la mer; **to set the table** mettre [**47**] le couvert

set off vb partir [**57**] ▷ We set off for London at 9 o'clock. Nous sommes partis pour Londres à neuf heures.

set out vb partir [**57**] ▷ We set out for London at 9 o'clock. Nous sommes partis pour Londres à neuf heures.

settee n canapé m

settle vb ❶ (problem) résoudre [**70**] ❷ (argument, account) régler [**34**]; **to settle on something** opter [**28**] pour quelque chose

settle down vb (calm down) se calmer [**28**]; **Settle down!** Du calme!

settle in vb s'installer [**28**]

seven num sept ▷ She's seven. Elle a sept ans.

seventeen num dix-sept ▷ He's seventeen. Il a dix-sept ans.

seventeenth adj dix-septième ▷ her seventeenth birthday son dix-septième anniversaire ▷ the seventeenth floor le dix-septième étage; **the seventeenth of August** le dix-sept août

seventh adj septième ▷ the seventh floor le septième étage; **the seventh of August** le sept août

seventy num soixante-dix

several adj, pron plusieurs ▷ several schools plusieurs écoles; **several of them** plusieurs ▷ I've seen several of them. J'en ai vu plusieurs.

sew vb coudre [**15**]

sew up vb (tear) recoudre [**15**]

sewing n couture f ▷ I like sewing. J'aime faire de la couture.; **a sewing machine** une machine à coudre

sewn vb see sew

sex n sexe m; **to have sex with somebody** coucher [**28**] avec quelqu'un; **sex education** l'éducation sexuelle f

sexism n sexisme m

sexist adj sexiste

sexual adj sexuel (f sexuelle) ▷ sexual discrimination la discrimination sexuelle ▷ sexual harassment le harcèlement sexuel

sexuality n sexualité f

sexy adj sexy

shabby adj miteux (f miteuse)

shade n ❶ ombre f; **in the shade** à l'ombre ▷ It was 35 degrees in the shade. Il faisait trente-cinq à l'ombre. ❷ (colour) nuance f ▷ a shade of blue une nuance de bleu

shadow n ombre f

shake vb ❶ secouer [**28**] ▷ She shook the rug. Elle a secoué le tapis. ❷ (tremble) trembler [**28**] ▷ He was shaking with cold. Il tremblait de froid.; **to shake one's head** (in refusal) faire [**36**] non de la tête; **to shake hands with somebody** serrer [**28**] la main à quelqu'un ▷ They shook hands. Ils se sont serré la main.

shaken adj secoué(e) ▷ I was feeling a bit shaken. J'étais un peu secoué.

shall vb **Shall I shut the window?** Vous voulez que je ferme la fenêtre?;

a b c d e f g h i j k l m n o p q r s t u v w x y z

Shall we ask him to come with us? Si on lui demandait de venir avec nous?

shallow adj (water, pool) peu profond(e)

shambles n pagaille f ▷ It's a complete shambles. C'est la pagaille complète.

shame n honte f ▷ The shame of it! Quelle honte!; **What a shame!** Quel dommage!; **It's a shame that ...** C'est dommage que ...

> c'est dommage que has to be followed by a verb in the subjunctive.

▷ It's a shame he isn't here. C'est dommage qu'il ne soit pas ici.

shampoo n shampo(o)ing m ▷ a bottle of shampoo une bouteille de shampo(o)ing

shandy n panaché m

shape n forme f

share n ❶ (in company) action f ▷ They've got shares in the company. Ils ont des actions dans la société. ❷ part f ▷ Everybody pays their share. Tout le monde paie sa part.

▶ vb partager [45] ▷ to share a room with somebody partager une chambre avec quelqu'un

share out vb distribuer [28] ▷ They shared the sweets out among the children. Ils ont distribué les bonbons aux enfants.

shark n requin m

sharp adj ❶ (razor, knife) tranchant(e) ❷ (spike, point) pointu(e) ❸ (clever) intelligent(e) ▷ She's very sharp. Elle est très

intelligente.; **at two o'clock sharp** à deux heures pile

shave vb (have a shave) se raser [28]; **to shave one's legs** se raser [28] les jambes

shaver n an electric shaver un rasoir électrique

shaving cream n crème à raser f

shaving foam n mousse à raser f

she pron elle ▷ She's very nice. Elle est très gentille.

shed n remise f

she'd = she had; she would

sheep n mouton m

sheepdog n chien de berger m

sheer adj pur(e) ▷ It's sheer greed. C'est de l'avidité pure.

sheet n (on bed) drap m; **a sheet of paper** une feuille de papier

shelf n ❶ (in house) étagère f ❷ (in shop) rayon m

shell n ❶ (on beach) coquillage m ❷ (of egg, nut) coquille f ❸ (explosive) obus m

she'll = she will

shellfish n fruits de mer mpl

shelter n to take shelter se mettre [47] à l'abri; **a bus shelter** un arrêt d'autobus

shelves npl see shelf

shepherd n berger m

sherry n xérès m

she's = she is; she has

shift n service m ▷ His shift starts at 8 o'clock. Il prend son service à huit heures. ▷ the night shift le service de nuit; **to do shift work** faire [36] les trois-huit

▶ vb (move) déplacer [12] ▷ I couldn't

shift the wardrobe on my own. Je n'ai pas pu déplacer l'armoire tout seul.; **Shift yourself!** *(informal)* Pousse-toi de là!

shin n tibia m

shine vb briller [**28**] ▷ *The sun was shining.* Le soleil brillait.

shiny adj brillant(e)

ship n ❶ bateau m (pl bateaux) ❷ *(warship)* navire m

shirt n ❶ *(man's)* chemise f ❷ *(woman's)* chemisier m

shiver vb frissonner [**28**]

shock n choc m; **to get a shock** **(1)** *(surprise)* avoir [**8**] un choc **(2)** *(electric)* recevoir [**67**] une décharge; **an electric shock** une décharge
▶ vb ❶ *(upset)* bouleverser [**28**] ▷ *They were shocked by the tragedy.* Ils ont été bouleversés par la tragédie. ❷ *(scandalize)* choquer [**28**] ▷ *I was rather shocked by her attitude.* J'ai été assez choqué par son attitude.

shocking adj choquant(e) ▷ *It's shocking!* C'est choquant!; **a shocking waste** un gaspillage épouvantable

shoe n chaussure f

shoelace n lacet m

shoe polish n cirage m

shoe shop n magasin de chaussures m

shone vb see **shine**

shook vb see **shake**

shoot vb ❶ *(kill)* abattre [**9**] ▷ *He was shot by a sniper.* Il a été abattu par un franc-tireur. ❷ *(execute)* fusiller [**28**] ▷ *He was shot at dawn.* Il

a été fusillé à l'aube. ❸ *(gun)* tirer [**28**] ▷ *Don't shoot!* Ne tirez pas!; **to shoot at somebody** tirer [**28**] sur quelqu'un; **He shot himself with a revolver.** *(dead)* Il s'est suicidé d'un coup de revolver.; **He was shot in the leg.** *(wounded)* Il a reçu une balle dans la jambe.; **to shoot an arrow** envoyer [**33**] une flèche ❹ *(film)* tourner [**28**] ▷ *The film was shot in Prague.* Le film a été tourné à Prague. ❺ *(in football)* shooter [**28**]

shooting n ❶ coups de feu mpl ▷ *They heard shooting.* Ils ont entendu des coups de feu.; **a shooting** une fusillade ❷ *(hunting)* chasse f ▷ *to go shooting* aller à la chasse

shop n magasin m ▷ *a sports shop* un magasin de sports

shop assistant n vendeur m, vendeuse f ▷ *She's a shop assistant.* Elle est vendeuse.

shopkeeper n commerçant m, commerçante f ▷ *He's a shopkeeper.* Il est commerçant.

shoplifting n vol à l'étalage m

shopping n *(purchases)* courses fpl ▷ *Can you get the shopping from the car?* Tu peux aller chercher les courses dans la voiture?; **I love shopping.** J'adore faire du shopping.; **to go shopping (1)** *(for food)* faire [**36**] des courses **(2)** *(for pleasure)* faire [**36**] du shopping; **a shopping bag** un sac à provisions; **a shopping centre** un centre commercial

shop window n vitrine f

shore n rivage m; **on shore** à terre

short adj ❶ court(e) ▷ a short skirt une jupe courte ▷ short hair les cheveux courts; **too short** trop court ▷ It was a great holiday, but too short. C'étaient des vacances super, mais trop courtes. ❷ (person, period of time) petit(e) ▷ She's quite short. Elle est assez petite. ▷ a short break une petite pause ▷ a short walk une petite promenade; **to be short of something** être [35] à court de quelque chose ▷ I'm short of money. Je suis à court d'argent.; **at short notice** au dernier moment; **In short, the answer's no.** Bref, la réponse est non.

shortage n pénurie f ▷ a water shortage une pénurie d'eau

short cut n raccourci m ▷ I took a short cut. J'ai pris un raccourci.

shortly adv bientôt

shorts npl short msg; **a pair of shorts** un short

short-sighted adj myope

shot vb see **shoot**
  ▶ n ❶ (gunshot) coup de feu m ❷ (photo) photo f ▷ a shot of Edinburgh Castle une photo du château d'Édimbourg ❸ (vaccination) vaccin m

shotgun n fusil de chasse m

should vb

  When 'should' means 'ought to', use **devoir**.

  devoir [26] ▷ You should take more exercise. Vous devriez faire plus d'exercice. ▷ That shouldn't be too hard. Ça ne devrait pas être trop difficile.; **should have** avoir dû ▷ I should have told you before. J'aurais dû te le dire avant.

  When 'should' means 'would', use the conditional tense.

  ▷ I should go if I were you. Si j'étais vous, j'irais. ▷ I should be so lucky! Ça serait trop beau!

shoulder n épaule f; **a shoulder bag** un sac à bandoulière

shouldn't = **should not**

shout vb crier [19] ▷ Don't shout! Ne criez pas! ▷ 'Go away!' he shouted. 'Allez-vous-en!' a-t-il crié.
  ▶ n cri m

shovel n pelle f

show n ❶ (performance) spectacle m ❷ (programme) émission f ❸ (exhibition) salon m
  ▶ vb ❶ montrer [28]; **to show somebody something** montrer [28] quelque chose à quelqu'un ▷ Have I shown you my new trainers? Je t'ai montré mes nouvelles baskets? ❷ faire [36] preuve de ▷ She showed great courage. Elle a fait preuve de beaucoup de courage.; **It shows.** Ça se voit. ▷ I've never been riding before. — It shows. Je n'ai jamais fait de cheval. — Ça se voit.

show off vb frimer [28] (informal)

show up vb (turn up) se pointer [28] ▷ He showed up late as usual. Il s'est pointé en retard comme d'habitude.

shower n ❶ douche f; **to have a shower** prendre [65] une douche

❷ (of rain) averse f
shown vb see **show**
show-off n frimeur m, frimeuse f
shrank vb see **shrink**
shriek vb hurler [28]
shrimps npl crevettes fpl
shrink vb (clothes, fabric) rétrécir [38]
Shrove Tuesday n mardi gras m
shrug vb to shrug one's shoulders hausser [28] les épaules
shrunk vb see **shrink**
shuffle vb to shuffle the cards battre [9] les cartes
shut vb fermer [28] ▷ What time do you shut? À quelle heure est-ce que vous fermez? ▷ What time do the shops shut? À quelle heure est-ce que les magasins ferment?
shut down vb fermer [28] ▷ The cinema shut down last year. Le cinéma a fermé l'année dernière.
shut up vb ❶ (close) fermer [28] ❷ (be quiet) se taire [82] ▷ Shut up! Tais-toi!
shuttle n navette f
shuttlecock n (badminton) volant m
shy adj timide
Sicily n Sicile f; in Sicily en Sicile; to Sicily en Sicile
sick adj ❶ (ill) malade ▷ He was sick for four days. Il a été malade pendant quatre jours. ❷ (joke, humour) de mauvais goût ▷ That's really sick! C'est vraiment de mauvais goût!; to be sick (vomit) vomir [38]; I feel sick. J'ai envie de vomir.; to be sick of something

en avoir [8] assez de quelque chose ▷ I'm sick of your jokes. J'en ai assez de tes plaisanteries.
sickness n maladie f
side n ❶ (of object, building, car) côté m ▷ He was driving on the wrong side of the road. Il roulait du mauvais côté de la route. ❷ (of pool, river, road) bord m ▷ by the side of the lake au bord du lac ❸ (of hill) flanc m ❹ (team) équipe f; He's on my side. (1) (on my team) Il est dans mon équipe. (2) (supporting me) Il est de mon côté.; side by side côte à côte; the side entrance l'entrée latérale; to take sides prendre [65] parti ▷ She always takes his side. Elle prend toujours son parti.
sideboard n buffet m
side-effect n effet secondaire m
sidewalk n (US) trottoir m
sideways adv ❶ (look, be facing) de côté ❷ (move) de travers; sideways on de profil
sieve n passoire f
sigh n soupir m
▶ vb soupirer [28]
sight n ❶ vue f ▷ to have poor sight avoir une mauvaise vue; to know somebody by sight connaître [14] quelqu'un de vue ❷ spectacle m ▷ It was an amazing sight. C'était un spectacle étonnant.; in sight visible; out of sight hors de vue; the sights (tourist spots) les attractions touristiques; to see the sights of London visiter [28] Londres
sightseeing n tourisme m; to go

sightseeing faire [36] du tourisme

sign n ❶ (notice) panneau m (pl panneaux) ▷ There was a big sign saying 'private'. Il y avait un grand panneau indiquant 'privé'.; **a road sign** un panneau ❷ (gesture, indication) signe m ▷ There's no sign of improvement. Il n'y a aucun signe d'amélioration.; **What sign are you?** (star sign) Tu es de quel signe?
▶ vb signer [28]

sign on vb ❶ (as unemployed) s'inscrire [30] au chômage ❷ (for course) s'inscrire [30]

signal n signal m (pl signaux)
▶ vb **to signal to somebody** faire [36] un signe à quelqu'un

signature n signature f

significance n importance f

significant adj important(e)

sign language n langage des signes m

signpost n poteau indicateur m

silence n silence m

silent adj silencieux (f silencieuse)

silk n soie f
▶ adj en soie ▷ a silk scarf un foulard en soie

silky adj soyeux (f soyeuse)

silly adj bête

silver n argent m ▷ a silver medal une médaille d'argent

similar adj semblable; **similar to** semblable à

simple adj ❶ simple ▷ It's very simple. C'est très simple. ❷ (simple-minded) simplet (f simplette) ▷ He's a bit simple. Il est un peu simplet.

simply adv simplement ▷ It's simply not possible. Ça n'est tout simplement pas possible.

sin n péché m
▶ vb pécher [28]

since prep, adv, conj ❶ depuis ▷ since Christmas depuis Noël ▷ since then depuis ce moment-là ▷ I haven't seen him since. Je ne l'ai pas vu depuis.; **ever since** depuis ce moment-là ❷ depuis que ▷ I haven't seen her since she left. Je ne l'ai pas vue depuis qu'elle est partie. ❸ (because) puisque ▷ Since you're tired, let's stay at home. Puisque tu es fatigué, restons à la maison.

sincere adj sincère

sincerely adv Yours sincerely … **(1)** (in business letter) Veuillez agréer l'expression de mes sentiments les meilleurs … **(2)** (in personal letter) Cordialement …

sing vb chanter [28] ▷ He sang out of tune. Il chantait faux.

singer n chanteur m, chanteuse f

singing n chant m

single adj (unmarried) célibataire; **a single room** une chambre pour une personne; **not a single thing** rien du tout
▶ n (ticket) aller simple m ▷ A single to Toulouse, please. Un aller simple pour Toulouse, s'il vous plaît.; **a CD single** un CD single

single parent n She's a single parent. Elle élève ses enfants toute seule.; **a single parent family** une famille monoparentale

singular n singulier m ▷ in the singular au singulier

sink n évier m
▷ vb couler [28]

sir n monsieur m; **Yes sir.** Oui, Monsieur.

siren n sirène f

sister n ❶ sœur f ▷ my little sister ma petite sœur ❷ (nurse) infirmière en chef f

sister-in-law n belle-sœur f (pl belles-sœurs)

sit vb s'asseoir [6]; **to sit on something** s'asseoir [6] sur quelque chose ▷ She sat on the chair. Elle s'est assise sur la chaise.; **to be sitting** être [35] assis; **to sit an exam** passer [58] un examen

sit down vb s'asseoir [6]

site n ❶ site m ▷ an archaeological site un site archéologique; **the site of the accident** le lieu de l'accident ❷ (campsite) camping m; **a building site** un chantier

sitting room n salon m

situation n situation f

six num six ▷ He's six. Il a six ans.

sixteen num seize ▷ He's sixteen. Il a seize ans.

sixteenth adj seizième ▷ the sixteenth floor le seizième étage; **the sixteenth of August** le seize août

sixth adj sixième ▷ the sixth floor le sixième étage; **the sixth of August** le six août

sixty num soixante

size n ❶ (of object, clothing) taille f ▷ What size do you take? Quelle taille est-ce que vous faites?; **I'm a size ten.** Je fais du trente-huit. ❷ (of shoes) pointure f; **I take size six.** Je fais du trente-neuf.

France uses the European system to show clothing and shoe sizes.

skate vb ❶ (ice-skate) faire [36] du patin à glace ❷ (roller-skate) faire [36] du patin à roulettes

skateboard n skateboard m

skateboarding n skateboard m ▷ to go skateboarding faire du skateboard

skates n patins mpl

skating n patin à glace m ▷ to go skating faire du patin à glace; **a skating rink** une patinoire

skeleton n squelette m

sketch n (drawing) croquis m
▷ vb to sketch something faire [36] un croquis de quelque chose

ski n ski m; **ski boots** les chaussures de ski fpl; **a ski lift** un remonte-pente; **ski pants** le fuseau sg; **a ski pole** un bâton de ski; **a ski slope** une piste de ski; **a ski suit** une combinaison de ski
▷ vb skier [19] ▷ Can you ski? Tu sais skier?

skid vb déraper [28]

skier n skieur m, skieuse f

skiing n ski m; **to go skiing** faire [36] du ski; **to go on a skiing holiday** aller [3] aux sports d'hiver

skilful adj adroit(e)

skill n talent m ▷ He played with great skill. Il a joué avec beaucoup de talent.

skilled adj **a skilled worker** un ouvrier spécialisé

skimmed milk n lait écrémé m

skin n peau f (pl peaux); **skin cancer** le cancer de la peau

skinhead n skinhead mf

skinny adj maigre

skip n (container) benne f
▶ vb sauter [28] ▷ **to skip a meal** sauter un repas; **to skip a lesson** sécher [34] un cours

skirt n jupe f

skive vb (be lazy) tirer [28] au flanc

skive off vb sécher [34] (informal) ▷ **to skive off school** sécher les cours

skull n crâne m

sky n ciel m

skyscraper n gratte-ciel m (pl gratte-ciel)

slam vb claquer [28] ▷ **The door slammed.** La porte a claqué. ▷ **She slammed the door.** Elle a claqué la porte.

slang n argot m

slap n claque f
▶ vb **to slap somebody** donner [28] une claque à quelqu'un

slate n ardoise f

sledge n luge f

sledging n **to go sledging** faire [36] de la luge

sleep n sommeil m; **I need some sleep.** J'ai besoin de dormir.; **to go to sleep** s'endormir [29]
▶ vb dormir [29] ▷ **I couldn't sleep last night.** J'ai mal dormi la nuit dernière.; **to sleep with somebody** coucher [28] avec quelqu'un

sleep around vb coucher [28] à droite et à gauche

sleep in vb ❶ (accidentally) ne pas se réveiller [28] ▷ **I'm sorry I'm late, I slept in.** Désolé d'être en retard: je ne me suis pas réveillé. ❷ (on purpose) faire [36] la grasse matinée

sleep together vb coucher [28] ensemble

sleeping bag n sac de couchage m

sleeping pill n somnifère m

sleepy adj **to feel sleepy** avoir [8] sommeil ▷ **I was feeling sleepy.** J'avais sommeil.; **a sleepy little village** un petit village tranquille

sleet n neige fondue f
▶ vb **It's sleeting.** Il tombe de la neige fondue.

sleeve n manche f ▷ **long sleeves** les manches longues

slept vb see **sleep**

slice n tranche f
▶ vb couper [28] en tranches

slide n ❶ (in playground) toboggan m ❷ (photo) diapositive f ❸ (hair slide) barrette f
▶ vb glisser [28]

slight adj léger (f légère) ▷ **a slight problem** un léger problème ▷ **a slight improvement** une légère amélioration

slightly adv légèrement

slim adj mince
▶ vb (be on a diet) faire [36] un régime ▷ **I'm slimming.** Je fais un régime.

sling n écharpe f ▷ **She had her arm in a sling.** Elle avait le bras en écharpe.

slip n ❶ *(mistake)* erreur f
❷ *(underskirt)* jupon m ❸ *(full-length underskirt)* combinaison f; **a slip of paper** un bout de papier; **a slip of the tongue** un lapsus
▶ vb glisser [**28**] ▷ *He slipped on the ice.* Il a glissé sur le verglas.

slip up vb *(make a mistake)* faire [**36**] une erreur

slipper n chausson m; **a pair of slippers** des chaussons

slippery adj glissant(e)

slip-up n erreur f

slope n pente f

slot n fente f

slot machine n ❶ *(for gambling)* machine à sous f ❷ *(vending machine)* distributeur automatique m

slow adj, adv ❶ lent(e) ▷ *We are behind a very slow lorry.* On est derrière un camion très lent.
❷ lentement ▷ *to go slow (person, car)* aller lentement ▷ *Drive slower!* Conduisez plus lentement!; **My watch is slow.** Ma montre retarde.

slow down vb ralentir [**38**]

slowly adv lentement

slug n limace f

slum n ❶ *(area)* quartier insalubre m ❷ *(house)* taudis m

smack n tape f
▶ vb **to smack somebody** donner [**28**] une tape à quelqu'un

small adj petit(e); **small change** la petite monnaie

smart adj ❶ *(elegant)* chic ❷ *(clever)* intelligent(e); **a smart idea** une idée astucieuse

smartphone n smartphone m

smashing adj formidable ▷ *I think he's smashing.* Je le trouve formidable.

smell n odeur f; **the sense of smell** l'odorat m
▶ vb ❶ sentir [**77**] mauvais ▷ *That old dog really smells!* Qu'est-ce qu'il sent mauvais, ce vieux chien!; **to smell of something** sentir [**77**] quelque chose ▷ *It smells of petrol.* Ça sent l'essence. ❷ *(detect)* sentir [**77**] ▷ *I can't smell anything.* Je ne sens rien.

smelly adj qui sent mauvais ▷ *He's got smelly feet.* Il a les pieds qui sentent mauvais.

smelt vb see **smell**

smile n sourire m
▶ vb sourire [**74**]

smiley n émoticon m

smoke n fumée f
▶ vb fumer [**28**] ▷ *I don't smoke.* Je ne fume pas.

smoker n fumeur m, fumeuse f

smoking n **to give up smoking** arrêter [**28**] de fumer; **Smoking is bad for you.** Le tabac est mauvais pour la santé.; **'no smoking'** 'défense de fumer'

smooth adj ❶ *(surface)* lisse ❷ *(person)* mielleux *(f* mielleuse)

SMS n SMS m ▷ *I'll send you an SMS.* Je t'enverrai un SMS.

smudge n bavure f

smuggle vb *(goods)* passer [**58**] en fraude ▷ *to smuggle cigarettes into a country* faire passer des cigarettes en fraude dans un pays; **They**

managed to smuggle him out of prison. Ils ont réussi à le faire sortir de prison clandestinement.

smuggler n contrebandier m, contrebandière f

smuggling n contrebande f

snack n en-cas m (pl en-cas); to have a snack prendre [65] un en-cas

snack bar n snack-bar m

snail n escargot m

snake n serpent m

snap vb (break) casser [28] net ▷ The branch snapped. La branche a cassé net.; to snap one's fingers faire [36] claquer ses doigts

snatch vb to snatch something from somebody arracher [28] quelque chose à quelqu'un ▷ He snatched the keys from my hand. Il m'a arraché les clés des mains.; My bag was snatched. On m'a arraché mon sac.

sneak vb to sneak in entrer [32] furtivement; to sneak out sortir [79] furtivement; to sneak up on somebody s'approcher [28] de quelqu'un sans faire de bruit

sneeze vb éternuer [28]

sniff vb ❶ renifler [28] ▷ Stop sniffing! Arrête de renifler! ❷ flairer [28] ▷ The dog sniffed my hand. Le chien m'a flairé la main.; to sniff glue sniffer [28] de la colle

snob n snob mf

snooker n billard m ▷ to play snooker jouer au billard

snooze n petit somme m ▷ to have a snooze faire un petit somme

snore vb ronfler [28]

snow n neige f
▶ vb neiger [45] ▷ It's snowing. Il neige.

snowball n boule de neige f

snowflake n flocon de neige m

snowman n bonhomme de neige m ▷ to build a snowman faire un bonhomme de neige

so conj, adv ❶ alors ▷ The shop was closed, so I went home. Le magasin était fermé, alors je suis rentré chez moi. ▷ So, have you always lived in London? Alors, vous avez toujours vécu à Londres?; So what? Et alors? ❷ (so that) donc ▷ It rained, so I got wet. Il pleuvait, donc j'ai été mouillé. ❸ (very) tellement ▷ It was so heavy! C'était tellement lourd! ▷ He was talking so fast I couldn't understand. Il parlait tellement vite que je ne comprenais pas.; It's not so heavy! Ça n'est pas si lourd que ça!; How's your father? — Not so good. Comment va ton père? — Pas très bien.; so much (a lot) tellement ▷ I love you so much. Je t'aime tellement.; so much ... tellement de ... ▷ I've got so much work. J'ai tellement de travail.; so many ... tellement de ... ▷ I've got so many things to do today. J'ai tellement de choses à faire aujourd'hui. ❹ (in comparisons) aussi ▷ He's like his sister but not so clever. Il est comme sa sœur mais pas aussi intelligent.; so do I moi aussi ▷ I love horses. — So do I. J'aime les chevaux. — Moi aussi.; so have

we nous aussi ▷ *I've been to France twice. — So have we.* Je suis allé en France deux fois. — Nous aussi.; **I think so.** Je crois.; **I hope so.** J'espère bien.; **That's not so.** Ça n'est pas le cas.; **so far** jusqu'à présent ▷ *It's been easy so far.* Ça a été facile jusqu'à présent.; **so far so good** jusqu'ici ça va; **ten or so people** environ dix personnes; **at five o'clock or so** à environ cinq heures

soak *vb* tremper [28]

soaking *adj* trempé(e) ▷ *By the time we got back we were soaking.* Nous sommes rentrés trempés.; **soaking wet** trempé ▷ *Your shoes are soaking wet.* Tes chaussures sont trempées.

soap *n* savon *m*

soap opera *n* feuilleton à l'eau de rose *m*

soap powder *n* lessive *f*

sob *vb* sangloter [28] ▷ *She was sobbing.* Elle sanglotait.

sober *adj* sobre

sober up *vb* dessoûler [28]

soccer *n* football *m* ▷ *to play soccer* jouer au football; **a soccer player** un joueur de football

social *adj* social(e) (*mpl* sociaux) ▷ *a social class* une classe sociale; **I have a good social life.** Je vois beaucoup de monde.

socialism *n* socialisme *m*

socialist *adj* socialiste
▶ *n* socialiste *mf*

social network *n* réseau social *m*

social security *n* ❶ (*money*) aide sociale *f*; **to be on social security** recevoir [67] de l'aide sociale ❷ (*organization*) sécurité sociale *f*

social worker *n* ❶ (*woman*) assistante sociale *f* ▷ *She's a social worker.* Elle est assistante sociale. ❷ (*man*) travailleur social *m* (*pl* travailleurs sociaux) ▷ *He's a social worker.* Il est travailleur social.

society *n* ❶ société *f* ▷ *We live in a multi-cultural society.* Nous vivons dans une société multiculturelle. ❷ club *m* ▷ *a drama society* un club de théâtre

sociology *n* sociologie *f*

sock *n* chaussette *f*

socket *n* prise de courant *f*

sofa *n* canapé *m*

soft *adj* ❶ (*fabric, texture*) doux (*f* douce) ❷ (*pillow, bed*) mou (*f* molle); **soft cheeses** les fromages à pâte molle ❸ (*hair*) fin(e); **to be soft on somebody** (*be kind to*) être [35] indulgent avec quelqu'un; **a soft drink** une boisson non alcoolisée; **soft drugs** les drogues douces *fpl*; **a soft option** une solution de facilité

software *n* logiciel *m*

soil *n* terre *f*

solar *adj* solaire; **a solar panel** un panneau solaire

solar power *n* énergie solaire *f*

sold *vb* see **sell**

soldier *n* soldat *m* ▷ *He's a soldier.* Il est soldat.

solicitor *n* ❶ (*for lawsuits*) avocat *m*, avocate *f* ▷ *He's a solicitor.* Il est avocat. ❷ (*for wills, property*)

a b c d e f g h i j k l m n o p q r s t u v w x y z

notaire m ▷ *She's a solicitor.* Elle est notaire.

solid adj ❶ (not hollow) massif (f massive) ▷ *solid gold* l'or massif ❷ solide ▷ *a solid wall* un mur solide; **for three hours solid** pendant trois heures entières

solo n solo m ▷ *a guitar solo* un solo de guitare

solution n solution f

solve vb résoudre [**70**]

some adj, pron

> When 'some' means 'a certain amount of', use **du**, **de la** or **des** according to the gender of the French noun that follows it. **du** and **de la** become **de l'** when they are followed by a noun starting with a vowel.

❶ du ▷ *Would you like some bread?* Voulez-vous du pain?

de la ▷ *Would you like some beer?* Voulez-vous de la bière?

de l' ▷ *Have you got some mineral water?* Avez-vous de l'eau minérale?

des ▷ *I've got some Madonna albums.* J'ai des albums de Madonna.; **Some people say that ...** Il y a des gens qui disent que ...; **some day** un de ces jours; **some day next week** un jour la semaine prochaine

❷ (some but not all) certains (f certaines) ▷ *Are these mushrooms poisonous? — Only some.* Est-ce que ces champignons sont vénéneux? — Certains le sont.; **some of them** quelques-uns ▷ *I only sold some of them.* J'en ai seulement vendu quelques-uns.; **I only took some**

of it. J'en ai seulement pris un peu **I'm going to buy some stamps. Do you want some too?** Je vais acheter des timbres. Tu en veux aussi?; **Would you like some coffee? — No thanks, I've got some.** Tu veux du café? — Non merci, j'en ai déjà.

somebody pron quelqu'un ▷ *Somebody stole my bag.* Quelqu'un a volé mon sac.

somehow adv **I'll do it somehow.** Je trouverai le moyen de le faire.; **Somehow I don't think he believed me.** Quelque chose me dit qu'il ne m'a pas cru.

someone pron quelqu'un

someplace adv (US) quelque part

something pron quelque chose ▷ *something special* quelque chose de spécial ▷ *That's really something!* C'est vraiment quelque chose! ▷ *It cost £100, or something like that.* Ça a coûté cent livres, ou quelque chose comme ça. ▷ *His name is Pierre or something.* Il s'appelle Pierre, ou quelque chose comme ça.

sometime adv un de ces jours ▷ *You must come and see us sometime.* Passez donc nous voir un de ces jours.; **sometime last month** dans le courant du mois dernier

sometimes adv quelquefois ▷ *Sometimes I think she hates me.* Quelquefois j'ai l'impression qu'elle me déteste.

somewhere adv quelque part ▷ *I left my keys somewhere.* J'ai laissé mes clés quelque part.

on n fils m

ong n chanson f

on-in-law n gendre m

oon adv bientôt ▷ **very soon** très bientôt; **soon afterwards** peu après; **as soon as possible** aussitôt que possible

ooner adv plus tôt ▷ *Can't you come a bit sooner?* Tu ne peux pas venir un peu plus tôt?; **sooner or later** tôt ou tard

soprano n (singer) soprano mf

sorcerer n sorcier m

sore adj **My feet are sore.** J'ai mal aux pieds.; **It's sore.** Ça fait mal.; **That's a sore point.** C'est un point sensible.
▶ n plaie f

sorry adj désolé(e) ▷ *I'm really sorry.* Je suis vraiment désolé. ▷ *I'm sorry I'm late.* Je suis désolé d'être en retard.; **sorry!** pardon!; **I'm sorry about the noise.** Je m'excuse pour le bruit.; **You'll be sorry!** Tu le regretteras!; **to feel sorry for somebody** plaindre [17] quelqu'un

sort n sorte f ▷ *What sort of bike have you got?* Quelle sorte de vélo as-tu?

sort out vb ❶ (objects) ranger [45] ❷ (problems) résoudre [70]

sought vb see **seek** vb

soul n ❶ (spirit) âme f ❷ (music) soul f

sound n ❶ (noise) bruit m ▷ *Don't make a sound!* Pas un bruit! ▷ *the sound of footsteps* des bruits de pas ❷ son m ▷ *Can I turn the sound down?* Je peux baisser le son?
▶ vb **That sounds interesting.** Ça a

l'air intéressant.; **It sounds as if she's doing well at school.** Elle a l'air de bien travailler à l'école.; **That sounds like a good idea.** C'est une bonne idée.
▶ adj, adv bon (f bonne) ▷ *That's sound advice.* C'est un bon conseil.; **sound asleep** profondément endormi

soundtrack n bande sonore f

soup n soupe f ▷ *vegetable soup* la soupe aux légumes

sour adj aigre

south adj, adv ❶ sud ▷ *the south coast* la côte sud ❷ vers le sud ▷ *We were travelling south.* Nous allions vers le sud.; **south of** au sud de ▷ *It's south of London.* C'est au sud de Londres.
▶ n sud m ▷ *in the south* dans le sud ▷ *the South of France* le sud de la France

South Africa n Afrique du Sud f; **in South Africa** en Afrique du Sud; **to South Africa** en Afrique du Sud

South America n Amérique du Sud f; **in South America** en Amérique du Sud; **to South America** en Amérique du Sud

South American n Sud-Américain m, Sud-Américaine f
▶ adj sud-américain(e)

southeast n sud-est m ▷ *southeast England* le sud-est de l'Angleterre

southern adj **the southern part of the island** la partie sud de l'île; **Southern England** le sud de l'Angleterre

South Pole n pôle Sud m

southwest n sud-ouest m
▷ *southwest France* le sud-ouest de
la France

souvenir n souvenir m; **a souvenir
shop** une boutique de souvenirs

Soviet adj **the former Soviet
Union** l'ex-Union Soviétique f

soya n soja m

soy sauce n sauce de soja f

space n ❶ place f ▷ *There isn't
enough space.* Il n'y a pas
suffisamment de place.; **a parking
space** une place de parking
❷ (universe, gap) espace m ▷ *Leave a
space after your answer.* Laissez un
espace après votre réponse.

spacecraft n engin spatial m

spade n pelle f; **spades** (in cards) le
pique sg ▷ *the ace of spades* l'as de
pique

Spain n Espagne f; **in Spain** en
Espagne; **to Spain** en Espagne

Spaniard n Espagnol m,
Espagnole f

spaniel n épagneul m

Spanish n (language) espagnol m;
the Spanish les Espagnols
▷ adj espagnol(e) ▷ *She's Spanish.*
Elle est espagnole.

spanner n clé anglaise f

spare adj de rechange ▷ *spare
batteries* des piles de rechange
▷ *a spare part* une pièce de
rechange; **a spare room** une
chambre d'amis; **spare time** le
temps libre ▷ *What do you do in your
spare time?* Qu'est-ce que tu fais
pendant ton temps libre?; **spare
wheel** une roue de secours

▷ vb **Can you spare a moment?**
Vous pouvez m'accorder un
instant?; **I can't spare the time.** Je
n'ai pas le temps.; **There's no
room to spare.** Il n'y a plus de
place.; **We arrived with time to
spare.** Nous sommes arrivés en
avance.
▷ n **a spare** un autre ▷ *I've lost my
key. — Have you got a spare?* J'ai perdu
ma clé. — Tu en as une autre?

sparkling adj (water) pétillant(e);
sparkling wine le mousseux

sparrow n moineau m (pl
moineaux)

spat vb see **spit**

speak vb parler [28] ▷ *Do you speak
English?* Est-ce que vous parlez
anglais?; **to speak to somebody**
parler [28] à quelqu'un ▷ *Have you
spoken to him?* Tu lui as parlé? ▷ *She
spoke to him about it.* Elle lui en a
parlé.

speak up vb parler [28] plus fort
▷ *Speak up, we can't hear you.* Parle
plus fort, nous ne t'entendons pas.

speaker n ❶ (loudspeaker) enceinte
f ❷ (in debate) intervenant m,
intervenante f

special adj spécial(e) (mpl spéciaux)

specialist n spécialiste mf

speciality n spécialité f

specialize vb se spécialiser [28]
▷ *We specialize in skiing equipment.*
Nous nous spécialisons dans les
articles de ski.

specially adv ❶ spécialement ▷ *It's
specially designed for teenagers.* C'est
spécialement conçu pour les

adolescents.; **not specially** pas spécialement ▷ *Do you like opera? — Not specially.* Tu aimes l'opéra? — Pas spécialement. ❷ <u>surtout</u> ▷ *It can be very cold here, specially in winter.* Il peut faire très froid ici, surtout en hiver.

pecies *n* <u>espèce</u> *f*

pecific *adj* ❶ *(particular)* <u>particulier</u> *(f* particulière*)* ▷ *certain specific issues* certains problèmes particuliers ❷ *(precise)* <u>précis(e)</u> ▷ *Could you be more specific?* Est-ce que vous pourriez être plus précis?

specs, spectacles *npl* <u>lunettes</u> *fpl*

spectacular *adj* <u>spectaculaire</u>

spectator *n* <u>spectateur</u> *m*, <u>spectatrice</u> *f*

speech *n* <u>discours</u> *m* ▷ *to make a speech* faire un discours

speechless *adj* <u>muet</u> *(f* muette*)* ▷ *speechless with admiration* muet d'admiration; **I was speechless.** Je suis resté sans voix.

speed *n* <u>vitesse</u> *f* ▷ *a three-speed bike* un vélo à trois vitesses ▷ *at top speed* à toute vitesse

speed up *vb* <u>accélérer</u> [**34**]

speedboat *n* <u>vedette</u> *f*

speeding *n* <u>excès de vitesse</u> *m* ▷ *He was fined for speeding.* Il a reçu une contravention pour excès de vitesse.

speed limit *n* <u>limitation de vitesse</u> *f*; **to break the speed limit** faire [**36**] un excès de vitesse

spell *vb* ❶ *(in writing)* <u>écrire</u> [**30**] ▷ *How do you spell that?* Comment est-ce que ça s'écrit? ❷ *(out loud)* <u>épeler</u> [**4**] ▷ *Can you spell that please?*

Est-ce que vous pouvez épeler, s'il vous plaît?; **I can't spell.** Je fais des fautes d'orthographe.

▶*n* **to cast a spell on somebody** jeter [**41**] un sort à quelqu'un; **to be under somebody's spell** être [**35**] sous le charme de quelqu'un

spelling *n* <u>orthographe</u> *f* ▷ *My spelling is terrible.* Je fais beaucoup de fautes d'orthographe.; **a spelling mistake** une faute d'orthographe

spelt *vb see* **spell**

spend *vb* ❶ *(money)* <u>dépenser</u> [**28**] ❷ *(time)* <u>passer</u> [**58**] ▷ *He spent a month in France.* Il a passé un mois en France.

spice *n* <u>épice</u> *f*

spicy *adj* <u>épicé(e)</u>

spider *n* <u>araignée</u> *f*

spill *vb* ❶ *(tip over)* <u>renverser</u> [**28**] ▷ *He spilled his coffee over his trousers.* Il a renversé son café sur son pantalon. ❷ *(get spilt)* <u>se répandre</u> [**9**] ▷ *The soup spilled all over the table.* La soupe s'est répandue sur la table.

spinach *n* <u>épinards</u> *mpl*

spine *n* <u>colonne vertébrale</u> *f*

spire *n* <u>flèche</u> *f*

spirit *n* ❶ *(courage)* <u>courage</u> *m*; **to be in good spirits** être [**35**] de bonne humeur ❷ *(energy)* <u>énergie</u> *f*

spirits *npl* <u>alcools forts</u> *mpl* ▷ *I don't drink spirits.* Je ne bois pas d'alcools forts.

spiritual *adj* <u>religieux</u> *(f* religieuse*)* ▷ *the spiritual leader of Tibet* le chef religieux du Tibet

a b c d e f g h i j k l m n o p q r s t u v w x y z

spit n salive f
▶ vb cracher [28]; **to spit something out** cracher [28] quelque chose
spite n **in spite of** malgré
▶ vb contrarier [19]
spiteful adj ❶ (action) méchant(e) ❷ (person) rancunier (f rancunière)
splash vb éclabousser [28]
▷ Careful! Don't splash me! Attention! Ne m'éclabousse pas!
▶ n plouf m ▷ I heard a splash. J'ai entendu un plouf.; **a splash of colour** une touche de couleur
splendid adj splendide
splinter n écharde f
split vb ❶ (break apart) fendre [88]
▷ He split the wood with an axe. Il a fendu le bois avec une hache. ❷ se fendre [88] ▷ The ship hit a rock and split in two. Le bateau a percuté un rocher et s'est fendu en deux.
❸ (divide up) partager [45] ▷ They decided to split the profits. Ils ont décidé de partager les bénéfices.
split up vb ❶ (couple) rompre [75]
▷ My parents have split up. Mes parents ont rompu. ❷ (group) se disperser [28]
spoil vb ❶ (object) abîmer [28]
❷ (occasion) gâcher [28] ❸ (child) gâter [28]
spoiled adj gâté(e) ▷ a spoiled child un enfant gâté
spoilsport n trouble-fête mf
spoilt adj gâté(e) ▷ a spoilt child un enfant gâté
▶ vb see **spoil**
spoken vb see **speak**

spokesman n porte-parole m (pl porte-parole)
spokesperson n porte-parole m (pl porte-parole)
spokeswoman n porte-parole m (pl porte-parole)
sponge n éponge f; **a sponge cake** un biscuit de Savoie
sponsor n donateur m, donatrice f
▶ vb parrainer [28] ▷ The festival was sponsored by ... Le festival a été parrainé par ...
spontaneous adj spontané(e)
spooky adj ❶ (eerie) sinistre; **a spooky story** une histoire qui fait froid dans le dos ❷ (strange) étrange ▷ a spooky coincidence une étrange coïncidence
spoon n cuiller f
sport n sport m ▷ What's your favourite sport? Quel est ton sport préféré?; **a sports bag** un sac de sport; **a sports car** une voiture de sport; **Go on, be a sport!** Allez, sois sympa!
sportsman n sportif m
sportswear n vêtements de sport mpl
sportswoman n sportive f
sporty adj sportif (f sportive) ▷ I'm not very sporty. Je ne suis pas très sportif.
spot n ❶ (mark) tache f ▷ There's a spot on your shirt. Il y a une tache sur ta chemise. ❷ (in pattern) pois m ▷ a red dress with white spots une robe rouge à pois blancs ❸ (pimple) bouton m ▷ He's covered in spots. Il est couvert de boutons. ❹ (place)

coin m ▷ It's a lovely spot for a picnic. C'est un coin agréable pour un pique-nique.; **on the spot** **(1)** (immediately) sur-le-champ ▷ They gave her the job on the spot. Ils lui ont offert le poste sur-le-champ. **(2)** (at the same place) sur place ▷ Luckily they were able to mend the car on the spot. Heureusement ils ont pu réparer la voiture sur place.
▶ vb repérer [**34**] ▷ I spotted a mistake. J'ai repéré une faute.

spotless adj immaculé(e)

spotlight n projecteur m ▷ The universities have been in the spotlight recently. Les universités ont été sous le feu des projecteurs ces derniers temps.

spotty adj (pimply) boutonneux (f boutonneuse)

sprain vb **to sprain one's ankle** se faire [**36**] une entorse à la cheville
▶ n entorse f ▷ It's just a sprain. C'est juste une entorse.

spray n (spray can) bombe f
▶ vb ❶ vaporiser [**28**] ▷ to spray perfume on one's hand se vaporiser du parfum sur la main ❷ (crops) traiter [**28**] ❸ (graffiti) peindre [**60**] avec une bombe ▷ Somebody had sprayed graffiti on the wall. Quelqu'un avait peint des graffiti avec une bombe sur le mur.

spread n **chocolate spread** le chocolat à tartiner
▶ vb ❶ étaler [**28**] ▷ to spread butter on a slice of bread étaler du beurre sur une tranche de pain ❷ (disease,

news) se propager [**45**] ▷ The news spread rapidly. La nouvelle s'est propagée rapidement.

spread out vb (people) se disperser [**28**]

spreadsheet n (computer program) tableur m

spring n ❶ (season) printemps m; **in spring** au printemps ❷ (metal coil) ressort m ❸ (water hole) source f

springtime n printemps m; **in springtime** au printemps

sprint n sprint m
▶ vb courir [**16**] à toute vitesse ▷ She sprinted for the bus. Elle a couru à toute vitesse pour attraper le bus.

sprouts npl **Brussels sprouts** les choux de Bruxelles mpl

spy n espion m, espionne f
▶ vb **to spy on somebody** espionner [**28**] quelqu'un

spying n espionnage m

square n ❶ carré m ▷ a square and a triangle un carré et un triangle ❷ place f ▷ the town square la place de l'hôtel de ville
▶ adj carré(e) ▷ two square metres deux mètres carrés; **It's 2 metres square.** Ça fait deux mètres sur deux.

squash n (sport) squash m ▷ I play squash. Je joue au squash.; **a squash court** un court de squash; **a squash racket** une raquette de squash; **orange squash** l'orangeade f; **lemon squash** la citronnade
▶ vb écraser [**28**] ▷ You're squashing me. Tu m'écrases.

squeak vb ❶ (mouse, child) pousser [28] un petit cri ❷ (creak) grincer [12]

squeeze vb ❶ (fruit, toothpaste) presser [28] ❷ (hand, arm) serrer [28]

squeeze in vb ❶ trouver [28] une petite place ▷ It was a tiny car, but we managed to squeeze in. La voiture était toute petite, mais nous avons réussi à trouver une petite place. ❷ (for appointment) caser [28] ▷ I can squeeze you in at two o'clock. Je peux vous caser demain à deux heures.

squirrel n écureuil m

stab vb poignarder [28]

stable n écurie f
▶ adj stable ▷ a stable relationship une relation stable

stack n pile f ▷ a stack of books une pile de livres

stadium n stade m

staff n ❶ (in company) personnel m ❷ (in school) professeurs mpl

staffroom n salle des professeurs f

stage n ❶ (in plays) scène f ❷ (for speeches, lectures) estrade f; at this stage (1) à ce stade ▷ at this stage in the negotiations à ce stade des négociations (2) pour l'instant ▷ At this stage, it's too early to comment. Pour l'instant, il est trop tôt pour se prononcer.; to do something in stages faire [36] quelque chose étape par étape

> Be careful not to translate **stage** by the French word **stage**.

stain n tache f
▶ vb tacher [28]

stainless steel n inox m

stair n (step) marche f

staircase n escalier m

stairs npl escalier msg

stale adj (bread) rassis (f rassie)

stalemate n (in chess) pat m

stall n stand m ▷ He's got a market stall. Il a un stand au marché.; the stalls (in cinema, theatre) l'orchestre msg

stammer n bégaiement m; He's got a stammer. Il bégaie.

stamp vb (letter) affranchir [38]; to stamp one's foot taper [28] du pied
▶ n ❶ timbre m ▷ My hobby is stamp collecting. Je collectionne les timbres.; a stamp album un album de timbres; a stamp collection une collection de timbres ❷ (rubber stamp) tampon m

stand vb ❶ (be standing) être [35] debout ▷ He was standing by the door. Il était debout à la porte. ❷ (stand up) se lever [43] ❸ (tolerate, withstand) supporter [28] ▷ I can't stand all this noise. Je ne supporte pas tout ce bruit.

stand for vb ❶ (be short for) être [35] l'abréviation de ▷ 'BT' stands for 'British Telecom'. 'BT' est l'abréviation de 'British Telecom'. ❷ (tolerate) supporter [28] ▷ I won't stand for it! Je ne supporterai pas ça!; to stand in for somebody remplacer [12] quelqu'un

stand out vb se distinguer [28]

▷ *None of the candidates really stood out.* Aucun des candidats ne s'est distingué.; **She really stands out in that orange coat.** Tout le monde la remarque avec ce manteau orange.

tand up vb (get up) se lever [**43**]; **to stand up for** défendre [**88**] ▷ *Stand up for your rights!* Défendez vos droits!

tandard adj ❶ courant(e) ▷ *standard French* le français courant ❷ (equipment) ordinaire; **the standard procedure** la procédure normale ▶ *n* niveau *m* (pl niveaux) ▷ *The standard is very high.* Le niveau est très haut.; **the standard of living** le niveau de vie; **She's got high standards.** Elle est très exigeante.

stands npl (at sports ground) tribune *fsg*

stank vb see **stink**

staple n agrafe *f* ▶ vb agrafer [**28**]

stapler n agrafeuse *f*

star n ❶ (in sky) étoile *f* ❷ (celebrity) vedette *f* ▷ *He's a TV star.* C'est une vedette de la télé.; **the stars** (horoscope) l'horoscope *m* ▶ vb être [**35**] la vedette ▷ *to star in a film* être la vedette d'un film; **The film stars Glenda Jackson.** Le film a pour vedette Glenda Jackson.; ... **starring Johnny Depp** ... avec Johnny Depp

stare vb **to stare at something** fixer [**28**] quelque chose

start n ❶ début *m* ▷ *It's not much,*

but it's a start. Ce n'est pas grand-chose, mais c'est un début.; **Shall we make a start on the washing-up?** On commence à faire la vaisselle? ❷ (of race) départ *m* ▶ vb ❶ commencer [**12**] ▷ *What time does it start?* À quelle heure est-ce que ça commence?; **to start doing something** commencer [**12**] à faire quelque chose ▷ *I started learning French three years ago.* J'ai commencé à apprendre le français il y a trois ans. ❷ (organization) créer [**18**] ▷ *He wants to start his own business.* Il veut créer sa propre entreprise. ❸ (campaign) organiser [**28**] ▷ *She started a campaign against drugs.* Elle a organisé une campagne contre la drogue. ❹ (car) démarrer [**28**] ▷ *He couldn't start the car.* Il n'a pas réussi à démarrer la voiture. ▷ *The car wouldn't start.* La voiture ne voulait pas démarrer.

start off vb (leave) partir [**57**] ▷ *We started off first thing in the morning.* Nous sommes partis en début de matinée.

starter n (first course) entrée *f*

starve vb mourir [**51**] de faim ▷ *People were literally starving.* Les gens mouraient littéralement de faim.; **I'm starving!** Je meurs de faim!

state n état *m*; **He was in a real state.** Il était dans tous ses états.; **the state** (government) l'État; **the States** (USA) les États-Unis *mpl*

a
b
c
d
e
f
g
h
i
j
k
l
m
n
o
p
q
r
s
t
u
v
w
x
y
z

▶vb ❶ (say) declarer [**28**] ▷ He stated his intention to resign. Il a déclaré son intention de démissionner. ❷ (give) donner [**28**] ▷ Please state your name and address. Veuillez donner vos nom et adresse.

statement n déclaration f

station n (railway) gare f; **the bus station** la gare routière; **a police station** un poste de police; **a radio station** une station de radio

stationer's n papeterie f

statue n statue f

stay n séjour m ▷ my stay in France mon séjour en France
▶vb ❶ (remain) rester [**71**] ▷ Stay here! Reste ici! ❷ (spend the night) loger [**45**] ▷ to stay with friends loger chez des amis ▷ Where are you staying? Où est-ce que vous logez?; **to stay the night** passer [**58**] la nuit; **We stayed in Belgium for a few days.** Nous avons passé quelques jours en Belgique.

stay in vb (not go out) rester [**71**] à la maison

stay up vb rester [**71**] debout ▷ We stayed up till midnight. Nous sommes restés debout jusqu'à minuit.

steady adj ❶ régulier (f régulière) ▷ steady progress des progrès réguliers ❷ stable ▷ a steady job un emploi stable ❸ (voice, hand) ferme ❹ (person) calme; **a steady boyfriend** un copain; **a steady girlfriend** une copine

steak n (beef) steak m ▷ steak and

chips un steak frites

steal vb voler [**28**]

steam n vapeur f ▷ a steam engine une locomotive à vapeur

steel n acier m ▷ a steel door une porte en acier

steep adj (slope) raide

steeple n clocher m

steering wheel n volant m

step n ❶ (pace) pas m ▷ He took a step forward. Il a fait un pas en avant. ❷ (stair) marche f ▷ She tripped over the step. Elle a trébuché sur la marche.
▶vb **to step aside** faire [**36**] un pas de côté; **to step back** faire [**36**] un pas en arrière

stepbrother n demi-frère m

stepdaughter n belle-fille f (pl belles-filles)

stepfather n beau-père m (pl beaux-pères)

stepladder n escabeau m (pl escabeaux)

stepmother n belle-mère f (pl belles-mères)

stepsister n demi-sœur f

stepson n beau-fils m (pl beaux-fils)

stereo n chaîne stéréo f (pl chaînes stéréo)

sterling adj £5 sterling cinq livres sterling

stew n ragoût m

steward n steward m

stewardess n hôtesse de l'air f

stick n ❶ bâton m ❷ (walking stick) canne f
▶vb (with adhesive) coller [**28**]
▷ Stick the stamps on the envelope.

Collez les timbres sur l'enveloppe.

stick out vb (project) sortir [**79**]
▷ A pen was sticking out of his pocket.
Un stylo sortait de sa poche.; **Stick
your tongue out and say 'ah'.**
Tirez la langue et dites 'ah'.

sticker n autocollant m

stick insect n phasme m

sticky adj ❶ poisseux (f poisseuse)
▷ to have sticky hands avoir les
mains poisseuses ❷ adhésif (f
adhésive) ▷ a sticky label une
étiquette adhésive

stiff adj, adv (rigid) rigide; **to have a
stiff neck** avoir [**8**] un torticolis; **to
feel stiff** avoir [**8**] des courbatures;
to be bored stiff s'ennuyer [**53**] à
mourir; **to be frozen stiff** être [**35**]
mort de froid; **to be scared stiff**
être [**35**] mort de peur

still adv ❶ encore ▷ I still haven't
finished. Je n'ai pas encore fini. ▷ Are
you still in bed? Tu es encore au lit?;
better still encore mieux ❷ (even
so) quand même ▷ She knows I don't
like it, but she still does it. Elle sait
que je n'aime pas ça, mais elle le
fait quand même. ❸ (after all) enfin
▷ Still, it's the thought that counts.
Enfin, c'est l'intention qui compte.
▶ adj **Keep still!** Ne bouge pas!; **Sit
still!** Reste tranquille!

sting n piqûre f ▷ a bee sting une
piqûre d'abeille
▶ vb piquer [**28**] ▷ I've been stung. J'ai
été piqué.

stink vb puer [**28**] ▷ It stinks! Ça pue!
▶ n puanteur f

stir vb remuer [**28**]

stitch vb (cloth) coudre [**15**]
▶ n ❶ (in sewing) point m ❷ (in
wound) point de suture m ▷ I had five
stitches. J'ai eu cinq points de
suture.

stock n ❶ (supply) réserve f ❷ (in
shop) stock m ▷ in stock en stock;
out of stock épuisé ❸ bouillon m
▷ chicken stock du bouillon de
volaille
▶ vb (have in stock) avoir [**8**] ▷ Do you
stock camping stoves? Vous avez des
camping-gaz?

stock up vb s'approvisionner [**28**]
▷ to stock up with something
s'approvisionner en quelque chose

stock cube n cube de bouillon m

stocking n bas m

stole, stolen vb see **steal**

stomach n estomac m

stomachache n **to have
stomachache** avoir [**8**] mal au
ventre

stone n ❶ (rock) pierre f ▷ a stone
wall un mur en pierre ❷ (in fruit)
noyau m (pl noyaux) ▷ a peach stone
un noyau de pêche
  In France, weight is expressed in
  kilos. A stone is about 6.3 kg.
I weigh eight stone. Je pèse
cinquante kilos.

stood vb see **stand**

stool n tabouret m

stop vb ❶ arrêter [**28**] ▷ a campaign
to stop whaling une campagne pour
arrêter la chasse à la baleine
❷ s'arrêter [**28**] ▷ The bus doesn't
stop there. Le bus ne s'arrête pas là.
▷ I think the rain's going to stop. Je

pense qu'il va s'arrêter de pleuvoir.;
to stop doing something arrêter
[**28**] de faire quelque chose ▷ *to
stop smoking* arrêter de fumer; **to
stop somebody doing something**
empêcher [**28**] quelqu'un de faire
quelque chose; **Stop!** Stop!
▶ *n* arrêt *m* ▷ *a bus stop* un arrêt de
bus; **This is my stop.** Je descends ici.
stopwatch *n* chronomètre *m*
store *n* ❶ *(shop)* magasin *m*
▷ *a furniture store* un magasin de
meubles ❷ *(stock, storeroom)*
réserve *f*
▶ *vb* ❶ garder [**28**] ▷ *They store
potatoes in the cellar.* Ils gardent des
pommes de terre dans la cave.
❷ *(information)* enregistrer [**28**]
storey *n* étage *m* ▷ *a three-storey
building* un immeuble à trois étages
storm *n* ❶ *(gale)* tempête *f*
❷ *(thunderstorm)* orage *m*
stormy *adj* orageux (*f* orageuse)
story *n* histoire *f*
stove *n* ❶ *(in kitchen)* cuisinière *f*
❷ *(camping stove)* réchaud *m*
straight *adj* ❶ droit(e) ▷ *a straight
line* une ligne droite ❷ raide
▷ *straight hair* les cheveux raides
❸ *(heterosexual)* hétéro; **straight
away** tout de suite; **straight on**
tout droit
straightforward *adj* simple
strain *n* stress *m*; **It was a strain.**
C'était éprouvant.
▶ *vb* se faire [**36**] mal à ▷ *I strained
my back.* Je me suis fait mal au dos.;
to strain a muscle se froisser [**28**]
un muscle

strange *adj* bizarre ▷ *That's strang*
C'est bizarre!
stranger *n* inconnu *m*, inconnue *f*
▷ *Don't talk to strangers.* Ne parle
pas aux inconnus.; **I'm a stranger
here.** Je ne suis pas d'ici.
strangle *vb* étrangler [**28**]
strap *n* ❶ *(of bag, camera, suitcase)*
courroie *f* ❷ *(of bra, dress)* bretelle *f*
❸ *(on shoe)* lanière *f* ❹ *(of watch)*
bracelet *m*
straw *n* paille *f*; **That's the last
straw!** Ça, c'est le comble!
strawberry *n* fraise *f* ▷ *strawberry
jam* la confiture de fraises
stray *n* a stray cat un chat perdu
stream *n* ruisseau *m* (*pl* ruisseaux)
street *n* rue *f* ▷ *in the street* dans la
rue
streetlamp *n* réverbère *m*
streetwise *adj* dégourdi(e)
strength *n* force *f*
stress *vb* souligner [**28**] ▷ *I would
like to stress that ...* J'aimerais
souligner que ...
▶ *n* stress *m*
stretch *vb* ❶ *(person, animal)* s'étirer
[**28**] ▷ *The dog woke up and stretched.*
Le chien s'est réveillé et s'est étiré.
❷ *(get bigger)* se détendre [**88**] ▷ *My
sweater stretched when I washed it.*
Mon pull s'est détendu au lavage.
❸ *(stretch out)* tendre [**88**] ▷ *They
stretched a rope between two trees.* Ils
ont tendu une corde entre deux
arbres.; **to stretch out one's arms**
tendre [**88**] les bras
stretcher *n* brancard *m*
stretchy *adj* élastique

trict adj strict(e)

trike n grève f; **to be on strike** être [35] en grève; **to go on strike** faire [36] grève
▸ vb ❶ (clock) sonner [28] ▷ *The clock struck three.* L'horloge a sonné trois heures. ❷ (go on strike) faire [36] grève ❸ (hit) frapper [28]; **to strike a match** frotter [28] une allumette

striker n ❶ (person on strike) gréviste mf ❷ (footballer) buteur m

string n ❶ ficelle f ▷ *a piece of string* un bout de ficelle ❷ (of violin, guitar) corde f

strip vb (get undressed) se déshabiller [28]
▸ n bande f; **a strip cartoon** une bande dessinée

stripe n rayure f

striped adj à rayures ▷ *a striped skirt* une jupe à rayures

stroke vb caresser [28]
▸ n attaque f ▷ *to have a stroke* avoir une attaque

stroll n **to go for a stroll** aller [3] faire une petite promenade

stroller n (US) poussette f

strong adj ❶ fort(e) ▷ *She's very strong.* Elle est très forte. ❷ (material) résistant(e)

strongly adv fortement ▷ *We recommend strongly that …* Nous recommandons fortement que …; **He smelt strongly of tobacco.** Il sentait fort le tabac.; **strongly built** solidement bâti; **I don't feel strongly about it.** Ça m'est égal.

struck vb see **strike**

struggle vb (physically) se débattre [9] ▷ *He struggled, but he couldn't escape.* Il s'est débattu, mais il n'a pas pu s'échapper.; **to struggle to do something** (1) (fight) se battre [9] pour faire quelque chose ▷ *He struggled to get custody of his daughter.* Il s'est battu pour obtenir la garde de sa fille. (2) (have difficulty) avoir [8] du mal à faire quelque chose
▸ n (for independence, equality) lutte f; **It was a struggle.** Ça a été laborieux.

stubborn adj têtu(e)

stuck vb see **stick**
▸ adj (jammed) coincé(e) ▷ *It's stuck.* C'est coincé.; **to get stuck** rester [71] coincé ▷ *We got stuck in a traffic jam.* Nous sommes restés coincés dans un embouteillage.

stuck-up adj coincé(e) (informal)

stud n ❶ (earring) boucle d'oreille f ❷ (on football boots) clou m

student n étudiant m, étudiante f

studio n studio m ▷ *a TV studio* un studio de télévision; **a studio flat** un studio

study vb ❶ (at university) faire [36] des études ▷ *I plan to study biology.* J'ai l'intention de faire des études de biologie. ❷ (do homework) travailler [28] ▷ *I've got to study tonight.* Je dois travailler ce soir.

stuff n ❶ (substance) truc m ▷ *I need some stuff for hay fever.* J'ai besoin d'un truc contre le rhume des foins. ❷ (things) trucs mpl ▷ *There's some stuff on the table for you.* Il y a des

a b c d e f g h i j k l m n o p q r s t u v w x y z

trucs sur la table pour toi.
❸ *(possessions)* affaires *fpl* ▷ *Have you got all your stuff?* Est-ce que tu as toutes tes affaires?

stuffy *adj (room)* mal aéré(e); **It's really stuffy in here.** On étouffe ici.

stumble *vb* trébucher [**28**]

stung *vb see* **sting**

stunk *vb see* **stink**

stunned *adj (amazed)* sidéré(e) ▷ *I was stunned.* J'étais sidéré.

stunning *adj* superbe

stunt *n (in film)* cascade *f*

stuntman *n* cascadeur *m*

stupid *adj* stupide ▷ *a stupid joke* une plaisanterie stupide; **Me, go jogging? Don't be stupid!** Moi, faire du footing? Ne dis pas de bêtises!

stutter *vb* bégayer [**59**]
▶ *n* **He's got a stutter.** Il bégaie.

style *n* style *m* ▷ *That's not his style.* Ça n'est pas son style.

subject *n* ❶ sujet *m* ▷ *The subject of my project was the internet.* Le sujet de mon projet était l'Internet. ❷ *(at school)* matière *f* ▷ *What's your favourite subject?* Quelle est ta matière préférée?

subjunctive *n* subjonctif *m*

submarine *n* sous-marin *m*

subscription *n (to paper, magazine)* abonnement *m*; **to take out a subscription to something** s'abonner [**28**] à quelque chose

subsidy *n* subvention *f*

substance *n* substance *f*

substitute *n (person)* remplaçant

m, remplaçante *f*
▶ *vb* substituer [**28**] ▷ *to substitute* for B substituer A à B

subtitled *adj* sous-titré(e)

subtitles *npl* sous-titres *mpl*
▷ *a French film with English subtitles* un film français avec des sous-titres en anglais

subtle *adj* subtil(e)

subtract *vb* retrancher [**28**] ▷ *to subtract 3 from 5* retrancher trois de cinq

suburb *n* banlieue *f* ▷ *a suburb of Paris* une banlieue de Paris

subway *n (underpass)* passage souterrain *m*

succeed *vb* réussir [**38**] ▷ *to succeed in doing something* réussir à faire quelque chose

success *n* succès *m* ▷ *The play was a great success.* La pièce a eu beaucoup de succès.

successful *adj* réussi(e)
▷ *a successful attempt* une tentative réussie; **to be successful in doing something** réussir [**38**] à faire quelque chose; **He's a successful businessman.** Ses affaires marchent bien.

successfully *adv* avec succès

such *adj, adv* si ▷ *such nice people* des gens si gentils; **such a lot of** tellement de ▷ *such a lot of work* tellement de travail; **such as** *(like)* comme ▷ *hot countries, such as India* les pays chauds, comme l'Inde; **not as such** pas exactement ▷ *He's not an expert as such, but ...* Ce n'est pas exactement un expert, mais ...;

There's no such thing. Ça n'existe pas. ▷ *There's no such thing as the yeti.* Le yéti n'existe pas.

uch-and-such *adj* tel ou tel (*f* telle ou telle) ▷ *such-and-such a place* tel ou tel endroit

uck *vb* sucer [**12**] ▷ *to suck one's thumb* sucer son pouce

sudden *adj* soudain(e) ▷ *a sudden change* un changement soudain; **all of a sudden** tout à coup

suddenly *adv* ❶ (stop, leave, change) brusquement ❷ (die) subitement ❸ (at beginning of sentence) soudain ▷ *Suddenly, the door opened.* Soudain, la porte s'est ouverte.

suede *n* daim *m* ▷ *a suede jacket* une veste en daim

suffer *vb* souffrir [**54**] ▷ *She was really suffering.* Elle souffrait beaucoup.; **to suffer from a disease** avoir [**8**] une maladie ▷ *I suffer from hay fever.* J'ai le rhume des foins.

suffocate *vb* suffoquer [**28**]

sugar *n* sucre *m* ▷ *Do you take sugar?* Est-ce que vous prenez du sucre?

suggest *vb* suggérer [**34**] ▷ *I suggested they set off early.* Je leur ai suggéré de partir de bonne heure.

suggestion *n* suggestion *f* ▷ *to make a suggestion* faire une suggestion

suicide *n* suicide *m*; **to commit suicide** se suicider [**28**]

suit *n* ❶ (man's) costume *m* ❷ (woman's) tailleur *m*
▶ *vb* ❶ (be convenient for) convenir [**89**] à ▷ *What time would suit you?* Quelle heure vous conviendrait?; **That suits me fine.** Ça m'arrange.; **Suit yourself!** Comme tu veux! ❷ (look good on) aller [**3**] bien à ▷ *That dress really suits you.* Cette robe te va vraiment bien.

suitable *adj* ❶ convenable ▷ *a suitable time* une heure convenable ❷ (clothes) approprié(e) ▷ *suitable clothing* des vêtements appropriés

suitcase *n* valise *f*

suite *n* (of rooms) suite *f*; **a bedroom suite** une chambre à coucher

sulk *vb* bouder [**28**]

sultana *n* raisin sec *m* (*pl* raisins secs)

sum *n* ❶ (calculation) calcul *m* ▷ *She's good at sums.* Elle est bonne en calcul. ❷ (amount) somme *f* ▷ *a sum of money* une somme d'argent

sum up *vb* résumer [**28**]

summarize *vb* résumer [**28**]

summary *n* résumé *m*

summer *n* été *m*; **in summer** en été; **summer clothes** les vêtements d'été; **the summer holidays** les vacances d'été; **a summer camp** (US) une colonie de vacances

summertime *n* été *m*; **in summertime** en été

summit *n* sommet *m*

sun *n* soleil *m* ▷ *in the sun* au soleil

sunbathe *vb* se bronzer [**28**]

sunblock *n* écran total *m*

sunburn *n* coup de soleil *m*

a
b
c
d
e
f
g
h
i
j
k
l
m
n
o
p
q
r
s
t
u
v
w
x
y
z

sunburnt adj I got sunburnt. J'ai attrapé un coup de soleil.

Sunday n dimanche m ▷ on Sunday dimanche ▷ on Sundays le dimanche ▷ every Sunday tous les dimanches ▷ last Sunday dimanche dernier ▷ next Sunday dimanche prochain

Sunday school n catéchisme m
　● le catéchisme, the French
　● equivalent of 'Sunday school',
　● takes place during the week
　● after school rather than on a
　● Sunday.

sunflower n tournesol m

sung vb see **sing**

sunglasses npl lunettes de soleil fpl

sunk vb see **sink**

sunlight n soleil m

sunny adj ensoleillé(e) ▷ a sunny morning une matinée ensoleillée; It's sunny. Il fait du soleil.; a sunny day une belle journée

sunrise n lever du soleil m

sunroof n toit ouvrant m

sunscreen n crème solaire f

sunset n coucher du soleil m

sunshine n soleil m

sunstroke n insolation f ▷ to get sunstroke attraper une insolation

suntan n bronzage m; **suntan lotion** le lait solaire; **suntan oil** l'huile solaire f

super adj formidable

supermarket n supermarché m

supernatural adj surnaturel (f surnaturelle)

superstitious adj superstitieux (f superstitieuse)

supervise vb surveiller [28]

supervisor n ❶ (in factory) surveillant m, surveillante f ❷ (in department store) chef de rayon m

supper n dîner m

supplement n supplément m

supplies npl (food) vivres mpl

supply vb (provide) fournir [38]; **to supply somebody with something** fournir [38] quelque chose à quelqu'un ▷ The centre supplied us with all the equipment. Le centre nous a fourni tout l'équipement.
　▶ n provision f ▷ a supply of paper une provision de papier; **the water supply** (to town) l'approvisionnement en eau m

supply teacher n suppléant m, suppléante f

support vb ❶ soutenir [83] ▷ My mum has always supported me. Ma mère m'a toujours soutenu. ❷ être [35] supporter de ▷ What team do you support? Tu es supporter de quelle équipe? ❸ (financially) subvenir [89] aux besoins de ▷ She had to support five children on her own. Elle a dû subvenir toute seule aux besoins de cinq enfants.
　▌ Be careful not to translate **to support** by **supporter**.
　▶ n (backing) soutien m

supporter n ❶ supporter m ▷ a Liverpool supporter un supporter de Liverpool ❷ sympathisant m, sympathisante f ▷ a supporter of the Labour Party un sympathisant du parti travailliste

uppose vb imaginer [**28**]
▷ I suppose he's late. J'imagine qu'il
est en retard.; **I suppose so.**
J'imagine.; **to be supposed to do
something** être [**35**] censé faire
quelque chose ▷ You're supposed to
show your passport. On est censé
montrer son passeport.

upposing conj si ▷ Supposing you
won the lottery ... Si tu gagnais à la
loterie ...

ure adj sûr(e) ▷ Are you sure? Tu es
sûr?; **Sure!** Bien sûr!; **to make sure
that ...** vérifier [**19**] que ... ▷ I'm
going to make sure the door's locked.
Je vais vérifier que la porte est
fermée à clé.

surely adv **Surely you've been to
London?** J'imagine que tu es allé à
Londres, non?; **The shops are
closed on Sundays, surely?**
J'imagine que les magasins sont
fermés le dimanche, non?

surf n ressac m
▶ vb surfer [**28**]; **to go surfing** faire
[**36**] du surf; **to surf the Net** surfer
[**28**] sur le Net

surface n surface f

surfboard n planche de surf f

surfing n surf m ▷ to go surfing faire
du surf

surgeon n chirurgien m ▷ She's a
surgeon. Elle est chirurgien.

surgery n (doctor's surgery) cabinet
médical m; **surgery hours** les
heures de consultation fpl

surname n nom de famille m

surprise n surprise f

surprised adj surpris(e) ▷ I was

surprised to see him. J'ai été surpris
de le voir.

surprising adj surprenant(e)

surrender vb capituler [**28**]

surrogate mother n mère
porteuse f

surround vb encercler [**28**] ▷ The
police surrounded the house. La police
a encerclé la maison.; **surrounded
by** entouré de ▷ The house is
surrounded by trees. La maison est
entourée d'arbres.

surroundings npl cadre msg
▷ a hotel in beautiful surroundings un
hôtel situé dans un beau cadre

survey n (research) enquête f

survivor n survivant m, survivante
f ▷ There were no survivors. Il n'y a pas
eu de survivants.

suspect vb soupçonner [**28**]
▶ n suspect m, suspecte f

suspend vb ❶ (from school, team)
exclure [**13**] ▷ He's been suspended. Il
s'est fait exclure. ❷ (from job)
suspendre [**88**]

suspense n ❶ (waiting) attente f
▷ The suspense was terrible. L'attente
a été terrible. ❷ (in story) suspense
m ▷ a film with lots of suspense un
film avec beaucoup de suspense

suspicious adj ❶ méfiant(e) ▷ He
was suspicious at first. Il était
méfiant au début. ❷ (suspicious-
looking) louche ▷ a suspicious person
un individu louche

swallow vb avaler [**28**]

swam vb see **swim**

swan n cygne m

swap vb échanger [**45**] ▷ to swap A

for B échanger A contre B

swear vb (make an oath, curse) jurer [**28**]

swearword n gros mot m

sweat n transpiration f
▶ vb transpirer [**28**]

sweater n pull m

sweatshirt n sweat m

Swede n (person) Suédois m, Suédoise f

Sweden n Suède f; **in Sweden** en Suède; **to Sweden** en Suède

Swedish n (language) suédois m
▶ adj suédois(e) ▷ She's Swedish. Elle est suédoise.

sweep vb balayer [**59**]; **to sweep the floor** balayer [**59**]

sweet n ❶ (candy) bonbon m ▷ a bag of sweets un paquet de bonbons ❷ (pudding) dessert m ▷ What sweet did you have? Qu'est-ce que vous avez mangé comme dessert?
▶ adj ❶ (not savoury) sucré(e) ❷ (kind) gentil (f gentille) ▷ That was really sweet of you. C'était vraiment gentil de ta part. ❸ (cute) mignon (f mignonne) ▷ Isn't she sweet? Comme elle est mignonne!; **sweet and sour pork** le porc à la sauce aigre-douce

sweetcorn n maïs doux m

swept vb see **sweep**

swerve vb faire [**36**] une embardée ▷ He swerved to avoid the cyclist. Il a fait une embardée pour éviter le cycliste.

swim n **to go for a swim** aller [**3**] se baigner
▶ vb nager [**45**] ▷ Can you swim? Tu

sais nager?; **She swam across the river.** Elle a traversé la rivière à la nage.

swimmer n nageur m, nageuse f ▷ She's a good swimmer. C'est une bonne nageuse.

swimming n natation f ▷ Do you like swimming? Tu aimes la natation?; **to go swimming** (in a pool) aller [**3**] à la piscine; **a swimming cap** un bonnet de bain; **a swimming costume** un maillot de bain; **a swimming pool** une piscine; **swimming trunks** le maillot de bain

swimsuit n maillot de bain m

swing n (in playground, garden) balançoire f
▶ vb ❶ se balancer [**12**] ▷ A bunch of keys swung from his belt. Un trousseau de clés se balançait à sa ceinture.; **Sam was swinging an umbrella as he walked.** Sam balançait son parapluie en marchant. ❷ virer [**28**] ▷ The canoe swung round sharply. Le canoë a viré brusquement.

Swiss n (person) Suisse mf; **the Swiss** les Suisses
▶ adj suisse ▷ Sabine's Swiss. Sabine est suisse.

switch n (for light, radio etc) bouton m
▶ vb changer [**45**] de ▷ We switched partners. Nous avons changé de partenaire.

switch off vb ❶ (electrical appliance) éteindre [**60**] ❷ (engine, machine) arrêter [**28**]

witch on *vb* ❶ *(electrical appliance)* allumer [**28**] ❷ *(engine, machine)* mettre [**47**] en marche

witzerland *n* Suisse *f*; in Switzerland en Suisse

wollen *adj (arm, leg)* enflé(e)

wop *vb* échanger [**45**] ▷ to swop A for B échanger A contre B

word *n* épée *f*

wore, sworn *vb see* **swear**

wot *n* bûcheur *m*, bûcheuse *f* ▶ *vb* bosser [**28**] dur ▷ I'll have to swot for my maths exam. Je vais devoir bosser dur pour mon examen de maths.

swum *vb see* **swim**

swung *vb see* **swing**

syllabus *n* programme *m* ▷ on the syllabus au programme

symbol *n* symbole *m*

sympathetic *adj* compréhensif (*f* compréhensive)

> Be careful not to translate **sympathetic** by **sympathique**.

sympathize *vb* to sympathize with somebody comprendre [**65**] quelqu'un

sympathy *n* compassion *f*

symptom *n* symptôme *m*

syringe *n* seringue *f*

system *n* système *m*

t

table *n* table *f* ▷ to lay the table mettre la table

tablecloth *n* nappe *f*

tablespoon *n* grande cuillère *f*; two tablespoons of sugar deux cuillerées à soupe de sucre

tablet *n* ❶ *(medicine)* comprimé *m* ❷ *(computer)* tablette *f*

table tennis *n* ping-pong *m* ▷ to play table tennis jouer au ping-pong

tact *n* tact *m*

tactful *adj* plein de tact (*f* pleine de tact)

tactics *npl* tactique *fsg*

tadpole *n* têtard *m*

tag *n (label)* étiquette *f*

tail *n* queue *f*; Heads or tails? Pile ou face?

tailor *n* tailleur *m*

take *vb* ❶ prendre [**65**] ▷ Are you

taking your new camera? Tu prends ton nouvel appareil photo? ▷ He took a plate from the cupboard. Il a pris une assiette dans le placard. ▷ It takes about an hour. Ça prend environ une heure. ❷ (person) emmener [**43**] ▷ When will you take me to London? Quand est-ce que tu vas m'emmener à Londres?; **to take something somewhere** emporter [**28**] quelque chose quelque part ▷ Do you take your exercise books home? Vous emportez vos cahiers chez vous? ▷ Don't take anything valuable with you. N'emportez pas d'objets de valeur. ▷ I'm going to take my coat to the cleaner's. Je vais donner mon manteau à nettoyer. ❸ (effort, skill) demander [**28**] ▷ That takes a lot of courage. Cela demande beaucoup de courage.; **It takes a lot of money to do that.** Il faut beaucoup d'argent pour faire ça. ❹ (tolerate) supporter [**28**] ▷ He can't take being criticized. Il ne supporte pas d'être critiqué. ❺ (exam, test) passer [**58**] ▷ Have you taken your driving test yet? Est-ce que tu as déjà passé ton permis de conduire? ❻ (subject) faire [**36**] ▷ I decided to take French instead of German. J'ai décidé de faire du français au lieu de l'allemand.

take after vb ressembler [**28**] à ▷ She takes after her mother. Elle ressemble à sa mère.

take apart vb **to take something apart** démonter [**28**] quelque chose

take away vb ❶ (object) emporter [**28**] ❷ (person) emmener [**43**]; **to take something away** (confiscate) confisquer [**28**] quelque chose; **hot meals to take away** des plats chauds à emporter

take back vb rapporter [**28**] ▷ I too it back to the shop. Je l'ai rapporté au magasin.; **I take it all back!** Je n'ai rien dit!

take down vb ❶ (poster, sign) enlever [**43**] ❷ (painting, curtains) décrocher [**28**] ❸ (tent, scaffolding) démonter [**28**] ❹ (make a note of) prendre [**65**] en note ▷ He took down the details in his notebook. Il a pris tous les détails en note dans son carnet.

take in vb (understand) comprendre [**65**] ▷ I didn't really take it in. Je n'ai pas bien compris.

take off vb ❶ (plane) décoller [**28**] ▷ The plane took off twenty minutes late. L'avion a décollé avec vingt minutes de retard. ❷ (clothes) enlever [**43**] ▷ Take your coat off. Enlevez votre manteau.

take out vb (from container, pocket) sortir [**79**]; **He took her out to the theatre.** Il l'a emmenée au théâtre.

take over vb prendre [**65**] la relève ▷ I'll take over now. Je vais prendre la relève.; **to take over from somebody** remplacer [**12**] quelqu'un

takeaway n (meal) plat à emporter m; **a Chinese takeaway** un restaurant chinois qui vend des plats à emporter

aken vb see **take**

akeoff n (of plane) décollage m

ale n (story) conte m

alent n talent m ▷ She's got lots of talent. Elle a beaucoup de talent.; **to have a talent for something** être [**35**] doué pour quelque chose ▷ He's got a real talent for languages. Il est vraiment doué pour les langues.

alented adj She's a talented pianist. C'est une pianiste de talent.

talk n ❶ (speech) exposé m ▷ She gave a talk on rock climbing. Elle a fait un exposé sur la varappe. ❷ (conversation) conversation f ▷ I had a talk with my Mum about it. J'ai eu une petite conversation avec ma mère à ce sujet. ❸ (gossip) racontars mpl ▷ It's just talk. Ce sont des racontars.
▶ vb parler [**28**] ▷ to talk about something parler de quelque chose; **to talk something over with somebody** discuter [**28**] de quelque chose avec quelqu'un

talkative adj bavard(e)

tall adj ❶ (person, tree) grand(e); **to be 2 metres tall** mesurer [**28**] deux mètres ❷ (building) haut(e)

tame adj (animal) apprivoisé(e) ▷ They've got a tame hedgehog. Ils ont un hérisson apprivoisé.

tampon n tampon m

tan n bronzage m ▷ She's got an amazing tan. Elle a un bronzage superbe.

tangerine n mandarine f

tangle n ❶ (ropes, cables) enchevêtrement m ❷ (hair) nœud m; **to be in a tangle (1)** (ropes, cables) être [**35**] enchevêtré **(2)** (hair) être [**35**] emmêlé

tank n ❶ (for water, petrol) réservoir m ❷ (military) char d'assaut m; **a fish tank** un aquarium

tanker n ❶ (ship) pétrolier m; **an oil tanker** un pétrolier ❷ (truck) camion-citerne m; **a petrol tanker** un camion-citerne

tap n ❶ (water tap) robinet m ❷ (gentle blow) petite tape f

tap-dancing n claquettes fpl ▷ I do tap-dancing. Je fais des claquettes.

tape vb (record) enregistrer [**28**] ▷ Did you tape that film last night? As-tu enregistré le film hier soir?
▶ n ❶ cassette f ❷ (sticky tape) scotch® m

tape measure n mètre à ruban m

tape recorder n magnétophone m

target n cible f

tart n tarte f ▷ an apple tart une tarte aux pommes

tartan adj écossais(e) ▷ a tartan scarf une écharpe écossaise

task n tâche f

taste n goût m ▷ It's got a really strange taste. Ça a un goût vraiment bizarre. ▷ a joke in bad taste une plaisanterie de mauvais goût; **Would you like a taste?** Tu veux goûter?
▶ vb goûter [**28**] ▷ Would you like to taste it? Vous voulez y goûter?; **to taste of something** avoir [**8**] un goût de quelque chose ▷ It tastes of

a
b
c
d
e
f
g
h
i
j
k
l
m
n
o
p
q
r
s
t
u
v
w
x
y
z

fish. Ça a un goût de poisson.; **You can taste the garlic in it.** Ça a bien le goût d'ail.

tasty adj savoureux (f savoureuse)

tattoo n tatouage m

taught vb see **teach**

Taurus n Taureau m ▷ I'm Taurus. Je suis Taureau.

tax n ❶ (on income) impôts mpl ❷ (on goods, alcohol) taxe f

taxi n taxi m; **a taxi driver** un chauffeur de taxi

taxi rank n station de taxis f

TB n tuberculose f

tea n ❶ thé m ▷ a cup of tea une tasse de thé; **a tea bag** un sachet de thé ❷ (evening meal) dîner m; **We were having tea.** Nous étions en train de dîner.

teach vb ❶ apprendre [65] ▷ My sister taught me to swim. Ma sœur m'a appris à nager. ❷ (in school) enseigner [28] ▷ She teaches physics. Elle enseigne la physique.

teacher n ❶ (in secondary school) professeur m ▷ a maths teacher un professeur de maths ▷ She's a teacher. Elle est professeur. ❷ (in primary school) instituteur m, institutrice f ▷ He's a primary school teacher. Il est instituteur.

teaching assistant n aide-éducateur m, aide-éducatrice f

team n équipe f ▷ a football team une équipe de football

teapot n théière f

tear n larme f ▷ She was in tears. Elle était en larmes.
▶ vb ❶ déchirer [28] ▷ Be careful or

you'll tear the page. Fais attention, tu vas déchirer la page. ❷ se déchirer [28] ▷ It won't tear, it's very strong. Ça ne se déchire pas, c'est très solide.

tear up vb déchirer [28] ▷ He tore up the letter. Il a déchiré la lettre.

tease vb ❶ (unkindly) tourmenter [28] ▷ Stop teasing that poor animal! Arrête de tourmenter cette pauvre bête! ❷ (jokingly) taquiner [28] ▷ He's teasing you. Il te taquine.; **I was only teasing.** Je plaisantais.

teaspoon n petite cuillère f; **two teaspoons of sugar** deux cuillerées à café de sucre

teatime n (in evening) heure du dîner f ▷ It was nearly teatime. C'était presque l'heure du dîner.; **Teatime!** À table!

tea towel n torchon m

technical adj technique; **a technical college** un lycée technique

technician n technicien m, technicienne f

technological adj technologique

technology n technologie f

teddy bear n nounours m

teenage adj ❶ pour les jeunes ▷ a teenage magazine un magazine pour les jeunes ❷ (boys, girls) adolescent(e) ▷ She has two teenage daughters. Elle a deux filles adolescentes.

teenager n adolescent m, adolescente f

teens npl She's in her teens. C'est une adolescente.

tee-shirt n tee-shirt m

teeth npl dents fpl

telephone n téléphone m ▷ on the telephone au téléphone; **a telephone box** une cabine téléphonique; **a telephone call** un coup de téléphone; **the telephone directory** l'annuaire m; **a telephone number** un numéro de téléphone

telescope n télescope m

television n télévision f; **on television** à la télévision; **a television licence** une redevance de télévision; **a television programme** une émission de télévision

tell vb dire [27]; **to tell somebody something** dire [27] quelque chose à quelqu'un ▷ Did you tell your mother? Tu l'as dit à ta mère? ▷ I told him that I was going on holiday. Je lui ai dit que je partais en vacances.; **to tell somebody to do something** dire [27] à quelqu'un de faire quelque chose ▷ He told me to wait a moment. Il m'a dit d'attendre un moment.; **to tell lies** dire [27] des mensonges; **to tell a story** raconter [28] une histoire; **I can't tell the difference between them.** Je n'arrive pas à les distinguer.

tell off vb gronder [28]

telly n télé f ▷ to watch telly regarder la télé; **on telly** à la télé

temper n caractère m ▷ He's got a terrible temper. Il a un sale caractère.; **to be in a temper** être

[35] en colère; **to lose one's temper** se mettre [47] en colère ▷ I lost my temper. Je me suis mis en colère.

temperature n (of oven, water, person) température f; **The temperature was 30 degrees.** Il faisait trente degrés.; **to have a temperature** avoir [8] de la fièvre

temple n temple m

temporary adj temporaire

temptation n tentation f

tempting adj tentant(e)

ten num dix ▷ She's ten. Elle a dix ans.

tend vb to tend to do something avoir [8] tendance à faire quelque chose ▷ He tends to arrive late. Il a tendance à arriver en retard.

tennis n tennis m ▷ Do you play tennis? Vous jouez au tennis?; **a tennis ball** une balle de tennis; **a tennis court** un court de tennis; **a tennis racket** une raquette de tennis

tennis player n joueur de tennis m, joueuse de tennis f ▷ He's a tennis player. Il est joueur de tennis.

tenor n ténor m

tenpin bowling n bowling m ▷ to go tenpin bowling jouer au bowling

tense adj tendu(e) ▶ n the present tense le présent; **the future tense** le futur

tension n tension f

tent n tente f; **a tent peg** un piquet de tente; **a tent pole** un montant de tente

tenth adj dixième ▷ the tenth floor le dixième étage; **the tenth of August** le dix août

term n ❶ (at school) trimestre m
❷ terme m ▷ a short-term solution
une solution à court terme; **to
come to terms with something**
accepter [**28**] quelque chose
terminal adj (illness, patient)
incurable
▸ n (of computer) un terminal; **an oil
terminal** un terminal pétrolier; **an
air terminal** une aérogare
terminally adv **to be terminally ill**
être [**35**] condamné
terrace n ❶ (patio) terrasse f ❷ (row
of houses) rangée de maisons f; **the
terraces** (at stadium) les gradins
mpl
terraced adj **a terraced house** une
maison mitoyenne
terrible adj épouvantable ▷ My
French is terrible. Mon français est
épouvantable.
terribly adv ❶ terriblement ▷ He
suffers terribly. Il souffre
terriblement. ❷ vraiment ▷ I'm
terribly sorry. Je suis vraiment
désolé.
terrific adj (wonderful) super
▷ That's terrific! C'est super!; **You
look terrific!** Tu es superbe!
terrified adj terrifié(e) ▷ I was
terrified! J'étais terrifié!
terrorism n terrorisme m
terrorist n terroriste mf; **a
terrorist attack** un attentat
terroriste
test n ❶ (at school) interrogation f
▷ I've got a test tomorrow. J'ai une
interrogation demain. ❷ (trial,
check) essai m ▷ nuclear tests les

essais nucléaires ❸ (medical)
analyse f ▷ a blood test une analyse
de sang ▷ They're going to do some
more tests. Ils vont faire d'autres
analyses.; **driving test** l'examen
du permis de conduire ▷ He's got his
driving test tomorrow. Il passe son
permis de conduire demain.
▸ vb ❶ essayer [**59**] ▷ to test
something out essayer quelque
chose ❷ (class) interroger [**45**] ▷ He
tested us on the vocabulary. Il nous a
interrogés sur le vocabulaire.; **She
was tested for drugs.** On lui a fait
subir un contrôle antidopage.
test tube n éprouvette f
text n ❶ texte m ❷ (on mobile phone)
SMS m
▸ vb **to text someone** envoyer [**33**]
un SMS à quelqu'un
textbook n manuel m ▷ a French
textbook un manuel de français
text message n SMS m
Thames n Tamise f
than conj que ▷ She's taller than me.
Elle est plus grande que moi.;
more than ten years plus de dix
ans; **more than once** plus d'une
fois
thank vb remercier [**19**] ▷ Don't
forget to write and thank them.
N'oublie pas de leur écrire pour les
remercier.; **thank you** merci;
thank you very much merci
beaucoup
thanks excl merci!; **thanks to**
grâce à ▷ Thanks to him, everything
went OK. Grâce à lui, tout s'est bien
passé.

hat adj, pron, conj

> Use **ce** when 'that' is followed by a masculine noun, and **cette** when 'that' is followed by a feminine noun. **ce** changes to **cet** before a vowel and before most words beginning with 'h'.

❶ ce ▷ *that book* ce livre; cet ▷ *that man* cet homme; cette ▷ *that woman* cette femme ▷ *that road* cette route; **THAT road** cette route-là; **that one (1)** celui-là m ▷ *This man? — No, that one.* Cet homme-ci — Non, celui-là. **(2)** celle-là f ▷ *Do you like this photo? — No, I prefer that one.* Tu aimes cette photo? — Non, je préfère celle-là. ❷ ça ▷ *You see that?* Tu vois ça?; **What's that?** Qu'est-ce que c'est?; **Who's that?** Qui est-ce?; **Is that you?** C'est toi?; **That's ...** C'est ... ▷ *That's my teacher.* C'est mon prof. ▷ *That's what he said.* C'est ce qu'il a dit.

> In relative phrases use **qui** when 'that' refers to the subject of the sentence, and **que** when it refers to the object.

❸ qui ▷ *the man that saw us* l'homme qui nous a vus ▷ *the man that spoke to us* l'homme qui nous a parlé ❹ que ▷ *the man that we saw* l'homme que nous avons vu ▷ *the man that we spoke to* l'homme à qui nous avons parlé

> **que** changes to **qu'** before a vowel and before most words beginning with 'h'.

▷ *the dog that she bought* le chien qu'elle a acheté ▷ *He thought that Henri was ill.* Il pensait qu'Henri était malade. ▷ *I know that she likes chocolate.* Je sais qu'elle aime le chocolat.; **It was that big.** Il était grand comme ça.; **It's about that high.** C'est à peu près haut comme ça.; **It's not that difficult.** Ça n'est pas si difficile que ça.

the art

> Use **le** with a masculine noun, and **la** with a feminine noun. Use **l'** before a vowel and most words beginning with 'h'. For plural nouns always use **les**.

le ▷ *the boy* le garçon; l' ▷ *the man* l'homme m ▷ *the air* l'air m ▷ *the habit* l'habitude f; la ▷ *the girl* la fille; les ▷ *the children* les enfants

theatre (US **theater**) n théâtre m

theft n vol m

their adj leur (pl leurs) ▷ *their house* leur maison ▷ *their parents* leurs parents

theirs pron le leur ▷ *It's not our garage, it's theirs.* Ce n'est pas notre garage, c'est le leur.
la leur ▷ *It's not our car, it's theirs.* Ce n'est pas notre voiture, c'est la leur.
les leurs ▷ *They're not our ideas, they're theirs.* Ce ne sont pas nos idées, ce sont les leurs.; **Is this theirs? (1)** (masculine owners) C'est à eux? **(2)** (feminine owners) C'est à elles? ▷ *This car is theirs.* Cette voiture est à eux.

them pron ❶ les ▷ *I didn't see them.* Je

a b c d e f g h i j k l m n o p q r s t u v w x y z

ne les ai pas vus.

Use **leur** when 'them' means 'to them'.

❷ leur ▷ *I told them the truth.* Je leur ai dit la vérité.

Use **eux** or **elles** after a preposition.

❸ eux *mpl* ▷ *It's for them.* C'est pour eux.; elles *fpl* ▷ *Ann and Sophie came — Graham was with them.* Ann et Sophie sont venues — Graham était avec elles.

theme park *n* parc d'attractions *m*

themselves *pron* ❶ se ▷ *Did they hurt themselves?* Est-ce qu'ils se sont fait mal? ❷ eux-mêmes *m*, elles-mêmes *f* ▷ *They did it themselves.* Ils l'ont fait eux-mêmes.

then *adv, conj* ❶ *(next)* ensuite ▷ *I get dressed. Then I have breakfast.* Je m'habille. Ensuite je prends mon petit déjeuner. ❷ *(in that case)* alors ▷ *My pen's run out. — Use a pencil then!* Il n'y a plus d'encre dans mon stylo. — Alors utilise un crayon! ❸ *(at that time)* à l'époque ▷ *There was no electricity then.* Il n'y avait pas l'électricité à l'époque.; **now and then** de temps en temps ▷ *Do you play chess? — Now and then.* Vous jouez aux échecs? — De temps en temps.; **By then it was too late.** Il était déjà trop tard.

there *adv* ❶ là ▷ *Put it there, on the table.* Mets-le là, sur la table.; **over there** là-bas; **in there** là; **on there** là; **up there** là-haut; **down there** là-bas; **There he is!** Le voilà! ❷ y

▷ *He went there on Friday.* Il y est allé vendredi.; **There is ...** Il y a ... ▷ *There's a factory near my house.* Il y a une usine près de chez moi.; **There are ...** Il y a ... ▷ *There are five people in my family.* Il y a cinq personnes dans ma famille.; **There has been an accident.** Il y a eu un accident.

therefore *adv* donc

there's = there is; there has

thermometer *n* thermomètre *m*

these *adj, pron* ❶ ces ▷ *these shoes* ces chaussures; **THESE shoes** ces chaussures-ci ❷ ceux-ci *m* ▷ *I want these!* Je veux ceux-ci!; celles-ci *f* ▷ *I'm looking for some sandals. Can I try these?* Je cherche des sandales. Je peux essayer celles-ci?

they *pron*

Check if 'they' stands for a masculine or feminine noun.

ils ▷ *Are there any tickets left? — No, they're all sold.* Est-ce qu'il reste des billets? — Non, ils sont tous vendus.

elles ▷ *Do you like those shoes? — No, they're horrible.* Tu aimes ces chaussures? — Non, elles sont affreuses.; **They say that ...** On dit que ...

they'd = they had; they would

they'll = they will

they're = they are

they've = they have

thick *adj* ❶ *(not thin)* épais *(f* épaisse); **The walls are one metre thick.** Les murs font un mètre d'épaisseur. ❷ (stupid) bête

hief n voleur m, voleuse f; **Stop
thief!** Au voleur!

high n cuisse f

hin adj ❶ (person, slice) mince
❷ (skinny) maigre

hing n ❶ chose f ▷ beautiful things
de belles choses ❷ (thingy) truc m
▷ What's that thing called?
Comment s'appelle ce truc?; **my
things** (belongings) mes affaires fpl;
You poor thing! Mon pauvre!

think vb ❶ (believe) penser [28]
▷ I think you're wrong. Je pense que
vous avez tort. ▷ What do you think
about the war? Que pensez-vous de
la guerre? ❷ (spend time thinking)
réfléchir [38] ▷ Think carefully before
you reply. Réfléchis bien avant de
répondre. ▷ I'll think about it. Je vais
y réfléchir.; **What are you
thinking about?** À quoi tu penses?
❸ (imagine) imaginer [28] ▷ Think
what life would be like without cars.
Imaginez la vie sans voitures.; **I
think so.** Oui, je crois.; **I don't
think so.** Je ne crois pas.; **I'll think
it over.** Je vais y réfléchir.

third adj troisième ▷ the third day le
troisième jour ▷ the third time la
troisième fois ▷ I came third. Je suis
arrivé troisième.; **the third of
March** le trois mars
▶ n tiers m ▷ a third of the population
un tiers de la population

thirdly adv troisièmement

Third World n tiers-monde m

thirst n soif f

thirsty adj **to be thirsty** avoir [8] soif

thirteen num treize ▷ I'm thirteen.
J'ai treize ans.

thirteenth adj treizième ▷ her
thirteenth birthday son treizième
anniversaire ▷ the thirteenth floor le
treizième étage; **the thirteenth of
August** le treize août

thirty num trente

this adj, pron

> Use **ce** when 'this' is followed
> by a masculine noun, and **cette**
> when 'this' is followed by a
> feminine noun. **ce** changes to
> **cet** before a vowel and before
> most words beginning with 'h'.

❶ ce ▷ this book ce livre; cet ▷ this
man cet homme; cette ▷ this
woman cette femme ▷ this road
cette route; **THIS road** cette
route-ci; **this one (1)** celui-ci m
▷ Pass me that pen. — This one?
Passe-moi ce stylo. — Celui-ci?
(2) celle-ci f ▷ Of the two photos, I
prefer this one. Des deux photos,
c'est celle-ci que je préfère. ❷ ça
▷ You see this? Tu vois ça?; **What's
this?** Qu'est-ce que c'est?; **This is
my mother.** (introduction) Je te
présente ma mère.; **This is Gavin
speaking.** (on the phone) C'est
Gavin à l'appareil.

thistle n chardon m

thorough adj minutieux (f
minutieuse) ▷ She's very thorough.
Elle est très minutieuse.

those adj, pron ❶ ces ▷ those shoes
ces chaussures; **THOSE shoes** ces
chaussures-là ❷ ceux-là m ▷ I want
those! Je veux ceux-là!

a
b
c
d
e
f
g
h
i
j
k
l
m
n
o
p
q
r
s
t
u
v
w
x
y
z

celles-là f ▷ *I'm looking for some sandals. Can I try those?* Je cherche des sandales. Je peux essayer celles-là?

though *conj, adv* bien que ▷ *Though it's raining …* Bien qu'il pleuve …

▮ **bien que** has to be followed by a verb in the subjunctive.

He's a nice person, though he's not very clever. Il est sympa, mais pas très malin.

thought *vb see* **think**
▷ *n* (idea) idée *f* ▷ *I've just had a thought.* Je viens d'avoir une idée.;
It was a nice thought, thank you. C'est gentil de ta part, merci.

thoughtful *adj* ❶ (deep in thought) pensif (*f* pensive) ▷ *You look thoughtful.* Tu as l'air pensif.
❷ (considerate) prévenant(e) ▷ *She's very thoughtful.* Elle est très prévenante.

thoughtless *adj* **He's completely thoughtless.** Il ne pense absolument pas aux autres.

thousand *num* **a thousand** mille
▷ *a thousand euros* mille euros;
£2000 deux mille livres;
thousands of people des milliers de personnes

thousandth *adj, n* millième *m*

thread *n* fil *m*

threat *n* menace *f*

threaten *vb* menacer [**12**] ▷ *to threaten to do something* menacer de faire quelque chose

three *num* trois ▷ *She's three.* Elle a trois ans.

threw *vb see* **throw**

thrilled *adj* **I was thrilled.** (pleased) J'étais absolument ravi.

thriller *n* thriller *m*

thrilling *adj* palpitant(e)

throat *n* gorge *f* ▷ *to have a sore throat* avoir mal à la gorge

through *prep, adj, adv* ❶ par
▷ *through the window* par la fenêtre
to go through a tunnel traverser [**28**] un tunnel ❷ à travers
▷ *through the crowd* à travers la foule; **a through train** un train direct; **'no through road'** impasse

throughout *prep* **throughout Britain** dans toute la Grande-Bretagne; **throughout the year** pendant toute l'année

throw *vb* lancer [**12**] ▷ *He threw the ball to me.* Il m'a lancé le ballon.; **to throw a party** organiser [**28**] une soirée; **That really threw him.** Ça l'a déconcentancé.

throw away *vb* ❶ (rubbish) jeter [**41**] ❷ (chance) perdre [**61**]

throw out *vb* ❶ (throw away) jeter [**41**] ❷ (person) mettre [**47**] à la porte ▷ *I threw him out.* Je l'ai mis à la porte.

throw up *vb* vomir [**38**]

thumb *n* pouce *m*

thumb tack *n* (US) punaise *f*

thump *vb* **to thump somebody** donner [**28**] un coup de poing à quelqu'un

thunder *n* tonnerre *m*

thunderstorm *n* orage *m*

Thursday *n* jeudi *m* ▷ *on Thursday* jeudi ▷ *on Thursdays* le jeudi ▷ *every Thursday* tous les jeudis ▷ *last*

Thursday jeudi dernier ▷ *next Thursday* jeudi prochain

ick n ❶ *(mark)* coche f ❷ *(of clock)* tic-tac m; **I'll be back in a tick.** J'en ai pour une seconde.
▶ vb ❶ cocher [28] ▷ *Tick the appropriate box.* Cochez la case correspondante. ❷ *(clock)* faire [36] tic-tac

ick off vb ❶ *(check)* cocher [28] ▷ *He ticked off our names on the list.* Il a coché nos noms sur la liste. ❷ *(tell off)* passer [58] un savon à ▷ *She ticked me off for being late.* Elle m'a passé un savon à cause de mon retard.

ticket n
Be careful to choose correctly between **le ticket** and **le billet**.
❶ *(for bus, tube, cinema, museum)* ticket m ▷ *an underground ticket* un ticket de métro ❷ *(for plane, train, theatre, concert)* billet m; **a parking ticket** un p.-v. *(informal)*

ticket inspector n contrôleur m, contrôleuse f

ticket office n guichet m

tickle vb chatouiller [28]

tide n marée f; **high tide** la marée haute; **low tide** la marée basse

tidy adj ❶ *(room)* bien rangé(e) ▷ *Your room's very tidy.* Ta chambre est bien rangée. ❷ *(person)* ordonné(e) ▷ *She's very tidy.* Elle est très ordonnée.
▶ vb ranger [45] ▷ *Go and tidy your room.* Va ranger ta chambre.

tidy up vb ranger [45] ▷ *Don't forget to tidy up afterwards.* N'oubliez pas

de ranger après.

tie n *(necktie)* cravate f; **It was a tie.** *(in sport)* Ils ont fait match nul.
▶ vb ❶ *(ribbon, shoelaces)* nouer [28]; **to tie a knot in something** faire [36] un nœud à quelque chose ❷ *(in sport)* faire [36] match nul ▷ *They tied three all.* Ils ont fait match nul, trois à trois.

tie up vb ❶ *(parcel)* ficeler [4] ❷ *(dog, boat)* attacher [28] ❸ *(prisoner)* ligoter [28]

tiger n tigre m

tight adj ❶ *(tight-fitting)* moulant(e) ▷ *tight clothes* les vêtements moulants ❷ *(too tight)* juste ▷ *This dress is a bit tight.* Cette robe est un peu juste.

tighten vb ❶ *(rope)* tendre [88] ❷ *(screw)* resserrer [28]

tightly adv *(hold)* fort

tights npl collant msg

tile n ❶ *(on roof)* tuile f ❷ *(on wall, floor)* carreau m *(pl* carreaux)

till n caisse f
▶ prep, conj ❶ jusqu'à ▷ *I waited till ten o'clock.* J'ai attendu jusqu'à dix heures.; **till now** jusqu'à présent; **till then** jusque-là ❷ avant
Use **avant** if the sentence you want to translate contains a negative such as 'not' or 'never'.
▷ *It won't be ready till next week.* Ça ne sera pas prêt avant la semaine prochaine.

time n ❶ *(on clock)* heure f ▷ *What time is it?* Quelle heure est-il? ▷ *What time do you get up?* À quelle heure tu te lèves?; **on time** à l'heure

▷ *He never arrives on time.* Il n'arrive jamais à l'heure. ❷ *(amount of time)* temps m ▷ *I'm sorry, I haven't got time.* Je suis désolé, je n'ai pas le temps.; **from time to time** de temps en temps; **in time** à temps ▷ *We arrived in time for lunch.* Nous sommes arrivés à temps pour le déjeuner.; **just in time** juste à temps; **in no time** en un rien de temps ▷ *It was ready in no time.* Ça a été prêt en un rien de temps.; **It's time to go.** Il est temps de partir.; **a long time** longtemps ▷ *Have you lived here for a long time?* Vous habitez ici depuis longtemps? ❸ *(moment)* moment m ▷ *This isn't a good time to ask him.* Ce n'est pas le bon moment pour lui demander.; **for the time being** pour le moment ❹ *(occasion)* fois f ▷ *this time* cette fois-ci ▷ *next time* la prochaine fois ▷ *two at a time* deux à la fois; **How many times?** Combien de fois?; **at times** parfois; **in a week's time** dans une semaine ▷ *I'll come back in a month's time.* Je reviendrai dans un mois.; **Come and see us any time.** Venez nous voir quand vous voulez.; **to have a good time** bien s'amuser [28] ▷ *Did you have a good time?* Vous vous êtes bien amusés?; **2 times 2 is 4** deux fois deux égalent quatre
time off n temps libre m
timetable n ❶ *(for train, bus)* horaire m ❷ *(at school)* emploi du temps m
tin n ❶ boîte f ▷ *a tin of soup* une

boîte de soupe ▷ *a biscuit tin* une boîte à biscuits ❷ boîte de conserve f ▷ *The bin was full of tins.* La poubelle était pleine de boîtes de conserve. ❸ *(type of metal)* étain m
tin opener n ouvre-boîte m
tiny adj minuscule
tip n ❶ *(money)* pourboire m ▷ *Shall I give him a tip?* Je lui donne un pourboire? ❷ *(advice)* tuyau m *(pl tuyaux)* ▷ *a useful tip* un bon tuyau *(informal)* ❸ *(end)* bout m ▷ *It's on the tip of my tongue.* Je l'ai sur le bout de la langue.; **a rubbish tip** une décharge; **This place is a complete tip!** Quel fouillis!
▶ vb donner [28] un pourboire à ▷ *Don't forget to tip the taxi driver.* N'oubliez pas de donner un pourboire au chauffeur de taxi.
tipsy adj pompette
tiptoe n **on tiptoe** sur la pointe des pieds
tired adj fatigué(e) ▷ *I'm tired.* Je suis fatigué.; **to be tired of something** en avoir [8] assez de quelque chose
tiring adj fatigant(e)
tissue n kleenex® m ▷ *Have you got a tissue?* Tu as un kleenex?®
title n titre m
to prep

à + **le** changes to **au**. à + **les** changes to **aux**.

❶ à ▷ *to go to Paris* aller à Paris ▷ *to go to school* aller à l'école ▷ *a letter to his mother* une lettre à sa mère ▷ *the answer to the question* la réponse à la question; au ▷ *to go to the theatre* aller au théâtre; aux ▷ *We said goodbye to the neighbours.* Nous avons dit au revoir aux voisins.; **ready to go** prêt à partir; **ready to eat** prêt à manger; **It's easy to do.** C'est facile à faire.; **something to drink** quelque chose à boire; **I've got things to do.** J'ai des choses à faire.; **from ... to ...** de ... à ... ▷ *from nine o'clock to half past three* de neuf heures à trois heures et demie ❷ de ▷ *the train to London* le train de Londres ▷ *the road to Edinburgh* la route d'Édimbourg ▷ *the key to the front door* la clé de la porte d'entrée; **It's difficult to say.** C'est difficile à dire.; **It's easy to criticize.** C'est facile de critiquer.

When referring to someone's house, shop or office, use **chez**.

❸ chez ▷ *to go to the doctor's* aller chez le docteur ▷ *to go to the butcher's* aller chez le boucher ▷ *Let's go to Anne's house.* Si on allait chez Anne?

When 'to' refers to a country which is feminine, use **en**; when the country is masculine, use **au**.

❹ en ▷ *to go to France* aller en France; au ▷ *to go to Portugal* aller au Portugal ❺ *(up to)* jusqu'à ▷ *to count to ten* compter jusqu'à dix ❻ *(in order to)* pour ▷ *I did it to help you.* Je l'ai fait pour vous aider. ▷ *She's too young to go to school.* Elle est trop jeune pour aller à l'école.

toad n crapaud m
toast n ❶ pain grillé m ▷ *a piece of toast* une tranche de pain grillé ❷ *(speech)* toast m ▷ *to drink a toast to somebody* porter un toast à quelqu'un
toaster n grille-pain m *(pl* grille-pain)
toastie n sandwich chaud m; **a cheese and ham toastie** un croque-monsieur
tobacco n tabac m
tobacconist's n bureau de tabac m *(pl* bureaux de tabac)
today adv aujourd'hui ▷ *What did you do today?* Qu'est-ce que tu as fait aujourd'hui?
toddler n bambin m
toe n doigt de pied m
toffee n caramel m
together adv ❶ ensemble ▷ *Are they still together?* Ils sont toujours ensemble? ❷ *(at the same time)* en même temps ▷ *Don't all speak together!* Ne parlez pas tous en même temps!; **together with** *(with person)* avec
toilet n toilettes fpl
toilet paper n papier hygiénique m
toiletries npl articles de toilette mpl
toilet roll n rouleau de papier hygiénique m *(pl* rouleaux de papier hygiénique)
told vb see tell
toll n *(on bridge, motorway)* péage m
tomato n tomate f ▷ *tomato sauce* la sauce tomate ▷ *tomato soup* la soupe à la tomate

a b c d e f g h i j k l m n o p q r s **t** u v w x y z

tomorrow adv demain ▷ tomorrow morning demain matin ▷ tomorrow night demain soir; **the day after tomorrow** après-demain

ton n tonne f ▷ That old bike weighs a ton. Ce vieux vélo pèse une tonne.
- ● In France measurements are in metric tonnes rather than tons. A ton is slightly more than a
- ● tonne.

tongue n langue f; **to say something tongue in cheek** dire [27] quelque chose en plaisantant

tonic n (tonic water) Schweppes® m; **a gin and tonic** un gin tonic

tonight adv ❶ (this evening) ce soir ▷ Are you going out tonight? Tu sors ce soir? ❷ (during the night) cette nuit ▷ I'll sleep well tonight. Je dormirai bien cette nuit.

tonsillitis n angine f

tonsils npl amygdales fpl

too adv ❶ (as well) aussi ▷ My sister came too. Ma sœur est venue aussi. ❷ (excessively) trop ▷ The water's too hot. L'eau est trop chaude. ▷ We arrived too late. Nous sommes arrivés trop tard.; **too much (1)** (with noun) trop de ▷ too much noise trop de bruit **(2)** (with verb) trop ▷ At Christmas we always eat too much. À Noël nous mangeons toujours trop. **(3)** (too expensive) trop cher ▷ Fifty euros? That's too much. Cinquante euros? C'est trop cher.; **too many** trop de ▷ too many hamburgers trop de hamburgers; **Too bad!** Tant pis!

took vb see **take**

tool n outil m; **a tool box** une boîte à outils

tooth n dent f

toothache n mal de dents m ▷ to have toothache avoir mal aux dents

toothbrush n brosse à dents f

toothpaste n dentifrice m

top n ❶ (of page, ladder, garment) haut m ▷ at the top of the page en haut de la page; **a bikini top** un haut de bikini ❷ (of mountain) sommet m ❸ (of table) dessus m; **on top of** (on) sur ▷ on top of the fridge sur le frigo; **There's a surcharge on top of that.** Il y a un supplément en plus.; **from top to bottom** de fond en comble ▷ I searched the house from top to bottom. J'ai fouillé la maison de fond en comble. ❹ (of box, jar) couvercle m ❺ (of bottle) bouchon m
  ▶ adj (first-class) grand(e) ▷ a top surgeon un grand chirurgien; **a top model** un top model; **He always gets top marks in French.** Il a toujours d'excellentes notes en français.; **the top floor** le dernier étage ▷ on the top floor au dernier étage

topic n sujet m ▷ The essay can be on any topic. Cette dissertation peut être sur n'importe quel sujet.

torch n lampe de poche f

tore, torn vb see **tear**

tortoise n tortue f

torture n torture f ▷ It was pure torture. C'était une vraie torture.
  ▶ vb torturer [28] ▷ Stop torturing

that poor animal! Arrête de torturer cette pauvre bête!

total adj total(e) (mpl totaux); **the total amount** le total

▶ n total m (pl totaux); **the grand total** le total

totally adv complètement ▷ He's totally useless. Il est complètement nul.

touch n **to get in touch with somebody** prendre [**65**] contact avec quelqu'un; **to keep in touch with somebody** ne pas perdre [**61**] contact avec quelqu'un; **Keep in touch!** Donne-moi de tes nouvelles!; **to lose touch** se perdre [**61**] de vue; **to lose touch with somebody** perdre [**61**] quelqu'un de vue

▶ vb toucher [**28**]; **Don't touch that!** N'y touche pas!

touchpad n pavé tactile m

tough adj **1** dur(e) ▷ It was tough, but I managed OK. C'était dur, mais je m'en suis tiré. ▷ It's a tough job. C'est dur.; **The meat's tough.** La viande est coriace. **2** (strong) solide ▷ She's tough. She can take it. Elle est solide. Elle tiendra le coup. **3** (rough, violent) dangereux (f dangereuse); **He thinks he's a tough guy.** Il se prend pour un gros dur.; **Tough luck!** C'est comme ça!

tour n **1** (of town, museum) visite f ▷ We went on a tour of the city. Nous avons visité la ville.; **a package tour** un voyage organisé **2** (by singer, group) tournée f ▷ **on tour** en tournée; **to go on tour** faire [**36**] une tournée

▶ vb **Robbie Williams is touring Europe.** Robbie Williams est en tournée en Europe.

tourism n tourisme m

tourist n touriste mf; **tourist information office** l'office du tourisme m

towards prep **1** (in the direction of) vers ▷ He came towards me. Il est venu vers moi. **2** (of attitude) envers ▷ my feelings towards him mes sentiments envers lui

towel n serviette f

tower n tour f; **a tower block** une tour

town n ville f ▷ a town plan un plan de ville; **the town centre** le centre-ville; **the town hall** la mairie

tow truck n (US) dépanneuse f

toy n jouet m ▷ a toy shop un magasin de jouets; **a toy car** une petite voiture

trace n trace f ▷ There was no trace of the robbers. Il n'y avait pas de trace des voleurs.

▶ vb (draw) décalquer [**28**]

tracing paper n papier calque m

track n **1** (dirt road) chemin m **2** (railway line) voie ferrée f **3** (in sport) piste f ▷ two laps of the track deux tours de piste **4** (song) chanson f ▷ This is my favourite track. C'est ma chanson préférée. **5** (trail) traces fpl ▷ They followed the tracks for miles. Ils ont suivi les traces pendant des kilomètres.

track down vb **to track somebody down** retrouver [**28**]

a b c d e f g h i j k l m n o p q r s t u v w x y z

quelqu'un ▷ *The police never tracked down the killer.* La police n'a jamais retrouvé l'assassin.

tracksuit n jogging m

tractor n tracteur m

trade n *(skill, job)* métier m ▷ *to learn a trade* apprendre un métier

trade union n syndicat m

tradition n tradition f

traditional adj traditionnel (f traditionnelle)

traffic n circulation f ▷ *The traffic was terrible.* Il y avait une circulation épouvantable.

traffic circle n *(US)* rond-point m (pl ronds-points)

traffic jam n embouteillage m

traffic lights npl feux mpl

traffic warden n contractuel m, contractuelle f

tragedy n tragédie f

tragic adj tragique

trailer n ❶ *(vehicle)* remorque f ❷ *(film advert)* bande-annonce f

train n ❶ train m ❷ *(on underground)* rame f
  ▶ vb *(sport)* s'entraîner [**28**] ▷ *to train for a race* s'entraîner pour une course; **to train as a teacher** suivre [**81**] une formation d'enseignant; **to train an animal to do something** dresser [**28**] un animal à faire quelque chose

trained adj *She's a trained nurse.* Elle est infirmière diplômée.

trainee n ❶ *(in profession)* stagiaire mf ▷ *She's a trainee.* Elle est stagiaire. ❷ *(apprentice)* apprenti m, apprentie f ▷ *a trainee plumber* un

apprenti plombier

trainer n ❶ *(sports coach)* entraîneur m ❷ *(of animals)* dompteur m, dompteuse f

trainers npl baskets fpl ▷ *a pair of trainers* une paire de baskets

training n ❶ formation f
  ▷ *a training course* un stage de formation ❷ *(sport)* entraînement m

tram n tramway m

tramp n clochard m, clocharde f

trampoline n trampoline m

transfer n *(sticker)* décalcomanie f

transit n transit m ▷ *in transit* en transit

transit lounge n salle de transit f

translate vb traduire [**23**] ▷ *to translate something into English* traduire quelque chose en anglais

translation n traduction f

translator n traducteur m, traductrice f ▷ *Anita's a translator.* Anita est traductrice.

transparent adj transparent(e)

transplant n greffe f ▷ *a heart transplant* une greffe du cœur

transport n transport m ▷ *public transport* les transports en commun
  ▶ vb transporter [**28**]

trap n piège m

trash n *(US)* ordures fpl; **the trash can** la poubelle

travel n voyages mpl
  ▶ vb voyager [**45**] ▷ *I prefer to travel by train.* Je préfère voyager en train.; **I'd like to travel round the world.** J'aimerais faire le tour du monde.;

We travelled over 800 kilometres.
Nous avons fait plus de huit cents
kilomètres.; **News travels fast!**
Les nouvelles circulent vite!

ravel agency n agence de
voyages f

ravel agent n She's a travel
agent. Elle travaille dans une
agence de voyages.

raveller (US **traveler**) n ❶ (on bus,
train, plane) voyageur m, voyageuse
f ❷ (gypsy) nomade mf

traveller's cheque (US **traveler's
check**) n chèque de voyage m

travelling (US **traveling**) n I love
travelling. J'adore les voyages.

travel sickness n mal des
transports m

tray n plateau m (pl plateaux)

tread vb marcher [28] ▷ to tread on
something marcher sur quelque
chose

treasure n trésor m

treat n ❶ (present) petit cadeau m
(pl petits cadeaux) ❷ (food) gâterie
f; **to give somebody a treat** faire
[36] plaisir à quelqu'un
▷ vb (well, badly) traiter [28]; **to
treat somebody to something**
offrir [54] quelque chose à
quelqu'un ▷ He treated us to an ice
cream. Il nous a offert une glace.

treatment n traitement m

treble vb tripler [28] ▷ The cost of
living there has trebled. Le coût de la
vie là-bas a triplé.

tree n arbre m

tremble vb trembler [28]

tremendous adj énorme ▷ a

tremendous success un succès énorme

trend n ❶ (fashion) mode f; **to set a
trend** lancer [12] une mode
❷ (tendency) tendance f

trendy adj branché(e)

trial n (in court) procès m

triangle n triangle m

tribe n tribu f

trick n ❶ tour m ▷ to play a trick on
somebody jouer un tour à quelqu'un
❷ (knack) truc m ▷ It's not easy:
there's a trick to it. Ce n'est pas
facile: il y a un truc.
▷ vb **to trick somebody** rouler [28]
quelqu'un

tricky adj délicat(e)

tricycle n tricycle m

trip n voyage m ▷ to go on a trip faire
un voyage; **a day trip** une
excursion d'une journée
▷ vb (stumble) trébucher [28]

triple adj triple

triplets npl triplés mpl, triplées fpl

trivial adj insignifiant(e)

trod, trodden vb see **tread**

trolley n chariot m

trombone n trombone m ▷ I play
the trombone. Je joue du trombone.

troops npl troupes mpl ▷ British
troops les troupes britanniques

trophy n trophée m ▷ to win a trophy
gagner un trophée

tropical adj tropical(e) ▷ The
weather was tropical. Il faisait une
chaleur tropicale.

trouble n problème m ▷ The trouble
is, it's too expensive. Le problème,
c'est que c'est trop cher.; **to be in
trouble** avoir [8] des ennuis;

What's the trouble? Qu'est-ce qui ne va pas?; **stomach trouble** troubles gastriques; **to take a lot of trouble over something** se donner [**28**] beaucoup de mal pour quelque chose; **Don't worry, it's no trouble.** Mais non, ça ne me dérange pas du tout.

troublemaker n élément perturbateur m

trousers npl pantalon msg

trout n truite f

truant n **to play truant** faire [**36**] l'école buissonnière

truck n camion m; **a truck driver** un camionneur ▷ He's a truck driver. Il est camionneur.

true adj vrai(e); **That's true.** C'est vrai.; **to come true** se réaliser [**28**] ▷ I hope my dream will come true. J'espère que mon rêve se réalisera.; **true love** le grand amour

truly adv vraiment ▷ It was a truly remarkable victory. C'était vraiment une victoire remarquable.; **Yours truly.** Je vous prie d'agréer mes salutations distinguées.

trumpet n trompette f ▷ She plays the trumpet. Elle joue de la trompette.

trunk n ❶ (of tree) tronc m ❷ (of elephant) trompe f ❸ (luggage) malle f ❹ (US: of car) coffre m

trunks npl **swimming trunks** le maillot de bain

trust n confiance f ▷ to have trust in somebody avoir confiance en quelqu'un
▶ vb **to trust somebody** faire [**36**]

confiance à quelqu'un ▷ Don't you trust me? Tu ne me fais pas confiance?

truth n vérité f

try n essai m ▷ his third try son troisième essai; **to have a try** essayer [**59**]; **It's worth a try.** Ça vaut la peine d'essayer.; **to give something a try** essayer [**59**] quelque chose
▶ vb ❶ (attempt) essayer [**59**] ▷ to try to do something essayer de faire quelque chose; **to try again** refaire [**36**] un essai ❷ (taste) goûter [**28**] ▷ Would you like to try some? Voulez-vous goûter?

try on vb (clothes) essayer [**59**]

try out vb essayer [**59**]

T-shirt n tee-shirt m

tube n tube m; **the Tube** (underground) le métro

tuberculosis n tuberculose f

Tuesday n mardi m ▷ on Tuesday mardi ▷ on Tuesdays le mardi ▷ every Tuesday tous les mardis ▷ last Tuesday mardi dernier ▷ next Tuesday mardi prochain; **Shrove Tuesday** (Pancake Tuesday) le mardi gras

tuition n cours mpl; **private tuition** les cours particuliers

tulip n tulipe f

tumble dryer n sèche-linge m (pl sèche-linge)

tummy n ventre m

tuna n thon m

tune n (melody) air m; **to play in tune** jouer [**28**] juste; **to sing out of tune** chanter [**28**] faux

unisia n Tunisie f; **in Tunisia** en Tunisie

unnel n tunnel m; **the Channel Tunnel** le tunnel sous la Manche

urk n Turc m, Turque f

urkey n Turquie f; **in Turkey** en Turquie; **to Turkey** en Turquie

urkey n ① (meat) dinde f ② (live bird) dindon m

urkish n (language) turc m
▶ adj turc (f turque)

turn n ① (bend in road) tournant m; **'no left turn'** défense de tourner à gauche' ② (go) tour m ▷ It's my turn! C'est mon tour!
▶ vb ① tourner [28] ▷ Turn right at the lights. Tournez à droite aux feux. ② (become) devenir [25] ▷ to turn red devenir rouge; **to turn into something** se transformer [28] en quelque chose ▷ The frog turned into a prince. La grenouille s'est transformée en prince.

turn back vb faire [36] demi-tour ▷ We turned back. Nous avons fait demi-tour.

turn down vb ① (offer) refuser [28] ② (radio, TV, heating) baisser [28] ▷ Shall I turn the heating down? Je baisse le chauffage?

turn off vb ① (light, radio) éteindre [60] ② (tap) fermer [28] ③ (engine) arrêter [28]

turn on vb ① (light, radio) allumer [28] ② (tap) ouvrir [55] ③ (engine) mettre [47] en marche

turn out vb **It turned out to be a mistake.** Il s'est avéré que c'était une erreur.; **It turned out that she**

was right. Il s'est avéré qu'elle avait raison.

turn round vb ① (car) faire [36] demi-tour ② (person) se retourner [72]

turn up vb ① (arrive) arriver [5] ② (heater) monter [48]; **Could you turn up the radio?** Tu peux monter le son de la radio?

turning n **It's the third turning on the left.** C'est la troisième à gauche.; **We took the wrong turning.** Nous n'avons pas tourné au bon endroit.

turnip n navet m

turquoise adj (colour) turquoise

turtle n tortue f

tutor n (private teacher) professeur particulier m

TV n télé f

tweezers npl pince à épiler f sg

twelfth adj douzième ▷ the twelfth floor le douzième étage; **the twelfth of August** le douze août

twelve num douze ▷ She's twelve. Elle a douze ans.; **twelve o'clock** (1) (midday) midi (2) (midnight) minuit

twentieth adj vingtième ▷ the twentieth time la vingtième fois; **the twentieth of May** le vingt mai

twenty num vingt ▷ He's twenty. Il a vingt ans.

twice adv deux fois; **twice as much** deux fois plus ▷ He gets twice as much pocket money as me. Il a deux fois plus d'argent de poche que moi.

twin n jumeau m (mpl jumeaux), jumelle f; **my twin brother** mon

frère jumeau; **her twin sister** sa
sœur jumelle; **identical twins** les
vrais jumeaux; **a twin room** une
chambre à deux lits

twinned adj jumelé(e) ▷ Stroud is
twinned with Châteaubriant. Stroud
est jumelée avec Châteaubriant.

twist vb ❶ (bend) tordre [**49**]
❷ (distort) déformer [**28**] ▷ You're
twisting my words. Tu déformes ce
que j'ai dit.

Twitter® n Twitter®

two num deux ▷ She's two. Elle a
deux ans.

type n type m ▷ What type of camera
have you got? Quel type d'appareil
photo as-tu?
▶ vb taper [**28**] à la machine ▷ Can
you type? Tu sais taper à la
machine?; **to type a letter** taper
[**28**] une lettre

typewriter n machine à écrire f

typical adj typique ▷ That's just
typical! C'est typique!

tyre n pneu m; **the tyre pressure** la
pression des pneus

UFO n OVNI m (= objet volant non
identifié)

ugly adj laid(e)

UK n (= United Kingdom)
Royaume-Uni m; **from the UK** du
Royaume-Uni; **in the UK** au
Royaume-Uni; **to the UK** au
Royaume-Uni

ulcer n ulcère m; **a mouth ulcer** un
aphte

Ulster n Irlande du Nord f; **in
Ulster** en Irlande du Nord

umbrella n ❶ parapluie m ❷ (for
sun) parasol m

umpire n ❶ (in cricket) arbitre m
❷ (in tennis) juge de chaise m

UN n (= United Nations) ONU f
(= Organisation des Nations Unies)

unable adj **to be unable to do
something** ne pas pouvoir [**64**]

faire quelque chose ▷ *I was unable to come.* Je n'ai pas pu venir.

unanimous *adj* unanime ▷ *a unanimous decision* une décision unanime

unavoidable *adj* inévitable

unbearable *adj* insupportable

unbelievable *adj* incroyable

unbreakable *adj* incassable

uncertain *adj* incertain(e) ▷ *The future is uncertain.* L'avenir est incertain.; **to be uncertain about something** ne pas être [**35**] sûr de quelque chose

uncle *n* oncle *m* ▷ *my uncle* mon oncle

uncomfortable *adj* pas confortable ▷ *The seats are rather uncomfortable.* Les sièges ne sont pas très confortables.

unconscious *adj* sans connaissance

uncontrollable *adj* incontrôlable

under *prep* ❶ sous ▷ *The cat's under the table.* Le chat est sous la table. ▷ *The tunnel goes under the Channel.* Le tunnel passe sous la Manche.; **under there** là-dessous ▷ *What's under there?* Qu'est-ce qu'il y a là-dessous? ❷ *(less than)* moins de ▷ *under 20 people* moins de vingt personnes ▷ *children under 10* les enfants de moins de dix ans

underage *adj* **He's underage.** Il n'a pas l'âge réglementaire.

underground *adj, adv* ❶ souterrain(e) ▷ *an underground car park* un parking souterrain ❷ sous terre ▷ *Moles live underground.* Les taupes vivent sous terre.
▶ *n* métro *m* ▷ *Is there an underground in Lille?* Est-ce qu'il y a un métro à Lille?

underline *vb* souligner [**28**]

underneath *prep, adv* ❶ sous ▷ *underneath the carpet* sous la moquette ❷ dessous ▷ *I got out of the car and looked underneath.* Je suis descendu de la voiture et j'ai regardé dessous.

underpants *npl* slip *msg*

underpass *n* ❶ *(for people)* passage souterrain *m* ❷ *(for cars)* passage inférieur *m*

undershirt *n (US)* maillot de corps *m*

understand *vb* comprendre [**65**] ▷ *Do you understand?* Vous comprenez? ▷ *I don't understand this word.* Je ne comprends pas ce mot. ▷ *Is that understood?* C'est compris?

understanding *adj* compréhensif *(f* compréhensive*)* ▷ *She's very understanding.* Elle est très compréhensive.

understood *vb see* **understand**

undertaker *n* entrepreneur des pompes funèbres *m*

underwater *adj, adv* sous l'eau ▷ *This sequence was filmed underwater.* Cette séquence a été filmée sous l'eau.; **an underwater camera** un appareil photographique de plongée; **underwater photography** la photographie subaquatique

underwear *n* sous-vêtements *mpl*

a
b
c
d
e
f
g
h
i
j
k
l
m
n
o
p
q
r
s
t
u
v
w
x
y
z

undo vb ❶ (buttons, knot) défaire [36] ❷ (parcel) déballer [28]

undress vb (get undressed) se déshabiller [28] ▷ The doctor told me to undress. Le médecin m'a dit de me déshabiller.

unemployed adj au chômage ▷ He's unemployed. Il est au chômage.; **the unemployed** les chômeurs mpl

unemployment n chômage m

unexpected adj inattendu(e) ▷ an unexpected visitor un visiteur inattendu

unexpectedly adv à l'improviste ▷ They arrived unexpectedly. Ils sont arrivés à l'improviste.

unfair adj injuste ▷ It's unfair to girls. C'est injuste pour les filles.

unfamiliar adj I heard an unfamiliar voice. J'ai entendu une voix que je ne connaissais pas.

unfashionable adj démodé(e)

unfit adj I'm rather unfit. Je ne suis pas en très bonne condition physique.

unfold vb déplier [19] ▷ She unfolded the map. Elle a déplié la carte.

unforgettable adj inoubliable

unfortunately adv malheureusement ▷ Unfortunately, I arrived late. Malheureusement, je suis arrivé en retard.

unfriendly adj pas aimable ▷ The waiters are a bit unfriendly. Les serveurs ne sont pas très aimables.

ungrateful adj ingrat(e)

unhappy adj malheureux (f malheureuse) ▷ He was very

unhappy as a child. Il était très malheureux quand il était petit.; **to look unhappy** avoir [8] l'air triste

unhealthy adj ❶ (person) maladif maladive) ❷ (place, habit) malsain(e) ❸ (food) pas sain(e)

uni n (university) fac f ▷ to go to uni aller à la fac

uniform n uniforme m ▷ school uniform l'uniforme scolaire

uninhabited adj inhabité(e)

union n (trade union) syndicat m

Union Jack n drapeau du Royaume-Uni m

unique adj unique

unit n ❶ unité f ▷ a unit of measurement une unité de mesure ❷ (piece of furniture) élément m ▷ a kitchen unit un élément de cuisine

United Kingdom n Royaume-Uni m

United Nations n Nations Unies fpl

United States n États-Unis mpl; **in the United States** aux États-Unis; **to the United States** aux États-Unis

universe n univers m

university n université f ▷ She's at university. Elle va à l'université. ▷ Do you want to go to university? Tu veux aller à l'université?

unleaded petrol n essence sans plomb f

unless conj unless he leaves à moins qu'il ne parte ▷ I won't come unless you phone me. Je ne viendrai pas à moins que tu ne me téléphones.

unlikely adj peu probable ▷ *It's possible, but unlikely.* C'est possible, mais peu probable.

unload vb décharger [**45**] ▷ *We unloaded the car.* Nous avons déchargé la voiture. ▷ *The lorries go there to unload.* Les camions y vont pour être déchargés.

unlock vb ouvrir [**55**] ▷ *He unlocked the door of the car.* Il a ouvert la portière de la voiture.

unlucky adj **to be unlucky**
(**1**) *(number, object)* porter [**28**] malheur ▷ *They say thirteen is an unlucky number.* On dit que le nombre treize porte malheur. (**2**) *(person)* ne pas avoir [**8**] de chance ▷ *Did you win? — No, I was unlucky.* Vous avez gagné? — Non, je n'ai pas eu de chance.

unmarried adj *(person)* célibataire ▷ *an unmarried mother* une mère célibataire; **an unmarried couple** un couple non marié

unnatural adj pas naturel (f pas naturelle)

unnecessary adj inutile

unpack vb ❶ défaire [**36**] ▷ *I unpacked my suitcase.* J'ai défait ma valise. ❷ déballer [**28**] ses affaires ▷ *I went to my room to unpack.* Je suis allé dans ma chambre pour déballer mes affaires. ▷ *I haven't unpacked my clothes yet.* Je n'ai pas encore déballé mes affaires.

unpleasant adj désagréable

unplug vb débrancher [**28**]

unpopular adj impopulaire

unrealistic adj peu réaliste

unreasonable adj pas raisonnable ▷ *Her attitude was completely unreasonable.* Son attitude n'était pas du tout raisonnable.

unreliable adj *(car, machine)* pas fiable ▷ *It's a nice car, but a bit unreliable.* C'est une belle voiture, mais elle n'est pas très fiable.; **He's completely unreliable.** On ne peut pas du tout compter sur lui.

unroll vb dérouler [**28**]

unscrew vb dévisser [**28**] ▷ *She unscrewed the top of the bottle.* Elle a dévissé le bouchon de la bouteille.

unsuccessful adj *(attempt)* vain(e); **to be unsuccessful in doing something** ne pas réussir [**38**] à faire quelque chose ▷ *an unsuccessful artist* un artiste qui n'a pas réussi

unsuitable adj *(clothes, equipment)* inapproprié(e)

untidy adj ❶ en désordre ▷ *My bedroom's always untidy.* Ma chambre est toujours en désordre. ❷ *(appearance, person)* débraillé(e) ▷ *He's always untidy.* Il est toujours débraillé. ❸ *(in character)* désordonné(e) ▷ *He's a very untidy person.* Il est très désordonné.

untie vb ❶ *(knot, parcel)* défaire [**36**] ❷ *(animal)* détacher [**28**]

until prep, conj ❶ jusqu'à ▷ *I waited until ten o'clock.* J'ai attendu jusqu'à dix heures.; **until now** jusqu'à présent ▷ *It's never been a problem* *until now.* Ça n'a jamais été un problème jusqu'à présent.; **until then** jusque-là ▷ *Until then I'd never been to France.* Jusque-là je n'étais jamais allé en France. ❷ avant

Use **avant** if the sentence you want to translate contains a negative, such as 'not' or 'never' ▷ *It won't be ready until next week.* Ça ne sera pas prêt avant la semaine prochaine.

unusual *adj* ❶ insolite ▷ *an unusual shape* une forme insolite ❷ rare ▷ *It's unusual to get snow at this time of year.* Il est rare qu'il neige à cette époque de l'année.

unwilling *adj* **to be unwilling to do something** ne pas être [**35**] disposé à faire quelque chose ▷ *He was unwilling to help me.* Il n'était pas disposé à m'aider.

unwrap *vb* déballer [**28**] ▷ *After the meal we unwrapped the presents.* Après le repas nous avons déballé les cadeaux.

up *prep, adv*

For other expressions with 'up', see the verbs 'go', 'come', 'put', 'turn' etc.

en haut ▷ *up on the hill* en haut de la colline; **up here** ici; **up there** là-haut; **up north** dans le nord; **to be up** *(out of bed)* être [**35**] levé ▷ *We were up at 6.* Nous étions levés à six heures. ▷ *He's not up yet.* Il n'est pas encore levé.; **What's up?** Qu'est-ce qu'il y a? ▷ *What's up with her?* Qu'est-ce qu'elle a?; **to get up** *(in the morning)* se lever [**43**] ▷ *What time do you get up?* À quelle heure est-ce que tu te lèves?; **to go up** monter [**48**] ▷ *The bus went up the hill.* Le bus a monté la colline.; **to go up to somebody** s'approcher [**28**] de quelqu'un ▷ *She came up to me.* Elle s'est approchée de moi.; **up to** *(as far as)* jusqu'à ▷ *to count up to fifty* compter jusqu'à cinquante ▷ *up to now* jusqu'à présent; **It's up to you.** C'est à vous de décider.

uphill *adv* **to go uphill** monter [**48**]

upper *adj* supérieur(e) ▷ *on the upper floor* à l'étage supérieur

upper sixth *n* **the upper sixth** la terminale ▷ *She's in the upper sixth.* Elle est en terminale.

upright *adj* **to stand upright** se tenir [**83**] droit

upset *n* **a stomach upset** une indigestion

▸ *adj* contrarié(e) ▷ *She's still a bit upset.* Elle est encore un peu contrariée.; **I had an upset stomach.** J'avais l'estomac dérangé.

▸ *vb* **to upset somebody** contrarier [**19**] quelqu'un

upside down *adv* à l'envers ▷ *That painting is upside down.* Ce tableau est à l'envers.

upstairs *adv* en haut ▷ *Where's your coat? — It's upstairs.* Où est ton manteau? — Il est en haut.; **to go upstairs** monter [**48**]

up-to-date *adj* ❶ *(car, stereo)* moderne ❷ *(information)* à jour ▷ *an up-to-date timetable* un horaire à jour; **to bring something up to**

date moderniser [**28**] quelque chose

upwards adv vers le haut ▷ to look upwards regarder vers le haut

urgent adj urgent(e) ▷ Is it urgent? C'est urgent?

US n USA mpl

us pron nous ▷ They helped us. Ils nous ont aidés.

USA n USA mpl

use n It's no use. Ça ne sert à rien. ▷ It's no use shouting, she's deaf. Ça ne sert à rien de crier, elle est sourde.; **It's no use, I can't do it.** Il n'y a rien à faire, je n'y arrive pas.; **to make use of something** utiliser [**28**] quelque chose

▶ vb utiliser [**28**] ▷ Can we use a dictionary in the exam? Est-ce qu'on peut utiliser un dictionnaire à l'examen?; **Can I use your phone?** Je peux téléphoner?; **to use the toilet** aller [**3**] aux W.C.; **I used to live in London.** J'habitais à Londres autrefois.; **I used not to like maths, but now …** Avant, je n'aimais pas les maths, mais maintenant …; **to be used to something** avoir [**8**] l'habitude de quelque chose ▷ He wasn't used to driving on the right. Il n'avait pas l'habitude de conduire à droite. ▷ Don't worry, I'm used to it. Ne t'inquiète pas, j'ai l'habitude.; **a used car** une voiture d'occasion

use up vb ❶ finir [**38**] ▷ We've used up all the paint. Nous avons fini la peinture. ❷ (money) dépenser [**28**]

useful adj utile

useless adj nul (f nulle) ▷ This map is just useless. Cette carte est vraiment nulle. ▷ You're useless! Tu es nul!; **It's useless!** Ça ne sert à rien!

user n utilisateur m, utilisatrice f

user-friendly adj facile à utiliser

username n nom d'utilisateur m

usual adj habituel (f habituelle); **as usual** comme d'habitude

usually adv ❶ (generally) en général ▷ I usually get to school at about half past eight. En général, j'arrive à l'école vers huit heures et demie. ❷ (when making a contrast) d'habitude ▷ Usually I don't wear make-up, but today is a special occasion. D'habitude je ne me maquille pas, mais aujourd'hui c'est spécial.

a
b
c
d
e
f
g
h
i
j
k
l
m
n
o
p
q
r
s
t
u
v
w
x
y
z

V

vacancy n **1** (job) poste vacant m
2 (room in hotel) chambre
disponible f; **'no vacancies'** (on
sign) 'complet'
vacant adj libre
vacation n (US) vacances fpl ▷ to be
on vacation être en vacances ▷ to
take a vacation prendre des vacances
vaccinate vb vacciner [**28**]
vacuum vb passer [**58**] l'aspirateur
▷ to vacuum the hall passer
l'aspirateur dans le couloir
vacuum cleaner n aspirateur m
vagina n vagin m
vague adj vague
vain adj vaniteux (f vaniteuse)
▷ He's so vain! Qu'est-ce qu'il est
vaniteux!; **in vain** en vain
Valentine card n carte de la
Saint-Valentin f

Valentine's Day n Saint-Valentin
valid adj valable ▷ This ticket is valid
for three months. Ce billet est
valable trois mois.
valley n vallée f
valuable adj **1** de valeur
▷ a valuable picture un tableau de
valeur **2** précieux (f précieuse)
▷ valuable help une aide précieuse
value n valeur f
van n camionnette f
vandal n vandale mf
vandalism n vandalisme m
vandalize vb saccager [**45**]
vanilla n vanille f ▷ vanilla ice cream
la glace à la vanille
vanish vb disparaître [**56**]
vape vb vapoter [**28**]
vaping n vapotage m, vape f
variety n variété f
various adj plusieurs ▷ We visited
various villages in the area. Nous avons
visité plusieurs villages de la région.
vary vb varier [**19**]
vase n vase m
VAT n (= value added tax) TVA f (= taxe
sur la valeur ajoutée)
VCR n (= video cassette recorder)
magnétoscope m
VDU n (= visual display unit)
moniteur m
veal n veau m
vegan n végétalien m, végétalienne
f ▷ I'm a vegan. Je suis végétalien.
vegetable n légume m ▷ vegetable
soup la soupe aux légumes
vegetarian adj végétarien (f
végétarienne) ▷ I'm vegetarian. Je
suis végétarien. ▷ vegetarian

lasagne les lasagnes végétariennes *fpl*
▸ *n* végétarien *m*, végétarienne *f*
▷ *I'm a vegetarian.* Je suis végétarien.
vehicle *n* véhicule *m*
vein *n* veine *f*
velvet *n* velours *m*
vending machine *n* distributeur automatique *m*
verb *n* verbe *m*
verdict *n* verdict *m*
vertical *adj* vertical(e) (*mpl* verticaux)
vertigo *n* vertige *m* ▷ *I get vertigo.* J'ai le vertige.
very *adv* très ▷ *very tall* très grand ▷ *not very interesting* pas très intéressant; **very much** beaucoup
vest *n* ❶ (*underclothing*) maillot de corps *m* ❷ (*US: waistcoat*) gilet *m*
vet *n* vétérinaire *mf* ▷ *She's a vet.* Elle est vétérinaire.
via *prep* en passant par ▷ *We went to Paris via Boulogne.* Nous sommes allés à Paris en passant par Boulogne.
vicar *n* pasteur *m* ▷ *He's a vicar.* Il est pasteur.
vicious *adj* ❶ brutal(e) (*mpl* brutaux) ▷ *a vicious attack* une agression brutale ❷ (*dog, person*) méchant(e); **a vicious circle** un cercle vicieux
victim *n* victime *f* ▷ *He was the victim of a mugging.* Il a été victime d'une agression.
victory *n* victoire *f*
video *vb* ❶ (*from TV*) enregistrer [28] ❷ (*with video camera*) filmer [28]

▸ *n* ❶ (*film*) vidéo *f* ▷ *to watch a video* regarder une vidéo ▷ *a video of my family on holiday* une vidéo de ma famille en vacances ❷ (*video cassette*) cassette vidéo *f* ▷ *She lent me a video.* Elle m'a prêté une cassette vidéo. ❸ (*video recorder*) magnétoscope *m*; **a video camera** une caméra vidéo; **a video game** un jeu vidéo ▷ *He likes playing video games.* Il aime les jeux vidéo.; **a video recorder** un magnétoscope; **a video shop** un vidéoclub
Vietnam *n* Viêt-Nam *m*; **in Vietnam** au Viêt-Nam
Vietnamese *adj* vietnamien (*f* vietnamienne)
view *n* ❶ vue *f* ▷ *There's an amazing view.* Il y a une vue extraordinaire. ❷ (*opinion*) avis *m* ▷ *in my view* à mon avis
viewer *n* téléspectateur *m*, téléspectatrice *f*
viewpoint *n* point de vue *m*
vile *adj* (*smell, food*) dégoûtant(e)
villa *n* villa *f*
village *n* village *m*
vine *n* vigne *f*
vinegar *n* vinaigre *m*
vineyard *n* vignoble *m*
viola *n* alto *m* ▷ *I play the viola.* Je joue de l'alto.
violence *n* violence *f*
violent *adj* violent(e)
violin *n* violon *m* ▷ *I play the violin.* Je joue du violon.
violinist *n* violoniste *mf*
virgin *n* vierge *f* ▷ *to be a virgin* être vierge

Virgo n Vierge f ▷ I'm Virgo. Je suis Vierge.

virtual reality n réalité virtuelle f

virus n (also computing) virus m

visa n visa m

visible adj visible

visit n ❶ (to museum) visite f ❷ (to country) séjour m ▷ Did you enjoy your visit to France? Ton séjour en France s'est bien passé?; **my last visit to my grandmother** la dernière fois que je suis allé voir ma grand-mère
▶ vb ❶ (person) rendre [7] visite à ▷ to visit somebody rendre visite à quelqu'un ❷ (place) visiter [28] ▷ We'd like to visit the castle. Nous voudrions visiter le château.

visitor n ❶ (tourist) visiteur m, visiteuse f ❷ (guest) invité m, invitée f; **to have a visitor** avoir [8] de la visite

visual adj visuel (f visuelle)

vital adj vital(e) (mpl vitaux)

vitamin n vitamine f

vivid adj (colour) vif (f vive); **to have a vivid imagination** avoir [8] une imagination débordante

vocabulary n vocabulaire m

vocational adj professionnel (f professionnelle); **a vocational course** un stage de formation professionnelle

vodka n vodka f

voice n voix f (pl voix)

voice mail n boîte vocale f

volcano n volcan m

volleyball n volley-ball m ▷ to play volleyball jouer au volley-ball

voluntary adj (contribution, statement) volontaire; **to do voluntary work** travailler [28] bénévolement

volunteer n volontaire mf
▶ vb **to volunteer to do something** se proposer [28] pour faire quelque chose

vomit vb vomir [38]

vote vb voter [28]

voucher n bon m ▷ a gift voucher un bon d'achat

vowel n voyelle f

vulgar adj vulgaire

W

wage n salaire m ▷ *He collected his wages.* Il a retiré son salaire.

waist n taille f

waistcoat n gilet m

wait vb attendre [7]; **to wait for something** attendre [7] quelque chose; **to wait for somebody** attendre [7] quelqu'un ▷ *I'll wait for you.* Je t'attendrai.; **Wait for me!** Attends-moi!; **Wait a minute!** Attends!; **to keep somebody waiting** faire [36] attendre quelqu'un ▷ *They kept us waiting for hours.* Ils nous ont fait attendre pendant des heures.; **I can't wait for the holidays.** J'ai hâte d'être en vacances.; **I can't wait to see him again.** J'ai hâte de le revoir.

wait up vb attendre [7] pour se coucher

waiter n serveur m; **Waiter!** Excusez-moi!

waiting list n liste d'attente f

waiting room n salle d'attente f

waitress n serveuse f

wake up vb se réveiller [28] ▷ *I woke up at six o'clock.* Je me suis réveillé à six heures.; **to wake somebody up** réveiller [28] quelqu'un ▷ *Please would you wake me up at seven o'clock?* Pourriez-vous me réveiller à sept heures?

Wales n pays de Galles m; **in Wales** au pays de Galles; **to Wales** au pays de Galles; **I'm from Wales.** Je suis gallois.; **the Prince of Wales** le prince de Galles

walk vb ❶ marcher [28] ▷ *He walks fast.* Il marche vite. ❷ (go on foot) aller [3] à pied ▷ *We walked 10 kilometres.* Nous avons fait dix kilomètres à pied.; **to walk the dog** promener [43] le chien ▶ n promenade f ▷ *to go for a walk* faire une promenade; **It's 10 minutes' walk from here.** C'est à dix minutes d'ici à pied.

walking n randonnée f ▷ *I did some walking in the Alps last summer.* J'ai fait de la randonnée dans les Alpes l'été dernier.

walking stick n canne f

Walkman® n baladeur m

wall n mur m

wallet n portefeuille m

wallpaper n ❶ papier peint m ❷ (for phone, PC) fond d'écran m

walnut n noix f (pl noix)

wander vb **to wander around**

flâner [**28**] ▷ *I just wandered around for a while.* J'ai flâné un peu.

want vb vouloir [**93**] ▷ *Do you want some cake?* Tu veux du gâteau?; **to want to do something** vouloir [**93**] faire quelque chose ▷ *I want to go to the cinema.* Je veux aller au cinéma.

war n guerre f

ward n (room in hospital) salle f

wardrobe n (piece of furniture) armoire f

warehouse n entrepôt m

warm adj ❶ chaud(e) ▷ *warm water* l'eau chaude; **It's warm in here.** Il fait chaud ici.; **to be warm** (person) avoir [**8**] chaud ▷ *I'm too warm.* J'ai trop chaud. ❷ chaleureux (f chaleureuse) ▷ *a warm welcome* un accueil chaleureux

warm up vb ❶ (for sport) s'échauffer [**28**] ❷ (food) réchauffer [**28**] ▷ *I'll warm up some lasagne for you.* Je vais te réchauffer des lasagnes.

warn vb prévenir [**89**] ▷ *Well, I warned you!* Je t'avais prévenu!; **to warn somebody to do something** conseiller [**28**] à quelqu'un de faire quelque chose

warning n avertissement m

wart n verrue f

was vb see be

wash n **to have a wash** se laver [**28**] ▷ *I had a wash.* Je me suis lavé.; **to give something a wash** laver [**28**] quelque chose ▷ *He gave the car a wash.* Il a lavé la voiture.
▶ vb ❶ laver [**28**] ▷ *to wash*

something laver quelque chose ❷ (have a wash) se laver [**28**] ▷ *Every morning I get up, wash and get dressed.* Tous les matins je me lève, je me lave et je m'habille.; **to wash one's hands** se laver [**28**] les mains; **to wash one's hair** se laver [**28**] les cheveux

wash up vb faire [**36**] la vaisselle

washbasin n lavabo m

washcloth n (US) gant de toilette m

washing n linge m ▷ *dirty washing* du linge sale; **Have you got any washing?** Tu as du linge à laver?; **to do the washing** faire [**36**] la lessive

washing machine n machine à laver f

washing powder n lessive f

washing-up n **to do the washing-up** faire [**36**] la vaisselle

washing-up liquid n produit à vaisselle m

wasn't = was not

wasp n guêpe f

waste n ❶ gaspillage m ▷ *It's such a waste!* C'est vraiment du gaspillage!; **It's a waste of time.** C'est une perte de temps. ❷ (rubbish) déchets mpl ▷ *nuclear waste* les déchets nucléaires
▶ vb gaspiller [**28**] ▷ *I don't like wasting money.* Je n'aime pas gaspiller de l'argent.; **to waste time** perdre [**61**] du temps ▷ *There's no time to waste.* Il n'y a pas de temps à perdre.

wastepaper basket n corbeille à papier f

watch n montre f
▶ vb ❶ regarder [28] ▷ to watch
television regarder la télévision
▷ Watch me! Regarde-moi! ❷ (keep a
watch on) surveiller [28] ▷ The police
were watching the house. La police
surveillait la maison.
watch out vb faire [36] attention;
Watch out! Attention!
water n eau f
▶ vb arroser [28] ▷ He was watering
his tulips. Il arrosait ses tulipes.
waterfall n cascade f
watering can n arrosoir m
watermelon n pastèque f
waterproof adj imperméable ▷ Is
this jacket waterproof? Ce blouson
est-il imperméable?; **a waterproof
watch** une montre étanche
water-skiing n ski nautique m ▷ to
go water-skiing faire du ski nautique
wave n ❶ (in water) vague f ❷ (of
hand) signe m ▷ We gave him a wave.
Nous lui avons fait signe.
▶ vb faire [36] un signe de la main
▷ to wave at somebody faire un signe
de la main à quelqu'un; **to wave
goodbye** faire [36] au revoir de la
main ▷ I waved her goodbye. Je lui ai
fait au revoir de la main.
wax n cire f
way n ❶ (manner) façon f ▷ She
looked at me in a strange way. Elle m'a
regardé d'une façon étrange.; **This
book tells you the right way to
do it.** Ce livre explique comment il
faut faire.; **You're doing it the
wrong way.** Ce n'est pas comme ça
qu'il faut faire.; **in a way ...** dans un

sens ...; **a way of life** un mode de
vie ❷ (route) chemin m ▷ I don't
know the way. Je ne connais pas le
chemin.; **on the way** en chemin
▷ We stopped on the way. Nous nous
sommes arrêtés en chemin.; **It's a
long way.** C'est loin. ▷ Paris is a long
way from London. Paris est loin de
Londres.; **Which way is it?** C'est
par où?; **The supermarket is this
way.** Le supermarché est par ici.;
**Do you know the way to the
station?** Vous savez comment aller
à la gare?; **He's on his way.** Il
arrive.; **'way in'** 'entrée'; **'way out'**
'sortie'; **by the way ...** au fait ...
we pron nous ▷ We're staying here for
a week. Nous restons une semaine
ici.
weak adj faible
wealthy adj riche
weapon n arme f
wear vb (clothes) porter [28] ▷ She
was wearing a hat. Elle portait un
chapeau.; **She was wearing
black.** Elle était en noir.
weather n temps m ▷ What was the
weather like? Quel temps a-t-il fait?
▷ The weather was lovely. Il a fait un
temps magnifique.
weather forecast n météo f
web n ❶ (spider) toile f ❷ (World Wide
Web) web m
web address n adresse web f
web browser n navigateur m
webcam n webcam f
website n site web m
we'd = we had; we would
wedding n mariage m; wedding

anniversary l'anniversaire de mariage *m*; **wedding dress** la robe de mariée

Wednesday *n* mercredi *m* ▷ *on Wednesday* mercredi ▷ *on Wednesdays* le mercredi ▷ *every Wednesday* tous les mercredis ▷ *last Wednesday* mercredi dernier ▷ *next Wednesday* mercredi prochain

weed *n* mauvaise herbe *f* ▷ *The garden's full of weeds.* Le jardin est plein de mauvaises herbes.

week *n* semaine *f* ▷ *last week* la semaine dernière ▷ *every week* toutes les semaines ▷ *next week* la semaine prochaine ▷ *in a week's time* dans une semaine; **a week on Friday** vendredi en huit

weekday *n* **on weekdays** en semaine

weekend *n* week-end *m* ▷ *at weekends* le week-end ▷ *last weekend* le week-end dernier ▷ *next weekend* le week-end prochain

weigh *vb* peser [**43**] ▷ *How much do you weigh?* Combien est-ce que tu pèses?; **to weigh oneself** se peser [**43**]

weight *n* poids *m*; **to lose weight** maigrir [**38**]; **to put on weight** grossir [**38**]

weightlifting *n* haltérophilie *f*

weird *adj* bizarre

welcome *n* accueil *m* ▷ *They gave her a warm welcome.* Ils lui ont fait un accueil chaleureux.; **Welcome!** Bienvenue! ▷ *Welcome to France!* Bienvenue en France!
  ▸ *vb* **to welcome somebody**

accueillir [**22**] quelqu'un; **Thank you! — You're welcome!** Merci! — De rien!

well *adj, adv* ❶ bien ▷ *You did that really well.* Tu as très bien fait ça.; **to do well** réussir [**38**] bien ▷ *She's doing really well at school.* Elle réussit vraiment bien à l'école.; **to be well** (*in good health*) aller [**3**] bien ▷ *I'm not very well at the moment.* Je ne vais pas très bien en ce moment.; **get well soon!** remets-toi vite!; **well done!** bravo! ❷ enfin ▷ *It's enormous! Well, quite big anyway.* C'est énorme! Enfin, c'est assez grand.; **as well** aussi ▷ *I decided to have dessert as well.* J'ai décidé de prendre aussi un dessert. ▷ *We went to Chartres as well as Paris.* Nous sommes allés à Paris et à Chartres aussi.
  ▸ *n* puits *m* (*pl* puits)

we'll = we will

well-behaved *adj* sage

wellingtons *npl* bottes en caoutchouc *fpl*

well-known *adj* célèbre ▷ *a well-known film star* une vedette de cinéma célèbre

well-off *adj* aisé(e)

Welsh *n* (*language*) gallois *m*
  ▸ *adj* gallois(e) ▷ *She's Welsh.* Elle est galloise.; **Welsh people** les Gallois *mpl*

Welshman *n* Gallois *m*

Welshwoman *n* Galloise *f*

went *vb see* go

were *vb see* be

we're = we are

weren't = were not

west n ouest m ▷ in the west dans l'ouest
▶ adj, adv ❶ ouest ▷ the west coast la côte ouest; **west of** à l'ouest de ▷ Stroud is west of Oxford. Stroud est à l'ouest d'Oxford. ❷ vers l'ouest ▷ We were travelling west. Nous allions vers l'ouest.; **the West Country** le sud-ouest de l'Angleterre

westbound adj **The truck was westbound on the M5.** Le camion roulait sur la M5 en direction de l'ouest.; **Westbound traffic is moving very slowly.** La circulation en direction de l'ouest est très ralentie.

western n (film) western m
▶ adj **the western part of the island** la partie ouest de l'île; **Western Europe** l'Europe de l'Ouest

West Indian n (person) Antillais m, Antillaise f
▶ adj antillais(e) ▷ She's West Indian. Elle est antillaise.

West Indies npl Antilles fpl; **in the West Indies** aux Antilles

wet adj mouillé(e) ▷ wet clothes les vêtements mouillés; **to get wet** se faire [36] mouiller; **dripping wet** trempé; **wet weather** le temps pluvieux; **It was wet all week.** Il a plu toute la semaine.

wetsuit n combinaison de plongée f

we've = we have

whale n baleine f

what adj, pron ❶ (which) quel (f quelle) ▷ What colour is it? C'est de quelle couleur? ▷ What's the capital of Finland? Quelle est la capitale de la Finlande? ▷ What a mess! Quel fouillis! ❷ qu'est-ce que ▷ What are you doing? Qu'est-ce que vous faites? ▷ What did you say? Qu'est-ce que vous avez dit? ▷ What is it? Qu'est-ce que c'est? ▷ What's the matter? Qu'est-ce qu'il y a? ❸ qu'est-ce qui ▷ What happened? Qu'est-ce qui s'est passé?

> In relative phrases use **ce qui** or **ce que** depending on whether 'what' refers to the subject or the object of the sentence.

❹ (subject) ce qui ▷ I saw what happened. J'ai vu ce qui est arrivé.; (object) ce que ▷ Tell me what you did. Dites-moi ce que vous avez fait.; **What?** (what did you say) Comment?

wheat n blé m

wheel n roue f; **the steering wheel** le volant

wheelchair n fauteuil roulant m

when adv, conj quand ▷ When did he go? Quand est-ce qu'il est parti? ▷ She was reading when I came in. Elle lisait quand je suis entré.

where adv, conj où ▷ Where's Emma today? Où est Emma aujourd'hui? ▷ Where do you live? Où habites-tu?

whether conj si ▷ I don't know whether to go or not. Je ne sais pas si je dois y aller ou non.

which adj, pron ❶ quel (f quelle) ▷ Which flavour do you want? Quel

a
b
c
d
e
f
g
h
i
j
k
l
m
n
o
p
q
r
s
t
u
v
w
x
y
z

parfum est-ce que tu veux?

> When asking 'which one' use **lequel** or **laquelle**, depending on whether the noun is masculine or feminine.

I know his brother. — Which one? Je connais son frère. — Lequel?; **I know his sister. — Which one?** Je connais sa sœur. — Laquelle?; **Which would you like?** Lequel est-ce que vous voulez?; **Which of these are yours?** Lesquels sont à vous?

> In relative phrases use **qui** or **que** depending on whether 'which' refers to the subject or the object of the sentence.

❷ (*subject*) qui ▷ *the CD which is playing now* le CD qui passe maintenant; (*object*) que ▷ *the CD which I bought yesterday* le CD que j'ai acheté hier

while *conj* ❶ pendant que ▷ *You hold the torch while I look inside.* Tiens la lampe électrique pendant que je regarde à l'intérieur. ❷ alors que ▷ *Isobel is very dynamic, while Kay is more laid-back.* Isobel est très dynamique, alors que Kay est plus relax.
▶ *n* moment *m* ▷ *after a while* au bout d'un moment; **a while ago** il y a un moment ▷ *He was here a while ago.* Il était là il y a un moment.; **for a while** pendant quelque temps ▷ *I lived in London for a while.* J'ai vécu à Londres pendant quelque temps.; **quite a while** longtemps ▷ *quite a while ago* il y a longtemps

whip *n* fouet *m*
▶ *vb* ❶ (*person, animal*) fouetter [28]
❷ (*eggs*) battre [9]
whipped cream *n* crème fouettée *f*
whiskers *npl* moustaches *fpl*
whisky *n* whisky *m* (*pl* whiskies)
whisper *vb* chuchoter [28]
whistle *n* sifflet *m*; **The referee blew his whistle.** L'arbitre a sifflé.
▶ *vb* siffler [28]
white *adj* blanc (*f* blanche) ▷ *He's got white hair.* Il a les cheveux blancs.; **white wine** le vin blanc; **white bread** le pain blanc; **white coffee** le café au lait; **a white man** un Blanc; **a white woman** une Blanche; **white people** les Blancs
whiteboard *n* tableau blanc *m*
Whitsun *n* Pentecôte *f*
who *pron* ❶ qui ▷ *Who said that?* Qui a dit ça?

> In relative phrases use **qui** or **que** depending on whether 'who' refers to the subject or the object of the verb.

❷ (*subject*) qui ▷ *the man who saw us* l'homme qui nous a vus; (*object*) que ▷ *the man who we saw* l'homme que nous avons vu
whole *adj* tout(e) ▷ *the whole class* toute la classe ▷ *the whole afternoon* tout l'après-midi; **a whole box of chocolates** toute une boîte de chocolats; **the whole world** le monde entier
▶ *n* **The whole of Wales was affected.** Le pays de Galles tout entier a été touché.; **on the whole** dans l'ensemble

wholemeal adj complet (f
complète); **wholemeal bread** le
pain complet

wholewheat adj (US) complet (f
complète)

whom pron qui ▷ Whom did you see?
Qui avez-vous vu? ▷ the man to
whom I spoke l'homme à qui j'ai
parlé

whose pron, adj ❶ à qui ▷ Whose is
this? À qui est-ce? ▷ I know whose it
is. Je sais à qui c'est. ❷ (after noun)
dont ▷ the girl whose picture was in
the paper la jeune fille dont la photo
était dans le journal

why adv pourquoi ▷ Why did you do
that? Pourquoi avez-vous fait ça?
▷ That's why he did it. Voilà pourquoi
il a fait ça. ▷ Tell me why. Dis-moi
pourquoi.; **I've never been to
France. — Why not?** Je ne suis
jamais allé en France. — Pourquoi?;
All right, why not? D'accord,
pourquoi pas?

wicked adj ❶ (evil) méchant(e)
❷ (really great) génial(e) (mpl
géniaux)

wide adj, adv large ▷ a wide road une
route large; **wide open** grand
ouvert ▷ The door was wide open. La
porte était grande ouverte.; **wide
awake** complètement réveillé

widow n veuve f ▷ She's a widow. Elle
est veuve.

widower n veuf m ▷ He's a widower.
Il est veuf.

width n largeur f

wife n femme f ▷ She's his wife. C'est
sa femme.

Wi-Fi n wifi m

wig n perruque f

wild adj ❶ (not tame) sauvage
▷ a wild animal un animal sauvage
❷ (crazy) fou (f folle) ▷ She's a bit
wild. Elle est un peu folle.

wildlife n nature f ▷ I'm interested in
wildlife. Je m'intéresse à la nature.

will n testament m ▷ He left me some
money in his will. Il m'a laissé de
l'argent dans son testament.
▶ vb **I'll show you your room.** Je
vais te montrer ta chambre.; **I'll
give you a hand.** Je vais t'aider.

Use the French future tense
when referring to the more
distant future.

I will finish it tomorrow. Je le
finirai demain.; **It won't take
long.** Ça ne prendra pas
longtemps.; **Will you wash up?
— No, I won't.** Est-ce que tu peux
faire la vaisselle? — Non.; **Will you
help me?** Est-ce que tu peux
m'aider?; **Will you be quiet!**
Voulez-vous bien vous taire!; **That
will be the postman.** Ça doit être
le facteur.

willing adj **to be willing to do
something** être [35] prêt à faire
quelque chose

win vb gagner [28] ▷ Did you win?
Est-ce que tu as gagné?; **to win a
prize** remporter [28] un prix
▶ n victoire f

wind vb ❶ (rope, wool, wire) enrouler
[28] ❷ (river, path) serpenter [28]
▷ The road winds through the valley.
La route serpente à travers la vallée.

▶ n vent m ▷ There was a strong wind.
Il y avait beaucoup de vent.; **a
wind instrument** un instrument à
vent; **wind power** l'énergie
éolienne f

window n ❶ (of building) fenêtre f
❷ (in car, train) vitre f; **a shop
window** une vitrine ❸ (window
pane) carreau m (pl carreaux) ▷ to
break a window casser un carreau
▷ a broken window un carreau cassé

windscreen n pare-brise m (pl
pare-brise)

windscreen wiper n essuie-glace
m (pl essuie-glace)

windshield n (US) pare-brise m (pl
pare-brise)

windshield wiper n (US)
essuie-glace m (pl essuie-glace)

windy adj (place) venteux (f
venteuse); **It's windy.** Il y a du
vent.

wine n vin m ▷ a bottle of wine une
bouteille de vin ▷ a glass of wine un
verre de vin; **white wine** le vin
blanc; **red wine** le vin rouge; **a
wine bar** un bar à vin; **a wine
glass** un verre à vin; **the wine list**
la carte des vins

wing n aile f

wink vb **to wink at somebody** faire
[36] un clin d'œil à quelqu'un ▷ He
winked at me. Il m'a fait un clin d'œil.

winner n gagnant m, gagnante f

winning adj **the winning team**
l'équipe gagnante; **the winning
goal** le but décisif

winter n hiver m; **in winter** en
hiver

wipe vb essuyer [53]; **to wipe one's
feet** s'essuyer [53] les pieds ▷ Wipe
your feet! Essuie-toi les pieds!

wipe up vb essuyer [53]

wire n fil de fer m

wisdom tooth n dent de sagesse f

wise adj sage

wish vb **to wish for something**
souhaiter [28] quelque chose
▷ What more could you wish for? Que
pourrais-tu souhaiter de plus?; **to
wish to do something** désirer [28]
faire quelque chose ▷ I wish to make
a complaint. Je désire porter
plainte.; **I wish you were here!** Si
seulement tu étais ici!; **I wish
you'd told me!** Si seulement tu
m'en avais parlé!
▶ n vœu m (pl vœux) ▷ to make a
wish faire un vœu; **'best wishes'**
(on greetings card) 'meilleurs vœux';
'with best wishes, Kathy' 'bien
amicalement, Kathy'

wit n (humour) esprit m

with prep ❶ avec ▷ Come with me.
Venez avec moi. ▷ He walks with a
stick. Il marche avec une canne.; **a
woman with blue eyes** une
femme aux yeux bleus ❷ (at the
home of) chez ▷ We stayed with
friends. Nous avons logé chez des
amis. ❸ de ▷ green with envy vert de
jalousie ▷ to shake with fear
trembler de peur ▷ Fill the jug with
water. Remplis la carafe d'eau.

without prep sans ▷ without a coat
sans manteau ▷ without speaking
sans parler

witness n témoin m ▷ There were no

witnesses. Il n'y avait pas de témoins.

vitty adj spirituel (f spirituelle)

vives npl see **wife**

voke up, woken up vb see **wake up**

wolf n loup m

woman n femme f ▷ a woman doctor une femme médecin

won vb see **win**

wonder vb se demander [28]
▷ I wonder why she said that. Je me demande pourquoi elle a dit ça.
▷ I wonder what that means. Je me demande ce que ça veut dire.
▷ I wonder where Caroline is. Je me demande où est Caroline.

wonderful adj formidable

won't = will not

wood n (timber, forest) bois m ▷ It's made of wood. C'est en bois. ▷ We went for a walk in the wood. Nous sommes allés nous promener dans le bois.

wooden adj en bois ▷ a wooden chair une chaise en bois

woodwork n menuiserie f ▷ My hobby is woodwork. Je fais de la menuiserie.

wool n laine f ▷ It's made of wool. C'est en laine.

word n mot m ▷ a difficult word un mot difficile; **What's the word for 'shop' in French?** Comment dit-on 'shop' en français?; **in other words** en d'autres termes; **to have a word with somebody** parler [28] avec quelqu'un; **the words** (lyrics) les paroles fpl ▷ I really like the words

of this song. J'adore les paroles de cette chanson.

word processing n traitement de texte m

word processor n machine de traitement de texte f

wore vb see **wear**

work n travail m (pl travaux) ▷ She's looking for work. Elle cherche du travail. ▷ He's at work at the moment. Il est au travail en ce moment.; **It's hard work.** C'est dur.; **to be off work** (sick) être [35] malade ▷ He's been off work for a week. Il est malade depuis une semaine.; **He's out of work.** Il est sans emploi.
▶ vb ❶ (person) travailler [28] ▷ She works in a shop. Elle travaille dans un magasin. ▷ to work hard travailler dur ❷ (machine, plan) marcher [28] ▷ The heating isn't working. Le chauffage ne marche pas. ▷ My plan worked perfectly. Mon plan a marché impeccablement.

work out vb ❶ (exercise) faire [36] de l'exercice ▷ I work out twice a week. Je fais de l'exercice deux fois par semaine. ❷ (turn out) marcher [28] ▷ In the end it worked out really well. Au bout du compte, ça a très bien marché. ❸ (figure out) arriver [5] à comprendre ▷ I just couldn't work it out. Je n'arrivais pas du tout à comprendre.; **It works out at £10 each.** Ça fait dix livres chacun.

worker n (in factory) ouvrier m, ouvrière f; **He's a factory worker.** Il est ouvrier.; **She's a good worker.** Elle travaille bien.

a
b
c
d
e
f
g
h
i
j
k
l
m
n
o
p
q
r
s
t
u
v
w
x
y
z

work experience n stage m ▷ I'm going to do work experience in a factory. Je vais faire un stage dans une usine.

working-class adj ouvrier (f ouvrière) ▷ a working-class family une famille ouvrière

workman n ouvrier m

worksheet n feuille d'exercices f

workshop n atelier m ▷ a drama workshop un atelier de théâtre

workspace n (computing) espace de travail m

workstation n poste de travail m

world n monde m; **He's the world champion.** Il est champion du monde.

worm n ver m

worn vb see wear

▶ adj usé(e) ▷ The carpet is a bit worn. La moquette est un peu usée.; **worn out** (tired) épuisé(e)

worried adj inquiet (f inquiète) ▷ She's very worried. Elle est très inquiète.; **to be worried about something** s'inquiéter [**34**] pour quelque chose ▷ I'm worried about the exams. Je m'inquiète pour les examens.; **to look worried** avoir [**8**] l'air inquiet ▷ She looks a bit worried. Elle a l'air un peu inquiète.

worry vb s'inquiéter [**34**]; **Don't worry!** Ne t'inquiète pas!

worse adj, adv ❶ pire ▷ It was even worse than that. C'était encore pire que ça. ❷ plus mal ▷ I'm feeling worse. Je me sens plus mal.

worst adj the worst le plus mauvais ▷ He got the worst mark in

the whole class. Il a eu la plus mauvaise note de toute la classe.; **my worst enemy** mon pire ennemi; **Maths is my worst subject.** Je suis vraiment nul en maths.

▶ n pire m ▷ The worst of it is that ... Le pire c'est que ...; **at worst** au pire; **if the worst comes to the worst** au pire

worth adj to be worth valoir [**87**] ▷ It's worth a lot of money. Ça vaut très cher. ▷ How much is it worth? Ça vaut combien?; **It's worth it.** Ça vaut la peine. ▷ Is it worth it? Est-ce que ça vaut la peine? ▷ It's not worth it. Ça ne vaut pas la peine.

would vb Would you like a biscuit? Vous voulez un biscuit?; **Would you like to go and see a film?** Est-ce que tu veux aller voir un film?; **Would you close the door please?** Vous pouvez fermer la porte, s'il vous plaît?; **I'd like ...** J'aimerais ... ▷ I'd like to go to America. J'aimerais aller en Amérique.; **I said I would do it.** J'ai dit que je le ferais.; **If you asked him he'd do it.** Si vous le lui demandiez, il le ferait.; **If you had asked him he would have done it.** Si vous le lui aviez demandé, il l'aurait fait.

wouldn't = would not

wound n blessure f

▶ vb blesser [**28**] ▷ He was wounded in the leg. Il a été blessé à la jambe.

wrap vb emballer [**28**] ▷ She's wrapping her Christmas presents. Elle est en train d'emballer ses cadeaux de Noël.; **Can you wrap it for me please?** (in shop) Vous pouvez me faire un papier cadeau, s'il vous plaît?

wrap up vb emballer [**28**]

wrapping paper n papier cadeau m

wreck n ❶ (vehicle, machine) tas de ferraille m ▷ That car is a wreck! Cette voiture est un tas de ferraille! ❷ (person) loque f ▷ After the exams I was a complete wreck. Après les examens j'étais une véritable loque.
▶ vb ❶ (building, vehicle) démolir [**38**] ▷ The explosion wrecked the whole house. L'explosion a démoli toute la maison. ❷ (plan, holiday) ruiner [**28**] ▷ The trip was wrecked by bad weather. Le voyage a été ruiné par le mauvais temps.

wrestler n lutteur m, lutteuse f

wrestling n lutte f

wrinkled adj ridé(e)

wrist n poignet m

write vb écrire [**30**] ▷ to write a letter écrire une lettre; **to write to somebody** écrire [**30**] à quelqu'un ▷ I'm going to write to her in French. Je vais lui écrire en français.

write down vb noter [**28**] ▷ I wrote down the address. J'ai noté l'adresse.; **Can you write it down for me, please?** Vous pouvez me l'écrire, s'il vous plaît?

writer n écrivain m ▷ She's a writer. Elle est écrivain.

writing n écriture f ▷ I can't read your writing. Je n'arrive pas à lire ton écriture.; **in writing** par écrit

written vb see **write**

wrong adj, adv ❶ (incorrect) faux (f fausse) ▷ The information they gave us was wrong. Les renseignements qu'ils nous ont donnés étaient faux.; **the wrong answer** la mauvaise réponse; **You've got the wrong number.** Vous vous êtes trompé de numéro. ❷ (morally bad) mal ▷ I think hunting is wrong. Je trouve que c'est mal de chasser.; **to be wrong** (mistaken) se tromper [**28**] ▷ You're wrong about that. Tu te trompes.; **to do something wrong** se tromper [**28**] ▷ You've done it wrong. Tu t'es trompé.; **to go wrong** (plan) mal tourner [**28**] ▷ The robbery went wrong and they got caught. Le cambriolage a mal tourné et ils ont été pris.; **What's wrong?** Qu'est-ce qu'il y a?; **What's wrong with her?** Qu'est-ce qu'elle a?

wrote vb see **write**

WWW n (= World Wide Web) Web m

a
b
c
d
e
f
g
h
i
j
k
l
m
n
o
p
q
r
s
t
u
v
w
x
y
z

Xmas *n* (= *Christmas*) <u>Noël</u>
X-ray *vb* **to X-ray something** faire
[**36**] une radio de quelque chose
▷ *They X-rayed my arm.* Ils ont fait
une radio de mon bras.
▶ *n* <u>radio</u> *f* ▷ *to have an X-ray* passer
une radio

yacht *n* ❶ (*sailing boat*) <u>voilier</u> *m*
❷ (*luxury motorboat*) <u>yacht</u> *m*
yawn *vb* <u>bâiller</u> [**28**]
year *n* an *m* ▷ *last year* l'an dernier
▷ *next year* l'an prochain; **to be 15
years old** avoir [**8**] quinze ans; **an
eight-year-old child** un enfant de
huit ans

● In French secondary schools,
● years are counted from the
●
● **sixième** (youngest) to **première**
● and **terminale** (oldest).

▷ *year 7* la sixième ▷ *year 8* la
cinquième ▷ *year 9* la quatrième
▷ *year 10* la troisième ▷ *year 11* la
seconde; **She's in year 11.** Elle est
en seconde.; **He's a first-year.** Il
est en sixième.
yell *vb* <u>hurler</u> [**28**]
yellow *adj* <u>jaune</u>

es adv ❶ oui ▷ *Do you like it? — Yes.* Tu aimes ça? — Oui.; **Would you like a cup of tea? — Yes please.** Voulez-vous une tasse de thé? — Je veux bien. ❷ si

Use **si** when answering negative questions.

▷ *Don't you like it? — Yes!* Tu n'aimes pas ça? — Si! ▷ *You're not Swiss, are you? — Yes I am!* Tu n'es pas suisse, si? — Si!

yesterday adv hier ▷ *yesterday morning* hier matin ▷ *yesterday afternoon* hier après-midi ▷ *yesterday evening* hier soir ▷ *all day yesterday* toute la journée d'hier

yet adv encore; **not yet** pas encore ▷ *It's not finished yet.* Ce n'est pas encore fini.; **not as yet** pas encore ▷ *There's no news as yet.* Nous n'avons pas encore de nouvelles.; **Have you finished yet?** Vous avez fini?

yoghurt n yaourt m
yolk n jaune d'œuf m
you pron

Only use **tu** when speaking to one person of your own age or younger. If in doubt use **vous**.

❶ *(polite form or plural)* vous ▷ *Do you like football?* Est-ce que vous aimez le football? ▷ *Can I help you?* Est-ce que je peux vous aider? ▷ *It's for you.* C'est pour vous. ❷ *(familiar singular)* tu ▷ *Do you like football?* Tu aimes le football?

vous never changes, but **tu** has different forms. When 'you' is the object of the sentence use

te not **tu**. **te** becomes **t'** before a vowel sound.

❸ te ▷ *I know you.* Je te connais. t' ▷ *I saw you.* Je t'ai vu. ❹ toi

toi is used instead of **tu** after a preposition and in comparisons.

▷ *It's for you.* C'est pour toi. ▷ *She's younger than you.* Elle est plus jeune que toi.

young adj jeune; **young people** les jeunes

younger adj plus jeune ▷ *He's younger than me.* Il est plus jeune que moi.; **my younger brother** mon frère cadet; **my younger sister** ma sœur cadette

youngest adj plus jeune ▷ *my youngest brother* mon plus jeune frère ▷ *She's the youngest.* C'est la plus jeune.

your adj

Only use **ton/ta/tes** when speaking to one person of your own age or younger. If in doubt use **votre/vos**.

❶ *(polite form or plural)* votre ▷ *your house* votre maison
vos pl ▷ *your seats* vos places
❷ *(familiar singular)* ton m ▷ *your brother* ton frère
ta f ▷ *your sister* ta sœur
tes pl ▷ *your parents* tes parents

ta becomes **ton** before a vowel sound

your friend (1) *(male)* ton ami
(2) *(female)* ton amie

Do not use **votre/vos** or **ton/ta/tes** with parts of the body.

▷ *Would you like to wash your hands?*
Est-ce que vous voulez vous laver
les mains?

yours *pron*

Only use **le tien/la tienne/les
tiens/les tiennes** when
talking to one person of your
own age or younger. If in doubt
use **le vôtre/la vôtre/les
vôtres**. The same applies to **à
toi** and **à vous**.

❶ le vôtre ▷ *I've lost my pen. Can I use
yours?* J'ai perdu mon stylo. Je peux
utiliser le vôtre?
la vôtre ▷ *I like that car. Is it yours?*
J'aime cette voiture-là. C'est la
vôtre?
les vôtres ▷ *my parents and yours*
mes parents et les vôtres; **Is this
yours?** C'est à vous? ▷ *This book is
yours.* Ce livre est à vous. ▷ *Whose is
this? — It's yours.* C'est à qui? — À
vous.; **Yours sincerely ...** Veuillez
agréer l'expression de mes
sentiments les meilleurs ... ❷ le
tien ▷ *I've lost my pen. Can I use yours?*
J'ai perdu mon stylo. Je peux utiliser
le tien?
la tienne ▷ *I like that car. Is it yours?*
J'aime cette voiture-là. C'est la
tienne?
les tiens ▷ *my parents and yours* mes
parents et les tiens
les tiennes ▷ *My hands are dirty,
yours are clean.* Mes mains sont
sales, les tiennes sont propres.; **Is
this yours?** C'est à toi? ▷ *This book is
yours.* Ce livre est à toi. ▷ *Whose is
this? — It's yours.* C'est à qui? — À toi.

yourself *pron*

Only use **te** when talking to
one person of your own age or
younger; use **vous** to everyone
else. If in doubt use **vous**.

❶ (*polite form*) vous ▷ *Have you hurt
yourself?* Est-ce que vous vous êtes
fait mal? ▷ *Tell me about yourself!*
Parlez-moi de vous! ❷ (*familiar
form*) te ▷ *Have you hurt yourself?*
Est-ce que tu t'es fait mal?
❸ (*familiar form*) toi

After a preposition, use **toi**
instead of **te**.

▷ *Tell me about yourself!* Parle-moi
de toi! ❹ toi-même ▷ *Do it yourself!*
Fais-le toi-même! ❺ vous-même
▷ *Do it yourself!* Faites-le
vous-même!
yourselves *pron* ❶ vous ▷ *Did you
enjoy yourselves?* Vous vous êtes
bien amusés? ❷ vous-mêmes ▷ *Did
you make it yourselves?* Vous l'avez
fait vous-mêmes?
youth club *n* centre de loisirs *m*
youth hostel *n* auberge de
jeunesse *f*
Yugoslavia *n* Yougoslavie *f*; **in the
former Yugoslavia** en
ex-Yougoslavie

Z

zany *adj* loufoque
zebra *n* zèbre *m*
zebra crossing *n* passage
clouté *m*
zero *n* zéro *m*
zip *n* fermeture éclair® *f* (*pl*
fermetures éclair®)
zip code *n* (US) code postal *m*
zipper *n* (US) fermeture éclair® *f* (*pl*
fermetures éclair®)
zodiac *n* zodiaque *m* ▷ *the signs of
the zodiac* les signes du zodiaque
zone *n* zone *f*
zoo *n* zoo *m*
zoom lens *n* zoom *m*
zucchini *n* (US) courgette *f*

VERB TABLES

Introduction

The verb tables in the following section contain 93 tables of French verbs (some regular and some irregular) in alphabetical order. Each table shows you the following form:

Present	*eg* je fais = **I do** *or* **I'm doing**
Present Subjunctive	*eg* je fasse = **I do**
Perfect	*eg* j'ai fait = **I did** *or* **I have done**
Imperfect	*eg* je faisais = **I was doing** *or* **I did**
Future	*eg* je ferai = **I will do**
Conditional	*eg* je ferais = **I would do**
Imperative	*eg* fais = **do**
Past Participle	*eg* fait = **done**
Present Participle	*eg* faisant = **doing**

On both sides of the dictionary, French verbs are usually followed by a number (e.g. **donner** [28] *vb* <u>to give</u>). This number corresponds to a verb table number in this verbs section, where the pattern followed by the model verb is shown. When you come across **aimer** [28] *vb* <u>to love</u>, for example, you will see that it follows the same pattern as that of model verb **donner**, shown in verb table **28**.

In order to help you use the verbs shown in the verb tables correctly, there are also a number of example phrases at the bottom of each page to show the verb as it is used in context.

Remember:

je/j'	=	I
tu	=	you (*to one person you know well*)
il	=	he/it
elle	=	she/it
on	=	we/one
nous	=	we
vous	=	you (*polite form or plural*)
ils/elles	=	they

PRESENT

j'	achète
tu	achètes
il/elle/on	achète
nous	achetons
vous	achetez
ils/elles	achètent

PRESENT SUBJUNCTIVE

j'	achète
tu	achètes
il/elle/on	achète
nous	achetions
vous	achetiez
ils/elles	achètent

PERFECT

j'	ai acheté
tu	as acheté
il/elle/on	a acheté
nous	avons acheté
vous	avez acheté
ils/elles	ont acheté

IMPERFECT

j'	achetais
tu	achetais
il/elle/on	achetait
nous	achetions
vous	achetiez
ils/elles	achetaient

FUTURE

j'	achèterai
tu	achèteras
il/elle/on	achètera
nous	achèterons
vous	achèterez
ils/elles	achèteront

CONDITIONAL

j'	achèterais
tu	achèterais
il/elle/on	achèterait
nous	achèterions
vous	achèteriez
ils/elles	achèteraient

IMPERATIVE

achète / achetons / achetez

PAST PARTICIPLE

acheté

PRESENT PARTICIPLE

achetant

--------- EXAMPLE PHRASES ---------

J'ai acheté des gâteaux à la pâtisserie.

I bought some cakes at the cake shop.

Qu'est-ce que tu lui **as acheté** pour son anniversaire?

What did you buy him for his birthday?

Je **n'achète** jamais de chips.

I never buy crisps.

Table
2

acquérir *to acquire*

PRESENT

j'	acquiers
tu	acquiers
il/elle/on	acquiert
nous	acquérons
vous	acquérez
ils/elles	acquièrent

PRESENT SUBJUNCTIVE

j'	acquière
tu	acquières
il/elle/on	acquière
nous	acquérions
vous	acquériez
ils/elles	acquièrent

PERFECT

j'	ai acquis
tu	as acquis
il/elle/on	a acquis
nous	avons acquis
vous	avez acquis
ils/elles	ont acquis

IMPERFECT

j'	acquérais
tu	acquérais
il/elle/on	acquérait
nous	acquérions
vous	acquériez
ils/elles	acquéraient

FUTURE

j'	acquerrai
tu	acquerras
il/elle/on	acquerra
nous	acquerrons
vous	acquerrez
ils/elles	acquerront

CONDITIONAL

j'	acquerrais
tu	acquerrais
il/elle/on	acquerrait
nous	acquerrions
vous	acquerriez
ils/elles	acquerraient

IMPERATIVE
acquiers / acquérons / acquérez

PAST PARTICIPLE
acquis

PRESENT PARTICIPLE
acquérant

EXAMPLE PHRASES

Elle **a acquis** la nationalité française en 2017.

She acquired French nationality in 2017.

PRESENT

je	vais
tu	vas
il/elle/on	va
nous	allons
vous	allez
ils/elles	vont

PRESENT SUBJUNCTIVE

j'	aille
tu	ailles
il/elle/on	aille
nous	allions
vous	alliez
ils/elles	aillent

PERFECT

je	suis allé(e)
tu	es allé(e)
il/elle/on	est allé(e)
nous	sommes allé(e)s
vous	êtes allé(e)(s)
ils/elles	sont allé(e)s

IMPERFECT

j'	allais
tu	allais
il/elle/on	allait
nous	allions
vous	alliez
ils/elles	allaient

FUTURE

j'	irai
tu	iras
il/elle/on	ira
nous	irons
vous	irez
ils/elles	iront

CONDITIONAL

j'	irais
tu	irais
il/elle/on	irait
nous	irions
vous	iriez
ils/elles	iraient

IMPERATIVE

va / allons / allez

PAST PARTICIPLE

allé

PRESENT PARTICIPLE

allant

— EXAMPLE PHRASES —

Vous **allez** au cinéma? — *Are you going to the cinema?*
Je **suis allé** à Londres. — *I went to London.*
Est-ce que tu **es** déjà **allé** en Allemagne? — *Have you ever been to Germany?*

Table
4

appeler *to call*

PRESENT

j'	appelle
tu	appelles
il/elle/on	appelle
nous	appelons
vous	appelez
ils/elles	appellent

PRESENT SUBJUNCTIVE

j'	appelle
tu	appelles
il/elle/on	appelle
nous	appelions
vous	appeliez
ils/elles	appellent

PERFECT

j'	ai appelé
tu	as appelé
il/elle/on	a appelé
nous	avons appelé
vous	avez appelé
ils/elles	ont appelé

IMPERFECT

j'	appelais
tu	appelais
il/elle/on	appelait
nous	appelions
vous	appeliez
ils/elles	appelaient

FUTURE

j'	appellerai
tu	appelleras
il/elle/on	appellera
nous	appellerons
vous	appellerez
ils/elles	appelleront

CONDITIONAL

j'	appellerais
tu	appellerais
il/elle/on	appellerait
nous	appellerions
vous	appelleriez
ils/elles	appelleraient

IMPERATIVE

appelle / appelons / appelez

PAST PARTICIPLE

appelé

PRESENT PARTICIPLE

appelant

--- EXAMPLE PHRASES ---

Elle **a appelé** le médecin.
J'**ai appelé** Richard à Londres.
Comment tu **t'appelles**?

She called the doctor.
I called Richard in London.
What's your name?

• *Note that **s'appeler** follows the same pattern, but takes **être** in the perfect tense. For an example of a reflexive verb in full, see verb table **6 s'asseoir**.*

PRESENT

j'	arrive
tu	arrives
il/elle/on	arrive
nous	arrivons
vous	arrivez
ils/elles	arrivent

PRESENT SUBJUNCTIVE

j'	arrive
tu	arrives
il/elle/on	arrive
nous	arrivions
vous	arriviez
ils/elles	arrivent

PERFECT

je	suis arrivé(e)
tu	es arrivé(e)
il/elle/on	est arrivé(e)
nous	sommes arrivé(e)s
vous	êtes arrivé(e)(s)
ils/elles	sont arrivé(e)s

IMPERFECT

j'	arrivais
tu	arrivais
il/elle/on	arrivait
nous	arrivions
vous	arriviez
ils/elles	arrivaient

FUTURE

j'	arriverai
tu	arriveras
il/elle/on	arrivera
nous	arriverons
vous	arriverez
ils/elles	arriveront

CONDITIONAL

j'	arriverais
tu	arriverais
il/elle/on	arriverait
nous	arriverions
vous	arriveriez
ils/elles	arriveraient

IMPERATIVE

arrive / arrivons / arrivez

PAST PARTICIPLE

arrivé

PRESENT PARTICIPLE

arrivant

--- EXAMPLE PHRASES ---

J'**arrive** à l'école à huit heures.
Le prof n'**est** pas encore **arrivé**.
Qu'est-ce qui **est arrivé** à Aurélie?

I arrive at school at 8 o'clock.
The teacher hasn't arrived yet.
What happened to Aurélie?

Table
6

s'asseoir *to sit down*

PRESENT		PRESENT SUBJUNCTIVE	
je	m'assieds/m'assois	je	m'asseye
tu	t'assieds/t'assois	tu	t'asseyes
il/elle/on	s'assied/s'assoit	il/elle/on	s'asseye
nous	nous asseyons/nous assoyons	nous	nous asseyions
vous	vous asseyez/vous assoyez	vous	vous asseyiez
ils/elles	s'asseyent/s'assoient	ils/elles	s'asseyent

PERFECT		IMPERFECT	
je	me suis assis(e)	je	m'asseyais
tu	t'es assis(e)	tu	t'asseyais
il/elle/on	s'est assis(e)	il/elle/on	s'asseyait
nous	nous sommes assis(es)	nous	nous asseyions
vous	vous êtes assis(e(s))	vous	vous asseyiez
ils/elles	se sont assis(es)	ils/elles	s'asseyaient

FUTURE		CONDITIONAL	
je	m'assiérai	je	m'assiérais
tu	t'assiéras	tu	t'assiérais
il/elle/on	s'assiéra	il/elle/on	s'assiérait
nous	nous assiérons	nous	nous assiérions
vous	vous assiérez	vous	vous assiériez
ils/elles	s'assiéront	ils/elles	s'assiéraient

IMPERATIVE   **PAST PARTICIPLE**

assieds-toi / asseyons-nous / asseyez-vous   assis

PRESENT PARTICIPLE

s'asseyant

─────────────── EXAMPLE PHRASES ───────────────

Assieds-toi, Nicole.	*Sit down Nicole.*
Asseyez-vous, les enfants.	*Sit down children.*
Je peux **m'asseoir**?	*May I sit down?*
Je **me suis assise** sur un chewing-gum!	*I've sat on some chewing gum!*

PRESENT

j'	attends
tu	attends
il/elle/on	attend
nous	attendons
vous	attendez
ils/elles	attendent

PRESENT SUBJUNCTIVE

j'	attende
tu	attendes
il/elle/on	attende
nous	attendions
vous	attendiez
ils/elles	attendent

PERFECT

j'	ai attendu
tu	as attendu
il/elle/on	a attendu
nous	avons attendu
vous	avez attendu
ils/elles	ont attendu

IMPERFECT

j'	attendais
tu	attendais
il/elle/on	attendait
nous	attendions
vous	attendiez
ils/elles	attendaient

FUTURE

j'	attendrai
tu	attendras
il/elle/on	attendra
nous	attendrons
vous	attendrez
ils/elles	attendront

CONDITIONAL

j'	attendrais
tu	attendrais
il/elle/on	attendrait
nous	attendrions
vous	attendriez
ils/elles	attendraient

IMPERATIVE

attends / attendons / attendez

PAST PARTICIPLE

attendu

PRESENT PARTICIPLE

attendant

EXAMPLE PHRASES

Attends-moi!	*Wait for me!*
Tu **attends** depuis longtemps?	*Have you been waiting long?*
Je l'**ai attendu** à la poste.	*I waited for him at the post office.*
Je **m'attends** à ce qu'il soit en retard.	*I expect he'll be late.*

- *Note that **s'attendre** follows the same pattern, but take **être** in the perfect tense.*
  *For an example of a reflexive verb in full, see verb table **6 s'asseoir**.*

Table
8

avoir *to have*

PRESENT		PRESENT SUBJUNCTIVE	
j'	ai	j'	aie
tu	as	tu	aies
il/elle/on	a	il/elle/on	ait
nous	avons	nous	ayons
vous	avez	vous	ayez
ils/elles	ont	ils/elles	aient

PERFECT		IMPERFECT	
j'	ai eu	j'	avais
tu	as eu	tu	avais
il/elle/on	a eu	il/elle/on	avait
nous	avons eu	nous	avions
vous	avez eu	vous	aviez
ils/elles	ont eu	ils/elles	avaient

FUTURE		CONDITIONAL	
j'	aurai	j'	aurais
tu	auras	tu	aurais
il/elle/on	aura	il/elle/on	aurait
nous	aurons	nous	aurions
vous	aurez	vous	auriez
ils/elles	auront	ils/elles	auraient

IMPERATIVE
aie / ayons / ayez

PAST PARTICIPLE
eu

PRESENT PARTICIPLE
ayant

—————————— EXAMPLE PHRASES ——————————

Il **a** les yeux bleus.	*He's got blue eyes.*
Quel âge **as**-tu?	*How old are you?*
Il **a eu** un accident.	*He's had an accident.*
J'**avais** faim.	*I was hungry.*
Il y **a** beaucoup de monde.	*There are lots of people.*

Table
9

to beat **battre**

PRESENT

je	bats
tu	bats
il/elle/on	bat
nous	battons
vous	battez
ils/elles	battent

PRESENT SUBJUNCTIVE

je	batte
tu	battes
il/elle/on	batte
nous	battions
vous	battiez
ils/elles	battent

PERFECT

j'	ai battu
tu	as battu
il/elle/on	a battu
nous	avons battu
vous	avez battu
ils/elles	ont battu

IMPERFECT

je	battais
tu	battais
il/elle/on	battait
nous	battions
vous	battiez
ils/elles	battaient

FUTURE

je	battrai
tu	battras
il/elle/on	battra
nous	battrons
vous	battrez
ils/elles	battront

CONDITIONAL

je	battrais
tu	battrais
il/elle/on	battrait
nous	battrions
vous	battriez
ils/elles	battraient

IMPERATIVE

bats / battons / battez

PAST PARTICIPLE

battu

PRESENT PARTICIPLE

battant

--- EXAMPLE PHRASES ---

On les **a battus** deux à un.
J'ai le cœur qui **bat**!
Arrêtez de **vous battre**!

We beat them 2-1.
My heart's beating (fast)!
Stop fighting!

- Note that **se battre** follows the same pattern, but takes **être** in the perfect tense.
  For an example of a reflexive verb in full, see verb table **82 se taire**.

Table
10

boire *to drink*

PRESENT

je	bois
tu	bois
il/elle/on	boit
nous	buvons
vous	buvez
ils/elles	boivent

PRESENT SUBJUNCTIVE

je	boive
tu	boives
il/elle/on	boive
nous	buvions
vous	buviez
ils/elles	boivent

PERFECT

j'	ai bu
tu	as bu
il/elle/on	a bu
nous	avons bu
vous	avez bu
ils/elles	ont bu

IMPERFECT

je	buvais
tu	buvais
il/elle/on	buvait
nous	buvions
vous	buviez
ils/elles	buvaient

FUTURE

je	boirai
tu	boiras
il/elle/on	boira
nous	boirons
vous	boirez
ils/elles	boiront

CONDITIONAL

je	boirais
tu	boirais
il/elle/on	boirait
nous	boirions
vous	boiriez
ils/elles	boiraient

IMPERATIVE

bois / buvons / buvez

PAST PARTICIPLE

bu

PRESENT PARTICIPLE

buvant

EXAMPLE PHRASES

Qu'est-ce que tu veux **boire**?
Il ne **boit** jamais d'alcool.
J'**ai bu** un litre d'eau.

What would you like to drink?
He never drinks alcohol.
I drank a litre of water.

PRESENT

je	bous
tu	bous
il/elle/on	bout
nous	bouillons
vous	bouillez
ils/elles	bouillent

PRESENT SUBJUNCTIVE

je	bouille
tu	bouilles
il/elle/on	bouille
nous	bouillions
vous	bouilliez
ils/elles	bouillent

PERFECT

j'	ai bouilli
tu	as bouilli
il/elle/on	a bouilli
nous	avons bouilli
vous	avez bouilli
ils/elles	ont bouilli

IMPERFECT

je	bouillais
tu	bouillais
il/elle/on	bouillait
nous	bouillions
vous	bouilliez
ils/elles	bouillaient

FUTURE

je	bouillirai
tu	bouilliras
il/elle/on	bouillira
nous	bouillirons
vous	bouillirez
ils/elles	bouilliront

CONDITIONAL

je	bouillirais
tu	bouillirais
il/elle/on	bouillirait
nous	bouillirions
vous	bouilliriez
ils/elles	bouilliraient

IMPERATIVE

bous / bouillons / bouillez

PAST PARTICIPLE

bouilli

PRESENT PARTICIPLE

bouillant

--- EXAMPLE PHRASES ---

L'eau **bout**.   *The water's boiling.*
Tu peux mettre de l'eau à **bouillir**?   *Can you boil some water?*

Table
12

commencer *to begin*

PRESENT

je	commence
tu	commences
il/elle/on	commence
nous	commençons
vous	commencez
ils/elles	commencent

PRESENT SUBJUNCTIVE

je	commence
tu	commences
il/elle/on	commence
nous	commencions
vous	commenciez
ils/elles	commencent

PERFECT

j'	ai commencé
tu	as commencé
il/elle/on	a commencé
nous	avons commencé
vous	avez commencé
ils/elles	ont commencé

IMPERFECT

je	commençais
tu	commençais
il/elle/on	commençait
nous	commencions
vous	commenciez
ils/elles	commençaient

FUTURE

je	commencerai
tu	commenceras
il/elle/on	commencera
nous	commencerons
vous	commencerez
ils/elles	commenceront

CONDITIONAL

je	commencerais
tu	commencerais
il/elle/on	commencerait
nous	commencerions
vous	commenceriez
ils/elles	commenceraient

IMPERATIVE

commence / commençons / commencez

PAST PARTICIPLE

commencé

PRESENT PARTICIPLE

commençant

—— EXAMPLE PHRASES ——

Il **a commencé** à pleuvoir.
It started to rain.

Les cours **commencent** à neuf heures.
Lessons start at 9 o'clock.

Tu **as** déjà **commencé** à réviser pour les examens?
Have you started revising for the exams?

PRESENT

je	conclus
tu	conclus
il/elle/on	conclut
nous	concluons
vous	concluez
ils/elles	concluent

PRESENT SUBJUNCTIVE

je	conclue
tu	conclues
il/elle/on	conclue
nous	concluions
vous	concluiez
ils/elles	concluent

PERFECT

j'	ai conclu
tu	as conclu
il/elle/on	a conclu
nous	avons conclu
vous	avez conclu
ils/elles	ont conclu

IMPERFECT

je	concluais
tu	concluais
il/elle/on	concluait
nous	concluions
vous	concluiez
ils/elles	concluaient

FUTURE

je	conclurai
tu	concluras
il/elle/on	conclura
nous	conclurons
vous	conclurez
ils/elles	concluront

CONDITIONAL

je	conclurais
tu	conclurais
il/elle/on	conclurait
nous	conclurions
vous	concluriez
ils/elles	concluraient

IMPERATIVE

conclus / concluons / concluez

PAST PARTICIPLE

conclu

PRESENT PARTICIPLE

concluant

――――――――――― EXAMPLE PHRASES ―――――――――――

Ils **ont conclu** un marché.
J'en **ai conclu** qu'il était parti.
Je **conclurai** par ces mots…

They concluded a deal.
I concluded that he had gone.
I will conclude with these words…

Table
14

connaître *to know*

PRESENT		PRESENT SUBJUNCTIVE	
je	connais	je	connaisse
tu	connais	tu	connaisses
il/elle/on	connaît	il/elle/on	connaisse
nous	connaissons	nous	connaissions
vous	connaissez	vous	connaissiez
ils/elles	connaissent	ils/elles	connaissent

PERFECT		IMPERFECT	
j'	ai connu	je	connaissais
tu	as connu	tu	connaissais
il/elle/on	a connu	il/elle/on	connaissait
nous	avons connu	nous	connaissions
vous	avez connu	vous	connaissiez
ils/elles	ont connu	ils/elles	connaissaient

FUTURE		CONDITIONAL	
je	connaîtrai	je	connaîtrais
tu	connaîtras	tu	connaîtrais
il/elle/on	connaîtra	il/elle/on	connaîtrait
nous	connaîtrons	nous	connaîtrions
vous	connaîtrez	vous	connaîtriez
ils/elles	connaîtront	ils/elles	connaîtraient

IMPERATIVE
connais / connaissons / connaissez

PAST PARTICIPLE
connu

PRESENT PARTICIPLE
connaissant

——————— EXAMPLE PHRASES ———————

Je ne **connais** pas du tout cette région. — *I don't know the area at all.*
Vous **connaissez** M. Amiot? — *Do you know Mr Amiot?*
Il n'**a** pas **connu** son grand-père. — *He never knew his grandad.*
Ils **se sont connus** à Rouen. — *They first met in Rouen.*

• Note that **se connaître** follows the same pattern, but takes **être** in the perfect tense. For an example of a reflexive verb in full, see verb table **82 se taire**.

PRESENT

je	couds
tu	couds
il/elle/on	coud
nous	cousons
vous	cousez
ils/elles	cousent

PRESENT SUBJUNCTIVE

je	couse
tu	couses
il/elle/on	couse
nous	cousions
vous	cousiez
ils/elles	cousent

PERFECT

j'	ai cousu
tu	as cousu
il/elle/on	a cousu
nous	avons cousu
vous	avez cousu
ils/elles	ont cousu

IMPERFECT

je	cousais
tu	cousais
il/elle/on	cousait
nous	cousions
vous	cousiez
ils/elles	cousaient

FUTURE

je	coudrai
tu	coudras
il/elle/on	coudra
nous	coudrons
vous	coudrez
ils/elles	coudront

CONDITIONAL

je	coudrais
tu	coudrais
il/elle/on	coudrait
nous	coudrions
vous	coudriez
ils/elles	coudraient

IMPERATIVE

couds / cousons / cousez

PAST PARTICIPLE

cousu

PRESENT PARTICIPLE

cousant

—————— EXAMPLE PHRASES ——————

Tu sais **coudre**?
Elle **a cousu** elle-même son
costume.

Can you sew?
She made her costume herself.

Table
16

courir *to run*

PRESENT

je	cours
tu	cours
il/elle/on	court
nous	courons
vous	courez
ils/elles	courent

PRESENT SUBJUNCTIVE

je	coure
tu	coures
il/elle/on	coure
nous	courions
vous	couriez
ils/elles	courent

PERFECT

j'	ai couru
tu	as couru
il/elle/on	a couru
nous	avons couru
vous	avez couru
ils/elles	ont couru

IMPERFECT

je	courais
tu	courais
il/elle/on	courait
nous	courions
vous	couriez
ils/elles	couraient

FUTURE

je	courrai
tu	courras
il/elle/on	courra
nous	courrons
vous	courrez
ils/elles	courront

CONDITIONAL

je	courrais
tu	courrais
il/elle/on	courrait
nous	courrions
vous	courriez
ils/elles	courraient

IMPERATIVE
cours / courons / courez

PAST PARTICIPLE
couru

PRESENT PARTICIPLE
courant

--- EXAMPLE PHRASES ---

Je ne **cours** pas très vite.	*I can't run very fast.*
Elle est sortie en **courant**.	*She ran out.*
Ne **courez** pas dans le couloir.	*Don't run in the corridor.*
J'**ai couru** jusqu'à l'école.	*I ran all the way to school.*

PRESENT

je	crains
tu	crains
il/elle/on	craint
nous	craignons
vous	craignez
ils/elles	craignent

PRESENT SUBJUNCTIVE

je	craigne
tu	craignes
il/elle/on	craigne
nous	craignions
vous	craigniez
ils/elles	craignent

PERFECT

j'	ai craint
tu	as craint
il/elle/on	a craint
nous	avons craint
vous	avez craint
ils/elles	ont craint

IMPERFECT

je	craignais
tu	craignais
il/elle/on	craignait
nous	craignions
vous	craigniez
ils/elles	craignaient

FUTURE

je	craindrai
tu	craindras
il/elle/on	craindra
nous	craindrons
vous	craindrez
ils/elles	craindront

CONDITIONAL

je	craindrais
tu	craindrais
il/elle/on	craindrait
nous	craindrions
vous	craindriez
ils/elles	craindraient

IMPERATIVE
crains / craignons / craignez

PAST PARTICIPLE
craint

PRESENT PARTICIPLE
craignant

——————————— EXAMPLE PHRASES ———————————

Tu n'as rien à **craindre**.
Je **crains** le pire.

You've got nothing to fear.
I fear the worst.

Table
18

créer *to create*

PRESENT

je	crée
tu	crées
il/elle/on	crée
nous	créons
vous	créez
ils/elles	créent

PRESENT SUBJUNCTIVE

je	crée
tu	crées
il/elle/on	crée
nous	créions
vous	créiez
ils/elles	créent

PERFECT

j'	ai créé
tu	as créé
il/elle/on	a créé
nous	avons créé
vous	avez créé
ils/elles	ont créé

IMPERFECT

je	créais
tu	créais
il/elle/on	créait
nous	créions
vous	créiez
ils/elles	créaient

FUTURE

je	créerai
tu	créeras
il/elle/on	créera
nous	créerons
vous	créerez
ils/elles	créeront

CONDITIONAL

je	créerais
tu	créerais
il/elle/on	créerait
nous	créerions
vous	créeriez
ils/elles	créeraient

IMPERATIVE
crée / créons / créez

PAST PARTICIPLE
créé

PRESENT PARTICIPLE
créant

EXAMPLE PHRASES

Il **a créé** une nouvelle invention.
Ce virus **crée** des difficultés dans le monde entier.
Le gouvernement **créera** deux mille emplois supplémentaires.

He's created a new invention.
This virus is creating difficulties all over the world.
The government will create an extra 2000 jobs.

PRESENT

je	crie
tu	cries
il/elle/on	crie
nous	crions
vous	criez
ils/elles	crient

PRESENT SUBJUNCTIVE

je	crie
tu	cries
il/elle/on	crie
nous	criions
vous	criiez
ils/elles	crient

PERFECT

j'	ai crié
tu	as crié
il/elle/on	a crié
nous	avons crié
vous	avez crié
ils/elles	ont crié

IMPERFECT

je	criais
tu	criais
il/elle/on	criait
nous	criions
vous	criiez
ils/elles	criaient

FUTURE

je	crierai
tu	crieras
il/elle/on	criera
nous	crierons
vous	crierez
ils/elles	crieront

CONDITIONAL

je	crierais
tu	crierais
il/elle/on	crierait
nous	crierions
vous	crieriez
ils/elles	crieraient

IMPERATIVE
crie / crions / criez

PAST PARTICIPLE
crié

PRESENT PARTICIPLE
criant

––––––––––––––––––– EXAMPLE PHRASES –––––––––––––––––––

Ne **crie** pas comme ça!
Elle **a crié** au secours.
Il **criait** de plus en plus fort.

Don't shout!
She cried for help.
He shouted louder and louder.

Table
20

croire *to believe*

PRESENT

je	crois
tu	crois
il/elle/on	croit
nous	croyons
vous	croyez
ils/elles	croient

PRESENT SUBJUNCTIVE

je	croie
tu	croies
il/elle/on	croie
nous	croyions
vous	croyiez
ils/elles	croient

PERFECT

j'	ai cru
tu	as cru
il/elle/on	a cru
nous	avons cru
vous	avez cru
ils/elles	ont cru

IMPERFECT

je	croyais
tu	croyais
il/elle/on	croyait
nous	croyions
vous	croyiez
ils/elles	croyaient

FUTURE

je	croirai
tu	croiras
il/elle/on	croira
nous	croirons
vous	croirez
ils/elles	croiront

CONDITIONAL

je	croirais
tu	croirais
il/elle/on	croirait
nous	croirions
vous	croiriez
ils/elles	croiraient

IMPERATIVE

crois / croyons / croyez

PAST PARTICIPLE

cru

PRESENT PARTICIPLE

croyant

--- EXAMPLE PHRASES ---

Je ne te **crois** pas.
J'**ai cru** que tu n'allais pas venir.
Elle **croyait** encore au père Noël.

I don't believe you.
I thought you weren't going to come.
She still believed in Santa.

PRESENT

je	croîs
tu	croîs
il/elle/on	croît
nous	croissons
vous	croissez
ils/elles	croissent

PRESENT SUBJUNCTIVE

je	croisse
tu	croisses
il/elle/on	croisse
nous	croissions
vous	croissiez
ils/elles	croissent

PERFECT

j'	ai crû
tu	as crû
il/elle/on	a crû
nous	avons crû
vous	avez crû
ils/elles	ont crû

IMPERFECT

je	croissais
tu	croissais
il/elle/on	croissait
nous	croissions
vous	croissiez
ils/elles	croissaient

FUTURE

je	croîtrai
tu	croîtras
il/elle/on	croîtra
nous	croîtrons
vous	croîtrez
ils/elles	croîtront

CONDITIONAL

je	croîtrais
tu	croîtrais
il/elle/on	croîtrait
nous	croîtrions
vous	croîtriez
ils/elles	croîtraient

IMPERATIVE

croîs / croissons / croissez

PRESENT PARTICIPLE

croissant

PAST PARTICIPLE

crû
(NB: crue, crus, crues)

--- EXAMPLE PHRASES ---

Les ventes **croissent** de 6% par an.
C'est une plante qui **croît** dans les pays chauds.

Sales are growing by 6% per year.
This plant grows in hot countries.

Table
22

cueillir *to pick*

PRESENT

je	cueille
tu	cueilles
il/elle/on	cueille
nous	cueillons
vous	cueillez
ils/elles	cueillent

PRESENT SUBJUNCTIVE

je	cueille
tu	cueilles
il/elle/on	cueille
nous	cueillions
vous	cueilliez
ils/elles	cueillent

PERFECT

j'	ai cueilli
tu	as cueilli
il/elle/on	a cueilli
nous	avons cueilli
vous	avez cueilli
ils/elles	ont cueilli

IMPERFECT

je	cueillais
tu	cueillais
il/elle/on	cueillait
nous	cueillions
vous	cueilliez
ils/elles	cueillaient

FUTURE

je	cueillerai
tu	cueilleras
il/elle/on	cueillera
nous	cueillerons
vous	cueillerez
ils/elles	cueilleront

CONDITIONAL

je	cueillerais
tu	cueillerais
il/elle/on	cueillerait
nous	cueillerions
vous	cueilleriez
ils/elles	cueilleraient

IMPERATIVE
cueille / cueillons / cueillez

PAST PARTICIPLE
cueilli

PRESENT PARTICIPLE
cueillant

EXAMPLE PHRASES

J'**ai cueilli** quelques fraises dans le jardin.
Il est interdit de **cueillir** des fleurs sauvages dans la montagne.

I've picked a few strawberries in the garden.
It's forbidden to pick wild flowers in the mountains.

PRESENT

je	cuis
tu	cuis
il/elle/on	cuit
nous	cuisons
vous	cuisez
ils/elles	cuisent

PRESENT SUBJUNCTIVE

je	cuise
tu	cuises
il/elle/on	cuise
nous	cuisions
vous	cuisiez
ils/elles	cuisent

PERFECT

j'	ai cuit
tu	as cuit
il/elle/on	a cuit
nous	avons cuit
vous	avez cuit
ils/elles	ont cuit

IMPERFECT

je	cuisais
tu	cuisais
il/elle/on	cuisait
nous	cuisions
vous	cuisiez
ils/elles	cuisaient

FUTURE

je	cuirai
tu	cuiras
il/elle/on	cuira
nous	cuirons
vous	cuirez
ils/elles	cuiront

CONDITIONAL

je	cuirais
tu	cuirais
il/elle/on	cuirait
nous	cuirions
vous	cuiriez
ils/elles	cuiraient

IMPERATIVE

cuis / cuisons / cuisez

PAST PARTICIPLE

cuit

PRESENT PARTICIPLE

cuisant

--- EXAMPLE PHRASES ---

Je les **ai cuits** au beurre. | *I cooked them in butter.*
En général, je **cuis** les légumes à la vapeur. | *I usually steam vegetables.*
Ce gâteau met environ une heure à **cuire**. | *This cake takes about an hour to bake.*

Table
24

descendre *to go down*

PRESENT

je	descends
tu	descends
il/elle/on	descend
nous	descendons
vous	descendez
ils/elles	descendent

PRESENT SUBJUNCTIVE

je	descende
tu	descendes
il/elle/on	descende
nous	descendions
vous	descendiez
ils/elles	descendent

PERFECT

je	suis descendu(e)
tu	es descendu(e)
il/elle/on	est descendu(e)
nous	sommes descendu(e)(s)
vous	êtes descendu(e)(s)
ils/elles	sont descendu(e)s

IMPERFECT

je	descendais
tu	descendais
il/elle/on	descendait
nous	descendions
vous	descendiez
ils/elles	descendaient

FUTURE

je	descendrai
tu	descendras
il/elle/on	descendra
nous	descendrons
vous	descendrez
ils/elles	descendront

CONDITIONAL

je	descendrais
tu	descendrais
il/elle/on	descendrait
nous	descendrions
vous	descendriez
ils/elles	descendraient

IMPERATIVE

descends / descendons / descendez

PAST PARTICIPLE

descendu

PRESENT PARTICIPLE

descendant

EXAMPLE PHRASES

Descendez la rue jusqu'au rond-point.
Go down the street to the roundabout.

Reste en bas: je **descends**!
Stay downstairs – I'm coming down!

Nous **sommes descendus** à la station Trocadéro.
We got off at the Trocadéro station.

Vous pouvez **descendre** ma valise, s'il vous plaît?
Can you get my suitcase down, please?

• Note that **descendre** takes *avoir* in the perfect tense when it is used with a direct object.

PRESENT

je	deviens
tu	deviens
il/elle/on	devient
nous	devenons
vous	devenez
ils/elles	deviennent

PRESENT SUBJUNCTIVE

je	devienne
tu	deviennes
il/elle/on	devienne
nous	devenions
vous	deveniez
ils/elles	deviennent

PERFECT

je	suis devenu(e)
tu	es devenu(e)
il/elle/on	est devenu(e)
nous	sommes devenu(e)s
vous	êtes devenu(e)(s)
ils/elles	sont devenu(e)s

IMPERFECT

je	devenais
tu	devenais
il/elle/on	devenait
nous	devenions
vous	deveniez
ils/elles	devenaient

FUTURE

je	deviendrai
tu	deviendras
il/elle/on	deviendra
nous	deviendrons
vous	deviendrez
ils/elles	deviendront

CONDITIONAL

je	deviendrais
tu	deviendrais
il/elle/on	deviendrait
nous	deviendrions
vous	deviendriez
ils/elles	deviendraient

IMPERATIVE

deviens / devenons / devenez

PAST PARTICIPLE

devenu

PRESENT PARTICIPLE

devenant

——— EXAMPLE PHRASES ———

Il **est devenu** médecin. — *He became a doctor.*
Ça **devient** de plus en plus difficile. — *It's becoming more and more difficult.*
Qu'est-ce qu'elle **est devenue**? — *What has become of her?*

Table
26

devoir *to have to; to owe*

PRESENT

je	dois
tu	dois
il/elle/on	doit
nous	devons
vous	devez
ils/elles	doivent

PRESENT SUBJUNCTIVE

je	doive
tu	doives
il/elle/on	doive
nous	devions
vous	deviez
ils/elles	doivent

PERFECT

j'	ai dû
tu	as dû
il/elle/on	a dû
nous	avons dû
vous	avez dû
ils/elles	ont dû

IMPERFECT

je	devais
tu	devais
il/elle/on	devait
nous	devions
vous	deviez
ils/elles	devaient

FUTURE

je	devrai
tu	devras
il/elle/on	devra
nous	devrons
vous	devrez
ils/elles	devront

CONDITIONAL

je	devrais
tu	devrais
il/elle/on	devrait
nous	devrions
vous	devriez
ils/elles	devraient

IMPERATIVE

dois / devons / devez

PAST PARTICIPLE

dû
(NB: due, dus, dues)

PRESENT PARTICIPLE

devant

------ EXAMPLE PHRASES ------

Je **dois** aller faire les courses ce matin.
À quelle heure est-ce que tu **dois** partir?
Il **a dû** faire ses devoirs hier soir.

Il **devait** prendre le train pour aller travailler.

I have to do the shopping this morning.
What time do you have to leave?

He had to do his homework last night.
He had to go to work by train.

PRESENT

je	dis
tu	dis
il/elle/on	dit
nous	disons
vous	dites
ils/elles	disent

PRESENT SUBJUNCTIVE

je	dise
tu	dises
il/elle/on	dise
nous	disions
vous	disiez
ils/elles	disent

PERFECT

j'	ai dit
tu	as dit
il/elle/on	a dit
nous	avons dit
vous	avez dit
ils/elles	ont dit

IMPERFECT

je	disais
tu	disais
il/elle/on	disait
nous	disions
vous	disiez
ils/elles	disaient

FUTURE

je	dirai
tu	diras
il/elle/on	dira
nous	dirons
vous	direz
ils/elles	diront

CONDITIONAL

je	dirais
tu	dirais
il/elle/on	dirait
nous	dirions
vous	diriez
ils/elles	diraient

IMPERATIVE

dis / disons / dites

PAST PARTICIPLE

dit

PRESENT PARTICIPLE

disant

———————————— EXAMPLE PHRASES ————————————

Qu'est-ce qu'elle **dit**?	*What is she saying?*
"Bonjour!", a-t-il **dit**.	*"Hello!" he said.*
Ils m'**ont dit** que le film était nul.	*They told me that the film was rubbish.*
Comment ça **se dit** en anglais?	*How do you say that in English?*

- *Note that **se dire** follows the same pattern, but takes **être** in the perfect tense. For an example of a reflexive verb in full, see verb table **82 se taire**.*

Table
28

donner *to give*

PRESENT		**PRESENT SUBJUNCTIVE**	
je	donne	je	donne
tu	donnes	tu	donnes
il/elle/on	donne	il/elle/on	donne
nous	donnons	nous	donnions
vous	donnez	vous	donniez
ils/elles	donnent	ils/elles	donnent

PERFECT		**IMPERFECT**	
j'	ai donné	je	donnais
tu	as donné	tu	donnais
il/elle/on	a donné	il/elle/on	donnait
nous	avons donné	nous	donnions
vous	avez donné	vous	donniez
ils/elles	ont donné	ils/elles	donnaient

FUTURE		**CONDITIONAL**	
je	donnerai	je	donnerais
tu	donneras	tu	donnerais
il/elle/on	donnera	il/elle/on	donnerait
nous	donnerons	nous	donnerions
vous	donnerez	vous	donneriez
ils/elles	donneront	ils/elles	donneraient

IMPERATIVE
donne / donnons / donnez

PAST PARTICIPLE
donné

PRESENT PARTICIPLE
donnant

——————————— EXAMPLE PHRASES ———————————

Donne-moi la main.
Give me your hand.
Est-ce que je t'**ai donné** mon adresse?
Did I give you my address?
L'appartement **donne** sur la place.
The flat overlooks the square.

PRESENT

je	dors
tu	dors
il/elle/on	dort
nous	dormons
vous	dormez
ils/elles	dorment

PRESENT SUBJUNCTIVE

je	dorme
tu	dormes
il/elle/on	dorme
nous	dormions
vous	dormiez
ils/elles	dorment

PERFECT

j'	ai dormi
tu	as dormi
il/elle/on	a dormi
nous	avons dormi
vous	avez dormi
ils/elles	ont dormi

IMPERFECT

je	dormais
tu	dormais
il/elle/on	dormait
nous	dormions
vous	dormiez
ils/elles	dormaient

FUTURE

je	dormirai
tu	dormiras
il/elle/on	dormira
nous	dormirons
vous	dormirez
ils/elles	dormiront

CONDITIONAL

je	dormirais
tu	dormirais
il/elle/on	dormirait
nous	dormirions
vous	dormiriez
ils/elles	dormiraient

IMPERATIVE

dors / dormons / dormez

PRESENT PARTICIPLE

dormant

PAST PARTICIPLE

dormi

——————————— EXAMPLE PHRASES ———————————

Tu **as** bien **dormi**?
Nous **dormons** dans la même
chambre.
À 9 heures, il **dormait** déjà.

Did you sleep well?
We sleep in the same bedroom.

He was already asleep by nine.

Table
30

écrire *to write*

PRESENT

j'	écris
tu	écris
il/elle/on	écrit
nous	écrivons
vous	écrivez
ils/elles	écrivent

PRESENT SUBJUNCTIVE

j'	écrive
tu	écrives
il/elle/on	écrive
nous	écrivions
vous	écriviez
ils/elles	écrivent

PERFECT

j'	ai écrit
tu	as écrit
il/elle/on	a écrit
nous	avons écrit
vous	avez écrit
ils/elles	ont écrit

IMPERFECT

j'	écrivais
tu	écrivais
il/elle/on	écrivait
nous	écrivions
vous	écriviez
ils/elles	écrivaient

FUTURE

j'	écrirai
tu	écriras
il/elle/on	écrira
nous	écrirons
vous	écrirez
ils/elles	écriront

CONDITIONAL

j'	écrirais
tu	écrirais
il/elle/on	écrirait
nous	écririons
vous	écririez
ils/elles	écriraient

IMPERATIVE

écris / écrivons / écrivez

PAST PARTICIPLE

écrit

PRESENT PARTICIPLE

écrivant

——————————— EXAMPLE PHRASES ———————————

Tu **as écrit** à ta correspondante récemment?

Have you written to your penfriend lately?

Elle **écrit** des romans.

She writes novels.

Comment ça **s'écrit**, "brouillard"?

How do you spell "brouillard"?

- Note that *s'écrire* follows the same pattern, but take *être* in the perfect tense. For an example of a reflexive verb in full, see verb table **6** *s'asseoir*.

PRESENT

j'	émeus
tu	émeus
il/elle/on	émeut
nous	émouvons
vous	émouvez
ils/elles	émeuvent

PRESENT SUBJUNCTIVE

j'	émeuve
tu	émeuves
il/elle/on	émeuve
nous	émouvions
vous	émouviez
ils/elles	émeuvent

PERFECT

j'	ai ému
tu	as ému
il/elle/on	a ému
nous	avons ému
vous	avez ému
ils/elles	ont ému

IMPERFECT

j'	émouvais
tu	émouvais
il/elle/on	émouvait
nous	émouvions
vous	émouviez
ils/elles	émouvaient

FUTURE

j'	émouvrai
tu	émouvras
il/elle/on	émouvra
nous	émouvrons
vous	émouvrez
ils/elles	émouvront

CONDITIONAL

j'	émouvrais
tu	émouvrais
il/elle/on	émouvrait
nous	émouvrions
vous	émouvriez
ils/elles	émouvraient

IMPERATIVE
émeus / émouvons / émouvez

PAST PARTICIPLE
ému

PRESENT PARTICIPLE
émouvant

——————— EXAMPLE PHRASES ———————

Ce film nous **a ému(e)s**. *This film moved us.*
Cette histoire m'**émeut** toujours beaucoup. *This story always moves me to tears.*

Table
32

entrer *to enter*

PRESENT

j'	entre
tu	entres
il/elle/on	entre
nous	entrons
vous	entrez
ils/elles	entrent

PRESENT SUBJUNCTIVE

j'	entre
tu	entres
il/elle/on	entre
nous	entrions
vous	entriez
ils/elles	entrent

PERFECT

je	suis entré(e)
tu	es entré(e)
il/elle/on	est entré(e)
nous	sommes entré(e)s
vous	êtes entré(e)(s)
ils/elles	sont entré(e)s

IMPERFECT

j'	entrais
tu	entrais
il/elle/on	entrait
nous	entrions
vous	entriez
ils/elles	entraient

FUTURE

j'	entrerai
tu	entreras
il/elle/on	entrera
nous	entrerons
vous	entrerez
ils/elles	entreront

CONDITIONAL

j'	entrerais
tu	entrerais
il/elle/on	entrerait
nous	entrerions
vous	entreriez
ils/elles	entreraient

IMPERATIVE

entre / entrons / entrez

PAST PARTICIPLE

entré

PRESENT PARTICIPLE

entrant

EXAMPLE PHRASES

Je peux **entrer**?
Essuie-toi les pieds en **entrant**.
Ils **sont** tous **entrés** dans la maison.

Can I come in?
Wipe your feet as you come in.
They all went into the house.

PRESENT

j'	envoie
tu	envoies
il/elle/on	envoie
nous	envoyons
vous	envoyez
ils/elles	envoient

PRESENT SUBJUNCTIVE

j'	envoie
tu	envoies
il/elle/on	envoie
nous	envoyions
vous	envoyiez
ils/elles	envoient

PERFECT

j'	ai envoyé
tu	as envoyé
il/elle/on	a envoyé
nous	avons envoyé
vous	avez envoyé
ils/elles	ont envoyé

IMPERFECT

j'	envoyais
tu	envoyais
il/elle/on	envoyait
nous	envoyions
vous	envoyiez
ils/elles	envoyaient

FUTURE

j'	enverrai
tu	enverras
il/elle/on	enverra
nous	enverrons
vous	enverrez
ils/elles	enverront

CONDITIONAL

j'	enverrais
tu	enverrais
il/elle/on	enverrait
nous	enverrions
vous	enverriez
ils/elles	enverraient

IMPERATIVE

envoie / envoyons / envoyez

PAST PARTICIPLE

envoyé

PRESENT PARTICIPLE

envoyant

EXAMPLE PHRASES

J'**ai envoyé** une carte postale à ma tante.
Envoie-moi un e-mail.
Je t'**enverrai** ton cadeau par la poste.

I sent my aunt a postcard.

Send me an email.
I'll send you your present by post.

Table
34

espérer *to hope*

PRESENT

j'	espère
tu	espères
il/elle/on	espère
nous	espérons
vous	espérez
ils/elles	espèrent

PRESENT SUBJUNCTIVE

j'	espère
tu	espères
il/elle/on	espère
nous	espérions
vous	espériez
ils/elles	espèrent

PERFECT

j'	ai espéré
tu	as espéré
il/elle/on	a espéré
nous	avons espéré
vous	avez espéré
ils/elles	ont espéré

IMPERFECT

j'	espérais
tu	espérais
il/elle/on	espérait
nous	espérions
vous	espériez
ils/elles	espéraient

FUTURE

j'	espérerai
tu	espéreras
il/elle/on	espérera
nous	espérerons
vous	espérerez
ils/elles	espéreront

CONDITIONAL

j'	espérerais
tu	espérerais
il/elle/on	espérerait
nous	espérerions
vous	espéreriez
ils/elles	espéreraient

IMPERATIVE
espère / espérons / espérez

PAST PARTICIPLE
espéré

PRESENT PARTICIPLE
espérant

EXAMPLE PHRASES

J'**espère** que tu vas bien.
Il **espérait** pouvoir venir.
Tu penses réussir tes examens?
– J'**espère** bien!

I hope you're well.
He was hoping he'd be able to come.
Do you think you'll pass your exams?
– I hope so!

PRESENT

je	suis
tu	es
il/elle/on	est
nous	sommes
vous	êtes
ils/elles	sont

PRESENT SUBJUNCTIVE

je	sois
tu	sois
il/elle/on	soit
nous	soyons
vous	soyez
ils/elles	soient

PERFECT

j'	ai été
tu	as été
il/elle/on	a été
nous	avons été
vous	avez été
ils/elles	ont été

IMPERFECT

j'	étais
tu	étais
il/elle/on	était
nous	étions
vous	étiez
ils/elles	étaient

FUTURE

je	serai
tu	seras
il/elle/on	sera
nous	serons
vous	serez
ils/elles	seront

CONDITIONAL

je	serais
tu	serais
il/elle/on	serait
nous	serions
vous	seriez
ils/elles	seraient

IMPERATIVE
sois / soyons / soyez

PAST PARTICIPLE
été

PRESENT PARTICIPLE
étant

─────── EXAMPLE PHRASES ───────

Mon père **est** professeur.
Quelle heure **est**-il? – Il **est** dix heures.
Ils ne **sont** pas encore arrivés.

My father's a teacher.
What time is it? – It's 10 o'clock.

They haven't arrived yet.

Table
36

faire *to do; to make*

PRESENT

je	fais
tu	fais
il/elle/on	fait
nous	faisons
vous	faites
ils/elles	font

PRESENT SUBJUNCTIVE

je	fasse
tu	fasses
il/elle/on	fasse
nous	fassions
vous	fassiez
ils/elles	fassent

PERFECT

j'	ai fait
tu	as fait
il/elle/on	a fait
nous	avons fait
vous	avez fait
ils/elles	ont fait

IMPERFECT

je	faisais
tu	faisais
il/elle/on	faisait
nous	faisions
vous	faisiez
ils/elles	faisaient

FUTURE

je	ferai
tu	feras
il/elle/on	fera
nous	ferons
vous	ferez
ils/elles	feront

CONDITIONAL

je	ferais
tu	ferais
il/elle/on	ferait
nous	ferions
vous	feriez
ils/elles	feraient

IMPERATIVE

fais / faisons / faites

PAST PARTICIPLE

fait

PRESENT PARTICIPLE

faisant

―――――――――――― EXAMPLE PHRASES ――――――――――――

Qu'est-ce que tu **fais**?	*What are you doing?*
Qu'est-ce qu'il **a fait**?	*What has he done? or What did he do?*
J'**ai fait** un gâteau.	*I've made a cake or I made a cake.*
Il **s'est fait** couper les cheveux.	*He's had his hair cut.*

• Note that *se faire* follows the same pattern, but takes *être* in the perfect tense. For an example of a reflexive verb in full, see verb table **82 se taire**.

PRESENT
    il   faut

PRESENT SUBJUNCTIVE
    il   faille

PERFECT
    il   a fallu

IMPERFECT
    il   fallait

FUTURE
    il   faudra

CONDITIONAL
    il   faudrait

IMPERATIVE
not used

PAST PARTICIPLE
    fallu

PRESENT PARTICIPLE
not used

—————————————— EXAMPLE PHRASES ——————————————

Il **faut** se dépêcher!	*We have to hurry up!*
Il me **fallait** de l'argent.	*I needed money.*
Il **faudra** que tu sois là à 8 heures.	*You'll have to be there at 8.*

Table
38

finir *to finish*

PRESENT

je	finis
tu	finis
il/elle/on	finit
nous	finissons
vous	finissez
ils/elles	finissent

PRESENT SUBJUNCTIVE

je	finisse
tu	finisses
il/elle/on	finisse
nous	finissions
vous	finissiez
ils/elles	finissent

PERFECT

j'	ai fini
tu	as fini
il/elle/on	a fini
nous	avons fini
vous	avez fini
ils/elles	ont fini

IMPERFECT

je	finissais
tu	finissais
il/elle/on	finissait
nous	finissions
vous	finissiez
ils/elles	finissaient

FUTURE

je	finirai
tu	finiras
il/elle/on	finira
nous	finirons
vous	finirez
ils/elles	finiront

CONDITIONAL

je	finirais
tu	finirais
il/elle/on	finirait
nous	finirions
vous	finiriez
ils/elles	finiraient

IMPERATIVE

finis / finissons / finissez

PAST PARTICIPLE

fini

PRESENT PARTICIPLE

finissant

EXAMPLE PHRASES

Finis ta soupe!   *Finish your soup!*
J'ai **fini**!   *I've finished!*
Je **finirai** mes devoirs demain.   *I'll finish my homework tomorrow.*

PRESENT

je	fuis
tu	fuis
il/elle/on	fuit
nous	fuyons
vous	fuyez
ils/elles	fuient

PRESENT SUBJUNCTIVE

je	fuie
tu	fuies
il/elle/on	fuie
nous	fuyions
vous	fuyiez
ils/elles	fuient

PERFECT

j'	ai fui
tu	as fui
il/elle/on	a fui
nous	avons fui
vous	avez fui
ils/elles	ont fui

IMPERFECT

je	fuyais
tu	fuyais
il/elle/on	fuyait
nous	fuyions
vous	fuyiez
ils/elles	fuyaient

FUTURE

je	fuirai
tu	fuiras
il/elle/on	fuira
nous	fuirons
vous	fuirez
ils/elles	fuiront

CONDITIONAL

je	fuirais
tu	fuirais
il/elle/on	fuirait
nous	fuirions
vous	fuiriez
ils/elles	fuiraient

IMPERATIVE

fuis / fuyons / fuyez

PAST PARTICIPLE

fui

PRESENT PARTICIPLE

fuyant

─────────── EXAMPLE PHRASES ───────────

Ils **ont fui** leur pays.
Le robinet **fuit**.

They fled their country.
The tap is dripping.

Table
40

haïr *to hate*

	PRESENT		PRESENT SUBJUNCTIVE
je	hais	je	haïsse
tu	hais	tu	haïsses
il/elle/on	hait	il/elle/on	haïsse
nous	haïssons	nous	haïssions
vous	haïssez	vous	haïssiez
ils/elles	haïssent	ils/elles	haïssent

	PERFECT		IMPERFECT
j'	ai haï	je	haïssais
tu	as haï	tu	haïssais
il/elle/on	a haï	il/elle/on	haïssait
nous	avons haï	nous	haïssions
vous	avez haï	vous	haïssiez
ils/elles	ont haï	ils/elles	haïssaient

	FUTURE		CONDITIONAL
je	haïrai	je	haïrais
tu	haïras	tu	haïrais
il/elle/on	haïra	il/elle/on	haïrait
nous	haïrons	nous	haïrions
vous	haïrez	vous	haïriez
ils/elles	haïront	ils/elles	haïraient

IMPERATIVE
hais / haïssons / haïssez

PAST PARTICIPLE
haï

PRESENT PARTICIPLE
haïssant

─────────────── EXAMPLE PHRASES ───────────────

Je te **hais**!	*I hate you!*
Elle **haïssait** tout le monde.	*She hated everyone.*
Ils **se haïssent**.	*They hate each other.*

- Note that **se haïr** follows the same pattern, but takes **être** in the perfect tense. For an example of a reflexive verb in full, see verb table **82 se taire**.

PRESENT

je	jette
tu	jettes
il/elle/on	jette
nous	jetons
vous	jetez
ils/elles	jettent

PRESENT SUBJUNCTIVE

je	jette
tu	jettes
il/elle/on	jette
nous	jetions
vous	jetiez
ils/elles	jettent

PERFECT

j'	ai jeté
tu	as jeté
il/elle/on	a jeté
nous	avons jeté
vous	avez jeté
ils/elles	ont jeté

IMPERFECT

je	jetais
tu	jetais
il/elle/on	jetait
nous	jetions
vous	jetiez
ils/elles	jetaient

FUTURE

je	jetterai
tu	jetteras
il/elle/on	jettera
nous	jetterons
vous	jetterez
ils/elles	jetteront

CONDITIONAL

je	jetterais
tu	jetterais
il/elle/on	jetterait
nous	jetterions
vous	jetteriez
ils/elles	jetteraient

IMPERATIVE

jette / jetons / jetez

PAST PARTICIPLE

jeté

PRESENT PARTICIPLE

jetant

─────────── EXAMPLE PHRASES ───────────

Ne **jette** pas tes vêtements par terre.

Elle **a jeté** son chewing-gum par la fenêtre.

Ils ne **jettent** jamais rien.

Don't throw your clothes on the floor.

She threw her chewing gum out of the window.

They never throw anything away.

Table
42

joindre *to join*

PRESENT		**PRESENT SUBJUNCTIVE**	
je	joins	je	joigne
tu	joins	tu	joignes
il/elle/on	joint	il/elle/on	joigne
nous	joignons	nous	joignions
vous	joignez	vous	joigniez
ils/elles	joignent	ils/elles	joignent

PERFECT		**IMPERFECT**	
j'	ai joint	je	joignais
tu	as joint	tu	joignais
il/elle/on	a joint	il/elle/on	joignait
nous	avons joint	nous	joignions
vous	avez joint	vous	joigniez
ils/elles	ont joint	ils/elles	joignaient

FUTURE		**CONDITIONAL**	
je	joindrai	je	joindrais
tu	joindras	tu	joindrais
il/elle/on	joindra	il/elle/on	joindrait
nous	joindrons	nous	joindrions
vous	joindrez	vous	joindriez
ils/elles	joindront	ils/elles	joindraient

IMPERATIVE
joins / joignons / joignez

PAST PARTICIPLE
joint

PRESENT PARTICIPLE
joignant

––––––––––––––– EXAMPLE PHRASES –––––––––––––––

Où est-ce qu'on peut te **joindre** ce week-end?
On **a joint** les deux tables.

Where can we contact you this weekend?
We put the two tables together.

PRESENT

je	lève
tu	lèves
il/elle/on	lève
nous	levons
vous	levez
ils/elles	lèvent

PRESENT SUBJUNCTIVE

je	lève
tu	lèves
il/elle/on	lève
nous	levions
vous	leviez
ils/elles	lèvent

PERFECT

j'	ai levé
tu	as levé
il/elle/on	a levé
nous	avons levé
vous	avez levé
ils/elles	ont levé

IMPERFECT

je	levais
tu	levais
il/elle/on	levait
nous	levions
vous	leviez
ils/elles	levaient

FUTURE

je	lèverai
tu	lèveras
il/elle/on	lèvera
nous	lèverons
vous	lèverez
ils/elles	lèveront

CONDITIONAL

je	lèverais
tu	lèverais
il/elle/on	lèverait
nous	lèverions
vous	lèveriez
ils/elles	lèveraient

IMPERATIVE

lève / levons / levez

PAST PARTICIPLE

levé

PRESENT PARTICIPLE

levant

=================== EXAMPLE PHRASES ===================

Lève la tête.	_Lift your head up._
Levez la main!	_Put your hand up!_
Je **me lève** tous les jours à sept heures.	_I get up at 7 every day._

- Note that **se lever** follows the same pattern, but takes **être** in the perfect tense. For an example of a reflexive verb in full, see verb table **82 se taire**.

Table
44

lire *to read*

PRESENT

je	lis
tu	lis
il/elle/on	lit
nous	lisons
vous	lisez
ils/elles	lisent

PRESENT SUBJUNCTIVE

je	lise
tu	lises
il/elle/on	lise
nous	lisions
vous	lisiez
ils/elles	lisent

PERFECT

j'	ai lu
tu	as lu
il/elle/on	a lu
nous	avons lu
vous	avez lu
ils/elles	ont lu

IMPERFECT

je	lisais
tu	lisais
il/elle/on	lisait
nous	lisions
vous	lisiez
ils/elles	lisaient

FUTURE

je	lirai
tu	liras
il/elle/on	lira
nous	lirons
vous	lirez
ils/elles	liront

CONDITIONAL

je	lirais
tu	lirais
il/elle/on	lirait
nous	lirions
vous	liriez
ils/elles	liraient

IMPERATIVE

lis / lisons / lisez

PAST PARTICIPLE

lu

PRESENT PARTICIPLE

lisant

EXAMPLE PHRASES

Vous **avez lu** "Madame Bovary"?
Je le **lirai** dans l'avion.
Elle lui **lisait** une histoire.

Have you read "Madame Bovary"?
I'll read it on the plane.
She was reading him a story.

PRESENT

je	mange
tu	manges
il/elle/on	mange
nous	mangeons
vous	mangez
ils/elles	mangent

PRESENT SUBJUNCTIVE

je	mange
tu	manges
il/elle/on	mange
nous	mangions
vous	mangiez
ils/elles	mangent

PERFECT

j'	ai mangé
tu	as mangé
il/elle/on	a mangé
nous	avons mangé
vous	avez mangé
ils/elles	ont mangé

IMPERFECT

je	mangeais
tu	mangeais
il/elle/on	mangeait
nous	mangions
vous	mangiez
ils/elles	mangeaient

FUTURE

je	mangerai
tu	mangeras
il/elle/on	mangera
nous	mangerons
vous	mangerez
ils/elles	mangeront

CONDITIONAL

je	mangerais
tu	mangerais
il/elle/on	mangerait
nous	mangerions
vous	mangeriez
ils/elles	mangeraient

IMPERATIVE

mange / mangeons / mangez

PAST PARTICIPLE

mangé

PRESENT PARTICIPLE

mangeant

───────────── EXAMPLE PHRASES ─────────────

Nous ne **mangeons** pas souvent ensemble.

We don't often eat together.

Tu **as** assez **mangé**?

Have you had enough to eat?

Je **mangerai** plus tard.

I'll eat later on.

Table
46

maudire *to curse*

PRESENT

je	maudis
tu	maudis
il/elle/on	maudit
nous	maudissons
vous	maudissez
ils/elles	maudissent

PRESENT SUBJUNCTIVE

je	maudisse
tu	maudisses
il/elle/on	maudisse
nous	maudissions
vous	maudissiez
ils/elles	maudissent

PERFECT

j'	ai maudit
tu	as maudit
il/elle/on	a maudit
nous	avons maudit
vous	avez maudit
ils/elles	ont maudit

IMPERFECT

je	maudissais
tu	maudissais
il/elle/on	maudissait
nous	maudissions
vous	maudissiez
ils/elles	maudissaient

FUTURE

je	maudirai
tu	maudiras
il/elle/on	maudira
nous	maudirons
vous	maudirez
ils/elles	maudiront

CONDITIONAL

je	maudirais
tu	maudirais
il/elle/on	maudirait
nous	maudirions
vous	maudiriez
ils/elles	maudiraient

IMPERATIVE
maudis / maudissons / maudissez

PAST PARTICIPLE
maudit

PRESENT PARTICIPLE
maudissant

─────── EXAMPLE PHRASES ───────

Ils **maudissent** leurs ennemis.
Ce **maudit** stylo ne marche pas!

They curse their enemies.
This blasted pen doesn't work!

PRESENT

je	mets
tu	mets
il/elle/on	met
nous	mettons
vous	mettez
ils/elles	mettent

PRESENT SUBJUNCTIVE

je	mette
tu	mettes
il/elle/on	mette
nous	mettions
vous	mettiez
ils/elles	mettent

PERFECT

j'	ai mis
tu	as mis
il/elle/on	a mis
nous	avons mis
vous	avez mis
ils/elles	ont mis

IMPERFECT

je	mettais
tu	mettais
il/elle/on	mettait
nous	mettions
vous	mettiez
ils/elles	mettaient

FUTURE

je	mettrai
tu	mettras
il/elle/on	mettra
nous	mettrons
vous	mettrez
ils/elles	mettront

CONDITIONAL

je	mettrais
tu	mettrais
il/elle/on	mettrait
nous	mettrions
vous	mettriez
ils/elles	mettraient

IMPERATIVE

mets / mettons / mettez

PAST PARTICIPLE

mis

PRESENT PARTICIPLE

mettant

──────── EXAMPLE PHRASES ────────

Mets ton manteau!
Où est-ce que tu **as mis** les clés?
J'**ai mis** le livre sur la table.
Elle **s'est mise** à pleurer.

Put your coat on!
Where have you put the keys?
I put the book on the table.
She started crying.

• Note that **se mettre** follows the same pattern, but takes **être** in the perfect tense. For an example of a reflexive verb in full, see verb table **82 se taire**.

Table
48

monter *to go up*

PRESENT

je	monte
tu	montes
il/elle/on	monte
nous	montons
vous	montez
ils/elles	montent

PRESENT SUBJUNCTIVE

je	monte
tu	montes
il/elle/on	monte
nous	montions
vous	montiez
ils/elles	montent

PERFECT

je	suis monté(e)
tu	es monté(e)
il/elle/on	est monté(e)
nous	sommes monté(e)s
vous	êtes monté(e)(s)
ils/elles	sont monté(e)s

IMPERFECT

je	montais
tu	montais
il/elle/on	montait
nous	montions
vous	montiez
ils/elles	montaient

FUTURE

je	monterai
tu	monteras
il/elle/on	montera
nous	monterons
vous	monterez
ils/elles	monteront

CONDITIONAL

je	monterais
tu	monterais
il/elle/on	monterait
nous	monterions
vous	monteriez
ils/elles	monteraient

IMPERATIVE

monte / montons / montez

PAST PARTICIPLE

monté

PRESENT PARTICIPLE

montant

─────── EXAMPLE PHRASES ───────

Je **suis montée** tout en haut de
la tour.
Monte dans la voiture, je t'emmène.
Il s'est tordu la cheville en
montant à une échelle.

I went all the way up the tower.

Get into the car, I'll take you there.
He twisted his ankle going up
a ladder.

- Note that **monter** takes **avoir** in the perfect tense when it is used with a direct object.
- The verb **surmonter** follows the same pattern as **monter**, but takes **avoir** in the
  perfect tense.

PRESENT

je	mords
tu	mords
il/elle/on	mord
nous	mordons
vous	mordez
ils/elles	mordent

PRESENT SUBJUNCTIVE

je	morde
tu	mordes
il/elle/on	morde
nous	mordions
vous	mordiez
ils/elles	mordent

PERFECT

j'	ai mordu
tu	as mordu
il/elle/on	a mordu
nous	avons mordu
vous	avez mordu
ils/elles	ont mordu

IMPERFECT

je	mordais
tu	mordais
il/elle/on	mordait
nous	mordions
vous	mordiez
ils/elles	mordaient

FUTURE

je	mordrai
tu	mordras
il/elle/on	mordra
nous	mordrons
vous	mordrez
ils/elles	mordront

CONDITIONAL

je	mordrais
tu	mordrais
il/elle/on	mordrait
nous	mordrions
vous	mordriez
ils/elles	mordraient

IMPERATIVE

mords / mordons / mordez

PAST PARTICIPLE

mordu

PRESENT PARTICIPLE

mordant

--- EXAMPLE PHRASES ---

Le chien m'**a mordu**.
Il ne va pas te **mordre**!

The dog bit me.
He won't bite!

Table
50

moudre *to grind*

PRESENT

je	mouds
tu	mouds
il/elle/on	moud
nous	moulons
vous	moulez
ils/elles	moulent

PRESENT SUBJUNCTIVE

je	moule
tu	moules
il/elle/on	moule
nous	moulions
vous	mouliez
ils/elles	moulent

PERFECT

j'	ai moulu
tu	as moulu
il/elle/on	a moulu
nous	avons moulu
vous	avez moulu
ils/elles	ont moulu

IMPERFECT

je	moulais
tu	moulais
il/elle/on	moulait
nous	moulions
vous	mouliez
ils/elles	moulaient

FUTURE

je	moudrai
tu	moudras
il/elle/on	moudra
nous	moudrons
vous	moudrez
ils/elles	moudront

CONDITIONAL

je	moudrais
tu	moudrais
il/elle/on	moudrait
nous	moudrions
vous	moudriez
ils/elles	moudraient

IMPERATIVE

mouds / moulons / moulez

PAST PARTICIPLE

moulu

PRESENT PARTICIPLE

moulant

--- EXAMPLE PHRASES ---

J'**ai moulu** du café pour demain matin.

I've ground some coffee for tomorrow morning.

PRESENT

je	meurs
tu	meurs
il/elle/on	meurt
nous	mourons
vous	mourez
ils/elles	meurent

PRESENT SUBJUNCTIVE

je	meure
tu	meures
il/elle/on	meure
nous	mourions
vous	mouriez
ils/elles	meurent

PERFECT

je	suis mort(e)
tu	es mort(e)
il/elle/on	est mort(e)
nous	sommes mort(e)s
vous	êtes mort(e)(s)
ils/elles	sont mort(e)s

IMPERFECT

je	mourais
tu	mourais
il/elle/on	mourait
nous	mourions
vous	mouriez
ils/elles	mouraient

FUTURE

je	mourrai
tu	mourras
il/elle/on	mourra
nous	mourrons
vous	mourrez
ils/elles	mourront

CONDITIONAL

je	mourrais
tu	mourrais
il/elle/on	mourrait
nous	mourrions
vous	mourriez
ils/elles	mourraient

IMPERATIVE

meurs / mourons / mourez

PAST PARTICIPLE

mort

PRESENT PARTICIPLE

mourant

=== EXAMPLE PHRASES ===

Elle **est morte** en 2015.
Ils **sont morts**.
On **meurt** de froid ici!

She died in 2015.
They're dead.
We're freezing to death in here!

Table 52 — **naître** *to be born*

PRESENT
je	nais
tu	nais
il/elle/on	naît
nous	naissons
vous	naissez
ils/elles	naissent

PRESENT SUBJUNCTIVE
je	naisse
tu	naisses
il/elle/on	naisse
nous	naissions
vous	naissiez
ils/elles	naissent

PERFECT
je	suis né(e)
tu	es né(e)
il/elle/on	est né(e)
nous	sommes né(e)s
vous	êtes né(e)(s)
ils/elles	sont né(e)s

IMPERFECT
je	naissais
tu	naissais
il/elle/on	naissait
nous	naissions
vous	naissiez
ils/elles	naissaient

FUTURE
je	naîtrai
tu	naîtras
il/elle/on	naîtra
nous	naîtrons
vous	naîtrez
ils/elles	naîtront

CONDITIONAL
je	naîtrais
tu	naîtrais
il/elle/on	naîtrait
nous	naîtrions
vous	naîtriez
ils/elles	naîtraient

IMPERATIVE
nais / naissons / naissez

PAST PARTICIPLE
né

PRESENT PARTICIPLE
naissant

EXAMPLE PHRASES

Je **suis née** le 12 février.
Le bébé de Delphine **naîtra** en mars.
Quand est-ce que tu **es né**?

I was born on 12 February.
Delphine is going to have a baby in March.
When were you born?

PRESENT

je	nettoie
tu	nettoies
il/elle/on	nettoie
nous	nettoyons
vous	nettoyez
ils/elles	nettoient

PRESENT SUBJUNCTIVE

je	nettoie
tu	nettoies
il/elle/on	nettoie
nous	nettoyions
vous	nettoyiez
ils/elles	nettoient

PERFECT

j'	ai nettoyé
tu	as nettoyé
il/elle/on	a nettoyé
nous	avons nettoyé
vous	avez nettoyé
ils/elles	ont nettoyé

IMPERFECT

je	nettoyais
tu	nettoyais
il/elle/on	nettoyait
nous	nettoyions
vous	nettoyiez
ils/elles	nettoyaient

FUTURE

je	nettoierai
tu	nettoieras
il/elle/on	nettoiera
nous	nettoierons
vous	nettoierez
ils/elles	nettoieront

CONDITIONAL

je	nettoierais
tu	nettoierais
il/elle/on	nettoierait
nous	nettoierions
vous	nettoieriez
ils/elles	nettoieraient

IMPERATIVE

nettoie / nettoyons / nettoyez

PAST PARTICIPLE

nettoyé

PRESENT PARTICIPLE

nettoyant

--- EXAMPLE PHRASES ---

Richard **a nettoyé** tout l'appartement.

Richard has cleaned the whole flat.

Elle **nettoyait** le sol en écoutant la radio.

She was cleaning the floor while listening to the radio.

Je ne **nettoie** pas souvent mes lunettes.

I don't clean my glasses very often.

Table
54

offrir *to offer*

PRESENT

j'	offre
tu	offres
il/elle/on	offre
nous	offrons
vous	offrez
ils/elles	offrent

PRESENT SUBJUNCTIVE

j'	offre
tu	offres
il/elle/on	offre
nous	offrions
vous	offriez
ils/elles	offrent

PERFECT

j'	ai offert
tu	as offert
il/elle/on	a offert
nous	avons offert
vous	avez offert
ils/elles	ont offert

IMPERFECT

j'	offrais
tu	offrais
il/elle/on	offrait
nous	offrions
vous	offriez
ils/elles	offraient

FUTURE

j'	offrirai
tu	offriras
il/elle/on	offrira
nous	offrirons
vous	offrirez
ils/elles	offriront

CONDITIONAL

j'	offrirais
tu	offrirais
il/elle/on	offrirait
nous	offririons
vous	offririez
ils/elles	offriraient

IMPERATIVE

offre / offrons / offrez

PAST PARTICIPLE

offert

PRESENT PARTICIPLE

offrant

EXAMPLE PHRASES

On lui **a offert** un poste de secrétaire.
They offered her a secreterial post.

Offre-lui des fleurs.
Give her some flowers.

Viens, je t'**offre** à boire.
Come on, I'll buy you a drink.

Je **me suis offert** un nouveau stylo.
I treated myself to a new pen.

- Note that *s'offrir* follows the same pattern, but takes **être** in the perfect tense. For an example of a reflexive verb in full, see verb table **6 s'asseoir**.

PRESENT

j'	ouvre
tu	ouvres
il/elle/on	ouvre
nous	ouvrons
vous	ouvrez
ils/elles	ouvrent

PRESENT SUBJUNCTIVE

j'	ouvre
tu	ouvres
il/elle/on	ouvre
nous	ouvrions
vous	ouvriez
ils/elles	ouvrent

PERFECT

j'	ai ouvert
tu	as ouvert
il/elle/on	a ouvert
nous	avons ouvert
vous	avez ouvert
ils/elles	ont ouvert

IMPERFECT

j'	ouvrais
tu	ouvrais
il/elle/on	ouvrait
nous	ouvrions
vous	ouvriez
ils/elles	ouvraient

FUTURE

j'	ouvrirai
tu	ouvriras
il/elle/on	ouvrira
nous	ouvrirons
vous	ouvrirez
ils/elles	ouvriront

CONDITIONAL

j'	ouvrirais
tu	ouvrirais
il/elle/on	ouvrirait
nous	ouvririons
vous	ouvririez
ils/elles	ouvriraient

IMPERATIVE

ouvre / ouvrons / ouvrez

PAST PARTICIPLE

ouvert

PRESENT PARTICIPLE

ouvrant

——————————— EXAMPLE PHRASES ———————————

Elle **a ouvert** la porte.	_She opened the door._
Est-ce que tu pourrais **ouvrir** la fenêtre?	_Could you open the window?_
Je me suis coupé en **ouvrant** une boîte de conserve.	_I cut myself opening a tin._
La porte **s'est ouverte**.	_The door opened._

• _Note that **s'ouvrir** follows the same pattern, but takes **être** in the perfect tense._
  For an example of a reflexive verb in full, see verb table **6 s'asseoir**.

Table
56

paraître *to appear*

PRESENT

je	parais
tu	parais
il/elle/on	paraît
nous	paraissons
vous	paraissez
ils/elles	paraissent

PRESENT SUBJUNCTIVE

je	paraisse
tu	paraisses
il/elle/on	paraisse
nous	paraissions
vous	paraissiez
ils/elles	paraissent

PERFECT

j'	ai paru
tu	as paru
il/elle/on	a paru
nous	avons paru
vous	avez paru
ils/elles	ont paru

IMPERFECT

je	paraissais
tu	paraissais
il/elle/on	paraissait
nous	paraissions
vous	paraissiez
ils/elles	paraissaient

FUTURE

je	paraîtrai
tu	paraîtras
il/elle/on	paraîtra
nous	paraîtrons
vous	paraîtrez
ils/elles	paraîtront

CONDITIONAL

je	paraîtrais
tu	paraîtrais
il/elle/on	paraîtrait
nous	paraîtrions
vous	paraîtriez
ils/elles	paraîtraient

IMPERATIVE

parais / paraissons / paraissez

PAST PARTICIPLE

paru

PRESENT PARTICIPLE

paraissant

EXAMPLE PHRASES

Elle **paraissait** fatiguée. / *She seemed tired.*
Gisèle **paraît** plus jeune que son âge. / *Gisèle doesn't look her age.*
Il **paraît** qu'il fait chaud toute l'année là-bas. / *Apparently it's hot all year round over there.*

• Note that the verb **apparaître** follows the same pattern as **paraître**, but takes **être** in the perfect tense.

PRESENT

je	pars
tu	pars
il/elle/on	part
nous	partons
vous	partez
ils/elles	partent

PRESENT SUBJUNCTIVE

je	parte
tu	partes
il/elle/on	parte
nous	partions
vous	partiez
ils/elles	partent

PERFECT

je	suis parti(e)
tu	es parti(e)
il/elle/on	est parti(e)
nous	sommes parti(e)s
vous	êtes parti(e)(s)
ils/elles	sont parti(e)s

IMPERFECT

je	partais
tu	partais
il/elle/on	partait
nous	partions
vous	partiez
ils/elles	partaient

FUTURE

je	partirai
tu	partiras
il/elle/on	partira
nous	partirons
vous	partirez
ils/elles	partiront

CONDITIONAL

je	partirais
tu	partirais
il/elle/on	partirait
nous	partirions
vous	partiriez
ils/elles	partiraient

IMPERATIVE

pars / partons / partez

PAST PARTICIPLE

parti

PRESENT PARTICIPLE

partant

——— EXAMPLE PHRASES ———

On **part** en vacances le 15 août.
Ne **partez** pas sans moi!
Elle **est partie** tôt ce matin.

We're going on holiday on 15 August.
Don't leave without me!
She left early this morning.

Table
58

passer *to pass*

PRESENT

je	passe
tu	passes
il/elle/on	passe
nous	passons
vous	passez
ils/elles	passent

PRESENT SUBJUNCTIVE

je	passe
tu	passes
il/elle/on	passe
nous	passions
vous	passiez
ils/elles	passent

PERFECT

j'	ai passé
tu	as passé
il/elle/on	a passé
nous	avons passé
vous	avez passé
ils/elles	ont passé

IMPERFECT

je	passais
tu	passais
il/elle/on	passait
nous	passions
vous	passiez
ils/elles	passaient

FUTURE

je	passerai
tu	passeras
il/elle/on	passera
nous	passerons
vous	passerez
ils/elles	passeront

CONDITIONAL

je	passerais
tu	passerais
il/elle/on	passerait
nous	passerions
vous	passeriez
ils/elles	passeraient

IMPERATIVE

passe / passons / passez

PAST PARTICIPLE

passé

PRESENT PARTICIPLE

passant

─────────── EXAMPLE PHRASES ───────────

Les mois **ont passé**.	*Months passed.*
Il **a passé** son examen en juin.	*He took his exam in June.*
Elle y **a passé** deux mois.	*She spent two months there.*
Elle **est passée** me dire bonjour.	*She came by to say hello.*
L'histoire **se passe** au Mexique.	*The story takes place in Mexico.*

- Note that *passer* can also take **être** in the perfect tense when it means "to call in" or "to go through"
- Note that *se passer* follows the same pattern, but takes **être** in the perfect tense. For an example of a reflexive verb in full, see verb table **6 s'asseoir**.

PRESENT

je	paye
tu	payes
il/elle/on	paye
nous	payons
vous	payez
ils/elles	payent

PRESENT SUBJUNCTIVE

je	paye
tu	payes
il/elle/on	paye
nous	payions
vous	payiez
ils/elles	payent

PERFECT

j'	ai payé
tu	as payé
il/elle/on	a payé
nous	avons payé
vous	avez payé
ils/elles	ont payé

IMPERFECT

je	payais
tu	payais
il/elle/on	payait
nous	payions
vous	payiez
ils/elles	payaient

FUTURE

je	paierai
tu	paieras
il/elle/on	paiera
nous	paierons
vous	paierez
ils/elles	paieront

CONDITIONAL

je	paierais
tu	paierais
il/elle/on	paierait
nous	paierions
vous	paieriez
ils/elles	paieraient

IMPERATIVE

paye / payons / payez

PAST PARTICIPLE

payé

PRESENT PARTICIPLE

payant

EXAMPLE PHRASES

Tu l'**as payé** combien? *How much did you pay for it?*
Ma patronne me **paiera** demain. *My boss will pay me tomorrow.*
Les étudiants **payent** moitié prix. *Students pay half price.*

Table
60

peindre *to paint*

PRESENT

je	peins
tu	peins
il/elle/on	peint
nous	peignons
vous	peignez
ils/elles	peignent

PRESENT SUBJUNCTIVE

je	peigne
tu	peignes
il/elle/on	peigne
nous	peignions
vous	peigniez
ils/elles	peignent

PERFECT

j'	ai peint
tu	as peint
il/elle/on	a peint
nous	avons peint
vous	avez peint
ils/elles	ont peint

IMPERFECT

je	peignais
tu	peignais
il/elle/on	peignait
nous	peignions
vous	peigniez
ils/elles	peignaient

FUTURE

je	peindrai
tu	peindras
il/elle/on	peindra
nous	peindrons
vous	peindrez
ils/elles	peindront

CONDITIONAL

je	peindrais
tu	peindrais
il/elle/on	peindrait
nous	peindrions
vous	peindriez
ils/elles	peindraient

IMPERATIVE

peins / peignons / peignez

PAST PARTICIPLE

peint

PRESENT PARTICIPLE

peignant

EXAMPLE PHRASES

On **a peint** l'entrée en bleu clair. *We painted the hall light blue.*
Ce tableau **a été peint** en 1913. *This picture was painted in 1913.*

PRESENT

je	perds
tu	perds
il/elle/on	perd
nous	perdons
vous	perdez
ils/elles	perdent

PRESENT SUBJUNCTIVE

je	perde
tu	perdes
il/elle/on	perde
nous	perdions
vous	perdiez
ils/elles	perdent

PERFECT

j'	ai perdu
tu	as perdu
il/elle/on	a perdu
nous	avons perdu
vous	avez perdu
ils/elles	ont perdu

IMPERFECT

je	perdais
tu	perdais
il/elle/on	perdait
nous	perdions
vous	perdiez
ils/elles	perdaient

FUTURE

je	perdrai
tu	perdras
il/elle/on	perdra
nous	perdrons
vous	perdrez
ils/elles	perdront

CONDITIONAL

je	perdrais
tu	perdrais
il/elle/on	perdrait
nous	perdrions
vous	perdriez
ils/elles	perdraient

IMPERATIVE

perds / perdons / perdez

PAST PARTICIPLE

perdu

PRESENT PARTICIPLE

perdant

——————————— EXAMPLE PHRASES ———————————

J'**ai perdu** mon porte-monnaie dans le métro.
L'Italie **a perdu** un à zéro.
Si tu **te perds**, appelle-moi.

I lost my purse on the underground.
Italy lost one-nil.
Call me if you get lost.

• Note that **se perdre** follows the same pattern, but takes **être** in the perfect tense. For an example of a reflexive verb in full, see verb table **82 se taire**.

Table
62

plaire *to please*

PRESENT

je	plais
tu	plais
il/elle/on	plaît
nous	plaisons
vous	plaisez
ils/elles	plaisent

PRESENT SUBJUNCTIVE

je	plaise
tu	plaises
il/elle/on	plaise
nous	plaisions
vous	plaisiez
ils/elles	plaisent

PERFECT

j'	ai plu
tu	as plu
il/elle/on	a plu
nous	avons plu
vous	avez plu
ils/elles	ont plu

IMPERFECT

je	plaisais
tu	plaisais
il/elle/on	plaisait
nous	plaisions
vous	plaisiez
ils/elles	plaisaient

FUTURE

je	plairai
tu	plairas
il/elle/on	plaira
nous	plairons
vous	plairez
ils/elles	plairont

CONDITIONAL

je	plairais
tu	plairais
il/elle/on	plairait
nous	plairions
vous	plairiez
ils/elles	plairaient

IMPERATIVE

plais / plaisons / plaisez

PAST PARTICIPLE

plu

PRESENT PARTICIPLE

plaisant

EXAMPLE PHRASES

Le menu ne me **plaît** pas.	*I don't like the menu.*
Ça te **plairait** d'aller à la mer?	*Would you like to go to the seaside?*
Ça t'**a plu**, le film?	*Did you like the film?*
s'il te **plaît**	*please*
s'il vous **plaît**	*please*

PRESENT

il pleut

PRESENT SUBJUNCTIVE

il pleuve

PERFECT

il a plu

IMPERFECT

il pleuvait

FUTURE

il pleuvra

CONDITIONAL

il pleuvrait

IMPERATIVE

not used

PAST PARTICIPLE

plu

PRESENT PARTICIPLE

not used

——————————— EXAMPLE PHRASES ———————————

Il **a plu** toute la journée.
Il **pleut** beaucoup à Glasgow.
J'espère qu'il ne **pleuvra** pas
demain.

It rained all day long.
It rains a lot in Glasgow.
I hope it won't be raining tomorrow.

Table
64

pouvoir *to be able*

PRESENT

je	peux
tu	peux
il/elle/on	peut
nous	pouvons
vous	pouvez
ils/elles	peuvent

PRESENT SUBJUNCTIVE

je	puisse
tu	puisses
il/elle/on	puisse
nous	puissions
vous	puissiez
ils/elles	puissent

PERFECT

j'	ai pu
tu	as pu
il/elle/on	a pu
nous	avons pu
vous	avez pu
ils/elles	ont pu

IMPERFECT

je	pouvais
tu	pouvais
il/elle/on	pouvait
nous	pouvions
vous	pouviez
ils/elles	pouvaient

FUTURE

je	pourrai
tu	pourras
il/elle/on	pourra
nous	pourrons
vous	pourrez
ils/elles	pourront

CONDITIONAL

je	pourrais
tu	pourrais
il/elle/on	pourrait
nous	pourrions
vous	pourriez
ils/elles	pourraient

IMPERATIVE

not used

PAST PARTICIPLE

pu

PRESENT PARTICIPLE

pouvant

EXAMPLE PHRASES

Je **peux** t'aider, si tu veux.   *I can help you if you like.*
J'ai fait tout ce que j'**ai pu**.   *I did all I could.*
Je ne **pourrai** pas venir samedi.   *I won't be able to come on Saturday.*

PRESENT

je	prends
tu	prends
il/elle/on	prend
nous	prenons
vous	prenez
ils/elles	prennent

PRESENT SUBJUNCTIVE

je	prenne
tu	prennes
il/elle/on	prenne
nous	prenions
vous	preniez
ils/elles	prennent

PERFECT

j'	ai pris
tu	as pris
il/elle/on	a pris
nous	avons pris
vous	avez pris
ils/elles	ont pris

IMPERFECT

je	prenais
tu	prenais
il/elle/on	prenait
nous	prenions
vous	preniez
ils/elles	prenaient

FUTURE

je	prendrai
tu	prendras
il/elle/on	prendra
nous	prendrons
vous	prendrez
ils/elles	prendront

CONDITIONAL

je	prendrais
tu	prendrais
il/elle/on	prendrait
nous	prendrions
vous	prendriez
ils/elles	prendraient

IMPERATIVE

prends / prenons / prenez

PAST PARTICIPLE

pris

PRESENT PARTICIPLE

prenant

—————— EXAMPLE PHRASES ——————

J'**ai pris** plein de photos.	*I took lots of pictures.*
N'oublie pas de **prendre** ton passeport.	*Don't forget to take your passport.*
Il **prendra** le train de 8h20.	*He'll take the 8.20 train.*
Pour qui est-ce qu'il **se prend**?	*Who does he think he is?*

- *Note that* **se prendre** *follows the same pattern, but takes* **être** *in the perfect tense. For an example of a reflexive verb in full, see verb table* **82 se taire**.

Table
66 **protéger** *to protect*

PRESENT

je	protège
tu	protèges
il/elle/on	protège
nous	protégeons
vous	protégez
ils/elles	protègent

PRESENT SUBJUNCTIVE

je	protège
tu	protèges
il/elle/on	protège
nous	protégions
vous	protégiez
ils/elles	protègent

PERFECT

j'	ai protégé
tu	as protégé
il/elle/on	a protégé
nous	avons protégé
vous	avez protégé
ils/elles	ont protégé

IMPERFECT

je	protégeais
tu	protégeais
il/elle/on	protégeait
nous	protégions
vous	protégiez
ils/elles	protégeaient

FUTURE

je	protégerai
tu	protégeras
il/elle/on	protégera
nous	protégerons
vous	protégerez
ils/elles	protégeront

CONDITIONAL

je	protégerais
tu	protégerais
il/elle/on	protégerait
nous	protégerions
vous	protégeriez
ils/elles	protégeraient

IMPERATIVE
protège / protégeons / protégez

PAST PARTICIPLE
protégé

PRESENT PARTICIPLE
protégeant

--- EXAMPLE PHRASES ---

Il **protège** sa petite sœur à l'école.
Protège ton livre de la pluie.
Le champ **est protégé** du vent par la colline.

He protects his little sister at school.
Protect your book from the rain.
The field is sheltered from the wind by the hill.

PRESENT

je	reçois
tu	reçois
il/elle/on	reçoit
nous	recevons
vous	recevez
ils/elles	reçoivent

PRESENT SUBJUNCTIVE

je	reçoive
tu	reçoives
il/elle/on	reçoive
nous	recevions
vous	receviez
ils/elles	reçoivent

PERFECT

j'	ai reçu
tu	as reçu
il/elle/on	a reçu
nous	avons reçu
vous	avez reçu
ils/elles	ont reçu

IMPERFECT

je	recevais
tu	recevais
il/elle/on	recevait
nous	recevions
vous	receviez
ils/elles	recevaient

FUTURE

je	recevrai
tu	recevras
il/elle/on	recevra
nous	recevrons
vous	recevrez
ils/elles	recevront

CONDITIONAL

je	recevrais
tu	recevrais
il/elle/on	recevrait
nous	recevrions
vous	recevriez
ils/elles	recevraient

IMPERATIVE

reçois / recevons / recevez

PAST PARTICIPLE

reçu

PRESENT PARTICIPLE

recevant

─────────── EXAMPLE PHRASES ───────────

Elle **a reçu** une lettre de Charlotte.	*She received a letter from Charlotte.*
Je ne **reçois** jamais de courrier.	*I never get any mail.*
Elle **recevra** une réponse la semaine prochaine.	*She'll get an answer next week.*

Table
68

rentrer *to go back; to go in*

PRESENT

je	rentre
tu	rentres
il/elle/on	rentre
nous	rentrons
vous	rentrez
ils/elles	rentrent

PRESENT SUBJUNCTIVE

je	rentre
tu	rentres
il/elle/on	rentre
nous	rentrions
vous	rentriez
ils/elles	rentrent

PERFECT

je	suis rentré(e)
tu	es rentré(e)
il/elle/on	est rentré(e)
nous	sommes rentré(e)s
vous	êtes rentré(e)(s)
ils/elles	sont rentré(e)s

IMPERFECT

je	rentrais
tu	rentrais
il/elle/on	rentrait
nous	rentrions
vous	rentriez
ils/elles	rentraient

FUTURE

je	rentrerai
tu	rentreras
il/elle/on	rentrera
nous	rentrerons
vous	rentrerez
ils/elles	rentreront

CONDITIONAL

je	rentrerais
tu	rentrerais
il/elle/on	rentrerait
nous	rentrerions
vous	rentreriez
ils/elles	rentreraient

IMPERATIVE

rentre / rentrons / rentrez

PAST PARTICIPLE

rentré

PRESENT PARTICIPLE

rentrant

EXAMPLE PHRASES

Ne **rentre** pas trop tard.
Don't come home too late.

Ils **sont rentrés** dans le magasin.
They went into the shop.

À quelle heure est-ce qu'elle **est rentrée**?
What time did she get in?

Je **rentre** déjeuner à midi.
I go home for lunch.

Il **a** déjà **rentré** la voiture dans le garage.
He's already brought the car into the garage.

- Note that **rentrer** takes **avoir** in the perfect tense when it is used with a direct object.

PRESENT

je	réponds
tu	réponds
il/elle/on	répond
nous	répondons
vous	répondez
ils/elles	répondent

PRESENT SUBJUNCTIVE

je	réponde
tu	répondes
il/elle/on	réponde
nous	répondions
vous	répondiez
ils/elles	répondent

PERFECT

j'	ai répondu
tu	as répondu
il/elle/on	a répondu
nous	avons répondu
vous	avez répondu
ils/elles	ont répondu

IMPERFECT

je	répondais
tu	répondais
il/elle/on	répondait
nous	répondions
vous	répondiez
ils/elles	répondaient

FUTURE

je	répondrai
tu	répondras
il/elle/on	répondra
nous	répondrons
vous	répondrez
ils/elles	répondront

CONDITIONAL

je	répondrais
tu	répondrais
il/elle/on	répondrait
nous	répondrions
vous	répondriez
ils/elles	répondraient

IMPERATIVE

réponds / répondons / répondez

PAST PARTICIPLE

répondu

PRESENT PARTICIPLE

répondant

EXAMPLE PHRASES

Lisez le texte et **répondez** aux questions.
C'est elle qui **a répondu** au téléphone.
Ça ne **répond** pas.

Read the text and answer the questions.
She answered the phone.
There's no reply.

Table
70

résoudre *to solve*

PRESENT

je	résous
tu	résous
il/elle/on	résout
nous	résolvons
vous	résolvez
ils/elles	résolvent

PRESENT SUBJUNCTIVE

je	résolve
tu	résolves
il/elle/on	résolve
nous	résolvions
vous	résolviez
ils/elles	résolvent

PERFECT

j'	ai résolu
tu	as résolu
il/elle/on	a résolu
nous	avons résolu
vous	avez résolu
ils/elles	ont résolu

IMPERFECT

je	résolvais
tu	résolvais
il/elle/on	résolvait
nous	résolvions
vous	résolviez
ils/elles	résolvaient

FUTURE

je	résoudrai
tu	résoudras
il/elle/on	résoudra
nous	résoudrons
vous	résoudrez
ils/elles	résoudront

CONDITIONAL

je	résoudrais
tu	résoudrais
il/elle/on	résoudrait
nous	résoudrions
vous	résoudriez
ils/elles	résoudraient

IMPERATIVE

résous / résolvons / résolvez

PAST PARTICIPLE

résolu

PRESENT PARTICIPLE

résolvant

EXAMPLE PHRASES

J'**ai résolu** le problème.	I've solved the problem.
La violence ne **résout** rien.	Violence doesn't solve anything.

• Note that the verb **dissoudre** follows the same pattern as **résoudre**, except for its past participle which is **dissous** (m), **dissoute** (f).

PRESENT

je	reste
tu	restes
il/elle/on	reste
nous	restons
vous	restez
ils/elles	restent

PRESENT SUBJUNCTIVE

je	reste
tu	restes
il/elle/on	reste
nous	restions
vous	restiez
ils/elles	restent

PERFECT

je	suis resté(e)
tu	es resté(e)
il/elle/on	est resté(e)
nous	sommes resté(e)s
vous	êtes resté(e)(s)
ils/elles	sont resté(e)s

IMPERFECT

je	restais
tu	restais
il/elle/on	restait
nous	restions
vous	restiez
ils/elles	restaient

FUTURE

je	resterai
tu	resteras
il/elle/on	restera
nous	resterons
vous	resterez
ils/elles	resteront

CONDITIONAL

je	resterais
tu	resterais
il/elle/on	resterait
nous	resterions
vous	resteriez
ils/elles	resteraient

IMPERATIVE

reste / restons / restez

PAST PARTICIPLE

resté

PRESENT PARTICIPLE

restant

——————————— EXAMPLE PHRASES ———————————

Cet été, je **reste** en Écosse.
Ils ne **sont** pas **restés** très longtemps.
Il leur **restait** encore un peu d'argent.

I'm staying in Scotland this summer.
They didn't stay very long.

They still had some money left.

Table
72

retourner *to return*

PRESENT
je	retourne
tu	retournes
il/elle/on	retourne
nous	retournons
vous	retournez
ils/elles	retournent

PRESENT SUBJUNCTIVE
je	retourne
tu	retournes
il/elle/on	retourne
nous	retournions
vous	retourniez
ils/elles	retournent

PERFECT
je	suis retourné(e)
tu	es retourné(e)
il/elle/on	est retourné(e)
nous	sommes retourné(e)s
vous	êtes retourné(e)(s)
ils/elles	sont retourné(e)s

IMPERFECT
je	retournais
tu	retournais
il/elle/on	retournait
nous	retournions
vous	retourniez
ils/elles	retournaient

FUTURE
je	retournerai
tu	retourneras
il/elle/on	retournera
nous	retournerons
vous	retournerez
ils/elles	retourneront

CONDITIONAL
je	retournerais
tu	retournerais
il/elle/on	retournerait
nous	retournerions
vous	retourneriez
ils/elles	retourneraient

IMPERATIVE
retourne / retournons / retournez

PAST PARTICIPLE
retourné

PRESENT PARTICIPLE
retournant

EXAMPLE PHRASES

Tu **es retournée** à Londres? — *Have you been back to London?*
J'aimerais bien **retourner** en Italie un jour. — *I'd like to go back to Italy one day.*
Elle **a retourné** la carte pour vérifier. — *She turned the card over to check.*
Zoë, **retourne-toi**! — *Turn around Zoë!*

- Note that **retourner** takes **avoir** in the perfect tense when it is used with a direct object.
- Note that **se retourner** follows the same pattern, and takes **être** in the perfect tense. For an example of a reflexive verb in full, see verb table **82 se taire**.

PRESENT

je	reviens
tu	reviens
il/elle/on	revient
nous	revenons
vous	revenez
ils/elles	reviennent

PRESENT SUBJUNCTIVE

je	revienne
tu	reviennes
il/elle/on	revienne
nous	revenions
vous	reveniez
ils/elles	reviennent

PERFECT

je	suis revenu(e)
tu	es revenu(e)
il/elle/on	est revenu(e)
nous	sommes revenu(e)s
vous	êtes revenu(e)(s)
ils/elles	sont revenu(e)s

IMPERFECT

je	revenais
tu	revenais
il/elle/on	revenait
nous	revenions
vous	reveniez
ils/elles	revenaient

FUTURE

je	reviendrai
tu	reviendras
il/elle/on	reviendra
nous	reviendrons
vous	reviendrez
ils/elles	reviendront

CONDITIONAL

je	reviendrais
tu	reviendrais
il/elle/on	reviendrait
nous	reviendrions
vous	reviendriez
ils/elles	reviendraient

IMPERATIVE

reviens / revenons / revenez

PAST PARTICIPLE

revenu

PRESENT PARTICIPLE

revenant

——————————— **EXAMPLE PHRASES** ———————————

Mon chat n'**est** toujours pas
revenu.

My cat still hasn't come back.

Je **reviens** dans cinq minutes!

I'll be back in five minutes!

Ça me **revient**!

It's coming back to me now!

Table
74

rire *to laugh*

PRESENT

je	ris
tu	ris
il/elle/on	rit
nous	rions
vous	riez
ils/elles	rient

PRESENT SUBJUNCTIVE

je	rie
tu	ries
il/elle/on	rie
nous	riions
vous	riiez
ils/elles	rient

PERFECT

j'	ai ri
tu	as ri
il/elle/on	a ri
nous	avons ri
vous	avez ri
ils/elles	ont ri

IMPERFECT

je	riais
tu	riais
il/elle/on	riait
nous	riions
vous	riiez
ils/elles	riaient

FUTURE

je	rirai
tu	riras
il/elle/on	rira
nous	rirons
vous	rirez
ils/elles	riront

CONDITIONAL

je	rirais
tu	rirais
il/elle/on	rirait
nous	ririons
vous	ririez
ils/elles	riraient

IMPERATIVE

ris / rions / riez

PAST PARTICIPLE

ri

PRESENT PARTICIPLE

riant

EXAMPLE PHRASES

On **a** bien **ri**.
Ne **ris** pas, ce n'est pas drôle!
C'était juste pour **rire**.

We had a good laugh.
Don't laugh, it's not funny!
It was only for a laugh.

PRESENT

je	romps
tu	romps
il/elle/on	rompt
nous	rompons
vous	rompez
ils/elles	rompent

PRESENT SUBJUNCTIVE

je	rompe
tu	rompes
il/elle/on	rompe
nous	rompions
vous	rompiez
ils/elles	rompent

PERFECT

j'	ai rompu
tu	as rompu
il/elle/on	a rompu
nous	avons rompu
vous	avez rompu
ils/elles	ont rompu

IMPERFECT

je	rompais
tu	rompais
il/elle/on	rompait
nous	rompions
vous	rompiez
ils/elles	rompaient

FUTURE

je	romprai
tu	rompras
il/elle/on	rompra
nous	romprons
vous	romprez
ils/elles	rompront

CONDITIONAL

je	romprais
tu	romprais
il/elle/on	romprait
nous	romprions
vous	rompriez
ils/elles	rompraient

IMPERATIVE

romps / rompons / rompez

PAST PARTICIPLE

rompu

PRESENT PARTICIPLE

rompant

─── EXAMPLE PHRASES ───

Elle **a rompu** le silence.
Paul et Jo **ont rompu**.

She broke the silence.
Paul and Jo have split up.

Table
76
savoir *to know*

PRESENT

je	sais
tu	sais
il/elle/on	sait
nous	savons
vous	savez
ils/elles	savent

PRESENT SUBJUNCTIVE

je	sache
tu	saches
il/elle/on	sache
nous	sachions
vous	sachiez
ils/elles	sachent

PERFECT

j'	ai su
tu	as su
il/elle/on	a su
nous	avons su
vous	avez su
ils/elles	ont su

IMPERFECT

je	savais
tu	savais
il/elle/on	savait
nous	savions
vous	saviez
ils/elles	savaient

FUTURE

je	saurai
tu	sauras
il/elle/on	saura
nous	saurons
vous	saurez
ils/elles	sauront

CONDITIONAL

je	saurais
tu	saurais
il/elle/on	saurait
nous	saurions
vous	sauriez
ils/elles	sauraient

IMPERATIVE
sache / sachons / sachez

PAST PARTICIPLE
su

PRESENT PARTICIPLE
sachant

EXAMPLE PHRASES

Tu **sais** ce que tu vas faire l'année prochaine?
Je ne **sais** pas.
Elle ne **sait** pas nager.
Tu **savais** que son père était pakistanais?

Do you know what you're doing next year?
I don't know.
She can't swim.
Did you know her father was Pakistani?

PRESENT

je	sens
tu	sens
il/elle/on	sent
nous	sentons
vous	sentez
ils/elles	sentent

PRESENT SUBJUNCTIVE

je	sente
tu	sentes
il/elle/on	sente
nous	sentions
vous	sentiez
ils/elles	sentent

PERFECT

j'	ai senti
tu	as senti
il/elle/on	a senti
nous	avons senti
vous	avez senti
ils/elles	ont senti

IMPERFECT

je	sentais
tu	sentais
il/elle/on	sentait
nous	sentions
vous	sentiez
ils/elles	sentaient

FUTURE

je	sentirai
tu	sentiras
il/elle/on	sentira
nous	sentirons
vous	sentirez
ils/elles	sentiront

CONDITIONAL

je	sentirais
tu	sentirais
il/elle/on	sentirait
nous	sentirions
vous	sentiriez
ils/elles	sentiraient

IMPERATIVE

sens / sentons / sentez

PAST PARTICIPLE

senti

PRESENT PARTICIPLE

sentant

— EXAMPLE PHRASES —

Ça **sentait** mauvais.
Je n'**ai** rien **senti**.
Elle ne **se sent** pas bien.

It smelt bad.
I didn't feel a thing.
She's not feeling well.

• Note that **se sentir** follows the same pattern, but takes **être** in the perfect tense. For an example of a reflexive verb in full, see verb table **82 se taire**.

Table
78

servir _to serve_

PRESENT		PRESENT SUBJUNCTIVE	
je	sers	je	serve
tu	sers	tu	serves
il/elle/on	sert	il/elle/on	serve
nous	servons	nous	servions
vous	servez	vous	serviez
ils/elles	servent	ils/elles	servent

PERFECT		IMPERFECT	
j'	ai servi	je	servais
tu	as servi	tu	servais
il/elle/on	a servi	il/elle/on	servait
nous	avons servi	nous	servions
vous	avez servi	vous	serviez
ils/elles	ont servi	ils/elles	servaient

FUTURE		CONDITIONAL	
je	servirai	je	servirais
tu	serviras	tu	servirais
il/elle/on	servira	il/elle/on	servirait
nous	servirons	nous	servirions
vous	servirez	vous	serviriez
ils/elles	serviront	ils/elles	serviraient

IMPERATIVE
sers / servons / servez

PAST PARTICIPLE
servi

PRESENT PARTICIPLE
servant

--- EXAMPLE PHRASES ---

On vous **sert**? _Are you being served?_
Ça **sert** à quoi, ce bouton? _What is this button for?_
Servez-vous en viande. _Help yourself to meat._

- Note that _se servir_ follows the same pattern, but takes **être** in the perfect tense. For an example of a reflexive verb in full, see verb table **82 se taire**.

PRESENT

je	sors
tu	sors
il/elle/on	sort
nous	sortons
vous	sortez
ils/elles	sortent

PRESENT SUBJUNCTIVE

je	sorte
tu	sortes
il/elle/on	sorte
nous	sortions
vous	sortiez
ils/elles	sortent

PERFECT

je	suis sorti(e)
tu	es sorti(e)
il/elle/on	est sorti(e)
nous	sommes sorti(e)s
vous	êtes sorti(e)(s)
ils/elles	sont sorti(e)s

IMPERFECT

je	sortais
tu	sortais
il/elle/on	sortait
nous	sortions
vous	sortiez
ils/elles	sortaient

FUTURE

je	sortirai
tu	sortiras
il/elle/on	sortira
nous	sortirons
vous	sortirez
ils/elles	sortiront

CONDITIONAL

je	sortirais
tu	sortirais
il/elle/on	sortirait
nous	sortirions
vous	sortiriez
ils/elles	sortiraient

IMPERATIVE

sors / sortons / sortez

PRESENT PARTICIPLE

sortant

PAST PARTICIPLE

sorti

EXAMPLE PHRASES

Je ne **suis** pas **sortie** ce week-end.
Aurélie **sort** avec Bruno.
Elle **est sortie** de l'hôpital hier.
Je n'**ai** pas **sorti** le chien parce qu'il pleuvait.

I didn't go out this weekend.
Aurélie is going out with Bruno.
She came out of hospital yesterday.
I didn't take the dog out for a walk because it was raining.

• Note that **sortir** takes **avoir** in the perfect tense when it is used with a direct object.

Table
80

suffire *to be enough*

PRESENT

je	suffis
tu	suffis
il/elle/on	suffit
nous	suffisons
vous	suffisez
ils/elles	suffisent

PRESENT SUBJUNCTIVE

je	suffise
tu	suffises
il/elle/on	suffise
nous	suffisions
vous	suffisiez
ils/elles	suffisent

PERFECT

j'	ai suffi
tu	as suffi
il/elle/on	a suffi
nous	avons suffi
vous	avez suffi
ils/elles	ont suffi

IMPERFECT

je	suffisais
tu	suffisais
il/elle/on	suffisait
nous	suffisions
vous	suffisiez
ils/elles	suffisaient

FUTURE

je	suffirai
tu	suffiras
il/elle/on	suffira
nous	suffirons
vous	suffirez
ils/elles	suffiront

CONDITIONAL

je	suffirais
tu	suffirais
il/elle/on	suffirait
nous	suffirions
vous	suffiriez
ils/elles	suffiraient

IMPERATIVE

suffis / suffisons / suffisez

PAST PARTICIPLE

suffi

PRESENT PARTICIPLE

suffisant

EXAMPLE PHRASES

Ça te **suffira**, 10 euros?   *Will 10 euros be enough?*
Ça **suffit**!   *That's enough!*
Il **suffisait** de me le demander.   *You only had to ask.*

• Note that the verb **frire** follows the same pattern as **suffire**, but that it is used mainly in the present singular and in compound tenses such as the perfect tense. Its past participle is **frit**.

PRESENT

je	suis
tu	suis
il/elle/on	suit
nous	suivons
vous	suivez
ils/elles	suivent

PRESENT SUBJUNCTIVE

je	suive
tu	suives
il/elle/on	suive
nous	suivions
vous	suiviez
ils/elles	suivent

PERFECT

j'	ai suivi
tu	as suivi
il/elle/on	a suivi
nous	avons suivi
vous	avez suivi
ils/elles	ont suivi

IMPERFECT

je	suivais
tu	suivais
il/elle/on	suivait
nous	suivions
vous	suiviez
ils/elles	suivaient

FUTURE

je	suivrai
tu	suivras
il/elle/on	suivra
nous	suivrons
vous	suivrez
ils/elles	suivront

CONDITIONAL

je	suivrais
tu	suivrais
il/elle/on	suivrait
nous	suivrions
vous	suivriez
ils/elles	suivraient

IMPERATIVE

suis / suivons / suivez

PAST PARTICIPLE

suivi

PRESENT PARTICIPLE

suivant

─── EXAMPLE PHRASES ───

Mon chat me **suit** partout dans la maison.
Il **a suivi** un cours d'allemand pendant six mois.
Elles n'arrivent pas à **suivre** en maths.

My cat follows me everywhere around the house.
He did a German course for 6 months.
They can't keep up in maths.

Table
82

se taire *to stop talking*

PRESENT		PRESENT SUBJUNCTIVE	
je	me tais	je	me taise
tu	te tais	tu	te taises
il/elle/on	se tait	il/elle/on	se taise
nous	nous taisons	nous	nous taisions
vous	vous taisez	vous	vous taisiez
ils/elles	se taisent	ils/elles	se taisent

PERFECT		IMPERFECT	
je	me suis tu(e)	je	me taisais
tu	t'es tu(e)	tu	te taisais
il/elle/on	s'est tu(e)	il/elle/on	se taisait
nous	nous sommes tu(e)s	nous	nous taisions
vous	vous êtes tu(e)(s)	vous	vous taisiez
ils/elles	se sont tu(e)s	ils/elles	se taisaient

FUTURE		CONDITIONAL	
je	me tairai	je	me tairais
tu	te tairas	tu	te tairais
il/elle/on	se taira	il/elle/on	se tairait
nous	nous tairons	nous	nous tairions
vous	vous tairez	vous	vous tairiez
ils/elles	se tairont	ils/elles	se tairaient

IMPERATIVE
tais-toi / taisons-nous / taisez-vous

PAST PARTICIPLE
tu

PRESENT PARTICIPLE
se taisant

--- EXAMPLE PHRASES ---

Il **s'est tu**.	*He stopped talking.*
Taisez-vous!	*Be quiet!*
Sophie, **tais-toi**!	*Be quiet Sophie!*

PRESENT

je	tiens
tu	tiens
il/elle/on	tient
nous	tenons
vous	tenez
ils/elles	tiennent

PRESENT SUBJUNCTIVE

je	tienne
tu	tiennes
il/elle/on	tienne
nous	tenions
vous	teniez
ils/elles	tiennent

PERFECT

j'	ai tenu
tu	as tenu
il/elle/on	a tenu
nous	avons tenu
vous	avez tenu
ils/elles	ont tenu

IMPERFECT

je	tenais
tu	tenais
il/elle/on	tenait
nous	tenions
vous	teniez
ils/elles	tenaient

FUTURE

je	tiendrai
tu	tiendras
il/elle/on	tiendra
nous	tiendrons
vous	tiendrez
ils/elles	tiendront

CONDITIONAL

je	tiendrais
tu	tiendrais
il/elle/on	tiendrait
nous	tiendrions
vous	tiendriez
ils/elles	tiendraient

IMPERATIVE

tiens / tenons / tenez

PAST PARTICIPLE

tenu

PRESENT PARTICIPLE

tenant

--- EXAMPLE PHRASES ---

Tiens-moi la main. — *Hold my hand.*
Elle **tenait** beaucoup à son chat. — *She was really attached to her cat.*
Tiens, prends mon stylo. — *Here, have my pen.*
Tiens-toi droit! — *Sit up straight!*

• Note that *se tenir* follows the same pattern, but takes **être** in the perfect tense.
  For an example of a reflexive verb in full, see verb table **82 se taire**.

Table
84

tomber *to fall*

PRESENT

je	tombe
tu	tombes
il/elle/on	tombe
nous	tombons
vous	tombez
ils/elles	tombent

PRESENT SUBJUNCTIVE

je	tombe
tu	tombes
il/elle/on	tombe
nous	tombions
vous	tombiez
ils/elles	tombent

PERFECT

je	suis tombé(e)
tu	es tombé(e)
il/elle/on	est tombé(e)
nous	sommes tombé(e)s
vous	êtes tombé(e)(s)
ils/elles	sont tombé(e)s

IMPERFECT

je	tombais
tu	tombais
il/elle/on	tombait
nous	tombions
vous	tombiez
ils/elles	tombaient

FUTURE

je	tomberai
tu	tomberas
il/elle/on	tombera
nous	tomberons
vous	tomberez
ils/elles	tomberont

CONDITIONAL

je	tomberais
tu	tomberais
il/elle/on	tomberait
nous	tomberions
vous	tomberiez
ils/elles	tomberaient

IMPERATIVE

tombe / tombons / tombez

PAST PARTICIPLE

tombé

PRESENT PARTICIPLE

tombant

--- EXAMPLE PHRASES ---

Attention, tu vas **tomber**!
Nicole **est tombée** de cheval.
Elle s'est fait mal en **tombant**
dans l'escalier.

Be careful, you'll fall!
Nicole fell off her horse.
She hurt herself falling down the
stairs.

PRESENT

je	trais
tu	trais
il/elle/on	trait
nous	trayons
vous	trayez
ils/elles	traient

PRESENT SUBJUNCTIVE

je	traie
tu	traies
il/elle/on	traie
nous	trayions
vous	trayiez
ils/elles	traient

PERFECT

j'	ai trait
tu	as trait
il/elle/on	a trait
nous	avons trait
vous	avez trait
ils/elles	ont trait

IMPERFECT

je	trayais
tu	trayais
il/elle/on	trayait
nous	trayions
vous	trayiez
ils/elles	trayaient

FUTURE

je	trairai
tu	trairas
il/elle/on	traira
nous	trairons
vous	trairez
ils/elles	trairont

CONDITIONAL

je	trairais
tu	trairais
il/elle/on	trairait
nous	trairions
vous	trairiez
ils/elles	trairaient

IMPERATIVE

trais / trayons / trayez

PAST PARTICIPLE

trait

PRESENT PARTICIPLE

trayant

————————— EXAMPLE PHRASES —————————

À la ferme, on a appris à **traire** les vaches.
We learnt to milk cows on the farm.

Elle **trait** les vaches à six heures du matin.
She milks the cows at 6 am.

Table
86

vaincre *to defeat*

PRESENT

je	vaincs
tu	vaincs
il/elle/on	vainc
nous	vainquons
vous	vainquez
ils/elles	vainquent

PRESENT SUBJUNCTIVE

je	vainque
tu	vainques
il/elle/on	vainque
nous	vainquions
vous	vainquiez
ils/elles	vainquent

PERFECT

j'	ai vaincu
tu	as vaincu
il/elle/on	a vaincu
nous	avons vaincu
vous	avez vaincu
ils/elles	ont vaincu

IMPERFECT

je	vainquais
tu	vainquais
il/elle/on	vainquait
nous	vainquions
vous	vainquiez
ils/elles	vainquaient

FUTURE

je	vaincrai
tu	vaincras
il/elle/on	vaincra
nous	vaincrons
vous	vaincrez
ils/elles	vaincront

CONDITIONAL

je	vaincrais
tu	vaincrais
il/elle/on	vaincrait
nous	vaincrions
vous	vaincriez
ils/elles	vaincraient

IMPERATIVE

vaincs / vainquons / vainquez

PAST PARTICIPLE

vaincu

PRESENT PARTICIPLE

vainquant

─────────── EXAMPLE PHRASES ───────────

L'armée **a été vaincue**.
La France **a vaincu** le Brésil trois
buts à deux.

The army was defeated.
France beat Brazil 3 goals to 2.

PRESENT

je	vaux
tu	vaux
il/elle/on	vaut
nous	valons
vous	valez
ils/elles	valent

PRESENT SUBJUNCTIVE

je	vaille
tu	vailles
il/elle/on	vaille
nous	valions
vous	valiez
ils/elles	vaillent

PERFECT

j'	ai valu
tu	as valu
il/elle/on	a valu
nous	avons valu
vous	avez valu
ils/elles	ont valu

IMPERFECT

je	valais
tu	valais
il/elle/on	valait
nous	valions
vous	valiez
ils/elles	valaient

FUTURE

je	vaudrai
tu	vaudras
il/elle/on	vaudra
nous	vaudrons
vous	vaudrez
ils/elles	vaudront

CONDITIONAL

je	vaudrais
tu	vaudrais
il/elle/on	vaudrait
nous	vaudrions
vous	vaudriez
ils/elles	vaudraient

IMPERATIVE

vaux / valons / valez

PAST PARTICIPLE

valu

PRESENT PARTICIPLE

valant

EXAMPLE PHRASES

Ça **vaut** combien?
Ça **vaudrait** la peine d'essayer.
Il **vaut** mieux ne pas y penser.

How much is it worth?
It would be worth a try.
It's best not to think about it.

Table
88

vendre *to sell*

PRESENT		**PRESENT SUBJUNCTIVE**	
je	vends	je	vende
tu	vends	tu	vendes
il/elle/on	vend	il/elle/on	vende
nous	vendons	nous	vendions
vous	vendez	vous	vendiez
ils/elles	vendent	ils/elles	vendent

PERFECT		**IMPERFECT**	
j'	ai vendu	je	vendais
tu	as vendu	tu	vendais
il/elle/on	a vendu	il/elle/on	vendait
nous	avons vendu	nous	vendions
vous	avez vendu	vous	vendiez
ils/elles	ont vendu	ils/elles	vendaient

FUTURE		**CONDITIONAL**	
je	vendrai	je	vendrais
tu	vendras	tu	vendrais
il/elle/on	vendra	il/elle/on	vendrait
nous	vendrons	nous	vendrions
vous	vendrez	vous	vendriez
ils/elles	vendront	ils/elles	vendraient

IMPERATIVE
vends / vendons / vendez

PAST PARTICIPLE
vendu

PRESENT PARTICIPLE
vendant

———————————— EXAMPLE PHRASES ————————————

Il m'**a vendu** son vélo pour 50 euros.   *He sold me his bike for 50 euros.*

Est-ce que vous **vendez** des piles?   *Do you sell batteries?*

Elle voudrait **vendre** sa voiture.   *She would like to sell her car.*

PRESENT

je	viens
tu	viens
il/elle/on	vient
nous	venons
vous	venez
ils/elles	viennent

PRESENT SUBJUNCTIVE

je	vienne
tu	viennes
il/elle/on	vienne
nous	venions
vous	veniez
ils/elles	viennent

PERFECT

je	suis venu(e)
tu	es venu(e)
il/elle/on	est venu(e)
nous	sommes venu(e)s
vous	êtes venu(e)(s)
ils/elles	sont venu(e)s

IMPERFECT

je	venais
tu	venais
il/elle/on	venait
nous	venions
vous	veniez
ils/elles	venaient

FUTURE

je	viendrai
tu	viendras
il/elle/on	viendra
nous	viendrons
vous	viendrez
ils/elles	viendront

CONDITIONAL

je	viendrais
tu	viendrais
il/elle/on	viendrait
nous	viendrions
vous	viendriez
ils/elles	viendraient

IMPERATIVE

viens / venons / venez

PAST PARTICIPLE

venu

PRESENT PARTICIPLE

venant

──────── EXAMPLE PHRASES ────────

Elle ne **viendra** pas cette année. / *She won't be coming this year.*
Fatou et Malik **viennent** du Sénégal. / *Fatou and Malik come from Senegal.*
Je **viens** de manger. / *I've just eaten.*

- Note that the verbs **convenir** and **prévenir** follow the same pattern as **venir**, but take **avoir** in the perfect tense.

Table
90

vêtir *to dress*

PRESENT

je	vêts
tu	vêts
il/elle/on	vêt
nous	vêtons
vous	vêtez
ils/elles	vêtent

PRESENT SUBJUNCTIVE

je	vête
tu	vêtes
il/elle/on	vête
nous	vêtions
vous	vêtiez
ils/elles	vêtent

PERFECT

j'	ai vêtu
tu	as vêtu
il/elle/on	a vêtu
nous	avons vêtu
vous	avez vêtu
ils/elles	ont vêtu

IMPERFECT

je	vêtais
tu	vêtais
il/elle/on	vêtait
nous	vêtions
vous	vêtiez
ils/elles	vêtaient

FUTURE

je	vêtirai
tu	vêtiras
il/elle/on	vêtira
nous	vêtirons
vous	vêtirez
ils/elles	vêtiront

CONDITIONAL

je	vêtirais
tu	vêtirais
il/elle/on	vêtirait
nous	vêtirions
vous	vêtiriez
ils/elles	vêtiraient

IMPERATIVE

vêts / vêtons / vêtez

PAST PARTICIPLE

vêtu

PRESENT PARTICIPLE

vêtant

--- EXAMPLE PHRASES ---

Il **était vêtu** d'un pantalon et d'un pull.
Il faut se lever, se laver et **se vêtir** en 10 minutes.

He was wearing trousers and a jumper.
You have to get up, get washed and get dressed in 10 minutes.

- Note that **se vêtir** follows the same pattern, but takes **être** in the perfect tense. For an example of a reflexive verb in full, see verb table **82 se taire**.

PRESENT

je	vis
tu	vis
il/elle/on	vit
nous	vivons
vous	vivez
ils/elles	vivent

PRESENT SUBJUNCTIVE

je	vive
tu	vives
il/elle/on	vive
nous	vivions
vous	viviez
ils/elles	vivent

PERFECT

j'	ai vécu
tu	as vécu
il/elle/on	a vécu
nous	avons vécu
vous	avez vécu
ils/elles	ont vécu

IMPERFECT

je	vivais
tu	vivais
il/elle/on	vivait
nous	vivions
vous	viviez
ils/elles	vivaient

FUTURE

je	vivrai
tu	vivras
il/elle/on	vivra
nous	vivrons
vous	vivrez
ils/elles	vivront

CONDITIONAL

je	vivrais
tu	vivrais
il/elle/on	vivrait
nous	vivrions
vous	vivriez
ils/elles	vivraient

IMPERATIVE

vis / vivons / vivez

PAST PARTICIPLE

vécu

PRESENT PARTICIPLE

vivant

——————————— EXAMPLE PHRASES ———————————

Ma sœur **vit** en Espagne.
Il **a vécu** dix ans à Lyon.
Les gorilles **vivent** surtout dans la forêt.

My sister lives in Spain.
He lived in Lyon for 10 years.
Gorillas mostly live in the forest.

Table
92

voir *to see*

PRESENT

je	vois
tu	vois
il/elle/on	voit
nous	voyons
vous	voyez
ils/elles	voient

PRESENT SUBJUNCTIVE

je	voie
tu	voies
il/elle/on	voie
nous	voyions
vous	voyiez
ils/elles	voient

PERFECT

j'	ai vu
tu	as vu
il/elle/on	a vu
nous	avons vu
vous	avez vu
ils/elles	ont vu

IMPERFECT

je	voyais
tu	voyais
il/elle/on	voyait
nous	voyions
vous	voyiez
ils/elles	voyaient

FUTURE

je	verrai
tu	verras
il/elle/on	verra
nous	verrons
vous	verrez
ils/elles	verront

CONDITIONAL

je	verrais
tu	verrais
il/elle/on	verrait
nous	verrions
vous	verriez
ils/elles	verraient

IMPERATIVE

vois / voyons / voyez

PAST PARTICIPLE

vu

PRESENT PARTICIPLE

voyant

───────────── EXAMPLE PHRASES ─────────────

Venez me **voir** demain.	*Come and see me tomorrow.*
Je ne **vois** rien sans mes lunettes.	*I can't see anything without my glasses.*
Est-ce que tu l'**as vu**?	*Did you see him? OR Have you seen him?*
Est-ce que cette tache **se voit**?	*Does that stain show?*

- *Note that **se voir** follows the same pattern, but takes **être** in the perfect tense. For an example of a reflexive verb in full, see verb table **82 se taire**.*
- *The verb **prévoir** follows the same pattern as **voir**, except for the future tense (**je prévoirai**, etc) and the conditional (**je prévoirais**, etc).*

PRESENT

je	veux
tu	veux
il/elle/on	veut
nous	voulons
vous	voulez
ils/elles	veulent

PRESENT SUBJUNCTIVE

je	veuille
tu	veuilles
il/elle/on	veuille
nous	voulions
vous	vouliez
ils/elles	veuillent

PERFECT

j'	ai voulu
tu	as voulu
il/elle/on	a voulu
nous	avons voulu
vous	avez voulu
ils/elles	ont voulu

IMPERFECT

je	voulais
tu	voulais
il/elle/on	voulait
nous	voulions
vous	vouliez
ils/elles	voulaient

FUTURE

je	voudrai
tu	voudras
il/elle/on	voudra
nous	voudrons
vous	voudrez
ils/elles	voudront

CONDITIONAL

je	voudrais
tu	voudrais
il/elle/on	voudrait
nous	voudrions
vous	voudriez
ils/elles	voudraient

IMPERATIVE

veuille / veuillons / veuillez

PAST PARTICIPLE

voulu

PRESENT PARTICIPLE

voulant

─────────────── EXAMPLE PHRASES ───────────────

Elle **veut** un vélo pour Noël.
She wants a bike for Christmas.
Ils **voulaient** aller au cinéma.
They wanted to go to the cinema.
Tu **voudrais** une tasse de thé?
Would you like a cup of tea?